scientific psychology
and social concern

scientific psychology and social concern

edited by
leonard w. schmaltz
the university of wisconsin

new york, evanston, san francisco, london
harper & row, publishers

This book is dedicated to my introductory
psychology students at The University of
Wisconsin, whose enthusiasm, sincerity,
and encouragement make teaching the joy
it can be.

Cover photos by Michel Cosson.

Scientific Psychology and Social Concern.
Copyright © 1971 by Leonard W. Schmaltz.
Printed in the United States of America. All rights reserved. No part of this book may be used or
reproduced in any manner whatsoever without written permission except in the case of brief quotations
embodied in critical articles and reviews. For information address Harper & Row, Publishers, Inc., 49
East 33rd Street, New York, N.Y. 10016.

Standard Book Number: 06-045778-3

LIBRARY OF CONGRESS CATALOG CARD NUMBER: 74-158544

contents

preface

My first semester of teaching introductory psychology at The University of Wisconsin was a disaster. Trained as a "hardheaded" physiological psychologist, my choice of a text and a collection of readings naturally reflected this bias. The 450-plus students enrolled in the course wasted little time in making their dissatisfaction with the assignments known to me. They demanded that the course be "socially relevant." Psychology, I was told, must have something to say about drugs, sexual behavior, race relations, and the multitude of problems that face our society today.

My initial reaction to such criticism was a defensive one. I carefully (and probably condescendingly) explained that psychology was a science and had to be taught with all the rigor that this involves. At that time and at present, I remained convinced of this view. Premature and unfounded solutions for society's ills obviously cannot be justified under any circumstances. On the other hand, psychologists have begun scientific exploration of research areas that today's student would consider relevant.

The articles in the present collection were chosen to meet two criteria: (1) they come from respected scholarly journals and texts and are written by scientists committed to furthering the science of behavior; (2) they deal with current social problems in a responsible fashion. I have assigned many of them to my own introductory classes, and the students found them comprehensible and profitable. The enthusiasm generated by the articles seemed to generalize to the entire course. I would hope that others using the collection have the same experience.

The collection is organized into eleven general areas, or topics. The order of presentation generally follows the sequence used in introductory texts. There are introductory remarks for each new topic and review questions at the end of each part. The author is close enough to his own undergraduate days to remember that it is common practice among students to ignore such introductory remarks or not bother with review questions. In many instances, this is at least partially the fault of the editor. I can only assure the student that substantial thought and effort went into the introductory statements and review questions in the present collection.

Many people have helped in the selection of the articles. Dr. Edward E. Smith of Stanford University, Dr. Charles Snowdon of The University of Wisconsin, and Dr. H. Philip Zeigler of Hunter College and the American Museum of Natural History were particularly helpful; and I am indeed grateful. I must also acknowledge the many authors and publishers who generously allowed their works to be reproduced here. Finally, Mr. George A. Middendorf and Miss Holly Detgen of the Harper & Row staff made the whole project a pleasant one from its inception to completion.

LEN SCHMALTZ
Madison, Wisconsin

part one
introduction

When asked the difference between
a psychologist and a psychiatrist, a colleague
of mine always replies "about $60,000 a
year." Erasmus Hoch, in his article "Psychology
Today: Conceptions and Misconceptions" (#1),
points out that the two professions also differ
in the nature of the required training and in
professional activities. A psychiatrist is a
medical doctor who has chosen as his particular
speciality the treatment of mental disorders.
Generally, he is "patient oriented," directing
his efforts toward elaborating the causes of
abnormal behavior and implementing
effective therapeutic measures for
an individual patient.

Psychology is a much broader discipline.
Its concern is all of behavior—both normal
and abnormal. Psychologists can be found in
elementary schools, factories, advertising
agencies, personnel offices, community centers,
government agencies, and in any setting
where there is need for the scientific analysis
of behavior. The Doctorate of Philosophy
(Ph.D.) in any field is a research degree.
Ph.D.'s in psychology are certainly no
exception. Professional psychologists devote
much of their time to formulating and testing
in a scientific way general laws or explanations
of behavior. In some sense, only after the
introductory psychology course is completed
will the student really know just how broad
the field of psychology is and how individual

psychologists utilize the scientific method in their particular fields of interest.

One source of confusion in the distinction between a psychiatrist and a psychologist is that a sizeable group of psychologists are called clinical psychologists. No one person could possibly be competent in all areas of a field as broad as psychology, and it is necessary to specialize or devote oneself to a particular aspect of behavior. Clinical psychologists, like psychiatrists, are interested in the causes and treatment of mental disorders. Many of them see patients on a regular basis and are as "patient oriented" as is the psychiatrist. They, of course, are not M.D.'s and cannot prescribe drugs, etc., in their practice. Clinical psychologists are, however, still psychologists and Ph.D.'s and, as a result, many of them keep a research orientation as well. A fairly new concept is that of the mental health team consisting of a psychiatrist, a clinical psychologist, and a psychiatric social worker. Each member of the team has his own job or area of speciality. The psychiatrist actually administers the therapy, the psychologist is concerned with diagnostic testing and long-term research programs, and the social worker tries to implement the therapeutic suggestions in the patient's day-to-day living.

The overwhelming majority of psychoanalysts are psychiatrists, although there are some few psychologists who are trained as analysts as well. The psychoanalyst chooses a particular theoretical approach in his treatment of mental disorders. In essence, analytic psychology centers around the writings and theories of Sigmund Freud. While the psychoanalytic school has certainly changed substantially and constantly since Freud proposed his theoretical framework, it retains this Freudian orientation even today.

Erasmus Hoch wrote his article in 1962 and concludes with a considera-

tion of the direction in which psychology will move in the future. Eight years have passed, and it is interesting to note that the field faces essentially the same dilemma though at present the issue seems to be more clearly in focus. It is undoubtedly an oversimplification, but young psychologists (under 35?) are faced with an agonizing decision—whether to devote their research efforts and talents directly to the solution of current social problems and hope for immediate solutions or continue to do more basic research with the view of long-term payoffs.

Edward L. Walker, in "Experimental Psychology and Social Responsibility" (#2), offers a possible solution for psychologists of all ages. The published article is an adaptation of Walker's Presidential Address to the Midwestern Psychological Association Convention in 1969. The convention was somewhat controversial from its beginning. It was held in Chicago, Illinois, some eight months after the turbulent Democratic Party National Convention of 1968. The past president of the organization did not attend the convention because it was being held in Chicago. Many psychologists in the Midwest shared this view. It was unclear in the minds of many in attendance why several "socially relevant" symposia were rejected and not allowed to be presented by the Program Committee of the convention. Against this backdrop, Walker departed from the tradition of presenting a summary of his current research activities. Instead, he chose to consider the general issue of the social responsibility of psychologists in their research activities. Walker begins by asserting that the essential difference between basic and applied research is remoteness of applicability. The merit or applicability of applied research is relatively easy to determine by both scientists and well-educated laymen. Basic research creates more of a problem and in fact, the assumption has been that such research "must be protected from close scrutiny because the greatest advances in knowledge frequently arise from research from which the potential applicability of the results is not foreseen or foreseeable." Walker accepts this assumption, yet points out that it has certain limits.

He argues that "basic research enjoys a freedom from accountability in terms of social values that is based on ignorance and is therefore unwarranted. However remote that applicability, I believe that ultimate human usefulness is the primary criterion on which the social support of psychological research should be based. I believe that the individual scientist should take social value into consideration in choosing his problems, and I believe that his colleagues should take social value into consideration in judging the merit of his work. Someone, either the individual scientist or his colleagues, must take the responsibility for assessing the potential social value of the research in question."

No one who attended the convention could have doubted Walker's sincerity and courage in delivering this address. It was well received. The response was particularly enthusiastic from younger psychologists. Essentially, they agreed with the new concept that even basic research must be considered in the light of possible social value. This fact should prove highly significant in psychology's next two or three decades.

Nevitt Sanford, in the selection "Will Psychologists Study Human Problems?" (#3), goes beyond the Walker position. He argues that very little of psychology —either basic or applied—is really relevant to human problems. Psychologists, in his opinion, lack sensitivity to human problems because of the nature of their professional training. "The plain fact is that our young psychological researchers do not know what

goes on in human beings, and their work shows it." Most "young" psychologists would quickly point out to Professor Sanford that it is the "older" generation that has trained this same group of young psychologists and would ask for evidence that senior psychologists know more about "what goes on in human beings" than do their junior colleagues.

In any event, Sanford outlines a series of steps that would lead psychology to more meaningful study of truly human problems. Everyone would agree that one of the first steps in the development of such a research program is discovering appropriate scientific techniques or methodologies. The history of any science shows that great strides occur shortly after some new research technique is perfected. Even given the existence of appropriate techniques, there still, however, remains the problem in psychology of getting psychologists interested in relevant research areas. It is to this problem that Sanford primarily addresses his article.

Protection of the privacy of individuals who serve as subjects in research is a current problem of psychology and conceivably will become even greater as psychology becomes more involved in human problems, as Sanford's article suggests. The Office of Science and Technology of the United States Government appointed a panel of behavioral scientists and other interested individuals to consider the general problem and propose specific recommendations. A preliminary report of their findings, entitled "Privacy and Behavioral Research" (#4), is reprinted here. The conclusions and recommendations presented are adequate safeguards for individual privacy while at the same time they do not impede the scientist in his research efforts.

Most students taking introductory psychology courses participate as subjects in ongoing research projects at their universities. The participant should find it reassuring to know that extensive precautions have been taken to protect his privacy. Perhaps government and other agencies in the future will follow the example of the behavioral scientist and adopt equally strict guidelines for protecting individual privacy.

1.
psychology today: conceptions and misconceptions

erasmus l. hoch

Small wonder that psychology and psychologists are often misunderstood. The field is old, yet new; it seems too mysterious to grasp, yet excites everyone's curiosity; its doctrines (or supposed doctrines) sound at once uncanny and self-evident; and the profession itself looks one day like society's Good Samaritan, the next like its Machiavelli.

There are good reasons for the perplexity. Although respecting his ability, most people seem to have relatively little personal investment in how the chemist fills his beakers or what the oceanographer dredges up from the ocean bottom. The psychologist, by contrast, is seen as doing things pretty directly *for* us, or even *to* us. He designs teaching machines; he is expected to give counsel; he samples public opinion. And there is more than a little feeling, it seems, about needing to pass a test to get a job, or hearing that advertisements are made "psychological," presumably to get us to buy products we may not really want.

It is precisely because psychology is seen as touching us so intimately that the public has developed ideas of its own about the profession, its members, and their objectives. If the ideas are sometimes faulty or actually untrue, it is partly because the field has not stood still long enough to let anyone get a good look at it. The psychology of 1960 is not the psychology of 1920; it is not even the psychology of 1940. Many things have happened to give the field a "new look" within the past two decades, and when

Excerpts reprinted from Wilse B. Webb (Ed.), *The Profession of Psychology*, New York, pp. 5–19. Copyright © 1962 by Holt, Rinehart and Winston, Inc. Reprinted by permission of Holt, Rinehart and Winston, Inc.

change takes place so rapidly, it may well breed some confusion.

True, one can watch a monkey in a laboratory cage; one can even "take" a test. It is not quite as easy to "see" how the psychologist gets at the basis of prejudice, studies problems of morale among refugees, or helps a person feel less uncomfortable in the presence of the opposite sex. The gadgets are few; the relationships often subtle (at least not easily represented); the jargon of the profession sometimes esoteric. Add to this the fact that the psychologist has not been around very long, as far as most people are concerned, and the discipline and its disciples begin to look like scientific Martians of a sort.

At least three circumstances have contributed to making psychology something of an enigma for the average person:

Popular misconceptions about the profession

The semantic problem of sharing terms and settings with other professions

The nature of the field

In this chapter, we shall examine some of the sources of misunderstanding and look at the difficulties inherent in getting across a clearer, truer picture of the field.

POPULAR MISCONCEPTIONS ABOUT THE PROFESSION

Let us back into our problem, correcting a number of common and somewhat fundamental misconceptions by running through a series of things psychology is *not*, the better to understand what it really is. We shall be concerned in turn with the focus of the field, the attributes of its members, and the scope of its problems.

Psychology Is Not Illness-Oriented

In the minds of most people, psychology is associated with correcting something that has gone wrong. Psychologists help people solve problems, find out why a child is doing poorly in school, attempt to patch up a marriage, and perform other psychological first aid. True, they do—not as directly or as simply as people hope they can, and not always successfully—but they do. The story, however, hardly ends there.

The psychological continuum. Psychologists deal not only with "sick" people. Theirs is the whole spectrum of behavior, from the very maladjusted to the very well adjusted, from earthworm to human being, from infancy to old age. They are concerned as much with potentialities as with limitations; their interest lies not only in traits that make life miserable but especially in the thoughts, feelings, aspirations, and actions that can ennoble and enrich and inspire.

This has not always been the case. Psychology, along with other disciplines, has needed time to realize that we know much more about sickness than about health. We realize many things about what makes people break down, fewer about what keeps them going. The slow learner has drawn our attention, his gifted classmate has been left, until recently, to shift largely for himself. A good deal is known about marital disharmony, far less about the happier side. We can keep the space voyager from going "stir-crazy," but find it much harder to help him keep his thoughts on the lofty plane at which he is cruising.

The situation holds not only for the "clinical" areas of knowledge. The social psychologist knows more about the foundations of prejudice than about the bases of international accord. Although able to shed considerable light on the problems of Suburbia, he would probably admit to knowing less about the impact of a Schweitzer on our culture. In any case, his interest too is coming increasingly to include the potentially creative forces at work in today's society.

The notion of "treatment." Probably no psychologist has escaped the experience of being edged into a corner at a party as soon as someone has found him out. Public information efforts notwithstanding, the field continues to be associated in the public mind with couch, distress, and advice to parents of problem children.

In point of fact, even the psychologist who works primarily in such treatment centers as mental hospitals does not only "treat" people. The term itself smacks of the practice of medicine, of which he desires no part. Technicalities aside, however, even the clinical psychologist does much more than provide such direct services as testing and psychotherapy. He conducts research, he provides in-service training, he serves as consultant to other professions, he studies the "therapeutic community," among others.

His colleague at the university may seldom if ever "treat" anyone except perhaps the monkeys being studied to determine which problems cause them ulcers and which situations help them get "cured." Psychologists working in other settings and performing other functions may have even less occasion to engage in treatment, unless it be statistical "treatment" of the data their research studies have netted. . . .

Psychologists Are Not Technicians

However incorrect it may be, the conception of the psychologist as technician is understandable. Psychologists do work in some very dissimilar and seemingly specialized settings—the university, the secondary school, the industrial plant, the hospital. Furthermore, people seek out a psychologist because they have, as they see it, an identifiable problem—their son is flunking, their product won't sell, their aviation cadets "wash out" too frequently in flight training. The presenting problem, it turns out, is usually part of a much larger situation, frequently not the real problem at all. But too often there is the hope that a psychologist can take a problem of a specific sort and come up with a solution of an immediate type.

The matter of specialization. Judging from typical inquiries, prospective psychologists are some of the prime offenders. Among enterprising high school and even college students, wishful think-ing has it that a set of rather specialized psychology courses qualifies one to be-come a "marriage counselor," a "child expert," a "psychological warfare spe-cialist," or a "test designer." Unfortu-nately, or fortunately, the thought is not father to the deed. The consummation, in terms of career, involves a less direct route to the goal and a delayed reward.

The psychologist is neither technician nor narrow specialist. His training em-phasizes general, over-all knowledge as the necessary condition for later speciali-zation. He is expected to be conversant with the several areas of knowledge which feed into his field; he must be a scientist first, a practitioner second (if at all); his training stresses the acquisi-tion of basic information and underlying concepts rather than *expertise* in tech-niques. Where such *expertise* exists, as in the case of the psychologist with special competence in the area of projective methods, the skills gain meaning only as parts of larger wholes. If one needed to speak of a basic skill, one common to all psychologists, it would be none other than a thoroughgoing conversance with scientific method. Any other is sub-sidiary.

At major conferences on education and training, there is still room for debate about the place of the nondoctoral per-son in psychology, the nature of the "core curriculum," and related considera-tions. The fact remains, however, that psychological training, at least in the early years, involves much that is broad and general rather than narrow and cir-cumscribed, and that specialization takes place later rather than sooner. The doc-toral degree, the saying goes, is a license to practice psychology, not an end in itself. If anything, it marks the begin-ning of the real kind of learning that takes place postdoctorally. All the while, psychologists remain psychologists first, "specialists" second. . . .

Psychological Problems Are Not Finite

Indebted as it is to its forebears, psy-chology is more than two parts biology, one part physics, three parts philosophy, and the like. Psychology is more than anything else simply psychology. It has

a language of its own (sometimes strange, to be sure), has developed tools and methods, and, most important, makes distinctive contributions to problems of its own choosing. This is not to say that it divorces itself from allied sciences and operates unilaterally. Psychologists find themselves working ever more closely alongside colleagues in other fields. In so doing, however, they retain their iden-tity as psychologists, members of a dis-tinct species of the genus scientist. Above all, they do not wait for problems to come to them; they search them out—and the latter are everywhere.

The notion of "common sense." One thing seems clear: Everyone fancies him-self a psychologist after a fashion. It is in the nature of man to have ideas on and feelings about how children are best reared, what makes for a successful mar-riage, how the student should study, and what motivates the Communist.

Whereas most people have relatively little inclination to tell the physician how he should practice or what he should prescribe (aside from suggestions that his fees may be too high or that he seems "too ready to operate"), the set toward the psychologist (and the psychiatrist, for that matter) is a different one. Terms such as "inferiority complex" and "re-pression" are common currency, and whole psychological philosophies seem to hinge on how the particular layman feels about a thing called "will power."

The result is an interesting, albeit somewhat perplexing, situation. Many of us may practice some favorite home rem-edies; few would fancy themselves physi-cians of sorts. Where problems of hu-man behavior are involved, however, there is noticeably less reluctance on the part of the average person to diagnose a situation, prescribe a solution, or even treat what seems like the problem. Iron-ically, when the trained psychologist pro-ceeds less boldly, his wisdom is often questioned, his motives impugned.

Small wonder, then, that some research findings strike the layman as something he "knew all along," whereas others im-press him as much scientific ado about nothing, and still others as outlandishly irrelevant to the business of living. The concept of "basic" research, as compared with the "applied" variety, is not the easiest to grasp. Nor are the problems psychologists choose to study always those which make most sense to the person concerned with the earthier problems of sleeping well at night and seeing the dawn of peace come upon the world. . . .

THE SEMANTIC PROBLEM OF SHARING TERMS AND SETTINGS WITH OTHER PROFESSIONS

Psychology Vis-à-vis Other Professions

No doubt many people cannot readily distinguish the meanings of such similar-sounding terms as "ethnologist," "ethologist," and "ecologist"; but a trip to the dictionary easily solves the problem. Not so when "psychologist," "psychiatrist," and "psychoanalyst" are at issue, let alone such a less well-known but phonetically allied term as "psychiatrist."

The layman is understandably confused. How does the psychologist fit into the professional picture generally? How are he and the psychiatrist alike? how different? Part of the problem lies in the similarity of terms used. But the attitudes and philosophies of the professions involved help compound the difficulty. Tradition plays a part in status, and the psychiatrist, with time and the prestige of medicine on his side, is certainly comfortable in the role of father of the hospital family of disciplines. The psychologist, newly arrived, as much research-oriented as clinically oriented and unencumbered by hospital lore, sees the relationship as something to be worked out rather than adjusted to. As his responsibilities in clinical settings broaden and diversify, he becomes even less inclined to accept ancillary status.

Several years ago Edith Stern (1956) wrote an article entitled "What Doctor for the Psyche?" In it she sought to unravel some of the semantic knots which keep the various "doctors" tied up with one another in the public mind. For the fact that the nonmedical psychologist comes by the title "Doctor" on the basis of his Ph.D. degree does not simplify matters. Deserved as the accolade may be (it antedates the "Doctor" of the

M.D. variety), it adds to the difficulty of explaining to the layman what a psychologist is and what he does.

Perhaps Dr. Adenauer and Dr. Oppenheimer suffer less in terms of having their title misunderstood. One assumes that the former has the Ph.D. degree in social or political science, the latter in physical science or mathematics; in any event, the former is seen as a statesman, the latter as a scientist, neither to be easily confused with the other or with other professions. The psychologist, working as he does in hospitals, among other places, and being called "Doctor," is faced repeatedly with the necessity of pointing out that he does not practice medicine; indeed, he has not studied medicine (except in the few cases where a psychologist has both a Ph.D. and an M.D. degree), and is a "doctor" of another sort.

Even when his nonmedical training is clear, people anticipate that the psychologist will somehow act like the more usual "doctor." He is expected to "do something" to a person, or at least show tangible evidence of ministration. While he is "giving" a test (or its scores), his role is perhaps not so confusing. When he is not imparting "answers" or "advice," the role becomes less clear. And when he is found working in a paint factory or in a legislator's office, his role seems completely puzzling to most people.

The existence of other "psyche" terms, such as "psychiatrist" or "psychoanalyst," simply adds to the confusion. Nor does it help matters when psychologists are found to be teaching (psychology) in medical schools, doing research at a school of aviation medicine, helping distinguish between "organic" and "functional" epilepsy, and trying to predict whether a patient will profit from shock therapy or from ataractic drugs.

No doubt some of the same confusion could be pointed out in other fields. For example, the average person is perhaps not quite clear as to the distinction between the civil and the mechanical engineer. But somehow these occupational roles seem to touch most people less directly than the ones with which we are concerned here.

We shall not carry the illustrations

further. We wish simply to suggest that the terms and language of the "psyche" fields are such as to mean many things to many men. The resultant (or causative) problems of semantics make the need all the greater for clarifying both what psychology is and what it is not.

Psychology Vis-à-vis the "Misprofessions"

As if distinguishing psychology from its legitimate fellow professions were not problem enough, there are an alarming number of illegitimate practitioners to be reckoned with. The reason is simple. As late as the close of 1961, only seventeen states had enacted any kind of legislation for dealing with the problem. Consequently, in thirty-three states it is still possible for anyone, regardless of training, to advertise himself with impunity as a "psychologist" and to sell his "services" to the public. Unsavory as the thought may be, it is a fact that there are any number of such "psychologists," completely or relatively untrained, often unscrupulous, "treating" people in the community. The existence of the "diploma mill" only intensifies the problem, lending a spurious note of prestige to the charlatan and making it more difficult for the average person to distinguish the competent from the incompetent.

To make matters worse, the services of the quack are, unfortunately, easy to come by. Under the heading "'psychologist," the classified telephone directory of most cities lists pretenders as well as it does qualified practitioners. The latter, if they advertise at all, do so with reserve and on a very limited scale. They neither solicit potential clients (something expressly forbidden by the "Ethical Standards of Psychologists") nor guarantee success or offer easy "cures." The charlatan, by contrast, makes his services infinitely more attractive to the person in distress. More frequently than not, he promises a quick, relatively effortless solution, very often holding out a technique such as hypnosis as the custom-tailored solution to a multiplicity of problems. In the hands of the well-trained, qualified person, hypnosis is indeed a reputable procedure, one to be used with discretion and one having admitted limitations. In the hands of the

untrained, it becomes a dangerous technique, often employed indiscriminately and held out as a panacea. Understandably, however, the client in the situation may comfort himself with feeling that a process of some consequence is going on in his behalf; that something is being done to and for him (as he has been wont to expect from a "doctor"); and that solutions are conveniently coming to him, sparing him the personal effort of working actively on his problems.

The charlatan is identifiable on several other counts. Given to boasting about his successes, he is not above divulging case material of actual clients he professes to have helped. Indeed, he is likely to do a good deal of talking himself, in contrast to the psychologist, who has been trained to listen skilfully, the better to help the client talk about and work out his own problems. Again, whereas the psychologist makes a special point of collaborating with physicians to provide for diagnosis and treatment of medical problems, the charlatan, though without medical training, may offer not only to diagnose but even to prescribe for medical conditions.

In the face of this situation, psychologists have felt not only justified in, but socially responsible for, seeking legislation that will protect the public from the untrained or unscrupulous practitioner masquerading as a psychologist. The intent is not to interfere with the practices of members of allied professions that likewise offer services to the public. Indeed, the American Psychological Association is on record as opposing "restrictive" legislation. The purpose is rather to ensure to the public psychologists who are fully trained, highly ethical, and deeply sensitive to the social responsibility which is theirs.

THE NATURE OF THE FIELD

It has become customary to speak, half facetiously, of the "hard" as compared with the "soft" sciences. (Within psychology itself there is sometimes reference to the "hard" psychologist—the experimentalist—and his "soft" confrere—the clinician.) In this vernacular classification, chemistry would be among the former, psychology among the latter. One can see what the chemist does as he prepares mixtures (which often change color before our eyes), boils solutions, and filters liquids. Furthermore, he can weigh and measure substances with incredible accuracy, controlling or allowing with exactness for such variables as temperature, pressure, and volume.

The psychologist is hard put to match the systematic, carefully regulated performance of the physical scientist. His measuring devices are not nearly so accurate, his materials not so tangible, his subjects less amenable to experimental manipulation, his results often less visible. Furthermore, the chemist's experiments can readily be replicated. Once the formula and procedures for making Saran Wrap are known, chemists everywhere can turn out the same product, uniform in thickness, strength, pliability, and whatever other characteristics are built into the material. Not so with the psychologist. The theory and practice of client-centered counseling, for example, have been presented in detail. Yet there is no guarantee that two clients, however similar, will follow the same course with the same therapist, or even that both will be helped. People are infinitely more complex than materials (though with the advent of more sophisticated kinds of chemistry, chemists are learning that their elements too may behave erratically). Even in the experimental laboratory, where conditions can be more carefully controlled, and where rats, with less extensive and less complicated repertories of behavior, serve as subjects, the experimenter cannot predict outcomes with anything like the confidence of the chemist.

If the subject matter of psychology is somehow unusual, so are its problems and procedures. The clinical psychologist seems to be trying to read minds or look through people, the experimental psychologist to insist that how rats learn mazes has some relation to why Johnny can't read. Add to this the fact that the psychologist, like the dentist, is often seen as someone to whom one goes only when one needs to, and then hardly willingly, and the public's slowness to understand becomes understandable.

As with most misperceptions, there is some basis for those surrounding psychologists. However inelegant the description may be, it is a fact that certain types of psychologists do in a sense try to "see through" people. Their inkblot tests attempt to get at what goes on beneath the surface. They pride themselves on their ability to "listen with the third ear" to what is *really* being said rather than only seeming to be said.

The procedures of the experimental psychologist are no less mysterious. He does, indeed, try to learn more about human behavior by investigating animal behavior. True, his generalizations are hedged about with proper precautions. At the same time, however, he is studying such peculiarly "human" problems as what makes monkeys develop ulcers, how sheep can be made "neurotic," and whether pigeons can learn to keep guided missiles on course.

While, then, the work of the chemist seems at once complicated and clear-cut, the procedures of the psychologist are, by contrast, relatively obscure. Even his approach and method seem not readily to make sense. Psychologists "sample" opinion, "measure" behavior, reduce statements to numbers. What is more, they seem to do elaborate research on problems to which most people know the answers—or believe they do. Then, when all is said and done, the psychologist proves ever so cautious about making seemingly simple predictions, apparently feeling the need for any number of qualifications.

The question of direction. If anything characterizes present-day psychology, it is its lively tempo, its alert recognition of new possibilities, its willingness to step into the breach, its dynamic, burgeoning spirit. Certainly this science does not yet have answers to many of its challenging problems; indeed, sometimes the questions themselves are not altogether clear. What should be understood by those contemplating a career in the field, however, is that society, although it looks with mixed awe and apprehension on the role of the psychologist, has come to expect all manner of things from this new-found scientist in its midst.

Portents of the future are everywhere, and their psychological implications are not hard to discern. Automation is already with us, bringing in its wake the twin problems of the use of leisure time and newer concepts of the meaning of retirement. Jet-age transportation creates a smaller world, population explosion a larger one; both spell new psychological problems. Young nations emerging from colonialism raise as yet unheard questions for the social psychologist. All the while psychology feels its own new restless stirrings in the form of psychopharmacological research, biophysical concepts, the birth of computer programs, teaching machines, and all manner of equally novel developments, each with its attendant host of new problems.

Even now the mélange of questions is incredible. A bank president asks psychologists to help him identify trustworthy tellers. A progressive congressman hopes psychology may be able to shed some light on problems of international peace. The traffic bureau of a large city inquires about psychological factors in highway safety. A commission of the federal government looks to psychology for an evaluation of the possibilities of subliminal advertising. A congressional committee asks that psychologists testify before it with reference to proposed legislation dealing with identification of the nation's talented youth. An embassy official requests references to psychological research on national stereotypes. The manager of a hospital wonders how psychological aspects of hospital architecture may affect patients' progress. A governor asks for help in setting up his state's testing program.

This sample of actual questions gives some little index of the miscellany of needs the psychologist is asked to help meet. Certainly the field will not allow itself to be shaped solely by the motley requests made of it, however significant the problems and well-intentioned the inquirers. The questions are invariably immediate ones and the hope is often for a speedy application of a psychological "technique."

The diversity of social needs out of which the queries arise undoubtedly helps shape in some measure the direction the field will take. At the same time, knowledge must be acquired before it can be put to use. The psychologist is admittedly interested in the manifold applications of his findings; he is as much, if not more, concerned about the theoretical structure that undergirds them. Whereas the community is perhaps most interested in applied research, the psychologist, as a scientist, is at least equally concerned with basic research.

Perhaps because they are relatively young members of the family of sciences and do not yet know their minds, or perhaps because psychologists are a lively lot and cannot always agree, there is no clear-cut "party line" as to the course the field should take. Indeed, at this point, there is some question whether a profession can really decree its course. Cook (1958) entitled his presidential address before the Eastern Psychological Association "The Psychologist of the Future: Scientist, Professional, or Both." The title may well have ended with a question mark. And Feigl (1959), in an invited address before the 1958 convention of the American Psychological Association, pointed out that the very methods of psychology still contain many "philosophical embarrassments" that need to be faced and overcome before we can clearly "assign to psychology its proper place in the uniting sciences."

Psychologists are clearer than most people as to what psychology is not and what it should not become. They are probably as unclear as most people how the field will look fifty years from now. What they are very clear about is that they want to discharge their social mission in the most responsible fashion.

REFERENCES

Cook, Stuart W., The psychologist of the future: Scientist, professional, or both. Amer. Psychologist, 1958, 13, 635–644.

Feigl, Herbert, Philosophical embarrass- ments of psychology. Amer. Psychologist, 1959, 14, 115–128.

Stern, Edith M., What doctor for the psyche? Saturday Rev., October 20, 1956.

2.
experimental psychology and social responsibility

edward l. walker

Experimental psychology is a social enterprise. It is an effort to attack problems of behavior in a controlled and rigorous fashion. The goal is the accumulation of data that are reproducible and the development of principles that work. These goals are common to any discipline with scientific aspirations.

Science is a social enterprise. Any effort to examine the problem of experimental psychology and social responsibility must place the problem in a context of the social responsibility of all science. In so doing, it becomes apparent to me that psychology has special problems in the realm of social responsibility that are not shared by other scientific disciplines. This paper is an attempt to explore the problems of social responsibility in an effort to begin the task of the development of a set of guiding principles. Those principles should preserve the integrity of experimental psychology while providing a basis for discussion and decision with respect to particular social realities when psychology is inescapably confronted with them or chooses to respond out of urgent necessity.

Science flourishes to the extent to which it receives social support, and its products may have profound social consequences. I believe that scientists have the responsibility for protecting, encouraging, and guiding social support of their disciplines. Since the products of science may have profound social consequences, I think that the problem of the scientist's responsibilities for the uses to which

Reprinted from *American Psychologist*, 1969, 24 (9), 862–864, 867–868. Published by the American Psychological Association. Abridged by permission of the author.

Presidential address delivered at the meeting of the Midwestern Psychological Association, Chicago, May 1969.

scientific principles are put requires reexamination.

The Roles of Scientist and Human Being

Some feel that the social responsibility of scientists extends far beyond the realm of the application of principles of science to human affairs. In a recent interview Noam Chomsky (1968) is quoted as saying, "I would not criticize a person as a physicist, in Nazi Germany, if he did only physics. But I'd criticize him as a human being. My argument would be that by being complacent and quiescent he's not preventing oppression and destruction."

There are at least two major difficulties with Chomsky's statement. (a) The first is that the roles of scientist and human being may not be as completely disassociatable as Chomsky implies. (b) The second is that the tasks he prescribes for the individual scientist may be physically and psychologically impossible.

While it may be clarifying in some respects to make the distinction between the role as scientist and the role as human being, the difficulty appears to me to arise from the quite unnecessary and invalid assumption that the two roles are in all respects different rather than merely being in some respects different. Specifically, it implies that the scientific enterprise is and should be free of social values. I believe this proposition to be false, and the belief in it to have arisen from false considerations.

There is sometimes confusion between the application of research findings and applied research. The first of these problems is the one that became traumatic for the atomic physicists. Is the individual scientist responsible for the nature of the use that is made of the knowledge he acquires? There is presumably nothing good or bad about knowledge of the structure of the atom. Atomic energy can be used for good purposes (power) and bad purposes (nuclear warfare). Yet individual physicists could not escape a feeling of profound guilt concerning Hiroshima and Nagasaki. The distinction, while useful for some purposes, turned out to be a specious one for individual physicists. Thus the answer the physicist has given us is that the individual scientist does, in fact, share the responsibility for the manner in which his knowledge is used, and physicists have created organizations in response to this problem.

It is often claimed that the criteria of social value are not relevant to basic research as they are to applied and socially relevant research in any discipline. It is implied that basic research is different from applied research in that its values are intrinsic rather than extrinsic. I believe this argument to be specious as well. The intrinsic value of research is independent of the dimension of basic versus applied. An applied problem can possess all of the features of intellectual intrigue of the most esoteric of basic conundrums.

Among the various characteristics that might be used to distinguish between basic and applied research, the functionally significant one may be remoteness of applicability. It is argued that basic research must be protected from close scrutiny because the greatest advances in knowledge frequently arise from research from which the potential applicability of the results is not foreseen or foreseeable. This is a value in the strategy of research in which I believe, yet it has certain limits. The dimension has basic research at one end and at the other end it has research that can be described as applied, relevant, or simply intelligible to the ordinary layman. Applied research is research that offers no mystery to any reasonably intelligent and well-educated individual. He can see how the results may be applied, and he can see the social implications of the results as well as the scientist who was responsible for the acquisition of the knowledge. A basic research study is one that the layman is not able to judge. The judgment must be made by colleagues.

I would argue that in judging the merit of basic research, colleagues have an obligation to evaluate the research in terms of relevance and social need in the broadest sense. The problem is similar to one addressed by Lytton (1863) about a century ago. He said, "In science, address the few, in literature, the many. In science, the few must dictate opinion to the many; in literature, the many, sooner or later, force their opinion on the few." By analogy, the basic research scientist must address himself to his colleagues, the few. The applied scientist, doing relevant research, must address himself to the many as well. And because he must address the many, he is subject to having the opinion of the many forced upon him.

I would argue that basic research enjoys a freedom from accountability in terms of social values that is based on ignorance and is therefore unwarranted. However remote that applicability, I believe that ultimate human usefulness is the primary criterion on which the social support of psychological research should be based. I believe that the individual scientist should take social value into consideration in choosing his problems, and I believe that his colleagues should take social value into consideration in judging the merit of his work. Someone, either the individual scientist or his colleagues, must take the responsibility for assessing the potential social value of the research in question.

Failure to perform this task adequately has led to the charge that experimental psychology too frequently addresses itself to *trivial* problems. I do not think the charge is just. I do, however, believe that the charge is a symptom of two failures on the part of scientific psychology. The first is that we have failed to interpret basic research in terms of social relevance declaring it to be impossible. I would agree that it is difficult, but I would argue that it is necessary. It is the responsibility of the scientist himself or his colleagues, since they are the only ones who understand the research, to perform the task, however difficult it may appear.

The second failure is a disproportionate emphasis on basic research at the expense of applied, or relevant, research. I think this occurs because basic research is not available to public scrutiny and its implications are not clear. It is therefore more comfortable to work on problems where the threat of public controversy is small. If there were more relevant research, there would be less of a tendency to regard basic research as trivial. I think scientific psychologists need to be supported in their basic research, but they also need to be encouraged to tackle the more controversial but more urgent problems.

Finally, it seems reasonable that the physicist can keep his work separate from his daily, nonprofessional life on the grounds that his scientific work involves inanimate matter and that his work is not therefore relevant to human affairs. However, knowledge is a human attribute, and the physicist could not be a physicist if he were not also human. Thus theoretical physics is a human, social form of behavior whether the immediate object of the theoretical physicist's work is living or nonliving. The inanimate character of his object of study does not make his work asocial in any significant sense. Thus the argument is that the work of a scientist working in physics is a social enterprise because all knowledge is social and of value only because of its social implications.

What *is* true is that the scientist working on nonliving matter enjoys a freedom of choice of problem and procedure that is not enjoyed by the scientist whose immediate subject matter is a living organism. Thus, the psychologist has an additional social dimension in his work in that his object of study is usually human. Therefore, he works under a set of varying social proscriptions that affect what he can and cannot do as a scientist. He may not carry out experiments that are obviously harmful to his subject, a proscription he shares with medicine.

In summary, then, I would argue that science cannot proceed as if the individual's roles as scientist and as human being are completely separate. In some respects, they are inseparable. No part of science is categorically free of social values. The scientist shares the responsibility for the uses that are made of his discoveries. Intrinsic values are equally applicable to basic and applied research, and social values are applicable to them in the same manner although they differ in remoteness of that applicability. The social difference between research on atoms and humans is a matter of social restrictions applicable when the object of the research is human but does not imply that one class of object of study makes science a social activity and the other asocial.

The Individual Scientist and the Scientific Organization

The second major difficulty in Chomsky's position is that, if a man is to be a social activist, it is very difficult for him to be a scientist. If a man is to be a scientist, he has little time and energy for social activism.

The successful scientist is often an individual who devotes an enormous number of hours to his scientific pursuits. He achieves a high level of scientific productivity by sacrificing a great many activities in which he would otherwise be engaged. He is likely to forego most social activities. He may neglect his family. He may teach sparingly and without substantial preparation. He may avoid involvement in committees and in administrative responsibilities. He attends meetings of scientific societies solely to exchange scientific information. He may do so even though he enjoys social affairs, has great affection for his family, believes in the need and value of teaching, realizes the necessity of administrative activities, and enjoys a party at the meetings as well as the next man. However, he loves science more than any of these, and his single-minded devotion to scientific enterprise is a choice among positively valenced activities. The same man may have deep concerns for social problems and issues, whether they appear to affect his scientific prospects or not. Yet he can no more devote himself to the solution to social problems than he can devote himself to effective university administration. There is only so much time in the day, and that time must be devoted to the scientific problem at hand, if progress is to be made. He cannot *do* science and *promote* science within the limits of his time and energy.

Furthermore, there is not always complete agreement among individual members of a discipline on what should be regarded as oppression that should therefore be opposed. For example, there may be in this audience some individuals who feel that the rabble in the park represented oppression and destruction so redolent of insurrection and threat of assassination that any preventive measures the Chicago police chose to take would be wholly justified. There may also be in this audience some who regard the behavior of the Chicago police as being so oppressive and destructive that very strong opposing action is required.

The only solution that I can see to this problem is for an organization or association of scientific psychologists to act for the individual psychologist. Such an association can determine the majority opinion of its constituency and it could act in the name of the individual scientist who has the will but not the time to devote to social action. . . .

SOCIAL AND POLITICAL OBLIGATIONS OF EXPERIMENTAL PSYCHOLOGY

In a recent speech, excerpts of which appeared in *Science*, Representative Daddario (1968) (D–Conn.) cited an Italian philosopher as saying, "There is nothing more difficult to take in hand, more perilous to conduct, or more uncertain of its success than to take the lead in the introduction of a new order of things." Yet my commitment to talk on this subject has led me to that perilous position. I would like to propose a new order of things for scientific psychology.

I have tried to argue that the new order of things with respect to the involvement of scientific psychology in certain political and social affairs is a task for a formal organization of scientists. The individual scholar must be left to pursue knowledge through individual scientific inquiry, for no organization originates knowledge. Some organizations *must* meet these obligations if we are to survive.

I would like to propose four sets of obligations experimental psychology owes to itself and to society as a whole. They amount to a preliminary formulation of a set of social and political goals, and I believe that an organization of psychologists should use every available means to advance the welfare of scientific psychology within that set of goals.

1. The first is a matter of communication. A convention such as this one provides a means of communication between scientist and scientist. It does not provide communication between scientist and layman. Such communication is an obligation of the profession and means must be developed to accomplish it. In brief, *experimental psychology has the responsibility to interpret its basic research to society as a whole.*

2. The second is the problem posed by the need for social support of experimental psychology. Representative Daddario (1968) sets this problem as a paradox. He says: "science is obviously affected by funding, funding is dependent on public policy, so science must affect public policy. The paradox is that science is characteristically aloof from politicking, feeling that it is in the best interests of the functioning of the scientific method to ignore the exigencies of politics." He also cites the outcome of a meeting that George Wald of Harvard helped to organize in August 1968 at Woods Hole. The problem was to discuss what action could be taken on Federal cutbacks in research support. The meeting seemed to produce the consensus that "the only way for scientists to work effectively for their cause is to become more active politically." I believe, then, that *experimental psychology has the responsibility to encourage its own social support through political action.*

3. The third goal has to do with pressing social problems. In the public mind, psychology, of all disciplines, should have something to offer that would aid in dealing with them. How can a discipline that has the scientific study of learning as one of its provinces be unable to offer any solution to the problem of educating children in such a manner that they do not turn to violence in the streets and punishment in the courts? How can a discipline that purports to include the scientific study of motivation be unable to provide understanding and control of the will to order the indiscriminate de-

struction of life that is modern war? Pressing social problems, such as the urban ghetto, police excesses, irrational violence in the name of dissent, racism, and poverty, are clearly matters of the execution of extremely stupid and irrational behavior on the part of intelligent and rational men. If the science of human behavior has too little to offer in the solution to these problems, then we had better reexamine our directions. It is not necessary for experimental psychology to take sides on controversial issues, but it is necessary for experimental psychology to provide the data and principles in terms of which rational solutions can be reached. The third goal is: *Experimental psychology must find a means of stepping up its attack on pressing social problems.*

4. The final goal that I would propose is perhaps the most remote from life in the laboratory, but perhaps the most important of all. Experimental psychology cannot survive in a repressive political atmosphere. It shares this vulnerability with other scientific and scholarly pursuits. However, political ideologies frequently contain dogma that is in direct conflict with the principle of freedom of inquiry with respect to human behavior. Thus there are forms of political milieu in which physics and mathematics can prosper and in which psychology cannot. Thus psychology, of all scientific disciplines, must remain alert to political weather signals and it must act within its power as a political force for freedom of scientific inquiry. Thus my fourth and final goal, and final words of the day are: *Experimental psychology has the responsibility to oppose political climates that would inhibit the progress of free psychological inquiry and to encourage political climates that permit or encourage such progress.*

REFERENCES

Chomsky, N. Quotation in *New York Times*, October 27, 1968.

Daddario, E. Q. Academic science and the federal government. *Science*, 1968, *162*, 1249–1251.

Lytton, E. B. *Caxtoniana: A series of essays on life, literature, and manners.* Edinburgh and London: W. Blackwood and Sons 1863.

Pitzer, K. S. University integrity. *Science* 1968, *162*, 228–230.

Seitz, F. Science, government and the university. *Stanford Alumni Almanac*, 1968, 7 5–6.

3.
will psychologists study human problems?

nevitt sanford

This paper started out to be a letter to Joseph M. Bobbitt in his capacity as Associate Director of the new National Institute of Child Health and Human Development. For some time it had seemed to me that certain unfortunate trends in psychology and social science were being aided and abetted by our great fund-granting agencies. Or was it that unfortunate trends in these agencies were being furthered by the "establishment" in psychology? Probably a chicken-and-egg situation. At any rate, it seemed that the inauguration of the new Institute was a good occasion for some analysis and criticism of the disciplines most directly concerned with research in psychological health and development. I warmed up to this subject, and went far enough in criticism so that it seemed I ought to undertake the more difficult task of offering some constructive suggestions.

And so my letter to Bobbitt has grown into an article, the main burden of which is that the new Institute—and other institutes and agencies—ought to encourage psychologists to study problems that people really worry about rather than only problems formulated on the basis of reading the professional journals.

If fund-granting agencies such as the new Institute were to insist that psychologists confront these human problems directly, they would be forced to examine longer sections of behavior, and larger areas of the person, than they usually attend to nowadays; they would have to deal with some really complex processes and, thus, they would be stimulated to devise methods for solving problems—

Reprinted from *American Psychologist*, 1965, 20 (3), 192–202. Published by the American Psychological Association. Abridged by permission of the author.

rather than confining themselves, as they do today, to problems to which existing methods are suited.

This would be good for psychology, and I for one am as much concerned about advancing this science as I am about finding a solution to any immediate problem.

Psychology is really in the doldrums right now. It is fragmented, overspecialized, method centered, and dull. I can rarely find in the journals anything that I am tempted to read. And when I do read psychological papers, as I must as an editorial consultant, I become very unhappy; I am annoyed by the fact that they all have been forced into the same mold, in research design and style of reporting, and I am appalled by the degree to which an inflation of jargon and professional baggage has been substituted for psychological insight and sensitivity.

I used to think, when I first noted the trend—10 years ago—that the authors' psychological knowledgeability had simply been edited out in the interests of saving space. I am now convinced that the trouble lies much deeper. The psychologists who are filling up the journals today just do not have sensivity to human experience, and the fault lies in their training—which is an expression of what academic psychology has become.

We have produced a whole generation of research psychologists who never had occasion to look closely at any one person, let alone themselves, who have never imagined what it might be like to be a subject in one of their experiments, who, indeed, have long since lost sight of the fact that their experimental subjects are, after all, people. (Let us leave the rats out of it for the moment.) They can define variables, state hypotheses, design experiments, manipulate data statistically, get publishable results—and miss the whole point of the thing. Reading their papers you get a strange sense of the unreality of it all; the authors' conceptions of variables and processes seem a bit off; and then you realize that the authors have never looked at human experience, they went straight from the textbook or journal to the laboratory, and thence into print—and thence into the business of getting research grants.

The plain fact is that our young psychological researchers do not know what goes on in human beings, and their work shows it. Not only is it dull, which psychology should never be, but it is often wrong, for that context of processes-in-the-person which they have been trained to ignore is usually doing more to determine what happens in the situation under study than the variables that have been "isolated experimentally."

What has happened is that the revolution in psychology that occurred during World War II, and in the 5 years thereafter, has been over for some time and we are in the midst of the reaction. Or perhaps one might better say that normal operating procedures have been restored, that it is only in times of crisis that the academic disciplines are brought into contact with real life and shaken out of their professional preoccupations.

The revolution reached its high-water mark in 1949 when Erik Erikson was appointed professor at Berkeley. Two years later this would not have been possible; nor has such a thing since been possible in any psychology department in the country. (The appointments at Harvard are special and do not really count. Harvard is special, too, in that it is the only place that can afford to make mistakes.)

The critique is not of the experimental approach in psychology or of general psychology as a discipline; it is of a state of affairs in which the advocates of a particular kind of psychology—psychology-without-a-person—have been able to gain and maintain power through putting across the idea that they are the representatives in psychology of *true science*.

It is quite possible that nothing can be done about the state of affairs I describe. Maybe we are just playthings of social forces that no one can control. The issues underlying the situation are ones that have divided psychologists for a long time. I believe, however, that there is a constructive alternative to the prevailing orientation, one that might be called a "human-problems" approach. It is an approach that has a highly respectable past, but today it is staunchly opposed and falls outside the main current of contemporary work in psychology. It has many silent supporters, but few spokesmen.

THE KIND OF APPROACH NEEDED

Psychology and social science have, of course, always been oriented to action, in the sense that they have proceeded on the assumption that their theories and empirical knowledge would eventually be applied. Psychology, when it has thought seriously about itself, has included among its aims "to promote human welfare." Sociology, traditionally has been concerned with the solution of social problems and with "building a better society." The National Institute of Mental Health, which has supported so much research in biology, psychology and the newer social sciences, has been guided by the principle that such research should be "mental-health relevant," but in practice any fundamental work in these fields has been considered to have this characteristic.

Yet there is no denying that at the present time there exists a wide gap between research and practice. Psychology participates fully in the trend toward specialization and disciplinary professionalism that dominates in the universities today. The discipline is still much concerned to establish itself as a science but the psychologists' naive conception of science has led them to adopt the more superficial characteristics of the physical sciences. This has made it difficult for them to study genuine human problems, since quantification, precision of measurement, elegance of experimental design, and general laws are so much more difficult to achieve once one goes beyond simple part processes.

There is, of course, a rationale for all this. It is not without some reason that the National Institute of Mental Health regards the so-called "pure science" of these disciplines as relevant to mental health. Science has always made progress through specialization. It can be argued, and it is argued, that findings concerning simple and isolated processes will eventually add up to systematic knowledge that can then be applied to human problems.

There are two things to be said about this. One is that the "adding up" function is rather neglected today, and the other is that many of these findings just do not add up. Concerning the first, the accent today is on the production of knowledge rather than on its organization. There are few attempts at systematization of the sort that would put particular facts in perspective and show their significance. More than that, there seem to be few attempts to organize knowledge in such a way that its relevance to practice or to policy becomes apparent. A college president might examine a large number of issues of educational or psychological journals without coming across anything that struck him as relevant to his purposes or helpful in the solution of his problem. It is not that all this material is irrelevant, but rather that the task of organizing and interpreting it so that it might be useful is so largely neglected. Scientists write for each other; and when they are looking for a problem to investigate, they turn to their professional journals rather than ask such questions as what might be troubling the college presidents.

When I say that the study of simple, isolated processes does not add up to an understanding of more complex ones, I am assuming that human and social processes are organized on different levels, and that processes on higher (more complex) levels have a character of their own, are just as "real" as processes on lower levels, and must be studied directly. It is just as "scientific" to study, say, self-esteem in its relations to other factors of equal complexity as it is to study the manifold conditioned responses into which self-esteem might be analyzed; it is just as scientific to study conditioned responses as it is to study by physiological methods the nerve processes that underlie them. The student of conditioning who

was somewhat contemptuous of the vague globalism of the students of such personality needs as self-esteem could be regarded in the same way by students of the action of the nervous system. I assume, further, that there is *interaction* between processes on different levels. Just as complex phenomena are to be explained in part in terms of the activities of constituent processes, so simple processes have to be understood as partly determined by the larger structures in which they have a place. Truth may be discovered by abstracting parts from the whole and studying them intensively, but the whole truth can never be discovered in this way. It is the whole truth, and particularly the truth about wholes, that is needed for practice. Thus it is that one has to be concerned about a trend in science that seems to put all the accent on the study of abstracted part functions. The main reason for this trend is that it is difficult to study complex processes by existing approved methods. In psychology it seems that theory making itself is often guided by consideration of what can be attacked by such methods rather than by an intellectual involvement with the problems of life. The kind of theory that is needed for the understanding of human problems is different from that which guides most laboratory research or is generated from it. Thus, instead of specialized personality theory and specialized social theory, a human-problems approach calls for a more general personality-social theory, a theory that is not formal or mechanistic but dynamic, not elementaristic but holistic, not narrow and specialized but comprehensive, not concrete and tangible but on a level of abstraction that is appropriate to the problem at hand. Each of these aspects of a human-problems approach may be taken up in turn.

Personality-Social Aspects

It seems clear enough that for an effective approach to human problems we must have an integration of personality theory and social theory. This is not as easy as might first appear. Most sociologists seem to get along quite well without giving much attention to the individual personality, and probably the great majority of clinical practitioners rely on an "individual-psychodynamic" approach that gives little attention to social and cultural factors. There is even a certain amount of interdisciplinary rivalry here: In discussions of problems such as prejudice or delinquency there is a tendency to oppose personality factors and social factors and argue about which is more important. But progress toward integration is being made. Certainly personality theory is far more "social" today than it was 25 years ago, and there is evidence, I think, that when sociologists note signs that their psychological colleagues are seeing the light they are willing to go halfway toward rapprochement. What is needed is more knowledge of the articulation of personality systems and social systems. This requires more, rather than less, attention to the relatively autonomous personality structures, and more searching analysis of social structures in terms that are psychologically relevant. The student of personality must, of course, focus on the internal structuring of personality, but he must grant that the hypothetical personality subsystems are not fully understood unless their situational relationships are specified. . . .

Dynamic Aspects

A personality, or an organized social group, seems best conceived as a system of interacting forces, a going concern in which energy is distributed among constituent parts and between the system (or its subsystems) and its environment. Dynamic organization refers to the way in which these forces or units of energy interact. Personalities and social systems also exhibit formal organization. They may be examined with attention to such overall features as number of different parts or the connectedness of parts, or with attention to such formal relationships among parts as similarity, proximity, or inclusion. In general, the analysis of systems into states, conditions, or arrangements prepares the way for explanation in terms of dynamic theory.

Dynamic theory is essential when it comes to consideration of how a system might be changed. The question here, typically, is how to bring force to bear upon a particular subsystem that one wishes to modify. One might think first of bringing to bear upon the subsystem in question a potent set of environmental stimuli, and this might indeed be effective sometimes. It usually turns out, however, that the particular subsystem is really being determined by other subsystems and by processes of the whole system. The problem, then, is to find out what within the larger system is determining of what, and then to get a purchase on the master processes. To take an example from the field of personality: An individual's prejudice toward minority groups may be due to a nagging but unrecognized sense of weakness in himself; in such a case it would do no good to give him correct information about minority groups; there would be no change in his prejudice until a way had been found to modify his sense of weakness. In an organization it might be generally recognized that a change in one of its processes would increase production without loss in other essential values, but this would not mean that the change would now take place as a matter of course—whoever wished to promote it would still have to reckon with the implicit values of various segments of the power structure.

All this is not to deny the importance of information or of the mechanisms by which it is acquired. It is to say that in dynamic theory information is instrumental to purpose. Just as in an organization the gathering, storing, and communication of information is put in the service of the organization's explicit and implicit functions, so in the individual perception and learning are organized in the interest of strivings. We should not expect learned factual content to be retained for long without becoming integrated with the individual's purposes. But how such integration occurs is a complex question; it could hardly be answered unless individuals were carefully observed over relatively long periods of time—hence, it receives little attention from psychologists. . . .

Holism

The essential idea was introduced above in our discussion of the neglect of com plex processes; particular phenomena such as a "perception" or a "conditioned response" are almost always in part determined by—their very nature depends upon—the larger organismic patterns and purposes within which they have a place.

The implications of this are great, and I would like to carry my argument further.

The first point to be made is that few psychologists care to deny, on principle, the holistic premise. It seems to be almost universally understood and agreed that how a stimulus is perceived depends on the context in which it exists at the moment, that whether or not an idea will be assimilated by a cognitive system depends on the degree of that idea's consistency with ideas that are already present there, that the meaning of a particular act depends on its place in a larger pattern of striving. It can be said with perfect safety that all personality theories are holistic in the sense that they are concerned with the relations of particular processes to larger personality functions.

What, then, is the argument about? It is not so much about high theory as it is about what is the best strategy for research. The basic complaint against holistic theory is that it does not lend itself to testing by empirical methods. The very term "whole" suggests something that cannot be analyzed, and American psychologists have been taught to be wary of anything "global." This argument would have force—complete force—if it were true that the study of part-whole relationships were impossible. But to confirm that this is not true one has only to point to the work of Klein (1951) on the relations of perception to the ego control system, of Rogers and his associates (Rogers & Dymond, 1959) on the relations of various attitudes and beliefs to the individual's self-concept, or to the results of Witkin, Lewis, Hertzman, Machover, Meissner, and Wagner (1954) on sex difference in perception. The whole research undertaking that issued in The Authoritarian Personality (Adorno, Frenkel-Brunswik, Levinson, & Sanford, 1950) was carried forward in accordance with a holistic orientation and, indeed, would have been impossible without

holistic theory. The F scale for measuring authoritarianism in personality was developed by a process of going back and forth from observed behavior to hypothetical inner structure. The coherence of overt behavior patterns led to the concept of an inner structure of personality, i.e., authoritarianism, and then this concept was used to predict other patterns of behavior.

It cannot, of course, be claimed that research carried out in accordance with the holistic orientation will soon achieve the standards of precision and elegance that are often attained in laboratory experiments involving a few simple variables. Such research can be improved in these respects, but it may never match the best laboratory experiments; it will have to aim at levels of rigor that are appropriate to the task at hand. It cannot be claimed, either, that this kind of research will be other than difficult and expensive. But the criticism of the current strategy of abstracting part functions for experimental study is more serious: It is that because of its very nature it is bound to fall short of the truth. It is not only that it avoids the big problems; it fails to achieve its own chosen goal, which is to establish general laws of behavior. But the main characteristic of such "laws" is their lack of generality. They break down as soon as a new variable is introduced into the picture. And since in real life new variables, or variables not taken into account in the laboratory experiment, are always in the picture, such laws are most limited in their applicability. . . .

The above is the main argument for holism as the best road to knowledge; there is as strong an argument from the point of view of practice. If parts really are determined by the wholes to which they belong, and one wishes to modify a part, then clearly his best course is to bring influence to bear upon the whole. Thus it is that in the psychotherapy of Carl Rogers (1959) the whole thrust is toward modifying the self-concept, because an inappropriate self-concept is believed to be determining of numerous specific unfortunate attitudes and patterns of overt behavior. The same would be true of a social institution such as a school or college. Practices with respect to grading, course requirements, the organization of teaching, and so on, are usually integral to the whole system and are not to be changed until after there has been some modification in the general character of the institution. This is far from being a hopeless prospect. Just as one may influence an individual's self-concept as readily as one of its constituent attitudes, so one might initiate a process of change in an institution's general climate with no more difficulty than would be involved in changing one of its most specific part functions. Success would depend upon knowledge of the individual's or the institution's dynamics. By the same token, a holistic approach to individual or social change involves for the change agent a considerable responsibility: He should not seek change in whole structures unless he is prepared for change in numerous particulars.

I have put the case for holism as strongly as I can; yet I do not see how we can do without the intensive study of abstracted part functions. The student of personality, after all, engages in this activity when he undertakes to explain the functioning of social groups. Here he might well be inclined to favor analysis in terms of the personality types of the group's members, but if he is a holist he would not be surprised or put off if a social theorist reminded him that there are things about personality that do not become apparent until the individual is seen in the context of the social group.

At a time when the holistic orientation seems rather neglected in psychology and social science, it seems proper to accent it as is done here. If we must abstract parts from wholes let us be fully aware of the fact that we *are abstracting,* and let us devote as much energy to finding out how special bits of knowledge fit into the larger picture as we do to analyzing wholes in the conventional scientific way.

Comprehensiveness

The holistic orientation requires that we consider in what respects living systems function as units. It says nothing about the size or complexity of the unit.

Such a unit might be the context of a perception, a pattern of striving that organizes particular acts, or the self that is expressed in numerous personality characteristics. The argument here is for bigger units; we must examine large areas of the person and of society, and long sections of behavior; and we must have theoretical models that permit us to do this.

The whole that helps to determine a particular personality characteristic may be the whole personality, and not merely the whole self or ego; hence, we need a theoretical model of the personality that permits us to deal with the relations of self to ego, and of these relatively large structures to others of like kind. Similarly for social structures. One may study holistically, a department of an industrial organization or a classroom in a school, but for full understanding he would have to see the department or classroom in relation to the whole institution, and the institution in relation to the whole society.

Another argument for comprehensiveness is that the determination of human events is almost always complex. Multiple factors are involved, and it is the task of the scientist to find them. This always takes some imagination, but the right kind of theory can be a big help. Consider, for example, the phenomenon of compulsive drinking. A formula for this could be written out in terms of rewards and punishments, and in such a formulation the reproaches of the drinker's spouse might in some cases be put down on the side of punishment. But what about the case of a man who drinks in order to express hostility toward his wife and who welcomes her reproaches as signs that he is achieving his purpose? One could still describe what happens in stimulus-response terms, after discovering what the effective internal stimuli are. But in finding the stimuli the usual sort of learning theory and the knowledge that proceeds from laboratory tests of it would be of no help; the quest would have to be guided by theory and knowledge concerning the complex interplay of forces within the personality. If we are to think comprehensively, must be with the use of gross units of analysis. The psychotherapist, for example, faced with the task of making sense of vast quantities of verbal material has no alternative to using coarse categories for bringing it all together. And it is thus that when we wish to speak of elements which together make up the whole personality—elements defined with attention to the theoretical structure of the whole—we can do no better today than to use the Freudian concepts of id, super-ego, and ego.

Suppose—to glance at a relatively broad aspect of the social scene—one wished to compare the culture of San Francisco with that of Los Angeles, a matter that might be of great importance for some aspects of California governmental policy. It would hardly do to employ the highly elaborated schemes and finely calibrated instruments that are used in research on small groups. The investigator who had something less than a lifetime to spend on this undertaking would decide upon a few gross categories that seemed to him important, and then content himself with rough estimates of them.

Most scientists, probably, would dislike the loss of rigor involved in this and would prefer to let George do it. And George, of course, has been very active. Decisions in big and important social matters are still based mainly on the observations and judgments of practical men. No doubt this will always be so to some extent since in practical matters there is a place for wisdom and judgments of value as well as for scientific knowledge. Still, scientists often feel free to criticize the day-to-day decisions that affect us all, and to complain that they are not consulted. This is an admission of their obligation to study complex problems and to show how their findings are relevant to practice. They may do this without being any the less scientific, in the best sense of the word, than the laboratory man. All they have to lose are the chains of respectability. Their procedure should be to suit their instruments to the task at hand, and to make sure that the gross categories used are consistent with what is known at

lower levels and lend themselves to reduction and systematic treatment.

LEVEL OF ABSTRACTION

When men are confronted with practical problems, their natural tendency is to focus on the concrete and particular. The psychotherapist, faced with the task of taking action on short notice, has to deal with what is happening to a particular patient in the situation of the moment; he cannot stop to translate his thoughts into the terms of a general theoretical system. The test specialist who wishes to develop an instrument for predicting some practically important pattern of overt behavior does not need abstract concepts to stand for general dispositions of personality; he can go far with a set of concrete test items that correlate with the behavior in which he is interested. And the business man or the administrator of an organization is likely to see his problems as particular, local, and pressing; he seeks solutions through manipulating plainly observable features of the immediate situation.

This kind of orientation to practical problems is a far cry from the most characteristic work of the scientist. The scientist interested in psychopathology must use terms for describing a patient that are sufficiently abstract so that one patient may be compared with others, and with nonpatients. The myriad specific acts of patients must be ordered to a conceptual scheme, so that future observations may be systematic, and general relationships among patients' processes may be established. As for organizations, one might say that we have hardly begun the scientific study of them until we have derived a set of abstract concepts—such as role, communication, power—that apply to organizations generally, so that we can carry over what we learn from one organization to the study of others. . . .

I am arguing that abstract theory is not only necessary to the development of a science of personality and social systems but also most use it in practice. Personality-social theory that is dynamic, holistic, and comprehensive, as practice demands, must be on a high level of abstraction. It is mainly through its use of hypothetical constructs that science gets beyond common sense, and it is in getting beyond common sense that its greatest usefulness lies. To revert to the example of prejudice: Most of what psychologists and social scientists have said about the situational, social, and economic determinants of prejudice conform well with what everybody knew already; to show that prejudice in some of its aspects springs from a hypothetical deeplying structure of personality is to go beyond the depth of the man in the street. At the same time it is to state a proposition whose implications for practice are very different from those that flow from the conventional wisdom.

My argument rests most heavily upon a conception of the nature of practical problems and of the role of science in efforts to solve them. We must inquire further into these matters. If we look at the history of psychology, it appears that there was a time when this science was far more concerned with practical problems than it is today, and that the results were not always to the good. For example, the early very practical concern with psychological tests led to many misapplications while contributing little to the advancement of psychology as a science. Again, the experiments of Thorndike and Woodworth (1901a, 1901b, 1901c) on "transfer of training" were carried on in an educational setting, with practice very much in mind. Their major conclusions, that learning was specific, that what was learned in one area of content or skill was not transferred to others, was immediately and very generally applied in the schools. This led to the introduction of all kinds of technical subjects into the schools, the proliferation of courses, the fragmentation of the curriculum. If children had not gone on transferring their training anyway, and if teachers had not continued to use their common sense, the results might have been even more serious. Experiences of this kind led the universities, in time, to become exceedingly wary of practice or "service," which were seen as restrictions upon the scientist's freedom to be

guided solely by his curiosity and to look for answers anywhere that he pleased. Hence the present accent on pure science, and the relegation of members of the professional schools to second-class citizenship.

I am arguing that the pendulum has now swung too far in the other direction, that psychology and social science have become too far removed from practice. Many early applications were premature, and science has gained from its period of withdrawal into "purity"; now it can afford to become involved with practice again, and in doing so it will fulfill its obligations and derive benefit for itself. . .

CHOICE OF PROBLEMS

A human-problems approach not only calls for a different theoretical orientation, it implies a different basis for choosing problems. I would like to see the new Institute include something of the following in its program:

1. Accent problems defined in terms of their human significance rather than in the terms of particular scientific disciplines. Study of these will require interdisciplinary theory and multidisciplinary research teams. It may work if the starting point is a human problem and not a disciplinary question or issue. And let us get away for the moment from the familiar psychiatric categories. I have in mind such problem areas as transitional stages, developmental crises, commitment (premature or delayed), institutional dependence, pleasure and play, problem drinking, aging.

2. Look at these problems in the perspective of long-range goals for the individual. If we want people to give up or get over some sort of problematic behavior we have to think of suitable alternatives to that behavior. Think about this for a while and we are bound to come to considerations of what is good for people and of what they might well become. Why not? There are good philosophical as well as practical reasons for this.

3. To think about long-range goals and how they might be reached we have to use a developmental perspective. We have

to consider present events with attention to their future consequences. Otherwise we can have no part in the planning of institutional arrangements for the development of young people. Nor can we have anything sensible to say about when is the best time to introduce young people to particular ideas or experiences.

4. If we adopt a developmental perspective there is no way to avoid attention to the whole life cycle. We cannot leave this whole area to Erik Erikson—and Charlotte Buhler. We have to have longitudinal studies, or suitable substitutes for them. At the least we must have studies of lives.

5. But study the conditions and processes of developmental change—in general, at any age. Assume that such changes can occur at any age. It is a matter of the right conditions being present. I say development in general—so I am interested in general laws. I mean organismic laws, which state relationships between part processes and the larger personal contexts in which they are imbedded.

6. This means study the general psychology of personality—particularly the general psychology of personality development. We have to conceive of structures in the person and we have to have theory to explain how these structures are modified through experience. Studies of structures—experimental studies or others—may of course be appropriately investigated in isolation, but there should be awareness of the fact that they *are* being studied in isolation and must eventually be related to persons.

7. Look at various kinds of social settings in which developmental changes occur, particularly settings that have been designed to modify people in some desired way: schools, training programs, correctional institutions, hospitals, psychotherapeutic programs, summer camps,

etc. Or, look at development in unnatural environments, forms of rigid institutionalization, for example, which result in regressive changes or fixations. Let all these settings be described and analyzed in sociological terms, but keep the focus of attention upon developmental change in individuals.

8. Give special attention to youth, but be flexible in defining its boundaries, and of course do not neglect its relation to earlier and later periods. Youth is a neglected area as compared with childhood and old age. It is not so much behavior of youth as development in youth that has been neglected. The theoretical bias has been that little or no development occurs during this period.

The study of development in youth is bound to force a confrontation of theoretical issues. It should lead to the production of new theory concerning the interaction of social and personality variables. If we assume that personality goes on developing, after the age of, say, 16, after the young person has been brought very much under the influence of factors outside the home, then we have to formulate such factors and conceive the ways in which they do their work. Classical personality theory has little to say on this subject—but it can be appropriately modified.

I have listed here special interests of my own. If the new Institute were to show that it really intends to support work of this kind, a great many other psychologists would take heart, believing that their interests would be served also. Proposals would come in from people who have not been heard from in Washington for some time; and new kinds of proposals would come in from scientists who saw a chance to do what they knew was important to the solution of human problems rather than what could be supported.

REFERENCES

Adorno, T. W., Frenkel-Brunswik, Else, Levinson, D. J., & Sanford, N. *The authoritarian personality.* New York: Harper, 1950.
Bridgman, P. W. *The logic of modern physics.* New York, Macmillan, 1927.

Klein, G. S. The personal world through perception. In R. R. Blake & G. V. Ramsey (Eds.), *Perception: An approach to personality.* New York: Ronald Press, 1951.
Rogers, C. R. A theory of therapy, person-

ality, and interpersonal relationships, as developed in the client-centered framework. In S. Koch (Ed.), *Psychology: A study of a science.* Vol. 3. New York: McGraw-Hill, 1959. Pp. 184–256.

Rogers, C. R., & Dymond, R. (Eds.) *Psychotherapy and personality change.* Chicago: Univer. Chicago Press, 1954.

Thorndike, E. L., & Woodworth, R. S. The influence of improvement in one mental function upon the efficiency of other functions. I. *Psychological Review,* 1901, *8,* 247–261. (a)

Thorndike, E. L., & Woodworth, R. S. The influence of improvement in one mental function upon the efficiency of other functions. II. The estimation of magnitudes. *Psychological Review,* 1901, *8,* 384–395. (b)

Thorndike, E. L., & Woodworth, R. S. The influence of improvement in one mental function upon the efficiency of other functions III. Functions involving attention, observation and discrimination. *Psychological Review,* 1901, *8,* 553–564. (c)

Witkin, H. A., Lewis, H. B., Hertzman, M. Machover, K., Meissner, Pearl B., & Wapner, S. *Personality through perception: An experimental and clinical study.* New York Harper, 1954.

4.
privacy and
behavioral research

preliminary summary
of the report of
the panel on privacy
and behavioral research

In recent years there have been growing threats to the privacy of individuals. Wiretapping, electronic eavesdropping, the use of personality tests in employment, the use of the lie detector in security or criminal investigations, and the detailed scrutiny of the private lives of people receiving public welfare funds all involve invasions of privacy. Although the social purpose is usually clear, the impact on the persons involved may be damaging. Our society has become more and more sensitive to the need to avoid such damage.

This concern has led to extensive discussion about the propriety of certain procedures in behavioral research, by the Congress, by officials in the various agencies of the government, by university officials, by the scientific community generally, and by leaders in professional societies in the behavioral sciences. The Office of Science and Technology appointed a panel, in January 1966, to examine these issues and to propose guidelines for those who are engaged in behavioral research or associated with its support and management.

The panel has restricted its attention to issues of privacy arising in connection with programs of data collection and study which are intimately associated with behavioral research. For example, it has not reviewed a number of the programs for data collection which are sponsored by the federal government, such as the various censuses, health and

Reprinted by permission from *Science*, February 3, 1967, *155* (3762), 535–538. Copyright 1967 by the American Association for the Advancement of Science.

welfare statistics, and financial information secured from business and industry. These programs may also encroach upon the privacy of individuals, either through the burden of disclosure which they impose on respondents or through their availability for unintended purposes.

It is our opinion that the principles described in this report for protection of privacy in behavioral research should apply equally to such inquiries. When response is mandatory, as in the case of information that must be furnished to the government, there is an even greater burden on the sponsoring agency to protect the individual against disclosure unless disclosure is specifically sanctioned by statute.

The panel has not reviewed in detail the wide variety of mechanical or electronic devices which make it possible to intrude into private lives. We have become acquainted with a few of the problems in that field, however, and are dismayed to observe the disregard for human values indicated by the advocacy or actual practice of eavesdropping, the use of lie detection without clear justification, and the frequent willingness to institute surveillance procedures to handle the problems of a small proportion of our population at the risk of eroding the rights and the quality of life for the majority.

Likewise, the panel has not reviewed in detail the propriety of procedures involved in employment or social welfare activities. Enough examples have been brought to our attention, however, to make us feel that examination of procedures in these spheres is needed also.

The attitudes of various segments of our society about proper procedures for the protection of privacy and the right to self-determination have been explored by the panel. It has reviewed relevant research in the behavioral sciences and the administrative practices of universities and government agencies. It has also consulted with the scientific community through its professional organizations.

THREATS TO PRIVACY

The right to privacy is the right of the individual to decide for himself how much he will share with others his thoughts, his feelings, and the facts of his personal life. It is a right that is essential to insure dignity and freedom of self-determination. In recent years there has been a severe erosion of this right by the widespread and often callous use of various devices for eavesdropping, lie detection, and secret observation in politics, in business, and in law enforcement. Indeed, modern electronic instruments for wiretapping and bugging have opened any human activity to the threat of illicit invasion of privacy. This unwholesome state of affairs has led to wide public concern over the methods of inquiry used by agencies of public employment, social welfare, and law enforcement.

Behavioral research, devoted as it is to the discovery of facts and principles underlying human activity of all types, comes naturally under scrutiny in any examination of possible threats to privacy. All of the social sciences, including economics, political science, anthropology, sociology, and psychology, take as a major object of study the behavior of individuals, communities, or other groups. In one context or another, investigators in all of these disciplines frequently need to seek information that is private to the men, women, and children who are the subjects of their study. In most instances this information is freely given by those who consent to cooperate in the scientific process. But the very nature of behavioral research is such that there is a risk of invasion of privacy if unusual care is not taken to secure the consent of research subjects, or if the data obtained are not given full confidentiality.

While the privacy problem in scientific research is small in comparison to that which exists in employment interviewing, social welfare screening, and law enforcement investigations, the opportunity for improper invasion is not negligible. About 35,000 behavioral scientists are engaged in research in the United States, 2,100 new Ph.D.'s are graduated each year, and the total number of students enrolled for advanced degrees in the behavioral sciences exceeds 40,000 at the present time.

It is probable that relatively few of the studies undertaken by these scientists raise serious questions of propriety in relation to privacy and human dignity. From a survey of articles published in professional journals and of research grant applications submitted to government agencies, we have concluded that most scientists who conduct research in privacy-sensitive areas are aware of the ethical implications of their experimental designs and arrange to secure the consent of subjects and to protect the confidentiality of the data obtained from them.

It cannot be denied, however, that in a limited number of instances, behavioral scientists have not followed appropriate procedures to protect the right of their subjects, and that in other cases recognition of the importance of privacy invading considerations has not been as sophisticated, or the considerations as affirmatively implemented, as good practice demands. Because of this failure there has been pressure from some quarters, both within the government and outside of it, to place arbitrary limits on the research methods which may be used. Behavioral scientists as a group do not question the importance of the right to privacy and are understandably concerned when suggestions are made that the detailed processes of science should be subjected to control by legislation or arbitrary administrative ruling. All scientists are opposed to restrictions which may curtail important research. At the same time they have an obligation to insure that all possible steps are taken to assure respect for the privacy and dignity of their subjects.

CONFLICTING RIGHTS

It is clear that there exists an important conflict between two values, both of which are strongly held in American society.

The individual has an inalienable right to dignity, self-respect, and freedom to determine his own thoughts and actions within the broad limits set by the requirements of society. The essential element in privacy and self-determination is the privilege of making one's own decision as to the extent to which one will reveal thoughts, feelings, and actions. When a person consents freely and fully to share himself with others—with a scientist, an employer, or a credit investigator—there is no invasion of privacy, regardless of the quality or nature of the information revealed.

Behavioral science is representative of another value vigorously championed by most American citizens, the right to know anything that may be known or discovered about any part of the universe. Man is part of this universe, and the extent of the federal government's financial support of human behavioral research (on the order of $300 million in 1966) testifies to the importance placed on the study of human behavior by the American people. In the past there have been conflicts between theological beliefs and the theoretical analyses of the physical sciences. These conflicts have largely subsided, but the behavioral sciences seem to have inherited the basic conflict that arises when strongly held beliefs or moral attitudes—whether theologically, economically, or politically based—are subjected to the free-ranging process of scientific inquiry. If society is to exercise its right to know, it must free its behavioral scientists as much as possible from unnecessary restraints. Behavioral scientists in turn must accept the constructive restraints that society imposes in order to establish that level of dignity, freedom, and personal fulfillment that men treasure virtually above all else in life.

The root of the conflict between the individual's right to privacy and society's right of discovery is the research process. Behavioral science seeks to assess and to measure many qualities of men's minds, feelings, and actions. In the absence of informed consent on the part of the subject, these measurements represent invasion of privacy. The scientist must therefore obtain the consent of his subject.

To obtain truly informed consent is often difficult. In the first place, the nature of the inquiry sometimes cannot be explained adequately because it involves complex variables that the nonscientist does not understand. Examples are the personality variables measured by questionnaires, and the qualities of cognitive processes measured by creativity tests. Secondly, the validity of an experiment is sometimes destroyed if the subject knows all the details of its conduct. Examples include drug-testing, in which the effect of suggestion (placebo effect) must be avoided, and studies of persuasability, in which the subjects remain ignorant of the influences that are being presented experimentally. Clearly, then, if behavioral research is to be effective, some modification of the traditional concept of informed consent is needed.

Such a change in no sense voids the more general proposition that the performance of human behavioral research is the product of a partnership between the scientist and his subject. Consent to participate in a study must be the norm before any subject embarks on the enterprise. Since consent must sometimes be given despite an admittedly inadequate understanding of the scientific purposes of the research procedures, the right to discontinue participation at any point must be stipulated in clear terms. In the meantime, when full information is not available to the subject and when no alternative procedures to minimize the privacy problem are available, the relationship between the subject and the scientist (and between the subject and the institution sponsoring the scientist) must be based upon trust. This places the scientist and the sponsoring institution under a fiduciary obligation to protect the privacy and dignity of the subject who entrusts himself to them. The scientist must agree to treat the subject fairly and with dignity, to cause him no inconvenience or discomfort unless the extent of the inconvenience and discomfort has been accepted by the subject in advance, to inform the subject as fully as possible of the purposes of the inquiry or experiment, and to put into effect all procedures which will assure the confidentiality of whatever information is obtained.

Occasionally, even this degree of consent cannot be obtained. Naturalistic observations of group behavior must sometimes be made unbeknownst to the subjects. In such cases, as well as in all others, the scientist has the obligation to insure full confidentiality of the research records. Only by doing so, and by making certain that published reports contain no identifying reference to a given subject, can the invasion of privacy be minimized.

Basically, then, the protection of privacy in research is assured first by securing the informed consent of the subject. When the subject cannot be completely informed, the consent must be based on trust in the scientist and in the institution sponsoring him. In any case the scientist and his sponsoring institution must insure privacy by the maintenance of confidentiality.

In the end, the fact must be accepted that human behavioral research will at times produce discomfort to some subjects, and will entail a partial invasion of their privacy. Neither the principle of privacy nor the need to discover new knowledge can supervene universally. As with other conflicting values in our society, there must be constant adjustment and compromise, with the decision as to which value is to govern in a given instance to be determined by a weighing of the costs and the gains—the cost in privacy, the gain in knowledge. The decision canot be made by the investigator alone, because he has a vested interest in his own research program, but must be a positive concern of his scientific peers and the institution which sponsors his work. Our society has grown strong on the principle of minimizing costs and maximizing gains and, when warmly held values are in conflict, there must be a thoughtful evaluation of the specific case. In particular we do not believe that detailed governmental controls of research

methods or instruments can substitute for the more effective procedures which are available and carry less risk of damage to the scientific enterprise.

ETHICAL ASPECTS OF HUMAN RESEARCH

Greater attention must be given to the ethical aspects of human research. The increase in scientists and in volume of research provides more chance for carelessness or recklessness and, in the hurried search for useful findings, can lead to abuses. Furthermore, if standards are not carefully maintained, there could develop an atmosphere of disregard for privacy that would be altogether alien to the spirit of American society. The increased potentials for damage and for fruitful outcomes from new knowledge are in no small part results of increased federal support of behavioral science. While no one would suggest that ethical standards should be different for scientists supported by public funds and for those supported by private funds, the government has an especially strong obligation to support research only under conditions that give fullest protection to individual human dignity. Government must avow and maintain the highest standards for the guidance of all.

To summarize, three parties—the investigator, his institution, and the sponsoring agency—have the responsibility for maintaining proper ethical standards with respect to government-sponsored research. The investigator designs the research and is in the best position to evaluate the propriety of his procedures. He has, therefore, the ultimate responsibility for insuring that his research is both effective and ethical.

The formalization of our ethics concerning privacy in connection with research is too recent, and perhaps too incomplete, to permit the assumption that all investigators have a full understanding of the proper methods for protecting the rights of subjects. Furthermore, the investigator is first and foremost a scientist in search of new knowledge, and it would not be in accord with our understanding of human motivation to expect him always to be as vigilant for his subject's welfare as he is for the productiveness of his own research.

We conclude, therefore, that responsibility must also be borne by the institution which employs the investigator. The employing institution is often a university or a government laboratory in which there are other scientists capable of reviewing the research plan. Such persons, drawn in part from disciplines other than the behavioral sciences, can present views that are colored neither by self-interest nor by the blind spots that may characterize the specific discipline of the investigator.

Finally, the sponsoring agency is obligated to make certain that both the investigator and his institution are fully aware of the importance of the ethical aspects of the research and that they have taken the necessary steps to discharge their responsibility to the human subjects involved. We believe that, in the majority of instances, it is neither necessary nor desirable for an agency to exceed this level of responsibility.

CONCLUSIONS

From our examination of the relation of behavioral science research to the right to privacy, we have been led to the following conclusions.

1) While most current practices in the field pose no significant threat to the privacy of research subjects, a sufficient number of exceptions have been noted to warrant a sharp increase in attention to procedures that will assure protection of this right. The increasing scale of behavioral research is itself an additional reason for focusing attention in this area.

2) Participation by subjects must be voluntary and based on informed consent to the extent that this is consistent with the objectives of the research. It is fully consistent with the protection of privacy that, in the absence of full information, consent be based on trust in the qualified investigator and the integrity of his institution.

3) The scientist has an obligation to insure that no permanent physical or psychological harm will ensue from the research procedures, and that temporary discomfort or loss of privacy will be remedied in an appropriate way during the course of the research or at its completion. To merit trust, the scientist must design his research with a view to protecting, to the fullest extent possible, the privacy of the subjects. If intrusion on privacy proves essential to the research, he should not proceed with his proposed experiment until he and his colleagues have considered all of the relevant facts and he has determined, with support from them, that the benefits outweigh the costs.

4) The scientist has the same responsibility to protect the privacy of the individual in published reports and in research records that he has in the conduct of the research itself.

5) The primary responsibility for the use of ethical procedures must rest with the individual investigator, but government agencies that support behavioral research should satisfy themselves that the institution which employs the investigator has effectively accepted its responsibility to require that he meet proper ethical standards.

6) Legislation to assure appropriate recognition of the rights of human subjects is neither necessary nor desirable if the scientists and sponsoring institutions fully discharge their responsibilities in accommodating to the claim of privacy. Because of its relative inflexibility, legislation cannot meet the challenge of the subtle and sensitive conflict of values under consideration, nor can it aid in the wise decision making by individuals which is required to assure optimum protection of subjects, together with the fullest effectiveness of research.

RECOMMENDATIONS

These conclusions lead us to make the following recommendations.

1) That government agencies supporting research in their own laboratories or in outside institutions require those institutions to agree to accept responsibility for the ethical propriety of human research performed with the aid of government funds.

2) That the methods used for institutional review be determined by the institutions themselves. The greatest possible flexibility of methods should be encouraged in order to build effective support for the principle of institutional responsibility within universities or other organizations. Institutions differ in their internal structures and operating procedures, and no single rigid formula will work for all.

3) That investigators and institutions be notified of the importance of consent and confidentiality as ethical requirements in research design, and that when either condition cannot be met, an explanation of the reasons be made in the application for funds.

4) That when research is undertaken directly by, or purchased on specification by, a government agency, responsibility for protection of privacy lies with the agency. When independent research is funded by the government, however, responsibility lies primarily with the scientist and his institution, and research instruments or design should not be subject to detailed review by government agencies with respect to protection of privacy.

5) That universities and professional associations be encouraged to emphasize the ethical aspects of behavioral research. When a training grant is made, a university should be requested to indicate its understanding that support of education on the ethics of research is one of the purposes of the grant.

REVIEW QUESTIONS

1. What is (are) the difference(s) in terms of training and professional activities among psychologists, psychiatrists, and psychoanalysts?
2. How does a clinical psychologist differ from a psychiatrist?
3. What does Walker say is the essential difference between basic and applied research?
4. Who, according to Walker, should evaluate the value of basic research and what criterion should be used?
5. What is the "holistic premise" as discussed in Sanford's article?
6. Has psychology in its entire history ever been concerned with practical problems? What does Sanford say caused psychology's present stance of being too far removed from human problems?
7. The Panel on Privacy and Behavioral Research describes two basic rights that seem to be in conflict in the case of psychological research. What are they and how does the panel suggest the conflict can be resolved?
8. Discuss the problems involved in obtaining consent from a participant serving as a subject in a psychological study.

part two
brain and behavior

Perhaps the most difficult topic in the introductory psychology course to generate enthusiasm for is physiological psychology. Students often feel that such material is more appropriately covered in a biology course and fail to see why its inclusion is important. That such reactions exist almost certainly is the fault of the instructor and introductory textbooks.

All behavior, of course, ultimately depends upon the underlying neural apparatus. Any meaningful study of psychology must include consideration of the workings of the brain and nervous system. The students' negative reaction probably stems from the fact that little or no attempt is made to point up the current social relevance of such research and its future possible application.

The social importance of Wilder Penfield's report, "The Interpretive Cortex" (#5), is not always obvious at first glance. The thoughtful student will, however, realize that Penfield's research presents the interesting possibility that a record of all of man's experiences and thoughts is permanently stored in the brain. The fact that man is unable to recall much of his previous experience is presumably due to his inability to activate or utilize appropriately great portions of the cortex. One can only speculate at this point as to what use(s) Penfield's basic findings will lead. After extensive research, it is possible that realistic and effective techniques will be developed enabling us to selectively remember any event of our past lives in great detail. Such techniques could involve artificial stimulating devices such as Penfield used in his brain surgery research or, possibly, man possesses within himself some presently unknown capacity for such precise memory. Many brain scientists find it extremely ironic that man must travel many millions of miles to explore his "last frontier." While space research is inherently interesting and important, one can only stress that within our own brains we certainly have a relatively unexplored frontier as well.

The discovery of "pleasure centers "in the rat brain is viewed by many brain scientists as one of the most significant research findings of this or any century. As noted by Jacques St. Laurent and James Olds (#6), rats will learn complex tasks and endure great pain simply to have stimulation (a small quantity of electrical current) applied to certain areas in the brain. This brain stimulation seems to be the most powerful or potent reinforcer that an experimental psychologist can utilize to motivate a rat in that these animals will choose it over food when they are hungry or water when thirsty. A male rat will also choose brain stimulation over a sexually receptive female rat. In one study, rats were allowed to stimulate their own brains by pushing a small bar. In such a situation, the animals will literally starve themselves to death, refusing to take time to eat or drink even though food and water are always available in the cage.

Located only a few millimeters away from these "pleasure centers" are areas which upon stimulation seem to produce extremely unpleasant sensations for the rat. Such "negatively reinforcing sites" can also be utilized extremely effectively to motivate or change the

animal's behavior. Rats will do almost anything—learn complex tasks, suffer great pain, etc.—simply to turn off the brain stimulation. In addition to rats, positive and negative brain sites have been found in a whole variety of species—including man!

Robert G. Heath, in his report "Electrical Self-Stimulation of the Brain in Man" (#7), describes the results from two human patients who have had electrodes permanently implanted in their brains. The subjective reports of these patients are surprisingly consistent with what would have been predicted from the animal studies. In presenting this material to my own introductory psychology classes over the years, I have always encountered both fear and hostility from large numbers of students. Such reactions, it seems to me, are justified and I personally share them to some extent. Fear, because the possibilities for social control in our society are immense utilizing such techniques; hostility stems from the fear reaction and also the humanistic tendency within all of us is offended by such research. It must be stressed, however, that the surgery and the resultant experimentation was only undertaken as a therapeutic measure. The entire scientific community would unanimously condemn any such research if it were undertaken for any but this reason.

The fact still remains that such techniques exist and there is really no certain way of predicting what the future will bring. Some students point out that there is no real need for concern because of our rather limited present technology. One can only respond that 20 years ago the feasibility of putting a man on the moon seemed remote as well.

The possible therapeutic applications of brain stimulation are further presented in the selection by José Delgado and his colleagues (#8). Technology has progressed to the point where it is no longer necessary to actually attach wire leads to the electrodes coming from the patient's brain. Radio waves can now be used to stimulate the appropriate brain areas. The patients also carry a small FM transmitter with them which can transmit the electrical activity occurring in the brain. By being able to both record and stimulate simultaneously and/or independently Delgado's work is particularly important for patients suffering from epileptic seizures and holds great therapeutic possibilities.

The final article in this part is by R. W. Sperry and is entitled "Hemisphere Deconnection and Unity in Conscious Awareness" (#9). The research described is a good example of how valuable animal research can be in the solution of human problems. The "split-brain" technique was developed and tested extensively on higher mammals before it was tried on human epileptics. The therapeutic success that has resulted must at least partially be attributed to the years of basic animal research.

The report also illustrates simultaneously the great progress that has been made in our understanding of brain function and how many basic unanswered questions still remain.

5.
the interpretive cortex
the stream of consciousness
in the human brain
can be electrically reactivated

wilder penfield

There is an area of the surface of the human brain where local electrical stimulation can call back a sequence of past experience. An epileptic irritation in this area may do the same. It is as though a wire recorder, or a strip of cinematographic film with sound track, had ben set in motion within the brain. The sights and sounds, and the thoughts, of a former day pass through the man's mind again.

The purpose of this article is to describe, for readers from various disciplines of science, the area of the cerebral cortex from which this neuron record of the past can be activated and to suggest what normal contribution it may make to cerebral function.

The human brain is the master organ of the human race. It differs from the brains of other mammals particularly in the greater extent of its cerebral cortex. The gray matter, or cortex, that covers the two cerebral hemispheres of the brain of man is so vast in nerve cell population that it could never have been contained within the human skull if it were not folded upon itself, and refolded, so as to form a very large number of fissures and convolutions (Figure 1). The fissures are so deep and so devious that by far the greater portion of this ganglionic carpet (about 65 percent) is hidden in them, below the surface.

The portion that is labeled "interpretive" in Figures 1 and 2 covers a part

Reprinted from *Science*, June 26, 1959, *129* (3365), 1719–1725. Copyright 1959 by the American Association for the Advancement of Science. Abridged by permission of the author.

of both temporal lobes. It is from these two homologous areas, and from nowhere else, that electrical stimulation has occasionally produced physical responses which may be divided into (i) experiential responses and (ii) interpretive responses.

EXPERIENTIAL RESPONSES

Occasionally during the course of a neurosurgical operation under local anesthesia, gentle electrical stimulation in this temporal area, right or left, has caused the conscious patient to be aware of some previous experience (1). The experience seems to be picked out at random from his own past. But it comes back to him in great detail. He is suddenly aware again of those things to which he paid attention in that distant

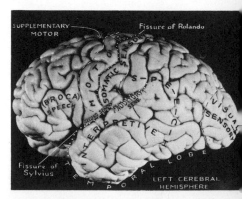

Figure 1. Photograph of the left hemisphere of a human brain. The frontal lobe is on the left, the occipital lobe on the right. The major motor and sensory areas are indicated, as well as the speech areas and the interpretive area. [Penfield and Roberts (18)]

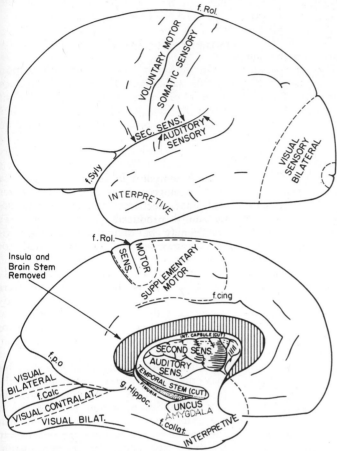

Figure 2. The left cerebral hemisphere; the lateral surface is shown above and the mesial surface below. In the lower drawing the brain stem with the island of Reil has been removed to show the inner banks of the fissure of Sylvius and the superior surface of the temporal lobe. The interpretive cortex extends from the lateral to the superior surface of the temporal lobe. [Penfield and Roberts (18)]

interval of time. This recollection of an experiential sequence stops suddenly when the electrical current is switched off or when the electrode is removed from contact with the cortex. This phenomenon we have chosen to call an experiential response to stimulation.

Case Examples (2). The patient S.Be. observed, when the electrode touched the temporal lobe (right superior temporal convolution), "There was a piano over there and someone playing. I could hear the song you know." When the cortex was stimulated again without warning, at approximately the same point, the pa-

tient had a different experience. He said: "Someone speaking to another, and he mentioned a name but I could not understand it . . . It was like a dream." Again the point was restimulated without his knowledge. He said quietly: "Yes, 'Oh Marie, Oh Marie'! Someone is singing it." When the point was stimulated a fourth time he heard the same song again and said it was the "theme song of a radio program."

The electrode was then applied to a point 4 centimeters farther forward on the first temporal convolution. While the electrode was still in place, S.Be. said:

"Something brings back a memory. I can see Seven-Up Bottling Company—Harrison Bakery." He was evidently seeing two of Montreal's large illuminated advertisements.

The surgeon then warned him that he was about to apply the electrode again. Then, after a pause, the surgeon said "Now," but he did not stimulate. (The patient has no means of knowing when the electrode is applied, unless he is told, since the cortex itself is without sensation.) The patient replied promptly, "Nothing."

A woman (D.F.) (3) heard an orchestra playing an air while the electrode was held in place. The music stopped when the electrode was removed. It came again when the electrode was reapplied. On request, she hummed the tune, while the electrode was held in place, accompanying the orchestra. It was a popular song. Over and over again, restimulation at the same spot produced the same song. The music seemed always to begin at the same place and to progress at the normally expected tempo. All efforts to mislead her failed. She believed that a gramaphone was being turned on in the operating room on each occasion, and she asserted her belief stoutly in a conversation some days after the operation.

A boy (R.W.) heard his mother talking to someone on the telephone when an electrode was applied to his right temporal cortex. When the stimulus was repeated without warning, he heard his mother again in the same conversation. When the stimulus was repeated after a lapse of time, he said, "My mother is telling my brother he has got his coat on backwards. I can just hear them."

The surgeon then asked the boy whether he remembered this happening. "Oh yes," he said, "just before I came here." Asked again whether this seemed like a dream, he replied: "No, it is like I go into a daze."

J.T. cried out in astonishment when the electrode was applied to the temporal cortex; "Yes doctor, yes doctor. Now I hear people laughing—my friends in South Africa!"

When asked about this, he explained the reason for his surprise. He seemed to be laughing with his cousins, Bessie and Ann Wheliow, whom he had left behind him on a farm in South Africa, although he knew he was now on the operating table in Montreal.

INTERPRETIVE RESPONSES

On the other hand, similar stimulation in this same general area may produce quite a different response. The patient discovers, on stimulation, that he has somehow changed his own interpretation of what he is seeing at the moment, or hearing or thinking. For example, he may exclaim that his present experience seems familiar, as though he had seen it or heard it or thought it before. He realizes that this must be a false interpretation. Or, on the contrary, these things may seem suddenly strange, absurd. Sights or sounds may seem distant and small, or they may come unexpectedly close and seem loud or large. He may feel suddenly afraid, as though his environment were threatening him, and he is possessed by a nameless dread or panic. Another patient may say he feels lonely or aloof, or as though he were observing himself at a distance.

Under normal circumstances anyone may make such interpretations of the present, and these interpretations serve him as guides to action or reaction. If the interpretations are accurate guides they must be based upon previous comparable experience. It is conceivable, therefore, that the recall mechanism which is activated by the electrode during an experiential response and the mechanism activated in an interpretive response may be parts of a common inclusive mechanism of reflex recognition or interpretation.

No special function had been previously assigned by neurologists to the area in each temporal lobe that is marked "interpretive" in Figures 1 and 2 though some clinicians have suggested it might have to do with the recall of music. The term *interpretive cortex*, therefore, is no more than slang to be employed for the purposes of discussion. The terms *motor cortex*, *sensory cortex*, and *speech cortex* began as slang phrases and have served such a purpose. But such phrases must not be understood to signify independence of action of separated units in the case of any of these areas. Localization of function in the cerebral cortex means no more than specialization of function as compared with other cortical regions, not separation from the integrated action of the brain.

Before considering the interpretive cortex further, we may turn briefly to the motor and sensory areas and the speech areas of the cortex. After considering the effects of electrical stimulation there, we should be better able to understand the results of stimulation in the temporal lobes.

SPECIALIZATION OF FUNCTION IN THE CORTEX

Evidence for some degree of localization within the brain was recognized early in the 19th century by Flourens. He concluded from experiment that functional subdivision of "the organ of the mind" was possible. The forebrain (4), he said [cerebral hemispheres and higher brain stem] had to do with thought and will power, while the cerebellum was involved in the coordination of movement.

In 1861, Paul Broca showed that a man with a relatively small area of destruction in a certain part of the left hemisphere

alone might lose only the power of speech. It was soon realized that this was the speech area of man's dominant (left) hemisphere. In 1870, Fritsch and Hitzig applied an electric current to the exposed cortex of one hemisphere of a lightly anesthetized dog and caused the legs of the opposite side to move. Thus, an area of cortex called motor was discovered.

After that, localization of function became a research target for many clinicians and experimentalists. It was soon evident that in the case of man, the precentral gyrus (Figure 3) in each hemisphere was related to voluntary control of the contralateral limbs and that there was an analogous area of motor cortex in the frontal lobes of animals. It appeared also that other separate areas of cortex (Figures 1 and 3) in each hemisphere were dedicated to sensation (one for visual sensation, others for auditory, olfactory, and discriminative somatic sensation, respectively).

It was demonstrated, too, that from the "motor cortex" there was an efferent bundle of nerve fibers (the pyramidal tract) that ran down through the lower brain stem and the spinal cord to be relayed on out to the muscles. Through this

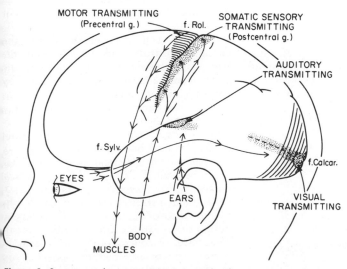

Figure 3. Sensory and motor projection areas. The sensory areas are stippled; and the afferent pathways to them from eyes, ears, and body are indicated by entering arrows. The motor cortex is indicated by parallel lines, and the efferent corticospinal tract is indicated by emerging arrows. [Penfield and Roberts (**18**)]

efferent pathway, voluntary control of these muscles was actually carried out. It was evident, too, that there were separate sensory tracts carrying nerve impulses in the other direction, from the principal organs of special sense (eye, ear, nose, and skin and muscle) into separate sensory areas of the cortex.

These areas, motor and sensory, have been called "projection areas." They play a role in the projection of nerve currents to the cortex from the periphery of the body, and from the cortex to the periphery. This makes possible (sensory) awareness of environment and provides the individual with a means of outward (motor) expression. The motor cortex has a specialized use during voluntary action, and each of the several sensory areas has a specialized use, when the individual is seeing, hearing, smelling, or feeling.

TRAVELING POTENTIALS

The action of the living brain depends upon the movement, within it, of "transient electrical potentials traveling the fibers of the nervous system." This was Sherrington's phrase. Within the vast circuits of this master organ, potentials travel, here and there and yonder, like meteors that streak across the sky at night and line the firmament with trails of light. When the meteors pass, the paths of luminescence still glow a little while, then fade and are gone. The changing patterns of these paths of passing energy make possible the changing content of the mind. The patterns are never quite the same, and so it is with the content of the mind.

Specialized areas in the cortex are at times active and again relatively quiet. But, when a man is awake, there is always some central integration and coordination of the traveling potentials. There must be activity within the brain stem and some areas of the cortex. This is centrencephalic integration (5).

SENSORY, MOTOR, AND PSYCHICAL RESPONSES TO CORTICAL STIMULATION

My purpose in writing this article is to discuss in simple words (free of tech-nical terms) the meaning of the "psychical" responses which appear only on stimulation of the so-called interpretive cortex. But before considering these responses let us consider the motor and sensory activity of the cortex for a moment.

When the streams of electrical potentials that pass normally through the various areas of sensory cortex are examined electrically, they do not seem to differ from each other except in pattern and timing. The essential difference is to be found in the fact that the visual stream passes to the visual cortex and then to one subcortical target and the auditory stream passes through the auditory cortex and then on to another subcortical target.

When the surgeon stimulates the intact sensory cortex he must be sending a current along the next "piece of road" to a subcortical destination. This electrode (delivering, for example, 60 "waves" per second of 2-millisecond duration and 1-volt intensity) produces no more than elementary sight when applied to visual cortex. The patient reports colors, lights, and shadows that move and take on crude outlines. The same electrode, applied to auditory cortex, causes him to hear a ringing or hissing or thumping sound. When applied to postcentral gyrus it produces tingling or a false sense of movement.

Thus, sensation is produced by the passage inward of electrical potentials. And when the electrode is applied to the motor cortex, movement is produced by passage of potentials outward to the muscles. In each case positive response is produced by conduction in the direction of normal physiological flow—that is, by dromic conduction (6).

Responses to electrical stimulation that may be called "psychical," as distinguished from sensory or motor, have been elicited from certain areas of the human cortex. But they have never been produced by stimulation in other areas. There are, of course, other large areas of cortex which are neither sensory nor motor in function. They seem to be employed in other neuron mechanisms that are also associated with psychical processes. But the function of these other areas cannot, it seems, be activated by so simple a stimulus as an electric current applied to the cortex.

DREAMY STATES OF EPILEPSY

"Epilepsy" may be defined, in Jackson's words, as "the name for occasional, sudden, excessive, rapid and local discharges of grey matter." Our aim in the operations under discussion was to remove the gray matter responsible for epileptic attacks if that gray matter could be spared. When the stimulating electrode reproduced the psychical phenomenon that initiated the fit, it provided the guidance sought (7).

During the 19th century clinicians had recognized these phenomena as epileptic. They applied the term *intellectual aura* to such attacks. Jackson substituted the expression *dreamy states* (see 8). These were, he said, "psychical states during the onset of certain epileptic seizures, states which are much more elaborate than crude sensations." And again, he wrote, "These are all voluminous mental states and yet of different kinds; no doubt they ought to be classified, but for my present purpose they may be considered together."

"The state," he said, "is often like that occasionally experienced by healthy people as a feeling of 'reminiscence.'" Or the patient has "dreamy feelings," "dreams mixing up with present thoughts," "double consciousness," a "feeling of being somewhere else," a feeling "as if I went back to all that occurred in my childhood," "silly thoughts."

Jackson never did classify these states, but he did something more important. He localized the area of cortex from which epileptic discharge would produce dreamy states. His localization was in the anterior and deep portions of the temporal lobes, the same area that is labeled "interpretive" cortex in Figure 2.

Case Example. Brief reference may be made to a specific case. The patient had seizures, and stimulation produced responses which were first recognized as psychical.

In 1936, a girl of 16 (J.V.) was admitted to the Montreal Neurological Institute complaining of epileptic attacks, each of which was ushered in by the same hallucination. It was a little dream, she said, in which an experience from early childhood was reenacted, always the same train of events. She would then cry out with fear and run to her mother. Occasionally this was followed immediately by a major convulsive seizure.

At operation, under local anesthesia, we tried to set off the dream by a gentle electrical stimulus in the right temporal lobe. The attempt was successful. The dream was produced by the electrode. Stimulation at other points on the temporal cortex produced sudden fear without the dream. At still other points, stimulation caused her to say that she saw "someone coming toward me." At another point, stimulation caused her to say she heard the voices of her mother and her brothers (9).

This suggested a new order of cortical response to electrical stimulation. When the neighboring visual sensory area of the cortex is stimulated, any patient may report seeing stars of light or moving colors or black outlines but never "someone coming toward me." Stimulation of the auditory sensory cortex may cause any patient to report that he hears ringing, buzzing, blowing, or thumping sounds, perhaps, but never voices that speak. Stimulation in the areas of sensory cortex can call forth nothing more than the elements of visual or auditory or tactile sensation, never happenings that might have been previously experienced.

During the 23 years that have followed, although practically all areas of the cerebral cortex have been stimulated and studied in more than 1000 craniotomies, performed under local anesthesia, psychical responses of the experiential or interpretive variety have been produced only from the temporal cortex in the general areas that are marked "psychical responses" in Figure 2 (10, 11).

CLASSIFICATION

It seems reasonable to subdivide psychical responses and psychical seizures (epileptic dreamy states) in the same way, classifying them as "interpretive" or "experiential." Interpretive psychical responses are those involving interpretations of the present experience, or emotions related to it; experiential psychical responses are reenactments of past experiences. Interpretive seizures are those accompanied by auras and illusions; experiential seizures are those accompanied by auras and hallucinations.

The interpretive responses and seizures may be divided into groups (11) of which the commonest are as follows: (i) recognition, the illusion that things seen and heard and thought are familiar (déjà vu phenomenon); (ii) visual illusion, the illusion that things seen are changing—for example, coming nearer; growing larger (macropsia); (iii) auditory illusion, the illusion that things heard are changing—for example, coming near, going away, changing tempo; (iv) illusional emotion, the emotion of fear or, less often, loneliness, sorrow, or disgust.

Experiential phenomena (hallucinations) are an awareness of experiences from the past that come into the mind without complete loss of awareness of the present.

DISCUSSION

What, then, is the function of the interpretive cortex? This is a physiological question that follows the foregoing observations naturally.

An electrode, delivering, for example, 60 electrical pulses per second to the surface of the motor cortex, causes a man to make crude movements. When applied to the various sensory areas of the cortex, it causes him to have crude sensations of sight or sound or body feeling. This indicates only that these areas have something to do with the complicated mechanism of voluntary action or conscious sensation. It does not reveal what contribution the cortex may make, or in what way it may contribute to skill in making voluntary movement or qualify the incoming sensory streams.

In the case of the interpretive cortex, the observations are similar. We may say that the interpretive cortex has something to do with a mechanism that can reactivate the vivid record of the past. It has also something to do with a mechanism that can present to consciousness a reflex

interpretation of the present. To conclude that here is the mechanism of memory would be an unjustified assumption. It would be too simple.

What a man remembers when he makes a voluntary effort is apt to be a generalization. If this were not so, he might be hopelessly lost in detail. On the other hand, the experiential responses described above are detailed reenactments of a single experience. Such experiences soon slip beyond the range of voluntary recall. A man may summon to mind a song at will. He hears it then in his mind, not all at once but advancing phrase by phrase. He may sing it or play it too, and one would call this memory.

But if a patient hears music in response to the electrode, he hears it in one particular strip of time. That time runs forward again at the original tempo, and he hears the orchestration, or he sees the player at a piano "over there." These are details he would have thought forgotten.

A vast amount of work remains to be done before the mechanism of memory, and how and where the recording takes place, are understood. This record is not laid down in the interpretive cortex, but it is kept in a part of the brain that is intimately connected with it.

Removal of large areas of interpretive cortex, even when carried out on both sides, may result in mild complaints of memory defect, but it does not abolish the capacity to remember recent events. On the other hand, surgical removals that result in bilateral interference with the underlying hippocampal zone do make the recording of recent events impossible, while distant memory is still preserved (12, 13).

The importance of the hippocampal area for memory was pointed out long ago in a forgotten publication by the Russian neurologist Bechterew (14). The year before publication Bechterew had demonstrated the case before the St Petersburg Clinic for Nervous and Mental Diseases. The man on whom Bechterew reported had "extraordinary weakness of memory, falsifications of memory and great apathy." These defects were shown at autopsy to be secondary to lesions of the mesial surface of the cortex of both temporal lobes. The English neurologists Glees and Griffith (15) reported similar defects, a half century later, in a patient who had symmetrical lesions of the hippocampus and of hippocampal and fusiform gyri on both sides.

The way in which the interpretive cortex seems to be used may be suggested by an example: After years of absence you meet, by chance, a man whose very existence you had forgotten. On seeing him, you may be struck by a sudden sense of familiarity, even before you have time to "think." A signal seems to flash up in consciousness to tell you that you've seen that man before. You watch him as he smiles and moves and speaks. The sense of familiarity grows stronger. Then you remember him. You may even recall that his name was Jones. The sight and the sound of the man has given you an instant access, through some reflex, to the records of the past in which this man has played some part. The opening of this forgotten file was subconscious. It was not a voluntary act. You would have known him even against your will. Although Jones was a forgotten man a moment before, now you can summon the record in such detail that you remark at once the slowness of his gait or a new line about the mouth.

If Jones had been a source of danger to you, you might have felt fear as well as familiarity before you had time to consider the man. Thus, the signal of fear as well as the signal of familiarity may come to one as the result of subconscious comparison of present with similar past experience.

One more example may be given from common experience. A sudden increase in the size of objects seen and in sounds heard may mean the rapid approach of something that calls for instant avoidance action. These are signals that, because of previous experience, we sometimes act upon with little consideration.

SUMMARY

The interpretive cortex has in it a mechanism for instant reactivation of the detailed record of the past. It has a mechanism also for the production of interpretive signals. Such signals could only be significant if past records are scanned and relevant experiences are selected for comparison with present experience. This is a subconscious process. But it may well be that this scanning of past experience and selection from it also renders the relevant past available for conscious consideration as well. Thus, the individual may refer to the record as he employs other circuits of the brain.

Access to the record of the past seems to be as readily available from the temporal cortex of one side as from that of the other. Auditory illusions (or interpretations of the distance, loudness, or tempo of sounds) have been produced by stimulation of the temporal cortex of either side. The same is true of illusional emotions, such as fear and disgust.

But, on the contrary, visual illusions (interpretations of the distance, dimension, erectness, and tempo of things seen) are only produced by stimulation of the temporal cortex on the nondominant (normally, right) side of the brain. Illusions of recognition, such as familiarity or strangeness, were also elicited only from the nondominant side, except in one case.

CONCLUSION

"Consciousness," to quote William James (16), "is never quite the same in successive moments of time. It is a stream forever flowing, forever changing." The stream of changing states of mind that James described so well does flow through each man's waking hours until the time when he falls asleep to wake no more. But the stream, unlike a river, leaves a record in the living brain.

Transient electrical potentials move with it through the circuits of the nervous system, leaving a path that can be followed again. The pattern of this pathway, from neuron to neuron along each nerve-cell body and fiber and junction, is the recorded pattern of each man's past. That complicated record is held there in temporal sequence through the principle of durable facilitation of conduction and connection.

A steady stream of electrical pulses applied through an electrode to some point in the interpretive cortex causes a stream of excitation to flow from the cortex to the place where past experience is recorded. This stream of excitation acts as a key to the past. It can enter the pathway of recorded consciousness at any random point, from childhood on through adult life. But having entered, the experience moves forward without interference from other experiences. And when the electrode is withdrawn there is a likelihood, which lasts for seconds or minutes, that the stream of excitation will enter the pathway again at the same moment of past time, even if the electrode is reapplied at neighboring points (17).

Finally, an electric current applied to the surface of what may be called the interpretive cortex of a conscious man (i) may cause the stream of former consciousness to flow again or (ii) may give him an interpretation of the present that is unexpected and involuntary. Therefore, it is concluded that, under normal circumcumstances, this area of cortex must make some functional contribution to reflex comparison of the present with related past experience. It contributes to reflex interpretation or perception of the present.

The combination and comparison of present experience with similar past experience must call for remarkable scanning of the past and classification of similarities. What contribution this area of the temporal cortex may make to the whole process is not clear. The term *interpretive cortex* will serve for identification until students of human physiology can shed more light on these fascinating findings.

REFERENCES AND NOTES

1. W. Penfield, *J. Mental Sci. 101*, 451 (1955).

2. These patients, designated by the same initials, have been described in previous publications in much greater detail. An index of patients (designated by initials) may be found in any of my books.

3. This case is reported in detail in W. Penfield and H. Jasper, *Epilepsy and the Functional Anatomy of the Human Brain* (Little, Brown, Boston, 1954) [published in abridged form in Russian (translation by N. P. Graschenkov and G. Smirnov) by the Soviet Academy of Sciences, 1958].

4. The forebrain, or prosencephalon, properly includes the diencephalon and the telencephalon, or higher brain stem, and hemispheres. Flourens probably had cerebral hemispheres in mind as distinguished from cerebellum.

5. "Within the brain, a central transactional core has been identified between the strictly sensory or motor systems of classical neurology. This central reticular mechanism has been found capable of grading the activity of most other parts of the brain"— H. Magoun, *The Waking Brain* (Thomas, Springfield, Ill., 1958).

6. W. Penfield, *The Excitable Cortex in Conscious Man* (Thomas, Springfield, Ill., 1958).

7. It did more than this; it produced illusions or hallucinations that had never been experienced by the patient during a seizure.

8. J. Taylor, Ed., *Selected Writings of John Hughlings Jackson* (Hodder and Stoughton, London, 1931), vol. 1, *On Epilepsy and Epileptiform Convulsions*.

9. Twenty-one years later this young woman, who is the daughter of a physician, was present at a meeting of the National Academy of Sciences in New York while her case was discussed. She could still recall the operation and the nature of the "dreams" that had preceded her seizures [W. Penfield, *Proc. Natl. Acad. Sci. U.S. 44*, 51 (1958)].

10. In a recent review of the series my associate, Dr. Phanor Perot, has found and summarized 35 out of 384 temporal lobe cases in which stimulation produced experiential responses. All such responses were elicited in the temporal cortex. In a study of 214 consecutive operations for temporal lobe epilepsy, my associate Sean Mullan found 70 cases in which interpretive illusion occurred in the minor seizures before operation, or in which an interpretive response was produced by stimulation during operation. In most cases it occurred both before and during operation.

11. S. Mullan and W. Penfield, *A.M.A. Arch. Neurol. Psychiat. 81*, 269 (1959).

12. This area is marked . . . "g. Hippoc." and "amygdala" in Figure 2.

13. W. Penfield and B. Milner, *A.M.A. Arch. Neurol. Psychiat. 79*, 475 (1958).

14. W. V. Bechterew, "Demonstration eines Gehirns mit Zerstörung der vorderen und inneren Theile der Hirnrinde beider

Schläfenlappen," *Neurol. Zentralbl. Leipzig* *19*, 990 (1900). My attention was called to this case recently by Dr. Peter Gloor of Montreal.

15. P. Glees and H. B. Griffith, *Monatsschr. Psychiat. Neurol. 123*, 193 (1952).

16. W. James, *The Principles of Psychology* (Holt, New York, 1910).

17. Thus, it is apparent that the beam of excitation that emanates from the interpretive cortex and seems to scan the record of the past is subject to the principles of transient facilitation already demonstrated for the anthropiod motor cortex [A. S. F. Grünbaum and C. Sherrington, *Proc. Roy. Soc. (London)* 72B, 152 (1901); T. Graham Brown and C. S. Sherrington, *ibid.* 85B, 250 (1912)].

Similarly subject to the principles of facilitation are the motor and the sensory cortex of man [W. Penfield and K. Welch, *J. Physiol. (London) 109*, 358 (1949)]. The patient D. F. heard the same orchestra playing the same music in the operating room more than 20 times when the electrode was reapplied to the superior surface of the temporal lobe. Each time the music began in the verse of a popular song. It proceeded to the chorus, if the electrode was kept in place.

18. W. Penfield and L. Roberts, *Speech and Brain Mechanisms* (Princeton Univ. Press, Princeton, N.J., 1959).

19. G. Jelgersma, *Atlas anatomicum cerebri humani* (Scheltema and Holkema, Amsterdam).

6.
alcohol and brain centers of positive reinforcement

jacques st. laurent and james olds

HISTORY

Our present understanding of centers in the brain where positive reinforcement of behavior is produced by direct electric stimulation may be conceived as having roots in the 1920's and 1930's with two nearly simultaneous methodological advances. In Switzerland, W. R. Hess (1954) began chronic implantation of electrodes in the brain to study awake, behaving animals by stimulating electrically small brain foci. At about the same time, B. F. Skinner (1938) in this country introduced response-reward conditioning. The major step occurred in the early 1950's when Miller (1957), Delgado (1955), Hebb (1955) and others began campaigns aimed at bringing together the chronic implantation methodology and psychological experimentation.

The self-stimulation studies began with an accidental observation made late in 1953 (Olds and Milner, 1954). A chronically implanted rat was free to move around relatively unimpeded in a field of about five feet by five feet. There were eight-inch wooden sides and a pair of light wires suspended from the ceiling which formed a loose leash and a connection to the electric stimulator. The animal was free to explore all parts of the field. The experimenter applied a sine wave stimulus of 60 cycles per second and about 100 microamperes root mean square by pressing a button.

More or less expecting to see some negative reinforcing effects of electric stimulation as had been observed earlier that year by Miller and Delgado, the

Reprinted from Ruth Fox (Ed.), *Alcoholism Behavior Research Therapeutic Approaches*, New York: Springer, 1967, pp. 80–101. Abridged by permission of the authors.

experimenter applied the stimulus each time the animal approached one of the corners.

The surprising observation was that the rat returned to that corner over and over again—much more often than one should have expected either on a negative reinforcement or even on a chance basis. At first one suspected interest or curiosity on the part of the rat with respect to the electric stimulus. But a few further tests quickly led to the belief that here was genuine positive reinforcement, a *brain stimulus with all the characteristics of a primary reward*.

The early tests involved first attracting the rat in any chosen direction by stimulating whenever the animal took a step in the right direction, and later provoking normal "T" maze learning and then reversal learning by shocking the brain whenever the animal reached the goal.

While all of these early tests provoked enthusiastic response from the rats, it was undoubtedly Skinner's method which put the experiments on a quantitative basis. A circuit was arranged so that each response of the animal produced a brief train of electric stimulation in the part of the brain which was to be studied. With this method, the rate at which the animal stimulated its brain turned out to be a relatively satisfactory method of measuring the reinforcing properties of the stimulus. We have found, in the various cases we have tried, that the stimulus which caused more rapid self-stimulation rates also causes more positive reinforcement in other tests we wished to apply (such as multiple choice and obstruction box tests).

A series of questions about this positive reinforcement phenomenon have been responsible for the series of further

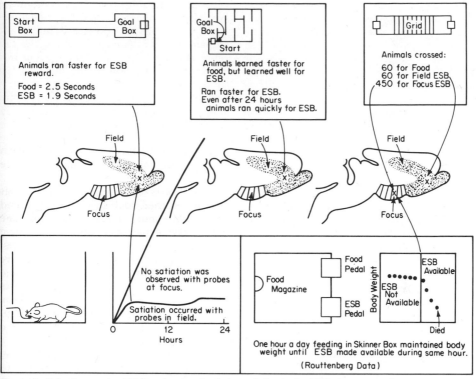

Figure 1. Behaviors rewarded by electric stimulation of the brain (ESB). Runway and maze experiments were reported by Olds (1956). Probes were in the rhinencephalic field where stimulation has mild effects. In gridcrossing experiments, animals crossed a 60-microampere foot-shock for food or for ESB via probes in the mild field; for ESB via probes in the hypothalamic focus where stimulation has intense positive effects they crossed a 450-microampere foot-shock. In satiation tests, animals sometimes self-stimulated continuously for 24 hours when ESB was applied at the focus (Olds, 1958b). In food-ESB competition experiments Aryeh Routtenberg in our laboratory found that animals often gave up needed food in order to self-stimulate via probes in the focus.

investigation in our laboratory and in others (Olds, 1962).

INTENSITY OF EFFECT

The first question had to do with the intensity of the effect. With electrodes correctly placed and with the current correctly set, it was possible to generate more motive force with a brain stimulus reward than with any other reward ordinarily used in animal experimentation (see Figure 1). With the current set lower, or with electrodes differently placed, far milder effects were achieved, comparable in every way to conventional rewards. These phenomena were demonstrated utilizing many different methods of be-

havior psychology, including runway maze, obstruction box, and the Skinner box. Electrodes were not placed in the area which we later found to be the focus but instead in the milder penultimate field in these early experiments; and yet, animals ran faster for brain stimulus reward than they did for food. They learned a maze faster for food but learned well for brain stimulus reward and ran faster for the brain stimulation. On the third and fourth days of training in the maze, good performance on the very first trial indicated overnight retention and, furthermore, indicated that no primer shock to the brain was necessary in order to instigate motivation on any given day.

For obstruction box tests, electrodes have been implanted in the focus and in the field. With electrodes in the focus, animals have crossed an obstruction more than seven times as strong as that which a normal hungry animal will cross for food. This same excess of motivation toward the brain stimulus reward has recently been shown by A. Routtenberg in our laboratory in a choice situation where animals had just time enough in the box to maintain body weight by pressing on the food pedal and eating at the magazine. Animals gave up food when the brain shock was made available thereby starving themselves to get the brain shock. And body weight has steadily declined on this schedule even to the point of death. Finally, in satiation tests with electrodes in the penultimate field, some satiation was observed. With electrodes at the focus, animals often responded continuously for 24-hour periods, responding under these conditions to the point of collapse; that is, to the point of physical exhaustion.

Topographic Organization

Possibly the question with the most ramifications is the anatomical one: Where in the brain does this happen? Where do the electrodes have to be placed to produce positive reinforcement?

Field and Focus. Positive reinforcement produced by electric stimulation of the brain was originally discovered with electrodes in a boundary system between the olfactory bulbs and the older olfactory parts of the cortex. It was first thought to be mainly related to this olfactory cortex; this cortex is called the rhinencephalon. Positive reinforcement could be produced by stimulating some parts of almost all rhinencephalic structures. In rats it became clear that more than half of the electrodes placed at random in the rhinencephalon would yield positive reinforcement when stimulated electrically. Later studies showed that the focus of the phenomenon, if maximum responding for a minimum of stimulation could be taken to indicate a focus, was not in olfactory cortex but rather in other olfactory projections directed toward the spinal cord through hypothalamus and midbrain tegmentum; that is, through the reticular activating system in its lower part. In fact, there is a pair of long tubes extending from the olfactory bulbs and rhinencephalon which pass along the two outer edges of the hypothalamus and into similar areas, the lower and medial areas of the midbrain. While much of the area between these tubes and surrounding them seems to yield positive reinforcement when electric stimulation of the brain is applied, the tubes themselves seem to compromise the focus of the phenomenon if maximum effect from minimum stimulation is used as the criterion.

A number of differences between the positive reinforcement produced by focus stimulation and that produced by field stimulation have been observed.

1. In experiments where each response was followed by one stimulus reward, response rates were far higher with hypothalamic than with rhinencephalic stimulation. Animals would press a lever 10,000 times an hour to stimulate lateral hypothalamus, but only about 500 times an hour under the same conditions to stimulate the areas of olfactory cortex.

2. As mentioned earlier, appetite for stimulation at the focus often seemed relatively insatiable, whereas a definite satiation point was usually reached in experiments with field stimulation. Animals stimulated themselves several thousand times in the olfactory subcortical area, and then stopped for the day. Animals stimulated themselves hour after hour in the lateral tube maintaining a rate of several thousand responses per hour and stopping only when a state of physical exhaustion appeared.

3. The reward produced by focus stimulation seemed to be accompanied by heightened general activity level (Roberts 1958), whereas the reward produced by olfactory cortex stimulation seemed often to be accompanied by more or less complete inhibition of general activity.

4. While there were some apparent pain or anxiety relieving effects of the rewarding stimulus near olfactory cortex there were places in hypothalamus where the reward stimulus did not have these effects.

What can be inferred from the anatomy?

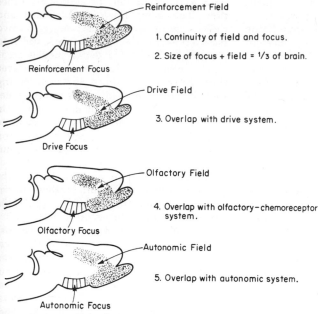

Reinforcement Field

1. Continuity of field and focus.

2. Size of focus + field = 1/3 of brain.

Reinforcement Focus

Drive Field

3. Overlap with drive system.

Drive Focus

Olfactory Field

4. Overlap with olfactory-chemoreceptor system.

Olfactory Focus

Autonomic Field

5. Overlap with autonomic system.

Autonomic Focus

Figure 2. Anatomical relations.

In the first place, the whole system of regions where electric stimulation causes positive reinforcement is continuous. The olfactory pathways directed from bulb toward tegmentum are continuous with the olfactory pathways directed from bulb toward the olfactory cortex. It appears, therefore, that one topographically continuous system of brain structures makes up the focus and the field of these regions. This seemed to suggest a common mechanism. In the second place, it is an extensive region making up almost one third of the brain in the rat, and while it is a smaller portion of the brain in the higher primates, still a substantial portion of the brain is involved even in the macaque and human.

Olfactory Relations. In the third place, there are three other functions which have been regularly ascribed to this whole series of structures (see Figure 2). The first is the olfactory or chemoreceptive function indicated by the names rhinencephalon and olfactory brain which have been applied. It was for a while in fashion to say that these structures make up an emotional brain once thought to be mainly olfactory. We believe that these structures make up an olfactory and chemoreceptor brain even now, but that chemoreception is not directed only toward smelling the environment, but also toward the sugars and hormones in blood which have so much to do with controlling high drive behaviors. It appears to be wise, therefore, to emphasize the phylogenetic and functional connection of these structures to the olfactory bulb and the widespread discovery of chemoreceptive functions within this system itself.

Drive Relations. This takes us directly into the second set of functions that have been generally ascribed to this set of areas. The hypothalamus and the rhinencephalon have for long been known to house a series of drive centers. For these it has been named the visceral brain by MacLean.

Not only was positive reinforcement regularly provoked by stimulating approximately the same areas as those previously implicated in studies of basic drives, but also, the positive reinforcement behavior provoked by stimulating any given brain point was usually sensitive to manipulation of at least one of the basic drives; and with stimulating probes at different brain points, different basic drives were effective (Olds 1958a).

With probes in the olfactory-tegmental focus, these differences made by drives were small, and difficult to demonstrate, possibly because the many drive systems are funneled through a very small area in this region and cannot be separated by the relatively gross electric stimulation methods. With probes in the olfactory-cortical boundary regions, however, different drive effects were more easily demonstrated. In one region it was clearly demonstrated that medial points were sensitive to hunger and lateral points sensitive to the levels of male sex hormone.

In other experiments it has regularly been demonstrated that in addition to positive reinforcement, the same brain probes often yielded the consummatory response appropriate to one of the basic drives if the stimulus was delivered by the experimenter and the response opportunity existed.

This brings to mind earlier experiments of 1940–1950 vintage by Anand and Brobeck (1951), Stellar (1954), Teitelbaum (1955), Klüver and Bucy (1939) in which these same areas were shown to have drive relevance because lesions here regularly caused disorganization of drive behaviors. Many reports of feeding "hyperphagia" and "aphagia" and aberrations in sexual and aversive behavior have been made on the basis of lesions in the lower focus and in the upper rhinencephalic field. An interesting difference between focus and field is worth mentioning: Lesions at the focus regularly upset control by the internal state of drive or satiation; lesions in the rhinencephalon, on the contrary, regularly upset the control of the animal by the reinforcing stimulus object. The animal with lesions in rhinencephalon could not discriminate food objects or sexual objects or dangerous objects.

Autonomic Relations. There are further anatomical overlaps. This reinforcement system is also the system of structures which has been shown to hold the higher control centers of autonomic function. The sympathetic and parasympathetic centers were discovered by W. R Hess (1954) in the earliest work utilizing chronically implanted depth probes.

It is interesting to consider that these three heavily-overlapped systems, that is the chemoreceptor olfactory mechanism the system of drive regulatory mechanisms, and the higher control centers of autonomic function should now turn out to be overlapped again by a new common denominator, namely the fact that reinforcement behavior can be elicited by stimulating almost all of these structures. In order to emphasize again the extreme ubiquity of reinforcement sites within this system of structures, we say this: We doubt if there are any points of the olfactory-visceral-autonomic brain which do not yield positive or negative reinforcement behavior. And the vast majority of points yield at least some reinforcement behavior of positive sign although some of these yield both negative and positive reinforcement behaviors.

POSITIVE AND NEGATIVE REINFORCEMENT

Anatomical Relations. Another major set of questions has concerned the relations of positive and negative reinforcement mechanisms in the brain; this is possibly the most fruitful area of our current research. There is, besides the overlaps mentioned, a heavy overlap of brain structures yielding positive reinforcement and brain structures yielding negative reinforcement behavior. This has gradually been brought home to us following the work of Roberts (1958) and Bower and Miller (1957). In many places electric stimulation causes both positive reinforcement behavior and negative reinforcement behavior simultaneously. Many people wonder how we observe this, how we can be sure of what is going on. And the answer is that it is very difficult to come to a clear conclusion. But often the animal will show avid pedal pressing behavior to initiate the brain stimulus and at the same time struggle to escape from the field where

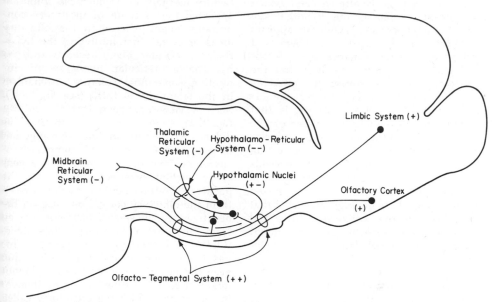

Figure 3. Locus of pure positive effects (+ and ++) in olfactory-tegmental fibers; pure negative effects (− and − −) in hypothalamo-reticular fibers; and mixed (±) effects in the hypothalamic nuclei where these two systems synapse with each other.

the pedal is available. These animals appear to be very confused. Our best way to demonstrate the conflicting effects of a probe is to test first for positive reinforcement behavior, confining the animal to an area where brain stimulation is available by pedal response but not forced. Under these circumstances, the animals which we will now call "ambivalent" will show a great deal of positive reinforcement behavior, pressing the pedal at substantial rates. Later, in other tests, often using the same chamber and the same pedal, the animal is subjected to forced stimulation which is now terminated by pedal responses. When a large number of brain areas were mapped (Olds, M. E. and Olds, J., 1963), all points being tested for both positive reinforcement behavior and negative reinforcement behavior caused by the electric stimulation, it was found that some areas yielded only positive reinforcement, other areas yielded only negative reinforcement and a third extensive set of structures yielded mixed effects (see Figure 3). We had originally anticipated that the mixed effects would appear with electrodes on

a boundary between areas yielding only positive and other areas yielding only negative reinforcement. We found instead, a synaptic boundary relation which quite surprised us at first. The main group of hypothalamic nuclei may be regarded from one gross point of view as a junction box which connects the large olfactory-hypothalamo-tegmental system of fibers to another large system of fibers running between hypothalamus and the reticular systems, the non-specific systems of thalamus and tegmentum. Our tests indicated that stimulation applied to the olfactory member of this synaptic relation caused positive reinforcement, stimulation of the reticular activating system member of the synapse caused negative reinforcement, and stimulation of the nuclei where the synapses between these two systems occur invariably caused the mixed phenomena. It was as though stimulation of the afferent fibers to these nuclei caused positive reinforcement; stimulation of the efferent fibers caused negative reinforcement; and stimulation at the synapses themselves caused a mixture of the two. However, we hasten to add that it is not at all clear which of the two fiber systems is afferent and which is efferent so far as the hypothalamic nuclei are concerned. While it appears that the reticular activating fibers and the olfactory fibers synapse in the hypothalamic nuclei, it is not clear that the olfactory fibers are always the afferents and the reticular fibers always the efferents. What is clear, however, is that stimulating the olfactory member of the synaptic relation yields positive reinforcement; stimulating the reticular activating member of the synaptic relation yields negative reinforcement; and stimulating the area of the synapse yields mixed phenomena. These findings suggested that inhibitory synapses between positive and negative reinforcement systems might exist in the hypothalamic nuclei themselves.

Interaction Experiment. The next question, therefore, was whether inhibitory relations might be demonstrated by simultaneous stimulation of the two systems. We can best describe this work briefly if we divide the reinforcement systems into three parts. First is the penultimate, positive reinforcement field which we spoke of earlier as residing in olfactory cortical regions. Second, there is the aversive or negative reinforcement mechanisms which we spoke of as being related to the reticular activating system. Third, there is the positive reinforcement focus which was described as residing in olfactory-hypothalamic-and-tegmental areas. We have tested the reinforcement behavior elicited by stimulating each of these areas while simultaneously applying a continuous train of stimulation to one of the others. By this method, we have found at least two sets of possible inhibitory relations. In the first case (Routtenberg and Olds, 1963) stimulation of the penultimate positive reinforcement field in olfactory cortex has depressed the negative reinforcement behavior caused by stimulation in hypothalamo-reticular fibers. In the second case (Olds, M. E. and Olds, J. 1962), stimulation of these same reticulo-hypothalamic negative reinforcement mechanism has regularly caused stopping of the positive reinforcement behavior caused by

stimulating the lateral hypothalamic olfactory mechanism. From these studies it appeared that a chain of inhibitory connections might exist with the olfactory areas of cortex first inhibiting the hypothalamo-reticular fibers second; and the hypothalamo-reticular fibers second inhibiting some final common mechanism in the lateral focus third (see Figure 4). Such a view has been fostered by the fact that stimulation in the lateral focus did not in its turn inhibit anything, but instead, stimulation of this supposed focus of positive reinforcement had a generally facilitatory effect not only on the positive reinforcement behavior driven from the olfactory cortex, but also on the negative reinforcement behavior driven from the hypothalamo-reticular fibers (Olds, M. E. and Olds, J., (1962). This has led to our current supposition that even the negative reinforcement behavior might in some way depend on excitement in this region which we previously called the positive reinforcement focus and which we now began to think of as possibly a general reinforcement focus, an area where augmented activity might play a part in the reinforcement of all antecedent behavior whether this was owing to an augmented reward condition or a depressed aversive condition.

Lesion Experiments. The next set of questions had to do with whether we could demonstrate in some way the dependence not only of olfactocortical positive reinforcement, but also reticulo-hypothalamic negative reinforcement on this supposed final common pathway in the lateral focus. In order to study this question, electrolytic lesions have been used in our laboratory and in the laboratory of H. P. Ward (1960), lesions were made in the olfactory-cortical parts of the positive reinforcement system, the penultimate positive reinforcement field. They consistently failed to eliminate positive reinforcement behavior which was driven by stimulating the focus. More recently in our laboratory (Olds, J. and Olds, M. E., 1964), we have made lesions at the tegmento-hypothalamic end of the olfactory-hypothalamic-tegmental system and it is clear that these posterior lesions substantially reduce or completely abolish

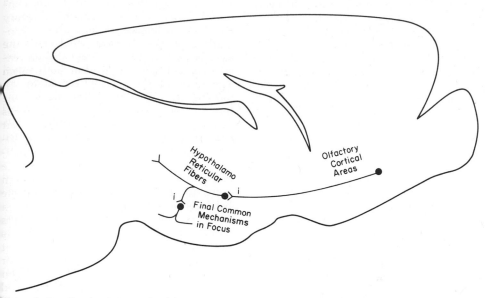

Figure 4. Postulated relations of inhibition (i) between olfactory cortical fibers, hypothalamo-reticular fibers innervating the focus of reinforcement.

positive reinforcement behavior produced by electric stimulation in the penultimate rhinencephalic field.

In a second set of experiments, we tested for effects lesions at the escape point on positive reinforcement behavior, and lesions at the positive reinforcement focus on escape behavior. This gave the strongest confirmation to date to the view that the focus is something of a common denominator in operant behavior, being involved in aversive as well as rewarded operants. The lesions in the lateral focus often abolished more or less completely the negative reinforcement behavior caused by stimulating the hypothalamo-reticular aversive area. However, lesions in the hypothalamo-reticular aversive area not only failed to antagonize positive reinforcement behavior, but in some circumstances even augmented it (Olds, J. and Olds, M. E., 1964).

It is, of course, not clear from these experiments that lateral hypothalamus is a final common path in control of operant behavior. They do seem to *suggest*, however, the view that aversive mechanism might act by inhibiting the focus.

It is clear that no simple pleasure center exists here, but rather in one way or another it is a complex integrating mechanism. For here is an area where electric stimulation produces a maximally intense form of positive reinforcement; and yet lesions produce distinct depressions in both positive and negative reinforcement behavior.

DRUG EXPERIMENTS

Two kinds of drugs have been most interesting in their effects on self-stimulation: 1) major tranquilizers and 2) the sedative-hypnotics which class, according to our view, includes the barbiturates, meprobamate, and alcohol.

The best known finding is the counteraction of self-stimulation by those major tranquilizers which counteract psychotic agitation. Very small doses of chlorpromazine, doses which have no obvious effect on behavior, counteract almost completely self-stimulation via olfactory/midbrain electrodes; reserpine may have similar effects but this is less clear. (Olds, Killam and Bach-y-Rita,

1956). Tranquilizers were more effective against the intense self-stimulation produced with electrodes in the posterior focus than against the less intense form produced with electrodes in the milder, anterior-modulating regions.

The most surprising aspect of these outcomes was that so strong a system of behavior was so totally antagonized by doses that seemed to have no other prominent effects on animal behavior. Of chlorpromazine, the question was repeatedly asked, "How can such small doses so completely counter a system of such apparent intensity?"

Alcohol, together with meprobamate and pentobarbital, was remarkable for just the opposite reason—it had practically no effect when electrodes were implanted in posterior, focal areas of the self-stimulation system, and this was true even when doses were raised to the point where an almost comatose state was produced.

With alcohol, therefore, the question was: How could a system of behavior survive a drug which so radically affected other behavior systems?

Animals were implanted with six probe electrodes either in the lateral hypothalamus or in the anterior area of the medial forebrain bundle. Each daily session involved 4 consecutive tests during each of which all electrodes were tested in turn for 2 minutes. The twelve days were divided in 3 periods of 4 days: four days precontrol, four days under the effect of ethanol, and four days postcontrol. The ethanol was injected intraperitoneally at a dosage of 2cc/kgm of body weight. This dosage always produced a marked state of intoxication which was assessed through a simple neurological examination. The steadiness of the gait, placing reaction, righting reflex and sense of equilibrium were in all cases markedly disturbed.

With the electrodes in the positive focus, i.e., the lateral hypothalamus, ethanol did not markedly affect the scores for any of the self-stimulating electrodes. There was only one effect—a slight attenuation in rate, which might be attributed to a loss of skill. We were led to conclude that behavior driven by direct stimulation of the posterior deep structures had a strong tendency to survive extreme doses of alcohol and we even surmised that there might be some tendency of such stimulation to counteract the influence of alcohol.

Most of the forward self-stimulating electrodes had their scores affected by ethanol, but the effects went both ways. The locus of the probes seemed to determine the direction of the alcohol effect. Why some probe-points caused behavior which was augmented while nearby points caused behavior which was depressed by alcohol was unclear. It was clear however that posterior probes yielded behavior which was immune to alcohol, anterior probes yielded behavior which was not.

Escape behavior was produced by posterior probes situation 1 mm. medial to those which yielded self-stimulation. Reasoning from earlier work on barbiturates (Olds, M. E. and Olds, J., 1964) we had expected the escape behavior to be relatively vulnerable to the debilitating effects of ethanol.

In fact the ethanol effects on posterior escape were disappointingly similar to the ethanol effects on posterior self-stimulation. Early in the period after injection, however, ethanol did antagonize escape behavior. No similar antagonism of self-stimulation appeared. During the later periods after injection when there would still be influences on anterior self-stimulation there were no effects on posterior escape.

In conclusion, with probes in the hypothalamic focus the self-stimulation scores were almost unaffected, and, when there was a minor depression in rate it could be attributed to a motor disability. With probes in the rhinencephalic field scores were depressed or augmented depending on the finer aspects of placement.

The considerably greater influence of alcohol with anterior electrodes, together with the fact that the influence might work both ways, has prompted a series of appealing speculations. One might guess that alcohol, influencing cortical mechanisms, modulates behavior only in cases where environment counts.

It might turn out, then, that when paleocortical areas are stimulated, these are points of access to deeper systems each access line being facilitated or inhibited by particular environments. These are places therefore where reinforcement produced by electric brain stimulation might be particularly influenced, positively or negatively, by environmental influences and therefore also by neighboring cortical structures.

It is these "input" pathways that appear to be particularly sensitive to alcohol. Deeper behavior systems are relatively intact. On the other hand, it would appear that the peculiar activity of the so-called tranquilizers is to attack directly the deeper mechanisms.

REFERENCES

Anand, B. K. and Brobeck, J. R. Localization of a "feeding center" in the hypothalamus of the rat. *Proc. Soc. Exper. Biol. Med.*, 77, 323–324, 1951.

Bower, G. H. and Miller, N. E. Rewarding and punishing effects from stimulating the same place in the rat's brain. *J. Comp. Physiol. Psychol.*, 51, 669–674, 1958.

Delgado, J. M. R. Cerebral structures involved in transmission and elaboration of noxious stimulation. *J. Neurophysiol.*, 18, 261–275, 1955.

Hebb, D. O. Drives and the conceptual nervous system. *Psychol. Rev.*, 62, 243–254, 1955.

Hess, W. R. *Diencephalon: Autonomic and Extraapyramidal Functions.* New York: Grune and Stratton, Inc., 1954.

Klüver, H. and Bucy, P. C. Preliminary analysis of functions of the temporal lobes in monkeys, *A.M.A. Arch. Neurol. Psychiat.*, 42, 979–1000, 1939.

Miller, N. E. Experiments on motivation. *Science*, 126, 1271–1278, 1957.

Olds, J. Runway and maze behavior controlled by basomedial forebrain stimulation in the rat. *J. Comp. Physiol. Psychol.*, 49, 507–512, 1956.

Olds, J. Effects of hunger and male sex hormones on self-stimulation of the brain, *J. Comp. Physiol. Psychol.*, 51, 320–324, 1958a.

Olds, J. Satiation effects in self-stimulation of the brain. *J. Comp. Physiol. Psychol.*, 51, 675–678, 1958b.

Olds, J. Hypothalamic substrates of reward. *Physiol. Rev.*, 42, 554–604, 1962.

Olds, J., Killam, K. F., and Bach-y-Rita, P. Self-stimulation of the brain used as a screening method for tranquilizing drugs. *Science*, 124, 265–266, 1956.

Olds, J. and Milner, P. Positive reinforcement produced by electrical stimulation of septal area and other regions of rat brain. *J. Comp. Physiol. Psychol.*, 47, 419–427, 1954.

Olds, J. and Olds, M. E. Mechanism of voluntary behavior. In *The Role of Pleasure in Behavior* (R. G. Heath ed.). New York: Hoeber Medical Division, Harper and Row, 1964, 23–53.

Olds, M. E. and Olds, J. Approach-escape interactions in rat brain. *Am. J. Physiol.*, 203, 803–810, 1962.

Olds, M. E. and Olds, J. Approach-avoidance analysis of rat diencephalon. *J. Comp. Neurol.*, 120, 259–295, 1963.

Olds, M. E. and Olds, J. Pharmacological patterns in subcortical reinforcement behavior. *Int. J. Neuropharmacol.*, 2, 309–325, 1964.

Roberts, W. W. Both rewarding and punishing effects from stimulation of posterior hypothalamus of cat with same electrode at same intensity. *J. Comp. Physiol. Psychol.*, 51, 400–407, 1958.

Routtenberg, A. and Olds, J. The attenuation of response to an aversive brain stimulus by concurrent rewarding septal stimulation. *Federation Proc.*, 22, 515 (Abstr.), 1963.

Skinner, B. F. *The Behavior of Organisms.* New York: Appleton-Century-Crofts, 1938.

Stellar, E. The physiology of motivation. *Psychol. Rev.*, 61, 5–22, 1954.

Teitelbaum, P. Sensory control of hypothalamic hyperphagia. *J. Comp. Physiol. Psychol.*, 48, 156–163, 1955.

Ward, H. P. Basal tegmental self-stimulation after septal ablation in rats. *Arch. Neurol.*, 158, 1960.

7.
electrical self-stimulation
of the brain in man

robert g. heath

At a symposium concerning depth electrode studies in animals and man in New Orleans in 1952, the Tulane investigators described (and illustrated with films of patients treated between 1950–1952) a pleasurable response with stimulation of specific regions of the brain (5). The pleasurable response to stimulation of some deep regions of the brain, first observed with electrical stimulation to the septal region, has proved a consistent finding in continuing studies (6, 7, 12). Since 1952 we have reported various aspects of the phenomenon including demonstration of relief of physical pain by stimulation to this pleasure-yielding area of the brain (11).

With the introduction of ingenious techniques for self-stimulation by Olds (14–17), the need to depend largely upon verbal reports of the subjective response was eliminated and it was possible to study apparent reward and aversive areas of the brain in animals. Subjective data, of course, were lacking in the animal studies.

Reprinted from The American Journal of Psychiatry, 1963, 120, 571–577. Copyright 1963, the American Psychiatric Association. Abridged by permission of the author.

Read at the 119th annual meeting of the American Psychiatric Association, St. Louis, Mo., May 6–10, 1963.

At the time of presentation, a 16 mm. sound film was shown demonstrating the effects of stimulation by the transistorized portable self-stimulator to a number of specific regions of the brain in Patients No. B-7 and No. B-10. The two subjects were interviewed to obtain subjective descriptions of the effects of stimulation.

Supported by funds provided by the Louisiana State Department of Hospitals. Charles J. Fontana, Electroencephalographic Technologist and Esther Blount, R.N., Research Nurse, Assistants.

During the last few years the Tulane researchers have incorporated and modified some animal intracranial self-stimulation (ICSS) methods for human investigation, permitting extension of the pleasurable phenomenon studies in man. An ICSS study recently published (3) was designed to explore human behavior under strict laboratory conditions of the type characteristically employed in animal studies. A study has also been described in which a patient was equipped with a small portable self-stimulator with 3 buttons, permitting delivery of electrical stimuli of fixed parameters to any one of 3 brain sites (8). The primary motivation in these studies, as in all depth electrode studies in man at Tulane, was therapeutic (5).

Study of reward areas in the brain of man, including use of induced reward for therapeutic purposes, is extensive and complex. This presentation will focus on a description of the subjective responses of two patients treated by the self-stimulation technique. Their reports provide information concerning the reasons for repeated ICSS—information that is not available from animal studies.

MATERIAL AND METHODS

Two patients were used in the study. Patient No. B-7, age 28, with a diagnosis of narcolepsy and cataplexy, had failed to respond to conventional treatments. He had electrodes implanted by the method developed in our laboratory (1, 2) into 14 predetermined brain regions and fixed to remain in exact position for prolonged study. These small silver ball electrodes (most of those used in this study consisted of 3 leads each separated by 2 mm.) were placed into the right anterior and posterior septal region, left anterior and posterior septal region, right anterior hypothalamus, mid-line mesencephalic tegmentum, left anterior and posterior hippocampus, left anterior and posterior caudate nucleus and over the right frontal cortex, right and left mid-temporal cortex, and left anterior temporal cortex.

Patient No. B-10, age 25, a psychomotor epileptic with episodic brief periods of impulsive behavior uncontrolled with the usual treatments, had 51 leads implanted into 17 brain sites: left and right centromedian, left caudate nucleus, right ventricle, left and right hippocampus, midline mesencephalic tegmentum, left and right septal region, left amygdaloid nucleus, left paraolfactory area, and over the left and right temporal cortex, left and right occipital cortex, and left and right frontal cortex. Twenty-four leads were of stainless steel .003 inch in diameter coated with Teflon; 27 were the small silver ball type electrode.[1]

ICSS studies were not initiated until a minimal period of 6 months following operation, assuring elimination of any variables introduced by operative trauma, e.g., edema, anesthetic effects.

Stimuli were delivered from a specially constructed transistorized self-contained unit[2] which was worn on the patient's belt. The unit generated a pre-set train of bidirectional stimulus pulses each time that one of the 3 control buttons was depressed. Each button directed the pulse train to a different electrode pair permitting the operator a possible selection of cerebral sites. A mechanical counter was coupled to each button to record the total number of stimuli directed toward a given area. An internal timer limited each pulse train to 0.5 second for each depression, thereby prohibiting the operator from obtaining continuous stimuli merely by keeping the button depressed. An additional feature of the unit pro-

vided 3 separate level potentiometers to give wide-range control of stimuli for each electrode pair. . . .

Studies conducted on the two patients differed somewhat because of therapeutic considerations. For studies with Patient No. B-7, the narcoleptic, the 3 buttons of the unit were attached to electrodes in the septal region, hippocampus, and mesencephalic tegmentum, and he was free to stimulate any of these sites as he chose. The patient wore the stimulator for a period of 17 weeks. Before he was equipped with the unit, baseline data concerning the time he spent sleeping during an arbitrary 6-hour period each day were charted by specified ward personnel. These data were later compared with sleeping time following attachment of the unit. This study was basically therapeutic (treatment results will be presented elsewhere) but from the experimental design we were able to obtain considerable subjective data regarding the effects of ICSS to several regions of the brain.

With Patient No. B-10, the psychomotor epileptic, a number of different experimental designs were employed to investigate the effects of ICSS. For illustrative purposes, the results of one study are presented herein as background for a description of the subjective responses. In the first part of the study a total of 17 different cerebral regions were stimulated. They were selected at random, the unit design permitting 3 sites to be hooked up at any one time. Each electrode was made available to the patient for stimulation for a minimal period of 2 hours. Various combinations of 3 sites were arranged. The purpose in making stimulation to different combinations of sites available was based on well-documented animal studies which indicate that rate of stimulation at a given site will vary somewhat depending upon the site stimulated beforehand. Data are presented in terms of the hourly stimulation to a given site as recorded with the automatic counter of the unit. Additionally, the same site of the brain was attached to different buttons to determine if the patient would relate a response to a given button. He reported, however, a consistent response to stimu-

---

[1]Stainless steel array constructed of No. 16 stainless steel wire, .003 inch in diameter, with quad Teflon-coated leads and 6 contact points 2 mm. apart. Electrode designed and fabricated by Henry A. Schryver, 10 W. Packard St., Fort Wayne, Indiana.

[2]Technical Associates of New Orleans.

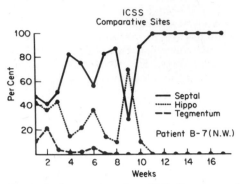

Figure 1. Comparative sites, ICSS. Frequency of stimulation to various intracranial sites expressed in percentages in patient with narcolepsy and cataplexy.

lation of a given electrode regardless of the button to which it was attached.

In the second part of the study the 3 sites of the brain which the subject had elected to stimulate most frequently during the first part of the study were compared over a 6-hour period.

RESULTS

Patient No. B-7. After randomly exploring the effects of stimulation with presses of each of the 3 buttons, Patient No. B-7 almost exclusively pressed the septal button (Figure 1).

Stimulation to the mesencephalic tegmentum resulted in a prompt alerting, but was quite aversive. The patient, complaining of intense discomfort and looking fearful, requested that the stimulus not be repeated. To make certain that the region was not stimulated, he ingeniously modified a hair pin to fit under the button which directed a pulse train to the mesencephalic tegmentum so it could not be depressed.

Hippocampal stimulation was mildly rewarding.

Stimulation to the septal region was the most rewarding of the stimulations and, additionally, it alerted the patient, thereby combatting the narcolepsy. By virtue of his ability to control symptoms with the stimulator, he was employed part-time, while wearing the unit, as an entertainer in a night club.

The patient's narcolepsy was severe. He would move from an alert state into a deep sleep in the matter of a second. Recognizing that button pressing promptly awakened him, fellow patients and friends occasionally resorted to pushing the button if he fell asleep so rapidly that he was unable to stimulate himself.

The patient, in explaining why he pressed the septal button with such frequency, stated that the feeling was "good"; it was as if he were building up to a sexual orgasm. He reported that he was unable to achieve the orgiastic end point, however, explaining that his frequent, sometimes frantic, pushing of the button was an attempt to reach the end point. This futile effort was frustrating at times and described by him on these occasions as a "nervous feeling."

Patient No. B-10. Studies conducted on the psychomotor epileptic patient were more varied and provided more information concerning subjective responses. The average number of button presses per hour for various regions of the brain is listed in Tables 1 and 2. Regions of the brain are listed in order of the frequency with which they were selectively stimulated by the subject. A summary of the principal subjective feelings is given.

The button most frequently pushed provided a stimulus to the centromedian thalamus. This stimulus did not, however induce the most pleasurable response; in fact, it induced irritability. The subject reported that he was almost able to recall a memory during this stimulation but he could not quite grasp it. The frequent self-stimulations were an endeavor to bring this elusive memory into clear focus.

The patient most consistently reported pleasurable feelings with stimulation to two electrodes in the septal region and one in the mesencephalic tegmentum With the pleasurable response to septal stimuli, he frequently produced associations in the sexual area. Actual content varied considerably, but regardless of his baseline emotional state and the subject under discussion in the room, the stimulation was accompanied by the patient's introduction of a sexual subject, usually with a broad grin. When questioned about

TABLE 1.   ICSS in Man—Reward (?) Sites

Region Stimulated	Average/Hour	Subjective Response
L. Centromedian	488.8	Partial memory recall; anger and frustration
R.P. Septal	394.9	"Feel great"; sexual thoughts; elimination of "bad" thoughts
L. Caudate	373.0	Cool taste; "like it OK"
Mesenceph. Teg.	280.0	"Drunk feeling"; "happy button"; elimination of "bad" thoughts
A. Amygdala	257.9	Indifferent feeling; somewhat pleasant, but feeling not intense
P. Amygdala	224.0	Moderately rewarding; increase of current requested

this, he would say, "I don't know why that came to mind—I just happened to think of it." The "happy feelings" with mesencephalic stimulation were not accompanied by sexual thoughts.

Patient No. B-10 also described as "good," but somewhat less in pleasurable-yielding quality, stimuli to two sites, the amygdaloid nucleus and the caudate nucleus. Several other septal electrodes and one other electrode in the amygdaloid nucleus were stimulated a moderate number of times. His reports concerning these stimulations suggested a lesser magnitude of pleasurable response, but definitely not an unpleasant feeling.

Minimal positive response was obtained with stimulation of several other septal electrodes. The most aversive response ("sick feeling") was obtained with stimulation to one hippocampal electrode and one lead in the paraolfactory area. With stimulation of the latter lead, he complained of light flashes, apparently due to spread to the optic nerve, and of general discomfort.

No consistent changes, either significantly aversive or rewarding, were displayed with stimulation to any of 12 cortical leads dispersed widely over the cortical surface, including the frontal, temporal, occipital, and parietal lobes.

In the second part of the study the 3 electrodes which were stimulated most during the first phase of the study were attached to the 3 buttons. The sites of these electrodes were the centromedian thalamus, the septal region, and the mesencephalic tegmentum. Data indicated that the combination of sites available influenced the number of times that a

given region of the brain was stimulated (Figure 2). When coupled with the subjective reports, the data also suggested that the over-all state of the subject at a given moment was an influential determinant for selecting the region to be stimulated. For example, the centromedian thalamus was stimulated up to 1,100 times per hour when in combination with relatively inactive sites of stimulation and only a maximum of 290 times per hour when in combination with two other highly rewarding areas, the septal region and the mesencephalic tegmentum.

The patient noted that the frustration and anger resulting from stimulation of the centromedian thalamus was allevi-

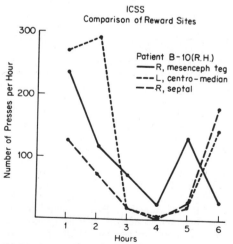

Figure 2. Comparison of frequency of stimulation to reward sites in the brain of patient with psychomotor epilepsy.

TABLE 2. ICSS in Man—Aversive Sites

Region Stimulated	Average/Hour	Subjective Response
R. Hippocampus	1.77	Strongly aversive; "feel sick all over"
L. Paraolfactory	0.36	Moderately aversive
R. Parietal Cortex	0.50	
R. Frontal Cortex	0.00	No significant subjective response
R. Occipital Cortex	0.00	
R. Temporal Cortex	0.00	

ated with stimulation to the septal region and to the mesencephalic tegmentum. As Figure 2 indicates, the patient during the first two hours stimulated the centromedian thalamus most frequently. This was associated with discomfort in his attempt to recapture a fleeting memory. He reported that stimulation of the other areas relieved this discomfort. There was little activity during the next two hours. Toward the end of the study, in the 5th and 6th hours, stimulation to septal and tegmental leads increased. During the 5th hour, the mesencephalic tegmentum was stimulated most frequently; during the 6th hour, the septal lead was stimulated most frequently. The patient evolved a pattern coupling the stimulus to the centromedian thalamus (which stirred his curiosity concerning the memory) with stimuli to the more pleasurable areas to lessen the feeling of frustration.[3]

[3]When the paper was presented, it was here that the 16 mm. sound film was shown. Clinical effects of stimulation to a variety of deep regions of the brain, as summarized herein, were demonstrated.

In the last sequence of the film, Patient No. B-10, the psychomotor epileptic, was stimulated in the septal region during a period when he was exhibiting agitated, violent psychotic behavior. The stimulus was introduced without his knowledge. Almost instantly his behavioral state changed from one of disorganization, rage, and persecution to one of happiness and mild euphoria. He described the beginning of a sexual motive state. He was unable, when questioned directly, to explain the sudden shift in his feelings and thoughts. This sequence of film was presented to demonstrate a phenomenon which appears to be consistent and which has been repeated in a large number of patients in our laboratories. This phenomenon is the ability to obliterate immediately painful emergency emotional feelings in a

DISCUSSION

Changes in parameters of stimuli to a given region of the brain, including current intensity, wave form, pulse width, and frequency, in many instances altered the patients' responses. This has similarly been reported with animal ICSS.

Information acquired from the patients' reporting of their reasons for button pressing indicates that all ICSS is not solely for pleasure. The highest rate of button pressing occurred with Patient No. B-7 when he was somewhat frustrated in his pleasurable pursuit and as he attempted to achieve an orgastic end point. In Patient No. B-10 the highest rate of button pressing also occurred with frustration, but of a different type, evolving with attempts to bring into focus a vague memory that ICSS had evoked. The subject's emotional state in this instance built into strong anger. It was interesting that the patient would button press to stimulate the region within the centromedian thalamus for a prolonged period, but at a slower rate when buttons providing more pleasurable septal and tegmental stimulation were also available. Depression of the septal button, with resultant pleasant feelings alleviated the painful emergency state according to the subject's report, and thereby provided him comfort to pursue his quest for the fleeting memory.

With septal stimulation in other patients, as well as the two subjects discussed here, a sexual motive state has frequently been induced in association with the pleasurable response. This sexual state has not developed in associa-

human subject through introduction of a pleasurable state by physical or chemical techniques.

tion with pleasurable feelings during stimulation to other regions. The consistent observation of a relation between sexual feelings and stimulation to the septal region has been described by MacLean in monkey experiments (13). These reports, in part, answer questions raised by Galambos regarding ICSS when he asked, "What motivates these animals to do such unheard-of-things? Is it some exquisite pleasure they receive, as several students of the problem staunchly contend, or the feeling of utter and complete well-being as others claim?" (4).

The ICSS techniques represent one of several methodologies that the Tulane researchers have used in man to investigate the pleasurable phenomenon associated with certain types of cerebral activity. These studies complement early subcortical electrical stimulation studies (5). The pleasurable response has also been induced in man with introduction of certain chemicals into specific deep brain regions (8–10). It is noteworthy that intense pleasurable responses induced with chemical stimulation of the brain occurred when a high amplitude spindling type of recording was set up in the septal region.

The observation that introduction of a stimulus which induces pleasure immediately eliminates painful emergency states is quite consistent. If our psychodynamic formulations are correct, this basic observation may have widespread implication for the development of therapeutic methods to alter favorably disordered behavior.

SUMMARY

Studies are described of two human patients under treatment with ICSS. Their subjective reports in association with stimulation to reward areas of the brain are presented. The data indicate that patients will stimulate regions of the brain at a high frequency for reasons other than to obtain a pleasurable response. These data extend information obtained from ICSS in animals.

BIBLIOGRAPHY

1. Becker, H. C., et al. In Studies in Schizophrenia. Cambridge: Harvard Univ. Press, 1954, p. 565.
2. Becker, H. C., et al. Electroenceph. Clin. Neurophysiol., 9: 533, 1957.
3. Bishop, M. P., et al. Science, 140: 394, 1963.
4. Galambos, Robert. Fed. Proc., 20: 603, 1961.
5. Heath, R. G., et al. Studies in Schizophrenia. Cambridge: Harvard Univ. Press, 1954, p. 42, 46, 47, 50, 560.
6. Heath, R. G. Psychosom. Med., 17: 383, 1955.
7. Heath, R. G. Confinia Neurol., 18: 305, 1958.
8. Heath, R. G. In Heath, R. G. (Ed.), Pleasure Integration and Behavior. New York: Hoeber. In press.
9. Heath, R. G., and deBalbian Verster, F. Am. J. Psychiat., 117: 980, 1961.
10. Heath, R. G., and Founds, W. L. Electroenceph. Clin. Neurophysiol., 12: 930, 1960.
11. Heath, R. G., et al. In Studies in Schizophrenia. Cambridge: Harvard Univ. Press, 1954, p. 555.
12. Heath, R. G., and Mickle, W. A. In Ramey, R. R., and O'Doherty, D. S. (Eds.), Electrical Studies on the Unanesthetized Brain. New York: Hoeber, 1960.
13. MacLean, P. D., et al. Trans. Am. Neurol. Ass., 84: 105, 1959.
14. Olds, J. Physiol. Rev., 42: 554, 1962.
15. Olds, J. Am. J. Physiol., 199: 965, 1960.
16. Olds, J., and Milner, P. J. Comp. Physiol. Psychol., 47: 419, 1954.
17. Olds, J., and Olds, M. E. In Heath, R. G. (Ed.), Pleasure Integration and Behavior. New York: Hoeber. In press.

8.
intracerebral radio stimulation and recording in completely free patients

josé m. r. delgado,
vernon mark,
william sweet,
frank ervin,
gerhard weiss,
george bach-y-rita,
and rioji hagiwara

Diagnosis and treatment of focal brain dysfunction associated with behavioral abnormalities are complex tasks which require more effective exploratory techniques. Intracerebral electrodes, electrocorticographical studies, and subsequent discrete neurosurgery have given the epileptologist and stereotaxic surgeon new possibilities for clinical investigation which as yet have been applied to only a small percentage of the patients suffering from neurological disorders including temporal lobe epilepsy and related episodic behavior problems. In these therapeutic studies, recordings and stimula-

Reprinted by permission from *The Journal of Nervous and Mental Disease* 1968, *147*, 329–340. Copyright 1968, The William & Wilkins Co., Baltimore, Md. 21202. Abridged by permission of the authors.

Research and instrumental development for the construction of the stimoceiver was supported by United States Air Force 6571st Aeromedical Research Laboratory F 29600–67–C–0058. Additional support for our research was provided by the United States Public Health Service, M 2004, and the Office of Naval Research, 609 (48).

The circuit for EEG recording is a modified version of the unit described by Meehan (21), and his help in providing us with information and with one of his units is gratefully acknowledged. The help of Mr. Per Hals in developing telestimulation instrumentation is also gratefully acknowledged.

tions of any chosen cerebral structure can be performed over a period of days or weeks, and neuronal sites identified as triggers for abnormal electrical patterns associated with behavioral disturbances can be destroyed by electrolysis or resection. Unfortunately, in some patients episodic behavior disorders may be more disabling than their epileptic seizures, and focal lesions may improve one syndrome without modifying the other. Furthermore, recording and stimulation are usually performed under conditions which qualify their usefulness, because the patients' mobility is limited by connecting leads, and their behavior is likewise altered by the stressful and artificial environment of the recording room.

During the last few years, methodology has been developed to stimulate and record the electrical activity of the brain in completely unrestrained monkeys and chimpanzees (10, 13). This procedure should be of considerable clinical interest because it permits exploration of the brain for unlimited periods in patients without disturbing their rest or normal spontaneous activities. This paper reports instrumentation used and clinical application in four patients with psychomotor epilepsy in whom electrodes had been implanted in the temporal lobes. To our knowledge, this is the first clinical use of intracerebral radio stimulation and recording in man.

Figure 1. Two patients instrumented for intracerebral radio stimulation and recording engage in spontaneous activities (one is playing the guitar) in the psychiatric ward in the presence of the doctor (VM). Explorations of the brain can be performed for as long as necessary without disturbing the patients.

METHODS

Implantation of Electrodes

Electrodes were constructed and stereotaxically implanted according to methods previously described *(20)*. The electrode assemblies, which were connected to a McPherson skull plug, consisted of a plastic stylet, 1.2 mm in diameter, with 15 stainless steel 3-mm wide contacts attached at 3-mm intervals, plus one thermistor and three other contacts at the tip. Using a McPherson type 2 stereotaxic machine *(20)*, electrode assemblies were implanted bilaterally into the anterior medial amygdala of each patient.

Radio Stimulation

This system consists of two instruments: 1) the RF transmitter which measures 30 by 25 by 15 cm and includes the circuitry for controlling the repetition rate, duration and amplitude (intensity) of the stimulating pulse. . . . 2) The receiver-stimulator which is carried by the sub-

ject, measures 3.7 by 3.0 by 1.4 cm, and weighs 20 g. The solid state circuitry is encapsulated in epoxy resin which provides it with very good mechanical strength and makes it waterproof. Space for the 7-volt Mercury battery is included in the size mentioned above. . . . Under average stimulation conditions, the battery life is approximately 1 week. Operating range is up to 100 ft. Three channels of stimulation are available. The pulse intensity of each channel can be controlled individually from the transmitter. The pulse duration and repetition rate are the same for all three channels.

Electroencephalographic (EEG) Telemetry

A miniature FM-FM amplifier-transmitter combination and a telemetry receiver are used for this purpose. . . .

The analogue output signals from the receiver were connected to the inputs of an EEG recorder and a magnetic tape recorder. A microphone was also mounted in the room with the subjects and conversation was recorded along with the EEG on magnetic tape.

Stimoceiver

The integration of the three-channel units for radio stimulation and EEG telemetry constitutes the stimoceiver (*stimulator and EEG receiver*). Several tests were conducted to ensure proper electronic and biological operation, as explained later. The complete instrument, which weighs only 70 g, can easily be taped onto the patient's head bandage (Figure 1). During part of her treatment, one patient wore a wig which covered her stimoceiver and all evidence of instrumentation.

Additional Equipment

Conversations with the patients were tape-recorded and synchronized with the EEG recordings and moments of stimulation. During interviews with the first two patients, time lapse photography was used to record possible changes in facial expression or behavior, according to a method employed for studies in monkey colonies (9).

Physical Location of the Studies

The first two patients were under treatment at the Boston General Hospital, and radio stimulations and recordings were performed in a curtained, shielded 12 by 12 ft room in which patients could walk around or remain seated. The other two cases were studied in their customary quarters within a closed psychiatric ward at Massachusetts General Hospital, and they could move freely around their bedrooms, bathroom, sitting room or dining room. Nurses and other patients were present during some of the recording and stimulation sessions, as seen in Figure 1.

Experimental Design

The purpose of this study was to identify sites of abnormal intracerebral electrical activity and to test brain excitability in order to guide contemplated therapeutic surgery. Patterns of electrical activity were correlated with behavioral performance, and alterations of conduct

evoked by brain stimulation were evaluated. Many hours of EEG recordings were taped and analyzed to determine the frequency, severity and propagation of spontaneous electrical discharges which could have pathological significance. Interviews were structured in order to elicit the patient's verbal expression without unduly influencing the ideological content. During these sessions, two intracerebral points were selected for more extensive study, and they were randomly stimulated at 3- to 5-min intervals according to a predetermined schedule. Neither the patient nor the therapist was informed of the exact moments of stimulation, and each point was stimulated seven times during three 60- to 90-min sessions. Tape-recorded conversations were transcribed, analyzed for number of words per minute and for ideological and emotional content, and correlated with the EEG activity recorded continuously during control periods and stimulations (17, 19).

Instrumenting the patient for telestimulation and recording is a simple and rapid procedure requiring only connection of the stimoceiver to the electrode assembly plug. The stimoceiver is so small and light that it can be concealed within the head bandage, as shown in Figure 1. The patient is thus continuously available, day and night, for brain exploration, and there is no interference with spontaneous behavior.

The entire instrumentation for these studies consisted of the stimoceiver, radio transmitter, FM receiver, electroencephalograph, tape recorder and oscilloscope. This equipment could be rapidly assembled in a small space and operates without any special physical or electrical requirements. These aspects are emphasized to indicate the feasibility of this type of research within minimum facilities of a hospital ward. . . .

Clinical Applications of the Stimoceiver

1. *L.K.* This 35-year-old white male design engineer had experienced attacks of staring and automatisms for 10 to 12 years. He also had frequent episodes of rage during which he assaulted and injured his wife and children. His driving was precarious because he became en-

raged if other cars cut in front of him and he would go miles out of his way to force them off the road.

The EEG revealed temporal lobe-spiking more prominent on the right side. Pneumo-encephalogram disclosed dilitation of the right lateral ventricle, and recording from inlying temporal lobe electrodes showed marked EEG abnormalities. Telemetered recordings were done to correlate the results of amygdala stimulation, EEG recording, and behavior without risking the danger of displacing the intracerebral electrodes by sudden, untoward movements of the patient which could not be compensated for with the usual method of EEG recording by means of direct leads.

2. M.R. This 25-year-old white male suffered from encephalitis as an infant and a severe head injury in the Navy. Following this he had 4 years of staring spells and automatisms. He was the driver of a car involved in a serious accident and had a police record for vagrancy and violence. He began assaulting his medical attendants on the neurology service of a local veterans' hospital and had to be confined in a mental institution while awaiting surgical evaluation.

The EEG showed bilateral temporal lobe abnormalities. Electrodes were implanted in both amygdalas and depth recordings revealed abnormalities particularly prominent on the right side. The clinical problem here was to decide if and where in the amygdala a focal destructive lesion should be made. The telemetered recording and stimulation allowed us to correlate the patient's behavior and electrical abnormalities without the structured rigidity of the EEG recording room.

3. J.P. This 20-year-old white female had a history of encephalitis at the age of 18 months. In addition, she had experienced temporal lobe seizures and occasional grand mal seizures for 10 years. She also had frequent rage attacks which on more than a dozen occasions resulted in an assault on another person. On one occasion she inserted a knife into a stranger's myocardium, and another time

she inserted scissors into the pleural cavity of a nurse.

The EEG showed occasional temporal lobe spikes and depth recordings revealed dramatic electrical abnormalities in both amygdala and hippocampus. The use of stimoceivers proved to be of crucial importance in selection of the temporal lobe site for a destructive lesion because it was difficult to confine the patient in the EEG recording room during a rage attack while recordings were easily made by telemetry.

4. G.C. This 14-year-old Negro girl was brought up in a foster home and was of borderline intelligence. On two separate occasions her violent behavior resulted in the death of a young foster sibling, and she subsequently assaulted a 7-year-old child at the state hospital where she was confined.

The EEGs, ventriculograms and arteriograms appeared normal, and extradural plates beneath the temporal lobes recorded normal brain waves. Depth electrodes were placed in each amygdala through the posterior approach. Recordings from the hippocampus showed marked focal electrical abnormalities. Telerecordings and telestimulations were used because of this patient's unpredictable behavior. She could not be relied on to sit quietly with the conventional EEG recording system. Stimulation in her right hippocampus produced a clinical and electrical temporal lobe seizure. In retrospect, the patient claimed to have had a number of these before electrode implantation but she had not communicated this information to her physicians.

RECORDING AND STIMULATION

. . . One of the main objectives in telemetric recording of intracerebral activity is the search for correlations between electrical patterns and behavioral manifestations. Computer analysis of the tape-recorded information is the best method for this purpose, and its results will be reported in the future. Visual inspection of ink writing recording may also give valuable data, as indicated in the following examples.

In patient J.P., spontaneous, brief peiods of aimless walking around the room coincided with an increase in high voltage sharp waves. At other times, spontaneous inhibition of speech lasting for several minutes was accompanied by a burst of spike localized activity. Psychological excitement of the same patient was related with an increase in the number and duration of 16-cps bursts. Emotionally charged conversation often modified the recordings from the amygdala, but this result was not as evident as the above mentioned changes. The possible significance of these correlations was increased by the fact that other behavioral manifestations did not produce detectable electrical changes. The patient walked around the room, used the toilet, read papers, and conversed without visible alterations in the telemetered depth recordings.

Radio stimulation of different points in the amygdala and hippocampus in the four patients produced a variety of effects including pleasant sensations, elation, deep thoughtful concentration, odd feelings, super relaxation, colored visions and other responses. In this article we will discuss only the following selected results:

During a recorded interview with patient G.C., point 9, located in the left hippocampus, was radio-stimulated for 5 sec with 100 cps, 0.5 msec, and 1 ma, resulting in an electrical after-discharge involving the amygdala, hippocampus and optic radiation, which lasted for 25 sec. During this time the patient's conversation stopped completely and she was unresponsive, without exhibiting motor convulsions, automatisms or other visible disturbances. When the after-discharge was over, the patient resumed conversation, remembered her speech arrest, but was not able to explain it. Spontaneous electrical activity of the brain was considerably modified for more than 2 min after stimulation. During this period, the patient expressed the successive sensations of fainting, fright and floating around. These "floating" feelings were repeatedly evoked on different days by stimulation of the same point even in the absence of after-discharges. Single shocks applied to the hippocampus induced bursts of high voltage activity in the optic

radiation and were accompanied by the perception of "funny feelings."

In patient J.P., crises of assaultive behavior reminiscent of her spontaneous bursts of anger could be elicited by radio stimulation of contact 3 in the right amygdala. Seven seconds after the onset of radio stimulation with 50 cps, 1.0 msec, and 1.2 ma, the patient interrupted spontaneous activities such as guitar playing, and in a fit of rage threw herself against the wall (never attacking the interviewer), paced around the room for several minutes, and then gradually reassumed her normal behavior. This effect was repeated on 2 days with similar results. During this elicited rage, no seizure activity was evident in the depth recording. The fact that only one contact gave this type of response suggested that the surrounding neuronal field was involved in the behavioral problems of the patient.

DISCUSSION

Important limitations of standard electroencephalographic recordings are as follows: 1) psychological stress of the recording room; 2) time required to attach leads to the patients; 3) restrictions imposed on individual mobility by the connecting leads; 4) limited period for the acquisition of data; and 5) the slim likelihood of taking recordings during spontaneous electrical or behavioral crises, which could provide the most important information for the patient's diagnosis and treatment.

These handicaps are eliminated by using telemetry. Extensive information has been published about different systems for radio telemetry in biological studies (4, 7, 15, 24). The disparity between the large number of technical papers and the few reports of results indicates the existence of methodological problems. There is some data on telemetered EEG obtained during space flights (1, 23); preliminary descriptions of scalp EEG studies in humans have been reported (6, 18), and there is also a technical paper on telemetered scalp EEG in disturbed children (25). Data is presented here to demonstrate that telemetry of EEG has already attained a degree of sophistication, miniaturization and reliability that render it suitable for widespread clinical application in both standard scalp and intracerebral electrical studies.

In the last decade, depth recording in man has become a major therapeutic tool in various medical centers (2, 3, 5, 16, 22, 26–28). The usefulness of intracerebral electrodes would be significantly increased if stimulations and recordings were performed by remote control. This technique, in addition to being more comfortable for the patients, would permit more detailed exploration and prolonged studies including periods of normal sleep.

Electrical stimulation of the brain, which is a standard procedure in neurosurgery, has been proposed by some authors as a therapeutic technique (16, 22, 27). For this purpose, programmed radio stimulation of ambulatory patients would be obviously advantageous.

The combination of both stimulation and EEG recording by radio telemetry offers a new tool for two-way clinical exploration of the brain, and it may be predicted that in the near future microminiaturization and more refined methodology will permit the construction of instruments without batteries and small enough to be permanently implanted underneath the patient's skin, for transdermal reception and transmission of signals through several channels. Part of the basic circuitry for this purpose has already passed satisfactory testing in our laboratory. While the use of cardiac pacemakers is well established in clinical medicine, methodological problems in the development of a similar instrument for cerebral pacemaking are far more difficult because of the requirements of multichanneling, external control of several parameters of stimulation, and the far greater functional complexity of the brain in comparison with the heart. These technical problems, however, are soluble, and the possibility of clinical application should attract the interest of more electronic and medical investigators.

Experimentation in animals has demonstrated the practicality of long term, programmed stimulation of the brain to inhibit episodes of assaultive behavior (8), to increase or decrease appetite (14),

to modify drives (10) and to modulate intracerebral reactivity (9). Some of these findings may be applicable to the treatment of cerebral disturbances in man.

With respect to the electrical information obtained in our four patients, analysis of their telemetered EEG supports the assumption that depth recordings reveal local activity rather than diffuse volume conductor fields in the brain, in agreement with previous work obtained by direct leads (12). The considerable independence of the electrical activity of different intracerebral points indicates that this electrographic information has anatomical significance. Caution is necessary, however, in a calculation of the origin of apparently abnormal waves, which could originate in the neuronal field around the contacts or could reflect merely the activity transmitted from a distant cerebral area, as demonstrated in animal experiments (11). The distinction between reactive and propagated activity which can be made by studying recorded electrical patterns may help to evaluate the origin of abnormal intracerebral activity.

SUMMARY

A new instrument called "stimoceiver" has been developed for the simultaneous multichannel recording and stimulation of the brain by FM radio waves in completely unrestrained subjects. This instrument is small enough to be worn comfortably and permanently by the patient.

Clinical application of the stimoceiver is reported in four patients with psychomotor epilepsy who had electrodes implanted in the amygdala and hippocampus for therapeutical reasons. The advantages of this methodology are: 1) the patient is instrumented for telestimulation and recording simply by plugging the stimoceiver into the electrode socket on the head; 2) the instrumentation does not limit or modify spontaneous behavior; 3) the patient is continuously available, day and night, for intracerebral recording or treatment; 4) studies are performed, without introducing factors of anxiety or stress, in the relatively normal environment of the hospital ward and during spontaneous social interactions; 5) cerebral explorations may be conducted in severely disturbed patients who would not tolerate the confinement of the recording room; 6) the lack of connecting wires eliminates the risk that during unpredictable behavior or convulsive episodes the patient may dislodge or even pull out the implanted electrodes; 7) programmed stimulation of the brain for therapeutic reasons may be continued for as long as necessary.

In four patients telemetric information obtained supports the following conclusions: 1) depth recordings reveal local activity rather than diffuse volume conductor fields, giving anatomical signifi-cance to the data; 2) abnormality in spontaneous behavior, including aimless walking, speech inhibition, and psychological excitement, coincided with abnormal EEG patterns: 3) arrest reaction accompanied by an after-discharge was evoked in one patient by radio stimulation of the hippocampus, and during the subsequent 2 min, abnormalities in brain waves coincided with successive sensations of fainting, fright and floating around; 4) assaultive behavior, reminiscent of spontaneous crises, was elicited in another patient by radio stimulation of the amygdala, and this fact was important in orienting therapeutic surgery.

REFERENCES

1. Adey, W. R. Potential for telemetry in the recording of brain waves from animals and men exposed to the stresses of space flight. In Slater, L., ed. Bio-Telemetry, pp. 289–300. Permagon Press, New York, 1963.

2. Alberts, W. W., Feinstein, B., Levin, G. and Wright, E. W., Electrical stimulation of therapeutic targets in waking dyskinetic patients. EEG Clin. Neurophysiol., 20: 559–566, 1966.

3. Ajmone Marsan, C. and Van Buren, J. Functional relationship between frontal cortex and subcortical structures in man. EEG Clin. Neurophysiol., 16: 80–87, 1964.

4. Barwick, R. E. and Fullager, P. J. A. bibliography of radio telemetry in biological studies. Proc. Ecol. Soc. Aust., 2: 27, 1967.

5. Bickford, R. G., Dodge, H. W., Jr. and Uihlein, A. Electrographic and behavioral effects related to depth stimulation in human patients. In Ramey, E. R. and O'Doherty, D. S., eds. Electrical Studies on the Unanesthetized Brain, pp. 248–259. Hoeber, New York, 1960.

6. Breakell, C. C., Parker, C. S. and Christopherson, F. Radio transmission of the human electroencephalogram and other electrophysiological data. EEG Clin. Neurophysiol., 1: 243–244, 1949.

7. Caceres, C. A., ed. Biomedical Telemetry. Academic Press, New York, 1965.

8. Delgado, J. M. R. Aggression and defense under cerebral radio control. In Clemente, C. D. and Lindsley, D. B., eds. Aggression and Defense. Neural Mechanisms and Social Patterns [Brain Function, vol. V], pp. 171–193. University of California Press, Berkeley, 1967.

9. Delgado, J. M. R. Free behavior and brain stimulation. In Pfeiffer, C. C. and Smythies, J. R., eds. International Review of Neurobiology, vol. 6, pp. 349–449. Academic Press, New York, 1964.

10. Delgado, J. M. R. Man's intervention in intracerebral functions. IEEE Int. Conv. Rec., 9: 143–150, 1967.

11. Delgado, J. M. R. and Hamlin, H. Depth electrography. Confin. Neurol., 22: 228–235, 1962.

12. Delgado, J. M. R. and Hamlin, H. Direct recording of spontaneous and evoked seizures in epileptics. EEG Clin. Neurophysiol., 10: 463–486, 1958.

13. Delgado, J. M. R. and Mir, D. Fragmental organization of emotional behavior in the monkey brain. N.Y. Acad. Sci. In press.

14. Fonberg, E. and Delgado, J. M. R. Avoidance and alimentary reactions during amygdala stimulation. J. Neurophysiol., 24: 651–664, 1961.

15. Geddes, L. A. A bibliography of biological telemetry. Amer. J. Med. Electronics, 1: 294–298, 1962.

16. Heath, R. G. Electrical self-stimulation of the brain in man. Amer. J. Psychiat., 120: 571–577, 1963.

17. Higgins, J. W., Mahl, G. F., Delgado, J. M. R. and Hamlin, H. Behavioral changes during intracerebral electrical stimulation. Arch. Neurol. Psychiat. (Chicago), 76: 339–419, 1956.

18. Kamp, A. and Van Leeuwen, W. S. A two-channel EEG radio telemetering system EEG Clin. Neurophysiol., 13: 803–806, 1961.

19. Mahl, G. F., Rothenberg, A., Delgado, J. M. R. and Hamlin, H. Psychological responses in the human to intracerebral electrical stimulation. Psychosom. Med., 26: 337–368, 1964.

20. Mark, V. H. and Ervin, F. The relief of chronic severe pain by stereotactic sur-

gery. In White, J. C. and Sweet, W. H., eds. *Pain and the Neurosurgeon: A Forty Years' Experience.* Thomas, Springfield, Ill. In press.

21. Meehan, J. P. and Rader, R. D. Multiple channel physiological data acquisition system for restrained and mobile subjects. Report to Air Force Systems Command on Contact AF04(695)-178, 1965.

22. Sem-Jacobsen, C. W. Electrical stimulation of the human brain. EEG Clin. Neurophysiol., *17:* 211, 1964.

23. Simons, D. G. and Prather, W. A personalized radio telemetry system for monitoring central nervous system arousal in aerospace flight. IEEE Trans. Biomed. Engin., *11:* 40, 1964.

24. Slater, L., ed. *Bio-Telemetry.* Pergamon Press, New York, 1963.

25. Vreeland, R., Collins, C., Williams, L., Yeager, C., Gianascol, A. and Henderson, J., Jr. A subminiature radio EEG telemeter for studies of disturbed children. EEG Clin. Neurophysiol., *15:* 327–329, 1963.

26. Walker, A. E. and Marshall, C. The contribution of depth recording to clinical medicine. EEG Clin. Neurophysiol., *16:* 88–99, 1964.

27. Walter, W. G. and Crow, H. J. Depth recording from the human brain. EEG Clin. Neurophysiol., *16:* 68–72, 1964.

28. White, J. C. and Sweet, W. H. eds. *Pain and the Neurosurgeon: A Forty Years' Experience.* Thomas, Springfield, Ill. In press.

9.
hemisphere deconnection and unity in conscious awareness

r. w. sperry

The following article is a result of studies my colleagues and I have been conducting with some neurosurgical patients of Philip J. Vogel of Los Angeles. These patients were all advanced epileptics in whom an extensive midline section of the cerebral commissures had been carried out in an effort to contain severe epileptic convulsions not controlled by medication. In all these people the surgical sections included division of the corpus callosum in its entirety, plus division also of the smaller anterior and hippocampal commissures, plus in some instances the massa intermedia. So far as I know, this is the most radical disconnection of the cerebral hemispheres attempted thus far in human surgery. The full array of sections was carried out in a single operation.

No major collapse of mentality or personality was anticipated as a result of this extreme surgery: earlier clinical observations on surgical section of the corpus callosum in man, as well as the results from dozens of monkeys on which I had carried out this exact same surgery, suggested that the functional deficits might very likely be less damaging than

Reprinted from *American Psychologist*, 1968, *23*, (10), 723–733. Published by the American Psychological Association. Abridged by permission of the author.

Invited address presented to the American Psychological Association in Washington, D. C., September 1967, and to the Pan American Congress of Neurology in San Juan, Puerto Rico, October 1967. Original work referred to in the text by the writer and his co-workers was supported by Grant MH-03372 from the National Institute of Mental Health, United States Public Health Service, and by the Hixon Fund of the California Institute of Technology.

some of the more common forms of cerebral surgery, such as frontal lobotomy, or even some of the unilateral lobotomies performed more routinely for epilepsy.

The first patient on whom this surgery was tried had been having seizures for more than 10 years with generalized convulsions that continued to worsen despite treatment that had included a sojourn in Bethesda at the National Institutes of Health. At the time of the surgery, he had been averaging two major attacks per week, each of which left him debilitated for another day or so. Episodes of *status epilepticus* (recurring seizures that fail to stop and represent a medical emergency with a fairly high mortality risk) had also begun to occur at 2- to 3-month intervals. Since leaving the hospital following his surgery over 5½ years ago, this man has not had, according to last reports, a single generalized convulsion. It has further been possible to reduce the level of medication and to obtain an overall improvement in his behavior and well being (see Bogen & Vogel, 1962).

The second patient, a housewife and mother in her 30s, also has been seizure-free since recovering from her surgery, which was more than 4 years ago (Bogen, Fisher & Vogel, 1965). Bogen related that even the EEG has regained a normal pattern in this patient. The excellent outcome in the initial, apparently hopeless, last-resort cases led to further application of the surgery to some nine more individuals to date, the majority of whom are too recent for therapeutic evaluation. Although the alleviation of the epilepsy has not held up 100% throughout the series (two patients are still having seizures, although their convulsions are much reduced in severity and frequency and tend to be confined to one side), the results on the whole continue to be predominantly beneficial, and the overall outlook at this time remains promising for selected severe cases.

The therapeutic success, however, and all other medical aspects are matters for our medical colleagues, Philip J. Vogel and Joseph E. Bogen. Our own work has been confined entirely to an examination of the functional outcome, that is, the behavioral, neurological, and psychological effects of this surgical disruption of all direct cross-talk between the hemispheres. Initially we were concerned as to whether we would be able to find in these patients any of the numerous symptoms of hemisphere deconnection that had been demonstrated in the so-called "split-brain" animal studies of the 1950s (Myers, 1961; Sperry, 1967a, 1967b). The outcome in man remained an open question in view of the historic Akelaitis (1944) studies that had set the prevailing doctrine of the 1940s and 1950s. This doctrine maintained that no important functional symptoms are found in man following even complete surgical section of the corpus callosum and anterior commissure, provided that other brain damage is excluded.

These earlier observations on the absence of behavioral symptoms in man have been confirmed in a general way to the extent that it remains fair to say today that the most remarkable effect of sectioning the neocortical commissures is the apparent lack of effect so far as ordinary behavior is concerned. This has been true in our animal studies throughout, and it seems now to be true for man also, with certain qualifications that we will come to later. At the same time, however—and this is in contradiction to the earlier doctrine set by the Akelaitis studies—we know today that with appropriate tests one can indeed demonstrate a large number of behavioral symptoms that correlate directly with the loss of the neocortical commissures in man as well as in animals (Gazzaniga, 1967; Sperry, 1967a, 1967b; Sperry, Gazzaniga & Bogen, 1968). Taken collectively, these symptoms may

be referred to as the syndrome of the neocortical commissures or the syndrome of the forebrain commissures or, less specifically, as the syndrome of hemisphere deconnection.

One of the more general and also more interesting and striking features of this syndrome may be summarized as an apparent doubling in most of the realms of conscious awareness. Instead of the normally unified single stream of consciousness, these patients behave in many ways as if they have two independent streams of conscious awareness, one in each hemisphere, each of which is cut off from and out of contact with the mental experiences of the other. In other words, each hemisphere seems to have its own separate and private sensations; its own perceptions; its own concepts; and its own impulses to act, with related volitional, cognitive, and learning experiences. Following the surgery, each hemisphere also has thereafter its own separate chain of memories that are rendered inaccessible to the recall processes of the other.

This presence of two minds in one body, as it were, is manifested in a large number and variety of test responses which, for the present purposes, I will try to review very briefly and in a somewhat streamlined and simplified form. First, however, let me take time to emphasize that the work reported here has been very much a team project. The surgery was performed by Vogel at the White Memorial Medical Center in Los Angeles. He has been assisted in the surgery and in the medical treatment throughout by Joseph Bogen. Bogen has also been collaborating in our behavioral testing program, along with a number of graduate students and postdoctoral fellows, among whom M. S. Gazzaniga, in particular, worked closely with us during the first several years and managed much of the testing during that period. The patients and their families have been most cooperative, and the whole project gets its primary funding from the National Institute of Mental Health.

Most of the main symptoms seen after hemisphere deconnection can be described for convenience with reference to a single testing setup—shown in

Figure 1. Apparatus for studying lateralization of visual, tactual, lingual, and associated functions in the surgically separated hemispheres.

Figure 1. Principally, it allows for the lateralized testing of the right and left halves of the visual field, separately or together, and the right and left hands and legs with vision excluded. The tests can be arranged in different combinations and in association with visual, auditory, and other input, with provisions for eliminating unwanted stimuli. In testing vision, the subject with one eye covered centers his gaze on a designated fixation point on the upright translucent screen. The visual stimuli on 35-millimeter transparencies are arranged in a standard projector equipped with a shutter and are then back-projected at 1/10 of a second or less—too fast for eye movements to get the material into the wrong half of the visual field. Figure 2 is merely a reminder that everything seen to the left of the vertical meridian through either eye is projected to the right hemisphere and vice versa. The midline division along the vertical meridian is found to be quite precise without significant gap or overlap (Sperry, 1968).

When the visual perception of these patients is tested under these conditions the results indicate that these people have not one inner visual world any longer, but rather two separate visual inner worlds, one serving the right half of the field of vision and the other the left half—each, of course, in its respective hemisphere. This doubling in the visual sphere shows up in many ways: For example, after a projected picture of an object has been identified and responded to in one half field, we find that it is recognized again only if it reappears in the same half of the field of vision. If the given visual stimulus reappears in the opposite half of the visual field, the subject responds as if he had no recollection of the previous exposure. In other words, things seen through the right half of the visual field (i.e., through the left hemisphere) are registered in mental experience and remembered quite separately from things seen in the other half of the field. Each half of the field of vision in the commissurotomized patient has its own train of visual images and memories.

This separate existence of two visual inner worlds is further illustrated in reference to speech and writing, the cortical mechanisms for which are centered in the dominant hemisphere. Visual material projected to the right half of the field—left-hemisphere system of the typical right-handed patient—can be described in speech and writing in an essentially normal manner. However, when the same visual material is projected into the left half of the field, and hence to the right hemisphere, the subject consistently insists that he did not see anything or that there was only a flash of light on the left side. The subject acts as if he were blind or agnostic for the left half of the visual field. If, however, instead of asking the subject to tell you what he saw, you instruct him to use his left hand to point to a matching picture or object presented among a collection of other pictures or objects, the subject has no trouble as a rule in pointing out consistently the very item that he has just insisted he did not see.

We do not think the subjects are trying to be difficult or to dupe the examiner in such tests. Everything indicates that the hemisphere that is talking to the examiner did in fact not see the left-field stimulus and truly had no experience with, nor recollection of, the given stimulus. The other, the right or nonlingual hemisphere, however, did see the projected stimulus in this situation and is able to remember and recognize the object and can demonstrate this by pointing out selectively the corresponding or matching item. This other hemisphere, like a deaf mute or like some aphasics, cannot talk about the perceived object and, worse still, cannot write about it either.

If two different figures are flashed simultaneously to the right and left visual fields, as for example a "dollar sign" on the left and a "question mark" on the right and the subject is asked to draw what he saw using the left hand out of sight, he regularly reproduces the figure seen on the left half of the field, that is, the dollar sign. If we now ask him what he has just drawn, he tells us without hesitation that the figure he drew was the question mark, or whatever appeared in the right half of the field. In other words, the one hemisphere does not know what the other hemisphere has been doing. The left and the right halves of the visual field seem to be perceived quite separately in each hemisphere with little or no cross-influence.

When words are flashed partly in the left field and partly in the right, the letters on each side of the midline are perceived and responded to separately. In the "key case" example shown in Figure 2 the subject might first reach for and select with the left hand a key from among a collection of objects indicating perception through the minor hemisphere. With the right hand he might then spell out the word "case" or he might speak the word if verbal response is in order. When asked what kind of "case" he was thinking of here, the answer coming from the left hemisphere might be something like "in *case* of fire" or "the *case* of the missing corpse" or "a *case* of beer," etc., depending upon the particular mental set of the left hemisphere at the moment. Any reference to "key case" under these conditions would be purely fortuitous, assuming that visual, auditory, and other cues have been properly controlled.

A similar separation in mental awareness is evident in tests that deal with stereognostic or other somesthetic discriminations made by the right and left hands, which are projected separately to

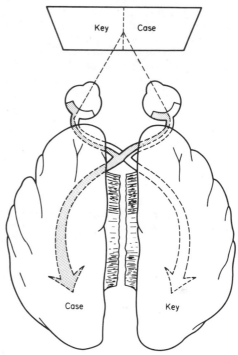

Figure 2. Things seen to the left of a central fixation point with either eye are projected to the right hemisphere and vice versa.

the left and right hemispheres, respectively. Objects put in the right hand for identification by touch are readily described or named in speech or writing, whereas, if the same objects are placed in the left hand, the subject can only make wild guesses and may often seem unaware that anything at all is present. As with vision in the left field, however, good perception, comprehension, and memory can be demonstrated for these objects in the left hand when the tests are so designed that the subject can express himself through nonverbal responses. For example, if one of these objects which the subject tells you he cannot feel or does not recognize is taken from the left hand and placed in a grab bag or scrambled among a dozen other test items, the subject is then able to search out and retrieve the initial object even after a delay of several minutes is deliberately interposed. Unlike the normal subject, however, these people are obliged to retrieve such an object with the same hand with which it was initially identified. They fail at cross-retrieval. That is, they cannot recognize with one hand something identified only moments before with the other hand. Again, the second hemisphere does not know what the first hemisphere has been doing.

When the subjects are first asked to use the left hand for these stereognostic tests they commonly complain that they cannot "work with that hand," that the hand "is numb," that they "just can't feel anything or can't do anything with it," or that they "don't get the message from that hand." If the subjects perform a series of successful trials and correctly retrieve a group of objects which they previously stated they could not feel, and if this contradiction is then pointed out to them, we get comments like "Well, I was just guessing," or "Well, I must have done it unconsciously.". . .

It is worth remembering that when you split the brain in half anatomically you do not divide in half, in quite the same sense, its functional properties. In some respects cerebral functions may be doubled as much as they are halved because of the extensive bilateral redundancy in brain organization, wherein most functions, particularly in subhuman species, are separately and rather fully organized on both sides. Consider for example the visual inner world of either of the disconnected hemispheres in these patients. Probably neither of the separated visual systems senses or perceives itself to be cut in half or even incomplete. One may compare it to the visual sphere of the hemianopic patient who, following accidental destruction of an entire visual cortex of one hemisphere, may not even notice the loss of the whole half sphere of vision until this has been pointed out to him in specific optometric tests. These commissurotomy patients continue to watch television and to read the paper and books with no complaints about peculiarities in the perceptual appearance of the visual field.

At the same time, I want to caution against any impression that these patients are better off mentally without their cerebral commissures. It is true that if you carefully select two simple tasks, each of which is easily handled by a single hemisphere, and then have the two performed simultaneously, there is a good chance of getting better than normal scores. The normal interference effects that come from trying to attend to two separate right and left tasks at the same time are largely eliminated in the commissurotomized patient. However, in most activities that are at all complex the normally unified cooperating hemispheres still appear to do better than the two disconnected hemispheres. Although it is true that the intelligence, as measured on IQ tests, is not much affected and that the personality comes through with little change, one gets the impression in working with these people that their intellect is nevertheless handicapped in ways that are probably not revealed in the ordinary tests. All the patients have marked short-term memory deficits, which are especially pronounced during the first year, and it is open to question whether this memory impairment ever clears completely. They also have orientation problems, fatigue more quickly in reading and in other tasks requiring mental concentration, and presumably have various other impairments that reduce the upper limits of performance in functions that have yet to be investigated. The patient that has shown the best recovery, a boy of 14, was able to return to public school and was doing passing work with B to D grades, except for an F in math, which he had to repeat. He was, however, a D student before the surgery, in part, it would seem for lack of motivation. In general, our tests to date have been concerned mostly with basic cross-integrational deficits in these patients and the kind of mental capacities preserved in the subordinate hemisphere. Studied comparisons of the upper limits of performance before and after surgery are still needed.

Much of the foregoing is summarized schematically in Figure 3. The left hemisphere in the right-handed patients is equipped with the expressive mechanisms for speech and writing and with the main centers for the comprehension and organization of language. This "major" hemisphere can communicate its experiences verbally and in an essentially normal manner. It can communicate, that is, about the visual experiences of the right half of the optic field and about the somesthetic and volitional experiences of the right hand and leg and right half of the body generally. In addition, and not indicated in the figure, the major hemisphere also communicates, of course, about all of the more general, less lateralized cerebral activity that is bilaterally represented and common to both hemispheres. On the other side we have the mute aphasic and agraphic right hemisphere, which cannot express itself verbally, but which through the use of nonverbal responses can show that it is not agnostic; that mental processes are indeed present centered around the left visual field, left hand, left leg, and left half of the body; along with the auditory, vestibular, axial somatic, and all other cerebral activities that are less lateralized and for which the mental experiences of the right and left hemispheres may be characterized as being similar but separate.

It may be noted that nearly all of the symptoms of cross-integrational impairment that I have been describing are easily hidden or compensated under the conditions of ordinary behavior. For example, the visual material has to be flashed at ⅒ of a second or less to one half of the field in order to prevent compensation by eye movements. The defects in manual stereognosis are not apparent unless vision is excluded; nor is doubling in olfactory perception evident without sequential occlusion of right and left nostril and elimination of visual cues. In many tests the major hemisphere must be prevented from talking to the minor hemisphere and thus giving away the answer through auditory channels. And, similarly, the minor hemisphere must be prevented from giving nonverbal signals of various sorts to the major hemisphere. There is a great diversity of indirect strategies and response signals, implicit as well as overt, by which the informed hemisphere can be used to cue-in the uninformed hemisphere (Levy-Agresti, 1968).

Normal behavior under ordinary con-

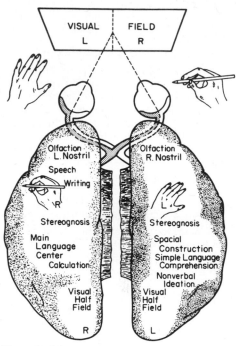

Figure 3. Schematic outline of the functional lateralization evident in behavioral tests of patients with forebrain commissurotomy.

ditions is favored also by many other unifying factors. Some of these are very obvious, like the fact that these two separate mental spheres have only one body, so they always get dragged to the same places, meet the same people, and see and do the same things all the time and thus are bound to have a great overlap of common, almost identical, experience. Just the unity of the optic image—and even after chiasm section in animal experiments, the conjugate movements of the eyes—means that both hemispheres automatically center on, focus on, and hence probably attend to, the same items in the visual field all the time. Through sensory feedback a unifying body schema is imposed in each hemisphere with common components that similarly condition in parallel many processes of perception and motor action onto a common base. To get different activities going and different experiences and different memory chains built up in the separated hemispheres of the bisected mammalian brain, as we do in the animal work, requires a considerable amount of experimental planning and effort.

In motor control we have another important unifying factor, in that either hemisphere can direct the movement of both sides of the body, including to some extent the movements of the ipsilateral hand (Hamilton, 1967). Insofar as a response involves mainly the axial parts and proximal limb segments, these patients have little problem in directing overall response from sensory information restricted to either single hemisphere. Control of the distal limb segments and especially of the finer finger movements of the hand ipsilateral to the governing hemisphere, however, are borderline functions and subject to considerable variation. Impairments are most conspicuous when the subject is given a verbal command to respond with the fingers of the left hand. The absence of the callosum, which normally would connect the language processing centers in the left hemisphere to the main left-hand motor controls in the opposite hemisphere, is clearly a handicap, especially in the early months after surgery. Cursive writing with the left hand presents a similar problem. It may be accomplished in time by some patients using shoulder and elbow rather than finger movement. At best, however, writing with the left hand is not as good after as before the surgery. The problem is not in motor coordination per se, because the subject can often copy with the left hand a word already written by the examiner when the same word cannot be written to verbal command.

In a test used for more direct determination of the upper limits of this ipsilateral motor control, a simple outline sketch of a finger posture (see Figure 4) is flashed to a single hemisphere, and the subject then tries to mimic the posture with the same or the opposite hand. The sample posture can usually be copied on the same side (i.e., through the main, contralateral control system) without difficulty, but the performance does not go so easily and often breaks down completely when the subject is

obliged to use the opposite hand. The closed fist and the open hand with all fingers extended seem to be the two simplest responses, in that these can most often be copied with the ipsilateral hand by the more adept patients.

The results are in accord with the thesis (Gazzaniga, Bogen, & Sperry, 1967) that the ipsilateral control systems are delicate and marginal and easily disrupted by associated cerebral damage and other complicating factors. Preservation of the ipsilateral control system in varying degree in some patients and not in others would appear to account for many of the discrepancies that exist in the literature on the symptoms of hemisphere deconnection, and also for a number of changes between the present picture and that described until 2 years ago. Those acquainted with the literature will notice that the present findings on dyspraxia come much closer to the earlier Akelaitis observations than they do to those of Liepmann or of others expounded more recently (see Geschwind, 1965).

To try to find out what goes on in that speechless agraphic minor hemisphere has always been one of the main challenges in our testing program. Does the minor hemisphere really possess a true stream of conscious awareness or is it just an agnostic automaton that is carried along in a reflex or trancelike state? What is the nature, the quality, and the level of the mental life of this isolated subordinate unknown half of the human brain—which, like the animal mind, cannot communicate its experiences? Closely tied in here are many problems that relate to lateral dominance and specialization in the human brain, to the functional roles mediated by the neocortical commissures, and to related aspects of cerebral organization.

With such in mind, I will try to review briefly some of the evidence obtained to date that pertains to the level and nature of the inner mental life of the disconnected minor hemisphere. First, it is clear that the minor hemisphere can perform intermodal or cross-modal transfer of perceptual and mnemonic information at a characteristically human level. For example, after a picture of some object, such as a cigarette, has been flashed to

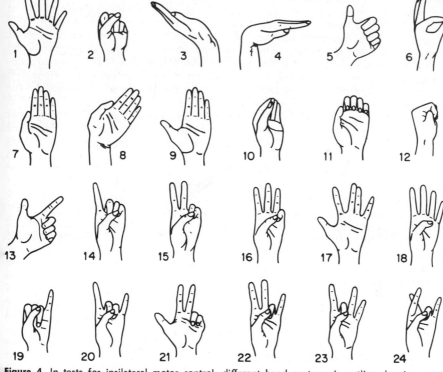

Figure 4. In tests for ipsilateral motor control, different hand postures in outline drawing are projected one at a time to left and right visual field (see Figure 1). Subject attempts to copy the sample hand pose with the homolateral and the contralateral hand.

the minor hemisphere through the left visual field, the subject can retrieve the item pictured from a collection of objects using blind touch with the left hand, which is mediated through the right hemisphere. Unlike the normal person, however, the commissurotomy patient is obliged to use the corresponding hand (i.e., the left hand, in this case) for retrieval and fails when he is required to search out the same object with the right hand. Using the right hand the subject recognizes and can call off the names of each object that he comes to if he is allowed to do so, but the right hand or its hemisphere does not know what it is looking for, and the hemisphere that can recognize the correct answer gets no feedback from the right hand. Hence, the two never get together, and the performance fails. Speech and other auditory cues must be controlled.

It also works the other way around: that is, if the subject is holding an object in the left hand, he can then point out a picture of this object or the printed name of the object when these appear in a series presented visually. But again, these latter must be seen through the corresponding half of the visual field; an object identified by the left hand is not recognized when seen in the right half of the visual field. Intermodal associations of this sort have been found to work between vision, hearing and touch, and, more recently, olfaction in various combinations within either hemisphere but not across from one hemisphere to the other. This perceptual or mnemonic transfer from one sense modality to another has special theoretical interest in that it is something that is extremely difficult or impossible for the monkey brain. The right hemisphere, in other words, may be animal-like in not being able to talk or write, but in performances like the foregoing and in a number of other respects it shows mental capacities that are definitely human.

Other responses from the minor hemisphere in this same testing situation suggest the presence of ideas and a capacity for mental association and at least some simple logic and reasoning. In the same visuo-tactual test described above, the minor hemisphere, instead of selecting objects that match exactly the pictured item, seems able also to select related items or items that "go with" the particular visual stimulus, if the subject is so instructed. For example, if we flash a picture of a wall clock to the minor side and the nearest item that can be found tactually by the left hand is a toy wrist watch, the subjects significantly select the watch. It is as if the minor hemisphere has an idea of a timepiece here and is not just matching sensory outlines. Or, if the picture of a dollar sign is flashed to the minor side, the subject searches through the list of items with the left hand and finally selects a coin such as a quarter or a 50¢ piece. If a picture of a hammer is presented, the subject may come up with a nail or a spike after checking out and rejecting all other items.

The capacity to think abstractly with symbols is further indicated in the ability of the minor hemisphere to perform simple arithmetical problems. When confronted with two numerals each less than 10, the minor hemisphere was able in four of six subjects so tested to respond with the correct sum or product up to 20 or so. The numbers were flashed to the left half of the visual field or presented as plastic block numerals to the left hand for identification. The answer was expressed by pointing to the correct number in columns of seen figures, or by left-hand signals in which the fingers were extended out of the subject's sight, or by writing the numerals with the left hand out of sight. After a correct left-hand response had been made by pointing or by writing the numeral, the major hemisphere could then report the same answer verbally, but the verbal report could not be made prior to the left-hand response. If an error was made with the left hand, the verbal report contained the same error. Two different pairs of numerals may be flashed to right and left fields simultaneously and the correct sum or products signaled separately by right and left hands. When verbal confirmation of correct left-hand signals is required under these conditions, the speaking hemisphere can only guess fortuitously, showing again that the answer must have been obtained from the minor and not from the major hemisphere. This has been demonstrated recently in a study still in progress by Biersner and the present writer. The findings correct an earlier impression (Gazzaniga & Sperry, 1967) in which we underestimated the capacity for calculation on the minor side. Normal subjects and also a subject with agenesis of the callosum (Saul & Sperry, 1968) were able to add or to multiply numerals shown one in the left and one in the right field under these conditions. The commissurotomy subjects, however, were able to perform such calculations only when both numerals appeared in the same half of the visual field.

According to a doctrine of long standing in the clinical writings on aphasia, it is believed that the minor hemisphere, when it has been disconnected by commissural or other lesions from the language centers on the opposite side, becomes then "word blind," "word deaf," and "tactually alexic." In contradiction to this, we find that the disconnected minor hemisphere in these commissurotomy patients is able to comprehend both written and spoken words to some extent, although this comprehension cannot be expressed verbally (Gazzaniga & Sperry, 1967; Sperry, 1966; Sperry & Gazzaniga, 1967). If the name of some object is flashed to the left visual field, like the word "eraser," for example, the subject is able then to search out an eraser from among a collection of objects using only touch with the left hand. If the subject is then asked what the item is after it has been selected correctly, his replies show that he does not know what he is holding in his left hand—as is the general rule for left-hand stereognosis. This means of course that the *talking* hemisphere does not know the correct answer, and we concluded accordingly that the minor hemisphere must, in this situation, have read and understood the test world.

These patients also demonstrate comprehension of language in the minor hemisphere by being able to find by blind touch with the left hand an object that has been named aloud by the examiner. For example, if asked to find a "piece of silverware," the subject may explore the array of test items and pick up a fork. If the subject is then asked what it is that he has chosen, he is just as likely in this case to reply "spoon" or "knife" as fork. Both hemispheres have heard and understood the word "silverware," but only the minor hemisphere knows what the left hand has actually found and picked up. In similar tests for comprehension of the spoken word, we find that the minor hemisphere seems able to understand even moderately advanced definitions like "shaving instrument" for razor or "dirt remover" for soap and "inserted in slot machines" for quarter.

Work in progress shows that the minor hemisphere can also sort objects into groups by touch on the basis of shape, size, and texture. In some tests the minor hemisphere is found to be superior to the major, for example, in tasks that involve drawing spatial relationships and performing block design tests. Perceptive mental performance in the minor hemisphere is also indicated in other situations in which the two hemispheres function concurrently in parallel at different tasks. It has been found, for example, that the divided hemispheres are capable of perceiving different things occupying the same position in space at the same time, and of learning mutually conflicting discrimination habits, something of which the normal brain is not capable. This was shown in the monkey work done some years ago by Trevarthen (1962) using a system of polarized light filters. It also required section of the optic chiasm, which of course is not included in the human surgery. The human patients, unlike normal subjects, are able to carry out a double voluntary reaction-time task as fast as they carry out a single task (Gazzaniga & Sperry, 1966).

Each hemisphere in this situation has to perform a separate and different visual discrimination in order to push with the corresponding hand the correct one of a right and left pair of panels. Whereas interference and extra delay are seen in normal subjects with the introduction of the second task, these patients with the two hemispheres working in parallel simultaneously perform the double task as rapidly as the single task.

The minor hemisphere is also observed to demonstrate appropriate emotional reactions as, for example, when a pinup shot of a nude is interjected by surprise among a series of neutral geometric figures being flashed to the right and left fields at random. When the surprise nude appears on the left side the subject characteristically says that he or she saw nothing or just a flash of light. However, the appearance of a sneaky grin and perhaps blushing and giggling on the next couple of trials or so belies the verbal contention of the speaking hemisphere. If asked what all the grinning is about, the subject's replies indicate that the conversant hemisphere has no idea at this stage what it was that had turned him on. Apparently, only the emotional effect gets across, as if the cognitive component of the process cannot be articulated through the brainstem.

Emotion is also evident on the minor side in a current study by Gordon and Sperry (1968) involving olfaction. When odors are presented through the right nostril to the minor hemisphere the subject is unable to name the odor but can frequently tell whether it is pleasant or unpleasant. The subject may even grunt, make aversive reactions or exclamations like "phew!" to a strong unpleasant smell, but not be able to state verbally whether it is garlic, cheese, or some decayed matter. Again it appears that the affective component gets across to the speaking hemisphere, but not the more specific information. The presence of the specific information within the minor hemisphere is demonstrated by the subject's correct selection through left-hand stereognosis of corresponding objects associated with the given odor. The minor hemisphere also commonly triggers emotional reactions of displeasure in the course of ordinary testing. This is evidenced in the frowning, wincing, and negative head shaking in test situations where the minor hemisphere, knowing the correct answer but unable to speak, hears the major hemisphere making obvious verbal mistakes. The minor hemisphere seems to express genuine annoyance at the erroneous vocal responses of its better half.

Observations like the foregoing lead us to favor the view that in the minor hemisphere we deal with a second conscious entity that is characteristically human and runs along in parallel with the more dominant stream of consciousness in the major hemisphere (Sperry, 1966). The quality of mental awareness present in the minor hemisphere may be comparable perhaps to that which survives in some types of aphasic patients following losses in the motor and main language centers. There is no indication that the dominant mental system of the left hemisphere is concerned about or even aware of the presence of the minor system under most ordinary conditions except quite indirectly as, for example,

through occasional responses triggered from the minor side. As one patient remarked immediately after seeing herself make a left-hand response of this kind, "Now I know it wasn't me did that!"

Let me emphasize again in closing that the foregoing represents a somewhat abbreviated and streamlined account of the syndrome of hemisphere deconnection as we understand it at the present time. The more we see of these patients and the more of these patients we see, the more we become impressed with their individual differences, and with the consequent qualifications that must be taken into account. Although the general picture has continued to hold up in the main as described, it is important to note that, with respect to many of the deconnection symptoms mentioned, striking modifications and even outright exceptions can be found among the small group of patients examined to date Where the accumulation evidence will settle out with respect to the extreme limits of such individual variations and with respect to a possible average "type" syndrome remains to be seen.

REFERENCES

Akelaitis, A. J. A study of gnosis, praxis, and language following section of the corpus callosum and anterior commissure. *Journal of Neurosurgery*, 1944, *1*, 94–102.

Bogen, J. E., Fisher, E. D., & Vogel, P. J. Cerebral commissurotomy: A second case report. *Journal of the American Medical Association*, 1965, *194*, 1328–1329.

Bogen, J. E., & Vogel, P. J. Cerebral commissurotomy: A case report. *Bulletin of the Los Angeles Neurological Society*, 1962, *27*, 169.

Gazzaniga, M. S. The split brain in man. *Scientific American*, 1967, *217*, 24–29.

Gazzaniga, M. S., Bogen, J. E., & Sperry, R. W. Dyspraxia following division of the cerebral commissures. *Archives of Neurology*, 1967, *16*, 606–612.

Gazzaniga, M. S., & Sperry, R. W. Simultaneous double discrimination following brain bisection. *Psychonomic Science*, 1966, *4*, 262–263.

Gazzaniga, M. S., & Sperry, R. W. Language after section of the cerebral commissures. *Brain*, 1967, *90*, 131–148.

Geschwind, N. Disconnexion syndromes in animals and man. *Brain*, 1965, *88*, 237–294, 584–644.

Gordon, H. W., & Sperry, R. W. Olfaction following surgical disconnection of the hemispheres in man. In, *Proceedings of the Psychonomic Society, 1968.* In press.

Hamilton, C. R. Effects of brain bisection on eye-hand coordination in monkeys wearing prisms. *Journal of Comparative and Physiological Psychology*, 1967, *64*, 434–443

Levy-Agresti, J. Ipsilateral projection systems and minor hemisphere function in man after neocommissurotomy. *Anatomical Record*, 1968, *160*, 384.

Myers, R. E. Corpus callosum and visual gnosis. In J. F. Delafresnaye (Ed.), *Brain mechanisms and learning.* Oxford: Blackwell, 1961.

Saul, R., & Sperry, R. W. Absence of commissurotomy symptoms with agenesis of th corpus callosum. *Neurology*, 1968, *17.* I press.

Sperry, R. W. Brain bisection and mechanisms of consciousness. In J. C. Eccle (Ed.), *Brain and conscious experience.* New York: Springer-Verlag, 1966.

Sperry, R. W. Mental unity following surgical disconnection of the hemisphere *The Harvey lectures.* Series 62. New York Academic Press, 1967. (a)

Sperry, R. W. Split-brain approach to learning problems. In G. C. Quarton, T. Melnechuk, & F. O. Schmitt (Eds.), *The neurosciences: A study program*. New York: Rockefeller University Press, 1967. (b)

Sperry, R. W. Apposition of visual half-fields after section of neocortical commissures. *Anatomical Record*, 1968, *160*, 498–499.

Sperry, R. W., & Gazzaniga, M. S. Language following surgical disconnection of the hemispheres. In C. H. Milikan (Ed.), *Brain mechanisms underlying speech and language*. New York: Grune & Stratton, 1967.

Sperry, R. W., Gazzaniga, M. S., & Bogen, J. E. Function of neocortical commissures: Syndrome of hemisphere deconnection. In P. J. Vinken & G. W. Bruyn (Eds.), *Handbook of neurology*. Amsterdam: North Holland, 1968. In press.

Trevarthen, C. B. Double visual learning in split-brain monkeys. *Science*, 1962, *136*, 258–259.

REVIEW QUESTIONS

1. Describe the difference between an experiential response and an interpretive response as reported by Penfield.

2. How do the responses elicited from the interpretive cortex differ from those elicited from sensory and motor cortex?

3. Briefly summarize the evidence indicating that rats find stimulation of certain brain areas more reinforcing than food and water.

4. How does intensity of brain stimulation interact with strength of reinforcement at a positive site?

5. What are the differences between the positive reinforcement produced by "focus stimulation" and that produced by "field stimulation?"

6. One patient described in the Heath article suffered from narcolepsy. What was the nature of the reported sensation resulting from stimulation of the septal area?

7. What other reasons outside of "pleasure" did the patients in Heath's article give for button pressing?

8. The report by Delgado and his colleagues utilized a new technique for brain stimulation. What were they able to accomplish in their patients that Heath was not?

9. What are some of the important limitations of standard electroencephalographic recordings as outlined by Delgado?

10. Under what circumstances can you find superior performance from patients with hemisphere deconnection?

11. Discuss the extent and types of behavioral impairment one finds in a patient with hemisphere deconnection.

12. What does Sperry mean when he talks about a "minor hemisphere" and of what is it capable?

drugs and
behavior

There is evidence that there are two components or aspects to any addiction: physiological and psychological. The physiological aspect refers to the fact that the system of the addicted person develops a physiological need for some foreign substance. The psychological component refers to the need for the sensory stimulation that accompanies the administering of the addicting substance.

Perhaps an example will help to make things clearer. The heroin addict in addition to a physiological dependency also seems to develop a psychological need for the accompanying sensory stimulation of heroin injection—the feel of the needle piercing the vein and the immediate sensation as the substance passes into the bloodstream, etc. Evidence for this psychological need comes from the fact that heroin addicts trying to "kick" the habit find that simply injecting a harmless, nonaddicting substance into a vein seems to partially satisfy the extreme craving they experience.

The possible strength of a psychological dependency can be seen in the common addiction of cigarette smoking. While the regular smoker develops some physiological need for nicotine, his addiction is primarily a psychological one. The feel of a cigarette in the hand, the striking of a match or lighter, the tactile stimulation of placing the cigarette in the mouth all become important and desired stimulation for the smoker. A good friend and colleague of mine gave up smoking a number of years ago, that is, he no longer is physiologically dependent upon nicotine. He is still psychologically hooked on cigarettes, however. He can be seen daily fondling an unlit cigarette, placing it repeatedly in his mouth, and drawing on it as if he were smoking. He may get a few strange looks each day, but as he says "at least I won't get lung cancer."

The definition of psychological addiction presented above is a limited one and certainly not totally adequate. One can develop a need or desire for the psychological state which follows the administration of the addicting substance. The relaxed, calm state that some people report after drinking several martinis can certainly become a desired state and, depending upon the strength of the desire, a psychological addiction as well.

The report by Weil, Zinberg, and Nelson, "Clinical and Psychological Effects of Marihuana in Man" (#10), is perhaps the best and most systematic study of the effects of marihuana in man. As these authors indicate, there had been virtually no controlled research done before their report which was published in 1968. The article explodes a number of myths about pot in a beautiful fashion and answers some important questions. What effects does marihuana have on heart rate, pupil size, respiratory rate, blood sugar level, etc.? What are the performance effects on intellectual and psychomotor tests in chronic and first-time users of the drug?

In a second work (#11), Weil and Zinberg extend their studies of the psychological effects of marihuana even further. They attempt to define just what being "high" is. The report is interesting and well worth reading.

The third article in this part is by Crancer and his colleagues, "A Comparison of the Effects of Marihuana and Alcohol on Simulated Driving Performance" (#12). This research directly follows from the earlier Weil, Zinberg, and Nelsen study (#10) and obviously has great practical importance.

In discussing marihuana use with my own introductory psychology classes, one question that is always asked is whether or not marihuana is physiologically addicting. Unfortunately, there is little or no scientific evidence on the long-term physiological effects of pot smoking. From a scientific point of view, the question must remain unanswerable at this time. Chronic users do, however, report that they can stop using the drug for long periods of time without suffering the withdrawal symptoms which accompany the stoppage of physiologically addicting substances. Anecdotal evidence such as this, of course, cannot possess the certainty of a scientific finding and hardly seems an appropriate basis for answering such an important question.

Another question which is always asked is whether pot is worse than alcohol. Again, there obviously is no certain answer. There is ample evidence, of course, that one can become physiologically addicted to alcohol, and this must be taken into account. A second consideration is which of these two drugs is it easier to become psychologically dependent upon. As a user of alcohol, I can give anecdotal evidence on this point, for whatever it is worth. Alcohol has a built-in negative reinforcer, that is, one can only drink so much before nausea, etc., occurs. The hangover the following day also serves as an effective negative reinforcer in that even the thought of a drink is unpleasant. This negative feeling toward alcohol can last for as long as a week—it is only then that a martini can be approached.

The extollers of pot smoking often

point out there is no nausea connected with heavy smoking and absolutely no hangover the following day. Is it conceivable that this very "virtue" of pot makes it more conducive to a psychological addiction? Obviously, answers to questions like this and many related ones await future research which hopefully will be undertaken shortly.

There can be little doubt that LSD-25 is a potent hallucinogenic and there is even some question whether it can ever be used safely even under proper conditions with qualified personnel. The schizophreniclike behavior, which sometimes results from LSD, and the limited number of reports of permanent behavioral abnormality resulting from a single dose indicate that it is foolish for anyone to take it until more is known about its effects. Irwin Feinberg, in the selection, "A Comparison of the Visual Hallucinations in Schizophrenia with Those Induced by Mescaline and LSD-25" (#13), describes the similarities and differences that exist between hallucinations induced by LSD and those occurring in schizophrenic patients. He tentatively concludes that it is not possible on the basis of the data reviewed to state that mescaline and LSD never produce visual hallucinations similar to those of schizophrenia. The more complex and organized induced hallucinations in some persons do resemble schizophrenic hallucinations. However, the visual phenomena occurring during the drug state are sufficiently different from those of schizophrenia to suggest that the two result from the operations of different mechanisms.

Jonathan O. Cole discusses the entire issue in his report "Drugs and Control of the Mind" (#14). He correctly asks what kinds of behavior are good and what kinds are bad. Cole stresses that we must answer this question before considering whether drugs can be used to facilitate the control of good behavior and the abolishment of bad behavior. He briefly reviews the various kinds of possible mind control drugs pointing out their limitations and their effects on individual patients.

Sherwin S. Radin's study, "Psychosocial Aspects of Drug Addiction" (#15), is the final one in this part. Radin considers whether there are certain personality characteristics that predispose one to addiction and possible changes in early school curriculum that could lead to fewer addicts.

10.
clinical and psychological effects of marihuana in man

andrew t. weil,
norman e. zinberg,
and judith m. nelsen

In the spring of 1968 we conducted a series of pilot experiments on acute marihuana intoxication in human subjects. The study was not undertaken to prove or disprove popularly held convictions about marihuana as an intoxicant, to compare it with other drugs, or to introduce our own opinions. Our concern was simply to collect some long overdue pharmacological data. In this article we describe the primitive state of knowledge of the drug, the research problems encountered in designing a replicable study, and the results of our investigations.

Marihuana is a crude preparation of flowering tops, leaves, seeds, and stems of female plants of Indian hemp *Cannabis sativa* L.; it is usually smoked. The intoxicating constituents of hemp are found in the sticky resin exuded by the tops of the plants, particularly the females. Male plants produce some resin but are grown mainly for hemp fiber, not for marihuana. The resin itself, when prepared for smoking or eating, is known as "hashish." Various *Cannabis* preparations are used as intoxicants throughout the world; their potency varies directly with the amount of resin

Reprinted from *Science*, December 13, 1968, *162*, 1234–1242, Copyright 1968 by the American Association for the Advancement of Science. Abridged by permission of the authors.

This work was conducted in the Behavioral Pharmacology Laboratory of the Boston University School of Medicine, sponsored and supported by its division of psychiatry, and at the Boston University Medical Center, Boston, Massachusetts.

present *(1)*. Samples of American marihuana differ greatly in pharmacological activity, depending on their composition (tops contain most resin; stems, seeds and lower leaves least) and on the conditions under which the plants were grown. In addition, different varieties of *Cannabis* probably produce resins with different proportions of constituents *(2)*. Botanists feel that only one species of hemp exists, but work on the phytochemistry of the varieties of this species is incomplete *(3)*. Chronic users claim that samples of marihuana differ in quality of effects as well as in potency, that some types cause a preponderance of physical symptoms, and that other types tend to cause greater distortion of perception or of thought.

Pharmacological studies of *Cannabis* indicate that the tetrahydrocannabinol fraction of the resin is the active portion. In 1965, Mechoulam and Gaoni *(4)* reported the first total synthesis of $(-)-\Delta^1trans$-tetrohydrocannabinol (THC) which they called "the psychotomimetically active constituent of hashish (marihuana)." Synthetic THC is now available for research in very limited supply.

In the United States, the use of *Cannabis* extracts as therapeutics goes back to the 19th century, but it was not until the 1920's that use of marihuana as an intoxicant by migrant Mexican laborers urban Negroes, and certain Bohemian groups caused public concern *(3)*. Despite increasingly severe legal penalties imposed during the 1930's, use of marihuana continued in these relatively small populations without great public uproar or apparent changes in numbers or type of users until the last few years. The fact that almost none of the studies devoted to the physiological and psychological effects of *Cannabis* in man was based on controlled laboratory experimentation escaped general notice. But with the explosion of use in the 1960's, at first on college campuses followed by a spread downward to secondary schools and upward to a portion of the established middle class, controversy over the dangers of marihuana generated a desire for more objective information about the drug.

Of the three known studies on human subjects performed by Americans, the first (see 5) was done in the Canal Zone with 34 soldiers; the consequences reported were hunger and hyperphagia, loss of inhibitions, increased pulse rate with unchanged blood pressure, a tendency to sleep, and unchanged performance of psychological and neurological tests. Doses and type of marihuana were not specified.

The second study, known as the 1944 LaGuardia Report (6), noted that 72 prisoners, 48 of whom were previous *Cannabis* users, showed minimum physiological responses, but suffered impaired intellectual functioning and decreased body steadiness, especially well demonstrated by nonusers after high doses. Basic personality structures remained unchanged as subjects reported feelings of relaxation, disinhibition, and self-confidence. In that study, the drug was administered orally as an extract. No controls were described, and doses and quality of marihuana were unspecified.

Williams et al. in 1946 (7) studied a small number of prisoners who were chronic users; they were chiefly interested in effects of long-term smoking on psychological functioning. They found an initial exhilaration and euphoria which gave way after a few days of smoking to indifference and lassitude that somewhat impaired performance requiring concentration and manual dexterity. Again, no controls were provided.

Predictably, these studies, each deficient in design for obtaining reliable physiological and psychological data, contributed no dramatic or conclusive results. The 1967 President's Commission

on Law Enforcement and the Administration of Justice described the present state of knowledge by concluding (3): ". . . no careful and detailed analysis of the American experience [with marihuana] seems to have been attempted. Basic research has been almost nonexistent. . . ." Since then, no other studies with marihuana itself have been reported, but in 1967 Isbell (8) administered synthetic THC to chronic users. At doses of 120 μg/kg orally or 50 μg/kg by smoking, subjects reported this drug to be similar to marihuana. At higher doses (300 to 400 μg/kg orally or 200 to 250 μg/kg by smoking), psychotomimetic effects occurred in most subjects. This synthetic has not yet been compared with marihuana in nonusers or given to any subjects along with marihuana in double-blind fashion.

Investigations outside the United States have been scientifically deficient, and for the most part have been limited to anecdotal and sociological approaches (9–12). So far as we know, our study is the first attempt to investigate marihuana in a formal double-blind experiment with the appropriate controls. It is also the first attempt to collect basic clinical and psychological information on the drug by observing its effects on marihuana-naive human subjects in a neutral laboratory setting.

RESEARCH PROBLEMS

That valid basic research on marihuana is almost nonexistent is not entirely accounted for by legislation which restricts even legitimate laboratory investigations or by public reaction sometimes verging on hysteria. A number of obstacles are intrinsic to the study of this drug. We now present a detailed description of our specific experimental approach, but must comment separately on six general problems confronting the investigator who contemplates marihuana research.

1) Concerning the route of administration, many pharmacologists dismiss the possibility of giving marihuana by smoking because, they say, the dose cannot be standardized (13). We consider it not only possible, but important to admin-

ister the drug to humans by smoking rather than by the oral route for the following reasons. (i) Smoking is the way nearly all Americans use marihuana. (ii) It is possible to have subjects smoke marihuana cigarettes in such a way that drug dosage is reasonably uniform for all subjects. (iii) Standardization of dose is not assured by giving the drug orally because little is known about gastrointestinal absorption of the highly water-insoluble cannabinols in man. (iv) There is considerable indirect evidence from users that the quality of the intoxication is different when marihuana or preparations of it are ingested rather than smoked. In particular, ingestion seems to cause more powerful effects, more "LSD-like" effects, longer-lasting effects, and more hangovers (12, 14). Further, marihuana smokers are accustomed to a very rapid onset of action due to efficient absorption through the lungs, whereas the latency for onset of effects may be 45 or 60 minutes after ingestion. (v) There is reported evidence from experiments with rats and mice that the pharmacological activities of natural hashish (not subjected to combustion) and hashish sublimate (the combustion products) are different (14).

2) Until quite recently, it was extremely difficult to estimate the relative potencies of different samples of marihuana by the techniques of analytical chemistry. For this study, we were able to have the marihuana samples assayed spectrophotometrically (15) for THC content. However, since THC has not been established as the sole determinant of marihuana's activity, we still feel it is important to have chronic users sample and rate marihuana used in research. Therefore, we assayed our material by this method as well.

3) One of the major deficiencies in previous studies has been the absence of negative control or placebo treatments, which we consider essential to the design of this kind of investigation. Because marihuana smoke has a distinctive odor and taste, it is difficult to find an effective placebo for use with chronic users. The problem is much less difficult with nonusers. Our solution to this dilemma was the use of portions of male hemp stalks (16), devoid of THC, in the placebo cigarettes.

4) In view of the primitive state of knowledge about marihuana, it is difficult to predict which psychological tests will be sensitive to the effects of the drug. The tests we chose were selected because, in addition to being likely to demonstrate effects, they have been used to evaluate many other psychoactive drugs. Of the various physiological parameters available, we chose to measure (i) heart rate, because previous studies have consistently reported increases in heart rate after administration of marihuana (for example, 5); (ii) respiratory rate, because it is an easily measured vital sign, and depression has been reported (11, 17); (iii) pupil size, because folklore on effects of marihuana consistently includes reports of pupillary dilatation, although objective experimental evidence of an effect of the drug on pupils has not been sought; (iv) conjunctival appearance, because both marihuana smokers and eaters are said to develop red eyes (11); and (v) blood sugar, because hypoglycemia has been invoked as a cause of the hunger and hyperphagia commonly reported by marihuana users, but animal and human evidence of this effect is contradictory (6, 10, 11). [The LaGuardia Report, quoted by Jaffe in Goodman and Gilman (18) described hyperglycemia as an effect of acute intoxication.] We did not measure blood pressure because previous studies have failed to demonstrate any consistent effect on blood pressure in man, and we were unwilling to subject our volunteers to a nonessential annoyance.

5) It is necessary to control set and setting. "Set" refers to the subject's psychological expectations of what a drug will do to him in relation to his general personality structure. The total environment in which the drug is taken is the setting. All indications are that the form of marihuana intoxication is particularly dependent on the interaction of drug, set and setting. Because of recent increase in the extent of use and in attention given this use by the mass media, it is difficult to find subjects with a neutral set toward marihuana. Our method of selecting subjects (described below), at the least, enabled us to identify the sub-

jects' attitudes. Unfortunately, too many researchers have succumbed to the temptation to have subjects take drugs in "psychedelic" environments or have influenced the response to the drug by asking questions that disturb the setting. Even a question as simple as, "How do you feel?" contains an element of suggestion that alters the drug-set-setting interaction. We took great pains to keep our laboratory setting neutral by strict adherence to an experimental timetable and to a prearranged set of conventions governing interactions between subjects and experimenters.

6) Medical, social, ethical, and legal concerns about the welfare of subjects are a major problem in a project of this kind. Is it ethical to introduce people to marihuana? When can subjects safely be sent home from the laboratory? What kind of follow-up care, if any, should be given? These are only a few specific questions with which the investigator must wrestle. Examples of some of the precautions we took are as follows. (i) All subjects were volunteers. All were given psychiatric screening interviews and were clearly informed that they might be asked to smoke marihuana. All nonusers tested were persons who had reported that they had been plannning to try marihuana. (ii) All subjects were driven home by an experimenter; they agreed not to engage in unusual activity or operate machinery until the next morning and to report any unusual, delayed effects. (iii) All subjects agreed to report for follow-up interviews 6 months after the experiment. Among other things, the check at 6 months should answer the question whether participation in the experiment encouraged further drug use. (iv) All subjects were protected from possible legal repercussions of their participation in these experiments by specific agreements with the Federal Bureau of Narcotics, the Office of the Attorney General of Massachusetts, and the Massachusetts Bureau of Drug Abuse and Drug Control (19).

SUBJECTS

The central group of subjects consisted of nine healthy, male volunteers,

21 to 26 years of age, all of whom smoked tobacco cigarettes regularly but had never tried marihuana previously. Eight chronic users of marihuana also participated, both to "assay" the quality of marihuana received from the Federal Bureau of Narcotics and to enable the experimenters to standardize the protocol, using subjects familiar with their responses to the drug. The age range for users was also 21 to 26 years. They all smoked marihuana regularly, most of them every day or every other day.

The nine "naive" subjects were selected after a careful screening process. An initial pool of prospective subjects was obtained by placing advertisements in the student newspapers of a number of universities in the Boston area. These advertisements sought "male volunteers, at least 21 years old, for psychological experiments." After nonsmokers were eliminated from this pool, the remaining volunteers were interviewed individually by a psychiatrist who determined their histories of use of alcohol and other intoxicants as well as their general personality types. In addition to serving as a potential screening technique to eliminate volunteers with evidence of psychosis, or of serious mental or personality disorder, these interviews served as the basis for the psychiatrist's prediction of the type of response an individual subject might have after smoking marihuana. (It should be noted that no marihuana-naive volunteer had to be disqualified on psychiatric grounds.) Only after a prospective subject passed the interview was he informed that the "psychological experiment" for which he had volunteered was a marihuana study. If he consented to participate, he was asked to sign a release, informing him that he would be "expected to smoke cigarettes containing marihuana or an inert substance." He was also required to agree to a number of conditions, among them that he would "during the course of the experiment take no psychoactive drugs, including alcohol, other than those drugs administered in the course of the experiment."

It proved extremely difficult to find marihuana-naive persons in the student population of Boston, and nearly 2

TABLE 1. Composition of the Dose

Dose	Marihuana in Each Cigarette	Total Dose Marihuana (2 Cigarettes)	Approximate Dose THC
Placebo	—	—	
Low	0.25	0.5	4.5 mg
High	1.0	2.0	18 mg

Note: The placebo cigarette consisted of placebo material, tobacco filler, and mint leaves for masking flavor. The low dose was made up of marihuana, tobacco filler, and mint leaves. The high dose consisted of marihuana and mint leaves.

months of interviewing were required to obtain nine men. All those interviewed who had already tried marihuana volunteered this information quite freely and were delighted to discuss their use of drugs with the psychiatrist. Nearly all persons encountered who had not tried marihuana admitted this somewhat apologetically. Several said they had been meaning to try the drug but had not got around to it. A few said they had no access to it. Only one person cited the current laws as his reason for not having experimented with marihuana. It seemed clear in the interviews that many of these persons were actually afraid of how they might react to marihuana; they therefore welcomed a chance to smoke it under medical supervision. Only one person (an Indian exchange student) who passed the screening interview refused to participate after learning the nature of the experiment.

The eight heavy users of marihuana were obtained with much less difficulty. They were interviewed in the same manner as the other subjects and were instructed not to smoke any marihuana on the day of their appointment in the laboratory.

Subjects were questioned during screening interviews and at the conclusion of the experiments to determine their knowledge of marihuana effects. None of the nine naive subjects had ever watched anyone smoke marihuana or observed anyone high on marihuana. Most of them knew of the effects of the drug only through reports in the popular press. Two subjects had friends who used marihuana frequently; one of these (No. 4)

announced his intention to "prove" in the experiments that marihuana really did not do anything; the other (No. 3), was extremely eager to get high because "everyone I know is always talking about it very positively."

SETTING

Greatest effort was made to create a neutral setting. That is, subjects were made comfortable and secure in a pleasant suite of laboratories and offices, but the experimental staff carefully avoided encouraging any person to have an enjoyable experience. Subjects were never asked how they felt, and no subject was permitted to discuss the experiment with the staff until he had completed all four sessions. Verbal interactions between staff and subjects were minimum and formal. At the end of each session, subjects were asked to complete a brief form asking whether they thought they had smoked marihuana that night; if so, whether a high dose or a low dose; and how confident they were of their answers. The experimenters completed similar forms on each subject.

MARIHUANA

Marihuana used in these experiments was of Mexican origin, supplied by the Federal Bureau of Narcotics (20). It consisted of finely chopped leaves of Cannabis, largely free of seeds and stems. An initial batch, which was judged to be of low potency by the experimenters on the basis of the doses needed to produce symptoms of intoxication in the chronic users, was subsequently found to contain only 0.3 percent of THC by weight. A second batch, assayed at 0.9 percent THC, was rated by the chronic users to be "good, average" marihuana, neither exceptionally strong nor exceptionally weak compared to their usual supplies. Users consistently reported symptoms of intoxication after smoking about 0.5 gram of the material with a variation of only a few puffs from subject to subject. This second batch of marihuana was used in the experiments described below: the low dose was 0.5 gram, and the high dose was 2.0 grams.

All marihuana was administered in the form of cigarettes of standard size made with a hand-operated rolling machine. In any given experimental session, each person was required to smoke two cigarettes in succession. (Table 1).

Placebo material consisted of the chopped outer covering of mature stalks of male hemp plants; it contained no THC. All cigarettes had a tiny plug of tobacco at one end and a plug of paper at the other end so that the contents were not visible. The length to which each cigarette was to be smoked was indicated by an ink line. Marihuana and placebos were administered to the naive subjects in double-blind fashion. Scented aerosols were sprayed in the laboratory before smoking, to mask the odor of marihuana. The protocol during an experimental session was as follows. The sessions began at approximately 5:30 p.m.

Time	Procedure
0:00	Physiological measurements; blood sample drawn
0:05	Psychological test battery No. 1 (base line)
0:35	Verbal sample No. 1
0:40	Cigarette smoking
1:00	Rest period
1:15	Physiological measurements; blood sample drawn
1:20	Psychological test battery No. 2
1:50	Verbal sample No. 2
1:55	Rest period (supper)
2:30	Physiological measurements
2:35	Physiological test battery No. 3
3:05	End of testing

EXPERIMENTAL SESSIONS

Chronic users were tested only on high doses of marihuana with no practice sessions. Each naive subject was required to come to four sessions, spaced about a week apart. The first was always a practice session, in which the subject learned the proper smoking technique and during which he became thoroughly acquainted with the tests and the protocol. In the practice session, each subject completed the entire protocol, smoking two hand-rolled tobacco cigarettes. He was instructed to take a long puff, to inhale deeply, and to maintain inspiration for 20 seconds, as timed by an experimenter with a stopwatch. Subjects were allowed 8 to 12 minutes to smoke each of the two cigarettes. One purpose of this practice smoking was to identify and eliminate individuals who were not tolerant to high doses of nicotine, thus reducing the effect of nicotine on the variables measured during subsequent drug sessions (21). A surprising number (five) of volunteers who had described themselves in screening interviews as heavy cigarette smokers, "inhaling" up to two packs of cigarettes a day, developed acute nicotine reactions when they smoked two tobacco cigarettes by the required method. Occurrence of such a reaction disqualified a subject from participation in the experiments.

In subsequent sessions, when cigarettes contained either drug or placebo, all smoking was similarly supervised by an experimenter with a stopwatch. Subjects were not permitted to smoke tobacco cigarettes while the experiment was in progress. They were assigned to one of the three treatment groups listed in Table 2.

PHYSIOLOGICAL AND PSYCHOLOGICAL MEASURES

The physiological parameters measured were heart rate, respiratory rate, pupil size, blood glucose level, and conjunctival vascular state. Pupil size was measured with a millimeter rule under constant illumination with eyes focused on an object at constant distance. Conjunctival appearance, was rated by an experienced experimenter for dilation of blood vessels on a 0 to 4 scale with ratings of 3 and 4 indicating "significant" vasodilatation. Blood samples were collected for immediate determinations of serum glucose and for the serum to be frozen and stored for possible future biochemical studies. Subjects were asked not to eat and not to imbibe a beverage containing sugar or caffeine during the 4 hours preceding a session. They were given supper after the second blood sample was drawn.

The psychological test battery con-

TABLE 2. Order of Treatment

Group	Drug Session		
	1	2	3
I	High	Placebo	Low
II	Low	High	Placebo
III	Placebo	Low	High

sisted of (i) the Continuous Performance Test (CPT)—5 minutes; (ii) the Digit Symbol Substitution Test (DSST)—90 seconds; (iii), CPT with strobe light distraction—5 minutes; (iv) self-rating bipolar mood scale—3 minutes; and (v) pursuit rotor—10 minutes.

The Continuous Performance Test was designed to measure a subject's capacity for sustained attention (22). The subject was placed in a darkened room and directed to watch a small screen upon which six letters of the alphabet were flashed rapidly and in random order. The subject was instructed to press a button whenever a specified critical letter appeared. The number of letters presented,

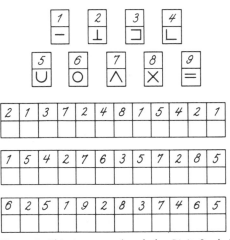

Figure 1. This is a sample of the Digit Symbol Substitution Test as used in these studies. On a signal from the examiner the subject was required to fill as many of the empty spaces as possible with the appropriate symbols. The code was always available to the subject during the 90-second administration of the test. [This figure appeared originally in **Psychopharmacologia 5,** 164 (1964)].

correct responses, and errors of commission and omission were counted over the 5-minute period. The test was also done with a strobe light flickering at 50 cycles per second. Normal subjects make no or nearly no errors on this test either with or without strobe distraction; but sleep deprivation, organic brain disease, and certain drugs like chlorpromazine adversely affect performance. Presence or absence of previous exposure to the task has no effect on performance.

The Digit Symbol Substitution Test is a simple test of cognitive function (see Figure 1). A subject's score was the number of correct answers in a 90-second period. As in the case of the CPT, practice should have little or no effect on performance.

The self-rating bipolar mood scale used in these experiments was one developed by Smith and Beecher (23) to evaluate subjective effects of morphine. By allowing subjects to rate themselves within a given category of moods, on an arbitrary scale from $+3$ to -3, it minimizes suggestion and is thus more neutral than the checklists often employed in drug testing.

The pursuit rotor measures muscular coordination and attention. The subject's task was to keep a stylus in contact with a small spot on a moving turntable. In these experiments, subjects were given ten 30-second trials in each battery. The score for each trial was total time in contact with the spot. There is a marked practice effect on this test, but naive subjects were brought to high levels of performance during their practice session, so that the changes due to practice were reduced during the actual drug sessions. In addition, since there was a different order of treatments for each of the three groups of naive subjects, any session-to-session practice effects were minimized in the statistical analysis of the pooled data.

At the end of the psychological test battery, a verbal sample was collected from each subject. The subject was left alone in a room with a tape recorder and instructions to describe "an interesting or dramatic experience" in his life until he was stopped. After exactly 5 minutes he was interrupted and asked how long he had been in the recording room. In this way, an estimate of the subject's ability to judge time was also obtained.

RESULTS

1. *Safety of Marihuana in Human Volunteers.* In view of the apprehension expressed by many persons over the safety of administering marihuana to research subjects, we wish to emphasize that no adverse marihuana reactions occurred in any of our subjects. In fact, the five acute nicotine reactions mentioned earlier were far more spectacular than any effects produced by marihuana.

In these experiments, observable effects of marihuana were maximum at 15 minutes after smoking. They were diminished between 30 minutes and 1 hour, and they were largely dissipated 3 hours after the end of smoking. No delayed or persistent effects beyond 3 hours were observed or reported.

2. *Intoxicating Properties of Marihuana in a Neutral Setting.* With the high dose of marihuana (2.0 grams), all chronic users became "high" (24) by their own accounts and in the judgment of experimenters who had observed many persons under the influence of marihuana. The effect was consistent even though prior to the session some of these subjects expressed anxiety about smoking marihuana and submitting to tests in a laboratory.

On the other hand, only one of the nine naive subjects (No. 3) had a definite "marihuana reaction" on the same high dose. He became markedly euphoric and laughed continuously during his first battery of tests after taking the drug. Interestingly, he was the one subject who had expressed his desire to get high.

3. *Comparison of Naive and Chronic User Subjects.* Throughout the experiments it was apparent that the two groups of subjects reacted differently to identical doses of marihuana. We must caution, however, that our study was designed to allow rigorous statistical analysis of data from the naive group— it was not designed to permit formal comparison between chronic users and

TABLE 3. Subjects' Appraisal of the Dose

Actual Dose	Guessed Dose			Fraction Correct
	Placebo	Low	High	
Placebo	8	1		8/9
Low	3	6		6/9
High	2	6	1	1/9

naive subjects. The conditions of the experiment were not the same for both groups: the chronic users were tested with the drug on their first visit to the laboratory with no practice and were informed that they were to receive high doses of marihuana. Therefore, differences between the chronic and naive groups reported below—although statistically valid—must be regarded as trends to be confirmed or rejected by additional experiments.

4. *Recognition of Marihuana Versus Placebo.* All nine naive subjects reported that they had not been able to identify the taste or smell of marihuana in the experimental cigarettes. A few subjects remarked that they noticed differences in the taste of the three sets of cigarettes but could not interpret the differences. Most subjects found the pure marihuana cigarettes (high dose) more mild than the low dose or placebo cigarettes, both of which contained tobacco.

The subjects' guesses of the contents of cigarettes for their three sessions are presented in Table 3. It is noteworthy that one of the two subjects who called the high dose a placebo was the subject (No. 4) who had told us he wanted to prove that marihuana really did nothing. There were three outstanding findings: (i) most subjects receiving marihuana in either high or low dose recognized that they were getting a drug; (ii) most subjects receiving placebos recognized that they were receiving placebos; (iii) most subjects called their high dose a low dose, but none called his low dose a high dose, emphasizing the unimpressiveness of their subjective reactions.

5. *Effect of Marihuana on Heart Rate.* The mean changes in heart rate from base-line rates before smoking the drug

to rates at 15 and 90 minutes after smoking marihuana and placebo were tested for significance at the .05 level by an analysis of variance; Tukey's method was applied for all possible comparisons. In the naive subjects, marihuana in low dose or high dose was followed by increased heart rate 15 minutes after smoking, but the effect was not demonstrated to be dose-dependent. The high dose caused a statistically greater increase in the heart rates of chronic users than in those of the naive subjects 15 minutes after smoking.

Two of the chronic users had unusually low resting pulse rates, but deletion of these two subjects still gave a significant difference in mean pulse rise of chronic users compared to naives. Because the conditions of the sessions and experimental design were not identical for the two groups, we prefer to report this difference as a trend that must be confirmed by further studies.

6. *Effect of Marihuana on Respiratory Rate.* In the naive group, there was no change in respiratory rate before and after smoking marihuana. Chronic users showed a small but statistically significant increase in respiratory rate after smoking, but we do not regard the change as clinically significant.

7. *Effect of Marihuana on Pupil Size.* There was no change in pupil size before and after smoking marihuana in either group.

8. *Effect of Marihuana on Conjunctival Appearance.* Significant reddening of conjunctivae due to dilatation of blood vessels occurred in one of nine subjects receiving placebo, three of nine receiving the low dose of marihuana, and eight of nine receiving the high dose. It occurred in all eight of the chronic users receiving the high dose and was rated as more prominent in them. The effect was more pronounced 15 minutes after the smoking period than 90 minutes after it.

9. *Effect of Marihuana on Blood Sugar.* There was no significant change in blood sugar levels after smoking marihuana in either group.

10. *Effect of Marihuana on the Continuous Performance Test.* Performance on the CPT and on the CPT with strobe distraction was unaffected by marihuana for both groups of subjects.

11. *Effect of Marihuana on the Digit Symbol Substitution Test.* The significance of the differences in mean changes of scores at the .05 level was determined by an analysis of variance by means of Tukey's method for all possible comparisons.

The results indicate that: (i) Decrements in performance of naive subjects following low and high doses of marihuana were significant at 15 and 90 minutes after smoking. (ii) The decrement following marihuana was greater after high dose than after low dose at 15 minutes after taking the drug, giving preliminary evidence of a dose-response relationship. (iii) Chronic users started with good base-line performance and improved slightly on the DSST after smoking 2.0 grams of marihuana, whereas performance of the naive subjects was grossly impaired. Experience with the DSST suggests that absence of impairment in chronic users cannot be accounted for solely by a practice effect. Still, because of the different procedures employed, we prefer to report this difference as a trend.

12. *Effect of Marihuana on Pursuit Rotor Performance.* Decrements in performance of naive subjects after both low and high doses of marihuana were significant at 15 and 90 minutes. This effect on performance followed a dose-response relation on testing batteries conducted at both 15 minutes and 90 minutes after the drug was smoked.

All chronic users started from good baselines and improved on the pursuit rotor after smoking marihuana. These data are not presented, however, because it is probable that the improvement was largely a practice effect.

13. *Effect of Marihuana on Time Estimation.* Before smoking, all nine naive subjects estimated the 5-minute verbal sample to be 5 ± 2 minutes. After placebo, no subject changed his guess. After

the low dose, three subjects raised their estimates to 10± 2 minutes, and after the high dose, four raised their estimates.

14. *Subjective Effects of Marihuana.* When questioned at the end of their participation in the experiment, persons who had never taken marihuana previously reported minimum subjective effects after smoking the drug, or, more precisely, few effects like those commonly reported by chronic users. Nonusers reported little euphoria, no distortion of visual or auditory perception, and no confusion. However, several subjects mentioned that "things seemed to take longer." Below are examples of comments by naive subjects after high doses.

Subject 1: "It was stronger than the previous time (low dose) but I really didn't think it could be marihuana. Things seemed to go slower."

Subject 2: "I think I realize why they took our watches. There was a sense of the past disappearing as happens when you're driving too long without sleeping. With a start you wake up to realize you were asleep for an instant; you discover yourself driving along the road. It was the same tonight with eating a sandwich. I'd look down to discover I'd just swallowed a bite but I hadn't noticed it at the time."

Subject 6: "I felt a combination of being almost-drunk and tired, with occasional fits of silliness—not my normal reaction to smoking tobacco.

Subject 8: "I felt faint briefly, but the dizziness went away, and I felt normal or slightly tired. I can't believe I had a high dose of marihuana."

Subject 9: "Time seemed very drawn out. I would keep forgetting what I was doing, especially on the continuous performance test, but somehow every time an "X" (the critical letter) came up, I found myself pushing the button."

After smoking their high dose, chronic users were asked to rate themselves on a scale of 1 to 10, 10 representing "the highest you've ever been." All subjects placed themselves between 7 and 10,

most at 8 or 9. Many of these subjects expressed anxiety at the start of their first battery of tests after smoking the drug when they were feeling very high. Then they expressed surprise during and after the tests when they judged (correctly) that their performance was as good as or better than it had been before taking the drug.

15. The effect of marihuana on the self-rating mood scale, the effect of marihuana on a 5-minute verbal sample, and the correlation of personality type with subjective effects of marihuana will be reported separately.

DISCUSSION

Several results from this study raise important questions about the action of marihuana and suggest directions for future research. Our finding that subjects who were naive to marihuana did not become subjectively "high" after a high dose of marihuana in a neutral setting is interesting when contrasted with the response of regular users who consistently reported and exhibited highs. It agrees with the reports of chronic users that many, if not most, people do not become high on their first exposure to marihuana even if they smoke it correctly. This puzzling phenomenon can be discussed from either a physiological or psychosocial point of view. Neither interpretation is entirely satisfactory. The physiological hypothesis suggests that getting high on marihuana occurs only after some sort of pharmacological sensitization takes place. The psychosocial interpretation is that repeated exposure to marihuana reduces psychological inhibition, as part of, or as the result of a learning process.

Indirect evidence makes the psychological hypothesis attractive. Anxiety about drug use in this country is sufficiently great to make worthy of careful consideration the possibility of an unconscious psychological inhibition or block on the part of naive drug takers. The subjective responses of our subjects indicate that they had imagined a marihuana effect to be much more profoundly disorganizing than what they experienced. For example, subject No. 4, who started with a bias against the possibility of becoming high on marihuana, was able to control subjectively the effect of the drug and report that he had received a placebo when he had actually gotten a high dose. As anxiety about the drug is lessened with experience, the block may decrease, and the subject may permit himself to notice the drug's effects.

It is well known that marihuana users, in introducing friends to the drug, do actually "teach" them to notice subtle effects of the drug on consciousness (25). The apparently enormous influence of set and setting on the form of the marihuana response is consistent with this hypothesis, as is the testimony of users that, as use becomes more frequent, the amount of drug required to produce intoxication decreases—a unique example of "reverse tolerance." (Regular use of many intoxicants is accompanied by the need for increasing doses to achieve the same effects.)

On the other hand, the suggestion arising from this study that users and nonusers react differently to the drug, not only subjectively but also physiologically, increases the plausibility of the pharmacological-sensitization hypothesis. Of course, reverse tolerance could equally well be a manifestation of this sensitization.

It would be useful to confirm the suggested differences between users and nonusers and then to test in a systematic manner the hypothetical explanations of the phenomenon. One possible approach would be to continue to administer high doses of marihuana to the naive subjects according to the protocol described. If subjects begin reporting high responses to the drug only after several exposures, in the absence of psychedelic settings, suggestions, or manipulations of mood, then the likelihood that marihuana induces a true physiological sensitization or that experience reduces psychological inhibitions, permitting real drug effects to appear, would be increased. If subjects fail to become high, we could conclude that learning to respond to marihuana requires some sort of teaching or suggestion.

An investigation of the literature of countries where anxieties over drug use are less prominent would be useful. If this difference between responses of users and nonusers is a uniquely American phenomenon, a psychological explanation would be indicated, although it would not account for greater effects with smaller doses after the initial, anxiety-reducing stage.

One impetus for reporting the finding of differences between chronic and naive subjects on some of the tests, despite the fact that the experimental designs were not the same, is that this finding agrees with the statements of many users. They say that the effects of marihuana are easily suppressed—much more so than those of alcohol. Our observation, that the chronic users after smoking marihuana performed on some tests as well as or better than they did before taking the drug, reinforced the argument advanced by chronic users that maintaining effective levels of performance for many tasks—driving, for example (26)—is much easier under the influence of marihuana than under that of other psychoactive drugs. Certainly the surprise that the chronic users expressed when they found they were performing more effectively on the CPT, DSST, and pursuit rotor tests than they thought they would is remarkable. It is quite the opposite of the false sense of improvement subjects have under some psychoactive drugs that actually impair performance.

What might be the basis of this suppressibility? Possibly, the actions of marihuana are confined to higher cortical functions without any general stimulatory or depressive effect on lower brain centers. The relative absence of neurological—as opposed to psychiatric—symptoms in marihuana intoxication suggests this possibility (7).

Our failure to detect any changes in blood sugar levels of subjects after they had smoked marihuana forces us to look elsewhere for an explanation of the hunger and hyperphagia commonly reported by users. A first step would be careful interviewing of users to determine whether they really become hungry after smoking marihuana or whether they simply find eating more pleasurable. Possibly, the basis of this effect is also central rather than due to some peripheral physiological change.

Lack of any change in pupil size of

subjects after they had smoked marihuana is an enlightening finding especially because so many users and law-
enforcement agents firmly believe that
marihuana dilates pupils. (Since users
generally observe each other in dim surroundings, it is not surprising that they
see large pupils.) This negative finding
emphasizes the need for data from carefully controlled investigations rather than
from casual observation or anecdotal reports in the evaluation of marihuana. It
also agrees with the findings of others
that synthetic THC does not alter pupil
size (8, 27).

Finally, we would like to comment on
the fact that marihuana appears to be
a relatively mild intoxicant in our studies.
If these results seem to differ from those
of earlier experiments, it must be remembered that other experimenters have given
marihuana orally, have given doses much
higher than those commonly smoked by
users, have administered potent synthe-
tics, and have not strictly controlled the
laboratory setting. As noted in our introduction, more powerful effects are
often reported by users who ingest preparations of marihuana. This may mean
that some active constituents which enter the body when the drug is ingested
are destroyed by combustion, a suggestion that must be investigated in man.
Another priority consideration is the extent to which synthetic THC reproduces
marihuana intoxication—a problem that
must be resolved before marihuana research proceeds with THC instead of the
natural resin of the whole plant.

The set, both of subjects and experimenters, and the setting must be recognized as critical variables in studies of
marihuana. Drug, set, and setting interact to shape the form of a marihuana
reaction. The researcher who sets out
with prior conviction that hemp is psychotomimetic or a "mild hallucinogen"
is likely to confirm his conviction experimentally (10), but he would probably confirm the opposite hypothesis if
his bias were in the opposite direction.

Precautions to insure neutrality of set
and setting, including use of a double-
blind procedure as an absolute minimum,
are vitally important if the object of investigation is to measure real marihuana-
induced responses.

CONCLUSIONS

1) It is feasible and safe to study the
effects of marihuana on human volunteers who smoke it in a laboratory.

2) In a neutral setting persons who
are naive to marihuana do not have
strong subjective experiences after smoking low or high doses of the drug, and
the effects they do report are not the
same as those described by regular users
of marihuana who take the drug in the
same neutral setting.

3) Marihuana-naive persons do demonstrate impaired performance on simple
intellectual and psychomotor tests after
smoking marihuana; the impairment is
dose-related in some cases.

4) Regular users of marihuana do get
high after smoking marihuana in a neutral setting but do not show the same
degree of impairment of performance on
the tests as do naive subjects. In some
cases, their performance even appears to
improve slightly after smoking marihuana.

5) Marihuana increases heart rate
moderately.

6) No change in respiratory rate follows administration of marihuana by inhalation.

7) No change in pupil size occurs in
short term exposure to marihuana.

8) Marihuana administration causes dilatation of conjunctival blood vessels.

9) Marihuana treatment produces no
change in blood sugar levels.

10) In a neutral setting the physiological and psychological effects of a single, inhaled dose of marihuana appear
to reach maximum intensity within one-
half hour of inhalation, to be diminished
after 1 hour, and to be completely dissipated by 3 hours.

REFERENCES AND NOTES

1. R. J. Bouquet, Bull. Narcotics 2, 14
(1950).
2. F. Korte and H. Sieper, in Hashish:
Its Chemistry and Pharmacology, G. E. W.
Wolstenholme and J. Knight, Eds. (Little,
Brown, Boston, 1965), pp. 15–30.

3. Task Force on Narcotics and Drug Abuse, the President's Commission on Law Enforcement and the Administration of Justice, *Task Force Report: Narcotics and Drug Abuse* (1967), p. 14.

4. R. Mechoulam, and Y. Gaoni, *J. Amer. Chem. Soc. 67*, 3273 (1965).

5. J. F. Siler, W. L. Sheep, L. B. Bates, G. F. Clark, G. W. Cook, W. A. Smith, *Mil. Surg.* (November 1933), pp. 269–280.

6. Mayor's Committee on Marihuana, *The Marihuana Problem in the City of New York*, 1944.

7. E. G. Williams, C. K. Himmelsbach, A. Winkler, D. C. Ruble, B. J. Lloyd, *Public Health Rep. 61*, 1059 (1946).

8. H. Isbell, *Psychopharmacologia 11*, 184 (1967).

9. I. C. Chopra and R. N. Chopra, *Bull. Narcotics 9*, 4 (1957).

10. F. Ames, *J. Ment. Sci. 104*, 972 (1958).

11. C. J. Miras, in *Hashish: Its Chemistry and Pharmacology*, G. E. W. Wolstenholme and J. Knight, Eds. (Little, Brown, Boston, 1965), pp. 37–47.

12. J. M. Watt, in *Hashish: Its Chemistry and Pharmacology*, G. E. W. Wolstenholme and J. Knight, Eds. (Little, Brown, Boston, 1965), pp. 54–66.

13. AMA Council on Mental Health, *J. Amer. Med. Ass. 204*, 1181 (1968).

14. G. Joachimoglu, in *Hashish: Its Chemistry and Pharmacology*, G. E. W. Wolstenholme and J. Knight, Eds. (Little, Brown, Boston, 1965), pp. 2–10.

15. We thank M. Lerner and A. Bober of the U.S. Customs Laboratory, Baltimore, for performing this assay.

16. We thank R. H. Pace and E. H. Hall of the Peter J. Schweitzer Division of the Kimberly-Clark Corp. for supplying placebo material.

17. S. Garattini, in *Hashish: Its Chemistry and Pharmacology*, G. E. W. Wolstenholme and J. Knight, Eds. (Little, Brown, Boston, 1965), pp. 70–78.

18. J. H. Jaffee, in *The Pharmacological Basis of Therapeutics*, L. S. Goodman and A. Gilman, Eds. (Macmillan, New York, ed. 3, 1965), pp. 299–301.

19. We thank E. L. Richardson, Attorney General of the Commonwealth of Massachu-setts for permitting these experiments to proceed and N. L. Chayet for legal assistance. We do not consider it appropriate to describe here the opposition we encountered from governmental agents and agencies and from university bureaucracies.

20. We thank D. Miller and M. Seifer of the Federal Bureau of Narcotics (now part of the Bureau of Narcotics and Dangerous Drugs, under the Department of Justice) for help in obtaining marihuana for this research.

21. The doses of tobacco in placebo and low-dose cigarettes were too small to cause physiological changes in subjects who qualified in the practice session.

22. K. E. Rosvold, A. F. Mirsky, I. Sarason, E. D. Bransome, L. H. Beck, *J. Consult. Psychol. 20*, 343 (1956); A. F. Mirsky and P. V. Cardon, *Electroencephalogr. Clin. Neurophysiol. 14*, 1 (1962); C. Kornetsky and G. Bain, *Psychopharmacologia 8*, 277 (1965).

23. G. M. Smith and H. K. Beecher, *J. Pharmacol. 126*, 50 (1959).

24. We will attempt to define the complex nature of a marihuana high in a subsequent paper discussing the speech samples and interviews.

25. H. S. Becker, *Outsiders: Studies in the Sociology of Deviance* (Macmillan, New York, 1963), chap. 3.

26. Although the motor skills measured by the pursuit rotor are represented in driving ability, they are only components of that ability. The influence of marihuana on driving skill remains an open question of high medico-legal priority.

27. L. E. Hollister, R. K. Richards, H. K. Gillespie. In preparation.

28. Sponsored and supported by Boston University's division of psychiatry, in part through PHS grants MH12568, MH06795–06, MH7753–06, and MH33319, and the Boston University Medical Center. The authors thank Dr. P. H. Knapp and Dr. C. Kornetsky of the Boston University School of Medicine, Department of Psychiatry and Pharmacology, for consistent support and excellent advice, and J. Finkelstein of 650 Madison Avenue, New York City, for his support at a crucial time.

11.
acute effects of marihuana on speech

andrew t. weil and norman e. zinberg

In a previous report of our double-blind experiments with marihuana in man,[1] we noted that chronic users of the drug became high in a neutral laboratory setting while marihuana-naive subjects did not. We did not, however, attempt to define what being "high" is.

The greatest puzzle about marihuana is the enormous discrepancy between its subjective and its objective mental effects. A person high on marihuana in a neutral setting may tell the experimenter that he is "stoned" and is having a major psychopharmacological experience, yet the experimenter is unable to show objectively that the subject is different in any way from one who is not high. In fact, all of the psychological testing done to date on high subjects has picked up only the non-specific effects of any intoxicant; it has not shown any specific or characteristic mental change associated with being high.

The experience of previous researchers[2] has been that if tasks are made complicated enough, subjects who are acutely intoxicated on marihuana will show across-the-board decrements in performance. Unusually high doses of marihuana given orally or of potent synthetic derivatives cause similar non-specific performance decrements, and the decrements are greatest in persons least familiar with the effects of the drug. But experienced users seem to be able to compensate for the acute effects of marihuana on ordinary kinds of performance (ref. 1, and R. T. Jones, work in progress; A. Cran-

cer, J. M. Dille, J. C. Delay, J. E. Wallace and M. D. Haykin, unpublished manuscript on marihuana and driving ability; L. Clark, unpublished manuscript).

At the moment, the only way to know someone is high on marihuana is for him to tell you so—hardly a satisfactory criterion for psychopharmacologists. It is therefore a matter of priority to find some specific, consistent change in mental function that can be taken as a reliable index of marihuana action.

On the basis of extensive interviews conducted with users of marihuana and of observations of volunteer subjects, we were led to look to speech as a possible territory in which to find such an indicative change.

Substantial indirect evidence makes this possibility likely. For example, even experienced marihuana users commonly report that they have difficulty talking to others when high. The essence of their difficulty is a fear of not making sense, of forgetting what one is saying and of saying "crazy things." Interestingly enough, very few non-users can actually detect any difficulty in a user's speech, but after listening to many high subjects we are convinced it is there. Consequently, we incorporated into our experiments the collection of a 5 min verbal sample. In this article we describe the technique of collection and analysis of the sample, outline the kinds of objective changes in speech we think occur under marihuana and offer suggestions for other experiments to document these changes more completely.

TESTING THE SUBJECTS

A full description of our experimental design has been reported previously (see ftn. 1). Briefly, chronic user subjects

Reprinted by permission from *Nature*, May 3, 1969, 222 (5153), 434–437.

[1]Weil, A. T., Zinberg, N. E., and Nelsen, J. M., *Science, 162*, 1234 (1968).

[2]Mayor's Committee on Marihuana, *The Marihuana Problem in the City of New York*, 1944.

were tested only once on high doses of marihuana (2–0 g of marihuana containing 0–9 per cent tetrahydrocannibinol). Naive subjects were tested three times on high dose, low dose (0–5 g) and placebo. Only the naive group was tested in double-blind fashion. All drugs and placebos were administered as cigarettes to be smoked in a prescribed manner.

Immediately before smoking and at 50 min after completion of smoking, a verbal sample was collected from each subject. The subject was left alone in a room with a tape recorder and instructions to describe "an interesting or dramatic experience" in his life until he was stopped. After exactly 5 min he was interrupted and asked how long he thought he had been in the recording room. The recordings were subsequently transcribed and analysed as follows.

(1) Cloze Method. In Cloze analysis,[3] verbal material (either recorded or transcribed) is mutilated by the deletion of every fifth (or *n*th) word. Judges are then asked to fill in the blanks as best they can. Because normal spoken language is highly redundant, it is possible to fill in blanks quite easily, and the ease with which it can be done is a measure of the understandability of the verbal sample. LSD has been shown to impair understandability as measured in this way.[4]

(2) Seven-Point Bipolar Scale.[5] Judges were also asked to rate the transcribed verbal samples on an arbitrary scale (− 3 to + 3) in each of nine categories. The following categories were used.

(a) Narrative quality: is the sample a formal narrative (+ 3) or not (− 3)? *(b)* Coherence: very coherent = + 3. *(c)* Unity: does the subject tell a complete story (+ 3) or does he wander from the

central theme (− 3)? *(d)* Awareness of a listener: is the subject aware of a listener and does he try to orient him (+3) or not (− 3)? *(e)* Thought completion: within the sample does the subject complete his thoughts (+ 3) or not (− 3)? *(f)* Time orientation: does the subject attempt to describe past events (+ 3) or is his attention caught by the present and his immediate environment (− 3)? *(g)* Free associative quality: is this weak (+ 3) or strong (− 3)? *(h)* Degree of intimacy: is this slight (+ 3) or great (− 3)? *(i)* Nature of imagery: is it very concrete (+ 3) or bizarre and dreamlike (−3)?

On the assumption that being high would be reflected by a shift toward the minus end of the scale in all categories, judges were then asked to guess whether the samples were pre- or post-drug and whether the naive subjects had taken a high dose, low dose, or placebo.

(3) Gottschalk–Glaser Content Analysis Scales. These scales[6] are standardized systems for rating the content of verbal samples for levels of anxiety, hostility, social alienation and so on.

RESULTS OF TESTS

In view of the fact that the naive subjects had minimal subjective effects after smoking low or high doses of marihuana, it is not especially useful to look for changes in their verbal behaviour. Even though changes did occur (to be described later), they cannot be taken as indices of being high simply because the subjects were not really high.

The chronic users, by contrast, all became quite high in their own judgment on the high dose of marihuana. In most instances their verbal samples changed grossly after smoking the drug; however, the changes were not consistent from subject to subject.

In neither group were Cloze scores affected by marihuana. That is, marihuana did not impair understandability as measured by this procedure. This result was somewhat surprising in view of the obvious distortion seen in transcripts

[3]Taylor, W. L., *Journalism Quart.*, 33, 42 (1956).

[4]Honigfeld, G., *J. Abnorm. Psychol.*, 70, 303 (1965).

[5]We thank Miss Carol Welch, of the Behavioral Pharmacology Laboratory, Boston University School of Medicine, for her help in constructing this scale.

[6]Winget, C. M., Gottschalk, L. M., and Gleser, G. C., *Verbal Behavior Manual*, 1963

of users post-drug. (See example given and Table 1.) What it means is that the distortion did not occur on the level at which words are combined into sentences according to the principles of English syntax; all the normally redundant patterns of English speech were retained even though the transcripts looked "strange" to the judges. With the seven-point bipolar scale correlations between scores and dose came out generally as anticipated; that is, neutral judges, in blind conditions, assigned greater minus scores to samples collected after marihuana from both groups, although the magnitude of change was greater for the chronic-user subjects. As a result, these judges were able to guess correctly most of the time which were the before and which the after samples of users and for naives on high dose. (See example given and Table 2.)

The trouble is that although the total score correlated well, no one category changed consistently for all subjects. Thus one subject used dreamlike imagery constantly but made fewer wanderings and better efforts to orient the listener on placebo. Another showed a marked increase in free association after marihuana, whereas before he tended to complete thoughts and resist free associations. Overall, the following patterns were noted: marihuana tended to cause greater and more vivid imagery, shift of time orientation from past or future to present, increased free associative quality and intimacy, and decreased awareness of a listener.

As an example of the kinds of changes seen, we reproduce below the full transcripts before and after a high dose of marihuana from one of our user subjects (subject 10) with scoring profiles from five judges.

(1) Pre-drug (dots indicate pauses): "Well, I guess the most interesting event recently that I can think of would have to do with turning my draft card in, which happened on January 29, 1968, and—uh—one of the most interesting things to be about handing in my draft card to the Resistance was that I hadn't planned to do so before I did it. In fact, the

TABLE 1. Results of Cloze Analysis on the Pre- and Post-drug Verbal Samples Reproduced

Blanks Correctly Filled in (out of Seventy-Five Total)		
Judge	Pre-drug	Post-drug
1	39	41
2	47	45
3	41	41
4	49	44
5	43	45

Note: The pre-drug sample was cut at the end so as to be exactly the same length as the post-drug sample. Every fifth word was deleted from the typed transcripts of the two samples; each then contained seventy-five blanks. The mutilated transcripts were presented independently to five judges, each of whom was asked to fill in the blanks as best he could. Judges were scientists and non-scientists who did not know how, why, or from whom the samples were collected.

In a similar way, no changes in Cloze scores were found pre-drug versus post-drug for the other chronic user subjects or for any of the naive subjects on drug.

29th was the day the—uh—Spock arraignment took place, and I had gone downtown to the Federal Building to the demonstration that was called for that event and—uh—went on to the Arlington Street Church without actually knowing that there was anything planned there. I just heard about it at the demonstration. And—uh—I had been anxious to turn my draft card in actually, just feeling that that was what I ought to be doing since October, but have been held back from it because I have this difficulty in my . . . my living situation where . . . where I'm raising my daughter myself. Uh— if I do happen to get arrested it could kind of mess up my life and hers a bit, and—uh—that had been holding me back up to that point, and I think that . . . I just began to feel more and more that . . . that . . . that that situation was really restricting my freedom to too great a degree and that I had to . . . I had to assert a freedom from their control over my life, and this really shifted my attitude after that . . . my attitude toward my situation and my existence was more one of that I had done something that I knew I

TABLE 2.   Results of the 7-Point Bipolar Scale Scoring on the Pre- and Post-drug Verbal Samples Reproduced

Judge	Actual Score									
	Pre-drug					Post-drug				
	1	2	3	4	5	1	2	3	4	5
Category										
A (narrative)	+3	+3	+3	+2	+3	−2	−3	−2	−3	−2
B (coherence)	+3	+3	+3	+2	+3	−2	−1	−1	−2	−1
C (unity)	+3	+2	+3	+2	+3	−2	−0	−1	−3	−2
D (listener)	+2	+2	+3	+2	+2	+2	+2	+3	+1	+2
E (completion)	+2	+1	+2	+1	+2	−1	−2	−2	−2	−2
F (time)	+3	+3	+3	+3	+2	−3	−3	−3	−3	−3
G (association)	+3	+2	+2	+2	+2	−2	−1	−1	−2	−1
H (intimacy)	−2	−2	−1	−2	−2	0	+1	−1	0	0
I (imagery)	+3	+3	+3	+2	+3	−2	−3	−1	−3	−2
Total	+20	+17	+21	+14	+18	−12	−10	−9	−17	−11

Judges were scientists and writers who were instructed in the use of the scale but who did not know the purpose of the scoring. They also did not know how or from whom the samples were collected.

Scoring patterns for the other chronic user subjects showed the same trend to minus values post-drug; the trend was also present for naive subjects on drug but was of much smaller magnitude. Further data will not be presented, however, because of the two serious deficiencies of this first collection of verbal samples: (1) the naive subjects were not high and (2) the chronic user subjects were not tested in double-blind conditions. Because the scale looks promising in this preliminary study, it will be used again on a chronic user population, this time in a double-blind series.

should do and really the next move now is up to them. If they want to try to mess me up, then I'll have to deal with it when it comes. At least I've made a statement. It was Father Dan Berigan . . . now let's see . . . Philip Berigan . . . the Berigan who's the priest from Baltimore who gave a talk that day. I think it's Philip Berigan. He's the fellow who's been indicted for pouring blood on the draft board records in Baltimore, and it was really, I think, his talk at that service that . . . that kind of convinced me because . . . well, his talk was different. It wasn't a terribly emotional or passionate appeal, and it wasn't very . . . it wasn't very sharply ideological. It was a kind of very matter-of-fact tone. I was first of all impressed by the fact that Berigan's appearance would really put him far from me. He looks like a very Irish sort of fellow, crew-cut—uh—and—uh—not at all the sort of fellow that would be sympathetic to me if I'd seen him on the street. But I was impressed with how matter-of-factly, how plainly he stated the case. There really didn't seem to be more than one thing to do. Uh . . . he talked

about being jailed in Baltimore for his little draft board episode and about how the Irish cops—Catholic cops—were rather appalled to find a priest in jail for this kind of thing and how it was his realization that they should have been appalled several years ago, that he wasn't there several years ago rather than that he was there now. And—uh—by the time his talk was over, I began to feel simply that he was kind of saying to me personally something like—uh—in a very low-keyed manner, something like, 'Well, you up there, what are you doing with your draft card in your pocket?' or 'Have you still got your draft card in your pocket? Why?' Something on that score."

(2) Post-drug: "Uh . . . yes . . . well the present is a kind of interesting event in my life with A. ―― [an experimenter] going out the open door. He's now closing it behind him with a kind of . . . how shall I say? . . . an endearing little smile, full of care, full of the doctor's care for his patient [laughs] . . . I guess . . . I guess that's about all the

interest I can drum up for that
little moment. What is he going to
do now with the door closing? . . . Yes,
well, an interesting or dramatic event.
. . . Hell, you know, they're all alike
[chuckles]. . . . Um . . . okay . . .
beginning of event . . . quote . . .
[apparently, subject goes to washbasin
and runs water at this point]. . . . You
think that's something, wait till you
hear the cold [runs water again]. . . .
Yes, well—uh—I'd better fill some
of this up, I guess, because you're
probably getting very bored listening
to it. Oh—[clears throat]—you know,
the tro- . . . the trouble is that—
uh—the present is more interesting
now than events in the past. I mean
the idea of sitting here and talking
about something that's already happened instead of—uh—you know—
instead of happening now—instead
of just being now—the present—is
kind of ridiculous. It doesn't
really make sense to do that, so I
guess I'll—uh—just sort of being
now—things that are going through
my mind—uh—[clears throat] . . .
okay . . . a lot of Yeats . . . a lot
of . . . Yeats going through my mind,
which is funny because I don't
usually think about that. Recently, . . .
it's just been a couple of years that
I think about that kind of thing
much. . . . 'A shudder in the loins
engenders there/The broken wall, the
burning roof and tower/And
Agamemnon dead.' Like that . . .
[long pause] . . . It's interesting to
wonder what you could tell from
the room. . . . The tape recorder has
been going rather steadily. The
room . . . the room is just so goddam
confused and noisy—noisy in a visual
sense. This whole thing—it's hard
to get any sense of it at all. It's just
kind of like an absolutely random
collection of things. It's hard to get
a sense of people living in here. This
is obviously a laboratory, where . . .
where nobody permanently has their
office, it would seem. It doesn't
look like any person really lives
in here all day. It looks just like a
general kind of room that a lot of
people use. . . . I think they're coming

after me. Yes, they're coming after
me. They're here. He's return——— . . .''

No consistent patterns in post-mari-
huana speech were detected with the
Gottschalk–Gleser content analysis scales.
In view of users' consistent reports that
marihuana acutely induces euphoria, we
attempted to assay mood by means of a
self-rating bipolar scale developed by
Smith and Beecher[7] to evaluate subjective
effects of morphine. By allowing subjects
to rate themselves within a given category of moods, on an arbitrary scale
from -3 to $+3$, it minimizes suggestion
and is thus more neutral than the checklists often used in drug testing. The
twelve categories include such entries as
uneasiness, alertness, dreaminess, cheer-
fulness, confidence, worry and so on.
Smith and Beecher showed that morphine
influenced those items in the scale associated with "mental clouding" and thus
caused shifts in mood in the direction of
greater slowness of thought, dreaminess
and grogginess. Using the same scale, we
found that marihuana caused no consistent changes in mood either in naive
subjects or in chronic users in our neutral laboratory setting where suggestion
was reduced to an absolute minimum.

SPEECH DIFFICULTY

The methods described here show
something of the nature of the difference
in speech samples before and after intoxication, but these differences would
not account for the difficulty marihuana
users report they feel in talking when
they are high. The difficulty was detected
by the judges on all samples and can be
noticed in the example given here. If the
existence of this subtle speech retardation is demonstrable, what, then, is the
source of it?

On the basis of careful listening to
users high on the drug, we think the
problem is this: a high individual appears to have to expend more effort than
when not intoxicated to remember from
moment to moment the logical thread of
what he is saying. Our subjects reported

[7]Smith, G. M., and Beecher, H. K., J.
Pharmacol., *126*, 50 (1959).

this need for increased effort whatever highly variable mood change occurred, which leads us to suspect an actual change in brain function rather than a change resulting from a difference in motivation because of an affectful response to drug intake. This speech difficulty has two principal manifestations: simple forgetting of what one is going to say next and a strong tendency to go off on irrelevant tangents because the line of thought is lost. As a result, in the post-drug speech sample given here, the subject typically sticks to the concrete present by commenting on the room. These comments have a greater free associative quality than in the pre-drug narrative about his draft card and, when the post-drug present oriented pattern falters, the flight is to a highly evocative poetic image which contrasts with his pre-drug concern with the priest's matter of fact tone. This post-drug sample maintains an awareness of the listener, which many do not, although the concern with the listener has a curious concrete quality. This sample does not have the quality of personal intimacy which many other samples showed. It must be emphasized, however, that these manifestations are fine and not readily apparent except to persons who listen very carefully for them.

Here are descriptions of the phenomenon by two heavy users of marihuana. (1) (24-year-old male medical student): "I've learned to do a lot of things when I'm stoned and seem to be able to function quite well in all spheres of activity. I can also 'turn off' a high when that seems necessary. The one problem I have, however, is talking to straight people when I don't want them to know I'm stoned. It's really scary, because you constantly imagine you're talking nonsense and that the other person is going to realize you're high. That's never happened, though, so I conclude that I don't sound as crazy to others as I do to myself. It's worst on the telephone. Someone will call up and be talking to me, and when he stops I'll have no idea what he just said. Then I don't know what I'm supposed to answer, and I have to stall until I get a clue as to what's expected of me. Again, even though this is very disconcerting, the other party never seems to notice that anything's wrong, unless he's a heavy grass smoker, too, and then it doesn't matter."

(2) (25-year-old male lawyer): "I very much agree with the idea that marihuana does something to memory when you're trying to talk normally. For one thing, I've noticed that conversations in groups where everyone has been smoking marihuana are peculiar in a specific way that supports this hypothesis. Very often, the last statement made by a member of the group is totally ignored, as if everyone had just forgotten it, and the next remark refers to something said a minute or so earlier. But, eventually, conversation returns to the forgotten statement. Also, I've found myself that if I'm distracted or interrupted in any way while talking when I'm high, I forget what I was saying and have to wait a minute or so to get it back. Most people I know have had the same experience."

The next step is to document these effects in the laboratory in appropriately controlled conditions. One of us is about to start another series of double-blind human experiments in San Francisco, a principal goal of which will be to show that persons high on marihuana have this kind of difficulty speaking. A simple test is suggested in the second description given: interrupting a subject during a narrative and then asking him what he was about to say.

If this effect can be demonstrated, it is likely that it is, itself, a manifestation of a more general acute effect of marihuana on a specific mental function, namely, an interference with ultra-short-term (or immediate) memory. By immediate memory we mean memory over the past few seconds. To be more precise, the interference seems to be with retrieval of information while it is in an immediate memory storage; once it passes into the next (recent-memory) storage, it again seems to be easily accessible to consciousness. Indirect evidence for this kind of interference is abundant. (1) (28-year-old male physician): "I often drive my automobile when I'm high on marihuana and have never had any actual problems doing so. But I do have some purely subjective difficulty, which perhaps you'l understand. My reflexes and perception seem to be O.K., but I have problems like this: I'll come to a stop light and have a moment of panic because I can't remember whether or not I've just put my foot on the brake. Of course, when I look down, it's there, but in the second or two afterwards I can't remember having done it. In a similar way, I can't recall whether I've passed a turn I want to take or even whether I've made the turn. So all of this difficulty must have something to do with some aspect of memory." (2) (26-year-old male graduate student—a naive subject in the previous experiments describing his reaction to the high doses): "Time seemed very drawn out. I would keep forgetting what I was doing, especially on the continuous performance test, but somehow every time an "X" [the critical letter] came up, I found myself pushing the button." (See ref. 1 for explanation of the test.)

We therefore propose to conduct experiments on user subjects (assuming we find a placebo for smoking acceptable to them) to document this hypothesized interference with immediate memory retrieval during a marihuana high. We will do this both by examining verbal behaviour more intensively and by using established psychological tests of immediate memory.[8] (It will also be useful to repeat the Bipolar Scale and Gottschalk–Gleser Scale analyses on user subjects who we know will become high in a neutral laboratory setting, this time in double-blind fashion.) If interference with immediate memory retrieval can be demonstrated in controlled conditions, it will be the first specific, objective psychological change found in persons high on marihuana and may serve as an index of marihuana effect in the design of more complicated experiments.[9]

[8]Keppel, G., *Psychol. Bull.*, *63*, 1 (1965).

[9]This work was conducted in the Behavioral Pharmacology Laboratory of the Boston University School of Medicine and at the Boston University Medical Center, Boston, Massachusetts. It was sponsored and supported by Boston University's Division of Psychiatry, in part through US Public Health Service grants. We thank Mr. J. Finkelstein of 650 Madison Avenue, New York City, for his support, and Dr. Peter H. Knapp, professor of psychiatry, Boston University School of Medicine, for his suggestion of the speech sample technique and for his suggestions on analysis of verbal samples.

12.
comparison of the effects
of marihuana and alcohol on
simulated driving performance

alfred crancer, jr.,
james m. dille,
jack c. delay,
jean e. wallace, and
martin d. haykin

We have determined the effect of a "normal social marihuana high" on simulated driving performance among experienced marihuana smokers. We compared the degree of driving impairment due to smoking marihuana to the effect on driving of a recognized standard—that is, legally defined intoxication at the presumptive limit of 0.10 percent alcohol concentration in the blood. This study focused attention on the effect of smoking marihuana rather than on the effect of ingesting Δ^9-tetrahydrocannabinol (Δ^9-THC), the principal active component.

Weil et al. (1) have studied the clinical and psychological effects of smoking marihuana on both experienced and inexperienced subjects. They suggest, as do others (2), that experienced smokers when "high" show no significant impairment as judged by performance on selected tests; they also establish the existence of physiological changes that are useful in determining whether a subject smoking marihuana is "high." A review of the relation of alcohol to fatal accidents (3) showed that nearly half of the drivers fatally injured in an accident had an alcohol concentration in the blood of 0.05 percent or more.

Crancer (4) found a driving simulator test to be a valid indicator for distinguishing driving performance; this result

Reprinted from Science, May 16, 1969, 164, 851–854. Copyright 1969 by the American Association for the Advancement of Science. Abridged by permission of the authors.

was based on a 5-year driving record. Further studies (5) indicated that a behind-the-wheel road test is not significantly correlated to driving performance. We therefore chose the simulator test, which presents a programmed series of emergency situations that are impractical and dangerous in actual road tests.

Subjects were required to be (i) experienced marihuana smokers who had been smoking marihuana at least twice a month for the past 6 months, (ii) licensed as a motor vehicle operator, (iii) engaged in a generally accepted educational or vocational pursuit, and (iv) familiar with the effects of alcohol. The subjects were given (i) a physical examination to exclude persons currently in poor health or under medication, and (ii) a written personality inventory (Minnesota Multi-phasic Personality Inventory) to exclude persons showing a combination of psychological stress and inflexible defense patterns. Seven of the subjects were females and 29 were males (mean age, 22.9).

We compared the effects of a marihuana "high," alcohol intoxication, and no treatment on simulated driving performance over a 4½-hour period. We used a Latin-square analysis of variance design (6) to account for the effects of treatments, subjects, days, and the order in which the treatments were given. To measure the time response effects of each treatment, simulator scores were obtained at three constant points in the course of each experimental period. A sample of 36 subjects was determined to be sufficient in size to meet the demands of this experimental design.

Three treatments were given to each subject. In treatment M (normal social marihuana "high"), the experimental subject stated that he experienced the physical and psychological effects of smoking marihuana in a social environment comparable to his previous experiences. This subjective evaluation of "high" was confirmed by requiring a minimum consumption of marihuana established with a separate test group, and by identifying an increase in pulse rate (1).

In treatment M, the subjects smoked two marihuana (7) cigarettes of approximately equal weight and totaling 1.7 g. They completed smoking in about 30 minutes and were given their first simulator test 30 minutes later.

Some confirmation that the amount of marihuana smoked was sufficient to produce a "high" is found in Weil's (1) study. His subjects smoked about 0.5 g of marihuana of 0.9 percent Δ^9-THC.

In treatment A, subjects consumed two drinks containing equal amounts of 95 percent alcohol mixed in orange or tomato juice. Dosage was regulated according to subject's weight with the intended result of a 0.10 blood alcohol concentration as determined by a Breathalyzer reading (8). Thus, a subject weighing 120 pounds received 84 ml of 95 percent laboratory alcohol equally divided between two drinks. This was equivalent to about 6 ounces of 86 proof liquor. The dosage was increased 14 ml or ½ ounce for each additional 15 pounds of body weight. A Breathalyzer reading was obtained for each subject about 1 hour after drinking began; most subjects completed drinking in 30 minutes.

Treatment C consisted of waiting in the lounge with no treatment for the same period of time required for treatments M and A. The experimental subject stated that his physiological and psychological condition was normal. Subjects were requested to refrain from all drug or alcohol use during the time they were participating in the experiment.

A driver-training simulator was specially modified to obtain data on the effect of the treatments. The car unit was a console mockup of a recent model containing all the control and instrument equipment relevant to the driving task. The car unit faced a 6 by 18 foot screen upon which the test film was projected. The test film gave the subject a driver's eye view of the road as it led him through normal and emergency driving situations on freeways and urban and suburban streets. From the logic unit, located to the rear of the driver, the examiner started the automated test, observed the subject driving, and recorded the final scores.

A series of checks was placed on the 23-minute driving film which monitored driver reactions to a programmed series of driving stimuli. The test variables monitored were: accelerator (164 checks), brake (106 checks), turn signals (59 checks), steering (53 checks), and speedometer (23 checks). There was a total of 405 checks, allowing driver scores to range from zero to 405 errors per test. Errors were accumulated as follows.

1) Speedometer errors: Speedometer readings outside the range of 15 to 35 mile/hour for city portion of film and 45 to 65 mile/hour for freeways. The speed of the filmed presentation is not under the control of the driver. Therefore, speedometer errors are not an indication of speeding errors, but of the amount of time spent monitoring the speedometer.

2) Steering errors: Steering wheel in other than the appropriate position.

3) Brake errors: Not braking when the appropriate response is to brake, or braking at an inappropriate time.

4) Accelerator errors: Acceleration when the appropriate response is to decelerate, or deceleration when it is appropriate to accelerate.

5) Signal errors: Use of turn signal at an inappropriate time or position.

6) Total errors: An accumulation of the total number of errors on the five test variables.

Two rooms were used for the experiment. The lounge, designed to provide a familiar and comfortable environment for the subjects, was approximately 12 feet square and contained six casual chairs, a refrigerator, a desk, and several small movable tables. The room was lighted by a red lava lamp and one indirect red

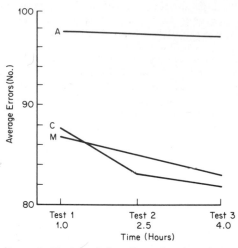

Figure 1. Display of the effect of each treatment on simulator error scores over a 4-hour period. Alcohol (A), marihuana (M), and control (C).

light, and contemporary rock music was played. Snacks, soft drinks, ashtrays, wastebaskets, and a supply of cigarettes were readily available. Subjects remained in this room except during simulator tests.

The driving simulator was located in a larger room about 50 feet from the lounge. The simulator room was approximately 20 by 30 feet and was kept in almost total darkness.

Each subject took three preliminary tests on the driving simulator to familiarize himself with the equipment and to minimize the effect of learning through practice during the experiment. Subjects whose error scores varied by more than 10 percent between the second and third tests were given subsequent tests until the stability criterion was met.

The experiment was conducted over a 6-week period. Six subjects were tested each week. On day 1, six subjects took a final test on the driving simulator to assure recent familiarity with the equipment. A "normal" pulse rate was recorded, and each was given two marihuana cigarettes of approximately 0.9 g each. Subjects smoked the marihuana in the lounge to become acquainted with the surroundings and other test subjects, and with the potency of the marihuana. A

second pulse reading was recorded for each subject when he reported that he was "high" in order to obtain an indication of the expected rate increase during the experiment proper. They remained in the lounge for approximately 4 hours after they had started smoking.

Three of the subjects were scheduled for testing in the early evening on days 2, 4, and 6; the remaining three subjects for days 3, 5, and 7. A single treatment was given each evening. Within a given week, all subjects received treatments in the same order. Treatment order was changed from week to week to meet the requirements of a Latin-square design. Procedure for each evening was identical except for the specific treatment.

Subject 1 arrived at the laboratory and took the simulator warm-up test. Treatment A, M, or C was begun at zero hour and finished about ½ hour later. One hour after treatment began, subject 1 took simulator test 1, returning to the lounge when he was finished. He took simulator test 2 2½ hours after treatment began, and test 3 4 hours after treatment began. Pulse or Breathalyzer readings, depending on the treatment, were taken immediately before each simulator test.

Subject 2 followed the same schedule, beginning ½ hour after subject 1. Time used in testing one subject each evening was 4½ hours, with a total elapsed time of 5½ hours to test three subjects.

The three simulator tests taken after each treatment establish a time response effect for the treatment. For each treatment the total error scores for each time period were subjected to an analysis of variance.

The simulated driving scores for subjects experiencing a normal social marihuana "high" and the same subjects under control conditions are not significantly different. However, there are significantly more errors ($P < .01$) for intoxicated than for control subjects (difference of 15.4 percent). This finding is consistent with the mean error scores of the three treatments: control, 84.46 errors, marihuana, 84.49 errors; and alcohol, 97.44 errors.

The time response curves for "high" and control treatments are comparable (Figure 1). In contrast, the curve for alcohol shows more total errors ($P < .01$). These higher error scores for alcohol persist across all three time periods with little evidence of the improvement shown under the other two treatments.

A separate Latin-square analysis of variance was completed for each test variable to supplement the analysis of total errors. In comparison of intoxicated and control subjects, significant differences ($P < .05$) were found for accelerator errors in periods 1 and 2, for signal errors in periods 1, 2, and 3, for braking errors in periods 2 and 3, and for speedometer errors in period 1. In the comparison of marihuana smokers and controls, a significant difference ($P < .05$) was found for speedometer errors in period 1. In all of these cases, the number of errors for the drug treatments exceeded the errors for the control treatment.

Other sources of variation are Latin squares, subjects, and days. In all of the analyses, the effect of subjects and Latin squares (representing groups of subjects) were significant ($P < .05$). In contrast, the effect of days was not significant, thus indicating that no significant amount of learning was associated with repeated exposure to the test material.

For normal drivers, Crancer (4) found a significant correlation ($P < .05$) between the three simulator test variables (signals, accelerator, and total errors) and driving performance. An increase in error scores was associated with an increase in number of accidents and violations on a driving record. In the same study, error scores for brake, speedometer, and steering were not correlated with driving performance.

It may not be valid to assume the same relationship for persons under the influence of alcohol or marihuana. However, we feel that, because the simulator task is a less complex but related task, deterioration in simulator performance implies deterioration in actual driving performance. We are less willing to assume that nondeterioration in simulator performance implies nondeterioration in actual driving. We therefore conclude that finding significantly more accelerator, signal, and total errors by intoxicated subjects implies a deterioration in actual driving performance.

Relating speedometer errors to actual driving performance is highly speculative because Crancer (4) found no correlation for normal drivers. This may be due in part to the fact that the speed of the filmed presentation is not under the control of the driver. However, speedometer errors are related to the amount of time spent monitoring the speedometer. The increase of speedometer errors by intoxicated or "high" subjects probably indicates that the subjects spent less time monitoring the speedometer than under control conditions.

This study could not determine if the drugs would alter the speed at which subjects normally drive. However, comments by marihuana users may be pertinent. They often report alteration of time and space perceptions, leading to a different sense of speed which generally results in driving more slowly.

Weil et al. (1) emphasize the importance and influence of both subject bias (set) and the experimental environment (setting). For this study, the environmental setting was conducive to good performance under all treatments.

Traditional methods for controlling potential subject bias by using placebos to disguise the form or effect of the marihuana treatment were not applicable. This is confirmed by Weil et al. (1); they showed that inexperienced subjects correctly appraised the presence or absence of a placebo in 21 of 27 trials.

The nature of selection probably resulted in subjects who preferred marihuana to alcohol and, therefore, had a set to perform better with marihuana. The main safeguard against bias was that subjects were not told how well they did on any of their driving tests, nor were they acquainted with the specific methods used to determine errors. Thus, it would have been very difficult intentionally and effectively to manipulate error scores on a given test or sequence of tests.

A further check on subject bias was made by comparing error scores on the warm-up tests given before each treatment. We found no significant difference in the mean error scores preceding the treatments of marihuana, alcohol, and control. This suggests that subjects were not "set" to perform better or worse on the day of a particular treatment.

In addition, an inspection of chance variation of individual error scores for treatment M shows about half the subjects doing worse and half better than under control conditions. This variability in direction is consistent with findings reviewed earlier, and we feel reasonably certain that a bias in favor of marihuana did not influence the results of this experiment.

A cursory investigation of dose response was made by retesting four subjects after they had smoked approximately three times the amount of marihuana used in the main experiment. None of the subjects showed a significant change in performance.

Four additional subjects who had never smoked marihuana before were pretested to obtain control scores, then given marihuana to smoke until they were subjectively "high" with an associated increase in pulse rate. All subjects smoked at least the minimum quantity established for the experiment. All subjects showed either no change or negligible improvement in their scores. These results suggest that impairment in simulated driving performance is not a function of increased marihuana dosage or inexperience with the drug.

A significant difference ($P < .01$) was found between pulse rates before and after the marihuana treatment. Similar results were reported (1) for both experienced and inexperienced marihuana subjects. We found no significant difference in pulse rates before and after drinking.

Thus, when subjects experienced a social marihuana "high," they accumulated significantly more speedometer errors on the simulator than under control conditions, but there were no significant differences in accelerator, brake, signal, steering, and total errors. The same subjects intoxicated from alcohol accumulated significantly more accelerator, brake, signal, speedometer, and total errors than under control conditions, but there was no significant difference in steering errors. Furthermore, impairment in simulated driving performance apparently is not a function of increased marihuana dosage or inexperience with the drug.

REFERENCES AND NOTES

1. A. T. Weil, N. E. Zinberg, J. M. Nelsen, Science 162, 1234 (1968).

2. Mayor's Committee on Marihuana, The Marihuana Problem in the City of New York (1944).

3. W. J. Haddon and V. A. Braddess, J. Amer. Med. Ass. 169, No. 14, 127 (1959); J. R. McCarroll and W. J. Haddon, J. Chronic Dis. 15, 811 (1962): J. H. W. Birrell, Med. J. Aust. 2, 949 (1965); R. A. Neilson, Alcohol Involvement in Fatal Motor Vehicle Accidents in Twenty-Seven California Counties in 1964, (California Traffic Safety Foundation, San Francisco, 1965).

4. A. Crancer, Predicting Driving Performance with a Driver Simulator Test (Washington Department of Motor Vehicles, Olympia, 1968).

5. J. E. Wallace and A. Crancer, Licensing Examinations and Their Relation to Subsequent Driving Record (Washington Department of Motor Vehicles, Olympia, 1968).

6. A. E. Edwards, Experimental Design in Psychological Research (Holt, Rinehart and Winston, New York, 1968), pp. 173–174.

7. The marihuana was an assayed batch (1.312 percent $\triangle^9$-THC) from NIH through the cooperation of Dr. J. A. Scigliano.

8. L. A. Greenberg, Quart. J. Studies Alcohol 29, 252 (1968).

13.
a comparison of the visual hallucinations in schizophrenia with those induced by mescaline and LSD-25

irwin feinberg

INTRODUCTION

In an autobiographical account of a schizophrenic episode, published recently (1), two kinds of spontaneous visual experiences were described by the author. One variety was likened to the projection of motion pictures on the wall. A second type of hallucination consisted of striking intensifications of color and light, a visual disturbance similar to those occurring in the early stages of mescaline and LSD intoxication. This account, by a well educated and apparently careful observer, raised the possibility that visual aberrations characteristic of the drug syndromes might also occur in schizophrenia. That these have not often been noted in the past might be due to a preoccupation of the patient with the more dramatic aspects of his hallucinatory experience, and to an absence of specific inquiry designed to elicit this information. It has often been noted that mescaline and LSD induce hallucinatory syndromes grossly different from schizophrenia in the predominant, if not exclusive, occurrence of

Reprinted from Louis J. West (Ed.), Hallucinations, New York: Grune & Stratton, 1962, pp. 64–73, 76. Reprinted by permission of Grune & Stratton, Inc. Abridged by permission of the author.
Patients included in this study were drawn from three mental hospitals. The author is indebted to Dr. Winfred Overholtzer of Saint Elizabeths Hospital, Dr. A. A. Kurland of Spring Grove Hospital, and Dr. I. Iitchman of Springfield State Hospital for permission to use their facilities.
The author is indebted to Dr. Edward V. Evarts for his helpful criticisms of the manuscript.

visual rather than auditory hallucinations. One may still wonder, however, if the visual hallucinations that do occur in schizophrenia resemble those evoked by psychotomimetic agents. The present study was designed to investigate this possibility. In addition, the study offered an opportunity to obtain further observations regarding the phenomenology of visual hallucination in schizophrenia.

SELECTION OF SUBJECTS

Since schizophrenic patients with visual hallucinations are so uncommon, it was not feasible to obtain a sufficient number of cases by random sampling. Instead, it was necessary to rely upon information made available by the staffs of several state hospitals. The patients were selected primarily from acute or subacute wards, where the staff/patient ratio was sufficiently high to provide accurate information with respect to mental state. Of the 19 patients studied, only 4 were from chronic wards. Therefore, the data obtained is biased in the direction of representing the more acute and communicative patient.

Nineteen patients, 8 male and 11 female, each with an established diagnosis of schizophrenia, were studied. Two patients included in this study had histories of positive spinal fluid serology. Neither had evidence of luetic activity other than some elevation of the colloidal gold curve. Both had been extensively treated with penicillin with reversion of the gold curve to normal. There was no history or present finding of neurologic defect. The nature of the hallucinations of these two patients in no way distinguished them from the remainder of the group.

METHODS

The visual phenomena induced by mescaline have been extensively described (2, 3); those produced by LSD appear to be essentially identical (4). A questionnaire based on these descriptions was devised, and it contained items designed to elicit the essential features of the drug syndromes. Klüver (3), in his investigations of mescaline intoxication, concluded that certain visual figures are invariably seen during the development of the drug-induced hallucinations. These figures he termed "form-constants"; included were lattice-work, cobwebs, tunnels, alleys, vessels and spirals, as well as a tendency toward geometrization of other shapes. Other common features of the drug state were: alterations of color, i.e., unusual brightness, saturation and texture; fluctuations of size, shape and number; a tendency toward the three dimensional appearance of flat figures; abnormalities of movement; and frequent synesthesiae. The questionnaire included items pertaining to the above features and, in addition, to the following: the relationship of the visual hallucinations to hallucinations in other modalities and to delusions; and, for visual hallucinations, duration, time of occurrence, subjective response (i.e., whether of pleasure or of fear), overt, behavioral response, and the degree to which the experience seemed real.

Each patient was interviewed by the author, who elicited information to complete the questionnaire during the course of one or several interviews, depending upon the willingness of the patient to cooperate. Patients were told the purpose of the study, i.e., that we wished to learn the details of their experiences in order to compare them with the experiences of other patients and of normal persons who received certain drugs. The statement that others have had similar experiences was most important in securing the patient's cooperation. It reassured many of them, apparently because it signified that we respected their experiences and considered them worthy of investigation.

Patients were invariably interested in the fact that others had undergone similar experiences, and this information seemed to reduce their feelings of isolation.

The 19 patients studied described a total of 22 hallucinatory experiences. The interviews were conducted within two weeks of the occurrence of the hallucination in 10 cases, within two months in five, and within one year in three. Four hallucinations were described after more than one year had elapsed (two after a period of one and one-half years, and two after a period of two and one-third years).

RESULTS

Comparison of Visual Hallucinations

None of the patients reported visual experiences generally similar to those occurring in the early stages of drug intoxications. Form-constants were almost invariably absent, and so were consistent distortions or exaggerations of color. Synesthesiae were not found. Distortion of movement, such as undulation of stationary objects, rarely was reported. There was no tendency for flat figures to appear three dimensional. However, certain visual phenomena that are characteristic of the drug states appeared as isolated findings among the patients. Unusually bright visions, particularly glowing objects, were reported by several. One patient saw the wall of his room wavering; another saw a woman undulate as though she were a snake. It must be emphasized that these scattered reports of alterations in luminosity or motion appeared to be a reflection of the delusional significance of the hallucinations, rather than a more general alteration of the visual environment. Thus it would appear that the visual hallucinations of schizophrenia differ from those of the drug syndromes by the absence of a number of features highly characteristic of, if not actually invariable in the latter condition.

Visual Hallucination in Schizophrenia

The present study offered an opportunity to make some general observations on the phenomenology of visual hallucination in schizophrenia. First, the appaent source of the visual experience varies in a manner quite similar to that found for auditory hallucinations. Auditory hallucinations may appear to the patient as the perception of his own thoughts within his head, or as the perception of these thoughts coming from without; or he may recognize no connection between the voices he hears and his own thoughts. Visual hallucinations display an analogous variation. It may seem to the patient that he is merely seeing his own "imagination" (such cases were encountered but were not included in this study); at the other extreme, it may appear to the patient that the events he "sees" are quite independent of his own thoughts.

Auditory hallucinations were prominent in the present series of patients. Seventeen of the 19 subjects heard voices and the remaining two patients believed that they could receive thought messages, though these were not auditorily perceived. In general, the auditory hallucinations occurred earlier in the course of the disease, were more protracted and seemed more real than did the visual experiences. It is interesting that when auditory and visual hallucinations occurred simultaneously, they usually were not integrated or else were very poorly so. When an hallucinated person appeared to speak, his lips would not be seen to move as in ordinary conversation, and, at best, the voice would appear to emanate from the direction of the hallucination. Even when hallucinations in all five sense modalities occurred contemporaneously there appeared to be no genuine sensory integration comparable to that of everyday life. One exception was the integration of visual and tactile sensations by a patient who saw spiders crawling on his arms.

It was possible to distinguish three kinds of hallucinatory content. In the first variety, the hallucinations were either directly related to the delusional material, or else appeared as eerie or weird events that had no ready interpretation but suggested to the individual severe, foreboding disruption of contact with reality. These occurred during acute stages of the illness, either at its inception or during exacerbations of a chronic course. They were brief, discrete episodes, lasting seconds to minutes, and they were vividly remembered. A second type of hallucination was similar to the phenomenon of the imaginary companion of childhood, e.g., patients who had been chronically hospitalized would catch brief glimpses of familiar persons. Such events were reassuring, were seldom confused with reality, and were usually independent of the delusional material. A third kind of hallucination was intermediate between the other two, possessing elements of each. In these cases, patients seemed to withdraw to a delusional world that was peopled by creatures of their imagination and that they occasionally asserted they actually saw. Much of this behavior satisfied the patients' need for companionship, but it was heavily colored, if not dominated, by delusional material.

The following relationships of the visual hallucination to the veridical environment were noted:

1. The veridical environment is intact, but a part of it undergoes change or distortion (see Figure 1).

2. The veridical environment remains unchanged, but something is added to it. For example, the figure of an angel may appear on a wall (see Figure 2).

3. Only hallucinated objects are seen, and the remainder of the environment is not seen or is obliterated. For example, one patient saw in the distance the faces of men who appeared to be laughing at him and ridiculing him; everything else was "blacked-out."

Any of these three types may be accompanied by a diffuse, delusional *misidentification* of the surroundings in which true hallucinations are interspersed.

DISCUSSION

It is not possible, on the basis of the above data, to conclude that mescaline and LSD never produce visual hallucinations similar to those of schizophrenia. The more complex and organized hallucinations (Stage IV of Klüver) induced in some persons by these drugs do resemble schizophrenic hallucinations. Nevertheless, the visual phenomena occurring during the course of the drug states are

Figure 1. This picture was painted in watercolor by the patient and illustrates hallucinatory change of a single aspect of the visual environment. The patient, a 38-year-old married white female, has suffered from a schizophrenic illness for the past five years. Her spontaneous description of the experience follows: "My husband's eyes looked very large. They were real deep blue, midnight blue, and as though they were full of fear. They looked almost six inches in diameter and almost covered his whole face. It lasted 5–10 seconds." Extensive questioning failed to elicit any other changes in the visual environment occurring at this time.

sufficiently different from those of schizophrenia to suggest that the two result from the operations of different mechanisms. An early study by Zucker (5) lends additional phenomenologic support to this assertion. He administered mescaline sulfate to schizophrenic patients who previously had experienced visual hallucinations. In 8 of the 9 cases, the subjects reported the mescaline reaction as dissimilar to the hallucinations produced in the course of their illness. Unfortunately, the differences were not specifically described.

In summary, the major differences between the visual hallucinations found in our patients, and those reported to occur in the mescaline-LSD syndrome, are as follows.

1. The visual hallucinations of schizophrenia appear suddenly and withou prodromata; those of mescaline and LSD are heralded by unformed visual sensations, simple geometric figures, and al terations of color, size, shape, movemen and number. Certain visual forms (form constants) almost invariably present dur ing the development of the drug-syn dromes, are almost invariably absent i schizophrenic hallucinations.

2. In schizophrenia, hallucinations oc cur in a psychic setting of intense affec tive need or delusional preoccupation and these features are either spontane ously reported or can be obtained throug brief questioning. The mescaline and LSD hallucinations appear to develop inde pendently of such emotional conditions or else they produce their own affectiv alterations. Another possibility is that th drugs possess manifold actions, alterin perception on the one hand and emotio: or cognition on the other, and that thes actions may be relatively independent o each other.

3. Schizophrenic hallucinations may b superimposed on a visual environmen that appears otherwise normal, or, mor rarely, they may appear with the re mainder of the environment excludec The drugs produce diffuse distortions c the existing visual world. One could like this distinction to the changes of visua agnosia, and consider hallucinations th result of a combination of peripheral an central impairment. If we accept as phe nomenologic evidence of peripheral im pairment the distortion of relativel simple stimuli, we could conclude tha the mescaline-LSD syndrome is heavil weighted in this direction, while th schizophrenic syndrome is not. Some e> perimental evidence would tend to suj port this assertion. Evarts (6) found th LSD interferes with transmission throug the lateral geniculate in the cat, an Carlson (7) has demonstrated in norm subjects that LSD raises the absolute vi ual threshold.

4. Schizophrenic hallucinations are ge erally seen with the eyes open; those mescaline and LSD are more readily see with the eyes closed or in darkened su roundings.

Our findings, apart from the differe

tiation of the visual hallucinatory syndromes of drug-induced psychoses and schizophrenia, may have some general implications. One can expect continuing efforts to discover psychotomimetic agents that will produce syndromes more closely resembling schizophrenia. But what criteria should be adopted in assessing the degree of resemblance of artificially induced psychoses to the naturally occurring disease? So long as we deal with perceptual, i.e., hallucinatory phenomena, the problem is relatively simple. The dimensions of variation of such phenomena (size, shape, color, movement, dimensionality) permit a ready consensus, and one may easily establish specific criteria for similarity. But other subjective experiences, no less important than false perceptions, occur in schizophrenia. What are the dimensions along which anxiety, depersonalization or cognitive distortion may vary? There are no obvious answers, but it would seem to be the responsibility of psychiatrists and psychologists to provide them.

In searching for schizophrenic patients who experience true visual hallucinations, one is struck by their rarity, compared with patients who have auditory hallucinations. A rough estimate of the frequency of visual hallucinations on the receiving wards of a large state hospital, based on our data, is that such hallucinations occur in 3 to 4 per cent of schizophrenic patients. Other studies suggest a considerably higher incidence (8), but there is no doubt that visual hallucinations in schizophrenia occur far less often than do auditory hallucinations. This symposium offers us an opportunity to share speculations on the causes of the relative rarity of visual hallucinations in schizophrenia. Several possibilities are apparent:

1. One may simply postulate that the neurophysiologic system underlying visual memory and images is less susceptible to derangement by, or involvement in, the schizophrenic process than is the system underlying verbal memory and images. This merely restates the problem in other terms, but it may specify the level at which a solution is to be found.

2. A second possibility is that stimulation in the auditory environment is more

Figure 2. This picture, painted by the patient described in Figure 1, illustrates an hallucination superimposed upon an intact visual environment. The spontaneous description follows: "I was saying prayers at the window of the hospital and I was looking into the back yard which was very dark. There was some light in the yard. I saw a figure of a man, thought it was the devil. He was standing very still. I was afraid to move. It lasted a few minutes."

fleeting and transitory than is that of the visual world. Relatively prolonged periods of exposure to the same stimuli are common in vision, but infrequent in audition. The visual background is one of patterned stimuli; the auditory background is, in general, less structured Thus, the latter may be considered more ambiguous and hence more open to misinterpretation, or reconstruction, in the direction of affective need.

3. A third possibility is that the information that must be communicated, for delusional reasons, is more readily expressed in words than in pictures. It is easier to hear, "You are a wicked person," or "You are a specially chosen person," than it is to conjure up a visual image which would convey the same message.

Dr. S. Morgenbesser (9) has suggested that hallucinations in schizophrenia may represent, in part, an attempt to find support for delusional beliefs through sense data. Morgenbesser hypothesizes that the schizophrenic is confronted with a situation in which a delusional idea is primary, for reasons which are unknown to us. Unable to give up this idea, but recognizing the absence of supporting evidence, the patient manufactures the required evidence through hallucinations. In this sense, hallucinations might be considered restitutional in that they restore the normal relationship between sense data and belief. However, this explanation would not encompass hallucinatory phenomena which appear unrelated to delusional material, or those that seem to occur prior to the establishment of delusions.

Auditory sense data, i.e., verbal material, may be simpler and more effective than pictorial data for supporting delusional beliefs. It is noteworthy that the majority of visual hallucinations encountered in this study were of stereotyped content, primarily religious, and were obvious in their implications and required little interpretation.

4. Psychoanalysts, following Isakower (10), have suggested that auditory hallucinations are preeminent because they represent criticism by the super-ego. This institution, the super-ego, develops through the incorporation into the psychic structure of normative values previously expressed through the verbal prohibitions or commands of the parents. In hallucinations, the super-ego speaks with these voices to an individual beset by the eruption into consciousness of intolerable impulses.

It is by no means certain, however, that verbally expressed censure is more potent than censure that is visually perceived, i.e., in facial expressions. Furthermore, Modell (11) has objected to Isakower's formulation on the grounds that hallucinated voices frequently give helpful advice or assist in decisions, and in this manner represent executive or ego, rather than super-ego, functions.

An alternative explanation, compatible with psychoanalytic theory, might be that the trauma or event responsible for the development of schizophrenic reactions in later life occurs at a critical period of development, and that this period coincides with the organization of that aspect of the ego concerned with verbal functioning or language mastery. "Ego" is used according to its specialized psychoanalytic sense (12), and includes the psychic processes that mediate between inner needs and external reality. The perceptual apparatus is particularly important in this regard. The critical period presumably would occur between the first and third years of life. Such an hypothesis requires an assumption that the organization of visual functions of the ego is largely completed by the end of the first year. While not implausible, this remains an assumption only.

The above speculations are not intended to be exhaustive. They are offered here in an attempt to provoke some discussion of the long observed, but still unexplained, difference in frequency between auditory and visual hallucinations in schizophrenia.

REFERENCES

1. Anonymous: An autobiography of a schizophrenic experience. J. Abnorm. & Soc. Psychol. 51:677–689, 1955.

2. Klüver, H.: Mescal; The 'Divine' Plant and Its Psychological Effects. London, K. Paul, Trench, Trubner & Co., Ltd., 1928.

3. Klüver, H.: Mechanisms of hallucinations. In Studies in Personality. New York, McGraw-Hill, 1942, chap. X, pp. 175–207.

4. Wikler, A.: The Relation of Psychiatry to Pharmacology. Baltimore, Williams and Wikins, 1957, pp. 80, 83–84.

5. Zucker, K.: Versuche mit Mescalin an Halluzinanten. Z. ges. Neurol. Psychiat. 127 108–161, 1930.

6. Evarts, E. V.: Neurophysiological cor relates of pharmacologically-induced beha vioral disturbances. In Res. Publ. A. Nerv. & Ment. Dis. 36:347–380, 1958.

7. Carlson, V. R.: Effect of lysergic aci diethylamide (LSD-25) on the absolute vis ual threshold. J. Comp. & Physiol. Psychol 51:528–531, 1958.

8. Bowman, K. M., and Raymond, A. F. A statistical study of hallucinations in th

manic-depressive psychoses. Am. J. Psychiat. 88:299–309, 1931.

9. Morgenbesser, S.: Personal communication.

10. Isakower, O.: On the exceptional position of the auditory sphere. Internat. J. Psycho-Analysis. 20:340–348, 1939.

11. Modell, A.: Hallucinatory experiences in schizophrenia. J. Am. Psychoan. A. 6: 442–480, 1958.

12. English, H. B., and English, A. D.: A Comprehensive Dictionary of Psychological and Psychoanalytical Terms. New York, London and Toronto, Longmans, Green & Co., 1958, p. 171.

14.
drugs and
control of the mind

jonathan o. cole

Since I have been asked to give a paper on the relationship of psychopharmacology to human behavior in a conference which focuses its attention on the control of the mind, I must conclude that those organizing this conference believed explicitly, or implicitly, that drugs could be used to control the mind. An alternative hypothesis, of course, would be that the group organizing this meeting believed that drugs could be used to enhance the freedom of the mind. I will examine the evidence relating to both hypotheses.

I also believe I detect in this conference an implicit assumption that control of the mind is bad and freedom of the mind is good. B. F. Skinner, the father of the operant approach to the study of behavior, has seriously questioned this assumption (7), believing that behavior can be controlled effectively, or is about to be able to be controlled effectively, and that it is the duty of our society to actively attempt to control human behavior in such a way as to achieve effects which we consider desirable before some group becomes more proficient at controlling behavior and directing it into paths which we consider undesirable. He assumes, of course, that human behavior can be controlled in an effective and precise manner, and that someone, somewhere, in this country or in the Western world, is capable of making value judgments concerning the kinds of behavior which are good and should be positively elicited and the kinds of behavior which are bad and should be suppressed. This,

of course, complicates the whole matter. We must consider whether drugs can be used to facilitate the control of "good" behavior and the abolishment of "bad" behavior, as well as the possibility that drugs may be used by enemies of our society to suppress desirable behavior and to elicit undesirable behavior. Can drugs do any of these things?

To answer this complex set of questions it would be necessary to define what kinds of behavior are bad and what kinds are good. This I feel uncomfortable doing, except in clinical situations, and will therefore retreat to the simpler question concerning the possibility of using drugs to control any behavior, noting in passing the effects of drugs on extremes of behavior which many people would unanimously consider to be clearly undesirable or clearly desirable. Skinner, of course, prefers to restrict himself to overt behavior. For the purpose of this conference, however, one must also consider less readily observable subjective phenomena, such as mood, creativity, imagination, etc.

Assuming one wished either to control or to free the mind, or to influence behavior, what classes of drugs are available for this purpose? Existing psychopharmacological agents fall rather nicely into five groups. First, one has the major tranquilizers (3), which include chlorpromazine and a variety of other phenothiazine derivatives, reserpine and a few related Rauwolfia alkaloids, and a few newer compounds such as haloperidol which are chemically unrelated to the other two groups but appear to share certain properties with them. These drugs are relatively effective in the control of the symptoms of schizophrenia and other psychotic states.

The second group consists of the minor tranquilizers and sedatives (3), a group

Reprinted by permission from Seymour M. Faber and Roger H. L. Wilson (Eds.), *Control of the Mind*, New York, pp. 110–120. Copyright © 1961 by McGraw-Hill, Inc. Used by permission of McGraw-Hill Book Company.

including such compounds as meprobamate (Equanil, Miltown) and methaminodiazepoxide (Librium), which may be effective in relieving neurotic anxiety at dosage levels that do not produce undesirable degrees of sedation, and sedatives such as the barbiturates and the bromides, whose clinically undesirable sedative properties may be more prominent than their anxiety-relieving properties.

The third discernible group is that of the stimulant drugs, including amphetamine (4). These drugs have a euphoriant action in some individuals. They also increase wakefulness, decrease fatigue-induced performance decrement under some conditions, and in addition sometimes causing jitteryness, tachycardia, and other relatively undesirable signs of central nervous system stimulation.

The fourth group is that of the antidepressive drugs (4), including iproniazid (Marsilid) and other monoamine oxidase inhibitors and imipramine (Tofranil). These drugs have some demonstrated effectiveness in the relief of depressive syndromes. In contrast to the stimulants, they are slow to act, requiring approximately 2 weeks for desirable clinical effects to manifest themselves. The monoamine oxidase inhibitors appear to share with the stimulants some euphoriant effect in some individuals and some capacity to speed reaction time, increase verbal productivity, and otherwise stimulate the organism. Imipramine does not seem to possess these particular properties.

The fifth group is that of the psychotomimetic drugs, including older compounds such as mescaline and LSD-25 and newer and more diverse compounds such as Sernyl and Ditran and psilocybin.

It may be that other classes or types of drugs with different, more discrete, more specific, or more varied effects will be found in the near future. Since all existing new types of drugs have been identified as having unique properties in man only on the basis of their observed effects in human subjects, rather than as a result of well-planned extrapolations from their effect in animals to their effects in man, it is extremely difficult to predict what kinds of drugs the future will bring. I suggest with some reluctance that it is unlikely, at present, that any chemical compounds with specific identifiable and predictable effects in human subjects can be developed on the basis of animal experimentation alone. In short, even if I felt that I could identify in man the psychological or behavioral function which I or anyone else wished to control, or for that matter to free, I would not be willing to predict that a rational and energetic attempt to create a drug which would have these specific effects would be particularly likely to be fruitful. This is not to say that investigation in man of compounds with new and different behavioral or neuropharmacological effects in animals may not lead to the discovery of drugs with new and surprising clinical properties, but I doubt that at this stage in our knowledge the discovery of such compounds can be systematically engineered. It is possible, of course, that having identified a drug with some specific desirable properties in animals one can by examining related compounds find one which possesses a particular property in greater degree while lacking some other undesirable or confounding properties. However, given the present state of drug development, it seems more appropriate to concern oneself with the effects of drugs we now have than to speculate further about the possible effects of possible drugs which might conceivably be developed to control specific mental functions or behaviors.

The physician, particularly the psychiatrist, is currently using the first four of the above five groups of drugs for the control of the mind. Most of the available evidence concerning the ability of drugs to control the mind or to control behavior comes from exactly this clinical use. The physician usually does not worry too much about the social goodness or badness of controlling behavior, since many patients come to him asking that their behavior, feelings, or thoughts be controlled. Other patients, of course, are brought to him by relatives or by society because their behavior is such that others feel it needs control. The need for such control is, in fact, not uncommonly legally certified by a court, and the patient is committed to a hospital for treatment until such time as the aberrant behavior has been brought under control. Physicians now have an extensive experience in using these drugs to control behavior, and I think most physicians would agree that the reliability with which existing drugs control specific behaviors leaves much to be desired.

Overwhelming doses of a barbiturate or an anesthetic will, of course, put anybody to sleep, and adequate doses of a drug like Metrazol will produce convulsions in anyone. Even with such clear-cut end-points, there is considerable individual variability in the doses required to produce these profound effects.

Moreover, our clinically most effective drugs, the phenothiazines and the antidepressives, appear to produce quite different effects in psychiatrically ill individuals from those they produce in normal subjects. Thus, a dose of chlorpromazine which renders a disturbed schizophrenic relatively calm and reduces the prominence of his delusions and hallucinations and improves the clarity of his thinking processes would leave a normal individual fatigued, lethargic, numb, and miserable. The evidence concerning the effects of the more potent antidepressives in normal subjects is very scanty, but again it seems likely that their effects are much less dramatic and much less desirable than they are in seriously depressed individuals.

The phenothiazines and Rauwolfia alkaloids could, of course, be used for the control of behavior in normal subjects by giving doses large enough to produce, in effect, a chemical straight jacket, in which the individual had his muscles so stiffened by the Parkinsonian-like effects of the drugs and his energies so reduced by their anergic properties as to render him ineffective for most purposes. But I would judge that the use of drugs to induce the temporary states of physical incapacity is of less interest to this group than their use in producing less dramatic and more socially meaningful alterations in thinking and behavior.

The milder tranquilizers and sedatives can cause, in some individuals, a decrease in anxiety when anxiety is present to a discernible degree, and the amphetamines may prevent the occurrence of a fatigue-induced decrement in performance at monotonous tasks such as airplane flying or radar-screen watching, in addition to producing mild euphoria and some increase in talkativeness in some subjects. The sedatives and mild tranquilizers are likely to produce temporary decrements in psychomotor performance, and some evidence has recently been presented by Beecher (2) to the effect that a barbiturate in athletes caused an impairment of athletic performance while causing the subjects to judge themselves to be doing much better than they usually did. Although it is suspected that the stimulants may also cause some alteration in judgment, this has not been clearly demonstrated.

All of the psychotomimetic agents can effectively impair behavior, if only through their autonomic side effects. Sernyl (6) can produce a complete anesthesia in adequate dosage, while Ditran (5) seems to be the one most capable of producing a severe and intense delirium with marked disorganization of thought, auditory and visual hallucinations, and complete loss of contact with reality.

The trouble with all existing psychopharmacologic agents as tools to be used in the control of the mind is that, even from the standpoint of the practicing psychiatrist, they are not completely satisfactory. Although both the phenothiazines and the antidepressive drugs may produce startling improvements, and even what appear to be complete remissions in some patients, these patients are usually in the minority. There is generally a larger proportion of patients in whom some change in the desired direction is produced, and such patients are usually classified as moderately improved, or slightly improved. There is always a residual group of patients, often in the neighborhood of 20 to 30 per cent who are unchanged or worse. Worse, in this sense, means movement in the opposite direction from that desired. To date, clinicians have been notably unsuccessful in predicting which patients will respond in which ways. For this reason, even if one were only attempting to control the minds of a homogeneous group of psychiatric patients with a drug with which one had had considerable experience, the desired effect would not be produced in all patients, and one would not be able to plan specifically that any particular effect would be produced in a particular patient.

With the milder stimulants and sedatives one runs into great difficulty in predicting their effects on normal subjects or patients. Some patients become more active, stimulated, and euphoric when given sedatives; some normal subjects find the effects of amphetamine unpleasant and undesirable and experience no euphoria whatever. In hyperactive, hyperkinetic children, amphetamine often has a tranquilizing, slowing effect, and I have known adult depressed patients to take Benzedrine to go to sleep at night.

Particularly in normal and neurotic subjects, there is considerable evidence that the individual's expectations, the cues provided by the milieu, and the attitudes of the therapist may significantly alter the effectiveness of the drug. In a pilot study recently made at Denison University in collaboration with the Psychopharmacology Service Center on the response of normal college students to d-amphetamine, on some psychological measures there was a tendency for subjects who believed they were getting d-amphetamine and actually received d-amphetamine to have typical amphetaminelike reactions in both mood and psychomotor performance, while subjects who received Dexedrine and believed they were receiving a barbiturate showed a tendency toward barbituratelike reactions, at least in some aspects of psychological functioning. This study is in the process of being replicated to see whether these preliminary trends will be strengthened. Although further work may show that specific combinations of social influences and pharmacological effects may be very powerful methods for producing specific types of results, I know of no strong evidence that this is in fact the case.

There has been considerable discussion in recent years of the capacity of psychomimetic agents, particularly LSD-25, mescaline, and psilocybin, to produce what may be described, in the context of this conference, as a "freeing" of the mind. Visual and auditory experiences may be made more vivid, and dramatic flights of fantasy, pleasurable or terrifying, may accompany the administration of these drugs. Artistic productions by persons in drugged states have elicited interest. These altered states of consciousness have also been reported to have been followed by profound and lasting changes in personality functioning and psychiatric symptomatology (1).

Two questions arise: First, do these psychotomimetic drugs "free" the mind in any useful manner during the period of their pharmacological activity? Second, do they have a useful effect in altering psychological functioning after the drug's acute effects have passed?

The first question is hard for me to answer. It is possible that artistic productions, poetry, or story plots conceived or executed under a psychotomimetic agent may, in some individuals, be superior to those produced in a drug-free or predrug state. I doubt this, being dubious that any interference with brain functioning is likely to produce an improvement in performance in a normal subject, but I suggest that the matter is susceptible to scientific test. A series of artistic productions by a series of artists produced predrug, during drug, and postdrug could be judged by other artists who were unaware of the conditions under which each production was executed. If the work produced during the influence of a drug such as LSD-25 were to be judged consistently superior, this would be powerfully convincing evidence indeed.

It should be noted, however, that the setting, including the expectations of the person administering the drug and the person receiving it, play a very powerful role here. There even is what I believe to be an artificial "geographical" effect on the response to the drug LSD-25 (1). Workers in the East Coast, such as Malitz and Klee, do not appear to obtain from their subjects much in the way of bizarre fantasy material. Occasional subjects may become paranoid, and most experience visual illusions and autonomic side effects, but none of the subjects have reported self-revelations or other dramatic personal experiences. Hartman and Chandler and other workers in the Los Angeles area, on the other hand, seem to be able to induce most subjects to experience cosmic events such as union with the sun or death and rebirth with comparative ease. Other investigators such as Jackson and Savage report similar, though less dramatic, results. Since it seems unlikely that the subjects on the West Coast are organically different from those on the East Coast, it is more reasonable to assume that something in the test situation produces the striking difference in response. Does LSD-25 really increase a subject's suggestability? Is the West Coast phenomenon entirely physician-induced or due to cultural differences in expectations of patients, or do investigators in the East somehow manage to create a situation in which flights of fantasy and dramatic emotional experiences are effectively, and perhaps unconsciously, suppressed?

As possible additional evidence in favor of LSD-25 as a tool for eliciting a response desired by the administrator, one may note Abramson's utilization of it as a method for getting patients to work on their resistances in an approved psychoanalytic manner with an almost complete absence of more exotic or fantastic productions.

I view recent work on LSD-25 and psychotherapy with very mixed feelings. The drug may really be enabling patients to obtain startling new insights into their problems and may be able to cause them to strikingly alter their behavior, but I am at a loss as to how much of this to attribute to a drug-induced "freeing" of the mind and how much to attribute to a therapist-induced mystical experience similar to religious conversion. Either effect conceivably could be therapeutically valuable, but the whole area is now so highly charged with emotion and so lacking in adequately controlled research as to make firm conclusions impossible. I am also concerned with the possibility of prolonged psychotic episodes being precipitated by psychotomimetic agents and the possibility of suicidal attempts or other aberrant behavior occurring during the drugged state.

There remains the unpleasant possibility that psychotomimetic agents or other drugs may make individuals overly responsive to the demands of another person and therefore may be usable as a means of altering loyalties or changing moral attitudes or political beliefs. Certainly these drugs could be used to incapacitate individuals temporarily, but can they be used to establish long-term control over minds? The published scientific literature is not at all informative. Both experimental and clinical reports deal chiefly with volunteer subjects or amenable patients, and I know of no experimental attempts to specifically alter beliefs, attitudes, or perceptions during or after the psychotomimetic drug experience. Chronic schizophrenic subjects certainly appear to be very resistant to reporting any subjective effects of LSD-25, but whether this resistance is secondary to any inner will to avoid responding is impossible to say.

Other drugs, intravenous barbiturates or amphetamine derivatives, can certainly alter verbal behavior, increase talkativeness and emotional expression, and occasionally enable patients to recall repressed experiences or talk about subjects which they had previously consciously avoided mentioning. The extent to which such procedures are useful outside the combat-neurosis type of situation is difficult to assess. The fact that three such otherwise diverse drugs as sodium amytal, desoxyephedrine, and LSD-25 are all used to facilitate psychotherapy by increasing emotional expression and activating unconscious material is, in itself, evidence of the confusion in this area of psychiatric practice.

In summary, I advance the proposition that drugs are not, in and of themselves, useful tools for the control of the mind nor are they particularly well suited to free the mind if one is primarily concerned with the subjective experiences, attitudes, or beliefs of relatively normal human subjects. Some drugs such as LSD-25 and psilocybin can enable subjects to experience bizarre and perhaps rewarding experiences, but usually only if the subjects are interested in having such experiences or if such experience are expected by those administering the drug. Barbiturates or stimulants (or alcohol for that matter) may increase emo tional displays or promote talkativeness, but again the drugs are probably only facilitating the expression of emotions or thoughts already present in the subject.

Drugs such as the phenothiazine tranquilizers or the antidepressives are often effective in altering psychiatric symptoms in some, but not all, patients presenting appropriate symptoms. These clinical effects, however limited, are the phenomena closest to specific drug effects on behavior and psychological functioning, but these effects are confined to psychiatrically ill individuals and do not have any obvious applications to the control of thought or behavior in normal individuals.

Large enough doses of almost any of these five groups of psychopharmacological agents can disorganize or suppress human behavior by generally incapacitating the subjects receiving them, but there is no real reason to believe that these acute effects would have any long-term effect on the minds of the subjects.

There remains the possibility that some drug or drugs combined with some structured situation, e.g., some type of brainwashing program, might make the latter more effective or might reduce the time or effort required to produce a desired effect. Although published research even vaguely relevant to this last problem is almost totally lacking, I see no reason to believe any drug would be more effective than social and psychological pressures or physical discomforts in producing changes in an individual.

The great interindividual variability in response to psychopharmacological agents in normal subjects and in patients makes it unlikely that any single drug would be a reliable aid in any planned program of mass thought control, although I accept the possibility that individual attempts at thought control may have something in common with psychotherapy, and skilled practioners of such a black art may find drugs tailored to the practitioner and the subject of some use.

Furthermore, I consider it unlikely that current methods can be used to develop a new drug with any specific and reliable effect on either the freedom or the control of human mental processes, although I confidentially expect that new types of drugs with different effects on brain functioning and behavior will be uncovered by present drug-development methods.

In short, present psychopharmacological agents, though often chemically useful, have relatively nonspecific and quite variable effects on human behavior. How much of this variability is attributable to existing physical and psychological differences among human beings and how much variability is produced by the setting and by the behavior of the person administering the drugs is impossible to estimate. The difficulties in developing and evaluating drugs for the control of clinical psychiatric states are many; the difficulties in developing and/or evaluating drugs for the control of mental functioning or for the freeing of mental functioning in normal human beings appear to be well-nigh insurmountable.

REFERENCES

1. Abramson, H. A. (ed.), The Use of LSD in Psychotherapy, *Transactions of a Conference on d-Lysergic Acid Diethylamide (LSD-25), Princeton, N.J., April, 1959,* New York, Josiah Macy, Jr., Foundation, 1960.

2. Beecher, H. K., and Smith, G. M., Amphetamine, Secobarbital, and Athletic Performance. III. Quantitative Effects on Judgment, *J. Amer. Med. Ass.,* 172:1629–1632, 1960.

3. Cole, J. O., Klerman, G. L., and Jones, R. T., Drug Therapy, in E. J. Spiegel (ed.), *Progress in Neurology and Psychiatry,* vol. XV, New York, Grune & Stratton, Inc., 1960, pp. 540–576.

4. Cole, J. O., Jones, R. T., and Klerman,

G. L., Drug Therapy, in E. J. Spiegel (ed.), *Progress in Neurology and Psychiatry,* vol. XVI, New York, Grune & Stratton, Inc. 1961.

5. Gershon, S., and Olariu, J., JB 329: A New Psychotomimetic, Its Antagonism by Tetrahydroaminacrin and Its Comparison with LSD, Mescaline and Sernyl, *J. Neuropsychiat,* 1960, 1:283–292.

6. Luby, E. D., Cohen, B. D., Rosenbaum, G., Gottlieb, J. S., and Kelley, R., Study of a New Schizophrenomimetic Drug—Sernyl, *A.M.A. Arch. Neurol. Psychiat.,* 1959, 81: 363–369.

7. Skinner, B. F., Freedom and the Control of Men, *Amer. Scholar,* 25:47–65.

15.
psychosocial aspects
of drug addiction

sherwin s. radin

Drug addiction is a complex issue involving physiological, sociological, psychological, medical and legal parameters. There are many questions raised by this problem:

What is drug addiction?

Why does it occur?

Where and under what circumstances does one become addicted?

Who is most likely to become addicted?

What is the relationship to genetics and to developmental phenomena?

Are there specific personality characteristics of drug addicts?

Is narcotic addiction a crime or a disease or neither or both?

What is the natural course?

How do the cultural and personality aspects relate to one another?

What are the problems of treatment?

Is there anything to be done to prevent drug addiction?

Many papers have been written by persons from a variety of disciplines attempting to answer these questions. Unfortunately far too few answers have emerged. The complexity of the problem itself makes it difficult to arrive at valid conclusions. I will stress some of the psychosocial phenomena related to drug usage.

From time immemorial man has sought to ease his tensions of living and to make life more bearable. His adaptive maneuvers may be sanctioned or not. People utilize realistic endeavors or resort to magic and to phantasy.

Reprinted by permission from *The Journal of School Health*, 1966, 36, 481–487.

Presented to Nurses, Health Educators, Public Health Workers, Administrators, May 10, 1966, at a session in Syracuse, sponsored by the New York State Departments of Mental Hygiene and Education.

The adaptive challenge may be met by the alteration of the environment. If one is unable to accomplish this or elects not to, he may alter his perception of the environment, or alter himself or his perception of himself.

There are available a variety of drugs that enable one to alter his perceptual stage. How tempting for someone with a depreciated self image to resort to a magical potion! The effortless miracle is accomplished simply by introducing a foreign object into the body. The ability to change one's private world by altering one's view of it is reminiscent of the state of infantile omnipotence. The cry of the helpless infant signals the feeding mother whose ministrations rapidly alter his state of tension and hunger to one of calmness, satiation and perhaps blissful drowsiness or sleep. It is postulated that this is the paradigm for drug addiction. Just as the infant is dependent upon his mother for need gratification the addict is dependent upon his drug. Not everyone is tempted to try drugs and of those who do or are required to for medical reasons, only a relatively small percentage become addicted. It is thus postulated that there must be some physical and or psychological predisposition necessary for addiction to take place. Drug addiction includes a compulsive need for the drug; an increase in tolerance and in intake; a withdrawal syndrome. The addict believes he cannot function without the drug and strives to obtain it regardless of the price. The period of elation during which the sense of self is grossly expanded and the individual's problems minimized lasts for a period of time and is then generally followed by depression as the drug wears off and the harsh realities of life are magnified. The addict vigorously seeks drugs to alter the depression and regain elation as rapidly as possible. Painful reality plus the memory of the state of bliss motivates him strongly to seek the drug. There has been a shift in the population using narcotics and in the cultural reasons for addiction in this country during the past 150 years. During the early part of the 19th century the addictive powers of opium and other drugs were not recognized. People of all ages and from all social strata were exposed to a variety of patent medicines as well as to doctor's prescriptions containing opium. These remedies were sold without restraint and were publicized as being a "cure-all" for practically "anything that ails you." Opium, morphine, codeine and cocaine were the main drugs. By the middle of the 19th century some 3–4% of the population were addicted. During the 1890's the dangers of addiction were recognized and institutions were opened to treat the patients. Toward the turn of the century heroin was discovered and promoted as a cure for morphine addiction. Heroin did relieve the withdrawal symptoms of morphine but was even more of a pernicious addictive agent in its own right.

Thus the first group of addicts in this country were predisposed persons who were medically or quasi-medically exposed via perfectly legal channels. During the past 50 years a series of events, both legal and social, have resulted in a shift in the nature of the problem.

The early addicts were considered patients and were primarily under medical care. Dr. Charles Towns of New York was one of the early doctors who realized how dangerous addiction was and used his influence to help control it. He helped draft the Boylan Law in 1904 designed to enable physicians to assist in the control of the narcotic problem. Although this law was passed, the section drafted by Towns concerning treatment was dropped. The Harrison Narcotic Act passed by Congress in 1914 was primarily for the purpose of control of production, manufacture and distribution of narcotic drugs. It too minimized the physician's role in treatment. The enforcement of the revenue act was placed under the Bureau of Internal Revenue within its Bureau of Narcotics.

The essence of this change was that not only enforcement of production and distribution but also medical treatment came under the sway of the Bureau. The enforcement of the law was quite severe so that doctors were even imprisoned for administering to their patients, now considered criminals. The net effect of all this was that many persons who previously, while using the drug with medical supervision, lived a fairly regular life, now had to go underground in order to obtain illegally that which had become necessary for their psychosocial and even physiological survival. The criminal associations and traffic in narcotics is familiar to everyone. Since the drugs have become more valuable and more difficult to obtain, forbidden fruit connotations in defiance of authority have provided additional motivation to obtain drugs. Thus there is a shift from patients to criminals and from all social strata to a preponderance of addicts in high incidence lower socio-economic areas: where in order to gain acceptance amongst one's peers it is necessary to join in. The few cigarettes of marijuana in the 9–10 year old frequently gives way to heroin in the teenager. Recently another shift is under way: to the college campus where morphine, marijuana, LSD and other drugs are currently in vogue as youth seeks psychedelic experiences.

The incidence of narcotic addiction in the United States today is difficult to determine because of its illegal aspects. Estimates vary from 60,000 to 1 million. The majority are found in the larger cities, particularly New York, Los Angeles, Detroit and Chicago. The number of addicts has increased some 5 to 10 fold over the past 15 years. Males outnumber females by 5 to 1. These figures are based upon the number of arrests. The majority are young adults from 21 to 30, but there is a significant increase in addiction in children.

Even though many people from deprived areas become addicted, others exposed to the same socio-economic milieu do not. Apparently these sociological conditions help to produce addiction only in those with physical or psychological vulnerabilities. Since addiction is flourishing in a variety of colleges, it is inaccurate to accent the lower socio-economic area as the breeding place for addiction. Some authors have stated that boredom, hopelessness and the need for immediate gratification frequently seen in slum areas lead to addiction. These traits might be prevalent upon a college campus despite the intellectually stimulating atmosphere with its abundant opportunities for creative endeavors and discourse. A number of college students disregard this atmosphere and seek answers in a world of altered self perceptions, created by their ingestation of drugs. Proponents of a mystique, such as Timothy Leary and Allen Ginzberg, reinforce and promote drug cults. Young sensitive people are particularly susceptible since their natural developmental dilemma is to search for a true sense of identity. When authority purports to be able to delve into the depths of the mind and to uncover the essence of mental revelations a ray of hope is afforded to many which may become their religion or philosophy of life. It thus appears that the social milieu per se is not a crucial determinant of addiction; although it may provide the individual with the opportunity to obtain the drug, it doesn't guarantee that he will.

Is there an addict personality type? Are there qualities that all or most addicts possess? Does addiction itself lead to the development of characteristics such as impulsive, aggressive, assaultive behavior or passive dependent behavior? There are studies in the literature where traits of character as diverse as those indicated are thought to be related in some way to drug addiction. The overall consensus, however, is that there isn't any succinct pattern that is readily identifiable as the "Narcotic Character."

Most studies indicate that the addict may be in one of several psychiatric diagnostic categories: psychotic, neurotic, character disorder. There are common personality qualities which are described in many studies. However they are not exclusively found in addicts or are not in any way pathognomonic of narcotic addiction.

During the addiction phase most addicts reveal emotional blunting, immaturity, and a narcissistic orientation primarily related to the drug rather than to his family. His mind is usually clear, rational, logical and coherent. These qualities may be drastically altered during periods of overdose or withdrawal.

Many studies of hospitalized male addicts describe non-aggressivity, sociability, closeness to mother, interests in the arts and in creativity, passivity, omnipotent ideals and narcissism, orality with regressive tendencies as the significant qualities of addicts. These traits refer primarily to opium and its derivatives.

Drugs such as marijuana and alcohol act by releasing inhibitions and therefore aggressive and sexual behavior is much more common than in the case of opium where relaxation of tensions usually results in a state of pleasure, euphoria and relaxation. Dexedrine is an exhilarating stimulant. Cocaine stimulates the central nervous system and may produce wild excitement with hallucinations and paranoid ideas. The latter may lead to retaliatory aggression and even homicide. Peyote or mescaline produces colored geometric hallucinations. Barbiturates may lead to poor motor control and speech that may be inarticulate. Emotional liability is common. He may suddenly change from a warm and friendly demeanor to an outburst of violence. His judgment is poor, resorting to inner fantasies is common.

Lysergic acid diethylamide (LSD-25) is a drug which recently has been the subject of much concern. Like mescaline or psilocybin it is a hallucinogenic drug. Some persons, such as Timothy Leary, advocate it as a mind stimulant enabling one to experience fantastic sensory impressions. Their influence has been primarily upon the college campus. The potential of this drug to induce an underlying psychosis has been frequently reported. Some claim that no permanent damage to the brain results from LSD, while others state the contrary. At any rate it is a dangerous drug which is still in its experimental stage and should be primarily reserved for the laboratory. It may have its prime function in action upon the integration mechanisms of the mind.

Lauretta Bender has found that addicts under 16 years of age are more disturbed in the psychosocial areas than are those from 16–21. In some hospitalized adolescents there is the possibility that addiction to opiates protects against the development of underlying psychosis.

In her informative book, "The Drug Addict as a Patient," Dr. Marie Nyswander reviews formulations which are related to drug addiction. She notes that addiction usually begins during adolescence and spends itself by the middle forties. These 30 years or so are the most active and productive ones for most people. It is postulated that morphine serves to quell the anxiety associated with normal sexual and aggressive drives. This enables the addict to avoid sexuality and aggression. His history generally reveals disappointment and failure in ordinary sexual experiences. Morphine provides in many a substitute orgastic experience. It obviates the need for sexual relations. When addicts indulge in opiates sexual activity is not sought. In some addicts sexual feelings are enhanced but at the expense of sexual performance. This not only refers to opiates but other drugs such as LSD, alcohol and marijuana. "Whether this avoidance of sexuality is a cause or a result of addiction is open to question. But regardless of this aspect, the addict's life does not include what could by any stretch of the imagination be called normal sexuality." (1)

According to the Avoidance of Aggression theory, the drug prevents the addict from assuming his normal role in life associated with mature assertive strivings toward responsible behavior. The diminished interest in aggression and in sexuality in the addict predates adolescence and reflects distorted family life and developmental phenomena.

Many of the addict's qualities are reminiscent of early childhood, such as immaturity, omnipotent strivings, narcissism, inability to give, etc. The closeness and the identification of the addict with the opposite sex parent forges a personality that is poorly equipped to deal with life's problems. Through the vehicle of the drug and the providers of the same he fashions for himself an illusory world where his infantile strivings are gratified. He triumphs in his magical drug dependency as his self expands in omnipotent grandeur.

It is no mystery that the relapse rate is well over 90% in most studies regardless of the treatment, ambulatory or hospitalized and with or without vigorous case work and psychiatric treatment. It is extremely difficult to substitute reality which is painful for pleasurable fantasy.

There is apparently greater success in dealing with the management of this problem in England than in the United States. The legal problems are minimized and the treatment is primarily in medical hands. This enables a greater number of people to function effectively while under medical supervision. The person is not considered a criminal and motivations such as defiance of authority are eliminated. Those suggestible persons who are influenced by "dope peddlers" are no longer fair bait. Thus in all the total number of addicts is less and those who are still addicted function in the main stream of life to a greater extent than those in this country who are forced to wear the criminal label. Since many of the drugs, when properly supervised, do not constitute a health hazard to the user or a menace to society, the English approach is a warranted one. These comments, of course, do not exclude a psycho-social and educational program to aid those addicted.

Freedman and Wilson outline an educational approach to the prevention of addiction. (2,3) They stress a program for the 16 year olds who leave schools in slum areas where they are frequently exposed to narcotics. According to these authors group and recreation workers should provide an opportunity for the children to identify with an attitude counter to the narcotic one. This is particularly important when the child's family provides little direction or education. An informative approach to the use of drugs in the schools is readily implemented. Small discussion groups rather than formal lectures are most effective. "Two kinds of attack through environmental change are indicated: first, a general strengthening of population resistance to the addictive disorders, and, second, amelioration or elimination of the contributary environmental factors." (3) Since the addiction problem seems to flourish under conditions of frustration and failure, and since the schools might inadvertently provide such experience for some disadvantaged children, special programming is indicated for them, in which a positive and non-frustrating environment is created.

Many of these children have emotional problems of great severity. It isn't theoretical that such children can be helped. My experiences with the Syracuse Scholastic Rehabilitation Program for children with emotional problems has dramatically demonstrated how educators and clinicians working together can effect the rehabilitation of many children with emotional and learning problems. (4,5) The overall approach is both clinical and educational. The two reinforce each other. The teacher learns to utilize the clinical knowledge of the child, his development and his family to aid him in overcoming his learning problems. The child may simultaneously be receiving psychotherapy. His family may be involved if they appear to be playing a significant role. Usually they do and it is necessary to treat a child-family unit, rather than the child alone. Both clinician and educator working together are able to accomplish what either alone might not. The child's sense of self worth expands as he succeeds in school. He now enjoys learning. The clinician helps free those parts of his mind which were directed at containing the emotional problems. The teacher learns from the clinician the best way of approaching the child and presenting the academic program. The end result of this is that many children who were chronic failures in school are now able to learn. A number of these children come from the same areas where drug addiction is a problem. Many of these children enter the program at a very early age, 6–9 or ten. This perhaps is early enough to prevent their later developing such psychosocial problems as addiction and delinquency.

This approach is not adequate enough to prevent these problems. We are dealing with only a small number of children. It is necessary to enrich the normal child's academic program by utilizing proper mental health principles and personnnel. The child must be viewed as a total person in order to accomplish this task. He has social and psychological needs as well as educational ones. How can we enable children to utilize their native equipment optimally? This is the area where new approaches are warranted. How much of the pressure on young people brought to bear today for the purpose of enabling them to learn and enter colleges is exacting an unnecessary and deleterious effect? The argument that we are living in a competitive world and they might as well start now may be valid for some but not for all. In addition this extra stress might lead to a variety of emotional disorders and breakdowns and possibly to drug addiction. If the sense of self worth is diminished significantly and drugs serve to elevate the sense of self then the latter possibility must be considered.

Let us use the potential inherent in the school structure for all children not just for those with emotional problems. The days of teaching just the 3R's are long past. This means more than just a quantitative change to the 20, 50 or 100 R's. The effectiveness of our educational systems must be broadened by the utilization of psychological knowledge in collaboration with educators. A more effective model for children to learn, develop and flourish under will emerge. Only then will psychosocial problems such as addiction be remedied.

BIBLIOGRAPHY

1. Nyswander, M. "The Drug Addict as a Patient," Grune & Stratton, New York, p. 65, 1956.

2. Freedman, A. M., and Wilson, E. A., "Childhood and Adolescent Addictive Disorders," Pediatrics, p. 273–290, August, 1964.

3. Freedman, A. M., and Wilson, E. A., "Childhood and Adolescent Addictive Disorders," Pediatrics, p. 425–430, September, 1964.

4. Radin, S. S., "Mental Health Problems of School Children," Journal of School Health, Vol. XXXII, No. 10, p. 250–257, December, 1962.

5. Radin, S. S., "The Teacher and the Rehabilitation of the Emotionally Disturbed Child," Journal of School Health, Vol. XXXV, No. 3, 1965.

REVIEW QUESTIONS

1. Define the following terms as discussed in Weil, Zinberg, and Nelsen: reverse tolerance, set, placebo, and hashish.
2. Outline for yourself the differences in physiological and psychological effects that occur between chronic and first-time users of marihuana.
3. What reasons do Weil, Zinberg, and Nelson offer for their finding that subjects naive to marihuana do not become subjectively "high" during their first exposure?
4. What is the nature of the speech difficulty which Weil and Zinberg report for chronic marihuana users?
5. What is the distinction between immediate and recent memory and how does marihuana effect these two aspects of memory?
6. Subjects experiencing a marihuana "high" made more speedometer errors on the driver-training simulator than under control conditions. What is a possible explanation for this?
7. What are four differences between visual hallucinations in schizophrenic patients and those induced by mescaline or LSD?
8. What are four possible reasons why visual hallucinations in schizophrenia occur far less often than do auditory hallucinations?
9. What is Cole's view on the possibility of drugs as controller's of the mind and their ability to "free" the mind? What does he say drugs can accomplish?
10. Is there an addict personality type? At what age does Radin's article state addiction usually begins and how long does it continue?

part four
sensation and perception

The story goes that a freshman in an introductory psychology course once asked whether a patient undergoing brain surgery could see a beam of light focused directly on the visual cortex. Whether the story is true is unimportant; it does illustrate rather dramatically that the brain exists in an isolated, "unreal" world. It is entirely dependent upon afferent nerves to bring it information about the external world. A beam of light focused directly on the visual cortex could not be seen.

The brain's hang-up is one of transduction. It cannot receive and process directly the many physical energies like light waves which exist in the outside world. There energies must first be converted or transduced into neural energy. Sensory psychology refers generally to the study of the cells (receptor cells) that perform the transduction process. Most introductory texts contain an entire chapter devoted to sensation or sensory processes. If one is going to study how an organism responds to stimuli, it is obviously important to have some familiarity with the characteristics and limitations of the processes by which these stimuli initially affect the organism.

An unsolved problem of psychology is the exact nature of the difference between sensation and perception. Some psychologists, in fact, argue that there is no realistic way of making such a distinction. James Gibson of Cornell University has, however, described the difference in these words: "Perception involves meaning, sensation does not. To see a color is not to see an object." In other words, sensation is the registering of an environmental event, while perception goes a step further —it involves giving the environmental event meaning. Of all the sensations man experiences, there is probably less known about pain than any of the others. Ernest R. Hilgard, in his article "Pain as a Puzzle for Psychology and Physiology" (#16), briefly reviews some of the unknown aspects of pain and then goes on to describe some of his own research utilizing hypnosis for pain reduction. He concludes with an illuminating discussion of the importance of laboratory studies of pain for dentists, obstetricians, surgeons, and others who are confronted with the practical problems of suffering people. Gardner, Licklider, and Weisz, in "Suppression of Pain by Sound" (#17), describe the possibilities of "Audio Analgesia" and offer several possible explanations for this phenomenon.

While one can legitimately question whether the eyes are the "windows of the soul," psychologists are presenting strong data indicating that pupil size can be used to measure the inherent interest and pleasure value of visual stimuli, as shown in "Pupil Size as Related to Interest Value of Visual Stimuli" (#18). Male homosexual subjects, for example, show greater pupillary dilation to representations of male figures than when looking at pictures of females. Hetereosexual males responded in the opposite direction in a study by Eckhard H. Hess and his colleagues (#19). The pupillary response is a reflexive one and is not under voluntary control. The measurement technique could be used in a whole variety of situations. Advertising agencies and automobile manufacturers are certainly interested in this research. More important, the technique might be able to help man in his desire to design a pleasant and pleasing environment on our crowded planet.

No course in introductory psychology is complete without a discussion of extrasensory perception (ESP). It is interesting and informative to note the change in attitude toward the existence of ESP among college students over the past 10 years. The emphasis on science and the rather mechanistic approach toward man which was prevalent during the early 1960s among many college students led them to reject even the possibility of ESP existing. Instructors had to urge students to keep an open mind and wait for more experimental evidence before making a decision.

It seems to me that today almost the reverse is true. Most students not only are at home with the concept of ESP but in some cases are certain of its existence. Evidently the emphasis on mysticism and spiritualism in contemporary society is quite compatible or conducive to a favorable attitude toward ESP. An alternative explanation is offered by one of my own students: "The Establishment doesn't believe in ESP, therefore we do."

In any event, an open mind still seems to be an appropriate stance. R. A. McConnell, in "ESP and Credibility in Science" (#20), first attempts an operational definition of ESP. He also asks the question "Why are psychologists not interested in ESP?" After reading the article, each student should try to answer the question for himself.

Most psychologists are convinced that perceptual processes can distort or falsify reality to a substantial degree. Introductory textbooks all contain examples of illusions that are ample proof of such distortion. Another important question is whether the values, wants, and needs of a person can influence perceptual processes to the extent that reality is distorted substantially.

One of the earliest studies found that children whose parents were poor viewed standard coins as being larger in size than did children from wealthy homes. The study touched off somewhat of a controversy which remains unresolved to this time. Various methodological criticisms were made of the original work and several experimenters were unable to replicate the findings.

The study reproduced here, "The Perceived Size of Coins in Normal and Hypnotically Induced Economic States" (#21), was an attempt to answer some of the earlier criticisms of this research. The hypnotic state is, of course, an unnatural one and it is reasonable to question just how close to the real world situation the experimenters were able to come. Still, however, the study does support the notion that our perception of the world around us is greatly influenced by our values and wants, a view which seems inherently obvious but which psychologists have had difficulties supporting experimentally.

S. E. Asch's report, "Effects of Group Pressure upon the Modification and Distortion of Judgments" (#22), is a classic study and illustrates one of the basic problems of perception research and psychological research in general. The problem is that of relying upon verbal report of the human subject as the critical data. The study illustrates rather dramatically that subjects do not necessarily report what they actually perceive. Group pressure in this instance prompted some subjects to report exactly the opposite.

16.
pain as a puzzle for psychology and physiology

ernest r. hilgard

Pain is so familiar that we take it for granted, but this does not lessen its importance. Pain reduction is a primary task of the physician, second only to the preservation of life. The ubiquity of pain is clear enough from the many advertisements which pit one pain killer against another. Because pain is so important, and interest in pain is so great, it is surprising how little firm knowledge there is about pain.

WHAT IS PUZZLING ABOUT PAIN?

The very familiarity of pain may cause us to acknowledge it without questioning it. Pain appears to warn us of tissue damage, and it is easy to assign a superficial interpretation that it is merely "the cry of an injured nerve." When one does begin to question pain, however, there are many mysteries that remain to be unraveled. I wish to mention some of these before reporting some of our own experiments on pain and its reduction.

1. *Is Pain a Sensory Modality?* The first question is this: Shall we consider pain to be a sensory modality like vision or audition? If you cut your finger or stub your toe, pain behaves very much as if it were an ordinary sensory modality. That is, there is a stimulus, there

Reprinted from *American Psychologist*, 1969, 24 (2), 103–105, 107–113. Published by the American Psychological Association. Abridged by permission of the author.

The preparation of this article and the investigations here reported have been supported by the National Institute of Mental Health, Public Health Service, Grant MH-3859, and by a contract with the United States Air Force Office of Research (Contract AF 49 [638]-1436).

is an afferent transmission of impulses, a central processing of data, a perceptual response appropriate to the stimulus, and perhaps some verbal accompaniment, such as "Ouch." The perceptual response of felt pain localized in a finger or a toe is analogous to seeing a light off to the left or of hearing a sound off to your right. Perceptual responses give knowledge of environmental events, and you guide your actions accordingly. Furthermore, the stimulus to pain can be graduated, as by an electric shock of varying intensity, or by water at different degrees of hot or cold, with subsequent changes in felt pain. All that I have said thus far qualifies pain as a sensory modality.

But there are other considerations which make it less easy to assign pain the status of a sensory modality. Most defined sensory modalities have definite stimuli, definite receptors, specific sensory tracts, and localized receptive areas within the cortex. Not so for pain. Any stimulus can qualify to produce pain if it is intense enough; loud sounds and very bright lights are painful. The receptors are unspecified, despite the role traditionally assigned to free nerve endings. While there are pathways for cutaneous pain, there are at least two afferent systems, and they operate quite differently (Melzack & Wall, 1965). And there is no one pain center that has been localized in the brain.

A further problem arises in that there are so many differences in the quality of felt pain that it may be as dubious to consider pain a single sense as to consider all cutaneous experiences as belonging to a single sense of touch. Even the attempt to define pain has met numerous obstacles (e.g., Beecher, 1959; Melzack, 1968). One of the puzzles is how to deal with the distinction between mild sensory pain and the intense pains that are described as suffering or anguish; under frontal lobe operations, for example, the anguish may be reduced even though the pain remains.

We must therefore give a qualified answer to the question whether or not pain can be counted as a sensory modality.

2. *Are There Any Satisfactory Physiological Indicators of Pain?* We know about pain through a subject's verbal reports, but if we expect to objectify the amount of pain he feels we would be happy to have some physiological indicators by which to compare his pain with that of others who suffer. Our second question is, then: Do satisfactory indicators exist?

A satisfactory physiological indicator of pain is one which is present (or increased) when pain is felt, and absent (or reduced) when pain is not felt. The correlation between the physiological indicator and the verbal report has to be established both positively and negatively if the indicator is to be used in confidence in the absence of supplementary verbal report. Without attempting at this time a literature review, may I simply summarize the state of our knowledge of the physiological correlates of pain by saying that there is at present *no single accepted indicator of pain* that can be counted to vary in an orderly way with degrees of pain and absence of pain.[1] While in many experiments some kind of average difference in a physiological response can be detected with increase in pain, individual differences in the patterning of responses, and some individual response stereotypy to different kinds of stress, complicate the problem.

3. *Where Is the Pain that Is Felt?* My third question about the puzzle of pain is this: Where is the pain that the subject reports? A subject locates the pain of an injury at the site of the injury or noxious stimulation by the same sorts of local signs and environmental references that he uses in localizing other sources of stimulation. I say: "I feel pain in my finger." My listener sees that the finger is bleeding, and replies: "No wonder you feel pain in your finger; you cut it." The pain is in my finger just as the word I read is on the printed page. The psychoneural *conditions* of feeling pain and of seeing words are within me, but it would be as uninformative to say that the pain is in my head as to say that the word I read is in my head. We have to distinguish between the *conditions* of the perception and the *informative aspect* of the perception itself. The *information* is of a pain in my finger and of a word on the printed page.

The trouble about pain as informative is that there are at least three kinds of pain which make us wonder whether or not to accept information conferred by the localized pain. The first of these is *referred* pain, in which the source of irritation is one place and the pain is felt at another place, as in heartburn as the result of indigestion. The second is *psychosomatic* pain, in which the stimulus conditions may be vague, as in a headache following a political argument. The third kind is *phantom-limb* pain, where the pain is felt in a part of the body which has been amputated from it. Of these, phantom-limb pain is particularly interesting. Our tendency to revert to a strict sensory analogy is very strong; hence we would expect phantom-limb pain to be the result of referring the limb from which it originally received its impulses. However, phantom-limb pain probably has more to do with body image than with local signs (Melzack, 1968; Sternbach, 1968; Szasz, 1957). The reply to our question must then be that, *as information* (even if it be false), the best we can do is to accept that the pains are where they are felt, including the phantom-limb pains; as *conditions* for pain, there are many complex events within the nervous system.

[1]There have been a great many reviews of the literature on pain, of which Melzack (1968) and Sternbach (1968) can serve as recent representatives and as sources of citations of earlier reviews.

4. *How to Account for the Great Individual Differences in Felt Pain?* My fourth and final question about the puzzle of pain has to do with the *lack* of relationship between the conditions of

noxious stimulation and the amount of pain that is felt. This is primarily a matter of individual differences, but they are very impressive. I am not talking about the extreme cases of people who are born with practically complete lack of sensitivity to cutaneous or other pains. These people correspond in their own way to the totally blind or the totally deaf. Within the normal population, however, there are widespread differences, and it is these which concern us now.

In the relief of postsurgical pain through morphine, Beecher (1959) and his associates have found results that may be summarized roughly as follows: about a third of the patients gain relief of pain through morphine that is greater than the relief following a placebo; about a third get as much relief from a placebo as they do from morphine; the final third are relieved neither by placebo nor by morphine in doses considered safe to use.

Differences in pain responses are found to be related to cognitive styles by Petrie (1967). She reports that subjects selected on the basis of a test of kinesthetic aftereffects can be classified as augmenters or reducers: the augmenters exaggerate their pain responses and the reducers tend to inhibit theirs.

Differences in pain responsiveness, particularly complaints about pain, have been found to be associated with social class, ethnic groups, and family constellation. For example, Gonda (1962a, 1962b) found that those from the working class complain more to the nurses in hospitals than do those from white-collar classes, an observation confirmed in England as well as in the United States.

Finally, pain responses in the laboratory appear to follow some of the theories of cognitive consistency, in that the pain corresponds to the amount of reward offered for participating in pain experiments—the greater the reward the greater the pain—as though some suffering is consistent with the higher pay for participating (Lewin, 1965; Zimbardo, Cohen, Weisenberg, Dworkin, & Firestone, 1966; Zimbardo, 1969).

By raising these four questions, about pain as a sensory modality, about the physiological indicators of pain, about where pain is felt, and about individual differences in pain responsiveness, I hope that you will now agree that there are sufficient unsolved problems to make a concerned attack on pain a fruitful scientific enterprise.

PAIN AS A SENSORY MODALITY: COLD PRESSURE RESPONSE AND ISCHEMIC PAIN IN THE NORMAL WAKING STATE

We have used two sources of noxious stimulation in the experiments I am about to report.[2] In the first of these pain is produced by placing the subject's hand and forearm in circulating cold water at several temperatures. This arrangement is commonly referred to as the *cold pressor test* (Greene, Boltax, Lustig, & Rogow, 1965; Hines & Brown, 1932; Wolf & Hardy, 1941). In the second method pain is produced by first placing a tourniquet just above the elbow, and then asking the subject to squeeze a dynamometer a standard number of times. After he quits working and is quiet, the pain begins to mount. This we call *ischemic pain*, following the practice of Beecher and his associates (Beecher, 1966; Smith, Lawrence, Markowitz, Mosteller, & Beecher, 1966). Their method is a modification of the method initiated by Lewis, Pickering, and Rothschild (1931). . . .

PHYSIOLOGICAL ACCOMPANIMENTS OF PAIN

. . . We have studied a number of measures, but I shall confine my discussion to one indicator, systolic blood pres-

[2] Among the professional workers in the Laboratory of Hypnosis Research who have contributed most directly to the pain studies reported here the author wishes to mention Leslie M. Cooper, Arthur F. Lange, John R. Lenox, Arlene H. Morgan, Lewis B. Sachs, Toshimasa Saito, and John Voevodsky. A number of others have assisted in the record reading and data analysis. The author wishes to express his appreciation to these co-workers for permitting him to make use of the results of joint efforts as they have appeared in reports already published, and as they will appear in other reports in which the participants will be coauthors.

sure as measured from a finger on the hand opposite to that which is suffering the pain. We place a small inflatable cuff around one finger, with a plethysmographic transducer on the finger tip to indicate when the pulse is occluded. Another plethysmograph on an adjacent finger helps us to monitor heart responses. An automatically operated air pump inflates the finger cuff until the circulation is cut off, as indicated by the record from the plethysmograph on that finger, and then a device automatically releases the air from the cuff until the pulse again appears and is restored to normal, when the cycle automatically repeats itself. Thus a record is obtained on the polygraph of the systolic blood pressure every 10 seconds or so. By connecting these measurements as they appear on the polygraph we have an essentially continuous record of the blood pressure.

The rise in pain in the cold water is accompanied by a rise in blood pressure, and the rise in ischemic pain is also accompanied by a rise in blood pressure. Thus, under appropriate conditions, blood pressure appears to be the kind of indicator of pain for which we have been searching. A record of the blood pressure rise within cold water at four temperatures is given in Figure 1. The average results hold also for individual subjects. That is, those who suffer less at a given temperature also show less rise in blood pressure. Thus, for water at 0 degrees Centigrade, a correlation between mean pain reports and blood pressure rise for 22 subjects reaches $r = .53$, a satisfactorily significant correlation ($p = .02$). Others have reported similar findings (e.g., Tétreault, Panisset, & Gouger, 1964).

Blood pressure also rises as pain rises in ischemia. Rise in pain reports and rise in blood pressure yield the curves shown in Figure 2. These are means for 11 subjects. The abscissa has been converted to ratios of time in ischemia in order to plot the several subjects in comparable units. The time to maximum tolerable pain (at which the tourniquet had to be removed) fell between 12 and 32 minutes, by contrast with the water pain which was measured over a fraction of a minute only.

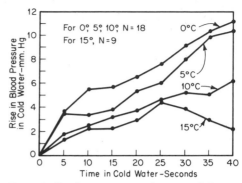

Figure 1. Blood pressure as a function of time in water at temperatures of 0, 5, 10, and 15 degrees Centigrade.

Thus we have established blood pressure as a candidate to serve as an indicator of pain. At least, in two stressful situations, it mounts as the pain mounts. As we shall see later, this does not satisfy all the requisites for a physiological pain indicator.

PAIN REDUCTION UNDER HYPNOSIS: COLD PRESSOR RESPONSE

. . . College students or high school students who come to the laboratory for their first experience of hypnosis differ widely in their responses to a standard induction procedure followed by a standard list of suggestions. By making use of some scales earlier standardized in our laboratory (Weitzenhoffer & Hilgard, 1959, 1962, 1967) we are able to sort our subjects according to their degree of hypnotic susceptibility before they take part in the experiments concerned with pain. Then, at some later time, they experience the cold pressor pain in the waking condition, and learn to use the verbal pain report to indicate how much pain they feel. On a subsequent occasion we may hypnotize them, without suggesting any pain reduction, and then expose them to immersion in the cold water, or we may hypnotize them and tell them that they will feel no pain in the cold water. This is the condition which we call attempted hypnotic analgesia. The subjects who entered the ice water experiments had had very little

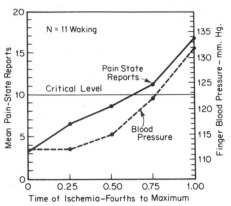

Figure 2. Pain reports and blood pressure as a function of time in ischemia. (The tourniquet was removed when pain became intolerable, which varied from 12 to 32 minutes for these 11 subjects. Hence the time to intolerable pain was divided into fourths for purposes of obtaining the means that are plotted.)

experience of hypnosis, and they were not trained in pain reduction. Our purpose was not to see how completely we could wipe out pain, but rather to see what individual differences in pain reduction would appear under standard conditions.

Because we did not have blood pressure measures on the subjects of our first reported experiment,[3] I shall turn to our second experiment which was partially a replication of the first one, but also introduced some modifications. We used high school students as subjects in this second investigation, instead of college students, largely because they were conveniently available in large numbers during the summer when the experiment was conducted. The subjects had already served in the experiment with water at different temperatures, in the normal

[3]Hilgard (1967). In this first experiment of the series with the cold pressor response, reactions from 55 college students were reported. The correlation between the amount of pain reduction under hypnotic analgesia and susceptibility to hypnosis was reported as $r = .37$ $(p = .01)$. If one very discordant subject is eliminated, this rises to $r = .46$. See also Hilgard, Cooper, Lenox, Morgan, and Voevodsky (1967).

waking state, so that they came to the hypnotic portion of the experiment well familiar with reports of pain on the verbal pain-state scale. They served three days, one in the normal waking condition, one in hypnosis without analgesia, and one in hypnosis with suggested analgesia; the orders of the latter two days were randomized, to correct for any demand characteristics associated with having the hand in ice water in the midst of hypnosis. The advantages of comparing a day of hypnosis *without* suggested analgesia and hypnosis *with* analgesia are twofold. In the first place, this arrangement separates out any physiological effects that are attributable to the hypnosis as distinct from those associated with the stressful stimulus, and, in the second place, it rules out the effect upon pain of whatever relaxation is associated with hypnotic induction. It is well known that relaxation may itself reduce pain. The results for the three days are shown in Figure 3, plotted separately for the subjects low in hypnotic susceptibility. What we see from the figure is that hypnosis alone did not reduce pain appreciably for either group, but the suggested analgesia did inded produce a reduction in verbally reported pain, slightly for the low hypnotizables, more for the high hypnotizables. In Figure 3 the high and low susceptibles are the extremes of a larger distribution, so that a correlational analysis is not appropriate. For a smaller group of 19 subjects, unselected for hypnosis, and including moderates as well as highs and lows, the correlation between hypnotic susceptibility as tested prior to the pain experiment and the pain reduction under hypnosis turned out to be $r = .60$ $(p = .01)$.

The verbal pain reports thus yield an orderly picture of pain reduction under hypnotic analgesia, with the greatest reduction found for those who are the most hypnotizable. Now what of the blood pressure measures? Will they continue to correlate with pain reports under these conditions? To our surprise, the blood pressure *rises* under hypnosis and is highest under the analgesic condition, for both high and low hypnotizable subjects. It may be noted that, particularly for the high hypnotizable subjects, the blood pressure rises before the hands are placed in the ice water, so that the initial readings are above those of the less hypnotizable.[4]

We are thus led to two propositions about the relationship between blood pressure and pain:

1. When pain is felt there is a tendency for blood pressure to rise in an amount correlated with the amount of experienced pain.

2. Blood pressure may rise in a stressful situation independent of the amount of felt pain.

The second of these statements is my reason for asserting that blood pressure is not a completely satisfactory physiological indicator of pain. It works in some situations, but not in others. There is nothing very surprising about this, because we know that there are many controls over blood pressure of which pain is but one. The two propositions, taken together, show that we have to be careful not to identify a *correlate* of pain, found in some special arrangement, with the pain itself. We may note also that we have to avoid a superficial interpretation of pain reduction under hypnosis by claiming that the effects of hypnotic analgesia rest entirely on the reduction of anxiety; it appears that excitation, possibly with some anxiety over the impending stress, may keep the blood pressure high, even while the pain is reduced.

PAIN REDUCTION UNDER HYPNOSIS: ISCHEMIC PAIN

The relationship between blood pressure and pain reduction under hypnosis turned out quite differently in ischemia. It is fortunate that we performed both experiments, for had we performed only one of them we might have produced misleading generalizations. There are several differences in the experiments to be noted. First, the cold water has the stress

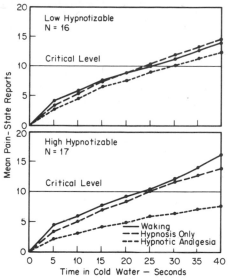

Figure 3. Pain as a function of time in water of 0 degrees Centigrade in waking state, and following attempted hypnotic induction without analgesia instructions and with analgesia instruction. (Low subjects, scores of 0–9 on combined Forms A and C—mean = 7.1; high subjects, scores of 18–24 on combined Forms A and C—mean = 21.6.)

of cold, in addition to pain, while the cold is lacking in the ischemia experiment. Second, ischemic pain tends to mount very slowly at first, so that there is time for the hypnotic subject to achieve a confident analgesic state, while the shock of the ice water is immediate. Third, in the experiments to be reported the subjects were much more highly selected for their ability to reduce pain in hypnosis than they were in the cold pressor experiment, in which they were not selected at all. Still, the subjects in the ischemia experiments were selected from those in the cold pressor experiment, so we are not dealing with idiosyncrasies that can be accounted for on the basis of subject differences. These subjects behaved differently in ischemia from the way that they themselves had behaved in the ice water experiment.

It turns out that in the ischemia experiment these highly responsive subjects were able not only to rid themselves completely of pain for a matter of 18–45 minutes, but their blood pres-

---

[4]The initial differences in blood pressure between waking and hypnosis days were not found in ischemia, and this discrepancy sets problems for further investigation. The conclusion holds, however, that blood pressure rises in the cold pressor test even when no pain is felt.

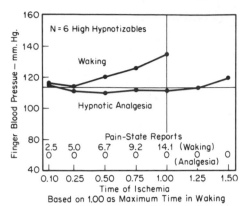

Figure 4. Blood pressure in ischemia, waking state and in hypnotic analgesia. (Mean, 6 subjects.)

sure, which rose sharply in the waking state, *did not rise in ischemia or rose very little* even though the stressful condition was continued for many minutes beyond the time, in the waking condition, when the pain was too severe to be further endured. Results for six subjects, all of whom suffered greatly in the waking state but were able to maintain their analgesia throughout in the hypnotic state, are shown in Figure 4. The time to unbearable pain in the waking state is taken as unity; under hypnotic analgesia the tourniquet was kept on well beyond the time at which the intolerable pain would have been found in the waking state. Two subjects were unable to remain analgesic throughout; their blood pressures showed changes beyond the subjects reported in Figure 4. While they were eliminated from Figure 4, statistical treatment with them left in shows a significant difference ($t = 3.12$, $df = 7$, $p = .01$) between the rise in blood pressure in the waking state over hypnotic analgesia for the whole group of subjects tested.

The three additional subjects, whose responses to ischemia in the waking state were reported earlier, were subjects refractory to hypnosis, who were intended to be used as simulators in the hypnotic analgesia experiment, according to the experimental design recommended by Orne (1959, 1962). It turned out that the stress was too great, however, and none of them could tolerate the pain for the

time required to parallel the behavior of the "true" hypnotic analgesia subjects. While this in some respects spoiled the experimental design, the conclusions are the same regarding the reality of the hypnotic analgesia for the "true" subjects, substantiated by the lack of any appreciable rise in blood pressure.

We are now prepared to add a third proposition regarding the relationship between blood pressure and pain:

3. When stressful conditions which normally lead both to reported pain and to an increase in blood pressure do not lead to an increase in blood pressure, it may be assumed that pain is absent.

This now brings us to a conclusion regarding the reality of hypnotic analgesia and to a summary assertion about the role of blood pressure. The absence of pain, reported by the hypnotically analgesia subject, is confirmed by the absence of a rise in blood pressure. Thus we have a physiological validation for the reality of hypnotic analgesia, but the validator works in one direction only. That is, *absence* of the blood pressure rise may be taken as an indication of absent pain under specified conditions, but pain may be absent *even if blood pressure rises*. This is a logical problem which has caused a good deal of confusion in earlier efforts to deal with the question of pain reduction under hypnotic analgesia (see especially Barber, 1963; Barber & Hahn, 1962; Sutcliffe, 1961).

CLINICAL RELEVANCE OF THE LABORATORY STUDY OF PAIN AND HYPNOTIC ANALGESIA

I wish to close my remarks with a few comments on the practical implications of the kind of experiments I have reported. There are continuing arguments over the relative amounts of money and energy to be expended on basic research and on research aimed at the applications of science. There are those who take the position that basic research is an end in itself, designed to satisfy curiosity, to seek the truth, to discover and order knowledge for its own sake. There are others who take the position that basic science will ultimately pay off in its contributions to society, although immediate payoff is not to be expected; this is the essence of the position that "there is nothing so practical as a good theory." On the more general issues, I take a moderate position: I believe that science has multiple aims, that there is a division of labor along the spectrum from pure science to the arts of practice, that there should be mutual respect and encouragement for those who work at any point along this spectrum, so long as their work is imaginative and sound.

When, however, there is an evident application for laboratory results I believe there is an obligation on the scientific enterprise as a whole to provide the bridging investigations that move from the laboratory to the real world. Thus the psychology of learning is incomplete if it is not reflected in educational practices, and the study of pain is incomplete if it does not contribute to the relief of pain outside the laboratory.

One may well ask how the experiments which I have reported bear upon the relief of pain through hypnosis by dentists, obstetricians, surgeons, and others who are confronted with the practical problems of suffering people. The answer is that the studies alone will not make much of a contribution unless they are extended to deal with the practical problems, either by those within laboratories such as ours, or by others who build upon our findings.

The potential contributions fall along the following lines:

1. First, our hypnotic susceptibility scales make it possible to determine what kinds of responsiveness to hypnosis are essential if a patient is to profit from the use of hypnosis in pain reduction. Not all people can be helped, and one obligation upon science is to be diagnostic regarding those who can be served by particular applications. It must be pointed out, however, that until normative data are obtained in the practical setting, the scales cannot be used effectively.

2. Second, the further study of the physiological consequences of pain, and the alterations of these consequences by hypnotic analgesia, can yield better understanding of what is happening in otherwise stressful conditions, such as the preparation for surgery or surgery itself. If hypnosis can reduce surgical pain or postoperative shock, it is important to know what is happening inside the body. Again, unless these studies are carried out eventually in the hospital, the information gained in the laboratory will tend to be idle and useless.

We have accepted this as part of the responsibility of our own laboratory, and have undertaken studies of some patients suffering the pains of terminal cancer, others with migraine headaches. Clinicians are at present far ahead of our laboratories in the hypnotic reduction of pain, but the laboratory worker has a contribution to make. The contribution will be made, however, only if he takes his obligation seriously, and goes to the necessary trouble to tailor his findings to the needs of the world outside the laboratory.

REFERENCES

Barber, T. X. The effects of "hypnosis" on pain: A critical review of experimental and clinical finding. *Psychosomatic Medicine,* 1963, *24,* 303–333.

Barber, T. X., & Hahn, K. W., Jr. Physiological and subjective responses to pain-producing stimulation under hypnotically suggested and waking-imagined "analgesia." *Journal of Abnormal and Social Psychology,* 1962, *65,* 411–418.

Barber, T. X., & Hahn, K. W., Jr. Experimental studies in "hypnotic" behavior: Physiologic and subjective effects of imagined pain. *Journal of Nervous and Mental Disease,* 1964, *139,* 416–425.

Beecher, H. K. *Measurement of subjective responses.* New York: Oxford University Press, 1959.

Beecher, H. K. Pain: One mystery solved. *Science,* 1966, *151,* 840–841

Brown, R. R., & Vogel, V. H. Psychophysiological reactions following painful stimuli under hypnotic analgesia contrasted with gas anesthesia and Novocain block. *Journal of Applied Psychology,* 1938, *22,* 408–420.

Doupe, J., Miller, W. R., & Keller, W. K. Vasomotor reactions in the hypnotic state. *Journal of Neurology and Psychiatry,* 1939, *2,* 97–106.

Dudley, D. L., Holmes, T. H., Martin,

C. J., & Ripley, H. S. Changes in respiration associated with hypnotically induced emotion, pain, and exercise. *Psychosomatic Medicine*, 1964, 24, 46–57.

Dudley, D. L., Holmes, T. H., Martin, C. J., & Ripley, H. S. Hypnotically induced facsimile of pain. *Archives of General Psychiatry*, 1966, 15, 198–204.

Dynes, J. B. Hypnotic analgesia. *Journal of Abnormal and Social Psychology*, 1932, 27, 79–88.

Gonda, T. A. The relation between complaints of persistent pain and family size. *Journal of Neurology, Neurosurgery, and Psychiatry*, 1962, 25, 277–281. (a)

Gonda, T. A. Some remarks on pain. *Bulletin, British Psychological Society*, 1962, 47, 29–35. (b)

Greene, M. A., Boltax, A. J., Lustig, G. A., & Rogow, E. Circulatory dynamics during the cold pressor test. *American Journal of Cardiology*, 1965, 16, 54–60.

Hilgard, E. R. A quantitative study of pain and its reduction through hypnotic suggestion. *Proceedings of the National Academy of Sciences*, 1967, 57, 1581–1586.

Hilgard, E. R., Cooper, L. M., Lenox, J., Morgan, A. H., & Voevodsky, J. The use of pain-state reports in the study of hypnotic analgesia to the pain of ice water. *Journal of Nervous and Mental Disease*, 1967, 144, 506–513.

Hines, E. A., & Brown, G. E. A standard stimulus for measuring vasomotor reactions: Its application in the study of hypertension. *Proceedings of Staff Meetings, Mayo Clinic*, 1932, 7, 332.

Levine, M. Psychogalvanic reaction to painful stimuli in hypnotic and hysterical anesthesia. *Bulletin Johns Hopkins Hospital*, 1930, 46, 331–339.

Lewin, I. The effect of reward on the experience of pain. In, *Dissertations in cognitive processes*. Detroit, Mich.: Center for Cognitive Processes, Wayne State University, 1965.

Lewis, T., Pickering, G. W., & Rothschild, P. Observations upon muscular pain in intermittent claudication. *Heart*, 1931, 15, 359–383.

Melzack, R. Pain. *International Encyclopedia of the Social Sciences*. Vol. 11. New York: Macmillan and Free Press, 1968. pp. 357–363.

Melzack, R., & Wall, P. D. Pain mechanisms: A new theory. *Science*, 1965, 150, 971–979.

Orne, M. T. The nature of hypnosis: Artifact and essence. *Journal of Abnormal and Social Psychology*, 1959, 58, 277–299.

Orne, M. T. On the social psychology of the psychological experiment: With particular reference to demand characteristics and their implications. *American Psychologist*, 1962, 17, 776–783.

Petrie, A. *Individuality in pain and suffering*. Chicago: University of Chicago Press, 1967.

Sears, R. R. Experimental study of hypnotic anesthesia. *Journal of Experimental Psychology*, 1932, 15, 1–22.

Shor, R. E. Physiological effects of painful stimulation during hypnotic analgesia under conditions designed to minimize anxiety. *International Journal of Clinical and Experimental Hypnosis*, 1962, 8, 151–163.

Smith, G. M., Lawrence, D. E., Markowitz, R. A., Mosteller, F., & Beecher, H. K. An experimental pain method sensitive to morphine in man: The sub-maximum effort tourniquet technique. *Journal of Pharmacology and Experimental Therapeutics*, 1966, 154, 324–332.

Sternbach, R. A. *Pain: A psychophysiological analysis*. New York: Academic Press, 1968.

Stevens, S. S. Matching functions between loudness and ten other continua. *Perception and Psychophysics*, 1966, 1, 5–8.

Sutcliffe, J. P. "Credulous" and "skeptical" views of hypnotic phenomena: Experiments on esthesia, hallucination, and delusion. *Journal of Abnormal and Social Psychology*, 1961, 62, 189–200.

Szasz, T. S. *Pain and pleasure*. New York: Basic Books, 1967.

Tétreault, L., Panisset, A., & Gouger, P. Étude des facteurs, émotion et douleur dans la réponse tensionnelle au "cold pressor test." *L'Union Médicale du Canada*, 1964, 93, 177–180.

Voevodsky, J., Cooper, L. M., Morgan, A. H., & Hilgard, E. R. The measurement of suprathreshold pain. *American Journal of Psychology*, 1967, 80, 124–128.

Weitzenhoffer, A. M., & Hilgard, E. R. *Stanford Hypnotic Susceptibility Scales, Forms A and B*. Palo Alto, Calif.: Consulting Psychologists Press, 1959.

Weitzenhoffer, A. M., & Hilgard, E. R. *Stanford Hypnotic Susceptibility Scales, Form C*. Palo Alto, Calif.: Consulting Psychologists Press, 1962.

Weitzenhoffer, A. M., & Hilgard, E. R. *Revised Stanford Profile Scales of Hypnotic Susceptibility, Forms I and II*. Palo Alto, Calif.: Consulting Psychologists Press, 1967.

West, L. J., Neill, K. C., & Hardy, J. D. Effects of hypnotic suggestions on pain perception and galvanic skin response. *Archives of Neurology and Psychiatry*, 1952, 68, 549–560.

Wolf, S., & Hardy, J. D. Studies on pain. Observations on pain due to local cooling and on factors involved in the "cold pressor" effect. *Journal of Clinical Investigation,* 1941, *20,* 521–533.

Wolff, H. G., & Goodell, H. The relation of attitude and suggestion to the perception of and reaction to pain. *Proceedings of the Association for Research in Nervous and Mental Disease,* 1943, *23,* 434–448.

Zimbardo, P. G., *Cognitive control of motivation.* Chicago: Scott, Foresman, 1969.

Zimbardo, P. G., Cohen, A. R., Weisenberg, M., Dworkin, L., & Firestone, I. Control of pain motivation by cognitive dissonance. *Science,* 1966, *151,* 217–219.

17.
suppression of pain by sound

wallace j. gardner,
j. c. r. licklider,
and a. z. weisz

Certain types of pain may be reduced or abolished by intense acoustic stimulation (1). We have studied "audio analgesia" in dental situations and, with others, have obtained preliminary results in hospitals and laboratories (2).

In Wallace J. Gardner's dental office, suppression of pain by sound has been fully effective for 65 percent of 1000 patients who previously required nitrous oxide or a local anesthetic in comparable operations. For 25 percent, sound-induced analgesia was sufficiently effective that no other analgesic or anesthetic agent was required. For 10 percent, it was less than adequate. In only a handful of cases has a patient reported experiencing objectionable pain while listening to the intense sound.

During the last year, audio analgesia equipments have been used by eight other dentists in the Boston area. Their experiences have paralleled those just summarized. In about 90 percent of 5000 operations, sound stimulation has been the only analgesic agent required. Gardner has extracted over 200 teeth without encountering any difficulty or report of objectionable pain. The other dentists, also, have extracted teeth under audio analgesia.

The procedure usually followed in inducing the analgesic condition involves the use of music and of noise. The patient wears headphones and controls the stimuli through a small control box in his hand. Before the operation, and until a potentially painful procedure has to be employed, the patient listens to stereo-

Reprinted by permission from *Science*, July 1, 1960, *132* (3418), 32–33. Copyright 1960 by the American Association for the Advancement of Science.

phonic music. As soon as he anticipates pain or feels incipient pain, he turns up the intensity of the noise stimulus. It is random noise with a spectrum shaped by lowpass filters to provide a compromise between analgesic effectiveness and pleasantness of quality.

The main function of the music is to relax the patient. For most patients, the noise is the main agent, the one that drowns out the pain.

Several factors operate simultaneously in producing the analgesia (3). The noise appears, in introspection, directly to suppress the pain caused by the dental operation. During cavity preparation, the noise also masks the sound of the dental drill, thereby removing a source of conditioned anxiety. The music promotes relaxation, and the noise, which sounds like a waterfall, also has a relaxing effect. When both music and noise are presented, the music can be followed only through concentration; it diverts attention from the dental operation. Patients enjoy having control over the massive acoustic stimulation; in their earlier experiences in dental offices, control of the situation had seemed entirely out of their hands. The procedure provides a needed channel of communication between the patient and the dentist: the dentist can judge the patient's state of anxiety or discomfort by noting whether the patient is using music or noise, and by observing the intensity level of the signal. All the foregoing factors appear to be important, different ones predominating in different situations and for different patients. Suggestion also plays a role, the significance of which has been difficult to estimate.

The results obtained in dental operations suggest that audio analgesia may be effective also in clinical medical situations. Preliminary observations have been made with the cooperation of physicians in the Boston area. The sources of pain included left heart catheterizations, removal of toenails, labor and childbirth, and the removal of a polyp from the shoulder of one of us. The audio procedure was effective in over two-thirds of these applications. When it was not effective, the patient was not relaxed, or the pain was well developed before the sound was turned on, or it was not feasible to continue intense stimulation throughout the operation. Exposure to intense acoustic stimulation must be carefully controlled in order to avoid the possibility of producing damage to hearing.

Audio analgesia is more effective against some kinds of pain than others. In the polyp removal, there was sharply localized pain ("pinprick") at the time of the incision and again when the suturing needle passed through the skin. The pain was clearly recognizable, but quite small and inconsequential. During the remainder of the operation, there was nothing that could be called pain— only pressure and tension. Some patients report no pain at all when the noise is on at high intensity. Others say that there is detectable pain, but that "it doesn't hurt."

Efforts to examine the phenomenon in the laboratory have encountered the difficulties noted in other nonclinical studies of analgesia (4). If the subject pays attention to the nociceptive stimulus and reports upon the magnitude of the resulting subjective pain, the effect of acoustic stimulation is usually small. It is possible, however, by duplicating the clinical context as nearly as possible, to set up demonstrations in which the subjective magnitude of a pain (deep pain of slow onset) is clearly modulated by the turning on and off of intense sound.

The pain-reducing effect of intense stimulation is not restricted to the auditory modality. Effect of vibratory stimulation has been observed by Weitz (5) and Wall (6). In our laboratory, Baruch and Fox recently demonstrated that a bright flash of light can inhibit the pain response to a localized electrodermal shock.

In thinking toward an explanation, we note that parts of the auditory and pain systems come together in several regions of the reticular formation and lower thalamus. The interactions between the two systems are largely inhibitory. Both the direct suppressive effect and the effects mediated through relaxation, reduction of anxiety, and diversion of attention, can be explained by assuming that acoustic stimulation decreases the "gain" of pain relays upon which branches of the auditory system impinge. The behavior of an analogue-computer simulation of the hypothesized process reflects the characteristics of audio analgesia observed in clinic and laboratory. Moreover, in a recent letter, Mountcastle reports that he has found, in the posterior group nuclei of the thalamus and in the cerebral cortex, pain-evoked neural activity that is suppressed by acoustic stimulation (7).

REFERENCES AND NOTES

1. W. J. Gardner and J. C. R. Licklider, J. Acoust. Soc. Am. 31, 177 (Abstr.), 850 (Abstr.), (1959). For details of initial observations, see W. J. Gardner and J. C. R. Licklider, J. Am. Dental Assoc. 59, 1144 (1959).

2. We use the word analgesia here in the sense of the dictionary definition, "insensibility to pain," which we interpret as "condition in which perceived pain is eliminated or significantly reduced, without implications concerning mechanism."

3. We are indebted to Dr. Ulric Neisser for his analysis of the psychological factors involved in auditory analgesia: "Auditory suppression of reactions to pain," unpublished manuscript, October 1958.

4. H. K. Beecher, Pharmacol. Rev. 9, 59 (1957).

5. J. Weitz, J. Exptl. Psychol. 30, 426 (1942).

6. P. D. Wall, personal communication, 25 May 1959.

7. V. Mountcastle, personal communication, 21 Nov. 1959.

18.
pupil size as related to interest value of visual stimuli

eckhard h. hess
and james m. polt

Qualities which have nothing to do with vision as such have long been attributed to the eyes. Perhaps the most poetical expression of this is found in the lines of Guillaume de Salluste: "These lovely lamps, these windows of the soul." Even if the eyes are not the "windows of the soul," there is an increasing amount of evidence that the eyes, more specifically the pupils, register directly certain activities of the nervous system, including, but not restricted to, the effects of visual stimulation.

Kuntz (1) discusses the control of the constriction and dilation of the pupil by the sympathetic and parasympathetic divisions of the autonomic nervous system. The light reflex, which is a change in pupil size due to changes in environmental light conditions, is controlled by the parasympathetic division through the action of the ciliary ganglion. The role of the sympathetic division in determining the size of the pupil is more complex, but Kuntz points out that "strong emotional states are accompanied by general sympathetic stimulation" and that "deep emotions of pleasure as well as fear are commonly accompanied by pupillary dilation."

Evidence that control of pupillary dilation by the sympathetic division of the autonomic nervous system is governed by hypothalamic centers is discussed by Gellhorn (2), who concludes that "pupillary dilation is one of the most constant symptoms observed on stimulation of the hypothalamus." Furthermore, Gibbs and

Reprinted by permission from *Science*, August 5, 1960, *132* (3423), 349–350. Published by the American Association for the Advancement of Science.

Gibbs (3) report that hypothalamic stimulation will elicit purring in cats, which is generally considered to be an emotional expression of pleasure.

These findings are, of course, consistent with the vast amount of research done by Cannon and his collaborators, and also with their hypothesis that emotion is based on discharge over the sympatheticoadrenal system.

Some preliminary studies have been conducted at the University of Chicago with cats reared as pets and with intact laboratory animals, which indicated that under constant light conditions there were marked pupillary dilations in response to such stimuli as a relatively strange cat introduced into the home territory, a familiar object of play, and food. When food was not recognized either because it was wrapped in paper or because it was an item foreign to the animal's normal diet, maximal dilation of the pupil did not occur until the scent of the food reached the animal.

To test the hypothesis that pupillary changes mediated by the sympathetic division, such as the changes we found in animals, could be used in human beings as both a quantitative and a qualitative measure of greater or less interest value and pleasure value of visual stimuli, we developed a technique for recording pupil size while the subject was shown visual material of different kinds.

Briefly, this technique involved obtaining exposures of the subject's eye on 16 mm film while he viewed a series consisting of test pictures alternated with a control pattern. Brightness was kept relatively constant in order to rule out any effect of changes in level of illumination on the size of the pupil. It was found

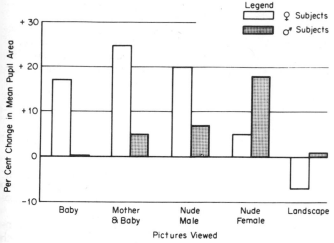

Figure 1. Changes in mean pupil size, in terms of percentage of decrease or increase in area, from size during viewing of control patterns, in response to various pictures.

that the most expedient way to analyze the film record was to project the 16-mm frames with a Percepto-Scope (4) and measure the pupil size in the projected image. In the pilot study reported here, the six subjects consisted of one single female, one married female, three single males, and one married male. Neither of the married subjects had children.

The figures shown in Figure 1 represent the mean area of the pupil in 20 exposures taken over a 10-second period during which a test picture was viewed in relation to the area in 20 exposures taken during the preceding 10-second presentation of the test pattern. This relationship is given for the six subjects for a picture of a baby, of a mother holding a young child, of a partially nude man, of a partially nude woman, and of a landscape.

These data show that there is a clear sexual dichotomy in regard to the interest value of the pictures, with no overlap between sexes for the first four pictures.

We purposely report the data for the small sample used in our first study to indicate the type of results obtainable with this technique with a minimum number of subjects. Further studies, in which we utilized similar materials and

more subjects, gave essentially the same results. Test-retest series, given after an interval of 1 day, show an extremely reliable result for the subjects tested. The probability of getting results of the degree of similarity by chance for any one subject falls below the .01 level.

The responses made to the picture of the baby and the picture of the mother and child substantiate an experiment conducted by Cann (5), who asked subjects to choose which picture they liked best in each of a series of pairs. Each pair consisted of an infant animal and an adult of the same species. Cann found that significantly more of the "baby" pictures were preferred by single women and by childless women than by single men and childless married men.

The responses to the pictures of the partially nude man and woman are what logically would be expected. Men are more interested in partially nude women, while women are more interested in partially nude men.

A comparison of the responses to the first four pictures with responses to the last emphasizes the possibilities for rating a wide range of material on the basis of interest value. It is also clear that differences in interest value of the various stimuli may be discerned within as well as between sexes.

Work now in progress deals with the range of visual materials for which reliable differences of pupil size can be found, as well as an exploration of how fine a discrimination will be possible with this technique. Further work deals with investigations of possible auditory effects on pupil size—for example, whether pleasant music causes pupillary dilation as compared to unpleasant sounds. Other avenues include the investigation of possible differences in pupil size when material dealing with experimental esthetics is presented.

The implications of this line of research seem to be far-reaching and could lead to a clearer understanding of behavior and its development at the human and infrahuman levels, through the study of a response with a basic mechanism which transcends gross species differences (6).

REFERENCES AND NOTES

1. A. Kuntz, *The Autonomic Nervous System* (Lea and Febiger, Philadelphia, 1929).
2. E. Gellhorn, *Autonomic Regulations* (Interscience, New York, 1943).
3. E. L. Gibbs and F. A. Gibbs, *J. Comp. Neurol.* 64, 209 (1943).
4. The Percepto-Scope is manufactured by Perceptual Development Laboratories, St. Louis, Mo.
5. M. A. Cann, thesis, University of Chicago (1953).
6. Part of this work was carried out at the Perception Research Laboratory of McCann-Erickson, Inc.

19.
pupil response of hetero- and homosexual males to pictures of men and women: a pilot study

eckhard h. hess,
allan l. seltzer,
and john m. shlien

Change in the size of the pupil of the human eye has been reported to vary with a subject's interest in various pictorial stimuli (Hess & Polt, 1960). Male subjects had a larger pupil while looking at pictures of women than when looking at pictures of men. The reverse was true for female subjects: they had larger pupils looking at men. Unpublished work with a large number of subjects has continued to substantiate the finding of this difference between the sexes.

If this difference in pupil response is truly a reflection of interest in the male or female figure as a sexual object then homosexuals would be expected to show a larger pupil response to pictures of their own sex. In the course of our work a few subjects have given a larger response to pictures of their own sex; as measured by pupil size, same-sex pictures seemed more interesting to them. Review of these anomalous cases increased the plausibility of the idea that this same-sex response might be typical of homosexuals. The present report, a pilot study of a small group of overt male homosexuals, strongly supports that hypothesis.

Reprinted from *Journal of Abnormal Psychology*, 1965, 70 (3), 165–168. Abridged by permission of the authors.

This research was supported in part by a grant from Social Sciences Research Committee of the University of Chicago and in part by Interpublic, New York, New York.

METHOD

Subjects

Ten young adult male subjects were tested. Five of these, students or workers in our laboratory—the heterosexual group—were well known to us over a period of several years. Their sexual outlet was judged to be exclusively heterosexual. The other five were known, through observation, interview, and in every case by their own voluntary admission to one of the authors who had gained their trust, to have overt homosexuality as their sole or primary sexual outlet. All 10 were of roughly the same age (between 24 and 34 years), same education (all but one were graduate students), and same social level. None was hospitalized or in therapy.

Procedure and Apparatus

In a dimly-lit room, a subject was seated before a viewing aperture, fitted with a headrest, which was inserted in a large plywood panel. The panel concealed the working of the apparatus from the subject. Resting his head against the aperture, the subject faced a rear-projection screen, set in an otherwise black box, at a distance of 2½ feet from his eyes. A 35-millimeter slide projector behind this screen projected a 9 x 12-inch picture onto it. Changing of slides was controlled by the experimenter from his position behind the panel where he also operated a concealed 16-millimeter camera fitted with a frame counter. As the slides were being viewed a half-silvered mirror placed at a 45-degree angle across the subject's line of vision permitted unobtrusive filming of the eye, at the rate of two frames per second. Illumination for this photography was furnished by a 100-watt bulb on rheostat control.

Stimuli

Fifteen picture slides, representations of the human figure, were shown in the following order:

Slide Content	Scoring Category
A. Painting, cubist, five figures	Art
B. Painting, realistic, crucifixion	Art
C. Painting, two nude males	Male
D. Painting, reclining female nude	Female
E. Photograph, nude man, head and upper torso	Male
F. Painting, seated nude female, rear view	Female
G. Painting, sailor, nude upper torso	Male
H. Painting, nude male and nude female	Art
I. Photograph, nude female torso	Female
J. Photograph, nude man, rear view	Male
K. Painting, nude female, head and upper torso	Female
L. Painting, two partly clothed males	Male
M. Painting, nude female, head and torso	Female
N. Painting, abstract, three figures	Art
O. Painting, cubist, three figures	Art

The presentation of each of these stimulus pictures was preceded by the presentation of a medium gray "control" slide. The total sequence was 30 slides in this order: Control A, Stimulus A, Control B, Stimulus B, etc., each shown for 10 seconds, with a total viewing time of 5 minutes for the entire sequence.

From the list of slides it can be seen that five were scored as being pictures of females and five were scored as pictures of males. The "male" pictures (C, E, G, J, and L), considered to be the homosexual equivalent of pinups, were culled from physique magazines and were generally more crude artistically than the pictures of females. These latter (D, F, I, K, and M) represented a rather lush con-

cept of the female figure: for example, "D" was a Titian "Venus," "K" an Ingres "Odalisque."

The five "art" slides (A, B, H, N, and O) ranged in style and period from a Michelangelo to a Picasso. None of these was a clearly male or clearly "female" picture; the abstracts (A, N, and O) were ambiguous sexually, "H" showed both sexes, "B" had a strong religious connotation. This group of slides was included in the series for several reasons. Firstly, it was deemed desirable to place the sexual pictures in an artistic setting to reduce the threat to some subjects that might inhere in the obviously sexual material. Secondly, an abnormally high response is frequently given to the first stimulus shown to a subject. By placing art slides "A" and "B" first in the sequence, the male and the female slides, which were of major interest, were protected from this artifact. Thirdly, homosexuals are often thought to have artistic interests and, indeed, most of the homosexuals in this study did verbally indicate such interests. It was useful, therefore, to include a group of slides which would permit appraisal of response to the artistic quality of pictures separate from their representation of sexual objects. Such a separation of pictorial content from its artistic mode of expression appears feasible since (a) the homosexuals, as a group, showed a high response to the artistically good but sexually ambiguous art slides but (b) they also showed a high response to the artistically crude male pictures yet (c) they showed a low response to the artistically good female pictures. Thus, in addition to the use made of it in this report, the data point also to the potential value of the pupil technique in esthetics research.

Measurement and Scoring

The processed 16-millimeter film was projected, frame by frame, onto the underside of an opal-glass insert in a table, to a magnification of approximately 20 times. The diameter of the pupil in each frame was measured with a millimeter rule and recorded, giving a set of 20 measurements for each control presentation and a set of 20 for each stimulus. Averages were then computed for each stimulus set and for each preceding control set. In order to compare average pupil size during viewing of a picture to the pupil size during the preceding control this method was used: for each control-stimulus pair the percentage of increase or decrease in average pupil size was computed by dividing the difference between stimulus average and control average by the control average. A positive percentage indicated a larger pupil size when the subject was viewing the stimulus than when he viewed the preceding control. A negative percentage meant a smaller average pupil size during stimulus viewing. For each subject, the five percentages of his response to each of the male pictures (C, E, G, J, and L) were added together to give his "response to 'male' picture" score (Table 1, first column). The total of percentages of his response to the female pictures (D, F, I, K, and M) gave his "response to 'female' picture" score (Table 1, second column). The algebraic subtraction of each subject's male picture total from his female picture total (column two minus column one) gave each subject's relative male-female response measure (Table 1, third column). Using this order of procedure for the table, a positive figure in the third column indicates that the subject had a greater total response to pictures of females than to pictures of males; a negative figure indicates lesser response to pictures of females but greater response to pictures of males.

RESULTS

These male-female response measures clearly discriminate between the subject groups, as is shown in the last column of Table 1. There is no overlap between the groups in that the lowest heterosexual response is + 05.7. All heterosexual males show a larger response to pictures of women than to pictures of men (positive scores). Four of the homosexuals show a larger response to pictures of men (negative scores).

DISCUSSION

Some of the female pictures drew a high-positive response from some of the

TABLE 1. Pupil Size Increase or Decrease When Comparing Stimuli to Controls Expressed in Percentage Totals

Subject	Total Response to "Male" Pictures	Total Response to "Female" Pictures	Relative "Male-Female" Response Score
Heterosexuals			
1	−00.4	+05.9	+06.3
2	−54.5	−22.4	+32.1
3	+12.5	+19.2	+06.7
4	+06.3	+39.0	+32.7
5	−01.5	+23.1	+24.6
Homosexuals			
6	+18.8	+11.2	−07.6
7	−04.6	−38.0	−33.4
8	+18.9	+18.1	−00.8
9	+18.2	−05.6	−23.8
10	+15.8	+21.5	+05.7

homosexuals and some of the male pictures drew a high-positive response from some of the heterosexuals. Therefore, response to any single stimulus did not serve to categorize individuals. The total response of a group of subjects to any single stimulus, however, usually served to categorize that stimulus. Total heterosexual response to three of the five female pictures was positive. Total homosexual response to each of the five male pictures was positive. The pictures used in this pilot study were chosen on an a priori basis. The information they have given us and more recent advances in our technique—especially in the matter of brightness matching of pictures—may now permit the formulation of a test battery of pictorial stimuli designed to give a more absolute reflection of a single subject's sex-object interest. It should be emphasized, however, that since *all* subjects in this study saw identical stimuli, the brightness factor could not in any way account for the reported difference between individuals and the resultant groups.

The cooperation of the homosexual subjects, it should be noted, was an unusual relaxation of their customary defense against identification as homosexuals. They were all effectively operating in a normal living environment, in school, at work, with friends. Their sexual preferences were not obvious, and they were ordinarily most reluctant to talk about or reveal them, yet the pupil technique, using a response that is nonverbal and beyond voluntary control, was able to differentiate them from the heterosexual subjects. This is not to say that the pupil response as an index of preference is a predictive substitute for the ultimate criterion of the behavior itself. It does mean that where both preference and behavior are homosexual, even though socially concealed, the pupil response has been shown in this sample to have discriminating power.

Pupil response has already seen application in the area of studies of cognition (Hess & Polt, 1964). In the study of some aspects of personality, compared with projective tests and other instruments and techniques that have been used, this technique appears to us to open up entirely new dimensions.

REFERENCES

Hess, E. H., & Polt, J. M. Pupil size as related to interest value of visual stimuli. *Science, 1960,* 132, 349–350.

Hess, E. H., & Polt, J. M. Pupil size in relation to mental activity during simple problem-solving. *Science,* 1964, *143,* 1190–1192.

20.
ESP and credibility in science

r. a. mc connell

In discussing extrasensory perception (ESP) before psychology students, it is not uncommon to stress the credulity of the public. Perhaps, instead, we ought to examine the credibility of scientists—including those on both sides of the controversy.

In ESP research whom shall we trust? One can rather easily imagine experimental precautions to keep participating subjects from cheating. But how do we know whether the experimenter is deliberately deceiving us? And in a world where people believe all kinds of nonsense, how can we be sure that the experimenter is not deceiving himself?

Let us suppose that 10 experimenters independently get the same result. Can we accept it? Ten is not a large number. There are about 150,000 names in *American Men of Science*. We may reasonably assume that at least 10,000 of these hold beliefs about the nature of reality that the majority of scientists would regard as wholly without foundation. Thus, on a subject like ESP, where there are no recognized authorities, why should we accept the word of 10 experimenters—or, for that matter, a thousand? Are we not, all of us, creatures of our culture? Is there any way we can be sure that a scientist in any field is as rational as he pretends to be?

Questions concerning the credibility of scientists are rarely asked in our classrooms. I have wondered why. Perhaps it

makes us uncomfortable to consider the possibility of incompetence, dishonesty, or mental illness among professional people. Whatever the reason, this is forbidden territory for study.

Once in a long while, these embarrassing ideas do come to the surface. Someone, a little bolder or a little more eccentric than the rest of us, may write an article that slips by the editorial censor. When that happens, we have a chance to learn what people really think.

When I accepted this invitation to talk to you, I was told I could give you an advance reading assignment. I asked that you read an eight-page article on ESP by G. R. Price (1955) that appeared in *Science* together with several letters to the editor (Soal; Rhine; Meehl & Scriven; Bridgman; Price; Rhine, 1956) written in reply to Price. These papers are currently available as part of the Bobbs-Merrill reprint series that is widely used for teaching psychology, and they have thus acquired a quasi-official status as source documents to which the very young may be exposed.

I also suggested that you read an analysis of Price's article (McConnell, 1955) that appeared in the *Journal of Parapsychology* and that was not included in the Bobbs-Merrill series. I hope that most of you have had a chance to study these references, which I shall now discuss briefly.

Price, a chemist by profession, presented a well-supported argument showing that existing experimental evidence constitutes conclusive proof of ESP if one accepts the good faith and sanity of the experimenters. But he went on to say that all of the otherwise convincing evidence for ESP can be easily explained away if one assumes that experimenters,

Reprinted from *American Psychologist*, 1969, 24 (5), 531–538. Published by the American Psychological Association. Abridged by permission of the author.

An invited lecture to the introductory psychology classes at Carnegie-Mellon University, December 18 and 19, 1967.

working in collaboration with their witnesses, have intentionally faked their results.

Perhaps the most interesting thing about this unsubstantiated suggestion of fraud is that it was published on the first page of the most influential scientific journal in the United States. I will not say whether Price intended what he wrote as a joke. That is a riddle that I leave to you to answer. The important question is not whether Price took himself seriously, but whether you and I ought to do so.

I believe, as apparently does Price, that all kinds of fraud, even by highly placed scientists, are possible and that it is conceivable that there might be collaboration between two scientists in perpetuating a scientific hoax. Nevertheless, I think that those who accept Price's argument fail to understand two important things about science as a social enterprise.

First, they fail to realize that the way to tell whether a number of scientists are collaborating in a hoax is to consider the intricate web of public and private motivation, belief, and retribution that determines the behavior of professional people in our culture. Price suggested that scientists, university teachers, medical doctors, and intellectually prominent persons who have assisted in the investigation of ESP may have engaged in conscious collusive fraud. Price answered the question of how one might get such people to become willing accomplices by saying: "In recruiting, I would appeal not to desire for fame or material gain but to the noblest motives, arguing that much good to humanity could result from a small deception designed to strengthen religious belief." An experienced lawyer or even a politician would laugh at this explanation of a supposed conspiracy among well-educated and fully engaged members of our society, but evidently quite a few scientists find it plausible.

Second, those scientists who take Price seriously do not understand scientific method. Price suggested that the way to establish the scientific truth of ESP is to carry out a fraudproof experiment. In his words: "What is needed is one completely convincing experiment." He described in specific detail how this might be done by using prominent scientists and stage magicians as witnesses, backed up by motion pictures of the entire proceedings, plus photomicrographs of welded seals, and so on. This is nonsense because it assumes that scientific proof is of the same nature as legal proof. On the contrary, the acceptance of a scientific principle does not, and never can, depend upon the honesty of individual scientists.

I wish I had time to pursue with you the subtle psychological question of the nature of scientific proof and of how the method of science deals with individual experimenter error as well as mass irrationality. Those of you who are especially interested may wish to read a book by T. S. Kuhn (1962) titled *The Structure of Scientific Revolutions*.[1] Here today, I can only say that in my opinion, wittily or unwittingly, Price's article is a hoax about hoaxes and about the nature of science.

If you were to ask: "What does it signify that Price successfully placed his article in our most important journal of science?" I would answer as follows: There is a facade of respectability and belief that covers all of the activities of society and makes it possible for men to work together and for society to exist. Most people—including those who are well educated—are unaware of this false front and lose their equilibrium when they are forced by circumstances to penetrate behind it. On the other hand, those of you who are intellectually alienated from our culture understand quite well that this pretense exists. I hope that some day you will also understand why it is necessary and that it is not the contrivance of a group of evil men but reflects what existential philosophers refer to as "the human condition."

This curtain of propriety and convention exists in science also, where it allows us to believe that all is well with our knowledge system. ESP or any other revolutionary discovery may seem to threaten science. From time to time, when such a challenge is offered, the stage hands nervously fumble, the curtain slips

[1]For a condensation of this book see Mc Connell (1968b).

and we see a little of the normally concealed machinery. We get a glimpse of underlying reality, a glimpse of the ignorance and fear that govern the inner affairs of the mind of man. Such was the case when *Science* published Price's critique of ESP. That is why his article is important.

EVIDENCE AND BELIEF

Then, what about ESP? If laboratory scientists lack sophistication about human nature and even about the methodology of science, how do we decide for ourselves whether ESP is real or imaginary, true or false?

Before we try to answer so difficult a question, let us go back to the beginning. I shall give you an operational definition of ESP that you may find a bit confusing. Then I shall describe a test for ESP that I hope will make the matter clear to you.

The definition goes this way: "Extrasensory perception is a response to an unknown event not presented to any known sense." I shall not try to explain it. Instead, let me describe the test.

I have brought with me a deck of ESP cards. These cards have five different kinds of symbols printed on them: a circle, a square, a plus, a star, and wavy lines. Altogether, there are 25 cards, 5 of each kind.

Suppose I shuffle these cards, hide them, and ask you to guess them. By the theory of chance probability, the number you would most often get right is five. Sometimes you would get four or six or seven. Only once in a long while would you get 15 right out of 25. In fact, if you got more than 10 right very often, you would begin to suspect that it was not just good luck. It might even be ESP.

Of course, you could not be sure. It might be luck—or it might be something else. If you look closely at the backs of these cards, sometimes you can see the symbol showing through. Perhaps in this way you recognized some of the cards when I shuffled them. Or again, every time I asked whether you were ready for your next guess, perhaps I gave you a hint without knowing it. Perhaps, un-

consciously, I raised the tone of my voice just a little when I came to each star—because I think of stars as being "higher" than the other symbols, or for some other trivial reason.

You can see that there are many subtle ways for information to leak through by sight or by sound. No serious scientist would try to conduct an ESP experiment in this fashion. My only purpose in showing you these cards is to let you know how some of the early tests for ESP were done at Duke University 35 years ago. I regard these cards as a museum piece, although they are a lot of fun and can be used in preliminary testing.

The experiments that are carried out today are often so complex that one cannot evaluate them without advanced training in statistics, physics, and psychology. For this reason, and because the field is too large to describe in one lecture, I have prepared a list of reading materials. Some of these are intended to show the scope of the subject (Heywood, 1964; Langdon-Davies, 1961; McConnell, 1966; Murphy & Dale, 1961); others are experimental reports (Anderson & McConnell, 1961; McConnell & Forwald, 1967a, 1967b, 1968; McConnell, Snowdon, & Powell, 1955; Sinclair, 1962; Soal & Bateman, 1954).

You will notice that I have listed only my own journal articles. For this I offer my apology along with the following explanation. In any frontier field of science there are experimental hazards. If someone questions the soundness of what I recommend to you as evidence, I can probably do a better job of explaining if I have chosen research with which I am most familiar. I also want to convey the idea that there has been a large amount of work done in this field. If you study my papers and cannot find anything wrong with them, you ought to remember that there have been perhaps a hundred other investigators who have found substantial evidence for ESP under controlled experimental conditions.

ESP is a controversial idea in psychology. Nevertheless, the psychologists whom I know personally agree with me on many things. I am sure we agree on what constitutes good quality experimental laboratory research. We also agree that there is a sizable body of high-grade evidence for ESP in the literature.

In 1947 I visited Duke University in North Carolina where a man by the name of Rhine was doing experiments on ESP. I wanted to get acquainted with Rhine and with the people who were working under him. Even more important, I wanted to talk to those faculty members who rejected Rhine's work. I rented a dormitory room, and during four weeks I interviewed everyone I could, beginning with the President of the University and working down to assistant professors in various departments. I shall not have time to describe that adventure, but I will tell you what I was told by one professor of psychology in a private interview.

He said that he was familiar with the experimental literature of ESP and that, in his opinion, if it were anything else *but* ESP, one-tenth of the published evidence would already have established the phenomenon. He also explained that he would not accept ESP himself because, as he put it, he found "a world without ESP a more comfortable place in which to live."

That trip to Duke University was part of a larger investigation that made me decide to leave engineering electronics, in which I had acquired some experience, and to devote my life to the investigation of ESP and related effects.

That was 20 years ago. What has happened in this field since then? Among other things, there has been time to publish 20 more volumes of the *Journal of Parapsychology*. That comes to about 4,000 pages of research. There have been several thousand additional pages in the *Journal of the American Society for Psychical Research* and in the English and Continental journals. You might think that the argument would be settled by now.

Only recently, a brilliant young psychologist, who is here on your campus, gave a lecture on ESP in which he said "I tend to believe the evidence is as good as it is for many of our other psychological phenomena." He also said that "Psychologists will not be interested in ESP until there is a repeatable experiment."

Where my psychologist friends and I disagree, is that I believe that the available evidence for ESP is sufficient to establish its reality beyond all reasonable doubt. My psychologist friends think that the evidence is not yet conclusive. I do not regard this difference of opinion as very important. I am happy to allow anyone the privilege of doubt.

How else does the position of professional psychologists whom I know differ from my own? Perhaps the main difference—the really important difference—lies in our interpretation of the history and methodology of science—in what today we call the philosophy of science.

For one thing, my friends seem to believe that the only good evidence for ESP must come from controlled experimentation in a laboratory. My own belief is that all available evidence must be weighed, taking into account its source and the conditions under which it was gathered.

Perhaps it will clarify the problem if I say that there are only two important kinds of scientific evidence in this world; our own evidence and someone else's. Since most of us are not in a position to gather evidence of ESP, my remarks apply especially to other people's evidence.

The first thing to remember is that, no matter how reputable the scientific journal, someone else's evidence is always suspect. And if the matter is important, we ought to be *aggressively* skeptical about it.

Whether we are listening to a tale of a ghost in a haunted house or reading the tightly edited *Journal of Experimental Psychology*, we have to concern ourselves with two questions: what is the content of the report and what are the competence and motivation of the observer?

What I am suggesting is that our attitude toward *all* supposedly scientific reports must be that of the psychologist in receiving an introspective account from a human subject in a laboratory experiment—for it must be remembered that as far as the reader is concerned, a journal article by a distant scientist is in some ways even less dependable than what psychologists, often condescendingly, refer to as a "verbal report."

From a study of the history of science

I have come to two conclusions in this connection: (a) the evidence presented in scientific journals by professional scientists for all kinds of ordinary phenomena is not as good as commonly supposed, and (b) on a controversial subject where the professionals do not agree, the evidence of the layman may have considerable scientific value. As corollaries, I suggest that the textbooks of science are often wrong and that contrary popular opinion is sometimes right. Let us examine these ideas.

STOREHOUSES OF KNOWLEDGE?

Textbooks are the storehouses of man's knowledge. They are presumed to contain all of the things we know to be true. If you are becoming a scientist, you will spend at least 18 years studying from books. It would be not entirely unfair to call most of this training a "brainwashing" process. Nearly everything you learn as factual reality must be accepted upon the word of some recognized authority and not upon your own firsthand experience. It should be a matter of concern to you whether you have been told the truth for those 18 years. Just how bad are the textbooks we use? Let me take an example from the field of geology.

Did you know that until the year 1800 the highest scientific authorities thought that there was no such thing as a meteorite? After all, there are no stones in the sky; so stones cannot fall out of the sky. Only a superstitious person would believe in meteorites.

Many of you are familiar with the work of Lavoisier. He was the founder of modern chemistry. He discovered that burning is the combining of oxygen with other things, and he helped to show that the formula for water is H_2O. He was one of the great scientists of all time.

In 1772 Lavoisier signed a report to the French Academy of Science in which he said he had examined a stone that was believed to have fallen from the sky in a great blaze of light. Lavoisier said in his report that this was just an ordinary stone that had been struck by lightning and had melted partly into glass while lying on the ground.

Eventually, of course, the leaders of science decided that meteorites do come from outer space, and they revised the textbooks accordingly. But in doing so, they forgot to mention that there had ever been any argument about the matter. So here we are, living in the space age, without realizing how hard it is to discover the truth about even a simple thing like meteorites, which can be seen as meteors in the sky on any clear night, and which have been found upon the surface of the earth since the dawn of history.

Even worse, as students, we have no way of estimating how many arguments are still going on in science and how many mistakes—truly serious mistakes— there are in the textbooks from which we study. It is my guess that we can safely believe nearly all of what is said in the physics and chemistry books. But we ought to believe only half of the ideas in the biological sciences—although I am not sure which half. And we should accept as final very little in the social sciences, which try to explain why groups of people behave as they do.

Our subject today is extrasensory perception, which belongs in psychology, one of the biological sciences. ESP is something about which the "authorities" are in error. Most psychology textbooks omit the subject entirely as unworthy of serious attention. But these books are mistaken, because ESP is a real psychological phenomenon.

Of course, I am only giving you my individual opinion about ESP. I do not want you to base your belief upon what I tell you. When you have studied advanced psychology and statistics, and when you come to realize that your professors cannot be expected to teach you everything you wish to know, then I hope you will go to the scientific journals and study the experiments that have been done and decide for yourself.

MENTAL RADIO

I have already discussed the credibility of experts and the errors we find in science textbooks. I would like to turn next to the other half of my thesis, namely, that evidence from a layman may sometimes have scientific value.

Example 1.

Most of you are familiar with the name Upton Sinclair, who was a socialist reformer and a writer active in the first half of the twentieth century. He died in 1968 at the age of 90. In his time he wrote nearly 90 books. One of the best known of these, published in 1906, was called *The Jungle*. It told about the cruel and unsanitary conditions in the processing of beef in the Chicago stock yards. As a result of that book, laws were passed, and today the situation is much improved. In a very real sense, all of us are indebted to this man.

Sinclair discovered that his wife had an unusual amount of what was then known as "psychic ability." (That was before the beginning of the ESP controversy.) After three years of serious experimentation, he wrote a book about it: *Mental Radio* (1962, orig. publ. 1930).

In his experiments, Sinclair, or someone else, would draw a secret picture and ask Mrs. Sinclair to draw another picture to match it. Some of the pairs of pictures are presented in the following examples.[2] The one on the left is always the original picture, and the one on the right is what Mrs. Sinclair got by ESP.

[2]Illustrations from *Mental Radio* by Upton Sinclair are reproduced by permission of the publisher, Charles C. Thomas, Springfield, Illinois.

Sometimes the pictures were made as far apart as 40 miles. At other times the target picture was held by Mrs. Sinclair in her hand—without looking, of course—while she concentrated before drawing her matching picture. The degree of success did not seem to depend upon distance.

Let us examine some of the pictures. In Example 1 we see an almost perfect ESP response. It is a knight's helmet. Notice that for every important line in the left-hand picture there is a corresponding line on the right.

Compare that with Example 2. Here, the response on the right is not quite the same as the target on the left, but the idea is the same.

The next slide is Example 3. Sinclair drew a football as a target. Mrs. Sinclair made the drawing on the right, but she thought it was "a baby calf with a belly band." Why did her ESP make this mistake? We cannot be sure, but we think it had something to do with the fact that in her childhood she had known a queer old man who raised calves as parlor pets and dressed them in embroidered belly bands. . . .

The last example is the American flag and a response to it that could hardly be called a chance coincidence (Example 4).

Out of the 290 tries, 23% were rated by Upton Sinclair as hits, 53% were partial hits, and 23% were failures.

Of course, before you can be sure that these pictures were made by ESP, many questions must be answered. Because Upton Sinclair and his wife were laymen, you will have to pay particular attention to their competence and motivation. On the other hand, one important feature of Sinclair's book is that you do not have to be a scientist to understand it. Even though you may not have studied statistics and psychology, you can read the book yourself and make up your mind as to its value on the basis of common sense. When you do, I think you will arrive at the same conclusion that many scientists have reached by entirely different kinds of experiments. I think you will decide that extrasensory perception is a reality regardless of the skepticism of the psychological profession.

Example 2.

A MATTER OF INTEREST

I have been told by my friends that psychologists will not be interested in ESP until someone discovers a repeatable experiment. Upton Sinclair repeated his experiments over a period of three years. In London, a mathematician by the name of Soal (Soal & Bateman, 1954) repeated certain card-guessing experiments again and again over a period of six years using two subjects and many different witnesses. What do psychologists mean by a repeatable experiment?

Evidently, they mean an experiment that is "repeatable by prescription." They want a standard experimental procedure that can be described on paper by which any qualified person—or at least some qualified persons—can guarantee to produce ESP upon demand. I must confess that we have not yet reached that stage in ESP research. And, until we do, I can sympathize with my skeptical friends. I can see why they, as busy individuals with other interests, are unwilling to reach a firm position about the reality of ESP.

What I cannot understand is why they say: "Psychologists will not be *interested* in ESP until there is a repeatable experiment."

It is a statement of fact that psychologists are *not* interested in ESP. Recently, I had occasion to examine a number of psychology textbooks. Only one of them mentioned ESP—that book, by Hilgard and Atkinson (1967). After reading the four pages which these authors devote to ESP, I have only two minor critical observations to offer.

The first is that the authors have given too much space to finding fault with unimportant papers. They go back 25 years to a journal article in which they accuse an ESP experimenter of overanalyzing his data. I am sure that comparable examples of weak statistical method could be found in any one of the quantitative journals of the APA—and we would not need to go back a generation in time to do it.

My second comment is that Hilgard and Atkinson may have tended to damage their own scholarly reputations by recommending as a "scholarly review" a book by C. E. M. Hansel (1966) titled *ESP: A Scientific Evaluation.*

Example 3.

This book has been reviewed by S. S. Stevens of Harvard, who regards ESP as a Rabelaisian joke and who gave Hansel his unqualified approval. If you like amusing book reviews, I suggest that you read Stevens (1967). I regret that I do not have time here today to document for you the basis of my unfavorable opinion of Hansel's book.[3]

I have wandered over many facets of ESP. I shall now summarize what I think are the most important ideas. Since the scientific study of ESP was begun by the London Society for Psychical Research in 1882, there have been hundreds and perhaps thousands of experiments done with a care typical of the journals of the APA. Many psychologists of high repute admit that the evidence is as good as that for other phenomena that are accepted by their profession.

Surprising though it may seem, most of this research on ESP has been done by people who were not psychologists. From this fact and from the usual psychology textbook treatment of the subject as well as from private discussion, we know that psychologists are *not* interested in ESP. This raises a question—a very mysterious question that I invite you to try to answer: Why are psychologists not interested in ESP?[4]

[3]This has since been done. See McConnell (1968a).

[4]Those who wish to answer this question might start their odyssey by visiting Clark et al. (1967) and Linder (1967).

Example 4.

REFERENCES

Anderson, M. L., & McConnell, R. A. Fantasy testing for ESP in a fourth and fifth grade class. *Journal of Psychology*, 1961, *52*, 491–503.

Clark, K. E., et al. The scientific and professional aims of psychology. *American Psychologist*, 1967, *22*, 49–76.

Hansel, C. E. M. *ESP: A scientific evaluation.* New York: Scribner's, 1966.

Heywood, R. *ESP: A personal memoir.* New York: Dutton, 1964.

Hilgard, E. R., & Atkinson, R. C. *Introduction to psychology.* New York: Harcourt, Brace & World, 1967.

Kuhn, T. S. *The structure of scientific revolutions* (Vol. II, No. 2, of the *International Encyclopedia of Unified Science*). Chicago: University of Chicago Press, 1962.

Langdon-Davies, J. *On the nature of man.* New York: New American Library Corporation, 1961.

Linder, R. *Light one candle. American Psychologist*, 1967, *22*. 804–805.

McConnell, R. A. Price in *Science. Journal of Parapsychology*, 1955, *19*, 258–261.

McConnell, R. A. ESP research at three levels of method. *Journal of Parapsychology*, 1966, *30*, 195–207.

McConnell, R. A. The ESP scholar. *Contemporary Psychology*, 1968, *13*, 41. (a)

McConnell, R. A. The structure of scientific revolutions: An epitome. *Journal of the American Society for Psychical Research*, 1968, *62*, 321–327. (b)

McConnell, R. A., & Forwald, H. Psychokinetic placement: I. A re-examination of the Forwald-Durham experiment. *Journal of Parapsychology*, 1967, *31*, 51–69. (a)

McConnell, R. A., & Forwald, H. Psychokinetic placement: II. A factorial study of successful and unsuccessful series. *Journal of Parapsychology*, 1967, *31*, 198–213. (b)

McConnell, R. A., & Forwald, H. Psychokinetic placement: III. Cube-releasing devices. *Journal of Parapsychology*, 1968, *32*, 9–38.

McConnell, R. A., Snowdon, R. J., & Powell, K. F. Wishing with dice. *Journal of Experimental Psychology*, 1955, *50*, 269–275.

Murphy, G., & Dale, L. A. *Challenge of psychical research.* New York: Harper, 1961.

Price, G. R. Science and the supernatural. *Science*, 1955, *122*, 359–367.

Sinclair, U. *Mental radio.* Springfield, Ill.: Charles C Thomas, 1962.

Soal, S. G., & Bateman, F. *Modern experiments in telepathy.* London: Faber & Faber, 1954.

Soal, S. G.; Rhine, J. B.; Meehl, P. E.; & Scriven, M.; Bridgman, P. W.; Price, G. R.; Rhine, J. B. (Letters to the editor in rejoinder to G. R. Price.) *Science*, 1956, *123*, 9–19.

Stevens, S. S. The market for miracles. *Contemporary Psychology*, 1967, *12*, 1–3.

21.
the perceived size of coins in normal and hypnotically induced economic states

wayne r. ashley,
robert s. harper,
and dale l. runyon

Psychologists have generally agreed, certainly since the days of the British Empiricists, that man makes some contribution to his own perceptions. Usually this contribution has been thought of as that influence from those memories, past experiences, or traces which, coupled with the immediate sensory stimulation, gives rise to the meaning of a particular object, localized in space, with particular characteristics and uses. The basic figural organization of the perception—the organization which is responsible for the object being perceived as having a particular size, shape, and color—has been considered, however, to be dependent on the stimulus-pattern and thus independent of any influence derived from the nature of the perceiver.

Occasionally a report has been published indicating that the organization of the perception is completely determined by the stimulus-pattern, and that the perceiver plays no part in the organization of the perception.[1] More frequently, observations of congenital cataract patients[2] and of dark-reared chimpanzees,[3] and experiments in which the perceivers' acquaintanceship with the stimulus-object is varied,[4] have indicated that man does contribute to the figural organization of his perceptions. These positive results, for one reason or another, have been minimized, however, and there is still the prevalent view that the perceiver can change the verbalized meaning of an object, but not the basic figural organization of the perception of that object.

Shortly before World War II a different approach was made to this problem. Ansbacher, following Brunswik's conclusions that monetary value through familiarity does influence perception under certain circumstances, presented his Ss [Subjects] with cards on which were pasted many stamps of one of several denominations, and asked them to estimate the number of stamps they perceived on each card.[5] He reported that the larger the denomination of the stamp, the less numerous they

Reprinted from *American Journal of Psychology*, 1953, *66*, 564–572. Abridged by permission of the authors.

[1]Kurt Gottschaldt, Ueber den Einfluss der Erfahrung auf die Wahrnehmung von Figuren: I. Ueber den Einfluss gehäufter Einprägung von Figuren auf ihre Sichtbarkeit in umfassenden Konfigurationen, *Psychol. Forsch.*, 8, 1926, 261–318; II. Vergleichende Untersuchungen über die Wirkung figuraler Einprägung und den Einfluss spezifischer Geschehensverläufe auf die Auffassung optischer Komplexe, *ibid.*, 12, 1929, 1–87.
[2]M. von Senden, *Ramm- und Gestaltauffassung bei operierten Blindgeborenen vor und nach der Operation*, 1932, 1–303.
[3]A. H. Riesen, The development of visual perception in man and chimpanzee, *Science*, 106, 1947, 107–108.
[4]For example, M. Henle, An experimental investigation of past experience as a determinant of visual form perception, *J. Exper. Psychol.*, 30, 1942, 1–21.
[5]Heinz Ansbacher, Perception of number as affected by the monetary value of objects, *Arch. Psychol.*, 30, 1937, (no. 215), 1–88.

appeared, and concluded, therefore, that the stamps of large denominations were perceived as larger than those of small. This experiment attracted little attention, but a few years later, in 1947, Bruner and Goodman performed an experiment in which they had a group of children whose parents were rich and a group whose parents were poor match a variable size spot of light to coins of different denominations.[6] They reported that the "poor" children matched the coins to larger spots of light than did the "rich" children, and concluded that, as a result of the difference in values, the "poor" children perceived the coins as larger in size than did the "rich" ones. This precipitated a controversy which, in connection with other work of Bruner and his collaborators, is still going on.[7] The contrary group, tacitly admitting that the figural organization of the perception could be modified by the perceiver's previous experience, set out to show that the figural organization of the perception could not be altered by the perceiver's values.[8] The "repetitions" of the Bruner and Goodman experiment, usually including a criticism of the original study because of the sampling or because of the use of a multi-sided light spot instead of a round spot or because of the method of presentation of the coins, generally have not provided any confirmation of Bruner and Goodman's original hypothesis.[9]

[6]J. S. Bruner and C. C. Goodman, Value and need as organizing factors in perception, *J. Abnor. & Soc. Psychol.*, 42, 1947, 33–44.

[7]Leo Postman, J. S. Bruner, and E. Mc-Ginnies, Personal values as selective factors in perception, *J. Abnor. & Soc. Psychol.*, 43, 1949, 142–155; Bruner and Postman, Perception under stress, *Psychol. Rev.*, 55, 1948, 314–323.

[8]D. H. Howes and R. L. Solomon, A note on McGinnies' "Emotionality and perceptual defense," *Psychol. Rev.*, 57, 1950, 229–234.

[9]L. F. Carter and K. Schooler, Value, need, and other factors in perception, *Psychol. Rev.*, 56, 1949, 200–207; B. G. Rosenthal and J. H. Levi, Value, need and attitude toward money as determinants of perception, *Amer. Psychol.*, 5, 1950, 313.

To tie up loose ends it is necessary to show clearly and unequivocally that the perceiver can contribute to the organization of his perception in a structured stimulus-situation. The Bruner and Goodman type of experiment would do this if the rich group and the poor group were identical in every other respect—in terms of their experiences with money, their life histories, their physiological conditions, in short, if the sole difference between the two groups was only that one group had the psychological organization (which is responsible for the attitudes, values, wants, needs, interests, etc.) of rich people and the other group the psychological organization of poor people. Actually, for our problem, it is irrelevant whether the Ss are economically as well as psychologically rich or poor, or whether they are only psychologically rich or poor. In either case, a difference in performance of the two groups would reflect a difference in the perception due to the psychological organization of the perceivers.

Matching of everything but the perceivers' psychological organization may seem impossible at first, but it can be done through the use of hypnosis. Even though we do not know fully what happens when we hypnotize a person, if we do hypnotize him and tell him he is rich and he behaves in one way in the coin-matching situation, and then, a few moments later, we tell him he is now poor and he behaves in another way, we can conclude that the observed difference is due to a change in his psychological organization. It is within this framework that the present experiment was done.

Procedure. The experiment was conducted in two phases—Phase I, the coin-absent phase, and Phase II, the coin-present phase. Phase I was carried out in the spring of 1950 and, when the included economic states were seen to influence the results, Phase II was conducted the following fall. In both phases the Ss were hypnotized, an artificial life history induced, and then, in the hypnotic state, the Ss were instructed to adjust the size of a spot of light until it looked to them to be the size of a coin (a penny, nickel, dime, quarter) that was (Phase I) *remembered* and that was (Phase II) directly perceived.

Subjects. The Ss were volunteers from the Knox College student body. Although the enrollment fees and traditions of private schools tend to insure a student body that is relatively homogenous as far as socio-economic status goes, plans were initially made to eliminate any student that was at either extreme of the socio-economic scale. Fortunately, none of the volunteers differed appreciably from any of the others in terms of socio-economic status. They were all from middle class homes. About half of the volunteers were enrolled in Elementary Psychology, and none had had more than one course in psychology. The volunteers were unaware of the experimental results and theorizing in this area and were warned not to discuss the experiment with anyone.

About 30 Ss volunteered in the spring, and an equal number again in the fall. In phase I, 9 Ss were obtained from the initial group of volunteers who showed evidence of experiencing visual hallucinations in the hypnotic state. Only 8 Ss reached this criterion in Phase II. Three of the Ss in Phase I also served in Phase II. When their results in Phase II were checked, they were indistinguishable from the new Ss.

The experimental data were collected during a single 1-hr. session—the first session after S had reached the criterion. At this session S was hypnotized, told that he could remember nothing of his former life except his name, and, since he could not remember his past, that his history would be told to him. Then, either the "poor" or "rich" history was described.

The life histories that were induced, although varying in the precise wording for different Ss, always followed a set pattern. The outline of the story that the S was told when he was given the "poor" history was as follows:

He had been born of poor parents and his childhood had been spent in poverty; his father had never had an adequate income and consequently could not afford many of life's necessities; his clothes had been rags, his diet meager, his allowance negligible; he could not go to high school because he had to help support his family; he was still very poor; he had no regular job; what money he did earn was used to help support his family and to pay some of his many debts.

The "rich" history was the antithesis of the "poor" one. The outline of the "rich" story was as follows:

He had been born of very wealthy parents; he lived in a large mansion in the best and wealthiest neighborhood; he had attended the very best schools; he had always had a large allowance and never had to wish for anything; his father had given him a car and a large expense account when he had entered high school; his clothes had always been of the best quality and very expensive; he had never had any financial worries; at present he had an extremely large income that was further supplemented by his father.

In no case was there any mention of the particular size, value or worth of coins. The only mention of coins specifically was to remind the "poor" Ss that, despite their poverty, they did remember seeing coins. (This was necessitated after one "poor" S, who said she could not remember what a quarter looked like but since a quarter was only one-fourth of a whole it must be very small, set the variable spot of light at 0.3-in. diameter and said it was equal to the size of the quarter.)

Apparatus. The Ss, in the "poor," in the "rich," and in the normal states, adjusted a variable size spot of light until it appeared to be the size of a specified coin. The apparatus used for this purpose was similar to that of Bruner and Goodman. In a small covered box a 40-w. bulb illuminated a 7-in. square of milk glass. In front of this was placed a black

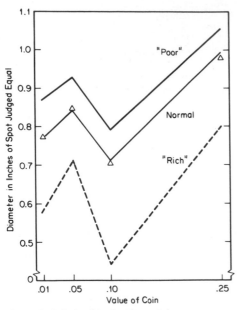

Figure 1. Relationship in Phase I between monetary value of four coins and the median diameter of a spot of light adjusted to equal each of the coins in size. (The triangles indicate the physical size of the coins.)

masking screen with a 1.75-in. diameter circular opening in the middle. In this opening was fitted a nineteen-vane iris diaphragm that could be varied in diameter from 0.3 in. The diaphragm was so fitted that only the vanes appeared in the opening of the masking screen. When S sat 2 ft. away, with the center of the opening at eye level, he saw a sharply defined circular spot of a white surface color in the center of a black field. The size of the spot was varied by pulling on one or the other side of a continuous long cord. (None of the Ss, incidentally, attempted to use the limiting sizes of the diaphragm as a reference point by opening or closing the diaphragm to its limits before beginning to make their adjustments.) The diameter of the spot was read from a concealed scale at the top of the box. To the left of this light spot, at the same level and in the same frontal plane, was a holder in to which could be slipped a 4-in. square of white cardboard. In the center of this card was mounted a new coin, countersunk so that its face was flush with the surface of the card. The center of the coin was 6 in. from the center of the light spot.

In Phase I, S made two adjustments of the remembered size of each of the four coins in all three states—the "rich," "poor," and normal states. One adjustment was made after the E had set the light spot at a much smaller diameter than the coin, and the other adjustment was made after the spot was set much larger than the coin. For some Ss the first adjustment was made with the spot smaller, for others with the spot larger. Some Ss made their initial adjustments in the "poor" state. Some Ss first adjusted the spot to be equal in size to a penny, others first to a quarter, or a dime, or a nickel. There was no systematic progression of events in the entire experiment, with the exception that all Ss made their final series of judgments in the normal state. Five of the Ss made initial adjustments, as well as final adjustments, in their normal state. The t-test for paired scores indicated these before and after judgments to be insignificantly different, so the before judgments were discontinued for the remainder of the experiment.

The procedure in Phase II differed in only three respects from that in Phase I. First, the coin was present on the card in the holder. Secondly, each S made four instead of two adjustments of the light spot for every coin, the adjustments being made in either a SLLS or an LSSL order. Thirdly, a supplemental series of judgments was added. In the supplemented series, a grayish metal slug from an electrical terminal box was fixed on a card in the same fashion as the coins. The Ss, in both the "rich" and "poor" states, were then told it was made of either lead, silver, white gold, or platinum, and to adjust the spot of light until it appeared to be the size of the slug. Again, the order in which the metals were named was non-systematic.

Results. The size of the light spot that the Ss set as equal to the coins differed markedly between the "rich" and "poor" states in both phases (I and II) of the experiment (see Figures 1 and 2). The difference between the judgments in the "rich" and "poor" states for both phases is significant, with one exception, at less than the 5% level of confidence, as shown by the t-test for paired scores. This exception is for the nickel in Phase I. Two Ss adjusted the light spot to the same size in both the "rich" and "poor" states, and one S even adjusted the spot to be slightly smaller when in the "poor" state than in the "rich" state. For this exception the difference is significant between the 5% and 10% levels of confidence. The hypnotically induced "rich" and "poor" states thus did make a real difference in the Ss' adjustments of the light spot. Still further confirmation of our hypothesis is provided by the fact that the results for our middle class Ss, when in the normal state, fell in between the results obtained from them in the induced extreme economic states.

The differences between the Ss' settings in Phase I and Phase II are probably due to the visual reference point provided by the presence of the coins in Phase II. The adjustments in Phase II, as might be expected, were less variable than in Phase I. The differences, in Phase II, between the adjustments in the normal state and the actual size of the coins can be explained, at least partially, by the difference in perceived size between a dark object seen on a light background (the coin on the white cardboard) and a light object seen on a dark background (the light spot in the black field). Since this illusion would result in the coin appearing slightly smaller than its physically equal spot of light, and in the light spot appearing slightly larger than its physically equal coin, there would be a consistent tendency for a particular coin to be judged as equal in size to a physically smaller light spot.

The results of the supplemental series of experiments in Phase II, i.e., with the metal slug, are even more convincing in indicating the importance of a person's psychological organization to his perceptions. As shown in Figure 3, in both the "rich" and "poor" states, the size of the light spot that was set as equal to the constant size slug increased with the cost of the metal of which S was told the slug was made. As usual, the judgments in the "poor" state were consist-

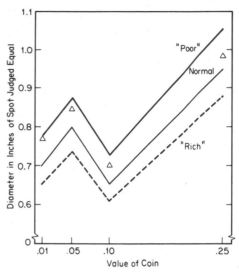

Figure 2. Relationship in Phase II between the monetary value of four coins and the median diameter of a spot of light adjusted to equal each of the coins in size. (The triangles indicate the physical size of the coins.)

ently larger than those in the "rich" state. An analysis of variance shows that both the state, either "rich" or "poor," and the name of the metal given the slug were significant sources of variance at less than the 0.1% level of confidence.

The effectiveness of the hypnotic technique in inducing "rich" and "poor" psychological organizations was further indicated by the behavior of the Ss toward the experiment when in the different states. The Ss, when "poor," were very deliberate and methodical in their performance. They sat erect in their chairs, made many small adjustments of the size of the spot, critically eyed it and the coin, and, in general, were earnest and cooperative. They behaved as different people, however, in the "rich" state. They slouched in their chairs, crossed their legs, made their settings rapidly with a few minor adjustments, and only condescendingly cooperated. Corresponding to their change in behavior there was a tendency for the judgments to be slightly more variable in the "rich" state.

These results confirm the hypothesis that the psychological organization of an individual does contribute to the figural

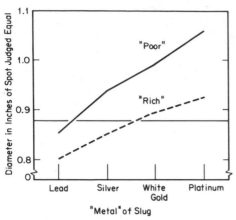

Figure 3. Relationship between the name of the metal given to the "slug" and the mean diameter of a spot of light adjusted to equal the "slug" in size. (The horizontal line indicates the physical size of the "slug.")

organization of his perception. The contemporary trend toward feed-back analogies, however, makes explicit the question: Does the psychological organization operate in a feed-back fashion so as to alter the basic sensory data of the perception, or does it alter the way in which the sensory data is organized within the perception? This question is being studied now and will be reported later.

SUMMARY

Nine Ss in Phase I and eight Ss in Phase II were hypnotized. Amnesia was induced in the Ss and "rich" or "poor" life histories substituted. Every S so adjusted a spot of light of variable size that it appeared to be equal to the remembered size of a penny, nickel, dime, or quarter (Phase I), or to the apparent size of a penny, nickel, dime, or quarter that actually was present (Phase II). In each phase every S made settings in the "rich," the "poor," and the normal states. The Ss, in the normal state, adjusted the light spot to be approximately equal to the physical size of the coins. In the "poor" state the Ss' settings were consistently smaller. The Ss were also shown a slug from an electrical terminal box, and, in both the "rich" and "poor" states, adjusted the spot to appear equal to the slug when they were told it was made of lead, silver, white gold, and platinum. The size of the spot that was called equal to the slug increased as the cost of the metal increased. The conclusion was that the psychological organization (which is responsible for the wants, needs, interests, attitudes, and values) of a person contributes to the figural organization of his perceptions.

22.
effects of group pressure
upon the modification
and distortion of judgments

s. e. asch

We shall here describe in summary form the conception and first findings of a program of investigation into the conditions of independence and submission to group pressure.[1]

Our immediate object was to study the social and personal conditions that induce individuals to resist or to yield to group pressures when the latter are perceived to be *contrary to fact*. The issues which this problem raises are of obvious consequence for society; it can be of decisive importance whether or not a group will, under certain conditions, submit to existing pressures. Equally direct are the consequences for individuals and our understanding of them, since it is a decisive fact about a person whether he possesses the freedom to act independently, or whether he characteristically submits to group pressures.

The problem under investigation requires the direct observation of certain individuals, and between individuals and groups. To clarify these seems necessary

Reprinted from Eleanor E. Maccoby, Theodore M. Newcomb, and Eugene L. Hartley (Eds.), *Readings in Social Psychology*, 3rd ed., New York: Holt, Rinehart and Winston, 1958, pp. 174–183. Prepared by the author from data previously reported in: S. E. Asch, "Effects of Group Pressure upon the Modification and Distortion of Judgments," in Harold Guetzkow (ed.), *Groups, Leadership and Men*, Pittsburgh: Carnegie Press, 1951. Reprinted by permission of Carnegie Press.
[1]The earlier experiments out of which the present work developed and the theoretical issues which prompted it are discussed in S. E. Asch, *Social Psychology* (New York: Prentice-Hall, Inc., 1952), Ch. 16. A full account of the procedures and data on which the present report is based will be published shortly.

if we are to make fundamental advances in the understanding of the formation and reorganization of attitudes, of the functioning of public opinion, and of the operation of propaganda. Today we do not possess an adequate theory of these central psycho-social processes. Empirical investigation has been predominantly controlled by general propositions concerning group influence which have as a rule been assumed but not tested. With few exceptions investigation has relied upon descriptive formulations concerning the operation of suggestion and prestige, the inadequacy of which is becoming increasingly obvious, and upon schematic applications of stimulus-response theory.

Basic to the current approach has been the axiom that group pressures characteristically induce psychological changes *arbitrarily*, in far-reaching disregard of the material properties of the given conditions. This mode of thinking has almost exclusively stressed the slavish submission of individuals to group forces, has neglected to inquire into their possibilities for independence and for productive relations with the human environment, and has virtually denied the capacity of men under certain conditions to rise above group passion and prejudice. It was our aim to contribute to a clarification of these questions, important both for theory and for their human implications, by means of direct observation of the effects of groups upon the decisions and evaluations of individuals.

THE EXPERIMENT AND FIRST RESULTS

To this end we developed an experimental technique which has served as the basis for the present series of studies. We employed the procedure of placing an individual in a relation of radical conflict with all the other members of a group, of measuring its effect upon him in quantitative terms, and of describing its psychological consequences. A group of eight individuals was instructed to judge a series of simple, clearly structured perceptual relations—to match the length of a given line with one of three unequal lines. Each member of the group announced his judgments publicly. In the midst of this monotonous "test" one individual found himself suddenly contradicted by the entire group, and this contradiction was repeated again and again in the course of the experiment. The group in question had, with the exception of one member, previously met with the experimenter and received instructions to respond at certain points with wrong—and unanimous—judgments. The errors of the majority were large (ranging between ½" and 1¾") and of an order not encountered under control conditions. The outstanding person—the critical subject—whom we had placed in the position of a *minority of one* in the midst of a *unanimous majority*—was the object of investigation. He faced, possibly for the first time in his life, a situation in which a group unanimously contradicted the evidence of his senses.

This procedure was the starting point of the investigation and the point of departure for the study of further problems. Its main features were the following: (1) The critical subject was submitted to two contradictory and irreconcilable forces—the evidence of his own experience of a clearly perceived relation, and the unanimous evidence of a group of equals. (2) Both forces were part of the immediate situation; the majority was concretely present, surrounding the subject physically. (3) The critical subject, who was requested together with all others to state his judgments publicly, was obliged to declare himself and to take a definite stand *vis-à-vis* the group. (4) The situation possessed a self-contained character. The critical subject could not avoid or evade the dilemma by reference to conditions external to the experimental situation. (It may be mentioned at this point that the forces generated by the given conditions acted so quickly upon the critical sub-

jects that instances of suspicion were infrequent.)

The technique employed permitted a simple quantitative measure of the "majority effect" in terms of the frequency of errors in the direction of the distorted estimates of the majority. At the same time we were concerned to obtain evidence of the ways in which the subjects perceived the group, to establish whether they became doubtful, whether they were tempted to join the majority. Most important, it was our object to establish the grounds of the subject's independence or yielding—whether, for example, the yielding subject was aware of the effect of the majority upon him, whether he abandoned his judgment deliberately or compulsively. To this end we constructed a comprehensive set of questions which served as the basis of an individual interview immediately following the experimental period. Toward the conclusion of the interview each subject was informed fully of the purpose of the experiment, of his role and of that of the majority. The reactions to the disclosure of the purpose of the experiment became in fact an integral part of the procedure. The information derived from the interview became an indispensable source of evidence and insight into the psychological structure of the experimental situation, and in particular, of the nature of the individual differences. It should be added that it is not justified or advisable to allow the subject to leave without giving him a full explanation of the experimental conditions. The experimenter has a responsibility to the subject to clarify his doubts and to state the reasons for placing him in the experimental situation. When this is done most subjects react with interest, and some express gratification at having lived through a striking situation which has some bearing on them personally and on wider human issues.

Both the members of the majority and the critical subjects were male college students. We shall report the results for a total of fifty critical subjects in this experiment. In Table 1 we summarize the successive comparison trials and the majority estimates. The reader will note that on certain trials the majority responded

TABLE 1. Lengths of Standard and Comparison Lines

Trial	Length of Standard Line (in inches)	Comparison Lines (in inches) 1	2	3	Correct Response	Group Response	Majority Error (in inches)
1	10	8¾	10	8	2	2	—
2	2	2	1	1½	1	1	—
3	3	3¾	4¼	3	3	1*	+¾
4	5	5	4	6½	1	2*	−1.0
5	4	3	5	4	3	3	—
6	3	3¾	4¼	3	3	2*	+1¼
7	8	6¼	8	6¾	2	3*	−1¼
8	5	5	4	6½	1	3*	+1½
9	8	6¼	8	6¾	2	1*	−1¾
10	10	8¾	10	8	2	2	—
11	2	2	1	1½	1	1	—
12	3	3¾	4¼	3	3	1*	+¾
13	5	5	4	6½	1	2*	−1.0
14	4	3	5	4	3	3	—
15	3	3¾	4¼	3	3	2*	+1¼
16	8	6¼	8	6¾	2	3*	−1¼
17	5	5	4	6½	1	3*	+1½
18	8	6¼	8	6¾	2	1*	−1¾

* Starred figures designate the erroneous estimates by the majority.

correctly; these were the "neutral" trials. There were twelve critical trials on which the responses of the majority responded incorrectly.

The quantitative results are clear and unambiguous.

1. There was a marked movement toward the majority. One third of all the estimates in the critical group were errors identical with or in the direction of the distorted estimates of the majority. The significance of this finding becomes clear in the light of the virtual absence of errors in the control group, the members of which recorded their estimates in writing. The relevant data of the critical and control groups are summarized in Table 2.

2. At the same time the effect of the majority was far from complete. The preponderance of estimates in the critical group (68 percent) was correct despite the pressure of the majority.

3. We found evidence of extreme individual differences. There were in the critical group subjects who remained independent without exception, and there were those who went nearly all the time with the majority. (The maximum possible number of errors was 12, while the actual range of errors was 0–11.) One fourth of the critical subjects was completely independent; at the other extreme, one third of the group displaced the estimates toward the majority in one half or more of the trials.

TABLE 2. Distribution of Errors in Experimental and Control Groups

Number of Critical Errors	Critical Group* (N = 50) F	Control Group (N = 37) F
0	13	35
1	4	1
2	5	1
3	6	
4	3	
5	4	
6	1	
7	2	
8	5	
9	3	
10	3	
11	1	
12	0	
Total	50	37
Mean	3.84	0.08

* All errors in the critical group were in the direction of the majority estimates.

The differences between the critical subjects in their reactions to the given conditions were equally striking. There were subjects who remained completely confident throughout. At the other extreme were those who became disoriented, doubt-ridden, and experienced a powerful impulse not to appear different from the majority.

For purposes of illustration we include a brief description of one independent and one yielding subject.

Independent. After a few trials he appeared puzzled, hesitant. He announced all disagreeing answers in the form of "Three, sir; two, sir"; not so with the unanimous answers on the neutral trials. At Trial 4 he answered immediately after the first member of the group, shook his head, blinked, and whispered to his neighbor: "Can't help it, that's one." His later answers came in a whispered voice, accompanied by a deprecating smile. At one point he grinned embarrassedly, and whispered explosively to his neighbor: "I always disagree—darn it!" During the questioning, this subject's constant refrain was: "I called them as I saw them, sir." He insisted that his estimates were right without, however, committing himself as to whether the others were wrong, remarking that "that's the way I see them and that's the way they see them." If he had to make a practical decision under similar circumstances, he declared, "I might be wrong." Immediately following the experiment the majority engaged this subject in a brief discussion. When they pressed him to say whether the entire group was wrong and he alone right, he turned upon them defiantly, exclaiming: "You're *probably* right, but you *may* be wrong!" To the disclosure of the experiment this subject reacted with the statement that he felt "exultant and relieved," adding, "I do not deny that at times I had the feeling: 'to heck with it, I'll go along with the rest.' "

Yielding. This subject went with the majority in 11 out of 12 trials. He appeared nervous and somewhat confused, but he did not attempt to evade discussion; on the contrary, he was helpful and tried to answer to the best of his ability. He opened the discussion with the statement: "If I'd been first I probably would have responded differently"; this was his way of stating that he had adopted the majority estimates. The primary factor in his case was loss of confidence. He perceived the majority as a decided group, acting without hesitation: "If they had been doubtful I probably would have changed, but they answered with such confidence." Certain of his errors, he explained, were due to the doubtful nature of the comparisons; in such instances he went with the majority. When the object of the experiment was explained, the subject volunteered: "I suspected about the middle—but tried to push it out of my mind." It is of interest that his suspicion did not restore his confidence or diminish the power of the majority. Equally striking is his report that he assumed the experiment to involve an "illusion" to which the others, but not he, were subject. This assumption too did not help to free him; on the contrary, he acted as if his divergence from the majority was a sign of defect. The principal impression this subject produced was one so caught up by immediate difficulties that he lost clear reasons for his actions, and could make no reasonable decisions.

A FIRST ANALYSIS OF INDIVIDUAL DIFFERENCES

On the basis of the interview data described earlier, we undertook to differentiate and describe the major forms of reaction to the experimental situation, which we shall now briefly summarize.

Among the *independent* subjects we distinguished the following main categories:

(1) Independence based on *confidence* in one's perception and experience. The most striking characteristic of these subjects is the vigor with which they withstand the group opposition. Though they are sensitive to the group, and experience the conflict, they show a resilience in coping with it, which is expressed in their continuing reliance on their perception and the effectiveness with which they shake off the oppressive group opposition.

(2) Quite different are those subjects who are independent and *withdrawn*. These do not react in a spontaneously emotional way, but rather on the basis of explicit principles concerning the necessity of being an individual.

(3) A third group of independent subjects manifests considerable tension and doubt, but adheres to their judgment on the basis of a felt necessity to deal adequately with the task.

The following were the main categories of reaction among the *yielding* subjects, or those who went with the majority during one half or more of the trials.

(1) *Distortion of perception* under the stress of group pressure. In this category belong a very few subjects who yield completely, but are not aware that their estimates have been displaced or distorted by the majority. These subjects report that they came to perceive the majority estimates as correct.

(2) *Distortion of judgment*. Most submitting subjects belong to this category. The factor of greatest importance in this group is a decision the subjects reach that their perceptions are inaccurate, and that those of the majority are correct. These subjects suffer from primary doubt and lack of confidence; on this basis they feel a strong tendency to join the majority.

(3) *Distortion of action*. The subjects in this group do not suffer a modification of perception nor do they conclude that they are wrong. They yield because of an overmastering need not to appear different from or inferior to others, because of an inability to tolerate the appearance of defectiveness in the eyes of the group. These subjects suppress their observations and voice the majority position with awareness of what they are doing.

The results are sufficient to establish that independence and yielding are not psychologically homogeneous, that submission to group pressure and freedom from pressure can be the result of different psychological conditions. It should also be noted that the categories described above, being based exclusively on the subjects' reactions to the experimental conditions, are descriptive, not presuming to explain why a given individual responded in one way rather than another. The further exploration of the basis for the individual differences is a separate task.

EXPERIMENTAL VARIATIONS

The results described are clearly a joint function of two broadly different sets of conditions. They are determined first by the specific external conditions, by the particular character of the relation between social evidence and one's own experience. Second, the presence of pronounced individual differences points to the important role of personal factors, or factors connected with the individual's character structure. We reasoned that there are group conditions which would produce independence in all subjects, and that there probably are group conditions which would induce intensified yielding in many, though not in all. Secondly, we deemed it reasonable to assume that behavior under the experimental social pressure is significantly related to certain characteristics of the individual. The present account will be limited to the effect of the surrounding conditions upon independence and submission. To this end we followed the procedure of experimental variation, systematically altering the quality of social evidence by means of systematic variation of the group conditions and of the task.

The Effect of Nonunanimous Majorities. Evidence obtained from the basic experiment suggested that the condition of being exposed *alone* to the opposition of a "compact majority" may have played a decisive role in determining the course and strength of the effects observed. Accordingly we undertook to investigate in a series of successive variations the effects of *nonunanimous* majorities. The technical problem of altering the uniformity of a majority is, in terms of our procedure, relatively simple. In most instances we merely directed one or more members of the instructed group to deviate from the majority in prescribed ways. It is obvious that we cannot hope to compare the performance of the same individual in two situations on the assumption that they remain independent of one another; at best we can investigate the effect of an earlier upon a later experimental condition. The comparison of different experimental situations therefore requires the use of different but comparable groups of critical subjects. This is the procedure we have followed. In the variations to be described we have maintained the conditions of the basic experiment (e.g., the sex of the subjects, the size of the majority, the content of the task, and so on) save for the specific factor that was varied. The following were some of the variations studied:

1. *The presence of a "true partner."* (a) In the midst of the majority were *two* naïve, critical subjects. The subjects were separated spatially, being seated in the fourth and eighth positions, respectively. Each therefore heard his judgments confirmed by one other person (provided the other person remained independent), one prior to, the other after announcing his own judgment. In addition, each experienced a break in the unanimity of the majority. There were six pairs of critical subjects. (b) In a further variation the "partner" to the critical subject was a member of the group who had been instructed to respond correctly throughout. This procedure permits the exact control of the partner's responses. The partner was always seated in the fourth position; he therefore announced his estimates in each case before the critical subject.

The results clearly demonstrate that a disturbance of the unanimity of the majority markedly increased the independence of the critical subjects. The frequency of promajority errors dropped to 10.4 percent of the total number of estimates in variation (a), and to 5.5 percent in variation (b). These results are to be compared with the frequency of yielding to the unanimous majorities in the basic experiment, which was 32 percent of the total number of estimates. It is clear that the presence in the field of *one other* individual who responded correctly was sufficient to deplete the power of the majority, and in some cases to destroy it. This finding is all the more striking in the light of other variations which demonstrate the effect of even

small minorities provided they are unanimous. Indeed, we have been able to show that a unanimous majority of 3 is, under the given conditions, far more effective than a majority of 8 containing 1 dissenter. That critical subjects will under these conditions free themselves of a majority of 7 and join forces with one other person in the minority is, we believe, a result significant for theory. It points to a fundamental psychological difference between the condition of being alone and having a minimum of human support. It further demonstrates that the effects obtained are not the result of a summation of influences proceeding from each member of the group; it is necessary to conceive the results as being relationally determined.

2. *Withdrawal of a "true partner."* What will be the effect of providing the critical subject with a partner who responds correctly and then withdrawing him? The critical subject started with a partner who responded correctly. The partner was a member of the majority who had been instructed to respond correctly and to "desert" to the majority in the middle of the experiment. This procedure permits the observation of the same subject in the course of the transition from one condition to another. The withdrawal of the partner produced a powerful and unexpected result. We had assumed that the critical subject, having gone through the experience of opposing the majority with a minimum of support, would maintain his independence when alone. Contrary to this expectation, we found that the experience of having had and then lost a partner restored the majority effect to its full force, the proportion of errors rising to 28.5 percent of all judgments, in contrast to the preceding level of 5.5 percent. Further experimentation is needed to establish whether the critical subjects were responding to the sheer fact of being alone, or to the fact that the partner abandoned them.

3. *Late arrival of a "true partner."* The critical subject started as a minority of 1 in the midst of a unanimous majority. Toward the conclusion of the experiment one member of the majority "broke" away and began announcing

TABLE 3. Errors of Critical Subjects with Unanimous Majorities of Different Size

Size of Majority	Control	1	2	3	4	8	10–15
N	37	10	15	10	10	50	12
Mean number of errors	0.08	0.33	1.53	4.0	4.20	3.84	3.75
Range of errors	0–2	0–1	0–5	1–12	0–11	0–11	0–10

correct estimates. This procedure, which reverses the order of conditions of the preceding experiment, permits the observation of the transition from being alone to being a member of a pair against a majority. It is obvious that those critical subjects who were independent when alone would continue to be so when joined by a partner. The variation is therefore of significance primarily for those subjects who yielded during the first phase of the experiment. The appearance of the late partner exerts a freeing effect, reducing the level of yielding to 8.7 percent. Those who had previously yielded also became markedly more independent, but not completely so, continuing to yield more than previously independent subjects. The reports of the subjects do not cast much light on the factors responsible for the result. It is our impression that some subjects, having once committed themselves to yielding, find it difficult to change their direction completely. To do so is tantamount to a public admission that they had not acted rightly. They therefore follow to an extent the precarious course they had chosen in order to maintain an outward semblance of consistency and conviction.

4. *The presence of a "compromise partner."* The majority was consistently extremist, always matching the standard with the most unequal line. One instructed subject (who, as in the other variations, preceded the critical subject) also responded incorrectly, but his estimates were always intermediate between the truth and the majority position. The critical subject therefore faced an extremist majority whose unanimity was broken by one more moderately erring person. Under these conditions the frequency of errors was reduced but not significantly. However, the lack of unanimity determined in a strikingly consistent way the *direction* of the errors. The preponderance of the errors, 75.7 percent of the total, was moderate, whereas in a parallel experiment in which the majority was unanimously extremist (i.e., with the "compromise" partner excluded), the incidence of moderate errors was 42 percent of the total. As might be expected, in a unanimously moderate majority, the errors of the critical subjects were without exception moderate.

The Role of Majority Size. To gain further understanding of the majority effect, we varied the size of the majority in several different variations. The majorities, which were in each case unanimous, consisted of 2, 3, 4, 8, and 10–15 persons, respectively. In addition, we studied the limiting case in which the critical subject was opposed by one instructed subject. Table 3 contains the mean and the range of errors under each condition.

With the opposition reduced to 1, the majority effect all but disappeared. When the opposition proceeded from a group of 2, it produced a measurable though small distortion, the errors being 12.8 percent of the total number of estimates. The effect appeared in full force with a majority of 3. Larger majorities did not produce effects greater than a majority of 3.

The effect of a majority is often silent, revealing little of its operation to the subject, and often hiding it from the experimenter. To examine the range of effects it is capable of inducing, decisive variations of conditions are necessary. An indication of one effect is furnished by the following variation in which the conditions of the basic experiment were simply reversed. Here the majority, consisting of a group of 16, was naïve; in the midst of it we placed a single individual who responded wrongly according to instructions. Under these conditions the members of the naïve majority reacted to the lone dissenter with amusement. Contagious laughter spread through the group at the droll minority of 1. Of significance is the fact that the members lacked awareness that they drew their strength from the majority, and that their reactions would change radically if they faced the dissenter individually. These observations demonstrate the role of social support as a source of power and stability, in contrast to the preceding investigations which stressed the effects of social opposition. Both aspects must be explicitly considered in a unified formulation of the effects of group conditions on the formation and change of judgments.

The Role of the Stimulus-Situation. It is obviously not possible to divorce the quality and course of the group forces which act upon the individual from the specific stimulus-conditions. Of necessity the structure of the situation molds the group forces and determines their direction as well as their strength. Indeed, this was the reason that we took pains in the investigations described above to center the issue between the individual and the group around an elementary matter of fact. And there can be no doubt that the resulting reactions were directly a function of the contradiction between the observed relations and the majority position. These general considerations are sufficient to establish the need to vary the stimulus-conditions and to observe their effect on the resulting group forces.

Accordingly we have studied the effect of increasing and decreasing the discrepancy between the correct relation and the position of the majority, going beyond the basic experiment which contained discrepancies of a relatively moderate order. Our technique permits the easy variation of this factor, since we can vary at will the deviation of the majority from the correct relation. At this point we can only summarize the trend of the results which is entirely clear. The degree of independence increases with the distance of the majority

from correctness. However, even glaring discrepancies (of the order of 3–6″) did not produce independence in all. While independence increases with the magnitude of contradiction, a certain proportion of individuals continues to yield under extreme conditions.

We have also varied systematically the structural clarity of the task, employing judgments based on mental standards. In agreement with other investigators, we find that the majority effect grows stronger as the situation diminishes in clarity. Concurrently, however, the disturbance of the subjects and the conflict-quality of the situation decrease markedly. We consider it of significance that the majority achieves its most pronounced effect when it acts most painlessly.

SUMMARY

We have investigated the effects upon individuals of majority opinions when the latter were seen to be in a direction contrary to fact. By means of a simple technique we produced a radical divergence between a majority and a minority, and observed the ways in which individuals coped with the resulting difficulty. Despite the stress of the given conditions, a substantial proportion of individuals retained their independence throughout. At the same time a substantial minority yielded, modifying their judgments in accordance with the majority. Independence and yielding are a joint function of the following major factors: (1) The character of the stimulus situation. Variations in structural clarity have a decisive effect: with diminishing clarity of the stimulus-conditions the majority effect increases. (2) The character of the group forces. Individuals are highly sensitive to the structural qualities of group opposition. In particular, we demonstrated the great importance of the factor of unanimity. Also, the majority effect is a function of the size of group opposition. (3) The character of the individual. There were wide and, indeed, striking differences among individuals within the same experimental situation.

REVIEW QUESTIONS

1. Is pain a sensory modality? Are there any satisfactory physiological indicators of pain?
2. Define the following terms: cold pressor test, ischemic pain, hypnotic analgesia.
3. What are three propositions about the relationship between blood pressure and pain?
4. Outline the psychological and physiological explanations offered by Gardner and his colleagues for their finding of audio analgesia.
5. Why is it important that all of the pictures used in the report by Hess and Polt be equally bright?
6. Why were Hess, Seltzer, and Shlien concerned with artistic quality in their pictures?
7. How does McConnell operationally define ESP?
8. McConnell's study of the history of science led him to two conclusions about evidence. What are they?
9. McConnell states that he does "not want you to base your belief [in ESP] upon what I tell you." What does he say you should base your belief or disbelief upon?
10. What additional evidence do Ashley, Harper, and Runyon offer for their view that hypnosis was actually able to induce psychological organizations of "rich" and "poor"?
11. What was the role of individual differences in the Asch study?
12. Summarize the effects of the presence of a "true partner," withdrawal of a "true partner," and the late arrival of a "true partner," in the Asch study.
13. What did Asch find was the role of majority size in his study?

part five
developmental processes

While the question sounds vaguely like a "chicken crossing the road" joke, have you ever asked yourself how a cat knows it is a cat and not a dog? Why do cats make appropriate sexual responses toward other cats and not to dogs? Psychologists and ethologists have studied this problem with interesting results. Imprinting refers to the strong attachment or emotional bond that the young of the species develop toward adult members of the same species. Imprinting usually occurs very early in the organism's life during a given critical period. The imprinting process in some species of birds, for example, occurs during the first few hours after hatching. The attachment which develops is a permanent one which presumably lasts throughout the organism's life.

There are ample examples in the literature of young animals imprinted to the wrong species or an inappropriate object. The classic case is that of a greylag goose who was imprinted to Konrad Lorenz, an ethologist who has devoted his life to the study of imprinting. The young goose followed Lorenz around in much the same way it would have followed its mother. At maturity, the animal made appropriate sexual responses toward Lorenz and not to other greylag geese.

The strength of the imprinting process can be seen in that it is possible to imprint a Bobwhite quail to a hawk (#23). The hawk is a natural predator to quail and through imprinting it is possible to change this prey-predator relationship—at least from the viewpoint of the quail.

Presumably, human children also imprint on their parents to some extent although the critical period is probably a much longer time interval. The concept of imprinting or a process like it can be used to explain great segments of adult behavior. A sexual abnormality like homosexuality could at least be partially due to improper imprinting processes. Although such an explanation must remain at the level of pure speculation, it is conceivable that a critical period for sexual identification in humans occurs during puberty. Assume that a male only has homosexual experiences during this time or that if he has heterosexual contacts, they are unpleasant and anxiety-producing. Such a person could imprint or develop strong sexual attachments only to other males. After the critical period was over, no amount of heterosexual experience would change this orientation if imprinting has the same permanence in humans that it has in lower animals.

R. Allen and Beatrice T. Gardner are a husband and wife team who have been "Teaching Sign Language to a Chimpanzee" (#24). An earlier attempt at teaching language to a chimp did not meet with much success, with the animal learning only a few words. In this instance, the chimp was required to vocalize. It is thought that chimps simply do not possess the vocal apparatus for spoken language, and this explains the poor performance. As the article indicates, the Gardners had tremendous success utilizing sign language and in the process provided some interesting insights into human speech acquisition.

Another husband and wife team who have spent considerable time working with primates are Harry F. and Margaret K. Harlow. The Harlows' work with the affectional systems in young rhesus monkeys is classic in every sense of the word. The article reproduced here, "Affection in Primates" (#25), summarizes their earlier findings and points out parallels to human socialization.

A practical problem which all parents face is that of excessive crying in their children. Such crying often is not the result of any sudden unexpected and/or painful stimulus, but seems to occur for long periods of time for no apparent reason. In its milder forms it can be extremely upsetting to the parents and in extreme cases can have very detrimental effects on the parent-child relationship. The "Effects of Social Reinforcement on Operant Crying" (#26) was an attempt by Betty M. Hart and her colleagues to investigate such behavior in preschool children and offers a possible technique for its control.

Another practical problem which parents face is that of toilet training. R. Keith Van Wagenen and Everett E. Murdock's study, "A Transistorized Signal-Package for Toilet Training of Infants" (#27), could be a great help. The act of urination or defecation causes a tone signal to be emitted, and the parent can immediately respond to the situation with either positive or negative reinforcement as outlined in the report.

We spend approximately one-third of our lives asleep. There can be little doubt, then, that this behavior is important and appropriate for psychological study. The student should read article #28, "A Night of Sleep", particularly carefully. It provides necessary background information for the next article, "The Development of Infant Sleep" (#29). Both selections describe a particular kind of sleep—the so-called REM period—during which man experiences his most vivid dreams. Article #28 also provides the background material for "The Meaning of Dreams" (#50) in Part Nine.

23.
imprinting of bobwhite quail to a hawk

kenneth b. melvin, f. thomas cloar, and lucinda s. massingill

Young precocial birds have been imprinted to such diverse stimuli as green footballs, flickering lights, and Konrad Lorenz. Thus it seemed possible that Bobwhite Quail might become imprinted to an avian predator. This social relationship could lead to interesting modifications of prey-predator interactions at a later time, especially since adult Bobwhite Quail show a strong "fear" response upon their first exposure to a hawk. (Martin & Melvin, 1964). The present exploratory study represents an attempt to imprint quail to a Sparrow Hawk.

METHOD

Subjects

The Ss were 21 Bobwhite Quail, Colinus virginianus, hatched in the laboratory and kept in individual containers in a brooder. The Ss were run 8–20 hr. after hatching, (except three birds tested at 30 hr.). Food and water were not available until S had completed the experimental sequence.

Apparatus

The apparatus was similar to that of Hess (1959), consisting of a circular runway 8 in. wide and 4 ft. in diameter with walls 5 in. high. An elevated arm radiated from the center of the apparatus and moved at a speed of .5 ft./sec. An

Reprinted from The Psychological Record, 1967, 17, 235–238. Abridged by permission of the authors.

This investigation was supported in part by National Institute of Health Grant MH 2573–01.

adult female Sparrow Hawk (Falco sparvarius) was trained to ride on this arm (Experiment 1) or a perch suspended from it.

Although this species of hawk primarily preys on mice and insects, it has been reported to take young quail (Stoddard, 1946). Since this particular hawk was not averse to eating Ss, it was fed some beef shortly before each imprinting session.

Procedure

In the search for optimal conditions, the procedure varied over several small experiments. The S was placed in the apparatus, and the hawk was moved intermittently during the first 20-min. session. Six to eight hours later a second and similar session took place. About 20 hours later a 20-min. testing session was given, in which the hawk moved at a constant speed. If S followed within one ft. of the hawk for 70 percent of the first eight min., it was considered imprinted.

In Experiment 1 (N = 3) a two-ft. piece of one-way film formed part of the outer wall of the apparatus. Since one quail seemed to imprint to its reflection, this material was replaced by metal. The hawk was rotated silently and E observed S in a mirror placed above the apparatus. Experiment 2 (N = 4) was similar, except the hawk rode on a perch adjusted so that its tail was ¼ in. above the runway. In Experiments 3, 4, and 5, taped quail distress calls, chirps, and tapping were sounded intermittently. In Experiment 5 (N = 4), an added session was introduced in which 6–10 hr. old quail were rotated for 20 min. at 14 r.p.m. in individual compartments 2 ft. from the perched hawk. Three hours later they were given the standard series in the circular runway. Another three Ss run at 30 hr. after hatching showed strong escape behavior and were given only one session.

RESULTS AND DISCUSSION

The number of Ss imprinted were as follows: Experiment 1 1S, Experiment 2: 1S, Experiment 3: 1S, Experiment 4: 2Ss, and Experiment 5: 2Ss. Three other birds showed a moderate amount of following, but did not meet the criterion. The imprinted birds gave "distress" calls when the hawk was out of sight, and typically ran to it when it appeared (on Day 2, non-imprinted birds typically ran the other way). Imprinted quail would often stay close under the hawk's tail, at times pecking it. Three imprinted birds were tested on Day 3. These quail approached the hawk rather than a model of a female Bobwhite Quail, when placed equi-distant from these two stimuli.

It is evident that quail can develop a strong following response to an avian predator, but there seem to be wide individual differences. Only 39% of these birds were imprinted—a fact that could be due to the variance in conditions, the attributes of the hawk, the species of S, etc. Even with Vantress Broiler chicks, however, Polt and Hess (1966), using a less stringent criterion for imprinting, report only 61–79% "followers." Other investigators have also reported considerable variability in following behavior (Sluckin, 1965, pp. 31–32).

The last imprinted bird provided an interesting and serendipitous demonstra-tion. The E had forgotten to feed the hawk, which sought to remedy this oversight. After about five minutes of following (first session), S ran past the perch and then stopped. Our "imprinting object" bent over and picked up S by the neck feathers, causing E to intervene. At this intrusion the hawk flew upwards about one in. (she was tethered to the perch), casting S out onto the floor. "Shaken" but unhurt, S was inserted into the apparatus after a 2 min. rest. The quail resumed following and showed very strong imprinting during sessions 2 and 3. This misplaced "maternal affection" may reflect a process similar to that found in the infant monkeys who clung tightly to Harlow's (1962) pain-inflicting "evil mothers." This observation seems also relevant to the finding that punishment may strengthen imprinting (e.g., Kovach & Hess, 1963).

This paradoxical effect of punishment is held to be one of several factors differentiating imprinting from associative learning (Hess, 1959). It should be noted, however, that in escape and avoidance learning, punishment administered during an ongoing locomotor response facilitates this response and prevents its extinction (e.g., Melvin, 1964; Melvin & Smith, in press). It is a common assumption that fear plays a role in both imprinting and aversive conditioning. If punishment increases fear, which is then reduced by nearness to the imprinting object (or entering a "safe" goal box), these facilitative effects of punishment are not paradoxical. Indeed, in terms of the effects of punishment on ongoing aversively-motivated responses, these findings are quite consistent.

REFERENCES

Harlow, H. F. 1962. The heterosexual affectional system in monkeys. Amer. Psycholog. 17:1–9.

Hess, E. H. 1959. Imprinting. Science, 130: 133–141.

Kovach, J. K. & Hess, E. H. 1963. Imprinting: Effects of painful stimulation upon the following response. J. comp. physiol. Psychol., 56:461–464.

Martin, R. C. & Melvin, K. B. 1964. Fear responses of Bobwhite Quail (Colinus vir-ginianus) to a live and a model Redtailed Hawk (Buteo jamaicensis). Psychol. Forsch. 27:323–336.

Melvin, K. B. 1964. Escape learning and "vicious-circle" behavior as a function of percentage of reinforcement. J. comp. physiol. Psychol., 58:248–251

Melvin, K. B. & Smith, F. H. Self-punitive avoidance behavior in the rat. J. comp. physiol. Psychol. In press.

Polt, J. M. & Hess, E. H. 1966. Effects of

social experience on the following response in chicks. *J. comp. physiol. Psychol.*, *61*: 268–270.

Sluckin, W. 1965. *Imprinting and early learning.* Chicago: Aldine.

Stoddard, H. L. 1946. *The Bobwhite Quail, its habits, preservation, and increase.* New York: Scribner's.

24.
teaching
sign language
to a chimpanzee
a standardized system
of gestures provides a means
of two-way communication
with a chimpanzee

r. allen gardner
and beatrice t. gardner

The extent to which another species might be able to use human language is a classical problem in comparative psychology. One approach to this problem is to consider the nature of language, the processes of learning, the neural mechanisms of learning and of language, and the genetic basis of these mechanisms, and then, while recognizing certain gaps in what is known about these factors, to attempt to arrive at an answer by dint of careful scholarship (1). An alternative approach is to try to teach a form of human language to an animal. We chose the latter alternative and, in June 1966, began training an infant female chimpanzee, named Washoe, to use the gestural language of the deaf. Within the first 22 months of training it became evident that we had been correct in at least one major aspect of method, the use of a gestural language. Additional aspects of method have evolved in the course of the project. These and some implications of our early results can now be described in a way that may be useful in other studies of communicative behavior. Accordingly, in this article we discuss the considerations which led us to use the chimpanzee as a subject and American Sign Language (the language used by the deaf in North America) as a medium of communication; describe the general methods of training as they were

Reprinted by permission from *Science*, August 15, 1969, *165* (3894), 664–672. Copyright 1969 by the American Association for the Advancement of Science.

initially conceived and as they developed in the course of the project; and summarize those results that could be reported with some degree of confidence by the end of the first phase of the project.

PRELIMINARY CONSIDERATIONS

The Chimpanzee as a Subject. Some discussion of the chimpanzee as an experimental subject is in order because this species is relatively uncommon in the psychological laboratory. Whether or not the chimpanzee is the most intelligent animal after man can be disputed; the gorilla, the orangutan, and even the dolphin have their loyal partisans in this debate. Nevertheless, it is generally conceded that chimpanzees are highly intelligent, and that members of this species might be intelligent enough for our purposes. Of equal or greater importance is their sociability and their capacity for forming strong attachments to human beings. We want to emphasize this trait of sociability; it seems highly likely that it is essential for the development of language in human beings, and it was a primary consideration in our choice of a chimpanzee as a subject.

Affectionate as chimpanzees are, they are still wild animals, and this is a serious disadvantage. Most psychologists are accustomed to working with animals that have been chosen, and sometimes bred for docility and adaptability to laboratory procedures. The difficulties presented by the wild nature of an experimental animal must not be underestimated. Chimpanzees are also very strong animals; a full-grown specimen is likely to weigh more than 120 pounds (55 kilograms) and is estimated to be from three to five times as strong as a man, pound-for-pound. Coupled with the wildness, this great strength presents serious difficulties for a procedure that requires interaction at close quarters with a free-living animal. We have always had to reckon with the likelihood that at some point Washoe's physical maturity will make this procedure prohibitively dangerous.

A more serious disadvantage is that human speech sounds are unsuitable as a medium of communication for the chimpanzee. The vocal apparatus of the chimpanzee is very different from that of man (2). More important, the vocal behavior of the chimpanzee is very different from that of man. Chimpanzees do make many different sounds, but generally vocalization occurs in situations of high excitement and tends to be specific to the exciting situations. Undisturbed, chimpanzees are usually silent. Thus, it is unlikely that a chimpanzee could be trained to make refined use of its vocalizations. Moreover, the intensive work of Hayes and Hayes (3) with the chimpanzee Viki indicates that a vocal language is not appropriate for this species. The Hayeses used modern, sophisticated, psychological methods and seem to have spared no effort to teach Viki to make speech sounds. Yet in 6 years Viki learned only four sounds that approximated English words (4).

Use of the hands, however, is a prominent feature of chimpanzee behavior; manipulatory mechanical problems are their forte. More to the point, even caged, laboratory chimpanzees develop begging and similar gestures spontaneously (5), while individuals that have had extensive contact with human beings have displayed an even wider variety of communicative gestures (6). In our choice of sign language we were influenced more by the behavioral evidence that this medium of communication was appropriate to the species than by anatomical evidence of structural similarity between the hands of chimpanzees and of men. The Hayes point out that

human tools and mechanical devices are constructed to fit the human hand, yet chimpanzees have little difficulty in using these devices with great skill. Nevertheless, they seem unable to adapt their vocalizations to approximate human speech.

Psychologists who work extensively with the instrumental conditioning of animals become sensitive to the need to use responses that are suited to the species they wish to study. Lever-pressing in rats is not an arbitrary response invented by Skinner to confound the mentalists; it is a type of response commonly made by rats when they are first placed in a Skinner box. The exquisite control of instrumental behavior by schedules of reward is achieved only if the original responses are well chosen. We chose a language based on gestures because we reasoned that gestures for the chimpanzee should be analogous to bar-pressing for rats, key-pecking for pigeons, and babbling for humans.

American Sign Language. Two systems of manual communication are used by the deaf. One system is the manual alphabet, or finger spelling, in which configurations of the hand correspond to letters of the alphabet. In this system the words of a spoken language, such as English, can be spelled out manually. The other system, sign language, consists of a set of manual configurations and gestures that correspond to particular words or concepts. Unlike finger spelling, which is the direct encoding of a spoken language, sign languages have their own rules of usage. Word-for-sign translation between a spoken language and a sign language yields results that are similar to those of word-for-word translation between two spoken languages: the translation is often passable, though awkward, but it can also be ambiguous or quite nonsensical. Also, there are national and regional variations in sign languages that are comparable to those of spoken languages.

We chose for this project the American Sign Language (ASL), which, with certain regional variations, is used by the deaf in North America. This particular sign language has recently been the subject of formal analysis (7). The ASL can be compared to pictograph writing in which some symbols are quite arbitrary and some are quite representational or iconic, but all are arbitrary to some degree. For example, in ASL the sign for "always" is made by holding the hand in a fist, index finger extended (the pointing hand), while rotating the arm at the elbow. This is clearly an arbitrary representation of the concept "always." The sign for "flower," however, is highly iconic; it is made by holding the fingers of one hand extended, all five fingertips touching (the tapered hand), and touching the fingertips first to one nostril then to the other, as if sniffing a flower. While this is an iconic sign for "flower," it is only one of a number of conventions by which the concept "flower" could be iconically represented; it is thus arbitrary to some degree. Undoubtedly, many of the signs of ASL that seem quite arbitrary today once had an iconic origin that was lost through years of stylized usage. Thus, the signs of ASL are neither uniformly arbitrary nor uniformly iconic: rather the degree of abstraction varies from sign to sign over a wide range. This would seem to be a useful property of ASL for our research.

The literate deaf typically use a combination of ASL and finger spelling; for purposes of this project we have avoided the use of finger spelling as much as possible. A great range of expression is possible within the limits of ASL. We soon found that a good way to practice signing among ourselves was to render familiar songs and poetry into signs; as far as we can judge, there is no message that cannot be rendered faithfully (apart from the usual problems of translation from one language to another). Technical terms and proper names are a problem when first introduced, but within any community of signers it is easy to agree on a convention for any commonly used term. For example, among ourselves we do not finger-spell the words *psychologist* and *psychology*, but render them as "think doctor" and "think science." Or, among users of ASL, "California" can be finger-spelled but is commonly rendered as "golden playland." (Incidentally, the sign for "gold"

is made by plucking at the earlobe with thumb and forefinger, indicating an earring—another example of an iconic sign that is at the same time arbitrary and stylized.)

The fact that ASL is in current use by human beings is an additional advantage. The early linguistic environment of the deaf children of deaf parents is in some respects similar to the linguistic environment that we could provide for an experimental subject. This should permit some comparative evaluation of Washoe's eventual level of competence. For example, in discussing Washoe's early performance with deaf parents we have been told that many of her variants of standard signs are similar to the baby-talk variants commonly observed when human children sign.

Washoe. Having decided on a species and a medium of communication, our next concern was to obtain an experimental subject. It is altogether possible that there is some critical early age for the acquisition of this type of behavior. On the other hand, newborn chimpanzees tend to be quite helpless and vegetative. They are also considerably less hardy than older infants. Nevertheless, we reasoned that the dangers of starting too late were much greater than the dangers of starting too early, and we sought the youngest infant we could get. Newborn laboratory chimpanzees are very scarce, and we found that the youngest laboratory infant we could get would be about 2 years old at the time we planned to start the project. It seemed preferable to obtain a wild-caught infant. Wild-caught infants are usually at least 8 to 10 months old before they are available for research. This is because infants rarely reach the United States before they are 5 months old, and to this age must be added 1 or 2 months before final purchase and 2 or 3 months for quarantine and other medical services.

We named our chimpanzee Washoe for Washoe County, the home of the University of Nevada. Her exact age will never be known, but from her weight and dentition we estimated her age to be between 8 and 14 months at the end of June 1966, when she first ar rived at our laboratory. (Her dentition has continued to agree with this initial estimate, but her weight has increased rather more than would be expected.) This is very young for a chimpanzee. The best available information indicates that infants are completely dependent until the age of 2 years and semi-dependent until the age of 4; the first signs of sexual maturity (for example, menstruation, sexual swelling) begin to appear at about 8 years, and full adult growth is reached between the ages of 12 and 16 (8). As for the complete life-span, captive specimens have survived for well over 40 years. Washoe was indeed very young when she arrived; she did not have her first canines or molars, her hand-eye coordination was rudimentary, she had only begun to crawl about, and she slept a great deal. Apart from making friends with her and adapting her to the daily routine, we could accomplish little during the first few months.

Laboratory Conditions. At the outset we were quite sure that Washoe could learn to make various signs in order to obtain food, drink, and other things. For the project to be a success, we felt that something more must be developed. We wanted Washoe not only to ask for objects but to answer questions about them and also to ask us questions. We wanted to develop behavior that could be described as conversation. With this in mind, we attempted to provide Washoe with an environment that might be conducive to this sort of behavior. Confinement was to be minimal, about the same as that of human infants. Her human companions were to be friends and playmates as well as providers and protectors, and they were to introduce a great many games and activities that would be likely to result in maximum interaction with Washoe.

In practice, such an environment is readily achieved with a chimpanzee: bonds of warm affection have always been established between Washoe and her several human companions. We have enjoyed the interaction almost as much as Washoe has, within the limits of human endurance. A number of human companions have been enlisted to participate in the project and relieve each other at intervals, so that at least one person would be with Washoe during all her waking hours. At first we feared that such frequent changes would be disturbing, but Washoe seemed to adapt very well to this procedure. Apparently it is possible to provide an infant chimpanzee with affection on a shift basis.

All of Washoe's human companions have been required to master ASL and to use it extensively in her presence, in association with interesting activities and events and also in a general way, as one chatters at a human infant in the course of the day. The ASL has been used almost exclusively, although occasional finger spelling has been permitted. From time to time, of course, there are lapses into spoken English, as when medical personnel must examine Washoe. At one time, we considered an alternative procedure in which we would sign and speak English to Washoe simultaneously, thus giving her an additional source of informative cues. We rejected this procedure, reasoning that, if she should come to understand speech sooner or more easily than ASL, then she might not pay sufficient attention to our gestures. Another alternative, that of speaking English among ourselves and signing to Washoe, was also rejected. We reasoned that this would make it seem that big chimps talk and only little chimps sign, which might give signing an undesirable social status.

The environment we are describing is not a silent one. The human beings can vocalize in many ways, laughing and making sounds of pleasure and displeasure. Whistles and drums are sounded in a variety of imitation games, and hands are clapped for attention. The rule is that all meaningful sounds, whether vocalized or not, must be sounds that a chimpanzee can imitate.

TRAINING METHODS

Imitation. The imitativeness of apes is proverbial, and rightly so. Those who have worked closely with chimpanzees have frequently remarked on their readiness to engage in visually guided imitation. Consider the following typical comment of Yerkes *(9)*: "Chim and Panzee would imitate many of my acts, but never have I heard them imitate a sound and rarely make a sound peculiarly their own in response to mine. As previously stated, their imitative tendency is as remarkable for its specialization and limitations as for its strength. It seems to be controlled chiefly by visual stimuli. Things which are seen tend to be imitated or reproduced. What is heard is not reproduced. Obviously an animal which lacks the tendency to reinstate auditory stimuli—in other words to imitate sounds—cannot reasonably be expected to talk. The human infant exhibits this tendency to a remarkable degree. So also does the parrot. If the imitative tendency of the parrot could be coupled with the quality of intelligence of the chimpanzee, the latter undoubtedly could speak."

In the course of their work with Viki, the Hayeses devised a game in which Viki would imitate various actions on hearing the command "Do this" *(10)*. Once established, this was an effective means of training Viki to perform actions that could be visually guided. The same method should be admirably suited to training a chimpanzee to use sign language; accordingly we have directed much effort toward establishing a version of the "Do this" game with Washoe. Getting Washoe to imitate us was not difficult, for she did so quite spontaneously, but getting her to imitate on command has been another matter altogether. It was not until the 16th month of the project that we achieved any degree of control over Washoe's imitation of gestures. Eventually we got to a point where she would imitate a simple gesture, such as pulling at her ears, or a series of such gestures—first we make a gesture, then she imitates, then we make a second gesture, she imitates the second gesture, and so on—for the reward of being tickled. Up to this writing, however, imitation of this sort has not been an important method for introducing new signs into Washoe's vocabulary.

As a method of prompting, we have been able to use imitation extensively to increase the frequency and refine the form of signs. Washoe sometimes fails to use a new sign in an appropriate situation, or uses another, incorrect sign. At such times we can make the correct sign to Washoe, repeating the performance until she makes the sign herself. (With more stable signs, more indirect forms of prompting can be used—for example, pointing at, or touching, Washoe's hand or a part of her body that should be involved in the sign; making the sign for "sign," which is equivalent to saying "Speak up"; or asking a question in signs, such as "What do you want?" or "What is it?") Again, with new signs, and often with old signs as well, Washoe can lapse into what we refer to as poor "diction." Of course, a great deal of slurring and a wide range of variants are permitted in ASL as in any spoken language. In any event, Washoe's diction has frequently been improved by the simple device of repeating, in exaggeratedly correct form, the sign she has just made, until she repeats it herself in more correct form. On the whole, she has responded quite well to prompting, but there are strict limits to its use with a wild animal—one that is probably quite spoiled, besides. Pressed too hard, Washoe can become completely diverted from her original object; she may ask for something entirely different, run away, go into a tantrum, or even bite her tutor.

Chimpanzees also imitate, after some delay, and this delayed imitation can be quite elaborate *(10)*. The following is a typical example of Washoe's delayed imitation. From the beginning of the project she was bathed regularly and according to a standard routine. Also, from her 2nd month with us, she always had dolls to play with. One day, during the 10th month of the project, she bathed one of her dolls in the way we usually bathed her. She filled her little bathtub with water, dunked the doll in the tub, then took it out and dried it with a towel. She has repeated the entire performance, or parts of it, many times since, sometimes also soaping the doll.

This is a type of imitation that may be very important in the acquisition of language by human children, and many of our procedures with Washoe were devised to capitalize on it. Routine activities—feeding, dressing, bathing, and so on—have been highly ritualized, with appropriate signs figuring prominently in the rituals. Many games have been invented which can be accompanied by appropriate signs. Objects and activities have been named as often as possible, especially when Washoe seemed to be paying particular attention to them. New objects and new examples of familiar objects, including pictures, have been continually brought to her attention, together with the appropriate signs. She likes to ride in automobiles, and a ride in an automobile, including the preparations for a ride, provides a wealth of sights that can be accompanied by signs. A good destination for a ride is a home or the university nursery school, both well stocked with props for language lessons.

The general principle should be clear: Washoe has been exposed to a wide variety of activities and objects, together with their appropriate signs, in the hope that she would come to associate the signs with their referents and later make the signs herself. We have reason to believe that she has come to understand a large vocabulary of signs. This was expected, since a number of chimpanzees have acquired extensive understanding vocabularies of spoken words, and there is evidence that even dogs can acquire a sizable understanding vocabulary of spoken words (11). The understanding vocabulary that Washoe has acquired, however, consists of signs that a chimpanzee can imitate.

Some of Washoe's signs seem to have been originally acquired by delayed imitation. A good example is the sign for "toothbrush." A part of the daily routine has been to brush her teeth after every meal. When this routine was first introduced Washoe generally resisted it. She gradually came to submit with less and less fuss, and after many months she would even help or sometimes brush her teeth herself. Usually, having finished her meal, Washoe would try to leave her highchair; we would restrain her, signing "First, toothbrushing, then you can go." One day, in the 10th month of the project, Washoe was visiting the Gard-

ner home and found her way into the bathroom. She climbed up on the counter, looked at our mug full of toothbrushes, and signed "toothbrush." At the time, we believed that Washoe understood this sign but we had not seen her use it. She had no reason to ask for the toothbrushes, because they were well within her reach, and it is most unlikely that she was asking to have her teeth brushed. This was our first observation, and one of the clearest examples, of behavior in which Washoe seemed to name an object or an event for no obvious motive other than communication.

Following this observation, the toothbrushing routine at mealtime was altered. First, initiative prompting was introduced. Then as the sign became more reliable, her rinsing-mug and toothbrush were displayed prominently until she made the sign. By the 14th month she was making the "toothbrush" sign at the end of meals with little or no prompting; in fact, she has called for her toothbrush in a peremptory fashion when its appearance at the end of a meal was delayed. The "toothbrush" sign is not merely a response cued by the end of a meal; Washoe retained her ability to name toothbrushes when they were shown to her at other times.

The sign for "flower" may also have been acquired by delayed imitation. From her first summer with us, Washoe showed a great interest in flowers, and we took advantage of this by providing many flowers and pictures of flowers accompanied by the appropriate sign. Then one day in the 15th month she made the sign, spontaneously, while she and a companion were walking toward a flower garden. As in the case of "toothbrush," we believed that she understood the sign at this time, but we had made no attempt to elicit it from her except by making it ourselves in appropriate situations. Again, after the first observation, we proceeded to elicit this sign as often as possible by a variety of methods most frequently by showing her a flower and giving it to her if she made the sign for it. Eventually the sign became very reliable and could be elicited by a variety of flowers and pictures of flowers.

It is difficult to decide which signs were acquired by the method of delayed imitation. The first appearance of these signs is likely to be sudden and unexpected; it is possible that some inadvertent movement of Washoe's has been interpreted as meaningful by one of her devoted companions. If the first observer were kept from reporting the observation and from making any direct attempts to elicit the sign again, then it might be possible to obtain independent verification. Quite understandably, we have been more interested in raising the frequency of new signs than in evaluating any particular method of training.

Babbling. Because the Hayeses were attempting to teach Viki to speak English, they were interested in babbling, and during the first year of their project they were encouraged by the number and variety of spontaneous vocalizations that Viki made. But, in time, Viki's spontaneous vocalizations decreased further and further to the point where the Hayeses felt that there was almost no vocal babbling from which to shape spoken language. In planning this project we expected a great deal of manual "babbling," but during the early months we observed very little behavior of this kind. In the course of the project, however, there has been a great increase in manual babbling. We have been particularly encouraged by the increase in movements that involve touching parts of the head and body, since these are important components of many signs. Also, more and more frequently, when Washoe has been unable to get something that she wants, she has burst into a flurry of random flourishes and arm-waving.

We have encouraged Washoe's babbling by our responsiveness; clapping, smiling, and repeating the gesture much as you might repeat "goo goo" to a human infant. If the babbled gesture has resembled a sign in ASL, we have made the correct form of the sign and have attempted to engage in some appropriate activity. The sign for "funny" was probably acquired in this way. It first appeared as a spontaneous babble that lent itself readily to a simple imitation game

—first Washoe signed "funny," then we did, then she did, and so on. We would laugh and smile during the interchanges that she initiated, and initiate the game ourselves when something funny happened. Eventually Washoe came to use the "funny" sign spontaneously in roughly appropriate situations.

Closely related to babbling are some gestures that seem to have appeared independently of any deliberate training on our part, and that resemble signs so closely that we could incorporate them into Washoe's repertoire with little or no modification. Almost from the first she had a begging gesture—an extension of her open hand, palm up, toward one of us. She made this gesture in situations in which she wanted aid and in situations in which we were holding some object that she wanted. The ASL signs for "give me" and "come" are very similar to this, except that they involve a prominent beckoning movement. Gradually Washoe came to incorporate a beckoning wrist movement into her use of this sign. In Table 1 we refer to this sign as "come-gimme." As Washoe has come to use it, the sign is not simply a modification of the original begging gesture. For example, very commonly she reaches forward with one hand (palm up) while she gestures with the other hand (palm down) held near her head. (The result resembles a classic fencing posture.)

Another sign of this type is the sign for "hurry," which, so far, Washoe has always made by shaking her open hand vigorously at the wrist. This first appeared as an impatient flourish following some request that she had made in signs; for example, after making the "open" sign before a door. The correct ASL for "hurry" is very close, and we began to use it often, ourselves, in appropriate contexts. We believe that Washoe has come to use this sign in a meaningful way, because she has frequently used it when she, herself, is in a hurry—for example, when rushing to her nursery chair.

Instrumental Conditioning. It seems intuitively unreasonable that the acquisition of language by human beings could be strictly a matter of reiterated instrumental conditioning—that a child acquires language after the fashion of a rat that is conditioned, first, to press a lever for food in the presence of one stimulus, then to turn a wheel in the presence of another stimulus, and so on until a large repertoire of discriminated responses is acquired. Nevertheless, the so-called "trick vocabulary" of early childhood is probably acquired in this way, and this may be a critical stage in the acquisition of language by children. In any case, a minimal objective of this project was to teach Washoe as many signs as possible by whatever procedures we could enlist. Thus, we have not hesitated to use conventional procedures of instrumental conditioning.

Anyone who becomes familiar with young chimpanzees soon learns about their passion for being tickled. There is no doubt that tickling is the most effective reward that we have used with Washoe. In the early months, when we would pause in our tickling. Washoe would indicate that she wanted more tickling by taking our hands and placing them against her ribs or around her neck. The meaning of these gestures was unmistakable, but since we were not studying our human ability to interpret her chimpanzee gestures, we decided to shape an arbitrary response that she could use to ask for more tickling. We tended to bring her arms together to cover the place being tickled. The result was a very crude approximation of the ASL sign for "more" (see Table 1). Thus, we would stop tickling and then pull Washoe's arms away from her body. When we released her arms and threatened to resume tickling, she tended to bring her hands together again. If she brought them back together, we would tickle her again. From time to time we would stop tickling and wait for her to put her hands together by herself. At first, any approximation to the "more" sign, however crude, was rewarded. Later, we required closer approximations and introduced imitative prompting. Soon, a very good version of the "more" sign could be obtained, but it was quite specific to the tickling situation.

In the 6th month of the project we were able to get "more" signs for a new game that consisted of pushing Washoe across the floor in a laundry basket. In this case we did not use the shaping procedure but, from the start, used imitative prompting to elicit the "more" sign. Soon after the "more" sign became spontaneous and reliable in the laundry-basket game, it began to appear as a request for more swinging (by the arms)—again, after first being elicited with imitative prompting. From this point on, Washoe transferred the "more" sign to all activities, including feeding. The transfer was usually spontaneous, occurring when there was some pause in a desired activity or when some object was removed. Often we ourselves were not sure that Washoe wanted "more" until she signed to us.

The sign for "open" had a similar history. When Washoe wanted to get through a door, she tended to hold up both hands and pound on the door with her palms or her knuckles. This is the beginning position for the "open" sign (see Table 1). By waiting for her to place her hands on the door and then lift them, and also by imititative prompting, we were able to shape a good approximation of the "open" sign, and would reward this by opening the door. Originally she was trained to make this sign for three particular doors that she used every day. Washoe transferred this sign to all doors; then to containers such as the refrigerator, cupboards, drawers, briefcases, boxes, and jars; and eventually—an invention of Washoe's—she used it to ask us to turn on water faucets.

In the case of "more" and "open" we followed the conventional laboratory procedure of waiting for Washoe to make some response that could be shaped into the sign we wished her to acquire. We soon found that this was not necessary; Washoe could acquire signs that were first elicited by our holding her hands, forming them into the desired configuration, and then putting them through the desired movement. Since this procedure of guidance is usually much more practical than waiting for a spontaneous approximation to occur at a favorable moment, we have used it much more frequently.

TABLE 1.   Signs Used Reliably by Chimpanzee Washoe
Within 22 Months of the Beginning of Training

Signs	Description	Context
Come-gimme	Beckoning motion, with wrist or knuckles as pivot.	Sign made to persons or animals, also for objects out of reach. Often combined: "come tickle," "gimme sweet," etc.
More	Fingertips are brought together, usually overhead. (Correct ASL form: tips of the tapered hand touch repeatedly.)	When asking for continuation or repetition of activities such as swinging or tickling, for second helpings of foods, etc. Also used to ask for repetition of some performance, such as a somersault.
Up	Arm extends upward, and index finger may also point up.	Wants to lift to reach objects such as grapes on vine, or leaves; or wants to be placed on someone's shoulders; or wants to leave potty-chair.
Sweet	Index or index and second fingers touch tip of wagging tongue. (Correct ASL form: index and second fingers extended side by side.)	For dessert; used spontaneously at end of meal. Also, when asking for candy.
Open	Flat hands are placed side by side, palms down, then drawn apart while rotated to palms up.	At door of house, room, car, refrigerator, or cupboard; on containers such as jars; and on faucets.
Tickle	The index finger of one hand is drawn across the back of the other hand. (Related to ASL "touch.")	For tickling or for chasing games.
Go	Opposite of "come-gimme."	While walking hand-in-hand or riding on someone's shoulders. Washoe usually indicates the direction desired.
Out	Curved hand grasps tapered hand; then tapered hand is withdrawn upward.	When passing through doorways; until recently, used for both "in" and "out." Also, when asking to be taken outdoors.
Hurry	Open hand is shaken at the wrist. (Correct ASL form: index and second fingers extended side by side.)	Often follows signs such as "come-gimme," "out," "open," and "go," particularly if there is a delay before Washoe is obeyed. Also, used while watching her meal being prepared.
Hear-listen	Index finger touches ear.	For loud or strange sounds; bells, car horns, sonic booms, etc. Also, for asking someone to hold a watch to her ear.
Toothbrush	Index finger is used as brush, to rub front teeth.	When Washoe has finished her meal, or at other times when shown a toothbrush.
Drink	Thumb is extended from fisted hand and touches mouth.	For water, formula, soda pop, etc. For soda pop, often combined with "sweet."
Hurt	Extended index fingers are jabbed toward each other. Can be used to indicate location of pain.	To indicate cuts and bruises on herself or on others. Can be elicited by red stains on a person's skin or by tears in clothing.
Sorry	Fisted hand clasps and unclasps at shoulder. (Correct ASL form: fisted hand is rubbed over heart with circular motion.)	After biting someone, or when someone has been hurt in another way (not necessarily by Washoe). When told to apologize for mischief.
Funny	Tip of index finger presses nose, and Washoe snorts. (Correct ASL form: index and second fingers used; no snort.)	When soliciting interaction play, and during games. Occasionally, when being pursued after mischief.

TABLE 1. (Continued)

Signs	Description	Context
Please	Open hand is drawn across chest. (Correct ASL form: fingertips used, and circular motion.)	When asking for objects and activities. Frequently combined: "Please go," "Out, please," "Please drink."
Food-eat	Several fingers of one hand are placed in mouth. (Correct ASL form: fingertips of tapered hand touch mouth repeatedly.)	During meals and preparation of meals.
Flower	Tip of index finger touches one or both nostrils. (Correct ASL form: tips of tapered hand touch first one nostril, then the other.)	For flowers.
Cover-blanket	Draws one hand toward self over the back of the other.	At bedtime or naptime, and, on cold days, when Washoe wants to be taken out.
Dog	Repeated slapping on thigh.	For dogs and for barking.
You	Index finger points at a person's chest.	Indicates successive turns in games. Also used in response to questions such as "Who tickle?" "Who brush?"
Napkin-bib	Fingertips wipe the mouth region.	For bib, for washcloth, and for Kleenex.
In	Opposite of "out."	Wants to go indoors, or wants someone to join her indoors.
Brush	The fisted hand rubs the back of the open hand several times (Adapted from ASL "polish.")	For hairbrush, and when asking for brushing.
Hat	Palm pats top of head.	For hats and caps.
I-me	Index finger points at, or touches, chest.	Indicates Washoe's turn, when she and a companion share food, drink, etc. Also used in phrases, such as "I drink," and in reply to questions such as "Who tickle?" (Washoe: "you"); "Who I tickle?" (Washoe: "Me.")
Shoes	The fisted hands are held side by side and strike down on shoes or floor. (Correct ASL form: the sides of the fisted hands strike against each other.)	For shoes and boots.
Smell	Palm is held before nose and moved slightly upward several times.	For scented objects: tobacco, perfume, sage, etc.
Pants	Palms of the flat hands are drawn up against the body toward waist.	For diapers, rubber pants, trousers.
Clothes	Fingertips brush down the chest.	For Washoe's jacket, nightgown, and shirts; also for our clothing.
Cat	Thumb and index finger grasp cheek hair near side of mouth and are drawn outward (representing cat's whiskers.)	For cats.
Key	Palm of one hand is repeatedly touched with the index finger of the other. (Correct ASL form: crooked index finger is rotated against palm.)	Used for keys and locks and to ask us to unlock a door.
Baby	One forearm is placed in the crook of the other, as if cradling a baby.	For dolls, including animal dolls such as a toy horse and duck.
Clean	The open palm of one hand is passed over the open palm of the other.	Used when Washoe is washing, or being washed, or when a companion is washing hands or some other object. Also used for "soap."

Note: The signs are listed in the order of their orginal appearance in her repertoire (see text for the criterion of reliability and for the method of assigning the date of original appearance).

RESULTS

Vocabulary. In the early stages of the project we were able to keep fairly complete records of Washoe's daily signing behavior. But, as the amount of signing behavior and the number of signs to be monitored increased, our initial attempts to obtain exhaustive records became prohibitively cumbersome. During the 16th month we settled on the following procedure. When a new sign was introduced we waited until it had been reported by three different observers as having occurred in an appropriate context and spontaneously (that is, with no prompting other than a question such as "What is it?" or "What do you want?"). The sign was then added to a checklist in which its occurrence, form, context, and the kind of prompting required were recorded. Two such checklists were filled out each day, one for the first half of the day and one for the second half. For a criterion of acquisition we chose a reported frequency of at least one appropriate and spontaneous occurrence each day over a period of 15 consecutive days.

In Table 1 we have listed 30 signs that met this criterion by the end of the 22nd month of the project. In addition, we have listed four signs ("dog," "smell," "me," and "clean") that we judged to be stable, despite the fact that they had not met the stringent criterion before the end of the 22nd month. These additional signs had, nevertheless, been reported to occur appropriately and spontaneously on more than half of the days in a period of 30 consecutive days. An indication of the variety of signs that Washoe used in the course of a day is given by the following data: during the 22nd month of the study, 28 of the 34 signs listed were reported on at least 20 days, and the smallest number of different signs reported for a single day was 23, with a median of 29 (12).

The order in which these signs first appeared in Washoe's repertoire is also given in Table 1. We considered the first appearance to be the date on which three different observers reported appropriate and spontaneous occurrences. By this criterion, 4 new signs first appeared during the first 7 months, 9 new signs during the next 7 months, and 21 new signs during the next 7 months. We chose the 21st month rather than the 22nd month as the cutoff for this tabulation so that no signs would be included that do not appear in Table 1. Clearly, if Washoe's rate of acquisition continues to accelerate, we will have to assess her vocabularly on the basis of sampling procedures. We are now in the process of developing procedures that could be used to make periodic tests of Washoe's performance on samples of her repertoire. However, now that there is evidence that a chimpanzee can acquire a vocabulary of more than 30 signs, the exact number of signs in her current vocabulary is less significant than the order of magnitude— 50, 100, 200 signs, or more—that might eventually be achieved.

Differentiation. In Table 1, column 1, we list English equivalents for each of Washoe's signs. It must be understood that this equivalence is only approximate, because equivalence between English and ASL, as between any two human languages, is only approximate, and because Washoe's usage does differ from that of standard ASL. To some extent her usage is indicated in the column labeled "Context" in Table 1, but the definition of any given sign must always depend upon her total vocabulary, and this has been continually changing. When she had very few signs for specific things, Washoe used the "more" sign for a wide class of requests. Our only restriction was that we discouraged the use of "more" for first requests. As she acquired signs for specific requests, her use of "more" declined until, at the time of this writing, she was using this sign mainly to ask for repetition of some action that she could not name, such as a somersault. Perhaps the best English equivalent would be "do it again." Still, it seemed preferable to list the English equivalent for the ASL sign rather than its current referent for Washoe, since further refinements in her usage may be achieved at a later date.

The differentiation of the signs for "flower" and "smell" provides a further illustration of usage depending upon size of vocabulary. As the "flower" sign became more frequent, we noted that it occurred in several inappropriate contexts that all seemed to include odors; for example, Washoe would make the "flower" sign when opening a tobacco pouch or when entering a kitchen filled with cooking odors. Taking our cue from this, we introduced the "smell" sign by passive shaping and imitative prompting. Gradually Washoe came to make the appropriate distinction between "flower" contexts and "smell" contexts in her signing, although "flower" (in the single-nostril form) (see Table 1) has continued to occur as a common error in "smell" contexts.

Transfer. In general, when introducing new signs we have used a very specific referent for the initial training—a particular door for "open," a particular hat for "hat." Early in the project we were concerned about the possibility that signs might become inseparable from their first referents. So far, however, there has been no problem of this kind: Washoe has always been able to transfer her signs spontaneously to new members of each class of referents. We have already described the transfer of "more" and "open." The sign for "flower" is a particularly good example of transfer, because flowers occur in so many varieties, indoors, outdoors, and in pictures, yet Washoe uses the same sign for all. It is fortunate that she has responded well to pictures of objects. In the case of "dog" and "cat" this has proved to be important because live dogs and cats can be too exciting, and we have had to use pictures to elicit most of the "dog" and "cat" signs. It is noteworthy that Washoe has transferred the "dog" sign to the sound of barking by an unseen dog.

The acquisition and transfer of the sign for "key" illustrates a further point. A great many cupboards and doors in Washoe's quarters have been kept secure by small padlocks that can all be opened by the same simple key. Because she was immature and awkward, Washoe had great difficulty in learning to use these keys and locks. Because we wanted her to improve her manual dexterity, we let her practice with these keys until she could open the locks quite easily (then we had to hide the keys). Washoe soon transferred this skill to all manner of locks and keys, including ignition keys. At about the same time, we taught her the sign for "key," using the original padlock keys as a referent. Washoe came to use this sign both to name keys that were presented to her and to ask for the keys to various locks when no key was in sight. She readily transferred the sign to all varieties of keys and locks.

Now, if an animal can transfer a skill learned with a certain key and lock to all types of key and lock, it should not be surprising that the same animal can learn to use an arbitrary response to name and ask for a certain key and then transfer that sign to new types of keys. Certainly, the relationship between the use of a key and the opening of locks is as arbitrary as the relationship between the sign for "key" and its many referents. Viewed in this way, the general phenomenon of transfer of training and the specifically linguistic phenomenon of labeling become very similar, and the problems that these phenomena pose for modern learning theory should require similar solutions. We do not mean to imply that the problem of labeling is less complex than has generally been supposed; rather, we are suggesting that the problem of transfer of training requires an equally sophisticated treatment.

Combinations. During the phase of the project covered by this article we made no deliberate attempts to elicit combinations or phrases, although we may have responded more readily to strings of two or more signs than to single signs. As far as we can judge, Washoe's early use of signs in strings was spontaneous. Almost as soon as she had eight or ten signs in her repertoire, she began to use them two and three at a time. As her repertoire increased, her tendency to produce strings of two or more signs also increased, to the point where this has become a common mode of signing for her. We, of course, usually signed to her in combinations, but if Washoe's use of combinations has been imitative, then it must be a generalized sort of limitation, since she has invented a number of combinations, such as "gimme tickle" (before we had ever asked her to tickle us), and "open food drink" (for the refrigerator—we have always called it the "cold box").

Four signs—"please," "come-gimme," "hurry," and "more"—used with one or more other signs, account for the largest share of Washoe's early combinations. In general, these four signs have functioned as emphasizers, as in "please open hurry" and "gimme drink please."

Until recently, five additional signs—"go," "out," "in," "open," and "hear-listen"—accounted for most of the remaining combinations. Typical examples of combinations using these four are, "go in" or "go out" (when at some distance from a door), "go sweet" (for being carried to a raspberry bush), "open flower" (to be let through the gate to a flower garden), "open key" (for a locked door), "listen eat" (at the sound of an alarm clock signaling mealtime), and "listen dog" (at the sound of barking by an unseen dog). All but the first and last of these six examples were inventions of Washoe's. Combinations of this type tend to amplify the meaning of the single signs used. Sometimes, however, the function of these five signs has been about the same as that of the emphasizers, as in "open out" (when standing in front of a door).

Toward the end of the period covered in this article we were able to introduce the pronouns "I-me" and "you," so that combinations that resemble short sentences have begun to appear.

CONCLUDING OBSERVATIONS

From time to time we have been asked questions such as, "Do you think that Washoe has language?" or "At what point will you be able to say that Washoe has language?" We find it very difficult to respond to these questions because they are altogether foreign to the spirit of our research. They imply a distinction between one class of communicative behavior that can be called language and another class that cannot. This in turn implies a well-established theory that could provide the distinction. If our objectives had required such a

theory, we would certainly not have been able to begin this project as early as we did.

In the first phase of the project we were able to verify the hypothesis that sign language is an appropriate medium of two-way communication for the chimpanzee. Washoe's intellectual immaturity, the continuing acceleration of her progress, the fact that her signs do not remain specific to their original referents but are transferred spontaneously to new referents, and the emergence of rudimentary combinations all suggest that significantly more can be accomplished by Washoe during the subsequent phases of this project. As we proceed, the problems of these subsequent phases will be chiefly concerned with the technical business of measurement. We are now developing a procedure for testing Washoe's ability to name objects. In this procedure, an object or a picture of an object is placed in a box with a window. An observer, who does not know what is in the box, asks Washoe what she sees through the window. At present, this method will have to be devised for other items. In particular, the ability to combine and recombine signs must be tested. Here, a great deal depends upon reaching a stage at which Washoe produces an extended series of signs in answer to questions. Our hope is that Washoe can be brought to the point where she describes events and situations to an observer who has no other source of information.

At an earlier time we would have been more cautious about suggesting that a chimpanzee might be able to produce extended utterances to communicate information. We believe now that it is the writers—who would predict just what it is that no chimpanzee will ever do—who must proceed with caution. Washoe's accomplishments will probably be exceeded by another chimpanzee, because it is unlikely that the conditions of training have been optimal in this first attempt. Theories of language that depend upon the identification of aspects of language that are exclusively human must remain tentative until a considerably larger body of intensive research with other species becomes available.

SUMMARY

We set ourselves the task of teaching an animal to use a form of human language. Highly intelligent and highly social, the chimpanzee is an obvious choice for such a study, yet it has not been possible to teach a member of this species more than a few spoken words. We reasoned that a spoken language, such as English, might be an inappropriate medium of communication for a chimpanzee. This led us to choose American Sign Language, the gestural system of communication used by the deaf in North America, for the project.

The youngest infant that we could obtain was a wild-born female, whom we named Washoe, and who was estimated to be between 8 and 14 months old when we began our program of training. The laboratory conditions, while not patterned after those of a human family (as in the studies of Kellogg and Kellogg and of Hayes and Hayes), involved a minimum of confinement and a maximum of social interaction with human companions. For all practical purposes, the only verbal communication was in ASL, and the chimpanzee was maximally exposed to the use of this language by human beings.

It was necessary to develop a rough-and-ready mixture of training methods. There was evidence that some of Washoe's early signs were acquired by delayed imitation of the signing behavior of her human companions, but very few if any, of her early signs were introduced by immediate imitation. Manual babbling was directly fostered and did increase in the course of the project. A number of signs were introduced by shaping and instrumental conditioning. A particularly effective and convenient method of shaping consisted of holding Washoe's hands, forming them into a configuration, and putting them through the movements of a sign.

We have listed more than 30 signs that Washoe acquired and could use spontaneously and appropriately by the end of the 22nd month of the project. The signs acquired earliest were simple demands. Most of the later signs have been names for objects, which Washoe has used both as demands and as answers to questions. Washoe readily used noun signs to name pictures of objects and has frequently called the attention of her companions to pictures and objects by naming them. Once acquired, the signs have not remained specific to the original referents but have been transferred spontaneously to a wide class of appropriate referents. At this writing, Washoe's rate of acquisition of new signs is still accelerating.

From the time she had eight or ten signs in her repertoire, Washoe began to use them in strings of two or more. During the period covered by this article we made no deliberate effort to elicit combinations other than by our own habitual use of strings of signs. Some of the combined forms that Washoe has used may have been imitative, but many have been inventions of her own. Only a small proportion of the possible combinations have, in fact, been observed. This is because most of Washoe's combinations include one of a limited group of signs that act as combiners. Among the signs that Washoe has recently acquired are the pronouns "I-me" and "you." When these occur in combinations the result resembles a short sentence. In terms of the eventual level of communication that a chimpanzee might be able to attain, the most promising results have been spontaneous naming, spontaneous transfer to new referents, and spontaneous combinations and recombinations of signs.

REFERENCES AND NOTES

1. See, for example, E. H. Lenneberg, *Biological Foundations of Language* (Wiley, New York, 1967).
2. A. L. Bryan, *Curr. Anthropol.* 4, 297 (1963).
3. K. J. Hayes and C. Hayes, *Proc. Amer. Phil. Soc.* 95, 105 (1951).
4. K. J. Hayes, personal communication. Dr. Hayes also informed us that Viki used a few additional sounds which, while not resembling English words, were used for specific requests.
5. R. M. Yerkes, *Chimpanzees* (Yale Univ. Press, New Haven, 1943).

6. K. J. Hayes and C. Hayes, in *The Non-Human Primates and Human Evolution*, J. A. Gavan, Ed. (Wayne Univ. Press, Detroit, 1955), p. 110; W. N. Kellogg and L. A. Kellogg, *The Ape and the Child* (Hafner, New York, 1967; originally published by McGraw-Hill, New York, 1933); W. N. Kellogg, *Science 162*, 423 (1968).

7. W. C. Stokoe, D. Casterline, C. G. Croneberg, *A Dictionary of American Sign Language* (Gallaudet College Press, Washington, D.C., 1965); E. A. McCall, thesis, University of Iowa (1965).

8. J. Goodall, in *Primate Behavior*, I. DeVore, Ed. (Holt, Rinehart & Winston, New York, 1965), p. 425; A. J. Riopelle and C. M. Rogers, in *Behavior of Nonhuman Primates*, A. M. Schrier, H. F. Harlow, F. Stollnitz, Eds. (Academic Press, New York, 1965), p. 449.

9. R. M. Yerkes and B. W. Learned, *Chimpanzee Intelligence and Its Vocal Expression* (William & Wilkins, Baltimore, 1925), p. 53.

10. K. J. Hayes and C. Hayes, *J. Comp. Physiol. Psychol. 45*, 450 (1952).

11. C. J. Warden and L. H. Warner, *Quart. Rev. Biol. 3*, 1 (1928).

12. The development of Washoe's vocabulary of signs is being recorded on motion-picture film. At the time of this writing, 30 of the 34 signs listed in Table 1 are on film.

13. The research described in this article has been supported by National Institute of Mental Health grants MH-12154 and MH-34953 (Research Scientist Development Award to B. T. Gardner) and by National Science Foundation grant GB-7432. We acknowledge a great debt to the personnel of the Aeromedical Research Laboratory, Holloman Air Force Base, whose support and expert assistance effectively absorbed all of the many difficulties attendant upon the acquisition of a wild-caught chimpanzee. We are also grateful to Dr. Frances L. FitzGerald of the Yerkes Regional Primate Research Center for detailed advice on the care of an infant chimpanzee. Drs. Emanual Berger of Reno, Nevada, and D. B. Olsen of the University of Nevada have served as medical consultants, and we are grateful to them for giving so generously of their time and medical skills. The faculty of the Sarah Hamilton Fleischmann School of Home Economics, University of Nevada, has generously allowed us to use the facilities of their experimental nursery school on weekends and holidays.

25.
affection
in
primates

m. k. harlow
and h. f. harlow

The importance of love or affection as both a binding and a disruptive social mechanism has been recognized as long as the existence of written literature and no doubt for countless millenia before. Credit for focusing scientific attention on love belongs to Sigmund Freud above all others. He conceived of a broad life force, the libido, as the basis of interpersonal attachments, and he traced its development from the cradle to adult-drives and their satisfactions as the underlying mechanisms. His dogged persistence in publicizing the libido or, in a broad sense, love as the socializing force in human behavior left an indelible imprint on psychiatrists, psychologists, and anthropologists.

Freud's source of data, the neurotic adult of the late nineteenth- and early twentieth-century Western Europe, gave him intimate knowledge of the aberrations produced by interferences with libidinal drives. Sexual deviations were prominent symptoms in his patients, and fears, anxieties, dreams, amnesias, conversion symptoms, and the like were in many instances so clearly relatable to frustration or suppression of the biological sex drive, that libido came more and more to connote sex drive and less and less his broader concept.

Cultural anthropologists particularly have stressed the satisfaction of the sex drive in their theories about the origin of human societies. Great emphasis has been placed on the importance of the receptivity of the human female throughout the menstrual cycle and even during

Reprinted from *Discovery*, 1966, 27, 11–17. By courtesy of *Science Journal* (London). Abridged by permission of the authors.

pregnancy and lactation. This phenomenon has been used to account for the formation of the family, because the continuous receptivity of the female assures the male of continuing sexual gratification through permanent association with a wife or wives. Apart from family organization, basic law has been widely attributed to the sex drive—a strong drive without natural inhibition. Control of this drive through rules and regulations has characterized every social group subjected to study. Circumstances under which young societies lived must have varied widely, and so must the restrictions. With time, rules became more divergent, more comprehensive, and more formalized, and their bases were progressively obscured. In the remaining primitive groups today, the mores show elaborate restrictions on sex and family relationships, but their origins are lost in antiquity.

SEARCHING FOR THE BASIS OF SOCIAL ORGANIZATION

To find simple groups in which to test the sexual theory of social organization, the cultural anthropologist turned to subhuman primates. The basic assumption has been that these close relatives of man share his biological origin and an environment comparable to that in which early man developed. In their simple nomadic existence, nonhuman primates today must encounter the problems of individual and species survival that early man once faced. Thus observation of the social organization of apes and monkeys should elucidate the social organization of early human groups. Field studies were not long in confirming that sex was the key to primary social organization, and the theory flourished as late as 1960. But about this time a new trend appeared. In 1961 Sherwood Washburn and Irven DeVore, in reporting their baboon field work, wrote: "Our data offer little support for the theory that sexuality provides the primary bond of the primate troop. It is the intensely social nature of the baboon expressed in a diversity of interindividual relationships, that keeps the troop together." Indeed, they noted the relative infrequency of receptivity in female baboons and theorized that, rather than being the magnet that holds the horde together, sex can disrupt the normal social organization.

Subsequent field studies have yielded data that also appear to conflict with the sexual theory of sociality. The chimpanzees observed by Jane Godall engaged in much sexual activity but showed low group stability. The intensive study of mountain gorillas by George Schaller revealed little sexual activity but extremely high group stability. Schaller found that females were receptive only in estrus, which does not occur during pregnancy or lactation. Since mature females were usually either pregnant or lactating, opportunity for copulation was infrequent, but group life proceeded peacefully. Schaller estimated that males might go a year or more without any opportunity for copulation, and even when a female came into estrus, her state aroused little troop interest and no fighting. She chose her partner without interference, and in each instance that Schaller observed, the partner happened to be a nondominant male.

The sex theory of primate social organization has apparently given way: the current interest is in social learning and interpersonal relationships to explain primate cohesiveness. Even before the demise of the sex theory, however, laboratory researchers into the social development of rhesus monkeys were well underway at the University of Wisconsin, and they independently pointed to a multiplicity of affectional bonds to account for the sociality of this species and, in a general way, of all primates. Although the laboratory cannot provide the richness of environment, either physical or social, that characterizes the natural habitat, it can introduce experimental controls, making possible a depth of analysis of affectional behavior that either cannot or has not been achieved on primates in the wild.

We believe that the role of affection in socialization of primates can only be understood by conceiving love as a number of love or affectional systems and not as a single emotion. We have identified five such systems in the rhesus monkey, each of which develops in a series of orderly stages. Anatomical and physiological characteristics underlying each system predispose the individual to react in particular ways, but the general capacity of the individual to learn with experience also plays an important part. In general, as the sequence of affectional systems develops in the life of the individual, the effects of prior social experience become more and more powerful in shaping affectional responsiveness. The affectional systems apparent in the rhesus monkey are also seen in other monkeys, in apes, and in man. Although the data are not complete for any affectional system, the exploratory work for most systems is well underway and the broad outlines are evident.

THE INFANT-MOTHER AFFECTIONAL SYSTEM

The rhesus monkey at birth is equipped with reflexes that enable it to cling tenaciously to its mother and to inch its way upward on her body until restrained by her arms, which automatically stop the infant at breast level if she is standing on all fours or moving about, as mothers usually are in the wild. Other reflexes cause it to orient toward the nipple, open its mouth, grasp the nipple, and suck. For the first two to three weeks of life, the infant's attachment to its mother is primarily reflex, and we refer to this period as the reflex stage. The infant only gradually enters the stage of attachment and comfort, characterized by increasing voluntary responses to replace the automatic ones. In this second stage of its relationships to its mother, the infant can move about awkwardly on a level surface and climb with some control, can and does voluntarily attach to the mother and seek out the nipple, and it becomes quiet when picked up by its mother. If the infant is raised with a pair of artificial mothers, one cloth-covered and one wire, it spends most of its time in contact with the cloth body even if it is fed on the wire mother (see Figure 1). Contact *per se* seems to be a primary factor in the infant-mother relationship, even superseding nursing.

Ape babies are less mature at birth and cannot cling as effectively as monkeys, and human babies have only the vestige of a clinging reflex. Both ape and human place an obligation on the mother to provide physical support for the newborn and to position it for nursing, but the normal mother's behaviour guarantees the infant the comforts of contact and nursing. These higher primates reach the stage of voluntary attachment much later.

The third stage in the infant's tie to its mother, a stage of security, is attained through some complex combination of maturation and learning. The newly born monkey shows no fear and can be readily handled without disturbance. But after the first few months, the monkey baby shows growing uneasiness when removed from its mother, real or artificial, and contacts her at the threat of removal and clings to her. With the contact, the infant relaxes. Strange objects soon become fear objects, and the infant away from its mother rushes to contact her, then relaxes. Gradually, the infant comes to contact the mother when frightened and then to go out and explore the fearsome object. Eventually, the infant needs only the sight of the mother to assure it in a strange situation. Ape and human babies show the same phenomena, but at more advanced ages in keeping with their slower maturation.

With the full development of security in the mother's presence, the infant becomes an active creature free to explore its environment—broadening its social contacts, and learning to solve the many problems of this new world. For the rhesus baby, this marks the start of a lengthy separation stage, the fourth stage of the infant-mother relationship, that eventually emancipates it from its mother physically and psychologically some time after the first year of life. For

Figure 1. Infant feeds from wire mother substitute while anchored to a cloth one. In the second stage of its relationship with the mother, the infant may voluntarily move away. But bodily contact remains important, even superseding nursing.

other monkeys the stage may come a little later. Apes attain this separation after three or four or more years and the human child is later still, how late being determined in large part by the culture. A full appreciation of the processes involved can only be obtained after consideration of the second and fourth affectional systems, which involve the relationship of the young monkey with other infants and the behaviour of the mother herself towards the baby monkey.

THE PEER AFFECTIONAL SYSTEM

In the laboratory we have studied the development of peer affection in two kinds of experimental situations. The first is the playpen, in which four infants live from birth in large cages with their own, adoptive, or artificial mothers but have sole access to adjoining play compartments where they can interact for fixed periods of time with their age-mates. Our second situation is a playroom equipped with ladders, artificial tree, ramps, swings, and toys where a

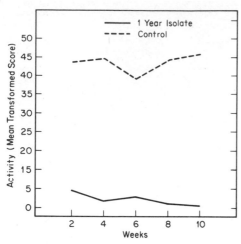

Figure 2. Depression of play in monkeys in the social playroom after 12 months of total social isolation. Three months leaves only rudiments of playfulness but 12 months of isolation destroys all potentialities for socialization. These latter monkeys are fearful and almost totally lacking in either aggression or play.

group of four monkeys is released during a fixed period each day for free play. In each of these situations, the pattern of play is in keeping with reports of monkey and ape play in the field. The principal difference is that laboratory monkeys play earlier, apparently because mothers in the wild tend to hold back their infants longer, whereas in the secure environment of the laboratory, mothers adjust sooner to having their infants leave to play or, in some situations, there are no mothers to exercise restraint.

Infants with real mothers may play earlier and more vigorously during the first six months than do infants with artificial mothers, but by the end of the first year, the groups are difficult to distinguish. A number of groups of adolescents have now been raised with peer associations but with mothering ranging from none to natural mothering, and they seem to be socially normal animals regardless of mothering condition. Infants raised with their own mothers for four or eight months before being permitted to see or play with peers come to play quickly and develop complex play

rapidly, but their play shows wariness of contact and more aggression than that of infants associating together from the first month of life. Moreover, the eight-month group is more fearful and more hostile than the four-month group, and these characteristics persist even in the third year of life and will probably be permanent. We also have a large number of monkeys lacking both mothering and peer experience in the first year, and without exception they are socially inadequate even though some females have been bred and have produced infants. Their behaviour will be discussed under the heterosexual and maternal affectional systems.

Several other studies emphasize further the importance of early peer experience. Monkeys raised from birth in total isolation and released at 3, 6, or 12 months of age and given regular playroom experience show different patterns. Three months of social isolation leaves no scars; the animals develop normally. Six months of isolation makes the monkeys extremely fearful and leaves them with only rudiments of playfulness. In adolescence they are both overly aggressive and overly fearful, responding to social situations in most inappropriate ways as compared with normal monkeys. Twelve months of isolation destroy all potential for socialization. The monkeys, after release and even in adolescence, are fearful and almost totally lacking in aggression and play (see Figure 2).

The affection which builds up between individuals in a play group is clearly shown by the cohesion of the group when brought into contact with other separately reared groups. It is also emphasized by the speed and enthusiasm of their contact with one another when released into the playroom or when barriers between playpen units are raised. In the wild and in large groupings in captivity monkeys and apes show clear friendship patterns from infancy through adulthood. Males and females associate together early in life, but gradually the sexes separate, probably because of inherent physical and physiological differences that tend to make males more active and aggressive and females more sedentary and more submissive.

THE HETEROSEXUAL
AFFECTIONAL SYSTEM

The origins of this system in the rhesus monkey lie in the play of infants. The laboratory data suggest that rhesus monkeys—and presumably other monkeys and apes—need to develop affectional attachments to their peers in infancy or, at least, by the early juvenile period if they are to develop an acceptance of bodily contact, a basic requirement for copulation and other heterosexual activities. Rhesus monkeys show maturation of fear by three months, mild aggression several months later, and true aggression in the second year. If their social experience is delayed so that they do not develop affectional ties before the emergence of fear and aggression, they may as adolescents and adults show both fear and hostility toward potential sexual partners as well as toward members of the same sex. Moreover, males, if they are to learn to integrate the various postural adjustments and motor skills required for their role in copulation, need practice. The female role is a more passive one and apparently some socially delayed females can eventually adjust posturally and accept male contact sufficiently to become passable sexual partners. Inhibition of fear and aggression with consequent acceptance of bodily contact is the major learning problem here.

An area of confusion in the study of heterosexual behaviour is the interpretation put upon the basic postural responses that eventually become part of the copulatory act. Mounting is a natural, unlearned response that through learning acquires not only sexual significance but broad social significance in monkeys and apes because it serves as an expression of either dominance or submission, depending upon the species, the sex and age of the individual, and the social situation. Similarly, presenting in both males and females is a common sign of submission or it is a sexual invitation by females, depending upon the circumstances. Both these responses must consequently be interpreted only in context.

Why in mating some potential partners are rejected and others accepted are questions not answered in the field studies. But it would be most unreasonable to assume that among animals as social as the primates the female in estrus is guided only by her hormones or that the male in the presence of an estrous female is excited only by her sexual state. We believe that the kind of affectional tie between infants or juveniles or between adult males or adult females also persists between members of the opposite sexes and plays a role in heterosexual behaviour. On this basis, we refer to the heterosexual ties as the "heterosexual affectional system," thus emphasizing the affectional aspects as well as the underlying biological sex drive. In most monkeys and apes, if there is very close association of males and females, it is confined to the female's estrus, but also among most of these primates and also among those that show no consort patterns, there are continuous casual and even friendly or avoidant contacts between males and females within a group, and it seems reasonable that these individuals should have preferences and aversions toward members of the opposite sex just as they have individual preferences and aversions among their own sex. In the laboratory breeding stock males and females show similar preferences, and through experience we have learned which pairings to avoid because they are apt to lead to an hour of inactivity instead of copulation.

Lest the reader assume that human and subhuman primates can be separated on the basis of differences in the development of heterosexual behaviour, it should be noted that children in permissive cultures openly show sex play long before puberty, and only when puberty sets in does adult authority control their behaviour. Moreover, reflexive erection is common in male babies from birth, as are reflexive thrusting and voluntary autoerotic behaviour in both males and females. Human adults generally set controls on voluntary infantile sexual behaviours and thus artificially obscure the developmental sequence. In fact, as in the subhuman primates, sex behaviour has its origins in infancy and develops according to the restrictions imposed by the culture. Just as mores control sexual behaviour among individuals in human groups from infancy onward, so in subhuman primates overall social conditions in the group seem to play a role in determining the nature and conditions of copulation among adolescents and adults.

THE MATERNAL AFFECTIONAL SYSTEM

Like the heterosexual affectional system, the maternal affectional system has its origins in infancy. The birth of a baby to a normal female sets in motion a sequence of behaviours that serve to nourish and protect the relatively helpless newborn. In the rhesus mother, this initial period is one of close physical attachment, the complement of the reflexive stage of the infant's attachment to the mother, and she willingly accepts all infants. As the infant gains control of its movements, the mother relaxes her hold somewhat, but her behaviour remains totally acceptant and affectionate, and she rarely lets the baby go beyond arm's reach. During the first three months, the mother gives almost continuous attention to her infant and rarely punishes it, although the amount of cradling and holding declines gradually as the infant demands more freedom to move about and exercise its developing motor skills. If the infant escapes, the mother shows intense disturbance and attempts to retrieve it. In the play-pen situation, where the mother is unable to retrieve the infant from the pen, she watches it and shows anxiety over its every contact with another infant or mother. If either the infant's playmate or the playmate's mother seems to be threatening or hurting her infant, she screams and threatens and may punish the other infant when it comes within her reach.

The second stage of rhesus maternal behaviour, the ambivalence stage, begins about three months after the birth of the baby. Even before this the mother shows many rejecting responses to babies not her own, but she now begins to punish her own infant from time to time although her overall treatment is positive and tender. Gradually the rejecting responses increase until the infant learns to anticipate her intentions and to avoid her when trouble threatens. Whether physiological factors or the growing nuisance character of the infant, or both, determine her behaviour is unknown, but the outcome is to encourage the infant to spend more of its time away from her and to find solace with its peers. At this period social play greatly accelerates and peer affectional ties build.

In the wild, the ambivalence stage leads to separation, but in the laboratory, we have never seen spontaneous separation of mother and infant or even alienation although some have lived together until the young were almost two. This is doubtless because we have not bred the mothers during this period nor offered them other companionship, and so the affectional ties of the mother for her offspring were not strained by competing social attractions. Close mother-offspring ties, especially between mothers and daughters, may well persist in the wild but have not been detected because of the short terms of study in the field. Only in the experimental colonies where marked animals are kept under semi-wild conditions is long-term tracing of genealogy certain. In Puerto Rico, where such a rhesus colony has been maintained for many years, mother-daughter groupings are common, and it has also been noted that male offspring, after they have left the female group, may show special friendly relations with their mothers. Goodall suspected that some subgroupings of chimpanzees containing a female with infant, juvenile, and adolescents and even young adults, might be mother-child groupings.

The mother-child interrelationship is the closest a primate experiences in its lifetime, and in subhuman primates it is closer and more intimate than in most human cultures although shorter in duration. Monkey and ape social groups permit mothers to give their full attention to infant care in the early stages of development while most human mothers by-pass infant care to a certain extent through cribs, playpens, nursing bottles —even bottle holders—nurses, fathers and baby-sitters. Were the close mother infant relationship of the monkeys and apes to persist in full strength when the infant is mature enough to run and climb and find food on its own, there would

Figure 3. Normal maternal behaviour (left) contrasts sharply with the abusive (right) behaviour of a motherless mother. These motherless monkeys were also allowed no social experience. So far only two of them have even approached normality. Four killed their infants and the others have been either excessively brutal or indifferent. Most surprising has been the behaviour of three abusive mothers and one indifferent mother that have had second and, in two cases, third babies—all four have been adequate mothers to these subsequent babies. They appear to have been socialized by their first infants.

be less desire to form other affectional ties, less chance for the young to be integrated into the larger social group, and consequently little reproduction outside a family group. Thus primate species and, indeed, all mammalian species, can survive only if the maternal ties are weakened and the young can form alliances with their own generation.

Under natural living conditions, the young eventually become part of the larger social group, develop friendships, mate, and the females become mothers and the males become the leaders and protectors of the group. Under the artificial conditions of the laboratory, however, we have been able to raise some infants without real mothers and with no social experience in the first year of life. We have already indicated that these animals were fearful or hostile or both when given opportunities to mate after maturity, but ten of the females have successfully produced babies through voluntary insemination and six have been inseminated while restrained in a rack.

As a group they have been cruel or indifferent mothers to their first infants (see Figure 3). Only two of them even approached normality, and both were mothers that had been part of a group allowed to live relatively freely during adolescence on an island in the Madison zoo. Four mothers killed their infants and one bit off six fingers of her baby within an hour of birth and would probably have killed it had it not been taken from her. Three more mothers were excessively brutal but the infants survived. The remaining four were indifferent, failed to nurse their babies so that artificial feeding was required to maintain them, and showed high rejection and punishment, although they did not seek out the babies to mistreat them. A gibbon in the Madison zoo showed similar rejection of its offspring and such behaviour is apparently quite common among gorillas in captivity.

However, most surprising to us is the behaviour of the motherless mothers that have had later babies. Thus far, three abusive and two indifferent mothers have had second babies and one of each group, third babies. Four have been adequate mothers to these subsequent babies. One indifferent mother has been indifferent to her second baby. Thus these females deprived of the early opportunity to form affectional ties appear to have become socialized by their first infants even though they treated them badly, so that they could with one exception treat their later babies adequately.

The physiological changes that accompany parturition are obviously not sufficient to insure good maternal behaviour in monkeys: some affectional experience is also necessary. Good maternal behaviour can even appear without the physiological support that accompanies parturition. In adoption studies we have found that females whose babies were taken from them at birth many months beforehand readily adopted young infants offered to them and treated them in a totally acceptant and protective manner as long as we have left the infants with them—a matter of months. Field studies also report instances of childless adult females picking up unattended infants in the wild, but the babies were always retrieved by their own mothers. How extensive this readiness to adopt infants may be, is not known yet, and further research is needed to define the necessary conditions and the limits for it. The importance of experience and prior observation of infants by females during their development within the social group is also left for future research. We hope soon to have some answers for the laboratory rhesus when our females raised with peers, or with mothers and peers, but without seeing or contacting monkeys younger than themselves, give birth to their own infants.

THE PATERNAL AFFECTIONAL SYSTEM

The paternal affectional system refers to the affection of adult males for the young of their species, whether the young are their offspring, as in most human cultures, more remote relatives as in some human cultural groups, or unrelated as in most nonhuman primates. There are no special physiological changes that occur in males when new babies are born to females, and so paternal behaviour cannot be explained by underlying physiological conditions. Both field and laboratory data are scanty yet observations clearly establish the existence of the pattern in human and subhuman primates, and what information we have suggests that it depends upon earlier establishment of affectional ties to members of the species.

Instances of reported paternal behaviour in group-living primates in the field usually involve large, highly dominant males. Among baboons there are observations of males adopting weak, displaced, or motherless older infants or young juveniles and transporting them and protecting them for long periods. There are observations of dominant males staying with new mothers unable to keep up with the group. Among Japanese macaques studied intensively in semi-wild conditions, there are data on the practice within some groups, but not all, for dominant males to adopt specific infants of about 10 to 12 months of age before the mothers give birth to new infants and to give special protection to the adoptees in the transitional period to juvenile living. Among various primates studied in the field there are observations of vicious attacks by males on intruders when infants have strayed from the group into the vicinity of the outsider or when the intruder was trying to steal the infant. There are also reports of males rushing to the aid of an injured infant or juvenile and protecting it from further harm until its mother could arrive to take over its care.

In almost all groups studied the gentle, tolerant attitude of dominant males toward infants is an outstanding characteristic of their behaviour. Acts that would elicit threat or attack if committed by older members of the group are either ignored or responded to positively by large adult males if the offender is a youngster. The species which would appear to be most deviant in this respect is the rhesus. Although little is known about the behaviour of the forest rhesus in India, there are observations of urban living rhesus in India and semi-wild rhesus in Puerto Rico which indicate that infants are not immune to abuse from adult males. While these males show many more instances of protective behaviour towards the youngsters and many evidences of acceptance of them, there are also reports of threats and even attacks made on older infants that got in the way of large males that were eating or that bumped into them inadvertently. This may reflect the generally more aggressive nature of the rhesus as compared with other monkeys (excepting possibly the baboons) and with all apes that have been studied. Attacks on infants by free-living adult males in other species are not reported in the literature.

Our laboratory data on paternal behaviour to date are limited. We do, however, have one study comparing the behaviour of adolescent rhesus males raised in isolation with that of adolescent males raised with mothers and peers in the first year of life. For each group a male was placed in a playroom with a young juvenile and observed. No socially raised male ever attacked the younger monkey, but the three males raised in social isolation for six months of their first year of life showed intense and unprovoked aggression against the juvenile. Thus, as in the study of maternal behaviour, early social deprivation appears to be a factor in abuse of the young.

AFFECTIONAL BONDS—
THE KEY TO PRIMATE EVOLUTION

These five affectional systems observed in monkeys in the laboratory seem to fit well with data collected in the field on both monkeys and apes and with the knowledge we have of human bonds. The aberrations of affectional behaviour that occur with social deprivation in subhuman primates in the laboratory and in zoos have their counterparts at the human level in the difficulties exhibited by many children and adults who were deprived of mothering or peer experience in infancy and childhood.

Human behaviour is far more complicated than ape or monkey behaviour, for human beings are more intelligent, more versatile, more subtle, and live in more complex societies. One cannot generalize from monkey or ape to man, but one may find parallels in the socialization process by observing these animals that evolved from the same remote ancestors as early man. Primates could not have evolved as we know them today if their only social bond were sex. The defence strength of living primates is in the group, not the individual, and to assure group living on a sex-bond basis females would have had to evolve as more frequently receptive creatures than are the living subhuman primate females. Without group living, primates would have had to develop specialized individual protection as, for example, have the cats, and they could not have afforded the luxury of a long developmental period prior to and after birth.

The evolution of the potentialities for forming strong affectional bonds must have played a role in the success of the Primate Order in the development of adaptable social organizations. With positive ties within and between sexes and within and between age ranges, the group could cohere, permitting animals relatively weak and poorly designed for individual defence to act co-operatively to hold predators in check. Insofar as intelligence and adaptability through learning contribute to co-operative defence and exploitation of the environment, so these traits rather than specializations for physical defence could be selective factors in survival of group-living creatures. Long gestation periods and long developmental periods after birth permitted increasingly greater intellectual development and learning, helping adaptation to changing environments, and these extended periods could only evolve in group-living animals that could protect the mothers and the young. If sex played the leading role in the cohesiveness of the earliest primates, it lost its strength early, for no living nonhuman primate species to our knowledge has females that show continuous sexual receptivity, and there is reason to believe that the human female's more or less continuous receptivity has a greater psychological than physiological basis.

26.
effects of social reinforcement on operant crying

betty m. hart, k. eileen allen,
joan s. buell, florence r. harris,
and montrose m. wolf

The application of reinforcement principles as a preschool guidance technique under field conditions has recently come under study (Allen et al., in press; Harris et al., 1964, Johnston et al., 1963). Other applications made under field conditions in hospital situations include Wolf's treatment of autism in a child (Wolf et al., 1964) and Ayllon's work with psychotic patients (Ayllon and Haughton, 1962). The present paper deals with the application of reinforcement principles to two cases of "operant crying."

Two classes of crying behavior seem readily discriminable on an "intuitive" basis by almost every teacher and parent: respondent crying and operant crying. Criteria for each class can be defined in terms of its dependent variables. Respondent crying occurs in response to a sudden unexpected and/or painful stimulus event. In general, preschool teachers assume crying to be respondent if the child has a hard or sudden fall; if he falls in an awkward position or is caught in equipment; if he is forced down and pummeled by a larger child; or if he has just faced a dire, unexpected event, such as a near accident. Teachers attend at once to respondent crying. Operant crying, on the other hand, is emitted and/or maintained depending upon its effects on the social environment. In general, the most clear-cut indication that a cry-

ing episode is operant rather than respondent is that the child looks around momentarily and makes eye-contact with an adult before he begins to cry. An increase in the volume and intensity of the child's cry when an adult fails to attend immediately, together with the child's neither calling nor coming for help, provides other criteria for operant crying. Crying that is initially respondent may readily become operant.

Since by 3 years of age children vary widely in their patterns of response to pain-fear situations, any reasonably exact discrimination between respondent and operant crying of an individual child can be made only on the basis of close daily observation of his crying behavior.

This paper presents two studies of the systematic use of positive social reinforcement to help children showing a high rate of operant crying to acquire more effective behavior in mildly distressful situations. Although the studies were conducted at different times, procedures and recording methods were the same in each.

METHOD

Subjects

Both subjects were enrolled in the Laboratory Preschool at the University of Washington. Both were in the same group, which included eight boys and eight girls of similar age (4–4½), socioeconomic level (upper middle class), and intelligence (above average). All children attended school five mornings a week for approximately 2½ hours.

Subject 1. The first subject, Bill, was 4 years and 1 month old when he en-

Reprinted from *Journal of Experimental Child Psychology*, 1964, 1, 145–163. Abridged by permission of the authors.

The authors acknowledge their indebtedness to Sidney W. Bijou, Donald M. Baer, and Jay S. Birnbrauer for frequent consultation and ready assistance with technical and procedural problems.

tered school. He was a tall, healthy, handsome child with well-developed verbal, social, and motor skills. Outdoors he ran, climbed, and rode a tricycle with energy and agility; indoors, he made use of all the available materials, though he appeared to prefer construction materials such as blocks, or imaginative play in the housekeeping corner, to activities such as painting or working with clay. His verbalizations to both teachers and children were characterized by persuasive and accurate use of vocabulary, and frequently demonstrated unusually sophisticated conceptualizations. He and many of the other children who entered nursery school at the same time had been together in a group situation the previous year and were thus fairly well acquainted. His former teachers had described Bill as a child eagerly sought by other children as a playmate. His capability and desirability as a playmate were immediately evident at the beginning of the second year. He moved almost directly into play with two other boys, and with his many good ideas structured one play situation after another with them, situations which often lasted an entire morning. Bill was frequently observed arbitrating differences of opinion between his playmates, insisting on his own way of doing things, or defending his own rights and ideas; nearly always, he did so verbally rather than physically.

In the first few days of school, teachers noted that in spite of Bill's sophisticated techniques for dealing with children, he cried more often during the morning than any other child in school. If he stubbed his toe while running or bumped his elbow on a piece of furniture, he cried until a teacher went to him. If he fell down, or if he was frustrated or threatened with any kind of physical attack by another child, he screamed and cried; all play, his and his companions', stopped until Bill had had several minutes of comfort from a teacher. In view of his advanced verbal and social skills, teachers questioned whether his crying was due to actual injury or maintained by adult attention.

Subject 2. The second subject, Alan, lacked 2 weeks of being 4 years old

when he entered the Preschool. He was enrolled in the same 4-year-old group as Bill. Unlike Bill, however, Alan was new to the group and therefore had had no previous acquaintance with any of the children. He spent most of the first month of school exploring with vigor all the equipment, materials, and social situations the school had to offer. He climbed, rode trikes, swung and dug, with skill and application. His use of creative materials was free and imaginative; his block-buildings were complex, intricately balanced structures. With children and adults he spoke confidently and assertively, often demanding that they listen to a lengthy story or fulfill his requests immediately. He defended himself both verbally and physically, holding on tenaciously to a possession or saying, "Don't!" over and over. Sometimes he forcibly appropriated an object from another child, calling names when the child resisted; but though he was the physical equal or superior of most of the others, he rarely attacked another child. He was attractive and vivacious as well as skillful. By the end of the first 6 weeks of school he was playing as an integral member of one or more groups of children every morning.

Though he did not cry quite as often as Bill, Alan cried equally as hard over much the same kinds of bumps and falls. Like Bill, he screamed and cried whenever another child succeeded in appropriating an object in his possession. He was observed to endure shoving and even hitting by a child smaller than he but to cry vociferously at a push by a child equal to him in size and strength. Though Alan's crying was noted from the beginning of school, the staff thought that Alan should fully adapt to the school situation and develop in play skills before any procedures were undertaken to deal directly with his crying behavior.

In dealing with both Alan and Bill, a distinction was made between respondent and operant crying. Teachers had observed that neither was unjustifiably aggressive; both could defend themselves, were physically strong and large relative to the group, and had better than average physical, verbal, and social skills. Neither had injured himself or been in-

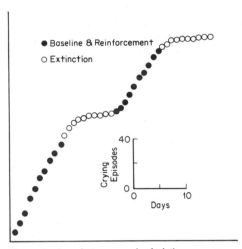

Figure 1. Cumulative record of daily operant crying episodes of Subject 1, Bill.

jured by another child in the group. Both were often observed to make momentary eye-contact with a teacher before beginning to cry, and the cries of both rapidly increased in volume until a teacher attended to them. Teachers agreed that both children would benefit if the frequency of crying episodes could be decreased and if more appropriate responses to mild pain and frustration could be developed.

Recording of Crying Episodes

In both cases the operant crying behavior was recorded by a teacher using a pocket counter. She depressed the lever on the counter once for each crying episode. A crying episode was defined as a cry (a) loud enough to be heard at least 50 feet away and (b) of 5 seconds or more duration. At the end of the day the total number of crying episodes was recorded and plotted on a cumulative graph.

Procedures for Presenting and Withdrawing Reinforces

For 10 days before initiating reinforcement-extinction procedures, the number of Bill's operant crying episodes per morning was to be recorded in order to obtain a baseline record of the operant level of the behavior. This was done at the end of his first month of school. A baseline record of Alan's daily crying episodes was similarly planned several months later, after Alan had attended school for 3 months.

For each child, extinction of operant crying was to be instituted immediately after these data had been secured. Teachers were to ignore each child's operant cries, neither going to him, speaking to him, nor looking at him while he was crying, except for an initial glance in order to assess the situation. If he was in close proximity to a teacher when he began to cry, she was to turn her back or walk away to be busy with another child. However, every time that either child responded in a more appropriate manner after a fall, scrape, push, or dispossession, however minor, he was immediately to be given much teacher attention and approval.

In order to substantiate the hypothesis that the operant crying of these children was truly a function of adult reinforcement, it was judged necessary, if the extinction process was successful, to reinstate the behavior. At first teachers were to give attention to every approximation to a cry, such as whimpering and sulking; then, if and when the behavior was re-established in strength, they were to go to the child immediately every time he began to cry and give him solicitous attention for several minutes.

If and when operant crying had again reached a level similar to that of the baseline period, it was again to be extinguished. The procedures of the first extinction period were to be re-instituted, teachers ignoring all operant cries by turning away or focusing their attention elsewhere. At the same time, they were to reinforce the boys for all verbal responses emitted during mild pain or frustration. As the second extinction progressed, teachers were gradually to refine the criteria for reinforcement to "appropriate" verbal behavior evoked by minor injuries and frustrations. Threats and name-calling were to be ignored, and attention given only for such verbalizations as "Stop that," "That hurts," "Ouch!" or explanation of prior possession.

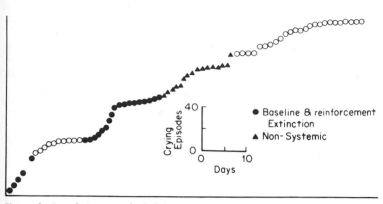

Figure 2. Cumulative record of daily operant crying episodes of Subject 2, Alan.

RESULTS

Subject 1. As can be seen in the baseline period for Bill (see Figure 1), at the beginning of the study he was crying 5–10 times every morning at school. Within 5 days after introduction of extinction procedures his operant crying decreased to between 0 and 2 episodes per day. When continuous adult attention was again given to all operant cries and approximations to cries, the baseline rate of crying episodes was soon reestablished. Then, 4 days after re-introduction of extinction for operant crying, the behavior was practically eliminated.

Subject 2. Alan's rate of operant crying during the baseline period (see Figure 2) averaged about 5 episodes per morning. As with Bill, Alan's crying episodes decreased to 2 or fewer per day within 5 days after the introduction of extinction procedures. The behavior again reached a level nearly as high as baseline 4 days after reinforcement of operant crying was re-instituted, and maintained approximately this level for 6 days. On the eleventh day of reinstatement of operant crying, the behavior suddenly decreased to one or fewer episodes per day (day 28, Figure 2). After continuing reinforcement procedures for more days, teachers decided that, though their attention may have initially reinstated the behavior, other uncontrolled factors in the environment had apparently led to its cessation. Therefore, systematic reinforcement techniques were discontinued (after day 35 on Figure 2).

However, very soon the behavior reappeared and gradually increased in frequency until on the 50th day it had reached a frequency almost double that of the baseline period. Extinction procedures were again introduced (on day 51, Figure 2). The rate of operant crying dropped much more gradually this time than had Bill's: there was a burst on the 56th day, and it was not until 10 days later that operant crying episodes stabilized at one or fewer per day.

DISCUSSION

During the extinction periods for both Bill and Alan, teachers noticed no unexpected side-effects. They had anticipated that play would become more rewarding to both children once the frequent interruptions for crying episodes were eliminated. Each of the children, during the extinction periods, sustained a cooperative, sometimes directing, role in play. Each appeared to become more constructively absorbed in such play, often to the point of appearing oblivious to persons outside the realm of the imaginative play situation.

Subject 1. After Bill's operant crying was reinstated and his play was again being interrupted six or seven times a morning for operant crying episodes, teachers began to notice occasional signs of impatience on his part. Even as teachers comforted him and he continued to shriek, he sometimes turned away from their comfort, though he did not leave. Also, the extent of the interruption of his play seemed more noticeable than it had during the baseline period. At that time his companions had often ignored, or retreated from, his crying episodes. During the reinstatement period they usually remained near Bill, watching him throughout the episode. Teachers thought that the powerful reinforcement that Bill obtained from play with his companions greatly contributed to the rapidity of the second extinction process.

Subject 2. After Alan's operant crying had risen during the reinstatement period to a rate equal to that of the baseline period, the sudden disappearance of the behavior was completely unexpected. Teachers continued to reinforce all cries and approximations to cries for 7 more days before deciding that some other factor in the environment had apparently decreased Alan's operant crying. Only after reinforcement procedures had been discontinued and the behavior had begun to reappear did teachers reflect on the possible significance of particular behaviors they had observed during the reinstatement period. At that time they had noticed that Alan often screwed up his face as though about to emit a loud cry when he was in close proximity to them. In accordance with the reinforcement procedures in effect, they immediately offered him comfort, and frequently he did not actually cry (only audible cries were counted in the data). One day, for example, Alan was climbing on an iron frame, a teacher watching him. As he climbed down from the frame he screwed up his face and clutched his ankle. The teacher approached at once, asked what had happened and comforted him. Alan explained that he had bumped his ankle, and then said, "I'm going to do that [climb the frame] again." As he descended the frame a second time, Allan bumped his leg and, looking at the teacher, emitted a low whimper. The teacher immediately comforted him,

whereupon he again climbed the frame, and again bumped himself descending. On none of these occasions did Alan actually cry. It appeared, upon subsequent reflection, that Alan did not need to cry: he had apparently effectively "shaped up" a teacher to give him comfort and attention whenever he merely looked as if he were about to cry.

When systematic reinforcement procedures were discontinued and Alan's "looking as if he were about to cry" was no longer given immediate adult attention and comfort, full-scale operant crying reappeared and was apparently reinforced in the period that followed, on some sort of unsystematic intermittent schedule. The rate of operant crying increased irregularly; the decline in rate after several days of a rise in rate might possibly be correlated with (a) teachers' having inadvertently put the behavior on extinction for a time after it became aversive to them, and (b) such frequent interruptions in Alan's play that his playmates moved away from him and into other activities. These intervals of extinction, if such they were, were not however, planned procedures.

After systematic extinction procedures were reinstated, Alan's operant crying behavior extinguished much more gradually than had Bill's. A possible cause was the preceding unsystematic intermittent schedule of reinforcement in Alan's case. In the literature (e.g., Ferster and Skinner, 1957) it has been well demonstrated that extinction after a continuous schedule of reinforcement is more rapid than after an intermittent schedule.

Though many of the findings concerning Alan's operant crying are still conjectural, the data from the studies seem to demonstrate that frequent crying may be largely a function of social reinforcement. The implications for parents and teachers in helping children to behave more appropriately appear evident.

REFERENCES

Allen, K. Eileen, Hart, Betty M., Harris, Florence R., and Wolf, M. M. Effects of social reinforcement on isolate behavior of a preschool child. *Child Develpm.* In press.

Ayllon, T., and Haughton, E. Control of the behavior of schizophrenic patients by food. *J. exp. anal. Behav.*, 1962, 5, 343–352.

Ferster, C. B., and Skinner, B. F. *Schedules of reinforcement.* New York: Appleton-Century-Crofts, 1957.

Harris, Florence R., Johnson, Margaret S., Kelley, C. Susan, and Wolf, M. M. Effects of positive social reinforcement on regressed crawling in a preschool child. *J. ed. Psychol.*, 1964, *55*, 35–41.

Johnston, Margaret S., Kelley, C. Susan, Buell, Joan S., Harris, Florence R., and

Wolf, M. M. Effects of positive social reinforcement on isolate behavior of a nursery school child. Unpublished manuscript, 1963.

Wolf, M., Mees, H., and Risley, T. Application of operant conditioning procedures to the behavior problems of an autistic child. *Behav. Res. Ther.*, 1964, *2*, 305–312.

27.
a transistorized signal-package for toilet training of infants

r. keith van wagenen
and everett e. murdock

In toilet training, one of the key features is that parents be able to immediately detect a urination or defecation event. A device has been developed for this purpose which mounts on the side of an infant and which places almost no restrictions on his movement. When the child produces an expulsion, a small speaker gives a clear tone signal which can be readily heard throughout an average-sized home. The tone signal is emitted when urine or moisture from fecal matter contacts a grid sewed into the child's training pants, thus closing the speaker circuit. The prototype package carried at waist level on the infant, weighs 4½ ounces and 2 x 2½ x 1¼ inches when contained in a polyethelene cigarette case. These dimensions could be reduced by employing a smaller speaker, which in the case of the prototype was 2 x ¾ inches. Power for the unit is supplied by a 4.2-volt radio battery that will satisfy the current requirement for several weeks. The reader who is familiar with the Mowrer (1939) device used in the treatment of enuresis will recognize certain similar characteristics in the present toilet-training circuit, the essential difference here being that a lightweight instrument is called for which demands a battery of limited size. This in turn suggests the need for a highly sensitive transistor circuit capable of operating on a small amount of current.

Of importance to the total is the requirement of an effective switching element that can set off the tone signal indicating urination has occurred. This is satisfied by a simple grid of special wire

that is not awkward when worn nor particularly visible. Dependability of the device rests largely on the design of the grid and its connection to the main package. The reader will be aided in following the description by reference to the drawing in Figure 1. Proceeding from the signal package, as shown mounted on the infant's side, are two insulated "tinsel" wires which run to the connector plug. The wires are the same as those joining a telephone receiver to its wall mount. It is recommended that the female part of the connector plug be sewed firmly to the rear of the training pants in order to reduce flexing of the grid as the pants are removed. Connecting to the plug from the opposite direction is the grid which is composed of two "tinsel" wires stripped of their insulation encapsulated in absorbent cloth, and sewed into the training pants. Care must be taken in covering the wires to insure that a thickness of cloth comes between them along their full length. A cross sectional view of the cloth would describe a figure eight with a wire in each enclosure. It is recommended that a strand of moderately flexible polyethelene plastic be sewed in with the wire in order to stiffen the grid somewhat and reduce the chance of crimping the wire. Placement of the stiffener is not of importance so long as it does not come between the two conductors nor significantly increase the distance between them. The result is a grid about half the diameter of a pencil and about ten (10) inches long. When attached, it extends from the rim of the pants in back downward through the crotch and up the front, approaching the rim. It should be emphasized that while "tinsel" wire is expressly designed to withstand flexing, it nevertheless wi

Reprinted from *Journal of Experimental Child Psychology*, 1966, 3, 312–314. Abridged by permission of the authors.

break, and particularly is this true since the normal insulation has been removed. For this reason, laundering of the training pants should avoid severe extraction of the water.

As an alternative to the grid just described, a more robust one has been tested and found satisfactory, but there is the possibility that it might become uncomfortable. However, no evidence of this appeared in tests made by the authors. The conductors in this case are 14-gauge, 23-strand, tinned-copper wires without insulation. These wires should be sewed into cloth in the same fashion as was described for the tinsel wires but leaving out the plastic stiffener.

The apparatus has been tried on both a male and a female subject of about 16 months of age and was found to function well. The authors employed a discrimination hierarchy based on proximity to the toilet facility. That is, the infant was initially reinforced at the occurrence of any expulsion, but on subsequent urinations or defecations, movement in the direction of the toilet was reinforced with confections, and the most distal areas of

Figure 1. Positioning of the signaling device showing the grid in exaggerated size.

the house successively removed from the possibility of reinforcement. Aspects of the response as movement toward the toilet and restraining of the expulsion were the focus of reinforcement.

REFERENCE

Mowrer, O. H., and Mowrer, Willie Mae. Enuresis: A method for its study and treatment. *Amer. J. Orthopsychiat.*, 1938, *8*, 436–459.

28.
a night of sleep

gay gaer luce

Each night at an accustomed time people begin to set the stage for sleep with small rituals that lead to bed and darkness. A dusk of consciousness will fall like a curtain on the day and soon, from outside, the body will seem still but for a shallow and even breathing. A twisting, a groan, fluttering of eyelids and perhaps muffled sounds may occasionally break the stillness, but for 7 or 8 hours the person seems to have departed, gone from the world into a silent internal communion from which he will rise like an amnesic. The forgetting, the sense of oblivion is so nearly complete that it is surprising how easily people accept this suspension from life, relinquishing themselves each night with little anxiety. Primitive people, understandably enough, often looked upon sleep as a temporary death, and remnants of their uncertainty and fear can be found in religious liturgies; one example is an Orthodox Jewish morning prayer, thanking the Lord for the return of the soul and therefore life. Although the sleeper is clearly animate, his prolonged stillness scarcely conveys to an observer any sense of the tides within.

Sleep, as we now know it, is not a state of unconsciousness, an oblivion punctuated by occasional dreams. It is not, indeed, a unitary state of being, but a progression of rhythmic cycles representing different phases of neural function. By watching a person sleep, the observer cannot see that the sleeper is rising and falling on the waves of a recurrent tide. Nor can he observe that the sleeper regularly enters long intervals so different from the rest of sleep that some scientists have called it another state—a state of frenzied internal activity, resembling

Reprinted from *Current Research on Sleep and Dreams*, Public Health Service Publication No. 1389, pp. 9–14.

in many ways alert wakefulness. The bedside observer cannot easily detect the signs of shifts within, for the place to watch a night of sleep is not in the bedroom—but in the recordings of laboratory polygraphs, the electroencephalograph, the cardiogram, myograph, and thermometer.

THE ELECTROENCEPHALOGRAPH

The progression of cycles that make up a night's sleep have been pieced together by numerous observers through nightlong vigils in sleep laboratories. There are perhaps 2 dozen sleep laboratories in the United States, in university buildings and hospitals. They vary somewhat in size and newness, and complexity of equipment, but laboratories designed for the study of human sleep basically resemble each other. In the control room the visitor will notice the fundamental polygraph instruments, consolidated in the big amplifier system, the electroencephalograph machine, a device through which researchers can watch brain activity. Small conductive electrodes, bits of metal pasted onto the scalp, or in some cases, needles implanted in the brain, transmit the natural beat of a brain region through changes of electric potential. The electroencephalograph (EEG) amplifies these shifts in potential, transmitting them to magnetic tape, or driving a row of ink pens on the desklike panel of the machine. Each pen, driven by a signal from a part of the brain, moves up when the electric charge is negative and down when the charge becomes positive. As a continuous sheet of graph paper moves forward on a roller, at a constant speed under the oscillating pens, the up-and-down pen movements are traced out as waves—brain waves. Their amplitude indicates the ever shifting amount of voltage generated in a brain region, and their shape can indicate the speed of the electrical changes within. Thus, a glance at the inked record will tell whether the potentials in the brain are shifting in a regular, synchronous fashion, with slow, large voltage changes, or whether the changes are fast and irregular, desynchronized.

Although some body functions can be detected by simply looking at a person, precise and reliable measures of blood pressure, pulse, respiration, muscle tone, temperature require sensing devices that can produce signals to be amplified and recorded in the manner of brain waves. In order to minimize interference with sleep, researchers now use some of the miniature instruments developed for space exploration. For example, a thermistor no bigger than a pin can be used to detect body temperature continuously. This kind of equipment enables simultaneous recordings of heart rate and temperature fluctuations on the same record as the EEG, showing how changes in brain wave patterns are related to changing body functions.

THE SLEEP LABORATORY

On any evening, when most people have settled down to an after-dinner entertainment or are preparing for bed, the sleep scientist has begun to check out his equipment. Inkwells are filled, pens cleaned, wire leads tested for insulation and possible breaks, and a thousand-foot sheet of folded EEG paper inserted between the rollers, reels of magnetic tape set in place. Continual adjustments, requiring some manual and electronic dexterity, are essential to reliable data collection, and before the arrival of a sleep subject, the control room resembles the cockpit of a plane during the instrument check for takeoff.

The aura of the sleep laboratory is similar, whether it is 10-below-zero on the snowbound University of Chicago campus where a solitary row of lights mark the brownstone containing the laboratory, or a balmy California night outside the vast and silent new hospital at UCLA. The sleep researcher collects his data largely during these lonely hours,

a strenuous pursuit, sometimes requiring vigils for many consecutive nights, weeks, or even months. It is an endeavor requiring physical and mental endurance, one that places a strain on all personal or social activity, for it may be necessary to monitor the sleep of others on many consecutive nights while fulfilling administrative and academic duties and analyzing the data by day.

Our current picture of a night's sleep is a composite of thousands of nights and thousands of volunteers, most of them young men in their twenties, generally students or professionals. Very often they are paid a small sum to sleep in the laboratory and abide by the rules of the study—which may prohibit napping, drinking coffee or alcohol, and taking drugs. Typically, the young volunteer will arrive before 10 p.m., change into pajamas, and seat himself in some corner of the laboratory to be decorated for the night.

Often, in the strong odor of acetone and collodion, used to fasten electrodes to the skin, the experimenter will conduct a quiet and soothing conversation as he carefully affixes the electrodes to the top of the head, at the temples, near the eyes. Each electrode disc has a brightly colored lead, following a color code, and the many-colored wires are often drawn through a ring at the top of the head like a pigtail. When the preparation is securely finished, the volunteer will go to bed in one of the quiet bedrooms adjacent to the control room. The room is ordinary enough, except for a jackboard at the head of the bed, and an intercom system. The wires from the volunteer's head are plugged into the jack-board, and he settles down. The lights go out. The bed is comfortable, and the volunteer can move freely, although he cannot get up and walk around ordinarily without being unplugged. If he wants anything, however, he can tell the experimenter through the intercom system.

The room is private, the volunteer is comfortable, the technical details of the study well in hand, and one might expect that data collection would be quite routine. In all human studies, however, there is an emotional component, and the somewhat predictable, somewhat elusive interplay of feelings adds a heavy burden to the sleep study. Even a well-balanced medical student may have a hard time falling asleep in his private bedroom although accustomed to being in laboratories; the gentlemen beyond the door are monitoring his brain waves, and although he knows that EEG patterns do not invade mental privacy in the sense that they cannot reveal thought or dream content, the laboratory situation is strange.

"THE LABORATORY EFFECT"

On their first night subjects often do not exhibit the sleep patterns that seem characteristic of them on later nights. A night or two of adjustment may be necessary, in full headdress. Sometimes as many as five or more consecutive nights will be necessary to obtain the baseline —the usual pattern of the individual's sleep—before the experimenter collects a sole night of data (Dement, Greenberg, and Klein, 1965). However trivial the bias may be in a particular study, and no matter what precautions have been taken, the so-called "laboratory effect" resides within all the generalizations being drawn from human studies —as illustrated by the fact that among hundreds of young men in the laboratories, nightmares and wet dreams have been extremely rare. Thus, in speaking of the typical night of sleep as we now see it, we must bear in mind some modifications for it is a composite of nights spent in a laboratory.

DROWSINESS

Usually, about 11 p.m., the acclimated volunteer will be relaxed. His body temperature is declining. His eyes are closed, and he is no longer moving. On the graph paper in the control room the jumble of rapid, irregular brain waves is beginning to form a new pattern, a regular rhythm known as the alpha rhythm. This pattern of 9–12 cycles a second indicates relaxed wakefulness. Subjectively, it is a serene and pleasant state, devoid of deliberate thought, into which images may float. A moment of tension

or attempt to solve a mental problem will disrupt it (Kamiya, 1962).

With further relaxation the alpha waves grow smaller, decreasing in amplitude. As alpha rhythm diminishes, a person's time perception seems to deteriorate, and two rapid flashes of light may seem to blend into one (Anliker, 1963). As his alpha rhythm diminishes, the young volunteer hovers on the borders of drowsiness and sleep, perhaps seeing images, experiencing dreamlike thoughts or fragments (Foulkes and Vogel).

STAGE 1

Another pattern begins to emerge on the EEG paper. This new script is smaller, indicating lower voltages. It is uneven, desynchronized, and it changes swiftly. At this point one may experience a floating sensation, drifting with idle images as the alpha rhythm gives way to the low voltage, fast irregular rhythm of the first stage of sleep. (Kamiya, 1961; Foulkes and Vogel). The volunteer, in this phase, can be easily awakened by a noise or spoken word. His body muscles are relaxing. Respiration is growing more even and heart rate is becoming slower (Snyder, 1960). If awakened at this point a person may assert that he was not really asleep. This phase of consciousness is like a port of entry, a borderland, and lasts only a few minutes. Soon the background rhythm of the EEG grows slower.

STAGE 2

The script grows larger and the pens trace out quick bursts known as spindles, rapid crescendos and decrescendos of waves. The eyes of the young volunteer may appear to be slowly rolling. He is quite soundly asleep, yet it is not hard to awaken him. By now there has been a fundamental change in his brain function. One aspect of this change is suggested by a study in which volunteers slept with their eyes half open; illuminated objects were suspended before their eyes. On the whole they were not awakened by the light, nor did they remember seeing anything, but when awakened by a voice a few seconds later the often insisted they had been wide awake and thinking thoughts that, as narrated, had a vague and dreamlike quality (Foulkes and Vogel; Rechtschaffen and Foulkes). If awakened at this point a person might feel he had been thinking or indulging in reverie. Left undisturbed, however, he will soon descend into another level of sleep.

STAGE 3

The spindle bursts and somewhat irregular brain wave rhythm begins to be interspersed with large slow waves. These occur at about one a second, and are high in amplitude. The electrical input may run as high as 300 microvolts in stage 3, as compared with the 60 microvolts of the waking alpha rhythm. Now it will take a louder noise to awaken the sleeping person or animal, perhaps a repetition of his name. His muscles are very relaxed. He breathes evenly, and his heart rate continues to slow down. His blood pressure is falling, and his temperature continues to decline. Innocuous sensory events are making almost no impression on the awareness of the sleeper, and were he among the people who do sleep with their eyes half open, he would not be seeing anything (Fuchs and Wu, 1948).

STAGE 4

This stage might be called a most oblivious sleep. The muscles are very relaxed, and the person rarely moves (Jacobson et al., 1964). It is hard to awaken him with the low noise or buzzer that would have aroused him earlier. His heart rate and temperature are still declining, and his respiration is slow and even. Waken the volunteer now with a loud noise or by calling his name and he may come into focus slowly, and may feel that he was not experiencing any mental activity (Rechtschaffen et al., 1962, 1963; Kales et al., 1963). The EEG pens scratch out a continuous train of low, high amplitude waves. The sleeper is utterly removed from the world, although his brain wave responses would indicate that every sound and the lightest touch are received in his brain. Indeed,

during this synchronous, slow-wave sleep the brain shows a very large response to outside stimuli such as sounds, but the brain systems that make this stimulation into conscious sensation appear not to be working in their usual way (Allison, 1965; Hernandez-Peon, 1963; Rosner et al., 1963; Williams et al., 1962, 1964; Weitzman and Kremen, 1965). This may account for the eerie apparition, the somnambulist, who will rise from bed in this stage of sleep, negotiate a room full of furniture, look straight at people with eyes open, yet appear not to perceive them, and return to bed, usually recalling nothing of the interlude when awakened (Jacobson et al., 1965). Stage 4 appears to be one of the times when children commonly wet their beds, a time when a person is, by some criteria, most deeply asleep (Pierce et al., 1961, 1963; Scott, 1964). Although people can be trained to discriminate between sounds, to press a button during another stage of sleep, their performance during stage 4 is not nearly so frequent (Granda and Hammack, 1961; Mandell et al., 1965; Williams et al., 1963).

A normal person will spend a considerable portion of the night in this stage, especially if he has lost sleep (Agnew et al., 1964). If annoyed from outside, he will tend to drift into a lighter phase of sleep, but if annoyances prevent him from spending a certain portion of his night in stage 4, on subsequent nights he will make it up by spending substantially more time in stage 4. Although he seems hard to awaken from this phase, paradoxically he may be even harder to awaken from the first stage of sleep—if he happens to be in the throes of dreaming.

STAGE 1 REM

About an hour or so after falling asleep, the sleeper may begin to drift back up into the lighter phases of sleep (Dement and Kleitman, 1957). Roughly 90 minutes have passed, and the volunteer's sleep has resumed the pattern of stage 2. Now, suddenly, the pens of the EEG begin to jabber, scratching out wild oscillations. He has turned over in bed, and moved. As the oscillations die away the brain wave record shows an irregular low-voltage, rapidly changing script like that of stage 1. Now two pens that are activated by movements of the eyes make rapid darts, as if the eyes had turned to look at something. Intermittedly the pens continue. The eyes move as if following a film (Aserinsky and Kleitman, 1955; Dement and Kleitman, 1957; Roffwarg et al., 1962). These rapid eye movements, known as REM's signal a phase of vivid dreaming, a most unique state of consciousness (Dement, 1965). In this phase, it will take a relatively huge amount of noise to awaken a person—yet a very slight noise, with significance, may quickly alert him (Goodenough, 1963).

Sound a click in the sleeper's ear, and his brain wave response will not resemble that of stage 4—but shows a great resemblance to the response during waking. Although it may be hard to awaken a person at this time, in many ways his brain activity paradoxically resembles waking, and REM sleep is often called paradoxical sleep. It is believed by some investigators to be a unique state, totally different from the rest of sleep, and subserved by different brain mechanisms.

The entire body shows pronounced changes now (Snyder, 1960, 1962, 1964, 1965). Gone is the even breath and pulse. The organs that show the most striking changes in sleep are those indicating fright or anger. Everyone is familiar with the blanched skin, wide eyes, rapid heart beat and knotted stomach of fright. These changes are controlled by the closely related nerves of the autonomic nervous system, which regulates the organs of the chest and viscera, changes in the skin and eyes, with the help of hormones secreted by the adrenal glands. The autonomic system modifies its organic domain in unison, and is tuned in to the emotional state of the creature. During slow-wave sleep the heart rate, respiration, and blood pressure fall to their lowest levels of the day, falling at sleep onset and continuing to drop until about an hour before awakening. During REM sleep, however, the heart rate, blood pressure, and respiration become exceedingly variable, sometimes fluctuating wildly. Usually there is a long interval of REM sleep during the latter part of the night, the time when a person's temperature has fallen to its nadir. During the REM period in the early hours of morning the activity of the autonomic system often becomes most intense, inducing what have been called "autonomic storms," which may account for the statistically frequent occurrence of heart attacks at this time, and further study of this period may make it possible to anticipate and prevent such coronaries.

Many of the physical changes that attend the REM state can be observed from watching the sleeper. At the onset the muscles of the head and chin will relax completely (Berger, 1961; Jouvet, 1963; Jacobson et al., 1964; Dement, 1965). This is so regular that the loss of tonus in the muscle under the chin can serve to activate an alarm, signalling the onset of REM sleep. Most teeth-grinding occurs at this time (Reding et al., 1964). From infancy through adulthood, the REM period is attended by penile erections in males (Fisher et al., 1965). Rapid, jerky movements of the eyes can be seen, even in many blind people (Berger et al., 1962; Gross et al., 1965).

Most striking of all, however, is the now substantial evidence that this is a period of vivid dreaming for all humankind, and the suggestion that it is a period of consciousness in which monkeys and perhaps other animals experience vivid imagery. Awakened during REM sleep, a person will almost inevitably report mentation that differs from waking thought, dramatic, and often bizarre—generally recognized as a dream (Dement and many others). Yet if he is awakened a few minutes after the rapid eye movements cease, when he has lapsed into another phase of sleep, the dream will have evaporated. The average individual spends a total of about 5 years of his life in such vivid dreaming, but for the most part he is amnesic, remembering very little.

The discovery of the REM phase of sleep and subsequent findings about the body and brain during this state have raised many fundamental questions about the organization and function of the central nervous system, and has stimulated a rapidly growing body of research which will be explored at greater length in later sections of this paper.

It has been said that the average adult dreams about every 90 minutes, and that the full cycle of sleep stages spans an interval of 90–120 minutes, corresponding to a subcycle within the circadian temperature rhythm.

This generalization is somewhat misleading, although it has been widely propagated in the press, for dreaming, dreamlike experiences, fragments, images, mentation occur in all phases of sleep, although recall varies. Sleep is a succession of repeated cycles. Nevertheless, one's progression through a night does not resemble the passage of a train on a circular track, arriving at different stations at a predictable time. People of about the same age do not follow such a rigid timetable of sleep, and all humanity does not rise and fall on the waves of a single tide.

THE WHOLE NIGHT

A reexamination of the nightly EEG patterns of sleep has been conducted recently with 16 medical students, each of whom spent four nights in the laboratory. Only two uniform patterns emerged. The entire group showed a greater incidence of REM periods during the last third of the night, and the slow-wave sleep of stage 4 predominated during the first third of the night. Not only was there no consistent time schedule of sleep stages for the group—but individuals showed slightly different patterns on different nights. Excepting for their REM periods they did not spend more than 10 minutes at a time in any EEG phase, and throughout the night stage 2 with its spindles occurred evenly, like a transition period, a bridge (Williams, Agnew, and Webb, 1964). Evidence from a number of studies suggests that each of us has a characteristic sleep pattern, an EEG script that is identifiable and individual, although we vary somewhat from night to night. So far no rules have been found for describing the succession of EEG phases that all people will pass through

in a night's sleep, but more sophisticated analyses may indeed reveal an inherent order in the sequence of cycles (Zung et al., 1965; Hammack et al., 1964).

However much people differ in detail, normal people show roughly the same overall pattern. They sleep for a long interval once in 24 hours, at the time of their lowest body temperature. They spend roughly the same proportion of the night in REM sleep and stage 4, distributing them over the night in roughly the same manner.

Marked deviations from this pattern are often signs of serious disorder. Encephalitis is an extreme instance, and its sufferers may suddenly find their daily temperature cycle inverted; they will sleep by day and remain awake at night. Or they may sleep for weeks after enduring periods of exhausting insomnia. Among some encephalitis patients, unusual EEG's have been noticed in sleep, such as extraordinarily slow spindles. Epileptics commonly have seizures during certain phases of sleep, and Drs. C. Markham and R. Walter at UCLA have observed bizarre EEG sleep patterns in some patients who alternated between stages 1 and 2 and never exhibited the patterns of deeper sleep. A characteristic abnormality of many narcoleptics is that REM activity begins at the onset of sleep instead of an hour or so later; while a tendency of some psychotic patients is to have delayed and reduced REM sleep. These deviations all speak of different disorders in the central nervous system, some of them perhaps of metabolic nature. Normative studies, encompassing individuals of all ages, may make it possible to clearly describe the protocols of the nighttime nervous system—yielding a diagnostic by which disorders can be pinpointed. Sleep is a convenient time for study, since the body is still and there are few distractions. It is not incongruous to use sleep EEGs in diagnosing many behavioral symptoms, for sleep is not separate from waking but seems to be a part of a neurophysiological continuum that ranges from coma to the high arousal of fierce rage.

REFERENCES

Agnew, H., Webb, W. B., and Williams, R. L. The effect of stage 4 sleep deprivation. *EEG Clin. Neurophysiol.*, 1964, 17:68–70.

Allison, T. Cortical and subcortical evoked responses to central stimuli during wakefulness and sleep. *EEG Clin. Neurophysiol.*, 1965, 18:131–139.

Anliker, J. Variations in alpha voltage of the EEG and time perception. *Science*, 1963, 140:1307–1309.

Aserinsky, E., and Kleitman, N. Two types of ocular motility occurring in sleep. *J. Appl. Physiol.*, 1955, 8:1–10.

Aserinsky, E., and Kleitman, N. A motility cycle in sleeping infants as manifested by ocular and gross bodily activity. *J. Appl. Physiol.*, 1955, 8:11–18.

Berger, R. J., Olley, P., and Oswald, I. The EEG, eye-movements and dreams of the blind. *Quart. J. Exp. Psychol.*, 1962, 14:183–186.

Berger, R. J., and Oswald, I. Effects of sleep variation on behavior, subsequent sleep, and dreaming. *J. Ment. Sci.*, 1962, 108:457–465.

Dement, W. C. An Essay on Dreams. In W. Edwards, H. Lindman, and L. D. Phillips (eds.), *New Directions in Psychology II*. New York: Holt, Rinehart & Winston, 1965.

Dement, W. C. Further studies on the function of rapid eye movement sleep. *Am. Psychiatric Assn.*, New York, 1965.

Dement, W. C., Greenberg, S., and Klein, R. The persistence of the REM deprivation effect. APSS, 1965, Washington, D.C.

Dement, W. C., and Kleitman, N. Cyclic variations in EEG during sleep and their relations to eye movements, body motility, and dreaming. *EEG Clin. Neurophysiol.*, 1957, 9:673–690.

Dement, W. C., and Kleitman, N. The relation of eye movements during sleep to dream activity: An objective method for the study of dreaming. *J. Exp. Psychol.*, 1957, 53:339–346.

Fischer, C., Gross, J., and Zuch, J. A cycle of penile erections synchronous with dreaming (REM) sleep. *Arch. Gen. Psychiatry*, 1965, 12:29–45.

Foulkes, D., and Vogel, G. Mental activity at sleep onset. *J. Abnorm. Psychol.* In press.

Fuchs and Wu. Sleep with half-open eyes. *Amer. J. Ophthal.*, 1948, 31.

Goodenough, D. R. Cyclical fluctuations in sleep-depth and eye-movement activity during the course of natural sleep. *Canad. Psychiat. J.*, 1963, 8:406–408.

Granda, A. M., and Hammack, J. T. Operant behavior during sleep. *Science*, 1961, 133:1485–1486.

Gross, J., Feldman, M., and Fisher, C. Eye movements during emergent stage 1 EEG in subjects with lifelong blindness. APSS, 1965, Washington, D.C.

Hammack, J. T., Williams, J. M., Weisberg, P., Brooks, Paula, and Gerald, Maryann. An experimental anlysis of behavior during sleep. U.S. Army Medical Research and Development Command, 1964, Contract No. Da–49–193–MD–2180.

Hernandez-Peon, R. Limbic cholinergic pathways involved in sleep and emotional behavior. *Exp. Neurol.*, 1963, 8:93–111.

Hernandez-Peon, R. Neurophysiological mechanisms of wakefulness and sleep. XVII International Congress of Psychology, 1963, Washington, D.C.

Jacobson, A., Kales A., Lehmann, D., and Hoedemaker, F. S. Muscle tonus in human subjects during sleep and dreaming. *Exp. Neurol.*, 1964, 10:418–424.

Jacobson, A., Kales, A., Lehmann, D., and Zweizig, J. R. Somnambulism: All night EEG studies. *Science*, 1965, 148:975–977.

Kales, A., Hoedemaker, F. S., and Jacobson, A. Reportable mental activity during sleep. APSS, 1963, New York.

Kamiya, J. Behavioral, subjective, and physiological aspects of drowsiness and sleep. In D. W. Fiske and S. R. Maddi (eds.), *Functions of Varied Experience*. Homewood: Dorsey, 1961.

Kamiya, J. Behavioral and physiological concomitants of dreaming. APSS, 1962, Chicago.

Mandell, M. P., Mandell, A. J., and Jacobson, A. Biochemical and Neurophysiological Studies of Paradoxical Sleep. *Recent Advances in Biological Psychiatry*, 7:115–124, J. Wortis (ed.), Plenum, N. Y., 1965.

Pierce, C. M., Whitman, R. R., Maas, J. W., and Gay, M. I. Enuresis and dreaming. *Arch. Gen. Psychiat.*, 1961, 4:166–170.

Pierce, C. M., Whitman, R. R., Maas, J. W., and Gay, M. I. Enuresis and dreaming. *Experimental Studies*, 1963.

Rechtschaffen, A., and Foulkes, D. The effect of visual stimuli on dream content. *Percept. Mot. Skills*, 1965, 20:149–160.

Rechtschaffen, A., Goodenough, D. R., and Shapiro, A. Patterns of sleep talking. *Arch. Gen. Psychiat.*, 1962, 7:418–426.

Rechtschaffen, A., Verdone, P., and Wheaton, Joy. Reports of mental activity during sleep. *Canad. Psychiat. Assn. J.*, 1963, 8:409–414.

Rechtschaffen, A., Vogel, G., and Shaikun, G. Interrelatedness of mental activity during sleep. *Arch. Gen. Psychiat.*, 1963, 9:536–547.

Rechtschaffen, A., Wolpert, E. A., Dement

W. C. Mitchell, S. A., and Fisher, C. Nocturnal sleep of narcoleptics. *EEG Clin. Neurophysiol.*, 1963, 15:599–609.

Reding, G. R., Rubright, W. C., Rechtschaffen, A., and Daniels, R. S. Sleep pattern of tooth-grinding: its relationship to dreaming. *Science*, 1964, 145:725–726.

Roffwarg, H. P. Dement, W. C., Muzio, J. N., and Fisher, C. Dream imagery: relationship to rapid eye movements of sleep. *Arch. Gen. Psychiat.*, 1962, 7:235–258.

Rosner, B. S., Goff, W. R., and Allison, T. Cerebral electrical responses to external stimuli. In *EEG and Behavior*, G. H. Glasser (ed.), 1963, New York: Basic Books.

Scott, J. Sleep patterns in normal and enuretic children (4–16 years). APSS, 1964, Palo Alto.

Snyder, F. Dream recall, respiratory variability and depth of sleep. Address, Symposium on Dreams, *Amer. Psychiat. Assn.*, 1960.

Snyder, F. Autonomic concomitants of REM and NREM sleep. APSS, 1962, Chicago.

Snyder, F. The REM state in a living fossil. APSS, 1964, Palo Alto.

Snyder, F. Progress in the new biology of dreaming. *Am. Psychiat. Assn.*, 1965.

Snyder, F. The organismic state associated with dreaming. In N. S. Greenfield and W. C. Lewis (eds.), *Psychoanalysis and Current Biological Thought*. University of Wisconsin Press, 1965, 275–315.

Weitzman, E. D., and Kremen, H. Auditory evoked responses during different stages of sleep in man. *EEG Clin. Neurophysiol.*, 1965, 18:65–70.

Williams, H. L., Granda, A. M., Jones, R. C., Lubin, A., and Armington, J. C. EEG frequency and finger pulse volume as predictors of reaction time during sleep loss. *EEG Clin. Neurophysiol.*, 1962, 14:64–70.

Williams, H. L., Hammack, J. T., Daly, R. L., Dement, W. C., and Lubin, A. Responses to auditory stimulation, sleep loss, and the EEG stages of sleep. *EEG Clin. Neurophysiol.*, 1964, 16:269–279.

Williams, H. L., Morlock, H. C., and Morlock, Jean V. Discriminative responses to auditory signals during sleep. APA, 1963, Philadelphia.

Williams, H. L., Morris, G. O., and Lubin, A. Illusions, hallucinations, and sleep loss. In L. J. West (ed.), *Hallucinations*, New York: Grune & Stratton, 1962.

Williams, H. L., Tepas, D. I., and Morlock, H. C. Evoked responses to clicks and electroencephalographic stages of sleep in man. *Science*, 1962, 138:685–686.

Williams, R. L., Agnew, H. W., and Webb, Wilse B. Sleep patterns in young adults: an EEG study. *EEG Clin. Neurophysiol.*, 1964, 17:376–381.

Zung, W. K., Naylor, T. Gianturco, D., and Wilson, W. P. Computer simulation of sleep EEG patterns using a Markov chain model. *Recent Advances in Biological Psychiatry*, vol. VIII, Plenum Press, New York, 1965.

29.
the development of infant sleep

gay gaer luce

Almost all autobiographies begin as close to the beginning as the author can remember, with a drama performed in early childhood in which he participated, the story of his molding, the explanation of his metamorphosis. As we try to explain, more systematically, the forces that shape behavior, to understand the process of development, we find ourselves looking for the earliest cues in infancy. But the young infant says little about himself in behavior, and furthermore, he is almost always asleep—one reason why studies of infant development are now including examinations of sleep patterns. The EEG patterns of sleep reflect activity of different neural structures in the brain and these may tell a good deal about the maturation process of the brain.

The infant's sleep differs from an adult's in several important ways. During his first weeks of life a human infant is asleep two-thirds of the time. Unlike his parents, and often to their chagrin, he does not sleep for one long siege at night, but rather for short intervals, interspersed with brief periods of waking, a polyphasic pattern that is characteristic of all newborn mammals. This cycle slowly changes, and he remains awake for longer periods and begins to sleep as his parents do, usually to their great relief. From the beginning the infant has had them at a great disadvantage, for he would awaken them easily enough with a yowl for food or attention, but infants are not so easy to arouse from sleep. At first, and to a lesser degree as they mature, infants are very often in a REM stage of sleep.

A number of anatomical studies on animals and behavioral studies of human infants have been directed toward answering an important question: Can we relate the maturation of sleep patterns to the maturation of the nervous system and to learning? What neural apparatus is necessary before an infant can begin to stay awake for long periods and sleep for long periods? What does the decline of REM sleep tell about the maturation of the infant's brain? Can the brain wave patterns of infant sleep serve as the earliest indicators of normal or abnormal development?

Since the 1930's babies had been known to sleep for roughly 50 minutes at a time. Within this interval there are minutes of slow, even breathing and quiescence, alternating with periods of fast uneven breathing and restless motions. Dr. Eugene Aserinsky watched from the cradle side for a relationship between slow rolling eye movements and body motion, and in 1952, when he transposed his study to adults, discovered the rapid eye movements that signify dreaming. On repeated inspection, infants also showed rapid jerky eye movements in sleep, and although we cannot imagine that the newborn infant experiences visual dreams, he appears to spend much of his sleep in the REM state (Dreyfus-Brisac et al.).

Judging from what we know about the REM state, as it may emanate from activity within the brain stem, exciting nearby regions associated with drives and emotions in the limbic system, it might be called a primitive activity of a primitive brain. The sleep of high amplitude, synchronous waves seems to depend upon the cortex and higher regions of the brain, as we have learned from decoticate accident victims and transected cats who no longer show slow-wave sleep.

Reprinted from *Current Research on Sleep and Dreams*, Public Health Service Publication No. 1389, pp. 91–95.

THE DECLINE
OF REM SLEEP WITH AGE

The regions associated with REM sleep seem to develop long before the cortex in its many folds and convolutions. In the embryo, the nervous system begins from nothing more than a tube of neural tissue. At the tail, the tube begins to form the spinal cord. At the head, the tube bulges into a forebrain, a midbrain and a hindbrain, and slowly these rudimentary bulges enlarge and fold. Slowly the cerebral hemispheres form, and last of all, during childhood, the outer layers of the cerebral cortex acquire their final convolutions. The hindbrain and midbrain develop long before the cortex and before the elaborate fiber network of communications is established between the cortex and the rest of the brain. Can we infer something about the rate of cortical development in an infant by watching his sleep, particularly the decline of the primitive REM state?

Only recently a number of investigators have indicated that the REM state does decline in infants as they mature (Parmelee et al., 1961–65; Roffwarg et al., 1963). By observing the sleep of young infants at progressive stages of development, they have all noted that the proportion of REM sleep declines during the first months of life, a clue that may help the pediatrician to chart the maturation of a baby's central nervous system and diagnose such abnormalities as retardation or schizophrenia at a very early stage of life.

It is interesting to note that monkeys follow a similar course. A recent polygraph study of newborn and infant rhesus monkeys indicated that for the first 7 days of life, the infant sleeps more, and a large proportion is REM sleep. After this critical seventh day the proportion of REM declined although total sleep time remained relatively constant throughout the first year (Meier and Berger, 1965).

From sleep studies of people of different ages including a premature infant born 10 weeks early and an old woman of 100 years, we can see approximately how much of one's sleep is spent in the dream state as one moves through life's timetable. In an infant, 10 weeks premature, 80 percent of sleep was REM sleep, but this ratio dropped as the infant approached full term, and in infants arriving only 2–4 weeks early the percentage of REM had dropped to 58 percent, and was 50 percent in the full term neonate. By 5 weeks REM sleep occupied only 40 percent; by a year only 35 percent; by 2–3 years, it had dropped to 30 percent, and by 5 years, 20 percent. Throughout later childhood and early adolescence, according to the limited observations available, the REM state dropped slightly, and in early adulthood rose slightly, ranging between 20–24 percent, again beginning to decline after about age 45 to about 13 percent in some of the aged persons studied. This is a very approximate schedule of the proportion of REM sleep occurring at any given age, but it suggests a developmental pattern of neural activity that begins in the cradle and follows a regular curve throughout life (Fisher, 1965).

A normative study of infant sleep may tell whether the decline of REM sleep is so precisely correlated with age that it might be used as a measurement in infant diagnostics. Such a study, begun in the UCLA laboratory of Dr. A. H. Parmelee, will encompass systematic observation of 100 infants from birth into childhood. New techniques for recording heart rate, EEGs, muscle tone, temperature, and respiration now permit such measurements even on very young infants and the premature. Recordings are being taken within the hospital nursery as soon as it is safe and comfortable for the baby, who is also watched by two observers. Once they leave the nursery the infants will periodically sleep in a special recording bedroom where they can be accompanied by their mothers. Then, as soon as they are old enough, they will receive graded batteries of behavioral tests at regular intervals.

An initial study of 46 infants has indicated the progress of the shift from polyphasic sleep to a diurnal pattern. This shift toward nightly sleep occurs in infants by about 16 weeks, even though they spend no more than about 3 hours awake in any 24 hour period (Parmelee et al., 1964).

Initial studies of premature infants, who must complete their embryonic development outside the womb, are beginning to show us something about the brain activity of the maturing unborn. Very premature infants (born 10 weeks early) do not show an EEG pattern like that of the full term baby. They seem to alternate between one state of drowsiness and another, and to exist in the REM state predominately. By taking EEG tracings during a 12-hour period of sleep, one such infant was observed to spend 80 percent of his time in the REM state. Less premature infants (6 or 7 weeks early) spent only 67 percent of their time in REM and the full term infants about 50 percent. By 8 months of age, this percentage dropped to 24 percent.

This steady and rapid decline in REM time was noted by Dement, Roffwarg, and Fisher, in studies conducted by watching the eye movements of infants in the nurseries of Chicago Lying In and Columbia Presbyterian Hospitals. Infants of many mammal species also have been observed to spend less sleeping time in the REM state as they matured. What might this decline of primitive activity mean in the anatomy of the developing infant brain? Could it mean that the growing tentacles of the cortex are beginning to gain greater contact and control, and that the brain stem is diminishing in its dominance?

CORTICAL DEVELOPMENT IN KITTENS

Some suggestive answers have been coming from the anatomical and behavioral studies of Drs. Arnold and Madge Schiebel at UCLA. They have been engaged in a long program of studies of kitten development, seeking the concomitants of gross behavioral maturation within the growing neural fibers of the brain. The newborn kitten has a messy EEG and it is hard to tell whether the creature sleeps or wakes. As it grows the EEG begins to show differentiation, corresponding with the growth of nerve fibers. Dendrites, receptor fibers of the cortex, can be stained conveniently, although the transmitter fibers, axons, cannot. Consequently, the dendrites or receivers have been the first to be studied.

The dendrites of the newborn kitten are very simple. They resemble plants with a single smooth root, incapable of multiple contacts with other cells. Within the first days of life these dendrites begin to sprout long strands in many directions, giving more surface for contact with other nerve cells. These fine rootlike spines grow more numerous and dense with age, putting out side excursions that may indicate multiplying contacts betweeen the cortex and reticular system.

The Scheibels have used pairs of littermates in their studies, recording the behavior and EEG measures of one kitten and simultaneously studying the brain tissue of its littermate. Within the same litter they found that kittens varied considerably in their rate of maturation. Characteristically, the slow kittens were born with smoother brains, an archaic and unarticulated cortex. The kittens who showed rapid development were often born with a more mature cortex, and their EEG patterns differed commensurately. The smoothbrained kittens gave slower rhythms in waking and showed the spindling of sleep much later than the kittens with convoluted cortex, maturer brains. This difference appeared in behavior as well. The more mature kittens snuggled against their mother and sought milk in a purposive fashion.

Roughly, as they observed kittens through the first 6 months of life, the Scheibels began to see EEG progressions that differentiated the "normal" kittens from those with developmental disturbances. At what stage in a kitten's life, or in a human infant's life, does brain development permit some voluntary control over waking? Is this a stage at which infants begin to shift to the diurnal sleep pattern of their parents? The Scheibels have performed conditioning experiments to determine at what age a kitten might learn to awaken. Kittens were trained to wake up and reach for a bottle of milk when their names were called.

The first kitten was tested by calling his name during slow-wave sleep when he was 68 days old. His EEG gave no sign of arousal. When the test was repeated at 117 days of age, the kitten's brain wave pattern quickly showed the desynchronized pattern of arousal, and he got up and began to suck at the nipple. However, he gave no sign of arousal when a meaningless name, one he had never heard before, was called. However, between about 9 weeks of age and about 16 weeks, the kitten had acquired the capacity to control his awakening.

The brain maturation of the kitten was clocked in yet another way, by direct stimulation of the reticular formation, the arousal area of the brain. Kittens, implanted in the reticular area and other deep brain sites, were stimulated during sleep at different ages. Newborn kittens did not awaken to rapid pulses; they only awakened after slow stimulation to the reticular formation. Moreover, their EEG response to brain stem stimulation appeared to fatigue quickly. After two repeated stimulations had aroused it, further stimulation failed to awaken the kitten. Similar behavior is seen among human infants, who do not arouse easily from sleep. The Scheibels have conjectured that the undeveloped enzyme systems of the newborn brain cannot supply the rudimentary neural contacts rapidly enough, and so after these nerve cells fire a few times, the supply of chemical transmitters may be exhausted. Lack of neurochemical supplies may explain why the infant can do what no adult can do—disregard repeated stimulation direct to the arousal centers of the reticular formation.

This rapid adaptation to stimulation, internal and external, is a talent that the infant loses with maturation, just as many of the sensitiveness and talents of the human child are, like eidetic imagery, lost by adulthood. These seem to decline during the very process of maturation by which voluntary controls are gained. Experience, itself, appears to be the teacher in a very literal sense, for repeated experience appears to alter the brain tissue and make it more responsive.

Ordinarily, experience does not come by electrical stimulation of the brain, but this is a kind of artificial experience. Brain stimulation does cause observable changes in the brain tissue of the kitten. Neurons connect with each other by sprouting boutons at the ends of their axons. These boutons then contact the receptor fibers, or dendrites, of other neurons. After electrical stimulation in an area, these boutons swell in size, an enlargement that can be seen under the microscope. The engorging of these boutons may be an accumulation of fluid, perhaps trapped by increased sodium ions. Similarly, it is supposed that after repeated stimulation an axon will grow in size and in its capacity for transmitting neural messages. Until now, the impact of experience, or stimulation upon the size of these contact fibers and links has been seen only after the fact, by placing specimens of brain tissue under the microscope. Now, however, an exceedingly elaborate microscope system with powerful lighting may make it possible to look into a living cat's or monkey's brain and watch the brain cells change as the animal is stimulated by repeated touches, light flashes, or sounds. If the technical obstacles are not insurmountable it may be possible to see into the brain and watch it grow during experience.

Here we may begin to see the anatomical changes, the neural growth that underlies the changing EEG patterns and behavior of the infant animal. By inference we may begin to understand what we are now observing from the surface, as we study the EEG changes of developing human infants during sleep. Perhaps we can begin to track the connections sprouted in the growing brain between the cortical areas and the recticular formation as we see maturing activity in the reduction of REM sleep, and the growing dominance of slow-wave sleep as well as the shift from a polyphasic sleep resembling that of the cat toward the strong diurnal rhythm of adult man.

DIAGNOSTIC POSSIBILITIES

The gathering of normative data and the process of interference from animal studies to human development are both very slow and expensive, but there is reason to hope that they will be exceedingly useful in diagnostics and for an understanding of the integrity of nervous function in infancy. The common story of mental retardation and malfunction is a tragic one, in many cases because it is detected late in childhood development when remedies are less and less potent and more elaborate. What amounts to mental retardation in late childhood could sometimes be prevented by the detection of a simple yet ramifying defect, during babyhood, which sometimes amounts to poor visual control, hearing, or to an insufficient rate of development that ends up in leaving a person toally behind. If such defects can be spotted in earliest infancy remedies can be applied at the time when they will do the most good, for each successive stage of development hinges to some extent upon the last.

Unfortunately most abnormal behaviors are difficult to see in young infants. Many pediatricians have had the feeling that activity patterns in the newborn can suggest the maturation progress that will follow, but infant behavioral tests are inadequate. Psychiatrists have reported that extremely underactive or overactive infants seem possible candidates for childhood schizophrenia. When such babies are brought into clinics they often have a history of unusual sleep patterns. Either they seemed to sleep too much, or they harried their mothers by crying incessantly and sleeping briefly and irregularly. If the normative studies of Dr. Parmelee, and his colleagues prove fruitful, we may have another yardstick for normal development in the rate of REM decline. Infants who are very slow in this decline may suffer metabolic problems, causing what we now call retardation, in a form that can be ameliorated before there are lifelong ramifications.

Recent designs for extremely sensitive polygraph equipment may indeed permit Parmelee and his group to trace the development of infant sleep patterns back into the womb, allowing us to track the brain activity and physiological development of the unborn. REM activity may indeed represent the first concerted workings of the brain, a fundamental rhythm into which all later activity becomes knit, the first pulsing from which experience and growth will shape the growing psyche. The dream state of infants, while unlike the subjective and complex dream of the adult, may be the first expression of all the forces of survival provided by nature within the very cells of the primitive brain, the first practice of the fundamental instinct and drive centers— and their first effector actions, seen as the sucking, smiling, kicking of REM sleep in the newly born.

REFERENCES

Dreyfus-Brisac, C., Samson, D., Blanc, C., and Monod, N. L'electro-encephalo-gramme de l'enfant normal demoins de 3 ans. *Etudes Neo-Natales*, 1958, 7:143.

Fisher, C. Psychoanalytic implications of recent research on sleep and dreaming. *J. Amer. Psychoanal. Ass.*, 1965, April.

Meier, G. W., and Berger, R. J. The development of sleep and wakefulness patterns in the infant rhesus monkey. APSS, 1965, Washington, D.C.

Parmelee, A. H., Akiyama, Y., Wenner, W., and Flescher, Jenny. Activated sleep in premature infants. APSS, 1966, Palo Alto.

Parmelee, A. H., Schulz, H. R., and Disbrow, M. A. Sleep patterns of the newborn. *J. Pediat.*, 1961, 58:241.

Parmelee, A. H., and Wenner, W. H. Sleep states in premature and full term newborn infants. APSS, 1965, Washington, D.C.

Parmelee, A. H., Wenner, W. H., and Schulz, H. R. Infant sleep patterns: from birth to 16 weeks of age. *J. Pediat.*, 1964, 65:576.

Roldan, E., Weiss, T., and Fifkova, E. Excitability changes during the sleep cycle of the rat. *EEG Clin. Neurophysiol.*, 1963 15:775–785.

REVIEW QUESTIONS

1. How do Melvin, Colar, and Massingill explain the possible finding that punishment strengthens imprinting?

2. Why did the Gardners choose to teach Washoe sign language rather than a spoken language?

3. What do the Gardners mean by delayed imitation, sign language babbling, and instrumental conditioning?

4. Was Washoe able to use signs in strings of two or more? How do the Gardners explain this ability?

5. What kinds of data have led to the rejection of the sex theory of primate social organization and what has taken its place?

6. Define briefly and give examples of the following affectional systems as outlined by the Harlows: infant-mother, peer, heterosexual, maternal, and paternal.

7. Speculate on which of these five affectional systems would be abnormally developed in a child brought up entirely in an orphanage and how this might influence adult behavior.

8. What is the distinction between respondent and operant crying?

9. Why was it important to determine a baseline record of the operant level of crying for each subject?

10. What were the positive and negative reinforcers in the operant crying study?

11. What does REM stand for, and why is this sleep called paradoxical?

12. What is the "laboratory effect" in sleep research?

13. What is an EEG record and how does it differ during the four stages of sleep?

14. What is the difference between a polyphasic sleep pattern and a monophasic one?

15. What is a possible explanation for the finding that REM sleep declines with age?

part six
sexual behavior

A professor of mine once began a lecture by stating that "there are four F's of life—fighting, fleeing, feeding, and . . . sex."

Any teacher knows that one of the most certain ways to get and keep student attention is to discuss sexual behavior—it is usually easy to get a laugh or two from the class as well!

Behavioral scientists have devoted serious study to sexual behavior for many years; it seems, however, that only recently the general public has become interested in and has seriously considered the research. Perhaps it is the publishing of the experimental findings in the popular press in conjunction with a more open and liberal view toward sex in general which is responsible.

Frank A. Beach summarizes "Experimental Studies of Mating Behavior in Animals" (#30) in fine fashion. The report illustrates the possibilities for exploring and analyzing human sexual behavior through research with lower animals where there are just fewer problems in general. Many a research problem that could not be undertaken with human subjects because of obvious moral and ethical considerations can be successfully attacked using animal subjects as the article indicates.

The work of Masters and Johnson has existed for at least 10 years, but it is only within the past year or so that its impact has been extensive upon the general public. Could it be that society was not ready for such research and analysis before this time? The article reproduced here (#31) is a summary of their research and contains much of the material found in their best-selling book, **The Human Sexual Response.** It seems to me that there has been much nonsense written about "sexual compatibility" in the popular press. There can be no doubt about its importance for a successful marriage; however, the important question which is always answered incorrectly—or not at all—is just what this involves. The Masters and Johnson study provides an important consideration for any person trying to achieve sexual compatibility with his or her partner. Immediately after an orgasm, the male experiences a refractory period during which the penis slowly returns to normal size. During this time period, sexual arousal is impossible and the male requires a "rest period" before sexual activity can continue. The female, on the other hand, experiences no such refractory period and can experience repeated orgasms without a rest. This clearly indicates that it is important for the female to experience her orgasm first or at the same time as the male. A premature orgasm on the part of the male must be followed by the refractory period during which he is not interested in further sexual activity. The unfortunate female in such a situation has not experienced her orgasm and will feel frustrated. The female, of course, can have an orgasm first and continue immediately with sexual activity until the male has an orgasm.

As S. Rachman and R. J. Hodgson, in "Experimentally Induced 'Sexual Fetishism': Replication and Development" (#32), indicate, it is possible to study unusual sexual behavior in a laboratory setting. The report provides a basic insight into and a possible explanation for the many sexual fetishisms which psychologists and others have described.

Elaine Walster and her colleagues are doing research on the role of physical attractiveness and dating choice in college students (#33). The article presented here may prove to be difficult reading for the student in introductory psychology; however, the material is so inherently interesting and important that the student should be willing to put forth the extra effort. Try to read the article for general concepts rather than get bogged down in the sophisticated statistical analyses.

Any research that helps in the understanding of homosexual behavior is obviously important. Very recently, many large college campuses have seen the establishment of militant homosexual organizations which are actively trying to change society's view of this behavior. It is obvious that a "gay revolution" is just beginning; an attempt at understanding and a true concern seems to be the most appropriate response by the "straight" world. Therefore, the final study of this part, "An Empirical Study of Some Relations Between Sexual Patterns and Gender Identity in Male Homosexuals" (#34), should be of particular interest.

30.
experimental studies of mating behavior in animals

frank a. beach

Sex research has a long history, but during the past few decades there have been several important and exciting advances. In part this is due to a marked increase in the number of scientists investigating problems of sexual behavior. Techniques have become more rigorous and sophisticated, and new theoretical formulations have been developed.

SEXUAL BEHAVIOR AND EVOLUTION

From the broad point of view, some of the most penetrating and fundamental questions that can be asked about sexual behavior have to do with its relationships to evolution. These problems do not concern psychologists in their day-to-day work, but they are problems that should not be forgotten.

Two questions are very important to many biologically oriented scientists. (1) How have evolutionary changes affected sexual behavior? (2) How has sexual behavior affected the course of evolution? As introductory reading for anyone interested in these questions, I recommend a book entitled *Behavior and Evolution* by Roe and Simpson (1958).

One way in which sexual behavior can influence the course of evolution is reflected in the concept of isolating mechanisms.

Evolution implies change. It demands the emergence of new species, but at the same time it demands a high degree of stability and integrity of existing groups.

If different kinds of animals were to interbreed and freely produce large numbers of viable and fertile hybrid offspring, the original genotypes could eventually be submerged and lost. This does not, in fact, occur. Two species may be prevented from interbreeding by one or a combination of types of barriers or isolating mechnaisms that have been classified by Dobzhansky (1941) and by Mayr (1942). These may be geographical, as when two species are separated by a body of water or a mountain range. They may be temporal, when the species live together but breed at different times of the year. Isolating mechanisms may also be behavioral or psychological. For example, it is sometimes possible to discover two hympatric species that can produce viable and fertile hybrids in artificial conditions but never do so in nature. Some instances of so-called psychological isolation present problems that are very familiar to the experimental psychologist. These may include species differences in sensory capacity, in perceptual organization, in motivational patterns, or even in early life experience, which contribute to the prevention of sexual mixture with the production of fertile hybrids which could successfully compete with the parental stocks.

In some instances, males and females of different species never attempt copulation although there seems to be some initial attraction. This can occur because one element in the premating courtship of one species is lacking in that of the other.

When a male Siamese fighting fish (*Betta splendens*) is ready to mate, he builds a bubble nest on the top of the water. When a female swims by, he executes certain courtship movements, the female approaches, and mating occurs under the bubble nest. There are closely related species of fish in which the male does not build the bubble nest, although the courtship pattern is much the same as that of *Betta splendens*. A female *Betta* may initially respond to the courtship invitations of a male from the nonnestbuilding species, but in the absence of a nest she soon loses interest and departs before the mating can be consummated.

Male frogs and toads of many species form breeding choruses that function to attract gravid females. Field and laboratory studies have shown that at least for some species females are attracted to and stimulated by calls of males of their own kind but do not react to the masculine vocalizations of a different species (Blair, 1956).

Some male birds announce their establishment of a breeding territory with a courtship song unique to their own species. New methods of recording and analyzing these songs have thrown light upon the role of vocal signals in sexual courtship as it relates to the evolutionary process. Such recordings are called sonograms or sound spectographs. . . .

Not only are there differences in the songs of different species, but within the same species there may be local dialects. For example, near the University of California white crown sparrows sing a Berkeley dialect, whereas white crown sparrows living three miles away sing a different dialect. Marler and his students have shown that dialects are learned by young birds during the fledgling period several months before they are capable of song production (Marler and Tamura, 1962).

It is conceivable that minor differences in the courtship song have an effect upon the choice of a mate. If this were true, local dialect differences might constitute a mechanism whereby new species start to emerge.

There have been several studies of isolating mechanisms in mammals, including the European vole (Godfrey, 1958) and various species of deer mice, *Peromycus* (Eisenberg, 1962). We are working with several species of these mice in my laboratory. They apparently do not interbreed, and we would like to find out why. Mr. Lyn Clemens is studying their mating patterns to see if some fundamental differences are present. We would like also to find out whether or not males or females of one kind are attracted to females of another species and vice versa. To answer this question Clemens has just begun to study what might be called "choice of neighbors."

The experimental situation permits a mouse to spend his time next door to an unoccupied compartment previously inhabited by an individual of his own species, a different compartment which previously housed a mouse of a foreign species, or a compartment in which no mice have been kept. Alternatively the stimulus compartments may contain mice of one or another species. Very preliminary observations on very few animals suggest that males of two species show little or no selectivity as far as their choice of neighbors is concerned. They may spend equal amounts of time in the vicinity of a female of their own kind and one of another species. In contrast some females do seem to exhibit discriminatory behavior over a period of twenty-four hours. A given female may spend twice as much time in a compartment that previously contained a male of her own type than she devotes to the exploration and occupation of a chamber that previously housed a male of a different species. We suspect that the discrimination is made on the basis of olfactory cues, but we are not sure and it will be necessary to test this hypothesis.

Thus far the discussion has dealt with the problem of how established species may be prevented from interbreeding. A different question deals with the ways in which species differences in sexual behavior may have evolved. It should be noted parenthetically that when biologists and psychologists ask apparently similar questions about behavior, they may be looking for quite dissimilar answers. For example, when a psychologist asks why an animal exhibits a particular type of behavior he is usually concerned with problems of motivation; whereas, when a zoologist asks the same question, he means how did the behavior "get that way," that is, what were the evolutionary origins? Important studies dealing with the second question have involved attempts to duplicate certain aspects of evolutionary change under controlled conditions. This has sometimes involved the use of controlled breeding techniques combined with careful study of behavior in successive generations.

HEREDITY AND SEXUAL BEHAVIOR

An outstanding example of this approach is represented by the work of Stella Crossley (Pearce, 1960) on two mutant types of the fruit fly, Drosophila. One mutant, known as Ebony, is a dark color. The other, called Vestigial, possesses very short, stubby wings that are inadequate for flight.

In 1956 Knight, Robertson, and Waddington allowed Ebony and Vestigial flies to interbreed for eighteen successive generations. The number of hybrid offspring progressively decreased and eventually dropped to zero. To determine why this occurred, Crossley repeated the original experiment with two important modifications. First she made direct observations of the sexual behavior. Second, in each generation, she eliminated the offspring that resulted from cross-mating between Ebony and Vestigal parents.

In the first generation, Ebony females mated equally with Ebony or Vestigial males. In contrast, from the very beginning, Vestigial females showed a measurable though not exclusive preference for mating with males of their own type. Direct observation of individual matings revealed that selective breeding over forty generations produced two progressive changes. (1) Both Ebony and Vestigial females showed an increase in the frequency and vigor of certain stereotyped movements which they used to repel the courting male. Since these movements were employed to reject males of the opposite type, they reduced the frequency of heterospecific matings. (2) At the same time, as the number of inbred generations increased, males became increasingly responsive to the females' repelling movements and tended to break off their initial attempts at courtship after shorter periods. The combined result was that no hybrid offspring were produced after forty generations.

Now, if we make the assumption that in their natural environment the offspring of heterospecific matings would be inferior in the capacity for survival or in reproductive potential, then Crossley's experiment can be taken as a model for the kind of changes which could conceivably lead to the emergence of two incipient species. It is important to stress the fact that these changes involve only behavior.

Other isolating mechanisms exist, of course, and the natural situation is much more complex than any laboratory experiment could reveal. Nonetheless, this particular study serves as an example of the way in which experimental methods can be applied to problems of behavioral evolution. At the same time it calls attention to the importance of genetical factors influencing sexual behavior.

There are two obvious ways of investigating the relationship between heredity and behavior. One is to begin with two populations which are known to have different genotypes and to examine them for behavioral differences. The second approach, often employed in conjunction with the first, and exemplified by the work of Crossley described above, involves selective breeding of successive generations to produce individuals of the desired behavioral phenotype.

During the past decade many psychologists have used the first method to show that inbred strains of mice differ from one another in terms of general activity, learning, aggressiveness, emotionality, and even in the preference for ethyl alcohol over branch water (McClearn and Rodgers, 1961). Years ago, Robert Tryon employed selective breeding to create strains of maze-bright and maze-dull rats (Tryon, 1929).

The literature includes very few relevant reports dealing with sexual behavior, and in this connection it is important to stress the fact that the most elaborate and detailed information concerning genotypical differences is valueless unless it is coupled with equally precise and reliable measures for behavior. Behavioral endpoints must be as objectively and quantitatively defined as are the genetical variables.

These desiderata have been approached within reasonable limits in few published studies. W. C. Young and his co-workers have measured the sexual behavior of three strains or families of guinea pigs. Two strains have been inbred for approximately eighty generations and the third is a heterogeneous strain, maintained without any attempt at genetic selection. Carefully devised measures of "sex drive" were applied to males of these three strains. It was found that the within-strain variance was small for inbred types and quite marked for the heterogeneous strain. In addition, "sex drive" was low for males of inbred strains as compared with males of the third strain, which had never been inbred (Valenstein, Riss and Young, 1955).

At the University of California in Berkeley, we maintain two strains of rats that are descendants of those bred by Tryon in his work on the inheritance of maze-learning ability. These strains, now known as S_1 and S_3, are the subject of intensive study on the differences in the biochemistry of various brain regions. Differences have been found in enzyme activity that correlate with differences in learning ability (Rosenzweig, Krech, and Bennet, 1960).

Working at Berkeley while on leave from Yale, R. Whalen (1961) conducted standardized sex tests on male rats from the S_1 and S_3 strains. He found that although they were closely similar in many respects, males from the two strains differed significantly in terms of certain standard measures of sexual behavior.

One of our most reliable indices to sexual activity in the male rat is the number of intromissions that precede the occurrence of ejaculation or orgasm. Whalen found that the S_3 males reached the threshold for ejaculation after fewer intromissions than were required by members of the S_1 strain. This is of more than incidental interest because the frequency of intromissions seems to influence the probability of successful pregnancy in this species.

Studies such as those of Young and of Whalen automatically lead to more detailed investigations. For example, one of the first questions that Dr. Young asked after discovering strain differences in the sex drive of guinea pigs was whether this could be due to differences in the output of androgen by the testes. Subsequent experiments showed that this was not the case. One cannot eradicate the strain difference by simply giving the strain that is low on sex drive large amounts of male hormone (Grunt and Young, 1952).

Whalen's experiments with the S_1 and S_3 males reminded me of earlier studies by McGaugh, who investigated maze learning in the same strains. He found that although S_3 rats tend to be inferior, they can be brought up to the performance level of S_1 animals if they are given diazadamantan—a drug which acts as a cerebral excitant. Under the influence of this drug S_3 rats do as well in a maze as the S_1 animals (McGough, Westbrook, and Burt, 1961). Preliminary experiments on mating behavior suggest that strain differences are temporarily eliminated by the same pharmacological agent. This work must be repeated with added controls and a larger N, but the problem seems worthy of investigation. . . .

HORMONES AND SEXUAL BEHAVIOR

My next topic has to do with gonadal hormones and sexual behavior. Instead of describing the effects of castration and subsequent administration of androgens or estrogens, I want to mention some relatively new developments that bear upon the problem of where, when, and how the so-called sex hormones have their effects.

. . . First, it is worthwhile to recall that gonadal hormones have long been known to exert specific effects upon the embryonic reproductive tract. The classic example is the freemartin. This is a female calf that has a twin brother. By reason of abnormalities in the prenatal blood supply, substances circulating in the male can pass into the vascular system of his female twin. Since the testes of the male fetus secrete androgen, the female is subjected to androgenic stimulation in the course of embryonic development. One result is that her external genitalia are greatly modified and in many respects resemble those of a male. There are additional indications of masculinization in the sex accessories.

In the early days of experimental embryology many studies were conducted to investigate the prenatal effects of gonadal hormones. In general, the results indicated that the differentiation and growth of the Wolffian ducts which give rise to much of the male reproductive apparatus depend upon stimulation by androgenic substances. In contrast, the Mullerian system, which provides the basis for female structures such as the fallopian tubes, the uterus, and vagina, undergoes normal development in the absence of gonadal secretions. . . .

A great deal of the credit for recent development of interest in the behavioral effects of hormones acting before birth belongs to Professor W. C. Young and his co-workers. The basic procedure consists of injecting pregnant guinea pigs with androgen or estrogen at a specific stage in gestation. The most interesting results pertain to the effects of testosterone on the female fetus. These females are ovariectomized soon after birth. When they reach adulthood they are injected with a combination of ovarian hormones known to produce sexual receptivity in spayed females that have not been exposed to androgen in the embryonic period. The experimental guinea pigs are strikingly unresponsive to the exogenous hormones. Many animals fail to become receptive, and the remainder show sluggish or attenuated mating responses to the male. . . .

The evidence suggests that gonadal hormones may exert part of their control over sexual behavior by directing the early differentiation and development of central nervous mechanisms which will mediate mating behavior in adulthood. In other words, certain behavioral differences between males and females may be related to differences in the CNS that are partly genetically controlled and partly due to the influence of hormones acting during the developmental period.

It is appropriate here to add some comments about the effects of gonadal hormones in adult animals. A question raised repeatedly is where and how these hormones exert their influence. One general assumption has been that they take effect in the CNS; that they may influence behavior by changing erotic excitability. Fuzzy notions of that sort have been advanced by a number of people, including myself. It has sometimes been argued that the gonadal steroids cannot pass the blood-brain barrier and therefore cannot affect the brain. The answer is that systemically administered steroids can and do pass this barrier, and that some gonadal hormones can act directly upon the brain.

One of the earliest relevant reports was that of Kent and Liberman (1949), dealing with the effects of ovarian hormones on sexual behavior in female golden hamsters. It was already known that such animals can be made sexually receptive by injecting them with an estrogenic hormone and following this with one injection of progesterone. Ordinarily the hormones are given intramuscularly or subcutaneously, and several hours must elapse between the progesterone injection and the onset of behavioral estrus. Kent and Liberman injected progesterone into the lateral brain ventricle and found that estrous responses appeared within one hour.

In 1956 Fisher published a brief but interesting report to the effect that sodium testosterone sulfate applied directly to the lateral hypothalamus of male rats produced the prompt appearance of intense masculine sexual behavior and, paradoxically enough, it also evoked maternal behavior on the part of males. More recently Fisher has suggested that this combination of male sex behavior and maternal behavior might have been brought about because the injection was made between two important centers (Fisher, 1960). Fisher has also stated that if he injects Versene in the brain, he obtains the same effect that is produced by androgen. This is important because Versene is not a hormone; it is a chelating agent that removes metallic ions. If this preliminary finding is verified by systematic experimentation it will be necessary to consider the possibility that hormonal effects on the brain do not involve stimulation, but may consist of removing chemical blocks and permitting the transmission of impulses from one center or system to another.

Another experiment which must be mentioned is that of Harris, Michael and Scott (1958). These workers used estrogen in a solid state. Crystals of stilbestrol were fused to the tip of a fine needle that could be permanently implanted at any desired location within the brain. Special tests revealed that the hormone diffuses only a short distance into the surrounding neural tissue. Nevertheless, when the implant was made in the dorsolateral hypothalamus of spayed cats sexual receptivity appeared within a few days. The same amount of hormone implanted in other brain regions or injected intramuscularly did not produce this effect. I have perhaps oversimplified the findings somewhat, and they yield no information concerning the mode of hormone action; but they do clearly point to certain hypothalamic regions as primary areas of involvement. . . .

BRAIN FUNCTION
AND SEXUAL BEHAVIOR

In discussing hormonal factors contributing to sexual performance I have unavoidably anticipated my final topic, which deals with brain function and mating behavior. The inextricable relationship between these problem areas is nicely illustrated by studies of localized changes in electrophysiological activity within the brain associated with changes in endocrinological condition or with the occurrence of certain hormone-dependent behavioral responses. One of the first such studies was reported in 1954 by Green, who recorded activity occurring in the anterior hypothalamus of female rabbits. He found that an increase occurred during mating behavior. Comparable changes were evoked in estrous rabbits by stimulating the vagina with a glass rod. It is important that Green got this result only when the females were in estrus and the estrogen level was high.

Immediately after mating the female cat shows a stereotyped behavior pattern known as the after-reaction. She disengages from the male, throwing him off if necessary, rolls over and over, squirming and twisting, and at intervals vigorously licks her vaginal area. Porter, Cavanaugh, Critchlow, and Sawyer (1957) implanted electrodes in the hypothalamus and recorded bursts of high amplitude activity that coincided with spontaneous display of after-reactions and could be artificially produced by mechanically stimulating the vagina of the receptive female.

These findings are particularly interesting when considered in conjunction with Fisher's report that injections of androgen into the lateral hypothalamus produce mating reactions in male rats. Other experiments reported from Sawyer's laboratory have shown that there are marked changes in neural activity within the preoptic region of female rabbits at the time of ovulation. This seems important because studies of labeled hormones indicate that the preoptic region is one of the brain areas in which injected estrogen accumulates (Michael, 1963). . . .

One counterpart of brain recording is brain stimulation, but there have been very few experiments that involved stimulating the brain and observing sexual activity in male or female animals. According to Vaughan and Fisher (1962) stimulation of the dorsolateral hypothalamus in male rats accelerates mating and the occurrence of ejaculation. Karinen and Law (1958) have reported that female rats in diestrus will permit copulation by the male when electrical stimulation is applied to the hypothalamus. There are other reports to suggest that isolated elements of the male's mating pattern can be evoked by brain stimulation. Thus, MacLean and his coworkers (MacLean and Ploog, 1962) have produced penile erection in squirrel monkeys by stimulating the septal, hippocampal, and cingulate areas.

Along similar lines Herberg (1963) has found that by stimulating male rats in the area of the median forebrain bundle he can elicit seminal emission. The emission usually occurs without erection and without any of the other signs of a complete ejaculation that have been produced by copulation. Electrically induced emission is not accompanied by any indication of sexual arousal, and the brain stimulus has no apparent effect upon the male's behavior toward an estrous female.

Published findings concerning brain stimulation and sexual reflexes are tantalizingly fragmentary, but they arouse my optimism because it should be a relatively easy and straightforward task to combine the techniques with others for measuring mating behavior and thus advance our knowledge of the ways in which activity in the CNS is related to sexual phenomena.

CONCLUSIONS

I began this presentation with the statement that research on sexual behavior is in a phase of rapid expansion. New techniques are being applied, new data are being collected, new points of view are emerging. I hope that the evidence I have had time to present in highly condensed form will convince you that substantial progress is being made.

It is too early to discern precisely what direction this progress eventually will take, but as one who has watched the development of this field for more than twenty-five years I am optimistic that we are on the verge of important discoveries, new insights, valuable syntheses, and productive theoretical formulations.

SUMMARY

Recent advances in the study of sexual behavior have been made on four major fronts. The first of these has to do with relationships between sexual behavior and the evolutionary process and includes study of ways in which evolution has affected behavior and vice versa. The second concerns the investigation of genetical determinants of sexual performance. Work in this area includes the detection and measurement of behavioral differences in various strains and subspecies. It also involves selective breeding for particular behavioral characters. The third area of advance centers upon the effects of gonadal hormones. It becomes increasingly clear that certain hormones act as organizing agents early in development, influencing the functional characteristics of neural mechanisms which later will mediate adult mating behavior. Other work reveals that the behavioral effects of hormones involve strictly localized responses in certain brain regions. Finally, techniques permitting continuous recording from selected areas of the brain or the application of stimuli to restricted brain regions have yielded important information concerning ways in which the central nervous system controls and directs sexual behavior.

REFERENCES

Blair, W. F. 1956. Call difference as an isolating mechanism in southwestern toads (*Genus Bufo*). *Texas J. Sci.* 8, 87–106.

Dobzhansky, T. 1941. *Genetics and the origin of species* (ed. 2). New York: Columbia Univ. Press.

Eisenberg, J. F. 1962. Studies on the behavior of *Peromyscus maniculatus gambelii* and *Peromyscus californicus parasiticus*. *Behaviour* 29, 177–207.

Fisher, A. E. 1956. Maternal and sexual behavior induced by intracranial chemical stimulation. *Science* 124, 228–229.

Fisher, A. E. 1960. Behavior as a function of certain neurobiochemical events. In *Current trends in psychological theory*. Pittsburgh: Univ. Pittsburgh Press.

Godfrey, J. 1958. The origin of visual isolation between bank voles. *Proc. royal physical Soc., Edinburgh* 27, 47–55.

Green, J. D. 1954. Electrical activity in hypothalamus and hippocampus of conscious rabbits. *Anat. Rec.* 118, 304.

Grunt, J. A., and Young, W. C. 1952. Differential reactivity of individuals and the response of the male guinea pig to testosterone propionate. *Endocrinology* 51, 237–248.

Harris, G. W., and Levine, S. 1962. Sexual differentiation of the brain and its experimental control. Proc. physiol. Soc., in *J. Physiol.* 163, 42–43P.

Harris, G. W., Michael, R. P., and Scott, P. P. 1958. Neurological site of action of stilboestrol in eliciting sexual behavior. In *Ciba foundation symposium on the neurological basis of behavior*. Boston: Little, Brown.

Herberg, L. J. 1963. Seminal ejaculation following positively reinforcing electrical stimulation of the rat hypothalamus. *J. comp. physiol. Psychol.* 56, 679–685.

Karinen, P., and Law, T. 1958. Changes in sexual behavior in female rats following subcortical electrical stimulation. *Amer. Psychologist* 13, 408 (abstract).

Kent, G. G., Jr., and Liberman, M. J. 1949. Induction of psychic estrus in the hamster with progesterone administered via the lateral brain ventricle. *Endocrinology* 45, 29–32.

Knight, G. R. Robertson, A., and Waddington, C. H. 1956. Selection for sexual isolation within a species. *Evolution 10*, 14–22.

McClearn, G. E., and Rodgers, D. A. 1961. Genetic factor in alcohol preference of laboratory mice. *J. comp. physiol. Psychol. 54*, 116–119.

McGaugh, J. L., Westbrook, W., and Burt, G. 1961. Strain differences in the facilitative effects of 5–7 diphenyl-1-3-diazadamantan-6-01 (1757 LS) on maze learning. *J. comp. physiol. Psychol. 54*, 502–505.

McGill, T. E., and Blight, W. C. 1963. The sexual behavior of hybrid male mice compared with the sexual behavior of males of the inbred parent strains. *Animal Behav. 11*, 480–483.

MacLean, P. D., and Ploog, D. W. 1962. Cerebral representation of penile erection. *J. Neurophysiol. 25*, 29–55.

Marler, P., and Tamura, M. 1962. Song "dialects" in three populations of white-crowned sparrows. *Condor 64*, 368–377.

Mayr, E. 1942. *Systematics and the origin of species.* New York: Columbia Univ. Press.

Michael, R. P. 1962. Estrogen sensitive neurons and sexual behavior in female cats. *Science 136*, 322.

Michael, R. P. 1963. Hormonal control of sexual behavior. Program of the Eighth International Ethological Conference, Leiden, Holland.

Pearce, Stela 1960. An experimental study of sexual isolation within the species *Drosophila melanogaster. Animal Behav. 8*, 232–233.

Porter, R. W., Cavanaugh, E. B. Critchlow, B. V., and Sawyer, C. H. 1957. Localized changes in electrical activity of the hypothalamus in estrous cats following vaginal stimulation. *Amer. J. Physiol. 189*, 145–148.

Rasmussen, E. W. 1953. The relation between strength of sexual drive and fertility in rats, cocks and mice. XVth International Veterinary Congress, Stockholm.

Roe, Anne, and Simpson, G. G. (Eds.) 1958. *Behavior and evolution.* New Haven: Yale Univ. Press.

Rosenzweig, M. R., Kreich, D., and Bennett, E. L. 1960. A search for relations between brain chemistry and behavior. *Psychol. Bull. 57*, 476–492.

Sawyer, C. H. 1960. Reproductive behavior. In J. Field (Ed.), *Handbook of physiology.* (Vol. II, Sec. I, Neurophysiology, pp. 1225–1240). Baltimore: Williams and Wilkins.

Tyron, R. C. 1929. Genetics of learning ability in rats. *University of California publications in psychology 4*, 71–89.

Valenstein, E. W. Riss, W., and Young, W. C. 1955. Experiential and genetic factors in the organization of sexual behavior in male guinea pigs. *J. comp. physiol. 48*, 397–403.

Vaughan, E., and Fisher, A. E. 1962. Male sexual behavior induced by intracranial stimulation. *Science 137*, 758.

Whalen, R. E. 1961. Strain differences in sexual behavior of the male rat. *Behaviour 28*, 199–204.

Young, W. C., Goy, R. W., and Phoenix, C. H. 1964. Hormones and sexual behavior. *Science 143*, 212–218.

31.
the sexual response cycles of the human male and female: comparative anatomy and physiology

william h. masters and virginia e. johnson

INTRODUCTION

During the past six years we have published a series of reports in which the anatomic responses of the human male and female to effective sexual stimulation were presented in detail. Drawing liberally from these reports, we shall present in this chapter a comparison between the reaction patterns of both sexes. Primary focus will be directed toward the marked similarities between men and women with respect to the anatomic and physiologic response to sexual tensions.

For decades the mores of our culture have thwarted objective scientific research in the multidisciplined areas of human sexual behavior. These taboos have been shattered with finality by the pioneering of Dickinson (1933), of Beach (1948, 1950), Ford and Beach (1951), of Kinsey, Pomeroy, and Martin (1948), and Kinsey, Pomeroy, Martin, and Gebhard (1953). The primary result of the incredible productivity of these investigators has been the creation of a firm scientific demand that psychologic concepts

Reprinted by permission from Frank A. Beach (Ed.), *Sex and Behavior*, New York, Wiley, 512–534.

These and a number of forthcoming reports represent some of the results of a long-term research program which was initiated in the Division of Reproductive Biology Department of Obstetrics and Gynecology, Washington University School of Medicine, and has been continued since January, 1964, under the auspices of the Reproductive Biology Research Foundation, St. Louis, Missouri.

of human sexual behavior find support in biologic fact.

Four Phases of the Cycle of Sexual Response

The cycle of sexual response has been divided arbitrarily into four phases by the Division of Reproductive Biology, in order to provide a framework for the description of anatomic reaction to sexual stimulation. Many of the reactions are of such brief duration that they may be confined to one phase of the cycle. Other reaction patterns develop with such magnitude that they may be observed throughout the entire cycle of sexual response.

The four phases of the human female's sexual response cycle have been termed excitement, plateau, orgasm, and resolution (Masters, 1959, 1960; Masters and Johnson, 1960, 1961). This terminology has been satisfactorily extended to the description of the human male's sexual response patterns by the simple expedient of adding a "refractory period" to the immediate postorgasmic onset of the resolution phase (Masters and Johnson, 1963, 1964). The successive phases are graphically represented in Figures 1 and 2.

Excitement Phase. For both sexes an excitement phase (Figures 1 and 2) may develop in response to any form of sexual stimulation regardless of whether it is primarily psychical or physical in origin. Variations in stimulative techniques may shorten, prolong, or even interrupt the excitement phase, particularly if the

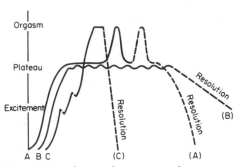

Figure 1. Female sexual response cycle.

stimulative variant is physically irritating and/or psychologically objectionable.

Plateau Phase. If sexual stimulation is maintained effectively, the second or plateau phase of the response cycle is entered by the aroused human female or male (Figures 1 and 2). At this level of stimulation the degree of sexual tension is intense and is marked by physical evidence of both superficial and deep vasocongestion, not only for the pelvic viscera but throughout the entire body. Receptivity to minor stimuli extraneous to sexual focus may be dulled or even lost as the body economy undergoes obvious physiologic strain. The plateau phase of sexual response is a base from which the individual usually moves with relative ease to orgasmic release of the psychologic and physiologic burdens of the accumulated sexual tensions. If effective stimulation is terminated at this level of sexual response, and the orgasmic phase release of sexual tensions is thus prevented, a long and frustrating resolution phase may be anticipated.

Orgasmic Phase. The orgasmic phase of the human female's sexual response cycle (Figure 1, Patterns A, C) is a suffusive, short-term reaction which usually includes contractile sensations of the pelvic viscera. There is a marked variation in the intensity of orgasmic reaction patterns, not only between different women, but within the same female's sexual experiences. The potential pattern of immediate return to orgasmic experience typical of more than 50 per cent of

human females[1] (Figure 1, Pattern A) is not observed frequently in the human male (Figure 2).

The human male's orgasmic phase extends from the onset of contractions in the prostate and the seminal vesicles until the last expulsive contractions of the penile urethra have been experienced. The severity of the male orgasmic phase is in direct proportion to the frequency and duration of contractions of both the primary and secondary organs of reproduction.

In connection with male-female comparisons, it should be emphasized that the human female's orgasmic experience can be terminated at any point by the unexpected introduction of strong extraneous sensory stimuli such as a loud noise, or a marked variation in lighting. On the other hand, we have unpublished evidence showing that once the male's ejaculatory process has been initiated, the orgasmic sequence will continue regardless of the severity of the extraneous sensory stimulation.

Resolution Phase. The resolution phase (Figures 1, 2) has as great a time variant as its counterpart (the excitement phase) in the sexual-response cycle. Physiologic residuals of sexual tension are dissipated slowly in the reacting human if there has been a correspondingly slow tension increment during the excitement phase. If the excitement phase has been a fulminating, short-lived experience, the resolution phase will tend to terminate rapidly.

As illustrated in Figure 2, the human male has an acute refractory period, comprising to a variable extent the first portion of the total resolution phase. During the refractory period any form of sexual stimulation will evoke at best a delayed erection reaction in men under 30 years of age. Men in older groups are frequently incapable of full erection until the refractory period has elapsed. Successive ejaculations are possible only after brief but obvious intervals during which resistance to sexual stimulation is severe and tension levels fall rapidly.

[1]See Davenport's ethnological evidence concerning multiple orgasm in women, chapter 8.

The human female does not develop a distinct refractory period. If she is immediately restimulated after termination of an orgasmic phase, the level of sexual tension may not drop below that of a plateau-phase response, and a repetitive orgasmic experience may develop rapidly and with ease. Many women may move directly from one orgasmic experience to the next under the influence of effective and constantly maintained stimulation.

Subject Population

The subject population available to this study has included, as of July 1, 1965, 382 women with an age range of 18 to 78 years and 312 men with an age range of 21 to 89. All of these individuals have undergone intensive investigation of their anatomic and physiologic responses to effective sexual stimulation All subjects have been studied as they passed through multiple complete and incomplete orgasmic cycles in response to controlled stimulation involving variations in both coital and manipulative techniques.

The female subject population included six postmenopausal women: five who had uterus and ovaries ablated surgically, and five with surgically created artificial vaginae (Masters and Johnson, 1961).

The data we have collected from older age-group males are too few to justify inclusion in this survey. To date no surgically castrated males have been available for study. Every male subject who has established a constant sexual-response pattern has at the same time frequently exhibited wide variation. Therefore our description of the anatomics of masculine sexual response actually constitutes a compilation of multiple basic reaction patterns. No evaluation of the male or female homosexual population has been reported during the nine years that have been devoted to this anatomic and physiologic study.

The individual investigator is at a marked disadvantage when attempting to evaluate human sexual-response patterns. Many response patterns are so fleeting that the most objective observation may fail to reveal all pertinent physiological and anatomical details. Therefore, cinematography has been employed exten-

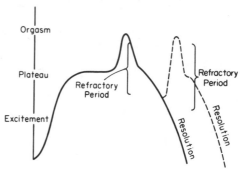

Figure 2. Male sexual response cycle.

sively as the most effective means of recording and interpreting finite details of male and female anatomic reaction to effective sexual stimulation. In addition, the man-woman team approach to the investigative recording and evaluation of male and female sexual reactions has been employed at all times and under all circumstances.

GENERAL BODY REACTIONS

The general body reactions associated with different phases of the cycle of sexual response in males and females are summarized in Table 1.

The Breasts

The first response of the female breast to sexual stimulation is erection of the nipples. Frequently the nipples do not achieve full erection simultaneously. Even though some cases of nipple inversion may be irreducible, many inverted nipples often reverse themselves to assume semierect positions.

There is no constant anatomic response of the male breast to effective stimulation, but specific nipple erection has been observed in approximately 30 per cent of our male sexual subjects. If nipple erection does occur, it usually develops late in the excitement phase and lasts through the remainder of the sexual-response cycle. Males nipples usually erect simultaneously.

The deep vasocongestive response of the female breast to sexual stimulation is evidenced by increased definition of the venous pattern. There is a concom-

TABLE 1.   General Body Reactions

Male	Female
Excitement Phase	
Nipple erection (30%)	Nipple erection
	Sex-tension flush (25%)
Plateau Phase	
Sex-tension flush (25%)	Sex-tension flush (75%)
Carpopedal spasm	Carpopedal spasm
Generalized skeletal muscle tension	Generalized skeletal muscle tension
Hyperventilation	Hyperventilation
Tachycardia (100 to 160/min)	Tachycardia (100 to 160/min)
Orgasmic Phase	
Specific skeletal muscle contractions	Specific skeletal muscle contractions
Hyperventilation	Hyperventilation
Tachycardia (100 to 180/min)	Tachycardia (110 to 180/min)
Resolution Phase	
Sweating reaction (30 to 40%)	Sweating reaction (30 to 40%)
Hyperventilation	Hyperventilation
Tachycardia (150 to 80/min)	Tachycardia (150 to 80/min)

itant increase in breast size and a marked tumescence of the areolae. The areolae usually achieve sufficient tumescence to create the impression that the nipples have lost their previously acquired full erection.

Deep vasocongestion of the female breasts progresses slowly during the plateau phase, and continues until immediately prior to orgasmic experience, when the breast may be from a fifth to a quarter enlarged over the sexually unstimulated baseline. This reaction is particularly evident in the nulliparous breast, and is not consistently apparent in the previously suckled breast. The sexually stimulated, vasocongestive increase in breast size may be supported by the fibrous tissue elements which invest breast lobules as supportive aids. These fibrous structures are frequently destroyed or rendered physiologically incompetent by the suckling process.

A superficial vasocongestive reaction (the sex-tension flush) develops late in the plateau phase over the anterior chest walls of both male and female subjects. This reaction will be discussed in detail in context.

The male exhibits no specific deep vasocongestive reaction which would result in increased breast size or areolar tumescence during either the plateau or orgasmic phases of the sexual-response cycle.

There is no distinct reaction of the female breast to the experience of orgasm. In the female resolution phase, involution of the breast progresses in reverse order from the sequence of anatomic response patterns seen during the original excitement phase. Loss of superficial vasocongestion is evidenced for both sexes by the rapid disappearance of the sex-tension flush which has spread over the breasts and the anterior chest wall. Next in order is reduction in integumental vasocongestion as evidenced in the female by loss of areolar tumescence, and rapid decrease in breast size. Finally, as areolar detumescence progresses, the nipples appear to stand erect, as if sexual stimulation had been reconstituted. This "false erection" of the nipples during the resolution phase has been observed repetitively.

In contrast to the rather rapid involution of the female breast during the resolution phase, in the male, if nipple erection has been established, it may take a matter of many minutes after ejaculation before total nipple retraction has been accomplished.

Vasocongestive Flush

Both male and female subjects have demonstrated a superficial vasocongestive sex-tension flush that may develop late in excitement or early in the plateau phase for the female, but in the male it appears only late in the plateau phase of sexual response. The flush achieves its widest distribution in the immediate preorgasmic period. There is marked variability in sex-flush production. It has been observed in approximately 75 per cent of all female and 25 per cent of all male subjects during individual sexual response cycles.

Numerous environmental and/or psychogenic factors appear to influence the development of male or female sex-tension flushes. Obviously the flush is more apt to develop in a heated than in a relatively cool environment. Certainly the appearance of the flush identifies severe levels of sexual tension. For instance, a subject may go through an entire orgasmic experience without manifesting a flush, yet in a subsequent encounter during which more severe levels of sexual tension develop, a widespread sex-tension flush may be evident in the same individual.

When the flush occurs in either sex, it originates over the epigastrium and spreads to the anterior chest wall. The face, neck, and forehead usually are involved progressively. In the female the flush frequently spreads over the lower abdomen, the thighs, and the low back in a more extensive reaction. With the occasional exception of the forearms and shoulders, the flush is rarely seen in the male other than in the primary sites of epigastrium, anterior chest, face, neck and forehead.

In both sexes the resolution-phase involution of the sex-tension flush closely follows an established sequence pattern. It disappears first from the epigastrium and anterior chest wall, secondarily but rapidly from the shoulders, extremities, thighs, and back, and finally, and much more slowly, from the face, neck, and forehead.

Skeletal Musculature

Skeletal muscles show numerous voluntary and involuntary reactions to progressive degrees of sexual tension. Musculature of the legs, arms, abdomen, as well as the neck and face contracts or contorts spasmodically as late plateau and orgasmic phases of sexual tension are

experienced. One of the most prominent of the muscle-tension reactions is that of carpopedal spasm which develops late in excitement or early in plateau-phase response. Carpopedal spasm is primarily observed in the female partner, if she is in the supine position during coitus. However, the same reaction has been observed regularly in male partners, when female-superior positioning was employed during intercourse. If the sexually stimulative techniques are manipulative rather than coital, both sexes develop severe carpopedal spasm with a high degree of frequency.

For the superior-positioned partner the physical activity of coition, with its normal employment of the voluntary musculature of the trunk, pelvis, and extremities precludes the frequent development of specific uncoordinated striated muscle spasm. However, many male partners have demonstrated specific contraction of the gluteal musculature immediately prior to ejaculation, when the female partner was in supine or knee-chest positioning. Specific preorgasmic contractions of the female gluteal musculature have been recorded on multiple occasions when the female partner was in female-superior coital positioning, but rarely when she was in supine or knee-chest positions.

During the orgasmic phase both sexes regularly demonstrate severe contraction of the recti abdominis, the sternocleidomastoid group, and the facial musculature. The orgasmic phase spasticity of these muscle groupings has been discussed in the literature for many years (Bauer, 1927; Block, 1908; Kinsey et al., 1948; Kinsey et al., 1953; Moll, 1912; Negri, 1949; Rauband, 1876; Siegler, 1944; Urbach, 1921).

Hyperventilation

Hyperventilation is a constant late plateau-phase reaction for both sexes regardless of the types of sexual stimulation or activity (Brown and Kempton, 1950; Klumbies and Kleinsorge, 1950a, b; Shock, 1950; Van de Velde, 1930). The physiologic intensity and duration of the reaction frequently provides a clinical indication of the degree of sexual tension that has developed.

When this physiologic evidence of physical or psychic strain develops in the male in the late plateau phase, it usually continues through the entire orgasmic phase and terminates during the refractory period of the resolution phase. Occasionally the female has been observed to return to orgasmic experience before hyperventilation has resolved. In other words, once the male ejaculates, he is refractory to sexual stimulation at least until his hyperventilative reaction has subsided; but the female may move from orgasm to orgasm without detectable loss in the intensity of her hyperventilation.

Tachycardia

The sexually responding human male and female achieve equal degrees of tachycardia during sexual stimulation. Recordable cardiac rates average from 100 to 160 beats per minute during plateau phases of sexual tension. During orgasmic phase cardiac rates have been recorded from 110 to 180 beats per minute. Tachycardia accompanying advanced degrees of sexual tension has been described many times (Boas, 1932; Klumbies and Kleinsorge, 1950a; Mendelson, 1896).

Specific investigative details of cardiorespiratory physiology in sexually responding human males and females will be reported in a separate monograph in the near future.

"Sweating Reaction"

Approximately 30 to 40 per cent of both sexes develop a "sweating reaction" in the immediate postorgasmic portion of the resolution phase. This reaction may develop whether or not there has been marked physical activity during the sexual encounter, and whether or not a sex-tension flush has appeared. In the male subjects this perspiratory reaction usually is confined to the soles of the feet and the palms of the hands, although occasionally it appears over the trunk and the head and neck. In the female, perspiration is more frequently distributed over the back, thighs, and chest wall, with occasional spread to the forehead and upper lip. The appearance of a postorgasmic perspiratory reaction has been described previously in the literature (El-

lis, 1936; Sadler and Sadler, 1944; Van de Velde, 1930).

PELVIC VISCERA

The various phases of the sexual response cycle are associated with a series of changes in the pelvic viscera. These are listed in Table 2.

Excitement Phase

The first responses of the pelvic viscera to the stimulation of sexual tensions are the erection of the male penis and the production of female vaginal lubrication. Full penile erection is accomplished in from three to eight seconds in the sexually responding male. As a general rule of thumb, the younger males (20 to 30 year age groupings) achieve full penile erection faster than men aged over 30. Vaginal lubrication, which appears as a "transudate-like" material on the walls of the vagina, is well established in from five to fifteen seconds. Human females from 20 to 30 years old generally do not accomplish full lubrication of the vaginal barrel as rapidly as women in the 30 to 40 year groups. Beyond the age of 40, the production rate of vaginal lubrication is significantly slowed,[2] and the average time for full penile erection also is prolonged.

Both of these physiologic phenomena become reversible processes as excitement-phase levels of sexual tension are prolonged. The male may lose full penile erection during long-maintained excitement-phase levels of sexual stimulation, and, under similar circumstances, the human female frequently almost ceases the production of vaginal lubrication, particularly when sex-tension levels are stimulated and/or maintained by manipulative rather than coital techniques.

The second excitement-phase response of the human pelvic viscera to sexual tension is again of vasocongestive origin. It is demonstrated in the male by thickening of the scrotal integument with resultant flattening, constriction, and eleva-

[2]In some societies women too old to produce vaginal secretions are considered sexually unresponsive and undesirable, Chapter 8.

TABLE 2. Pelvic Viscera

Male	Female
Excitement Phase	
Penile erection (3 to 8 seconds)	Vaginal lubrication (5 to 15 seconds)
↓ as phase is prolonged	↓ as phase is prolonged
Thickening, flattening, and elevation of scrotal integument	Thickening of vaginal walls, flattening and elevation of major labia
↑ as phase is prolonged	↓ as phase is prolonged
Moderate testicular elevation and size increase	Expansion of inner ⅔ vaginal barrel and elevation of cervix and corpus
↓ as phase is prolonged	↓ as phase is prolonged
Plateau Phase	
Increase in penile coronal circumference and testicular tumescence (½ to 1 × enlarged)	Orgasmic platform in outer ⅓ of vagina
Full testicular elevation and rotation (30 to 35 degrees)	Full inner ⅔ vaginal expansion, uterine, and cervical elevation
Purple cast to corona of penis (inconsistent, even if orgasm is to ensue)	"Sex-skin" discoloration of minor labia (constant, if orgasm is to ensue)
Mucoid-like emission (Cowper's gland)	Mucoid-like emission (Bartholin's gland)
Orgasmic Phase	
Ejaculation	Pelvic Response

1. Contraction of accessory organs of reproduction
    a. Vas deferens
    b. Seminal vesicles
    c. Ejaculatory duct
    d. Prostate
	1. Contractions of uterus from fundus toward lower uterine segment

2. Relaxation of external bladder sphincter	2. Minimal relaxation of external cervical os (nullipara)
3. Contractions of penile urethra 8/10 second for 2 to 3 contractions (slowing thereafter for 2 to 4 more contractions)	3. Contraction of orgasmic platform 8/10 second for 4 to 8 contractions (slowing thereafter for 2 to 4 more contractions)
4. External rectal sphincter contractions (2 to 4 contractions at 8/10-second intervals)	4. External rectal sphincter contractions (2 to 4 contractions at 8/10-second intervals)
	External urethral sphincter contractions [2 to 3 contractions at irregular intervals (10 to 15%)]
Resolution Phase	
1. Refractory period with rapid loss of pelvic vasocongestion	1. Ready return to orgasm with retarded loss of pelvic vasocongestion
2. Loss of penile erection in primary (rapid) and secondary (slow) stages	2. Loss of "sex-skin" color and orgasmic platform in primary (rapid) stage Remainder of pelvic vasocongestion as secondary (slow) stage

tion of the scrotal sac. The normal scrotal folding pattern is soon lost, as vasocongestion of the Dartos tunic progresses. The corresponding reaction in the female has a double application. First, there is a vasocongestive thickening of the vaginal walls and a flattening and elevation of the major labia. Second, the minor labia develop a two- or threefold vasocongestive increase in diameter which provides far more effective coital accommodation by lengthening the vaginal barrel with the obvious exception of the fourchette.

As the excitement phase progresses toward plateau, the male responds to increasing sexual tension by moderate elevation of the testes. Simultaneously the testes display a vasocongested size increase. Correspondingly, in the female the inner two-thirds of the vagina expands adding 2 to 3 centimeters to the length of the vaginal barrel and developing a two- to threefold increase in width at the transcervical diameter. The cervix of the anteriorly placed uterus moves back from its midvaginal positioning, and, with the uterus, is elevated toward the false pelvis. Full uterine elevation provides a tenting effect of the anterior vaginal wall. Thus, further distension of the vaginal barrel is accomplished by the additional separation of the anterior and posterior vaginal walls.

As is true for penile erection and vaginal lubrication, the physiologic responses of enlargement and elevation of the testes and expansion and extension of the vaginal barrel are reversible reactions if the excitement-phase levels of sexual stimulation are electively prolonged. Under these circumstances, the testes will return to the depths of a relaxed scrotal sac that partially has lost the vasocongested tensing of its integument, and the normal scrotal folding patterns may reappear. These reversible reactions of the testes and scrotum will occur even if a moderate to severe penile erection is maintained constantly.

During extended excitement-phase stimulation (provided mounting has not been accomplished), certain female anatomic reactions also are reversible. The cervix will return to the vaginal axis, and the transcervical expansion and concomitant extension of the vaginal barrel will be reduced. These reactions will occur even though advanced vasocongestion of the vaginal walls and the minor labia is well maintained.

Plateau Phase

If sexual tension is elevated to plateau-phase levels, the male reflects the high tension in further vasocongestion as evidenced by increase in penile circumference at the corona despite the fact that the penis has appeared in full erection during the excitement phase. Vasocongestive tumescence of the testicles (first evident in late excitement phase)

continues until they are from a half to one time enlarged. Finally, as tension mounts toward orgasm, the testes elevate and rotate in a thirty to thirty-five degree arc anteriorally so that the posterior testicular wall comes into direct apposition with the perineum.

The female's plateau-phase response also provides further evidence of pelvic vasocongestion in the form of the development of an orgasmic platform in the outer third of the vagina. The vasocongestive reaction usually progresses to such an extent that the outer third of the vaginal barrel may be obtunded by at least a fifty-per cent reduction in diameter. With achievement of plateau-phase sexual tension levels, full vaginal barrel expansion and uterine and cervical elevation are completed.

Further physiologic parallels in both sexes to plateau-phase levels of sexual tension are associated with perineal color changes. The male response is an increased purple cast to the coronal area of the penis. This color change is inconsistent even if orgasm is to ensue. Many men never demonstrate the color change while others do so only occasionally. The purple color change is apparently a reflection of high sexual tension levels.

The female develops such a marked discoloration of the minor labia that it has resulted in the designation of these tissues as "sex skin."[3] The minor labia of nulliparous women turn a deep cardinal red, and those of the multipara almost a burgundy-wine color as sexual tension advances toward orgasmic expression. Once the minor labia go through this sex-tension color change, orgasm is inevitable if effective sexual stimulation is maintained without interruption. Many women achieve plateau-phase sexual tension levels but do not experience orgasmic phase release; and these females do not show "sex-skin" discoloration of the minor labia.

Additional parallel physiologic phenomena which develop clinically during the plateau phase are evidenced in both

[3]Not to be confused with the swelling and reddening of the circumperineal areas seen in female monkeys and apes during estrus (Ed.).

sexes by mucoid-like secretory emissions. The male has a pre-ejaculatory emission from the urethral meatus that tentatively has been identified with Cowper's glands. This material usually is restricted to two or three drops in amount. Occasionally, during long-maintained plateau-phase levels of sexual tension, approximately half a cubic centimeter has been secreted and collected. On multiple occasions microscopic examination has demonstrated the presence of active spermatozoa.[4]

The female counterpart of the plateau-phase mucoid-like emission is provided by Bartholin's glands. The function of these glands previously has been described as providing vaginal lubrication (Stone and Stone, 1952; Talmey, 1912). The Bartholin secretions do not contribute to the lubrication of the vaginal barrel except for the immediate fourchette area, and then only subsequent to long-maintained plateau-phase levels of sexual stimulation. With prolonged coital activity the production of lubrication of the vaginal barrel is slowed, and continued fourchette lubrication is accomplished by the Bartholin's glands. From the timing sequence, however, it is obvious that this material has nothing to do with lubrication of the vaginal barrel during the initial excitement phase.

Orgasmic Phase

Male. The ejaculatory phenomenon is unique in the entire cycle of sexual response and is the essence of the male-orgasmic experience. Orgasm in the male is initiated by contraction of the accessory organs of reproduction. The vas deferens, seminal vesicles, ejaculatory duct, and prostate contract regularly to provide the seminal plasma and testicular fluid necessary for the ejaculate total. Contraction of the secondary organs of reproduction is experienced in the male as an anticipatory sign of imminent ejaculation. The sensation develops over a 2- to 3-second time interval, and has been described by many males as a feeling that the ejaculation is coming, and that it can no longer be voluntarily con-

[4]This underscores the fact that intercourse without male orgasm, in the usual sense, can result in impregnation (Ed.).

trolled. This anticipatory sensation coincides with the actual internal ejaculation of seminal plasma into the prostatic urethra.

As the seminal plasma is compressed in the prostatic urethra, the internal sphincter of the bladder contracts to avoid retrograde flow into the urinary bladder. The external sphincter and the membranous portion of the penile urethra relax, and the entire seminal pool is ejected along the penile urethra and through the urethral meatus under significant ejaculatory pressure. The ejaculatory contractions are established by the peri-urethral muscles as well as the ischio- and the bulbocavernosis musculature. The contractions have onset intervals of eight-tenths of a second and continue at this spacing for two to three expulsive efforts. Thereafter, the contractions are slowed, not only in interval timing but in expulsive force. However, they have been observed to continue on an irregular basis and with little expulsive force for two to four more occasions. The male orgasmic phase is terminated with the cessation of expulsive contractions of the penile urethra.

Female. The female's orgasmic experience usually is expressed over a longer time sequence. It has onset with contractions of the uterine musculature which originate in the fundus and move toward the lower uterine segment. The nulliparous external cervical os relaxes minimally, but this reaction cannot be reliably established in the parous individual. Concomitant with the onset of uterine contractions is the development of contractions of the orgasmic platform. These two physiologic reactions provide the sensations of pelvic visceral contraction that the sexually oriented human female identifies with orgasmic expression.

Both uterine and orgasmic-platform contractions have simultaneous onset in an overall pelvic-response pattern. At their onset the orgasmic-platform contractions occur at intervals of eight-tenths of a second and continue for four to eight times before there is recordable slowing in the intercontractile interval. Two to four additional contractions may be observed thereafter at irregular intervals and with diminishing muscle tone. They correspond to the nonexpulsive, slowed contractions of the penile urethra at the termination of the male orgasmic phase.

The duration of uterine contractions, their potential expulsive force, or the possible secretory activity of the uterine glands have not been established to justify their discussion here. This material will be presented in a subsequent monograph on the subject of uterine reaction to sexual stimulation.

Other Parallels. Further parallels of pelvic visceral response have been observed in both sexes during orgasmic expression. In the male the rectal sphincter contracts two to four times with onset intervals of eight-tenths of a second. These contractions have been observed to occur in a parallel time sequence with the expulsive contractions of the penile urethra. For the female the external rectal sphincter also contracts two to four times at eight-tenths of a second intervals, again in parallel time sequence with contractions of the orgasmic platform. An additional female response is the occasional (10 to 15 per cent) development of irregular contractions of the external urethra which occur without recordable rhythmicity and recur at the most two to three times. Loss of urine never has been observed in an orgasmically responding human female.

Resolution Phase

The male has a unique refractory period which develops as the last, irregular nonexpulsive contractions of the penile urethra occur, and is maintained until sexual tension has been reduced to low excitement phase levels of response. The female has no such refractory reaction. She generally maintains higher levels of immediate postgasmic sexual tension and susceptibility to stimulation. As previously stated, she is usually capable of repetitive return to orgasmic experience without postgasmic loss of sexual tension past plateau-phase levels of response.

Due to the loss of immediate postgasmic sexual susceptibility, the male pelvic viscera tend to lose their vasoconges-

tion more rapidly than those of the female. Loss of penile erection in the male occurs in two stages. The first stage evidences rapid loss of vasocongestion until the penis is perhaps one to one and one-half times enlarged. Second stage penile involution is a slow development, particularly if the excitement and/or plateau-phase levels of the specific sex-response cycle have been prolonged markedly. As a general rule of thumb, if penile erection has been maintained for long intervals before ejaculation, the second stage involution of penile vasocongestion is usually an extended process.

Loss of testicular vasocongestion and return of the testicles to the depth of the scrotum, together with the reappearance of the scrotal folding pattern and loss of congestion of the scrotal integument occur parallel in time sequence with the rapid primary involution stage of the vasocongested penis.

The female loses the vasocongestion of the orgasmic platform and the sexskin discoloration of the minor labia more rapidly than any other postgasmic involutionary process. Yet, these resolution reactions do not occur as rapidly as primary involution of the male's penile erection. Thereafter loss of minor labial vasocongestion and the return of the walls of the vaginal barrel to unstimulated width is frequently extended over many minutes despite a most satisfying orgasmic experience. Both the return of the cervix to normal vaginal positioning and the loss of the vaginal barrel's vasocongestion are slowed in comparison to the quick resolution reaction time of testicular descent and loss of scrotal vasocongestion. There have been occasional observations of continued production of vaginal lubrication well past the termination of an orgasmic-phase experience. This observation would parallel roughly in time sequence the frequently extended second stage involution of penile erection.

SUMMARY

Parallels between the anatomic responses of the human male and female to effective sexual stimulation have been established. As a comparison aid, Table 1 and 2 have been provided and are self explanatory. It is obvious from the descriptions and discussions presented in this paper that the primary physiologic reaction of either the male or female to sexual stimulation is superficial and/or deep vasocongestion. Hyperventilation, tachycardia, muscle spasm, pelvic musculature contraction, etc., are of secondary import when compared to the basic physiologic process of vasodistention. The marked similarities in the response patterns of the human male and female to effective sexual stimulation have been emphasized in context.

REFERENCES

Bauer, B. A. 1927. *Women and Love* (E. S. Jerden and E. C. Paul, trans.). New York: Liveright Publ. Corp.

Beach, F. A. 1948. *Hormones and Behavior.* New York: Paul B. Hoeber, Inc.

Beach F. A. 1950. Sexual behavior in animals and men. Harvey Society Lectures (1947–1948), Series 43. Springfield, Illinois: Charles C. Thomas.

Block, I. 1908. *The Sexual Life of Our Times in Its Relation to Modern Civilization* (M. E. Paul, trans.). London: Rebman and Co.

Boas, E. P. and Goldschmidt, E. F. 1932. *The Heart Rate.* Springfield, Illinois: Charles C. Thomas.

Brown, F. and Kempton, R. I. 1950. *Sex Questions and Answers.* New York: McGraw-Hill Book Co.

Dickinson, R. L. 1933. *Human Sex Anatomy* (2nd Ed.). Baltimore: Williams and Wilkins.

Ellis, H. 1936. *Studies in the Psychology of Sex.* New York: Random House.

Ford, C. S. and Beach, F. A. 1951. *Patterns of Sexual Behavior.* New York: Paul B. Hoeber, Inc.

Kinsey, A. C., Martin, C. E., and Pomeroy, W. B. 1948. *Sexual Behavior in the Human Male.* Philadelpia and London: W. B. Saunders Co.

Kinsey, A. C., Pomeroy, W. B., Martin, C. E., and Gebhard, P. H. 1953. *Sexual Behavior in the Human Female.* Philadelphia and London: W. B. Saunders Co.

Klumbies, G. and Kleinsorge, H. 1950. Das Herz in Orgasmuc, *Medizinische Klinik, 45,* 952–958 (a).

Klumbies, G. and Kleinsorge, H. 1950. Circulatory dangers and prophylaxis during orgasm, *Int. J. Sexol., 4,* 61–66 (b).

Masters, W. H. 1959. The sexual response cycle of the human female. II. Vaginal lubrication, *Ann. N.Y. Acad. Sci., 83,* 301–317.

Masters, W. H. 1960. The sexual response cycle of the human female. I. Gross anatomic considerations, *West. J. Surg., Obstet. and Gynec., 68,* 57–72.

Masters, W. H. and Johnson, V. E. 1960. The human female. Anatomy of sexual response, *Minnesota Med., 43,* 31–46.

Masters, W. H. and Johnson, V. E. 1961. Orgasm, anatomy of the female, *Ency. Sexual Behavior,* Vol. 2, 788–793. New York: Hawthorne Books, Inc.

Masters W. H. and Johnson, V. E. 1963. The sexual response cycle of the human male. I. Gross anatomic considerations, *West. J. Surg., Obstet. and Gynec., 71,* 85–95.

Masters, W. H. and Johnson, V. E. 1964. The anatomy and physiology of human sexual response. In C. Lloyd (Ed.), *Human Reproduction and Sexual Behavior.* Philadelphia: Lea and Febiger.

Masters W. H. and Johnson, V. E. 1961. The artificial vagina: Anatomic, physiologic and psychosexual function, *West. J. Surg., Obstet. and Gynec., 69,* 192–212.

Mendelson, M. 1896. Ist das Radfahren als eine Gesundheitsgemässe Webung anzusehen und aus artzlichen Gesichtpunkten zu empfehlen? *Dtsch. Med. Wehnschr., 22,* 381–384.

Moll, A. 1912. *The Sexual Life of the Child.* New York: Macmillan.

Negri, V. 1949 *Psychoanalysis of Sexual Life.* Los Angeles: Western Institute of Psychoanalysis.

Rauband, F. 1876. Traite de l'impuissance et de la sterilite chez l'homme et chez la femme. Paris: J. B. Bailliere et Fils.

Sadler, W. S. and Sadler, L. K. 1944. *Living a Sane Sex Life.* Chicago: Wilcox and Follett Co.

Shock, N. W. 1950. Physiological manifestations of chronic emotional states, The Mooseheart Symposium (M. L. Reymert, Ed.). New York: McGraw-Hill Book Co.

Siegler, S. L. 1944. *Fertility in Women.* Philadelphia: J. B. Lippincott Co.

Stone, H. M. and Stone, A. S. 1952. *A Marriage Manual.* New York: Simon and Schuster.

Talmey, B. S. 1912. *Neurasthenia Sexualis.* New York: Practitioner's Publishing Co.

Urbach, K. 1921. Uber die zeitliche Gefühls differenz der Geschlechter während der Kohabitation. *Ztschr. f. Sexualwiss, 8,* 124–138.

Van de Velde, T. H. 1930. *Ideal Marriage.* New York: Covici Freide.

32.
experimentally induced "sexual fetishism": replication and development

s. rachman
and
r. j. hodgson

An earlier experiment (Rachman, 1966) described how a sexual response could be conditioned to a picture of a pair of boots. The present paper describes a further small-scale experiment in which the possibility of pseudo-conditioning was controlled for. Pseudo-conditioning is defined as the appearance of a sequence of responses to the CS even though conditioning has not occurred (e.g. due to sensitization of the sexual response or concurrent sexual fantasies). In the control condition, the UCS was presented prior to the CS (i.e. backward conditioning) so that conditioning would be minimal and yet pseudo-conditioning would be as likely to occur in this control situation as in the experimental situation (i.e. forward conditioning).

METHOD

As in the previous experiment, the unconditioned stimuli were colored slides of nude or scantily-dressed women projected on to a screen (3ft. x 2ft.). The conditioned stimulus was a slide of a pair of knee-length, fur-lined boots. Five other slides of shoes and boots were used to test for stimulus generalization. The extent of the sexual response was measured on a phallo-plethysmograph which consisted of a fine-bore, extensible rubber tube containing mercury. As the length of the tube increases, the length of the

Reprinted from *The Psychological Record*, 1968, *18*, 25–27. Abridged by permission of the authors.
We are grateful to Professor H. J. Eysenck for his advice and assistance.

mercury thread is also extended (but decreased in cross-section). This decreases its resistance and the deflections are recorded electronically.

In the experimental condition (i.e. forward conditioning) the CS was presented for 30 sec. followed immediately by the UCS for 10 sec. The brief presentation of the UCS insured that "satiation" of the sexual response did not occur over a three-quarter hour session. Interest in the UCS was also maintained by having a large number of different pictures (40) so that a S did not see a particular UCS in the same session. A period of from 1 to 5 minutes was interspersed after the presentation of the UCS to allow the sexual response to subside. If the response did not show signs of subsiding after one minute, then a few easy arithmetical calculations were given in order to inhibit ongoing fantasies. Conditioning proceeded up to a criterion of five successive responses—a response being defined as a deflection of at least one unit of the scale. When this criterion was reached, extinction trials were initiated and continued until there were five successive failures to respond. Extinction trials consisted of repeated presentation of the CS for 30 sec. with intervals of at least one minute to allow the sexual response to subside.

In the control condition (i.e. backward conditioning the UCS was presented for 10 sec. followed by an interval to allow the response to subside and a few easy arithmetical calculations, to act as distraction, if the response persisted. The CS was then presented for 30 sec. followed by an interval of one minute

TABLE 1. Conditioning and Extinction Data in Five Subjects

S	Number of Presentations of CS-UCS to Reach Criterion	Number of Presentations to CS to Extinguish	Average Latency of Response During Conditioning	Proportion of Zero Responses to CS Extinction
1	35	8	19.5	0
2	36	18	18.4	0.38
3	21	50	6.9	0.44
4	45	12	10.0	0.43
5	38	29	17.4	0.33

before the next presentation of the UCS. Stimulus generalization was tested for immediately after the criterion was reached by presenting the following slides: brown short boots; high-heeled black shoes; low-heeled black shoes; brown string sandals; golden sandals. Response latencies were recorded to the nearest second during forward and backward conditioning and extinction trials.

Five naive Ss completed the experiment, three of them starting with forward conditioning followed by extinction and backward conditioning (condition A); the other two started with backward conditioning followed by forward conditioning and extinction (condition B). In condition A, backward conditioning proceeded until the number of pairings of UCS—CS was the same as the number of pairings of CS—UCS which were needed to reach the criterion during forward conditioning. In condition B, backward conditioning proceeded up to 40 pairings of the UCS—CS; the two Ss in this group then went on to condition after 35 and 36 presentations of CS—UCS. On the average, each S had five three-quarter hour sessions. Three other Ss did not complete the experiment. One of these showed very few reactions to any of the stimuli; the other two failed to condition after 60 presentations of CS—UCS and were therefore dismissed.

RESULTS

All five Ss who completed the experiment reached the criterion of five successive responses to the CS with forward conditioning but none of them reached this criterion with backward conditioning. Some of the Ss did respond occa-

sionally to the CS during the backward conditioning trials; often they reported, after a response to the CS, that they had been imagining the previous UCS or that they had been imagining some sexual scene involving boots. A stimulus variability theory of conditioning (e.g. Estes and Burke, 1953) would predict that rapid conditioners would have little stimulus fluctuation. This would lead to the hypothesis that the CR's of the rapid conditioners would be easily extinguished that they would have quick response latencies, and that they would have fewer zero responses during the extinction trials. Table 1 presents data relevant to these hypotheses. The number of subjects involved is, of course, not sufficient to permit rigorous testing of these hypothesized relationships; however, on inspection, there are no apparent covariations.

Two Ss did not show any evidence of stimulus generalizations. The other three all showed responses to the brown furlined boots, and two also responded to the high-heeled black shoes. One S responded to the golden sandals. The S showing the most generalization was the one who took longest to condition.

DISCUSSION

Firstly, the study was successful in reproducing the findings of the earlier report (Rachman, 1966). Apparently, it *is* possible to establish an experimental model of sexual fetishism. Secondly, we can now exclude the possibility that the earlier results were a reflection of "sensitization" or pseudo-conditioning. Our inability to evoke sexual responses to the boots under a backward conditioning procedure provides support for the conclusion that we were in fact establishing a genuine conditioned reaction in the forward conditioning procedure. These results also exclude the possibility that the subjects participating in the study were "faking," either in a voluntary or involuntary sense.

Having shown that this "abnormal" sexual reaction can be acquired by a process of conditioning, we now propose to investigate the influence of various conditions and events on this misdirected sexual reaction. One long-term aim is to use this model of fetishism as a test-condition for the study of parameters involved in aversion therapy (Eysenck and Rachman, 1965; Marks and Gelder, 1967).

REFERENCES

Estes, W. & Burke, C. 1953. A theory of stimulus variability in learning. *Psychol. Rev.*, *60*, 276–286.

Eysenck, H. J. & Rachman, S. 1965. *The Causes and Cures of Neurosis*. San Diego: R. Knapp.

Marks, I. & Gelder, M. 1967. Transvestism and fetishism: clinical and psychological changes during faradic aversion. *Brit. J. Psychiat.*, *113*, 711–730.

Rachman, S. 1966. Sexual fetishism an experimental analogue. *Psychol. Rec.*, *16*, 293–296.

33.
importance of
physical attractiveness
in dating behavior

elaine walster, vera aronson, darcy abrahams, and leon rottmann

In one of his delightful articles Goffman (1952) said that: "A proposal of marriage in our society tends to be a way in which a man sums up his social attributes and suggests to a woman that hers are not so much better as to preclude a merger or a partnership in these matters [p. 456]." Goffman's proposal suggests that one's romantic feelings and choices are affected both by the objective desirability of the romantic object and by one's perception of the possibility of attaining the affection of the other. Rosenfeld (1964) has demonstrated that an individual's choice of a *work* partner was affected by his assumptions about whether or not the partner would reciprocate his choice.

The following field experiment was conducted to see if one's romantic aspirations are influenced by the same factors that affect one's level of aspiration in other areas. (Level of aspiration theory is presented in Lewin, Dembo, Festinger, & Sears, 1944.) We wish to point out that this study concentrates on *realistic* social choices. In their discussion of *"ideal choices"* Lewin et al. conclude that an individual's ideal goals are usually based entirely on the desirability of the goal, with no consideration of the possibility of attaining this goal. Probably an individual's fantasy romantic choices are also based entirely on the desirability of the

object. One's *realistic* level of aspiration, on the other hand, has been shown by Lewin et al. to depend both on the objective desirability of the goal and on one's perceived possibility of attaining that goal.

We propose that one's realistic romantic choices will be affected by the same practical considerations that affect other realistic goal setting. Lewin et al. note that since the attractiveness of a goal and the probability of attaining that goal are negatively correlated, the goal an individual can expect to attain is usually less attractive than the one he would desire to attain. In romantic choices, attractiveness and availability would also seem to be negatively correlated. The more abstractly desirable a potential romantic object is, the more competition there probably is for him (or her), and the less likely it is that a given individual will be able to attain his friendship. Thus, one's *realistic* social choices should be less "socially desirable" than one's fantasy social choices. In addition, Lewin et al. note that one's realistic level of aspiration is affected by his perception of his skills. In the romantic area, we would expect that the individual's own social attractiveness would affect his level of aspiration. On the basis of the above reasoning, we would propose the following specific hypotheses:

1. Individuals who are themselves very socially desirable (physically attractive, personable, or possessing great material assets) will require that an appropriate partner possess more social desirability than will a less socially desirable individual.

Reprinted from *Journal of Personality and Social Psychology*, 1966, 4, (5), 508–516. Published by the American Psychological Association. Abridged by permission of the authors.

This study was financed by the Student Activities Bureau, University of Minnesota.

2. If couples varying in social desirability meet in a social situation, those couples who are similar in social desirability will most often attempt to date one another.

3. In addition, we propose that an individual will not only *choose* a date of approximately his own social desirability, but also that after actual experience with potential dates of various desirabilities an individual will express the most *liking* for a partner of approximately his own desirability. This prediction is not directly derived from level of aspiration formulations. Lewin et al. predict only that an individual will choose a goal of intermediate attractiveness and difficulty; they do not propose that an individual will come to *like* goals of intermediate difficulty. We thought that unattainably desirable individuals might be derogated (although inappropriately difficult tasks are not) for the following reasons:

1. If a man chooses an inappropriately difficult task and then fails to attain it, all he suffers is defeat. The task cannot point out to him that he has been presumptuous in choosing a goal so far beyond his level of ability. We speculated, however, that an extremely desirable date can be counted on to make it clear to a somewhat undesirable individual that he is foolish to try to win her friendship and that he should not embarrass her by asking her out.

2. We thought that perhaps an extremely attractive date would not be as considerate of an unattractive date as with a date more average in appearance.

PROCEDURE

Subjects were 376 men and 376 women who purchased tickets to a Friday night dance held on the last day of "Welcome Week." (Welcome Week is a week of cultural, educational, and social events provided for incoming University of Minnesota freshmen.) The dance was advertised along with 87 other events in a handbook all incoming freshmen received. In fact, however, the dance was not a regular Welcome Week event and had been set up solely to test our hypotheses. The handbook advertisement describing a Computer Dance said:

"Here's your chance to meet someone who has the same expressed interests as yourself." Freshmen were told that if they would give the computer some information about their interests and personalities, the computer would match them with a date. Tickets were $1.00 per person; both men and women purchased their own tickets. Long lines of subjects appeared to buy tickets on the opening day—only the first 376 male and 376 female students who appeared were accepted.

For experimental purposes, ticket sales and information distribution were set up in extremely bureaucratic style. The subject walked along a table in the foyer of the Student Union. First, a student sold him a ticket. He moved down the table, and a second student checked his identification card to make sure he was a student and told him to report to a large room two flights above. When the subject arrived at the upstairs room, a third student met him at the door and handed him a questionnaire with his student code number stamped on it and asked him to complete the questionnaire at an adjoining table. A fourth student directed him to a seat. (Proctors around the room answered the subject's questions and discouraged talking.)

Physical Attractiveness Rating

The four bureaucrats were actually college sophomores who had been hired to rate the physical attractiveness of the 752 freshmen who purchased tickets to the dance.[1]

We assumed that one's social desirability would include such attributes as physical attractiveness, personableness, and material resources and that these aspects would be positively correlated with one another. We chose physical attractiveness to be the indicator of the subject's social desirability since this trait was more quickly asssessed under standard conditions.

[1] David Kusher, John B. Kelly, Susan Lampland, and Victoria Noser rated the attractiveness of all the subjects. These students were simply told to use their own judgment in rating the subjects and to be careful not to communicate their ratings to the other raters.

As each subject passed, the four raters rapidly and individually evaluated the subject's physical attractiveness on an 8-point scale, going from 1 ("Extremely unattractive") to 8 ("Extremely attractive"). Obviously, these attractiveness ratings had to be made very quickly; usually the rater had less than 1 or 2 seconds to look at the subject before making his evaluation, and rarely did the rater get to hear the subject say more than "OK" or "Thank you." The briefness of this contact was by design. Since we had chosen to use one aspect of social desirability, as an index of total desirability, as far as possible, we wanted to be sure that the raters were assessing only that aspect. We did not want our ratings of attractiveness to be heavily influenced by the subject's personableness, intelligence, voice quality, etc.

Once the subjects were seated in the large upstairs room, they began filling out the questionnaire. The subject first answered several demographic questions concerning his age (nearly all were 18), height, race, and religious preference. The next measures were designed to assess how considerate the subject felt he would be of a fairly attractive date.

The remainder of the booklet contained material which we wanted to encourage the subjects to answer honestly. For this reason, a section prefacing the questions assured participants that their answers to the questions would not be used in selecting their date. We explained that we were including these questions only for research purposes and not for matching purposes. In addition, the subjects were reassured that their statements would be kept confidential and associated only with their ticket number, never their name. Four pages of questions followed this introduction. In the pages following this introduction, four variables were measured:

Subject's Popularity (Self-report). The subject was asked how popular he was with members of the opposite sex, how easy it was to get a date with someone he thought was exceptionally attractive, and how many dates he had had in the last 6 months.

Subject's Nervousness. The subject was asked how nervous or awkward he felt about the idea of going on a blind date.

Measure of the Subject's Expectations in a Computer Date. The subject was asked how physically attractive, how personally attractive, and how considerate he expected his date to be.

Subject's Self-Esteem. Questions from a scale developed by Berger (1952) ended the questionnaire. The subject was asked how true 36 different statements were of himself. The subject was once again reassured that this information was confidential and would not be used in selecting his computer date. (A typical question is: "When I'm in a group, I usually don't say much for fear of saying the wrong things.") This test was scored so that a high score indicated high self-acceptance and high self-esteem.

From the University's state-wide testing service program at the University of Minnesota,[2] several additional measures were secured for the subject whenever possible. The subject's high school academic percentile rank, his Minnesota Scholastic Aptitude test (MSAT) score, and his score on the MMPI or the Minnesota Counseling Inventory (MCI) were secured.

Two days after the subject completed his questionnaire, he was assigned to a date. Dates were randomly assigned to the subjects with one limitation: a man was never assigned to a date taller than himself. On the few occasions when the assigned female date would have been taller than the male, the IBM card next in the shuffled deck was selected as the partner. When subjects picked up their dates' name, the experimenter advised them to meet their dates at the dance. Many couples, however, met at the girl's home.

The dance was held in a large armory, the subjects had to turn in their numbered tickets at the door. In this way,

[2]We would like to thank Theda Hagenah and David Wark of the Student Counseling Bureau, University of Minnesota, for providing access to this information.

we could check on whether or not a given couple had attended the dance. Of the 376 male and 376 female students who signed up for the dance and were assigned a partner, 44 couples did not attend.[3] The subjects generally arrived at the dance at 9:00 p.m. and danced or talked until the 10:30 p.m. intermission.

Assessing Subjects' Attitudes Toward One Another

Subject's attitudes toward their dates were assessed during intermission. Several times during Welcome Week, we had advertised that couples should hold onto their ticket stubs until intermission, because these stubs would be collected during intermission and a $50 drawing would be held at that time. When the subjects bought their tickets, we reminded them that they would need to save their tickets for an intermission lottery. They were also told that during the dance they would have a chance to tell us how successful our matching techniques had been.

During the 10:30 p.m. intermission, the subjects were reminded that tickets for the lottery would be collected while they filled out a brief questionnaire assessing their dates and the dance. The purpose of the lottery was simply to insure that the subjects would retain their ticket stubs, which contained an identifying code number, and would report to an assigned classroom during intermission to evaluate their dates. Men were to report to one of seven small rooms to rate their dates and to turn in their stubs; women were to remain in the large armory to evaluate their partners.

The forms on which the subjects rated their partners were anonymous except that the subjects were asked to record their ticket numbers in the right-hand corner. This number, of course, identified the subjects perfectly to us, while not requiring the subjects to sign their name to their evaluation. A crew of experimenters rounded up any subjects who had wan-

dered to rest rooms, fire escapes, or adjoining buildings and asked them to turn in their ticket stubs and to complete the evaluation questionnaires.

In the eight rooms where the subjects were assembled to evaluate their dates, the experimenters[4] urged the subjects to take the questionnaire seriously and to answer all questions honestly. All but 5 of 332 couples attending the dance completed a questionnaire, either during intermission or in a subsequent contact 2 days later.

The intermission questionnaire asked the subject about the following things: (a) how much the subject liked his date, (b) how socially desirable the date seemed to be ("How physically attractive is your date?" "How personally attractive is your date?"), (c) how uncomfortable the subject was on this blind date, (d) how much the date seemed to like the subject, (e) how similar the date's values, attitudes, and beliefs seemed to the subject's own, (f) how much of an effort the subject made to insure that the date had a good time, and how much of an effort the date made on the subject's behalf, (g) whether or not the subject would like to date his partner again.

How often couples actually dated was determined in a follow-up study. All participants were contacted 4–6 months after the dance and asked whether or not they had tried to date their computer date after the dance. If the experimenter was unable to contact either the subject or the subject's date in 2 months of attempts, the couple was excluded from the sample. Only 10 couples could not be contacted.

RESULTS

Physical Attractiveness and Social Desirability

We assumed that we could use our ratings of physical attractiveness as a rough index of a person's social desir-

---

[3]By far the most common reason given by the subjects for not attending the dance was that the date was of a different religion than the subject and that their parents had objected to their dating.

[4]Darcy Abrahams, James Bell, Zita Brown, Eugene Gerard, Jenny Hoffman, Darwyn Linder, Perry Prestholdt, Bill Walster, and David Wark served as the experimenters. Male experimenters interviewed male subjects; female experimenters interviewed female subjects.

ability. Is there any evidence that these outside ratings are related to the subject's own perception of his social desirability? When we look at the data, we see that there is. The more attractive an individual is, the more popular he says he is. The correlation between physical attractiveness and popularity for men is .31 and for women is .46. (Both of these r's are significant at $p < .001$.)[5]

Hypothesis 1

Our first prediction was that a very socially desirable (attractive) subject would expect a "suitable" or "acceptable" date to possess more physical and personal charm and to be more considerate than would a less socially desirable subject.

We had two ways of testing whether or not attractive subjects did, in fact, have more rigorous requirements for an acceptable date than did less attractive individuals. Before the subject was assigned a date, he was asked how physically attractive, and how considerate he expected his date to be. His answers to these three questions were summed, and an index of degree of the perfection he expected was computed. From the data, it appears that the more attractive the subject is, the more attractive, personable, and considerate he expects his date to be. The correlation between physical attractiveness and total expectations in a date is .18 for men and .23 for women.

A second way an individual's stringency of requirements could have been tested was by seeing whether or not the subject refused to go out with an "unsuitable" date. We wanted to eliminate the possibility that attractive and unattractive subjects would attend the dance with different frequencies, so we encouraged subjects to meet one another at the dance. However, it is possible that a few individuals were ingenious enough to get a preview of their dates before their public appearance together. We tried to determine whether or not attractive individuals rejected their partners

[5]With an N of 327, a correlation of .10 is significant at $p < .05$, a correlation of .15 at $p < .01$, and a correlation of .18 at $p < .01$, and a correlation of .18 at $p < .001$.

before the dance more often than did unattractive ones.

It will be recalled that four raters rated each subject on an 8-point scale of attractiveness. We then separated subjects into three approximately equal-sized groups on the basis of these ratings. Men receiving an average rating of from 1.50 to 4.75 were classified as *Ugly* individuals; men receiving an average rating of from 5.25 to 6.00 and women rated 5.00 —5.75 were classified as *Average* individuals; and men rated 6.25—8.00 and women rated 6.00—8.00 were classified as *Attractive* individuals. We then contacted the 44 couples who did not attend the computer dance and interviewed them about their reasons for not attending. Attractive subjects did not reject their dates before the dance any more often than did unattractive subjects.

Behavioral Measures of Rejection

After men had arrived at the dance, or at their date's home, they met the partner who had been randomly assigned to them. Then during intermission, the subjects rated their liking for their dates. Since partners were randomly assigned, very attractive individuals should be assigned to just as attractive partners, on the average, as are average or ugly individuals. Thus, if during intermission, very handsome individuals rate their dates as less attractive, less personable, and less considerate than do less attractive men, this would indicate that attractive men are more harsh in their standards and ratings than are less attractive men. Also, if attractive individuals are more harsh in their standards they should, on the average, like their dates less, express less of a desire to date their partner again, and should actually try to date their computer partner less often than do less attractive individuals. When we look at the data, we see that this first hypothesis is confirmed.

The more attractive a man is, the less physically and personally attractive he thinks his date is ($F = 8.88$, $df = 1/318$, $p < .01$), the less he likes her ($F = 6.69$, $p < .01$), the less he would like to date her again ($F = 14.07$, $p < .001$), and the less often the date says he actually did ask her out again ($F - 3.15$, ns). Similarly, the more attractive a woman is, the less physically and personally attractive she thinks her date is ($F = 5.71$, $df = 1/318$, $p < .05$), the less she likes her date ($F = 2.23$, ns). and the less she would like to date him again ($F = 13.24$, $p < .001$).

Though it is clear that the more attractive subjects do appear to judge their dates more harshly than do unattractive subjects, we would like to note that this variable does *not* account for the very large portion of the total variance. For example, the relationships we have demonstrated between the subject's attractiveness and his expectations and evaluations of a date are strongly significant in five of the seven cases reported. However, correlations for the above variables range from only .07 to .20.

Hypothesis II proposed that an individual would most often choose to date a partner of approximately his own attractiveness. Hypothesis III stated that if individuals were to interact with partners of varying physical attractiveness, in a naturalistic setting, an individual would be better liked and would more often want to continue to date a partner similar to himself in attractiveness. . . .

Statistically, we test Hypotheses II and III by testing the significance of the interaction between date's attractiveness in influencing the subject's *attempts* to date the partner, and his liking for his date. . . .

Hypotheses II and III are not supported. The subject's attractiveness does not significantly interact with the date's attractiveness in determining his attempt to date her, his desire to date her, or his liking for her. In *no case* is there a significant interaction. If we look at the *actual* attempts of men to date their partners, we find that men did not more often ask out dates similar to themselves in attractiveness. (These data were secured in a follow-up study.) The only important determinant of whether or not the date was asked out again was how attractive the *date* was. The most attractive girls are most often asked out ($F = 12.02$, $df = 1/318$, $p < .001$). This is generally true *regardless of the attractiveness of the man* who is asking her out. There is *not* a significant tendency

for subjects to try to date partners of approximately their own physical desirability. The interaction F which is necessary to demonstrate such a tendency is very small ($F = .07$).

Our hypothesis (III) that individuals would best *like* dates similar to themselves in attractiveness also fails to be supported by the data. During intermission, individuals indicated how much they liked their dates on a scale ranging from 2.5 ("Like extremely much") to — 2.5 ("Dislike extremely much"). It is apparent that by far the greatest determinant of how much liking an individual feels for his partner is simply how attractive the partner is, the better liked she is ($F = 59.26$, $df = 1/318$) and the more often the man says that he would like to date her ($F = 49.87$). Men do not overrate women at their own attractiveness level. (Interaction Fs for liking and desire to date $= 2.53$ and .69, respectively.) Very surprising to us was the fact that a *man's* physical attractiveness is also by far the largest determinant of how well *he* is liked. We had assumed that physical attractiveness would be a much less important determinant of liking for men than for women. However, it appears that it is just as important a determinant. The more attractive the man, the more his partner likes him ($F = 55.79$, $df = 1/318$) and the more often she says she wants to date him again ($F = 37.24$). As before, we see that women do not tend to overrate partners at their own attractiveness level. (Interaction Fs for liking and desire to date $= .07$ and .08, respectively.)

In order to get a better idea of the extent to which liking was related to the date's physical attractiveness, we examined the correlation between these two variables. The correlations between the date's attractiveness and the partner's liking is almost as high as the reliability of the attractiveness ratings.

Our measure of physical attractiveness is not highly reliable. When rating the subject's physical attractiveness, raters saw the subject for only a few seconds as the subject moved along in a line. In addition, raters had to devise their own standards of attractiveness. Probably as a consequence of the preceeding factors, the attractiveness ratings made by the four raters of the same individual intercorrelate .49—.58. In addition, there is a factor which may further reduce the reliability of our attractiveness measure from the time of the rating to the time of the dance. At the time of the rating, the subjects were in school clothes casually dressed, while on the day of the dance they were dressed for a date. It is possible that this difference would have produced a change in the subject's relative attractiveness orderings. In spite of these limitations, the correlation between a *woman's* average physical attractiveness rating and her male partner's liking for her is .44; the correlation between her attractiveness and whether or not he wants to continue to date her is .39; and between her attractiveness and how much he actually does ask her out subsequently is .17. The correlations between a *man's* average physical attractiveness rating and his partner's liking for him and desire to date him are .36 and .31, respectively.

When we examine the relationship between the *individual's* own estimation of the date's physical attractiveness and his expression of liking for her, the correlations are still higher. The correlation between liking of the date and evaluation of the date's physical attractiveness is .78 for male subjects and .69 for female subjects.

It appears that the more attractive the date, the more he was liked, and the more the subject desired to date him regardless of how attracted the date was to the subject. The happy accommodation that we proposed between what an individual desires and what he can realistically hope to attain appears not to exist. The lack of symmetry between the individual's liking for his date and the date's liking for the individual is striking. The correlation between how much the man says he likes his partner and how much she likes him is virtually zero: $r = .03$. Nor is there a significant correlation between whether or not the subject wants to date his partner again and whether she wants to date him: $r = .07$. Clearly, a variable that we assumed would be very important—how much the date likes individual—does not appear to

be an important determinant of the individual's ratings. Sheer physical attractiveness appears to be the overriding determinant of liking.

How can we account for the singular importance of physical attractiveness in determining the individual's liking for the other? There seem to be several plausible explanations:

1. Perhaps it could be argued that in the relationships we have discussed it is not really physical attractiveness that is so crucial, but one of the *correlates* of attractiveness. For example, we know from developmental studies of intelligent individuals (Terman, 1925, 1947, 1959) that intelligence, physical attractiveness, creativity, and certain personality traits are often positively correlated. Perhaps it is one of these correlated variables that is really important in determining liking.

From the other evidence we have on this point and which we will present in the next paragraphs, it appears that "intelligence" and "personality" are *not* better predictors of liking than physical attractiveness.

Intelligence and Achievement Measures

Student's high school percentile ranks and MSAT scores are undoubtedly much more reliable measures than is our measure of physical attractiveness. Yet, these measures have only a very weak relationship to liking. The higher the male's high school percentage rank, the less his partner likes him ($r = -.18$) and the less she wants to date him again ($r = -.04$) ($N = 303$). Male's MSAT scores correlate .04 with both the woman's liking for him and her desire to date him ($N = 281$). The higher the female's high school percentile rank, the less her partner likes her ($r = -.07$) and the less he desires to date her again ($r = -.09$). High school rank is uncorrelated with his actual attempt to date her again ($r = .00$) ($N = 323$). Females' MSAT scores correlate $-.05$, $-.06$, and $-.06$ with these same variables ($N = 306$). It is clear then that intelligence is clearly not a variable of the same importance as physical attractiveness in determining liking. In no case did a subject's intellectual achievement or ability test scores have a significant relationship to the liking his date expressed for him.

Personality Measures

The subjects also completed several personality measures which could reasonably be expected to predict the liking one would engender in a social situation.[6]

MCI: Social Relationships (SR). Low scorers are said to have good social skills, have acceptable manners, and be courteous, mature individuals (Berdie, Layton, Swanson, Hagenah, & Merwin, 1962).

MMPI: Masculinity-Femininity (Mf). Low scorers are said to be more masculine in their values, attitudes, interest, styles of expression and speech, and in their sexual relationships than high scorers (Dahlstrom & Welsh, 1962).

MMPI: Social Introversion (Si). Low scorers are said to be more extroverted in their thinking, social participation, and emotional involvement.

Berger's Scale of Self-acceptance (1952)

When we look at the correlations between an individual's scores on these personality measures and the liking his date expresses for him, we see that these personality measures are not as good predictors of liking as is our crude measure of physical attractiveness. When we look at the data, we see that the low scoring individuals on the MCI (SR), on the MMPI (Mf), and on the MMPI (Si) or high scorers on Berger's Scale of Self-acceptance are only slightly better liked by their dates than are high scoring individuals. Men's scores on these tests correlate − .11, − .12, −.10, and .14 with their dates' liking for them. Women's scores on these tests correlate only − .18, − .10, − 08, and .03 with their dates' liking. Our personality measures, then, like our intelligence measures, appear to

be very inadequate predictors of liking.

It is, of course, possible that intelligence and personality determinants would have been more important had individuals had more time to get acquainted. It may be that 2½ hours is too short a time for individuals to discover much about their partner's intelligence or personality, while physical attractiveness is obvious from the start. It is not likely, however, that intelligence or personality variables are "really" underlying the correlations we obtained between attractiveness and romantic liking.

2. It may be that in this situation, individuals were not very affected by their dates' liking for them because the dates were so polite that it was impossible for the individual to know if he was accepted or rejected. Or, perhaps individuals were so eager to be liked that they did not want to correctly perceive the available cues.

The only available evidence for this position is ambiguous. The correlation between the partner's stated liking for the subject and the subject's perception of the partner's liking for him is .23 for male subjects and .36 for female subjects. The subject, thus, has some, though not a great deal of, ability in estimating how much his partner likes him. . . .

3. It may be that our findings are limited to large group situations, where young people are in very brief contact with one another. Perhaps if individuals had been exposed to one another for *long* periods of time, similarity of interests, beliefs, and reciprocal liking would come to be more important than physical appearance in determining liking. Finally, it might also be true that physical attractiveness loses some of its importance as individuals get to be *older* than the 18-year-olds interviewed in our study.

We should note that, even though further contact may have decreased the importance of physical attractiveness, whether or not the subject attempted to continue to date his partner depended on the partner's physical attractiveness. Similarly, though our findings may well be limited to the youthful population that we interviewed (average age: 18 years), it is also true that this is the

---

[6]MCI scores were secured for 234 of the male subjects and 240 of the female subjects during freshman testing. In addition, the MMPI had been adminstered to a sample including 50 of the men and 41 of the women.

age at which many individuals make their lifelong romantic choices.

4. Finally, it may be that if we had arranged more conventional single dates, the date's personality and conversational abilities would have been more important. It may have been that just getting to display a very attractive date compensated for any rejection on the date's part.

REFERENCES

Berdie, R. F., Layton, W. L., Swanson, E. O., Hagenah, T., & Merwin, J. C. *Counseling and the use of tests.* Minneapolis: Student Counseling Bureau, 1962.

Berger, E. M. The relation between expressed acceptance of self and expressed acceptance of others. *Journal of Abnormal and Social Psychology,* 1952, 47, 778–782.

Dahlstrom, W. G., & Welsh, G. S. *An MMPI handbook: A guide to use in practice and research.* Minneapolis: University of Minnesota Press, 1962.

Goffman, E. On cooling the mark out: Some aspect of adaptation to failure. *Psychiatry,* 1952, 15, 451–463.

Lewin, K., Dembo, T., Festinger, L., & Sears, P. Level of aspiration. In J. McV. Hunt (Ed.), *Personality and the behavior disorders.* Vol. 1. New York: Ronald Press, Pp. 333–378.

Rosenfeld, H. M. Social choice conceived as a level of aspiration. *Journal of Abnormal and Social Psychology,* 1964, 68, 491–499.

Terman, L. M. *Genetic studies of genius.* Vol. 1. Stanford: Stanford University Press, 1925.

Terman, L. M. *Genetic studies of genius.* Vol. 4. Stanford: Stanford University Press, 1947.

Terman, L. M. *Genetic studies of genius.* Vol. 5. Stanford: Stanford University Press, 1959.

34.
an empirical study of some relations between sexual patterns and gender identity in male homosexuals

evelyn hooker

The psychosexual identities of male homosexuals have long been a perplexing problem for research workers in the field of sex deviation. Efforts to resolve the problem have often resulted in the positing of two distinct types, on the basis of the preferred form of sexual activity and its relation to nonsexual aspects of gender roles.[1] Thus, Ferenczi (1914) distinguished between the "invert, or passive male homoerotic," who "feels himself to be a woman, and this not only

Excerpts reprinted from John Money (Ed.), *Sex Research: New Developments*, New York, 1965, 24–51. Copyright © 1965 by Holt, Rinehart and Winston, Inc. Reprinted by permission of Holt, Rinehart and Winston, Inc.

This investigation was supported by Research Grants M–839 and M–6452 and a Research Career Award from the National Institute of Mental Health of the National Institutes of Health, United States Public Health Service.

This chapter is a revision of the paper read by invitation at the symposium on sex research of the New England Psychological Association. The full development and documentation of this brief account is a task to be accomplished in two volumes on homosexuality on which I am now at work. I am indebted to Dr. Martin Orme and Dr. John Money for a careful reading of an original draft and many helpful suggestions.

[1] The terms *gender role* and *sex role* are often used interchangeably, and with resulting confusion. Sex role conventionally includes expected attitudes and behavior that distinguish males from females, including sexual performance. *Gender role* is often used with the same referents. For purposes of clarity, the term *sex role*, when homosexual practices are described, should be

in genital intercourse, but in all relations of life," and the "active homosexual," who "feels himself a man in every respect. . . . The object of his inclination alone is exchanged. . . ." (p. 300). Terman and Miles (1936) employed this distinction between the "passive male homosexual, or invert" and the "active, or masculine" homosexual, as defined by sexual practice, with results that tended to confirm the psychological gender (M–F) differences between the two types. Brown (1958, 1961) has reviewed the use of the concepts of inversion and homosexuality. He suggests that the term "sexual inversion" be applied to those individuals who have an "identification with, preference for, and adoption of the sex role of the other sex . . ." (1961, p. 1018). The term "homosexual" should then be used to refer to individuals who seek sexual satisfaction predominantly with members of their own sex. He asserts that "inversion is only *one* condition that may be related to *one* form of homosexuality." "*Passive, feminine* male homosexuality and *active, masculine* female homosexuality will often be found among male and female inverts respectively" (1961, p. 1019).

A number of writers, including Brown (1958), Terman and Miles (1936), and Rado (1949), while emphasizing the active–passive dichotomy in sexual patterns and the corresponding masculine–feminine dichotomy in gender identity in

restricted to *typical sexual performance.* The gender (M-F) connotations of these performances need not then be implicitly assumed.

some individuals, have noted that the patterns of many homosexuals cannot be characterized by such dichotomous concepts, but represent variable combinations or intermediate grades. Recently, Westwood (1960), Bieber, Dain, Dince, Drellich, Grand, Gundlach, Kremer, Rifkin, Wilbur, and Bieber (1962), and Hooker (1961) have questioned the accuracy of the terms "active" and "passive," when used to describe homosexual acts, and, either explicitly or by implication, have questioned the long-accepted gender role connotations of these terms.

The perspective of the two-sexed heterosexual society has dominated all attempts to classify the patterned relationships between sexual performance and psychological gender in male homosexuals. Many male homosexuals, however, who develop working solutions to the problems with which they are confronted by virtue of their sexual object-choice, live in two worlds, the larger society and homosexual subcultures that are, in the main, one-sexed societies. I propose that, in the context of their subcultures in relation to the larger society, homosexuals develop working solutions to problems of sexual performance and psychological gender which cannot be understood in the perspective of the two-sexed heterosexual world.

Is there a relation between what male homosexuals do sexually and how they feel about themselves as men? Is it possible for the male homosexual to "feel himself a man in every respect," not only in sexual activity but in his work life, erotic fantasies, social relations with nonhomosexual males, and in his domestic activities and love relationships? Does the status of being a male homosexual in our society inevitably produce problems about masculinity in a man who identifies himself as one? What is the influence on sexual patterns and a conscious sense of being masculine or feminine, of the fact that many male homosexuals participate in some sector of the homosexual subculture? If identity is discovered in interaction with others and is therefore not fixed and immutable but changes over time—a thesis which Strauss (1959) and others have developed—what transformations of psychosexual identity

occur with progressive involvement in the homosexual way of life? These questions suggest an expanded frame of reference, within which some of the problems of the psychosexual identities of male homosexuals will be examined.

RESEARCH SUBJECTS AND METHOD

The primary data have been obtained from thirty men, about whom I have previously reported other research findings (1957, 1958). They are adult homosexual males who are erotically and emotionally attracted to, and engage in overt sexual behavior exclusively or predominantly with, other males.[2] Detailed accounts of how they were obtained as research subjects, and of the criteria used in their selection, have already been reported; therefore only a brief summary will be given here. They were obtained by gaining access to homosexual groups and networks of friends, and by establishing a viable research role with them as one who was completely trustworthy and morally nonjudgmental. They were originally selected as "normal"; that is, they were not seeking psychological help, were gainfully employed, and, in an initial screening interview, showed no gross signs of psychological disturbance. To assess the kind and degree of normality or psychopathology is one of the objectives of the research.

They were committed to homosexuality, albeit with varying degrees of acceptance of that status. I use the term *committed* here to refer to the fact that they rejected the possibility of a change in sexual pattern to that of heterosexuality and, in most instances, did not see such a change as being desirable—although some expressed the opinion that if change were possible and could have occurred before they had adjusted to a homosexual way of life, they would have pre-

[2]At the time these subjects were first interviewed in 1954, all but three of the thirty were exclusively homosexual, and these three had had a maximum of three overt heterosexual experiences each. On the Kinsey scale, twenty-seven would be rated as 6, and there three would be rated as 5. All of them identified themselves as homosexual in their patterns of desire and behavior.

ferred it. As already indicated, they were erotically and emotionally attracted to, and engaged in overt sexual behavior predominantly or exclusively with, other males. I first interviewed them and administered a battery of psychological tests in 1954,[3] and have re-interviewed them twice since, the last time in 1962. Some of them have been interviewed at much more frequent intervals.

The complete and generous cooperation of these thirty men over a period of eight years—which continues at the present time—thus made possible a 100 percent follow-up. Most follow-up studies report a sizable loss of subjects over time. Some comments by way of explanation of the long-sustained motivation of these men to cooperate with the research may be appropriate. Their cooperation was completely voluntary, since they were not paid. For some individuals, the primary motivation was to make a contribution to a scientific inquiry into homosexuality. Having read a good deal of the literature, they knew that samples of homosexuals who had been studied were, for the most part, clinic patients, and that our knowledge of homosexuality is therefore fragmentary. The opportunity to talk with a trained professional person who had a genuine interest in them as individuals and in every aspect of their life patterns was, as some frequently reported, a rewarding experience, especially because of my completely accepting a morally nonjudgmental attitude toward homosexual behavior. Over the course of the years, many of them have come to see me not only as a friend rather than a detached scientist—and correctly so—but also as a person with knowledge of psychiatric, legal, and other expert resources in the community from which assistance in times of trouble can be obtained. It will be apparent that the motivations are much more complex than indicated in these brief statements.

When the research was begun in 1954, the primary objectives were to study the developmental sequences in the life history of the individual leading to adult identification as a male homosexual and

to determine the correlates in personality structure and adjustment of such an identification. It very quickly became apparent that in order to understand the adjustment patterns of such individuals, it would be necessary to study the sectors of the homosexual subculture in which many of them participated. A study of homosexual subcultures soon became a project in its own right. As I have described in greater detail in previous reports the procedures and difficulties involved in this ethnographic or field study method (1961, 1963), I shall repeat here only the fact that my effort is to look with the subject at his life and his world through his eyes as he sees it; to be as fully an "insider" or participant as one who is "wise" but not a member can be. Looking with him at his world is a multiphasic process, involving going with him to scenes, occasions, or social settings in which the activities are occurring that constitute some of the essential features of his homosexual world, and interviewing him about those activities before and after such occasions. Thus I have participated with most of the thirty subjects, and many additional ones, in a wide variety of social activities in their homes and/or other social settings, as well as interviewing and testing them in my home study.

Because of the long-sustained character of the inquiry, the repeated checks on life history data at intervals, the participation with the research subjects in other social activities, and the positive relationship with them, I have a high degree of confidence that the data are to be trusted.

In my initial interviews, which were relatively unstructured and tape recorded, I formulated the task as a joint enterprise between the subject and myself, in which the objective was to understand as much about his life history, including the present, as possible. A general statement was made to the effect that this would include, among other things, his relations with his parents, siblings, and friends; his educational career; occupational career; sexual history; health history; fantasies; and his hopes, worries, and satisfactions. Sometimes I was asked whether I was doing another Kinsey study, to which I always replied that I

[3]When first interviewed in 1954, the age range was 25–57, with a mean age of 34.5.

was not, and that although I wanted to learn about their sexual histories and current sexual activities, I was at least equally interested, if not more so, in other aspects of their lives. Unless information about sexual experience was given spontaneously in the course of relating other information, direct questions were not asked until a given period in the life history had been completed, such as childhood to age twelve, or adolescence to age eighteen.

The initial interviews varied from two to four sessions of two or three hours' duration. Five years later, all thirty subjects were re-interviewed, in order to fill gaps in the data, to follow the changes occurring in their lives, and to check on the reliability of the first interview. At this time, the entire sexual history was reviewed with the subject. In the third series of interviews, three years later, one area of intensive probing was the sexual, with a series of questions that focused on the total cycle of experience and behavior from the beginning of a given dyadic sexual sequence to its completion. If, for example, a subject reported that he went out to look for a sexual partner, I asked him to describe in detail what happened from the time he met the sexual partner until they separated, including every detail, if possible, of the sexual activity. This step-by-step procedure not only produced new information about feelings, fantasies, sexual practices, and problems, but also made it difficult for the subject to reply with evasive generalities.

These interviews produced extreme discomfort in many subjects. Often expressed at the end of the interview was the statement, "It's a good thing you didn't ask these questions in the first interview." The questions, "What is your preferred method of achieving sexual gratification?" or "What kind of sexual activities do you and your partner engage in?" or "Do you prefer fellatio or anal intercourse?" were answered without apparent discomfort. The question— if a preferred method is fellatio—"*How* do you perform fellatio?" is a much more disturbing one. One subject who had described sexual patterns without noticeable anxiety or evasion could not

respond to this request, and said, "In all the years and the many hours in which I have talked with you, this is the first time I have been ashamed. I simply cannot do it." I did not press it.[4]

SEXUAL PATTERNS

The range of erotic sensitivity, the preferred or accepted mode and conditions for achieving sexual gratification, the nature of sexual gratification, and the frequency with which it is sought, vary from one individual to another.[5] Some general patterns may, however, be distinguished. The major modes of achieving sexual gratification are fellatio, anal intercourse, masturbation, and body friction—or any combination thereof.

In my sample of thirty, 43 percent (thirteen) prefer and predominantly practice fellatio. Two of these men prefer and predominantly perform fellatio on the partner, but on occasion accept anal insertion by the partner. One man prefers and predominantly performs reciprocal or mutual fellatio, but also occasionally engages in anal intercourse, without preference for position or role. Ten men will not now practice any form of anal activity, although all have done so, with vary-

[4]The cooperation of these subjects, and their willigness to allow me to probe the most private aspects of their experience in great detail during extended hours of interview, were remarkable, in view of the fact that they were not clinical patients. Their disturbance, when asked about the details of *how* they performed particular sexual acts, is puzzling. I am indebted to Dr. Harold Garfinkel for the suggestion that it may be due to the fact that I asked them to make sexuality a *technically* describable project. I did not press this particular subject because I already had extensive material from him concerning his sexual behavior and erotic fantasies. In this necessarily brief paper, it is not possible to document the detail and depth of the interview material. In the full published report, this documentation will be provided.

[5]Data on the frequency with which sexual experience is sought and/or obtained are not presented in this paper, but will be included in the full published report, as will a discussion of the data on variations in the meaning and nature of sexual gratification.

ing frequencies, in the past. They now reject such practices for a variety of reasons—including fear of venereal disease, lack of sexual and/or emotional pleasure, experience of pain, or feelings of revulsion. Eight of the ten prefer and predominantly practice reciprocal or mutual fellatio with the partner; and the other two prefer to perform fellatio on the partner. The nine individuals who prefer mutual or reciprocal fellatio also engage in mutual masturbation, either as forepleasure or as an alternate form of achieving orgasm. Bieber and his co-authors (1962) use the term "insertee" to describe the sex roles of accepting the penis of the partner in either the oral or anal orifice, and the term "insertor" for the role of inserting the penis in either orifice of the partner. Using this terminology, four of the thirteen men who prefer fellatio are predominantly oral insertees; and nine assume both the insertee and insertor roles, simultaneously as in mutual fellatio ("69"), or in succession.

Seven of the thirty (23 percent) express no preference for any particular form of sexual activity, and engage in and enjoy all of the major forms of homosexual practices. An additional seven (23 percent) express preferences, but engage in and enjoy all forms, accommodating to the situation—which includes the wishes of the partner, the emotional response to the partner, and the duration of the relationship with the partner. Preferences may shift with a change of partner, so that, for example, if the partner is perceived as "more masculine," the preference may be to assume the insertee role. If, on the other hand, the partner is perceived as "less masculine," the preference may be to assume the insertor role. (This example should not be generalized to all subjects.) Thus, fourteen of the thirty (46 percent) either have no preference or adjust their preference to the situation, so that the terms, predominantly insertee or predominantly insertor, cannot be used to characterize them.

Only two of the thirty (6 percent) prefer and predominantly assume the insertor role in both anal and oral sexual activity. Both have living relationships with partners who prefer the insertee

role. Very rarely, these two men assume the insertee role, usually with other partners.

Finally, one man in the group prefers mutual masturbation, and will engage in mutual fellatio on occasion, but rejects any form of anal practice.

In summary, then: (1) for only six (20 percent) of the sample can the sexual preference and predominant practice be characterized as fitting into an insertee or insertor sex role (four are oral insertees, and two are insertors with no preference for anal or oral orifices); (2) nine (30 percent) of the group, who prefer and predominantly practice fellatio, assume both the insertee and the insertor roles, simultaneously or in succession with the same partner; (3) fourteen (46 percent) either express no preference and engage in all of the major forms of homosexual activity or, in spite of expressed preferences, adjust and accommodate to the situation, so that, depending on the partner, both the insertee and insertor roles are assumed, and no predominant role can be assigned. Perhaps the most striking finding is the fact that so few individuals prefer and predominantly engage in modes of sexual gratification for which any term defining a typical "sex role" can be assigned. Variability, interchangeability, and interpartner accommodation seem to preclude role categorizations for the majority. . . .

In this discussion of preferences and predominant sexual practices, I have deliberately avoided the terms *active* and *passive*. Commenting on the fact that *activity* and *passivity* are psychological concepts and that to relate them to sexual activities is misleading, Bieber and his co-authors (1962) (as already noted) have substituted the terms *insertor* and *insertee*. "In the act of fellatio, for example," they write (pp. 238–239), "it is incorrect to judge one participant as 'active' and the other 'passive.' Is the individual who is using his mouth as receptor in the act of sucking, passive? From a kinetic orientation he is not. It becomes clear that concepts of activity and passivity to describe role behavior are not operationally useful."

I agree that the terms *active* and *passive* to describe sex roles of homosexuals should be discarded because they are inaccurate and misleading. Also, their continued use perpetuates a stereotyped dichotomy not only of sexual preferences or roles but of associated psychological attitudes as well. The individual who assumes the insertee role, either orally or anally, may not only be the initiator of the activity and the more active one from a kinetic standpoint but may also control it in the most actively aggressive way. The insertor, on the other hand, may submit to action performed on him with relatively little activity, from a kinetic standpoint, or control of the action. Even in those instances in which the individual assumes one or the other sex role exclusively or predominantly, the way in which he performs the role can vary so greatly that the one constant is whether the penis of one is or is not in an oral or anal orifice of the other. Who is active or passive, controlled or controlling, possessor or possessed cannot be determined merely by designating the act performed. The terms *active* and *passive* may be as inaccurate in describing sex roles and correlated psychological attitudes in heterosexual dyads as in homosexual ones. Although the terms *passivity* and *activity* may be useful in referring to psychological states, their correlation with gender and sex roles is at least questionable, in the light of cross-cultural evidence; for example, Ford and Beach (1951) and Mead (1961).

GENDER IDENTITY AND SEXUAL PATTERNS

Let us consider now some problems of gender identity, as found in my highly selected sample of male homosexuals. That they are not representative of all homosexuals, nor that all "types" are represented, has already been indicated and will become even more clear in the discussion which follows. I shall use the term *male gender identity* to refer to *all* that distinguishes males from females: including patterns of skills, occupation, dress and adornment, gestures, demeanor, emotional expression, erotic fantasies, and sexual behavior. Many of these patterns show such wide cultural variation that it is generally assumed that a large portion

of psychological masculinity or femininity, or of the psychological attributes of gender identity, are culturally determined. To behave as a man or to assume the masculine gender role in one cultural setting may thus, as Mead (1961) and others have shown, require attitudes and behavior that are almost the polar opposite of those in another cultural setting. The problem of determining the basic psychological attributes of masculinity and femininity that cut across all cultural variations is one for which there are few answers on which behavioral or social scientists would agree.

In our society, irrespective of the degree to which the male homosexual fulfils the male gender role expectations in at least one; he is inappropriately erotically focused on males, not females. It is probably true that gender identity problems result in the failure to fulfil male gender role expectations, and that additional ones are created by the failure. How he resolves these problems, or whether he resolves them, is therefore a matter of considerable interest.

The working solution,[6] as the subject perceives it, is, of course, only part of the story, because, as is self-evident, there are many components of gender identity of which the subject is unaware. In this paper, however, we shall look primarily at the solutions from the subjective standpoint of the individual, recognizing that it is an incomplete account. From that standpoint there are, it seems to me, three major types of working solutions to the problem of masculine gender identity in these subjects.[7]

---

[6]The term *solution* may convey more to the reader than I intend, and may be ill-chosen. Although some coming to terms with problems is implied, no inferences should be made about the degree to which a particular "solution" represents a full resolution of the problem.

[7]All the subjects have been given a battery of psychological tests, which includes the TAT, Rorschach, and Sentence Completion, as well as standard psychological inventories with M–F subscales, and other measures of psychological femininity-masculinity. Erotic fantasies and some dream material have been obtained in interviews. All these materials provide rich sources of data

All of these men perceive themselves appropriately as biological males, and all now consciously prefer to be males. It should be made clear that none would surrender his biological maleness. For this group, however, the problem of psychological gender (that is, masculinity–femininity) is a complex one.

The first solution is to accept the masculine–feminine psychological gender dichotomy *for homosexuality* and place oneself at one or the other of these poles. The man who accepts this dichotomy and places himself at the masculine pole usually chooses between two alternatives. He may define himself as a *masculine* homosexual and point to occupation or athletic interests, emotional ease, or satisfaction and success in occupational and social associations with nonhomosexual males, to show that he is masculine. In sexual practice he predominantly engages in anal intercourse in the insertor position or accepts fellation, and he points to this fact as additional evidence that he is a masculine homosexual. Only two individuals in my sample adopt this solution. As indicated in the discussion of sexual patterns, both have living relationships with partners who prefer the insertee role. Both have occupations that would be rated as masculine. In manner, demeanor, gesture, and speech they present a masculine appearance. Neither of them has pronounced esthetic interests; one, in fact, is preoccupied almost exclusively, outside his occupation, with participant or spectator sports. I should make it clear that although they take pride in their masculinity, there does not appear to be any defensive exaggeration of the fact. (It may be pointed out parenthetically that there are sectors of the homosexual subculture in which masculinity is caricatured in the affectation of symbols of masculine toughness, as, for example, in the "motorcycle" or "leather" set.) One man appears to accept and enjoy his homosexuality without anxiety and guilt and has no wish, or sees no reason why he should want, to change his pattern. The other is consciously remorseful and guilty about his homosexuality, although he does not believe that it would be possible for him to change and has made no conscious effort to do so.

The other alternative for the man who accepts the masculine–feminine dichotomy for homosexuals and places himself at the masculine pole, is to separate the sexual and nonsexual aspects of the masculine role; and while pointing to "male" qualities such as aggressiveness, domination, decision-making, and control of emotionality, to assert that he is the masculine partner in any homosexual relationship, despite the fact that he engages in a variety of sexual practices. His occupation would be rated as highly masculine, and he occupies a position of considerable authority, involving the supervision of many men. Like the first two already described, his general bearing, speech, and manner are not effeminate in any way. He combines, to an unusual degree, leisure-time pursuits indicating high esthetic interest and talent, and ones requiring what would ordinarily be considered to be masculine skills. It is unfortunate that I cannot specify his interests in greater detail, but to do so would be to run the risk of identifying him. His preference and predominant sexual practice is mutual fellatio, and he does not and will not engage in anal activity, for medical and esthetic reasons. Although he sees himself as a masculine homosexual, he is quite conscious of his own culturally defined femininity, in terms of his esthetic interests, and does not appear to exaggerate his masculinity in any defensive way. His feelings about being homosexual are in conflict and are ambivalent.

For the man who accepts the masculine–feminine dichotomy and places himself in the feminine half, the most extreme position closely approaches transvestism; and perhaps the most vivid description is that given by Rechy (1963) of "Miss Destiny." He may insist on the insertee role in anal intercourse or fellatio, and in manner, occupation, and interest display his femininity. None of

---

for the other components of gender identity in these subjects. A detailed account of the intensive interview procedures used in eliciting the data from which the three types of solution have been formulated cannot be given in this brief paper.

these individuals is in my sample. Nine individuals in the sample, however, describe themselves as feminine homosexuals, and display this femininity in varying degrees. Although they see themselves as clearly and unmistakably male, they do not see themselves as masculine; and most of them express the wish to be more masculine. All of them are now in occupations in which there are probably as many women as men, and these occupations do not carry a distinctive gender connotation. In general, it is characteristic of this group that they feel uncomfortable in the presence of markedly heterosexual men, especially in social situations, and very often in work situations. With one exception, they have pronounced esthetic and/or feminine interests. With the same exception, all of them have gone through a period of dressing in women's clothing, either in private or on social occasions involving other homosexuals. Some of them continue to do so on such occasions. In careful questioning about conscious fantasies and motivations experienced during such cross-dressing, all of them make it clear that they were *pretending* to be women but that they did not have conscious wishes to be women or biological females. It is essential, however, that the question of unconscious motivations or fantasies in such behavior remain open for examination. When, for example, an individual goes to a Halloween party dressed as a pregnant woman, even though he does not make strenuous efforts to conceal the fact that he is a man-dressed-as-a-pregnant-woman, the motivational problems become very complex. It is also important to note at this point that attitudes toward femininity and display of femininity in homosexual societies are very much influenced by social factors operating in the group as well as in the individual motivations of the members. The sexual patterns of these nine individuals are predominantly oral. Four of them are predominantly oral insertees, and five assume both the insertee and insertor roles in reciprocal or mutual fellatio. . . .

The second major working solution to the gender identity problems is that adopted by those who do not accept the masculine–feminine dichotomy for themselves and reject it as undesirable in others. They then define themselves as male *and* homosexual: they reject sexual performance and erotic object choice as the critical criterion of maleness and masculinity; they accept the concept of the masculine–feminine *continuum* (not dichotomy) on the basis of psychological attributes; and they place themselves somewhere toward the masculine end of this continuum. Seventeen of the sample are in this category. (A description of one pair of men who are in this group, and who have established a living relationship of some duration, is given in a later section of this paper.) The majority are individuals who, as previously described, either have no preference for particular forms of sexual activity and engage in and enjoy most forms, or, in spite of preference, accommodate to the situation. The stability of this solution varies greatly. For some, there is a constant struggle to maintain the position. One man, for example, who in the early interviews equated homosexuality with "not being a man, and being feminine," no longer makes this equation—but the struggle to maintain a self-image as masculine and homosexual continues. Some others in the group seem not to have had any struggle in reaching this solution or maintaining it. For some of these, this may be accounted for in part by the fact that they have masculine occupations, and in appearance, manner, and interests show no evidence of conspicuous femininity. For some individuals who have achieved this solution, the primary problems cannot be described as gender problems but as problems involving control, domination, power, aggression, and initiative with their love and/or sexual partners. They may have once defined the wish to be possessed or to be dominated or to be controlled as feminine. Many of these are now able to see these motivations in their own right, apart from their imputed gender connotations.

The third working solution is the one which has been characterized as the "third sex" or "intermediate sex." This is the position expressed by only one person in the sample, who perceives himself, and thinks of other male homosexuals, as being both male and female, psychologically. In his manner, gestures, and speech there is nothing which could be described as effeminate. He is a professional man, in an occupational field which is preponderantly entered by men. He has high esthetic interests and talents. He is one of those who express no preference for any particular mode of sexual activity and engage in all forms, with equal pleasure.

From the data presented in the preceding discussion, it is clear that for the majority of the individuals in this particular sample there is no apparent correspondence between a conscious sense of gender identity and a preferred or predominant role in sexual activity. For the four individuals who are predominantly oral insertees in sexual practice and who accept the masculine–feminine dichotomy for homosexuality, their perception of themselves as being in the feminine half of that dichotomy shows a congruence between psychological gender and sex role. The two individuals who are predominantly insertors and who perceive themselves as masculine homosexuals also show the presumed congruence. For the remainder, however, as we have seen the sexual pattern cannot be categorized in terms of a predominant role, and the consciousness of masculinity or femininity appears to bear no clear relation to particular sexual patterns.

HOMOSEXUAL SUBCULTURE EFFECTS

For an interpretation of these findings, it may be helpful to remind ourselves that all of these men were obtained from homosexual groups and friendship networks; that they are committed to a homosexual way of life; and that their personal and social identities as homosexuals have been defined, in part, over the course of continuous social interaction with other homosexuals. Their entry into an active homosexual life may occur in a large variety of ways, and the particular group, setting, or sector of that life which they enter, or into which they subsequently move, may vary enormously. There are many homosexual worlds or subcultures, loosely linked by friendship and acquaintance networks, but differing greatly in normative expectations, which may in part determine the degree of gender and sex role differentiation, the criteria for and indices of masculinity, the expectation of effeminate behavior in gesture, speech, dress, and gait, the criteria for selection of appropriate sex or love partners, and the modes of sexual gratification.

The world of the hustler, as described by Rechy (1963) (also by Reis [1961] and Ross [1959], with some variations), in which sex roles for the hustler and his "score" are rigidly defined, in which the appearance of "tough masculinity" must be cultivated assiduously by the hustler, and sexual gratification for the hustler is understood to be a by-product in a monetary transaction, is completely foreign to and rejected by most of the men whom I have interviewed. In strongest contrast is the world of a group of men organized for social purposes, most of whom are college graduates and members of a fraternity. Informal standards of selection maintain a loose membership of individuals who take pride in the fact that they are masculine in appearance and manner and indistinguishable from their business and professional heterosexual associates. Effeminacy in gesture, dress, or speech excludes a prospective applicant, or provides grounds for quiet expulsion if it occurs in a member. Love and/or sex partners must meet the same standards in appearance and behavior, and a social introduction (in contrast to anonymous casual pickups) is a necessary prelude to an affair. Sex role differentiation between partners is unusual, and gender connotations of sexual practice are minimized or tend to disappear because both partners engage in most or all of the major forms of homosexual practice. In other informal social groups composed of one or more clique and/or friendship or acquaintance networks, sex role differentiation, with clear-cut gender connotations that are generalized to nonsexual aspects of the relations between temporary or more permanent partners, may be usual. There is some reason to believe that this is more common in lower socioeconomic groups, and, if so, would correspond to the clearer differentiation in the hetero-sexual world at that class level—but the evidence is too slight to be more than speculative.

Between these rather sharp extremes, social groups form in which there are few, if any, normative expectations and in which all degrees of gender and sex role differentiation occur. In some of these groups, the concern with masculinity—femininity is reflected in frequent discussions of who is "the husband" and who is "the wife" in a given pair, the assumption being that there is some differential in masculinity between the two and/or a corresponding difference in preferred sex role. Very often, even among intimate friends, the fact that the sexual practices do not correspond to the presumed differences in masculinity—femininity between members of the pair is a closely guarded secret. In other groups, while comparisons of masculinity—femininity may be frequently made, the assignment of gender role in any terminology borrowed from the two-sexed heterosexual world is derogated, and every effort is made to resist comparisons with heterosexual marriage and its differential gender and sex role prescriptions.

Homosexual bars also play a large part in the social life of many homosexuals, both for those who have an active social life in groups outside and for others who have few such associations. The bars vary greatly in the clientele that they attract and the informal rules or standards that they promote concerning effeminate display. In some bars, for example, obvious effeminacy in dress or demeanor is not only frowned upon but may be a sufficient reason for the refusal of admission. In other bars, there are no standards of admission, and the most obvious display of effeminacy may be found, so that the clues to biological maleness and femaleness are blurred and judgments are uncertain.

Individuals may move from one sector of the homosexual world to another at different stages in their homosexual careers, so that rather striking changes in behavior patterns and accompanying psychological gender identity may occur. For example, some of the men in my sample who are now in their forties, and who are masculine appearing in their general demeanor and deplore obvious display of femininity, report that when they first entered into an active homosexual life they were highly effeminate and frequently dressed in elaborate feminine costumes for ceremonial occasions in the homosexual world.

The many homosexual worlds or sub-cultures in which a homosexual may spend a large part of his social, leisure, or recreational life outside his work are only briefly sketched in the foregoing account. They form a very loose aggregate of deviant collectivities. An individual may move back and forth, from one to another, with or without full participation in any one.

This account is intended to draw attention to the importance of homosexual milieux or subcultures in helping to determine attitudes toward homosexuality, consciousness of and manifestations of masculinity and femininity, and the connotations attached to particular sex roles. It is clear that subculture effects constitute only one set of variables, which interact with many other variables, such as personality dynamics and structure, personal appearance (including body build, gesture, demeanor), age, and occupation, to produce these attitudes, self-concepts, and behavior. Most accounts of gender identity and sex roles in male homosexuals focus on personality traits and psychodynamics and ignore the important contribution of the shared perspectives of homosexual subcultures.

INDIVIDUAL PAIRS

Although reference has been made in the foregoing account to differences in homosexual pairs with respect to differentiation of sex and gender role in relation to the subculture context, it should be noted that individual pairs work out individual solutions, although influenced by that context.

It has often been said that the homosexual is unable to sustain continuous relationships for any period of time. To quote Bieber and his co-authors (1962, p. 317):

Some homosexuals tend to seek out a single relationship, hoping to gratify all emotional needs within a one-to-one exclusive relationship. Such twosomes are usually based on unrealistic expectations, often accompanied by inordinate demands; in most instances, these pairs are caught up in a turbulent, abrasive attachment. These liaisons are characterized by initial excitement which may include exaltation and confidence in the discovery of a great love which soon alternates with anxiety, rage, and depression as magical expectations are inevitably frustrated. Gratification of magical wishes is symbolically sought in homosexual activity which is intense in the early phase of a new "affair." These relationships are generally disrupted after a period of several months to a year or so; they are generally sought anew with another partner and the cycle starts again.

Although this is an accurate characterization of many homosexual liaisons, it does not apply to a number of pairs whom I have interviewed.

First some data from my sample on the duration of relationships. Of the thirty subjects, eight are at present in living relationships that they have sustained for periods of from nine to fifteen years. One of these has sustained a monogamous relationship for ten years. Five have sustained sexual relationships with the partner, although they are not monogamous. One maintained a monogamous relationship for four years; and although he still has occasional sexual experience with his living-partner, most of his sexual relations during the past eleven years have occurred outside. One man in this group sustained a sexual relationship with his partner for eleven years, with occasional outside contacts, but for the last three years sexual experience with his partner has ceased.

An additional eight individuals in the sample have sustained relationships, either in the past or at the present time, for from five to eight years. In one of these relationships, which lasted five years, there was continuous monogamy.

In the other seven, the sexuality between the members of each pair continued, but they also engaged in sexual contacts outside the relationship. Four of the thirty subjects have had a series of living relationships lasting from two to four years. For one individual only, monogamy was sustained in each relationship. None of the remaining ten individuals has sustained a living-relationship that was sexual in character for more than a few months.

All but three of the thirty individuals are seekers of dyadic relationships. They express an intense longing for relationships with stability, sexual continuity, intimacy, love, and affection. It is beyond the scope of this paper to analyze the complex personality and social variables that prevent so many from achieving their expressed objective. . . .

CONCLUDING COMMENT

I have proposed in this paper that our concepts of sex roles and their relationship to psychological gender identity in male homosexuals who are committed to a homosexual way of life require revision. I have also proposed that an expanded theoretical framework that will include variations in homosexual subcultures and social interaction between members of pairs may be useful.

The data which have given rise to these proposals have indicated that for the majority of the individuals in my particular sample there is no apparent correspondence between a conscious sense of gender identity and a preferred or predominant role in sexual activity. Except for a small minority, the sexual pattern cannot be categorized in terms of a predominant role, and the consciousness of masculinity or femininity appears to bear no clear relation to particular sexual patterns. Comparisons of homosexual subcultures indicate that the degree to which sex roles and gender roles are clearly differentiated varies greatly with the subculture. Cultural variables, as well as personality variables, appear to be important in defining prescribed or acceptable masculinity or femininity and/or sex roles. The relations between individual pairs appear to be additional determinants of the variations in sexual patterns and gender identity.

SUMMARY

Data are presented on sexual patterns and psychological gender identities of thirty predominantly or exclusively homosexual males who have been intensively interviewed at intervals over a period of eight years. The research subjects were obtained from homosexual cliques and friendship networks; they were committed to homosexuality and were not seeking therapeutic assistance.

The sexual patterns of a majority of these subjects cannot be categorized into clearly differentiated sex roles because of the variability and interchangeability of practices with the same partner or different partners. Psychological gender identity as perceived by these subjects appears to bear little relation to sexual practice. A variety of working solutions to the problem of psychological gender identity in homosexual males is discussed.

Comparisons of homosexual subcultures indicate that the degree to which sex roles and gender roles are clearly differentiated varies greatly with the subculture. The relations between individual pairs—especially those who sustain a living relationship of some duration—appear to be additional determinants of the variations in sexual patterns and gender identity.

It is proposed that concepts of sex roles and their relations to psychological gender identities in male homosexuals require revision, and that an expanded theoretical framework which will include variations in homosexual subcultures and social interaction between members of pairs may be useful.

REFERENCES

Bieber, I., Dain, H. J., Dince, P. R., Drellich, M. G., Grand, H. G., Gundlach, R. H., Kremer, M. W., Rifkin, A. H., Wilbur, C. B., and Bieber, T. B. 1962. *Homosexuality*. New York: Basic Books, Inc.

Brown, D. G. 1958. Inversion and homosexuality. *Amer. J. Orthopsychiat.* 28, 424–429.

Brown, D. G. 1961. Transvestism and sex-role inversion. In A. Ellis, and A. Abarbanel (Eds.), *The encyclopedia of sexual behavior*, Vol. II. New York: Hawthorn Books, Inc.

Ferenczi, S. 1914. The nosology of male homosexuality (homoeroticism). (Translated by Ernest Jones.) In *Sex in psychoanalysis* (1950). New York: Basic Books, Inc.

Ford, C. S., and Beach, F. A. 1951. *Patterns of sexual behavior*. New York: Harper & Row.

Hooker, E. 1957. The adjustment of the male overt homosexual. *J. proj. Tech. 21*, 18–31.

Hooker, E. 1958. Male homosexuality in the Rorschach. *J. proj. Tech. 22*, 33–54.

Hooker, E. 1961. The homosexual community. Paper read at the XIV International Congress of Applied Psychology. Published 1962 in *Personality research* (Vol. 2 of *Proceedings of the XIV International Congress of Applied Psychology*. Copenhagen: Munksgaard Press.

Hooker, E. 1962. Life styles of male homosexuals and venereal disease. Paper read at World Forum on Syphilis and Other Treponoematoses. In press, U. S. Public Health Reports.

Hooker, E. 1963. Male homosexuality. In N. L. Farberow (Ed.), *Taboo topics*. New York: Atherton Press.

Mead, M. 1961. Cultural determinants of sexual behavior. In W. C. Young (Ed.), *Sex and internal secretions*, Vol. II (ed. 3). Baltimore: Williams and Wilkins.

Rado, S. 1949. An adaptational view of sexual behavior. In P. H. Hoch and J. Zubin (Eds.), *Psychosexual development in health and disease*. New York: Grune & Stratton.

Rechy, J. 1963. *City of night*. New York: Grove Press, Inc.

Reiss, A. J., Jr. 1961. The social integration of queers and peers. *Soc. Prob. 9*, 102–120.

Ross, H. L. 1959. The "hustler" in Chicago. *J. Student Research 1*, 13–19.

Strauss, A. L. 1959. *Mirrors and masks*. New York: Free Press.

Terman, L. M., and Miles, C. C. 1936. *Sex and personality*. New York: McGraw-Hill.

Westwood, G. 1960. *A minority*. London: Longmans, Green.

REVIEW QUESTIONS

1. Discuss and give examples of how different species may be prevented from interbreeding.
2. How do the gonadal hormones exert their control over sexual behavior according to the latest research?
3. What effect does the unexpected introduction of strong extraneous stimuli have upon the human male's and female's orgasmic phase?
4. What is the importance of the human male's refractory period for "sexual compatibility?"
5. What is the vasocongestive flush? When does it occur in men and women? What does it indicate about the level of sexual tension?
6. What were the CS, CR, UCS, and UCR in the study of experimentally induced sexual fetishism? How were the CR and UCR measured?
7. What is pseudo-conditioning and how did Rachman and Hodgson control for this possibility?
8. What was found to be the only important determinant of the subject's liking for his (her) date in the dating study? Does this seem reasonable to you in terms of your own dating behavior?
9. Try to criticize the dating study—after all "ugly" people do get dates and marry. Has the article failed to answer any of your objections?
10. What is meant by "male gender identity" and do homosexuals all show it to the same extent?
11. "The homosexual is unable to sustain continuous relationships for any period of time." How should this statement be qualified according to the evidence presented in article #34?

heredity, measurement, and intelligence

In an absolute sense, an IQ is nothing more than the score one achieves on an intelligence test. Students often forget this and attribute some mystical power to an IQ score as the ultimate measure of their intellectual ability. A student's IQ can vary substantially, depending upon the particular IQ test he takes and his present emotional state. There is also evidence that IQ scores vary with age, depending upon the individual's educational and cultural experiences.

Small differences in IQ probably mean very little. There is really no justification for saying that a student with an IQ of 128 is brighter or more intelligent than a student with a score of 126. All one can really say is that the former student scored two points higher on an intelligence test. If the two students took different intelligence tests, there is even less justification for making such comparisons.

Perhaps the above is a little hard on intelligence testing in general, but better this extreme than the other. It seems to me that too many of my own students have hang-ups over their IQ's. Students who were told in high school they had high IQ's sometimes assume they need to do less work in college and as a result do not do well. On the other hand, someone who learns his IQ is not as high as his classmates often gives up and assumes that he could never achieve academic excellence so why try. It is trite but nevertheless true to say that one should put the necessary study time in each day and be content with the results if he feels he is working as hard as he should be.

Article #35, "The Nature of Intelligence" by David Wechsler, attempts a general definition of intelligence and considers the relationship of ability to intelligence.

One of the age-old questions which psychologists and others have asked is the relative role of hereditary and environmental factors in the production of intelligence. There are two extreme positions, with most psychologists falling somewhere in between. The hereditary position would be that intelligence is totally determined by the genetic composition of the individual while the environmentalists would hold that with proper education and so on it is possible to make an "intelligent" person out of almost anyone.

There can be little doubt that minority groups in the United States score lower on IQ tests than the white majority. The question, of course, is why. Is it because of the relative cultural deprivation and inferior education that these minorities groups experience or are the lower scores the result of genetic inferiority? It should come as no surprise to the reader that such a complex question will have no simple answer, assuming at some point psychologists will be able to provide any answer at all.

Arthur R. Jensen is certainly closer to the genetic end of the continuum in his theorizing than most psychologists. He recently published an article in the Harvard Educational Review that set off a controversy the likes of which psychology has not seen in many years. The section dealing with racial differences is reprinted here (#36). The article was so controversial that in the following issue of the journal five prominent psychologists were asked to discuss the research and its conclusions. The article most directly related to the race question is also presented here, "Inadequate Evidence and Illogical Conclusions" by Jerome S. Kagan (#37).

Jerry Hirsch points out some additional considerations for the study of the interaction between genetics and behavior (#38). He also has some comments on the Jensen research. He concludes his discussion with the following statement: "I believe that in order to study behavior, we must understand genetics quite thoroughly. Then, and only then, can we as psychologists forget about it intelligently."

The final selection deals with the practical problem of understanding and interpreting statistics in general. The student might find it fun and profitable to hunt for the "statistical tricks" mentioned in Darrell Huff's "How To Talk Back to a Statistic" (#39). One can find them everywhere—government documents, newspapers, and yes, even in psychological journals.

35.
the nature of intelligence

david wechsler

The word intelligence, in spite of its wide current usage and ancient roots, is a relatively recent term in psychological literature. It is met with rarely before the turn of the century, and in Baldwin's encyclopedic *Dictionary of Philosophy and Psychology*, published in 1901, it did not rate a separate entry but was merely given as an alternate to or synonym of *intellect*. Even the textbooks of psychology of a generation or two ago seldom used the term and, when they did, never discussed it as a separate topic.[1] We must not infer from this that these authors were not concerned with what we now think of as intelligence, but bound as they were to the old faculty psychology they still relegated the treatment of the subject under such terms as intellect, judgment and reason which they seemingly considered synonymous with it. Thus, Baldwin defines intellect (intelligence) as "the faculty or capacity of knowing." Our present day concepts of intelligence have expanded considerably. They are broader, more pragmatic, more concerned with learning and adaptive human behavior. The chief trouble with them is that few psychologists are willing to spell out what they mean by intelligence and, when they do, seldom agree.[2]

The great interest in intelligence as a

basic subject matter of psychology began with the publication of Binet's *Le développement de l'intelligence chez les enfants (2)*. Although Binet himself on several occasions made attempts to delimit the term, his primary concern was not with the definition but with the measurement or appraisal of intelligence, and this has been the main approach of psychologists since. A tremendous amount of research has been carried on in the area, actually more than 40 years of continuous endeavor. We can now measure intelligence in many more ways than Binet did, that is with many more different kinds of tests, and what is more important we know much more about what it is we are measuring, namely, the elements or factors that enter into our measures. Most important of all, two revolutionary discoveries have been made; the first is that these elements or factors of intelligence do not coincide with the historic attributes of intelligence and, second, that it is not possible to express them in a simple formulation. One of the results has been that some psychologists have come to doubt whether these laborious analyses have contributed anything fundamental to our understanding of intelligence while others have come to the equally disturbing conclusion that the term intelligence, as now employed, is so ambiguous that it ought to be discarded altogether. Psychology now seems to find itself in the paradoxical position of devising and advocating tests for measuring intelligence and then disclaiming responsibility for them by asserting that "nobody knows what the word really means."[3]

The view that we do not know what we are talking about when we speak of intelligence is unfortunate not only because it is not true by any comparative

Reprinted from *David Wechsler, The Measurement and Appraisal of Adult Intelligence*, 1958, pp. 3–17. Copyright 1958 by David Wechsler, New York, N. Y. 10028. By permission of the author and The Williams and Wilkins Company, Publishers.

[1] As late as 1927, C. Spearman complained, "Right up to the present day a large number, perhaps even the majority, of the best accredited books on psychology do not so much as bother to mention the word 'intelligence' from cover to cover" (7).

[2] On this point see article by R. B. Cattell (4).

[3] C. Spearman and L. Jones (8), p. 2.

standards—actually we now know more about intelligence than we do about any other mental function—but because it has nurtured a confusing pessimism and a profitless kind of account taking which almost completely misses the issue at hand. The issue is not, as is commonly supposed, the lack of agreement by psychologists on a standard definition of intelligence. If this were so, the problem might conceivably be resolved by an international convention, as has been done by physicists in defining various units of measurement. Unfortunately, the problem with which psychologists are concerned in defining intelligence is quite different from that which the physicist deals with when he defines amperes, farads and watts, or the biologist when he classifies living things as plants and animals. The difficulty involved is similar to what the physicist encounters when asked to state what he means by time or energy, or the biologist what he means by life. The fact is that energy and life are not tangible entities but limiting constructs. You cannot touch them or see them under a microscope even though you are able to describe them. We know them by their effects or properties. The same is true of general intelligence. It is not a material fact but an abstract construct. What we can reasonably expect of any attempt at definition is only a sufficiently clear and broad connotation as to what it comprehends. Mind you, not what it is but what it involves and eventually, what it distinguishes. Now that is precisely what the more effective definitions of intelligence have sought to do, though sometimes too tersely and sometimes with too special emphasis. Thus, intelligence has been defined as the ability to learn, the capacity to adapt to new situations, the ability to educe correlates, and so on. All these attempts to define intelligence as some broad function comprehend varieties of behavior which might reasonably be called "intelligent," although each from particular points of reference. The first might be more useful to the educator, the second to the biologist and the third to the psychologist. The pertinent question, however, is not whether intelligence is the ability to learn rather than the ability to adapt or to

educe relationships. It is all these and, as we shall see later, much more. Learning, adapting, reasoning and other forms of goal directed behavior are only different ways in which intelligence manifests itself. But while intelligence may manifest itself in a variety of ways, one must assume there is some communality or basic similarity between those forms of behavior which one identifies as intelligent. For example, we must assume there is something common to learning to count, avoiding danger and playing chess which makes it possible for us to say that they are evidence of intelligent behavior as against learning to walk, being accident prone and playing bingo, which seemingly have little if anything to do with it.

Much of the productive work done on the measurement of intelligence during the past decades has been devoted to the problem of identifying the basic elements or common factors of intelligence, and we shall presently consider how fruitful that has been. But three points need to be made at once. The first is that discovery and isolation of the "vectors of the mind" is only part of the problem involved in the definition of general intelligence; the second, that it is not possible to identify general intelligence with sheer intellectual ability; and the third, that general intelligence cannot be treated as an entity apart, but must be envisaged as an aspect of a greater whole, namely, the total personality structure with which it shares common elements and with which it is integrally related.

One of the important aspects of intelligent behavior is that it is goal directed, that is to say, purposive with respect to some intermediate or ulterior end. Purposiveness, however, is only a necessary condition for and not an exclusive condition of, intelligent behavior. When the decerebrated frog scratches its leg in response to an irritating stimulus, when the newborn babe starts suckling at its mother's breast and when a worker at an automatic stamping machine presses a lever, each may be said to be performing some goal directed act, but none of these though purposeful, could be taken as examples of intelligent behavior. They are what the physiologist would designate as reflex or automatic acts. But the situation is not so clear in instances involving complex reflex action, and ultimately a large segment of both human and animal behavior is commonly summed up by the term instinct.

Instincts are usually differentiated from learned acts as inherited rather than acquired patterns of behavior, but whether they also involve "intelligence" has been a matter of dispute. The side one espouses will largely depend on how one defines instinct and what one wishes to comprehend under the term of intelligence. Clearly, goal direction (purposiveness) and complexity of behavior alone are insufficient differentiae; otherwise the social behavior of the ants and bees, the nesting and homing habits of birds and a great many of the activities of the higher animals, and we might also add of human beings, would *ipso facto* be considered as evidence of intelligence. Some are. But biologists and psychologists have usually insisted that intelligent behavior meet two other conditions, namely, that it should involve insight and ratiocination. Whether the most complex behavior of higher animals meets these criteria is still a matter of opinion. Writers in the last quarter of the 19th century believed that they did, and expressed this opinion by saying that animals were able to think. Beginning with the turn of the century, particularly following the studies of Loeb, Jennings, Pavlou and the experimental biologist, this view gave way to the opinion that even the most complex of animal behavior was explicable in terms of stimulus response reactions (tropisms, conditioned reflexes, etc.). The term instinct itself fell into much disfavor and the question whether animals could think became a question which scientific investigators systematically avoided. The stimulus response psychology, however, received some severe knocks from the *Gestalt School*, especially from the studies of Köhler (6), who demonstrated that monkeys at least can show insight when they are confronted with novel situations. The question that now confronts psychology is whether the terms insight, learning and reasoning when used to describe behavior of animals are identical

with or similar to processes so designated when they are applied to the behavior of human beings. Our view of this matter is that the higher mental processes in man and animals are on a psychological continuum. This does not mean that "mental" processes in the higher animals are identical in all respects to those of human beings, but that, so far as one can see, they are distinguishable primarily in terms of degree of complexity, communicability and level of awareness. When a chimpanzee solves a problem he cannot tell us how he does it, and we can only infer how he arrived at a solution. By our standards there is a limit to the kind of problem he can solve. There is also reason to believe that a chimpanzee is not aware (conscious) of what he is doing as he works at his problem, but that is a matter of speculation. In any event, his behavior is both rational and intelligent.

The question of whether animals are able to reason and think is of interest not only in and of itself, but because of the influence it has had on the definition of intelligence. Historically, the so-called higher mental processes, and abstract reasoning in particular, have often been posited as the sole *sui generis* to man, and accordingly have often been posited as the sole criteria of intelligent behavior. More important, however, than whether animals can reason is whether this ability is all that is needed to account for intelligence. The view adopted in this book is that it is not. Reasoning, to be sure, is often required for intelligent behavior but frequently only to a minimal degree and sometimes, alas (or perhaps fortunately), not at all. Intelligence embraces many other abilities.

Intelligence, operationally defined, is the aggregate or global capacity of the individual to act purposefully, to think rationally and to deal effectively with his environment. It is aggregate or global because it is composed of elements or abilities which, though not entirely independent, are qualitatively differentiable. By measurement of these abilities, we ultimately evaluate intelligence. But intelligence is not identical with the mere sum of these abilities, however inclusive. There are three important reasons for this: 1) The ultimate products of intelligent behavior are a function not only of the number of abilities or their quality but also of the way in which they are combined, that is, their configuration. 2) Factors other than intellectual ability, for example, those of drive and incentive, are involved in intelligent behavior. 3) Finally, while different orders of intelligent behavior may require varying degrees of intellectual ability, an excess of any given ability may add relatively little to the effectiveness of the behavior as a whole. It would seem that, so far as general intelligence is concerned, intellectual ability, *per se*, merely enters as a necessary minimum. Thus, to act intelligently one must be able to recall numerous items, *i.e.*, have a retentive memory. But beyond a certain point this ability will not help much in coping with life situations successfully. This is true of even more important capacities, such as the ability to reason, particularly when specialized. The unusual reasoning abilities of the mathematician are more highly correlated with the thing that we ultimately measure as intelligence than sheer memory is, but possession of this ability is no guarantee that behavior as a whole will be very intelligent in the sense defined above. Every reader will be able to recall persons of high intellectual ability in some particular field whom they would unhesitatingly characterize as below average in general intelligence.

Although intelligence is not a mere sum of intellectual abilities, the only way we can evaluate it quantitatively is by the measurement of the various aspects of these abilities. There is no contradiction here unless we insist upon the identity of general intelligence and intellectual ability. We do not, for example, identify electricity with our modes of measuring it. Our measurements of electricity consist of quantitative records of its chemical, thermal and magnetic effects. But these effects are not identical with the "stuff" which produced them. We do not know what the ultimate nature of the "stuff" is which constitutes intelligence but, as in the case of electricity, we know it by the "thing" it enables us to do—such as making appro-

priate associations between events, drawing correct inferences from propositions, understanding the meaning of words, solving mathematical problems or building bridges. These are the effects of intelligence in the same sense that chemical dissociation, heat and magnetic fields are the effects of electricity;[4] but psychologists prefer the term mental products. We know intelligence by what it enables us to do.

E. L. Thorndike was the first to develop clearly the idea that the *measurement* of intelligence consists essentially of a quantitative evaluation of mental productions in terms of number, and the excellence and speed with which they are effected. Abilities are merely mental products arranged in different classes or types of operation. Thus, the class of operations which consists of effectually associating one fact with another and recalling either or both at an appropriate time is called learning; that of drawing inferences or educing relations between them, reasoning ability; that of merely retaining them, memory. The older psychologists were inclined to use a relatively small number of such classes based primarily on the kind of mental process supposedly involved. More recently, psychologists have altered their classifications to include subdivisions based on material content or factorial analyses. They speak not only of memory but of auditory memory, not only of reasoning but of abstract, verbal or arithmetical reasoning. In a like manner some psychologists have begun to distinguish various kinds of intelligence. Thorndike, for example, suggested subdividing intelligence into three main types: 1) abstract or verbal intelligence, involving facility in the use of symbols; 2) practical intelligence, involving facility in manipulating objects; 3) social intelligence, involving facility in dealing with human beings. The significant thing about this classification is that it emphasizes *what* a per-

---

[4]The analogy to electricity must not be carried too far. Also, in contrast to the views expressed in the earlier conditions we no longer think it correct or even useful to look upon intelligence as a kind of energy.

son can do, as well as *how* he can do it. This distinction between function and content is fully justified by experimental evidence. The rating which an individual attains on an intelligence examination depends to a considerable degree on the type of test used. His score on a test made up largely of verbal items may differ significantly from that obtained on a test involving questions of social comprehension and still more from another test made up of items involving predominantly psychomotor reactions and the perception of spatial relationships.

Though test results show that the rating which an individual attains will frequently depend upon the type of intelligence test used, they also show a contrary tendency. When large numbers of individuals are examined with a variety of intelligence tests, those who make high scores on any one of them tend to make high scores on the remaining ones, and the same holds true for those who make low and intermediate scores. This dual characteristic of human abilities—their specificity on the one hand and interdependence on the other—has been a long standing problem in psychology but is now approaching solution thanks to the contribution of factor analysis. The first and most important of these contributions was made by the great English psychologist Spearman some 50 years ago. It consisted of two parts: 1) He introduced a method for accounting for the variance between paired sets of correlated measures, and 2) he showed, or at least sought to show by this method,[5] that all intellectual abilities could be expressed as functions of two factors, one a general or intellectual factor (*g*) common to every ability, and another a specific factor (*s*), specific to any particular ability and "in every case different from that of all others." Both parts have been the subject of a great deal of discussion, criticism and investigation. Spearman's original methods of factoring a correlational table have now given way to broader and more refined techniques, and his concept of one central or unifactor theory has been largely abandoned by psychologists. The evidence is now quite clear that other factors besides *g* are required to account for intercorrelations between tests of intelligence, and the famous tetrad equation was shown by Thurstone (*10*), to be only a special case of a more general factor theorem. Nevertheless, Spearman's demonstration of the existence of at least one pervasive factor in all performances requiring intellectual ability remains one of the great discoveries of psychology.

As has often been the case in the history of science, the proof of the two factor theory, in addition to being a discovery, was also an explicit formulation of an hypothesis which workers in the field had unknowingly been assuming for some time. The fact is, that from the day psychologists began to use a series of tests for measuring intelligence, they necessarily assumed the existence of a general or common factor. This becomes immediately apparent if one recalls what the actual contents of intelligence tests are. They consist of various intellectual tasks which we call tests that require the subject to do such things as define words, reproduce facts from memory, solve problems in arithmetic and recognize likenesses and differences. The variety of tasks used, their difficulty and the manner of presentation vary with the type of scale employed. But so far as measuring intelligence is concerned, these specific tasks are only means to an end. Their object is not to test a person's memory, judgment or reasoning ability, but to measure something which it is hoped will emerge from the sum total of the subject's performance, namely, his general intelligence. One of the greatest contributions of Binet was his intuitive assumption that in the selection of tests, it made little difference what sort of task you used, provided that in some way it was a measure of the child's general intelligence. This explains in part the large variety of tasks employed in the original Binet scale. It also accounts for the fact that certain types of items which were found useful at one age level were not necessarily employed at other age levels. More important than either of these details is the fact that for all practical purposes, the combining of a variety of tests into a single measure of intelligence, *ipso*

[5]The method of tetrad differences.

facto, presupposes a certain functional unity or equivalence between them.

The functional equivalence of the test items, an assumption implicit not only in the Binet Scale but in any scale which is composed of a variety or pool of intellectual tasks, is absolutely necessary for the validation of the arithmetic employed in arriving at a final measure of intelligence. This arithmetic consists, first, of assigning some numerical value to every correct response; secondly, of adding the partial credits so obtained into a simple sum; and, thirdly, of treating equal sums as equivalent, regardless of the nature of the test items which contribute to the total. For example, every test passed on the Stanford-Binet (between ages 3 and 10) contributes two months to the mental age (M.A.) score of the subject, irrespective of whether the test passed calls for the repetition of a series of digits, the copying of a square, the definition of a word or the correct reply to a common-sense question. To all intents and purposes, therefore, the simple addition of these groups necessarily assumes an arithmetical equivalence of the test elements so combined. If the different tests were taken to represent generically different entities, one could no more add the values assigned to them in order to obtain an M.A. total than one could add 2 dogs, 3 cats and 4 elephants and expect the unqualified answer of 9. That, of course, does not mean that their addition is impossible. If, instead of being concerned with the characteristics of the dog, the cat and the elephant that differentiate them one from another, we restrict our interest to those which they all have in common, we can say that 2 dogs, 3 cats and 4 elephants make 9 animals. The reason we can get an answer of 9 here is because dogs, cats and elephants are in fact all animals. The addition would no longer be possible if for cats we were to substitute turnips.

The same principle is involved when we attempt to add up the number of tests correctly passed on an intelligence scale into a simple sum. The reason we can add together scores obtained from tests requiring such seemingly different abilities as those involved in solving arithmetic problems, repeating digits and

defining words is because they are alike in certain ways. They are similar in that they are all measures of general intelligence. This means that all must have a common characteristic, or to use the current psychological term *a common factor*, or factors. We might assume this *a priori*, and indeed such an hypothesis has been implicit in all tests of general intelligence whether acknowledged or not. But the assumption needed empirical validation—a validation which was eventually furnished by factor analysis.

Factor analysis is a statistical technique for separating common sources of variance between intercorrelated measures when these measures are arranged in certain ways. Its aims are to determine the smallest number of variables that must be posited in order to account for the observed variance and to calculate the degree to which they enter into the measures used. The independent variables or "reference" abilities thus defined are what the innovators of factor analysis have variously called central, common, primary and group factors. Their importance to psychology is that they testify to the probable existence of what are seemingly basic mental abilities capable of accounting for the way the mind operates. Similar intellectual entities are implied in the old concept of mental faculties, but the historic faculties were at best descriptive classifications with little proof of their uniqueness and no implication that they were functional unities. It is, of course, true that the modern factors may also be interpreted or even primarily construed as principles of classification (3). But factors are facts not just theoretical categories. Nor are they merely mathematical quantities intended to explain the correlations that exist between the most diverse sources of intellectual performance, as Spearman initially interpreted *g* (7). If mental factors were only mathematical quantities they would have no great importance for psychology. Mental factors, if they exist are descriptive of actual modes of mental operation. The great contribution of factor analysis has been to show that they do exist.

Factors of the mind are most readily

construed as native[6] tendencies and, in the field of cognition, as basic kinds of ability. More fundamentally, they are modalities of mental functioning which define these abilities—in the sense, as Thurstone (9) has pointed out, that vision, touch, hearing, etc. are modalities of sensation, but with no parallel assumption as regards cortical localization. It is probable that they are to some extent physiologically and anatomically determined but this is not a necessary condition for their acceptance. By hypothesis, primary abilities are generally conceived as independent variables, and are presumably identified as such only when they meet this criterion statistically. Nevertheless, in practice the posited independent factors almost invariably show some degree of positive correlation. This is due in part to a concomitant variance produced by the heterogeneity of any tested population,[7] and in part to the broader compass of the interaction principle which implies that no two forces (in our case, abilities) can exist side by side without in some way interacting to produce a resultant effect.[8]

Apart from the problems already considered, the most important question which confronts the application of factor theory to the concept of general intelligence is the definition of the nature of the factors, both as to number and identity, and as determinants of intellectual functioning. According to Spearman, only one general or central factor g was needed to account for basic intellectual ability: This factor he defined originally as a mathematical quantity "intended to explain the correlations that exist between most diverse sorts of cognitive performance." But, in the light of subsequent evaluation and application, it soon

became clear that g stood for something more important. It is not only a mathematical but a psychological quantity; g is a measure of the mind's capacity to do intellectual work.

It is universally agreed that the capacity to do intellectual work is a necessary and important sign of general intelligence. The question is whether it is the only important or paramount factor. In this writer's opinion it is not. Spearman seemingly thought it was, although on this point he failed to declare himself unequivocally. On the one hand, he wrote, "Such a factor as this (g) can scarcely be given the title of intelligence at all." But after having said this, he devoted several chapters (7) to an attempt to prove that the best tests of intelligence are precisely those which contain the largest amounts of g. If this is so, then for all practical purposes, g and general intelligence may be said to be equivalent. This equivalence, indeed, is implied by the mathematical relationship of the g and s factors in the two factor theory. According to this relationship an intelligence scale made up of a large number of tests especially rich in g would in the end be a measure of g exclusively.[9] In the writer's opinion, such a scale would not be a very good measure of general intelligence because it would eliminate a number of abilities essential for effective behavior.

The view that other salient factors besides g enter into measures of intelligence is based on several sources of evidence. The first is clinical. We know from experience that individuals attaining identical scores on intelligence tests cannot always be classified in the same way. This is perhaps most obvious in cases where test results call for practical action, as for example when they are used as a basis for deciding whether or not a subject should be committed to an institution for mental defectives. In such cases, the test results, e.g., a Binet IQ, cannot be used as the sole criterion. One child with an IQ of 75 may be definitely de-

[6] This is the author's opinion. Factor theory does not require that factors be innate.

[7] For a discussion of the ways in which population heterogeneity affects inter-test correlation, see T. L. Kelley (5).

[8] Thus, verbal and spatial ability will be concomitantly involved in abstract reasoning in the same way that hearing and vision combine in the perception of depth, even though both are conceived as independent functions.

[9] For, by pooling such tests, the g factor (being common) becomes cumulative, whereas the specific factors (being incidental) tend to cancel each other.

fective while another with an identical IQ, or indeed one 5 or 10 points lower, may be far from so classifiable. Of course, the objection may be made that the classification of mental deficiency is in part a social diagnosis. But is not the capacity for social adaptation also a sign of intelligence? Should not the capacity to avoid mischief and the ability to persevere at a task enter into one's definition of general intelligence, just as much as the ability to define words and perceive analogies? The clinician's answer has always been "yes." With this affirmation he implicitly assumes that there are other factors besides the intellective ones which enter into intelligent behavior. Hitherto he was unable to demonstrate their existence experimentally. In recent years, however, because of new correlational techniques, especially the methods of factorial analysis, a beginning has been made. Among the first and of particular significance is the study of W. P. Alexander, whose monograph on *Intelligence, Concrete and Abstract* (1) is in many ways basic.

Alexander set himself the problem of testing experimentally the evidence for and against the main theories until lately favored in psychological circles. The first of these is Professor Spearman's two factor theory to which we have already referred. The other is the unique traits theory, according to which intelligence involves several abilities or factors, each independent of one another. More specifically, his investigation took the form of an experimental study to determine whether test results supported the view that "practical" intelligence and "verbal" intelligence were each distinct and independent capacities, or the view of Spearman that both were essentially the same in that they were not independent capacities but only differed with respect to their non-intellective or specific factors.

Alexander's findings were extremely interesting. They confirmed Spearman's contention that there was one and only one common factor in *all* measures of intelligence and, at the same time, showed that this factor alone is not sufficient to explain the total correlational variance which existed between the tests used to measure intelligence. In addition to the common factor there are seemingly other broad factors which, while not showing the same generality, are nonetheless recurrent in a significant number of abilities which form subgroups or "communal clusters." The individual tests by which these abilities are measured contain a common factor of their own with respect to which they function in much the same way. Alexander has termed abilities involved in tests showing such similarity of function *functional unities.* Thus, verbal ability is one functional unity, practical ability another, and so on. But while each of these functional unities requires a separate factor to take care of its respective contribution to any global measure of intelligence, they are nevertheless "definitely related," that is, correlated with one another.[10] This means that they cannot be unitary traits in the sense implied by the unique traits theory. On the other hand, neither can they be considered as specific factors in the sense required by Spearman's two factor theory. For, these factors, unlike the *s* factors, actually contribute a considerable amount to the correlation variance of the test composites of which they form a part.

Another important conclusion suggested by Alexander's investigation was that in order to account for the complete intercorrelation variance found in any large battery of intelligence tests, one has to posit other factors in addition to purely intellectual ones. After eliminating the general factor (g), and such other factors[11] as were contributed by the "functional unities" described above, Alexander found that a considerable amount of his total intercorrelational variance was still unaccounted for. In addition to these factors there were apparently certain other supplementary global ones which, though not directly measurable, nevertheless contributed significant amounts to the total variance o

[10] Thus verbal ability correlates with practical ability to the extent of 0.50.

[11] These were primarily the factors v, common to tests involving verbal ability, and *f* common to tests purporting to measure practical ability.

the observed data. These factors he has provisionally labeled X and Z. They cover such items as the subject's interest in doing the tasks set, his persistence in attacking them and his zest and desire to succeed—items which might more familiarly be described as temperamental or personality factors, but which nevertheless must be recognized as important in all actual measures of intelligence. For this reason, one might appropriately refer to them as the non-intellective factors or, more specifically, as the *non-intellective factors* in general intelligence.[12]

It appears, therefore, that the entity or quantity which we are able to measure by intelligence tests is not a simple quantity. Certainly, it is not something which can be expressed by one single factor alone, for example, the ability to educe relations or the level of mental energy. Intelligence is all this and something more. It is the ability to utilize this energy or to exercise this ability in contextual situations, situations that have content and purpose as well as form and meaning. To concede as much is to admit that any practical definition of intelligence must be fundamentally a biological one in the widest sense of the term. That has been the hypothesis assumed in the construction of the author's intelligence scales. We think that they measure general intelligence in the context defined above. We shall not, however, claim that they measure all that goes to make up general intelligence, because no tests at present are capable of doing this. The only thing we can ask of an intelligence scale is that it measure sufficient portions of intelligence to enable us to use it as a fairly reliable index of the individual's global capacity.

THE RELATION OF ABILITY TO INTELLIGENCE

All measures of intelligence eventually are derived from measures of ability, that is to say, from tests of specific types of performance. In practice, an individual

[12]For further evidence as to the existence of these factors, see D. Wechsler: The non-intellective factors in general intelligence. (11).

is given a battery of such tests and on the basis of his scores is rated as showing such and such a level of intelligence. We begin with a series of aptitude measures but somehow end up with an IQ. How is this possible? The suggested answer is that in the process we are using measures of ability primarily as a tool, that is, not as an end in itself but as a means for discovering something more fundamental. Thus, when one employs an arithmetic or a vocabulary test as part of an intelligence scale, the object of the examiner is not to discover the subject's aptitude for arithmetic or extent of his word knowledge, although these are inevitably involved, but his capacity to function in over-all areas which are assumed to require intelligence. The term ability is here used in its most general sense, namely, that of "the power to perform responsive acts" (Warren) or as the manifestation of a human trait or attribute "in terms of what an individual can do" (Thurstone).

The tentative answer we are suggesting is that intelligence can be measured by way of abilities because what we are concerned with eventually is not the abilities themselves but what enters into or emerges from them. This hypothesis implies several postulates. 1) Intelligence, however defined, is not a simple entity but a complex function. 2) Intelligence is of the nature of a resultant effect. 3) The resultant effect depends upon the interaction of a theoretically infinite but practically limited number of qualitatively different but additive components or factors. These factors manifest themselves objectively in different forms of behavior. A factorially defined segment of behavior constitutes an ability. Such segments of behavior may be descriptively grouped into such broad classifications as verbal, spatial, numerical and other kinds of abilities, in the sense that they describe overlapping or similar modes of function.

A test is a device for evaluating a fragment of behavior; an intelligence test is one in which one seeks to appraise this bit of behavior insofar as it may be called intelligent. The abilities measured are of consequence only insofar as they permit the examiner to identify the behavior as intelligent. For this purpose some abilities are more generally or more readily available and, therefore, can be more profitably untilized in test construction. This is generally the case with verbal ability, which accordingly is oftener and more effectively made use of for measuring intelligence than other abilities, such as speed of motor response. But Vocabulary is a better test of intelligence than a Form Board, primarily because people can express themselves more meaningfully in verbal than in geometric symbols. This, of course, would not hold in the case of deaf-mutes or individuals who are in the habit of thinking spatially, manipulatively or in any other way. Hence, as a general principle, an effective test of intelligence should be made up of tasks calling upon as many "abilities" as possible. This was intuitively perceived by Binet, who was the first to devise an effective test of *general* intelligence.

The great merit of Binet's Scale is that it permits individuals to manifest their intelligence in many ways. Of course, some of his tests are better suited for some levels of functioning than others, but (contrary to Binet's belief) this fact involves no hierarchical concept of mental abilities. In the Binet Scale, copying a diamond is equally as "good" a test of intelligence at age 7 as detecting absurdities at age 10 or defining abstract words at age 15. The same may be said, *pari passu*, of the different subtests of the Wechsler Adult Intelligence Scales (WAIS) and the Wechsler-Bellevue (W–B) Scales. Of course, bases of selection other than age criteria can be employed to equate difficulty or level of task, but the specific abilities utilized are only of secondary importance, not only for the reasons already indicated but also because they are influenced to varying degrees by such things as culture and training as well as by differences in special endowment. What makes it possible to utilize them at all in appraising intelligence is that they do in fact permit the individual to evidence his capacity for directed, purposeful and adaptive behavior.

To sum up, human abilities are utilizable for measuring intelligence because when applied to goal directed activity they depend for their effectiveness on certain connate attributes or factors which constitute the basic components of intelligent behavior. These basic attributes are what contemporary psychologists, in searching for the "vectors of the mind," have described as general factors. The thing we seek to measure when we measure intelligence is the net result of the complex interaction between the various factors entering into intelligent behavior. In practice we measure this resultant fact by means of tests of ability. An intelligence scale is an assembled battery of such tests; the intelligence rating obtained from them is a numerical expression of their combined contribution. Although the amounts contributed by each test may be, and usually are, expressed as a simple sum, the factors which determine the scores ought not, strictly speaking, to be so combined, since the result is not a linear function of these factors. More likely it is what mathematicians call a complex functional, but the exact form of this function is yet to be determined.

REFERENCES

1. Alexander, W. P. Intelligence, concrete and abstract. *Brit. J. Psychol.*, Monog. Suppl., 1935, No. 19.
2. Binet, A., and Simon, T. Le développment de l'intelligence chez les enfants. *Ann. Psychol.*, 1908, *14*, 1–94.
3. Burt, Cyril. The structure of mind; a review of the results of factor analysis. *Brit. J. educ. Psychol.*, 1949, *19*, 100–111.
4. Cattell, R. B. The measurement of adult intelligence. *Psychol. Bull.*, 1943, *40*, 153–193.

5. Kelley, T. L. *Crossroads of the Mind.* Palo Alto, California: Stanford University Press, 1928.
6. Köhler, W. Relational determination in perception. In Jeffress, L. A. (Ed.) *Cerebral Mechanisms in Behavior.* New York: John Wiley & Sons, 1951, pp. 200–230.
7. Spearman, C. *The Abilities of Man.* New York: The Macmillan Co., 1927.
8. Spearman, C., and Jones, L. *Human Abilities.* London: The Macmillan Co., 1950.
9. Thurstone, L. L. *Multiple-Factor Anal-*

ysis. Chicago: University of Chicago Press, 1947.

10. Thurstone, L. L., and Thurstone, T. G. Factorial Studies in Intelligence. *Psychomtr. Monogr.*, No. 2, 1941.

11. Wechsler, D. *Measurement of Adult Intelligence.* Ed. 3. Baltimore: The Williams & Wilkins Co., 1944.

36.
race differences

arthur r. jensen

The important distinction between the *individual* and the *population* must always be kept clearly in mind in any discussion of racial differences in mental abilities or any other behavioral characteristics. Whenever we select a person for some special educational purpose, whether for special instruction in a grade-school class for children with learning problems, or for a "gifted" class with an advanced curriculum, or for college attendance, or for admission to graduate training or a professional school, we are selecting an *individual*, and we are selecting him and dealing with him as an individual for reasons of his individuality. Similarly, when we employ someone, or promote someone in his occupation, or give some special award or honor to someone for his accomplishments, we are doing this to an individual. The variables of social class, race, and national origin are correlated so imperfectly with any of the valid criteria on which the above decisions should depend, or, for that matter, with any behavioral characteristic, that these background factors are irrelevant as a basis for dealing with individuals—as students, as employees, as neighbors. Furthermore, since, as far as we know, the full range of human talents is represented in all the major races of man and in all socioeconomic levels, it is unjust to allow the mere fact of an individual's racial or social background to affect the treatment accorded to him. All persons rightfully must be regarded on the basis of their individual qualities and merits, and all social, educational, and economic institutions must have built into them the mechanisms for insuring

Reprinted from *Harvard Educational Review*, 1969, *39*, (1), 78–88. Copyright © 1969 by President and Fellows of Harvard College. All rights reserved. Reprinted by permission of the author.

and maximizing the treatment of persons according to their individual behavior.

If a society completely believed and practiced the ideal of treating every person as an individual, it would be hard to see why there should be any problems about "race" per se. There might still be problems concerning poverty, unemployment, crime, and other social ills, and, given the will, they could be tackled just as any other problems that require rational methods for solution. But if this philosophy prevailed in practice, there would not need to be a "race problem."

The question of *race* differences in intelligence comes up not when we deal with individuals as individuals, but when certain identifiable *groups* or subcultures within the society are brought into comparison with one another *as groups or populations*. It is only when the groups are disproportionately represented in what are commonly perceived as the most desirable and the least desirable social and occupational roles in a society that the question arises concerning average differences among groups. Since much of the current thinking behind civil rights, fair employment, and equality of educational opportunity appeals to the fact that there is a disproportionate representation of different racial groups in the various levels of the educational, occupational, and socioeconomic hierarchy, we are forced to examine all the possible reasons for this inequality among racial groups in the attainments and rewards generally valued by all groups within our society. To what extent can such inequalities be attributed to unfairness in society's multiple selection purpose? ("Unfair" meaning that selection is influenced by intrinsically irrelevant criteria, such as skin color, racial or national origin, etc.) And to what extent are these inequalities attributable to really relevant selection criteria which apply equally to all individuals but at the same time select disproportionately between some racial groups because there exist, in fact, real average differences among the groups—differences in the population distributions of those characteristics which are indisputably relevant to educational and occupational performance? This is certainly one of the most important questions confronting our nation today. The answer, which can be found only through unfettered research, has enormous consequences for the welfare of all, particularly of minorities whose plight is now in the foreground of public attention. A preordained, doctrinaire stance with regard to this issue hinders the achievement of a scientific understanding of the problem. To rule out of court, so to speak, any reasonable hypotheses on purely ideological grounds is to argue that static ignorance is preferable to increasing our knowledge of reality. I strongly disagree with those who believe in searching for the truth by scientific means only under certain circumstances and eschew this course in favor of ignorance under other circumstances, or who believe that the results of inquiry on some subjects cannot be entrusted to the public but should be kept the guarded possession of a scientific elite. Such attitudes, in my opinion, represent a danger to free inquiry and, consequently, in the long run, work to the disadvantage of society's general welfare. "No holds barred" is the best formula for scientific inquiry. One does not decree beforehand which phenomena cannot be studied or which questions cannot be answered.

Genetic Aspects of Racial Differences. No one, to my knowledge, questions the role of environmental factors, including influences from past history, in determining at least some of the variance between racial groups in standard measures of intelligence, school performance, and occupational status. The current literature on the culturally disadvantaged abounds with discussion—some of it factual, some of it fanciful—of how a host of environmental factors depresses cognitive development and performance. I recently co-edited a book which is largely

concerned with the environmental aspects of disadvantaged minorities (Deutsch, Katz, & Jensen, 1968). But the possible importance of genetic factors in racial behavioral differences has been greatly ignored, almost to the point of being a tabooed subject, just as were the topics of venereal disease and birth control a generation or so ago.

My discussion with a number of geneticists concerning the question of a genetic basis of differences among races in mental abilities have revealed to me a number of rather consistently agreed-upon points which can be summarized in general terms as follows: Any groups which have been geographically or socially isolated from one another for many generations are practically certain to differ in their gene pools, and consequently are likely to show differences in any phenotypic characteristics having high heritability. This is practically axiomatic, according to the geneticists with whom I have spoken. Races are said to be "breeding populations," which is to say that matings within the group have a much higher probability than matings outside the group. Races are more technically viewed by geneticists as populations having different distributions of gene frequencies. These genetic differences are manifested in virtually every anatomical, physiological, and biochemical comparison one can make between representative samples of identifiable racial groups (Kuttner, 1967). There is no reason to suppose that the brain should be exempt from this generalization. (Racial differences in the relative frequencies of various blood constituents have probably been the most thoroughly studied so far.)

But what about behavior? If it can be measured and shown to have a genetic component, it would be regarded, from a genetic standpoint, as no different from other human characteristics. There seems to be little question that racial differences in genetically conditioned behavioral characteristics, such as mental abilities, should exist, just as physical differences. The real questions, geneticists tell me, are not whether there are or are not genetic racial differences that affect behavior, because there undoubtedly are. The proper questions to ask, from a scientific standpoint, are: What is the direction of the difference? What is the magnitude of the difference? And what is the significance of the difference—medically, socially, educationally, or from whatever standpoint that may be relevant to the characteristic in question? A difference is important only within a specific context. For example, one's blood type in the ABO system is unimportant until one needs a transfusion. And some genetic differences are apparently of no importance with respect to any context as far as anyone has been able to discover— for example, differences in the size and shape of ear lobes. The idea that all genetic differences have arisen or persisted only as a result of natural selection, by conferring some survival or adaptive benefit on their possessors, is no longer generally held. There appear to be many genetic differences, or polymorphisms, which confer no discernible advantages to survival.[1]

Negro Intelligence and Scholastic Performance. Negroes in the United States are disproportionately represented among groups identified as culturally or educationally disadvantaged. This, plus the fact that Negroes constitute by far the largest racial minority in the United States, has for many years focused attention on Negro intelligence. It is a subject with a now vast literature which has been quite recently reviewed by Dreger and Miller (1960, 1968) and by Shuey (1966), whose 578 page review is the most comprehensive, covering 382 studies. The basic data are well known: on the average, Negroes test about 1 standard deviation (15 IQ points) below the average of the white population in IQ, and this finding is fairly uniform across the 81 different tests of intellectual ability used in the studies reviewed by Shuey. This magnitude of difference gives a median overlap of 15 percent, meaning that 15 percent of the Negro population exceeds the white average. In terms of proportions of variance, if the

numbers of Negroes and whites were equal, the differences *between* racial groups would account for 23 percent of the total variance, but—an important point—the differences *within* groups would account for 77 percent of the total variance. When gross socioeconomic level is controlled, the average difference reduces to about 11 IQ points (Shuey, 1966, p. 519), which, it should be recalled, is about the same spread as the average difference between siblings in the same family. So-called "culture-free" or "culture-fair" tests tend to give Negroes slightly lower scores, on the average, than more conventional IQ tests such as the Stanford-Binet and Wechsler scales. Also, as a group, Negroes perform somewhat more poorly on those subtests which tap abstract abilities. The majority of studies show that Negroes perform relatively better on verbal than on nonverbal intelligence tests.

In tests of scholastic achievement, also, judging from the massive data of the Coleman study (Coleman et al., 1966), Negroes score about 1 standard deviation (SD) below the average for whites and Orientals and considerably less than 1 SD below other disadvantaged minorities tested in the Coleman study—Puerto Rican, Mexican-American, and American Indian. The 1 SD decrement in Negro performance is fairly constant throughout the period from grades 1 through 12.

Another aspect of the distribution of IQs in the Negro population is their lesser variance in comparison to the white distribution. This shows up in most of the studies reviewed by Shuey. The best single estimate is probably the estimate based on a large normative study of Stanford-Binet IQs of Negro school children in five Southeastern states, by Kennedy, Van De Riet, and White (1963). They found the SD of Negro children's IQs to be 12.4, as compared with 16.4 in the white normative sample. The Negro distribution thus has only about 60 percent as much variance (i.e., SD^2) as the white distribution.

There is an increasing realization among students of the psychology of the disadvantaged that the discrepancy in their average performance cannot be completely or directly attributed to dis-

[1]The most comprehensive and sophisticated discussion of the genic-behavior analysis of race differences that I have found is by Spuhler and Lindzey (1967).

crimination or inequalities in education. It seems not unreasonable, in view of the fact that intelligence variation has a large genetic component, to hypothesize that genetic factors may play a part in this picture. But such an hypothesis is anathema to many social scientists. The idea that the lower average intelligence and scholastic performance of Negroes could involve, not only environmental, but also genetic, factors has indeed been strongly denounced (e.g., Pettigrew, 1964). But it has been neither contradicted nor discredited by evidence.

The fact that a reasonable hypothesis has not been rigorously proved does not mean that it should be summarily dismissed. It only means that we need more appropriate research for putting it to the test. I believe such definitive research is entirely possible but has not yet been done. So all we are left with are various lines of evidence, no one of which is definitive alone, but which, viewed all together, make it a not unreasonable hypothesis that genetic factors are strongly implicated in the average Negro-white intelligence difference. The preponderance of the evidence is, in my opinion, less consistent with a strictly environmental hypothesis than with a genetic hypothesis, which, of course, does not exclude the influence of environment or its interaction with genetic factors.

We can be accused of superficiality in our thinking about this issue, I believe, if we simply dismiss a genetic hypothesis without having seriously thought about the relevance of typical findings such as the following:

Failure to Equate Negroes and Whites in IQ and Scholastic Ability. No one has yet produced any evidence based on a properly controlled study to show that representative samples of Negro and white children can be equalized in intellectual ability through statistical control of environment and education.

Socioeconomic Level and Incidence of Mental Retardation. Since in no category of socioeconomic status (SES) are a majority of children found to be retarded in the technical sense of having an IQ below 75, it would be hard to claim that

TABLE 1. Estimated Prevalence of Children with IQs Below 75, by Socioeconomic Status (SES) and Race Given as Percentages (Heber, 1968)

SES	White	Negro
High 1	0.5	3.1
2	0.8	14.5
3	2.1	22.8
4	3.1	37.8
Low 5	7.8	42.9

the degree of environmental deprivation typically associated with lower-class status could be responsible for this degree of mental retardation. An IQ less than 75 reflects more than a lack of cultural amenities. Heber (1968) has estimated on the basis of existing evidence that IQs below 75 have a much higher incidence among Negro than among white children at every level of socioeconomic status, as shown in Table 1. In the two highest SES categories the estimated proportions of Negro and white children with IQs below 75, are in the ratio of 13.6 to 1. If environmental factors were mainly responsible for producing such differences, one should expect a lesser Negro-white discrepancy at the upper SES levels. Other lines of evidence also show this not to be the case. A genetic hypothesis, on the other hand, would predict this effect, since the higher SES Negro offspring would be regressing to a lower population mean than their white counterparts in SES, and consequently a larger proportion of the lower tail of the distribution of genotypes for Negroes would fall below the value that generally results in phenotypic IQs below 75.

A finding reported by Wilson (1967) is also in line with this prediction. He obtained the mean IQs of a large representative sample of Negro and white children in a California school district and compared the two groups within each of four social class categories: (1) professional and managerial, (2) white collar, (3) skilled and semiskilled manual, and (4) lower class (unskilled, unemployed, or welfare recipients). The mean IQ of Negro children in the first category was 15.5 points below that of the corresponding white children in SES category 1. But the Negro mean for SES 1 was also 3.9 points below the mean of white children in SES category 4. (The IQs of white children in SES 4 presumably have "regressed" upward toward the mean of the white population.)

Wilson's data are not atypical, for they agree with Shuey's (1966, p. 520) summarization of the total literature up to 1965 on this point. She reports that in all the studies which grouped subjects by SES, upper-status Negro children average 2.6 IQ points *below* the low-status whites. Shuey comments: "It seems improbable that upper and middle-class colored children would have no more culture opportunities provided them than white children of the lower and lowest class."

Duncan (1968, p. 69) also has presented striking evidence for a much greater "regression-to-the-mean" (from parents to their children) for high status occupations in the case of Negroes than in the case of whites. None of these findings is at all surprising from the standpoint of a genetic hypothesis, of which an intrinsic feature is Galton's "law of filial regression." While the data are not necessarily inconsistent with a possible environmental interpretation, they do seem more puzzling in terms of strictly environmental causation. Such explanations often seem intemperately strained.

Inadequacies of Purely Environmental Explanations. Strictly environmental explanations of group differences tend to have an ad hoc quality. They are usually plausible for the situation they are devised to explain, but often they have little generality across situations, and new ad hoc hypotheses have to be continually devised. Pointing to environmental differences between groups is never sufficient in itself to infer a causal relationship to group differences in intelligence. To take just one example of this tendency of social scientists to attribute lower intelligence and scholastic ability to almost any environmental difference that seems handy, we can look at the evidence regarding the effects of "father

absence." Since the father is absent in a significantly larger proportion of Negro than of white families, the factor of "father absence" has been frequently pointed to in the literature on the disadvantaged as one of the causes of Negroes' lower performance on IQ tests and in scholastic achievement. Yet the two largest studies directed at obtaining evidence on this very point—the only studies I have seen that are methodologically adequate—both conclude that the factor of "father absence" versus "father presence" makes no independent contribution to variance in intelligence or scholastic achievement. The sample sizes were so large in both of these studies that even a very slight degree of correlation between father-absence and the measures of cognitive performance would have shown up as statistically significant. Coleman (1966, p. 506) concluded: "Absence of a father in the home did not have the anticipated effect on ability scores. Overall, pupils without fathers performed at approximately the same level as those with fathers—although there was some variation between groups" (groups referring to geographical regions of the U.S.). And Wilson (1957, p. 177) concluded from his survey of a California school district: "Neither our own data nor the preponderance of evidence from other research studies indicate that father presence or absence, *per se*, is related to school achievement. While broken homes reflect the existence of social and personal problems, and have some consequence for the development of personality, broken homes do not have any systematic effect on the overall level of school success."

The nationwide Coleman study (1966) included assessments of a dozen environmental variables and socioeconomic indices which are generally thought to be major sources of environmental influence in determining individual and group differences in scholastic performance—such factors as: reading material in the home, cultural amenities in the home, structural integrity of the home, foreign language in the home, preschool attendance, parents' education, parents' educational desires for child, parents' interest in child's school work, time spent on homework, child's self-concept (self-esteem), and so on. These factors are all correlated—in the expected direction—with scholastic performance within each of the racial or ethnic groups studied by Coleman. Yet, interestingly enough, they are not systematically correlated with differences *between* groups. For example, by far the most environmentally disadvantaged groups in the Coleman study are the American Indians. On every environmental index they average *lower* than the Negro samples, and overall their environmental rating is about as far below the Negro average as the Negro rating is below the white average. (As pointed out by Kuttner [1968, p. 707], American Indians are much more disadvantaged than Negroes, or any other minority groups in the United States, on a host of other factors not assessed by Coleman, such as income, unemployment, standards of health care, life expectancy, and infant mortality.) Yet the American Indian ability and achievement test scores average about half a standard deviation higher than the scores of Negroes. The differences were in favor of the Indian children on each of the four tests used by Coleman: non-verbal intelligence, verbal intelligence, reading comprehension, and math achievement. If the environmental factors assessed by Coleman are the major determinants of Negro-white differences that many social scientists have claimed they are, it is hard to see why such factors should act in reverse fashion in determining differences between Negroes and Indians, especially in view of the fact that *within* each group the factors are significantly correlated in the expected direction with achievement.

Early Developmental Differences. A number of students of child development have noted the developmental precocity of Negro infants, particularly in motoric behavior. Geber (1958) and Geber and Dean (1957) have reported this precocity also in African infants. It hardly appears to be environmental, since it is evident in nine-hour-old infants. Cravioto (1966, p. 78) has noted that the Gesell tests of infant behavioral development, which are usually considered suitable only for children over four

weeks of age, "can be used with younger African, Mexican, and Guatemalan infants, since their development at two or three weeks is similar to that of Western European infants two or three times as old." Bayley's (1965a) study of a representative sample of 600 American Negro infants up to 15 months of age, using the Bayley Infant Scales of Mental and Motor Development, also found Negro infants to have significantly higher scores than white infants in their first year. The difference is largely attributable to the motor items in the Bayley test. For example, about 30 percent of white infants as compared with about 60 percent of Negro infants between 9 and 12 months were able to "pass" such tests as "pat-a-cake" muscular coordination, and ability to walk with help, to stand alone, and to walk alone. The highest scores for any group on the Bayley scales that I have found in my search of the literature were obtained by Negro infants in the poorest sections of Durham, North Carolina. The older siblings of these infants have an average IQ of about 80. The infants up to 6 months of age, however, have a Developmental Motor Quotient (DMQ) nearly one standard deviation above white norms and a Developmental IQ (i.e., the non-motor items of the Bayley scale) of about half a standard deviation above white norms (Durham Education Improvement Program, 1966–67, a, b).

The DMQ, as pointed out previously, correlates negatively in the white population with socioeconomic status and with later IQ. Since lower SES Negro and white school children are more alike in IQ than are upper SES children of the two groups (Wilson, 1967), one might expect greater DMQ differences in favor of Negro infants in high socioeconomic Negro and white samples than in low socioeconomic samples. This is just what Walters (1967) found. High SES Negro infants significantly exceeded whites in total score on the Gesell developmental schedules at 12 weeks of age, while low SES Negro and white infants did not differ significantly overall. (The only difference, on a single subscale, favored the white infants.)

It should also be noted that developmental quotients are usually depressed by adverse prenatal, perinatal, and postnatal complications such as lack of oxygen, prematurity, and nutritional deficiency.

Another relationship of interest is the finding that the negative correlation between DMQ and later IQ is higher in boys than in girls (Bayley, 1966, p. 127). Bronfenbrenner (1967, p. 912) cites evidence which shows that Negro boys perform relatively less well in school than Negro girls; the sex difference is much greater than is found in the white population. Brenfenbrenner (1967, p. 913) says, "It is noteworthy that these sex differences in achievement are observed among Southern as well as Northern Negroes, are present at every socioeconomic level, and tend to increase with age."

Physiological Indices. The behavioral precocity of Negro infants is also paralleled by certain physiological indices of development. For example, x-rays show that bone development, as indicated by the rate of ossification of cartilage, is more advanced in Negro as compared with white babies of about the same socioeconomic background, and Negro babies mature at a lower birth-weight than white babies (Naylor & Myrianthopoulos, 1967, p. 81).

It has also been noted that brain wave patterns in African newborn infants show greater maturity than is usually found in the European newborn child (Nilson & Dean, 1959). This finding especially merits further study, since there is evidence that brain waves have some relationship to IQ (Medical World News, 1968), and since at least one aspect of brain waves—the visually evoked potential—has a very significant genetic component, showing a heritability of about .80 (uncorrected for attenuation) (Dustman & Beck, 1965).

Magnitude of Adult Negro-White Differences. The largest sampling of Negro and white intelligence test scores resulted from the administration of the Armed Forces Qualification Test (AFQT) to a national sample of over 10 million men between the ages of 18 and 26. As of 1966, the overall failure rate for Negroes was 68 percent as compared with 19 percent for whites (*U.S. News and World Report,* 1966). (The failure cut-off score that yields these percentages is roughly equivalent to a Stanford-Binet IQ of 86.) Moynihan (1965) has estimated that during the same period in which the AFQT was administered to these large representative samples of Negro and white male youths, approximately one-half of Negro families could be considered as middle-class or above by the usual socioeconomic criteria. So even if we assumed that all of the lower 50 percent of Negroes on the SES scale failed the AFQT, it would still mean that at least 36 percent of the middle SES Negroes failed the test, a failure rate almost twice as high as that of the white population for all levels of SES.

Do such findings raise any question as to the plausibility of theories that postulate exclusively environmental factors as sufficient causes for the observed differences?

REFERENCES

Bayley, N. Comparisons of mental and motor test scores for ages 1–15 months by sex, birth order, race, geographical location, and education of parents. *Child Developm.,* 1965, *36,* 379–411. (a)

Bayley, N. Learning in adulthood: The role of intelligence. In H. J. Klausmeier & C. W. Harris (Eds.), *Analyses of concept learning.* New York: Academic Press, 1966. Pp. 117–138.

Bronfenbrenner, U. The psychological costs and equality in education. *Child Developm.,* 1967, *38,* 909–925.

Coleman J. S., et al. *Equality of educational opportunity.* U.S. Dept. of Health, Education, & Welfare, 1966.

Cravioto, J. Malnutrition and behavioral development in the preschool child. *Preschool child malnutrition.* National Health Science, Public., 1966, No. 1282.

Deutsch, M., Katz, I., & Jensen, A. R. (Eds.) *Social class, race, and psychological development.* New York: Holt, Rinehart & Winston, 1968.

Dreger, R. M., & Miller, K. S. Comparative psychological studies of Negroes and whites in the United States: 1959–1965. *Psychol. Bull.*, 1968 *(Monogr. Suppl. 70, No. 3, Part 2).*

Duncan, O. D., Featherman, D. L., & Duncan, B. Socioeconomic background and occupational achievement: Extensions of a basic model. Final Report, Project No. 5–0074 (EO–191) U.S. Dept. of Health, Education, and Welfare, Office of Education, Bureau of Research, May, 1968.

Durham Education Improvement Program, 1966–1967. (a)

Durham Education Improvement Program, Research, 1966–1967. (b)

Dustman, R. E., & Beck, E. C. The visually evoked potential in twins. *Electroenceph. clin. Neurophysiol.*, 1965, *19*, 570–575.

Geber, M. The psycho-motor development of African children in the first year, and the influence of maternal behavior. *J. soc. Psychol.*, 1958, *47*, 185–195.

Geber, M., & Dean, R. F. A. The state of development of newborn African children. *Lancet*, 1957, 1216–1219.

Kuttner, R. E. *Biochemical anthropology.* In R. E. Kuttner (Ed.), *Race and modern science.* New York: Social Science Press, 1967. Pp. 197–222.

Medical World News. Using speed of brain waves to test IQ. 1968, *9*, 26.

Moynihan, D. P. *The Negro family.* Washington, D.C.: Office of Policy Planning and Research, United States Department of Labor, 1965.

Naylor, A. E., & Myrianthopoulos, N. C. The relation of ethnic and selected socioeconomic factors to human birth-weight. *Ann. Hum. Genet.*, 1967, *31*, 71–83.

Shuey, A. M. *The testing of Negro intelligence.* (2nd ed.) New York: Social Science Press, 1966.

Spuhler, J. N., & Lindzey, G. Racial differences in behavior. In J. Hirsch (Ed.), *Behavior-genetic analysis.* New York: McGraw-Hill, 1967. Pp. 366–414.

U.S. News and World Report, Mental tests for 10 million Americans—what they show. October 17, 1966. Pp. 78–80.

Walters, C. E. Comparative development of Negro and white infants. *J. genet. Psychol.*, 1967, *110*, 243–251.

Wilson, A. B. Educational consequences of segregation in a California community. In *Racial isolation in the public schools*, Appendices, Vol. 2 of a report by the U.S. Commission on Civil Rights. Washington, D.C.: U.S. Government Printing Office, 1967.

37.
inadequate evidence and illogical conclusions

jerome s. kagan

Professor Kagan is critical of the logic of Dr. Jensen's article and presents evidence that any IQ data collected in the standardized manner may not reflect the actual potential of lower class children. In Kagan's opinion, Jensen's major fallacies are (1) his inappropriate generalization from within-family IQ differences to an argument that separate racial gene pools are necessarily different and (2) his conclusion that IQ differences are genetically determined, although he glosses over evidence of strong environmental influences on tested IQ—even between identical twins. Kagan cites new studies which suggest that part of the perceived intellectual inadequacy of lower class children may derive from a style of mother-child interaction that gives the lower class child less intense exposure to maternal intervention. Finally, Kagan argues, present compensatory education programs have been neither adequately developed nor evaluated. We cannot, therefore, use current evaluations of them to dismiss all possible compensatory programs.

Arthur Jensen's essay on IQ scholastic achievement, and heredity contains a pair of partially correct empirical generalizations wedded to a logically incorrect conclusion. Professor Jensen notes first that scores on a standard intelligence test are more similar for people with similar genetic constitutions. The more closely related two people are, the more similar their IQ scores, suggesting that there is

Reprinted from *Harvard Educational Review*, 1969, *39* (2), 126–129. Copyright © 1969 by President and Fellows of Harvard College. All rights reserved. Reprinted by permission of the author.

a genetic contribution to intelligence test performance. The second fact is that black children generally obtain lower IQ scores than whites. Unfortunately, Jensen combines the two facts to draw the logically faulted conclusion that there are genetic determinants behind the lower IQ scores of black children. The error in his logic can be illustrated easily, using stature as an example. There is no doubt that stature is inherited. Height is controlled by genetic factors. The more closely related two people are, the more similar their height. It is also true that Indian children living in the rural areas of most Central or South American countries are significantly shorter than the Indian children living in the urban areas of those countries. Jensen's logic would suggest that the shorter stature of the rural children is due to a different genetic constitution. However, the data indicate otherwise. The shorter heights of the rural children do not seem to be due to heredity but to disease and environmental malnutrition. The heights of children in many areas of the world, including the United States, have increased considerably during the past twenty years due to better nutrition and immunization against disease, not as a result of changes in genetic structure. Yet a person's height is still subject to genetic control. The essential error in Jensen's argument is the conclusion that if a trait is under genetic control, differences between two populations on that trait must be due to genetic factors. This is the heart of Jensen's position, and it is not persuasive.

Professor I. I. Gottesman, a leading behavioral geneticist, also questions the validity of Jensen's ideas. He notes that, ". . . even when gene pools are known to be matched, appreciable differences in mean IQ can be observed that could only have been associated with environmental differences." In a study of 38 pairs of identical twins reared in *different environments*, the average difference in IQ for these identical twins was 14 points, and at least one quarter of the identical pairs of twins reared in different environments had differences in IQ score *that were larger than 16 points*. This difference is larger than the average difference betwen black and white populations. Gottesman concludes, "The differences observed so far between whites and Negroes can hardly be accepted as sufficient evidence that with respect to intelligence the Negro American is genetically less endowed."

Let us consider some additional empirical evidence that casts doubt on the validity of Jensen's position. Longitudinal studies being conducted in our laboratory reveal that lower class white children perform less well than middle class children on tests related to those used in intelligence tests. These class differences with white populations occur as early as one to two years of age. Detailed observations of the mother-child interaction in the homes of these children indicate that the lower class children do not experience the quality of parent-child interaction that occurs in the middle class homes. Specifically, the lower class mothers spend less time in face to face mutual vocalization and smiling with their infants; they do not reward the child's maturational progress, and they do not enter into long periods of play with the child. Our theory of mental development suggests that specific absence of these experiences will retard mental growth and will lead to lower intelligence test scores. The most likely determinants of the black child's lower IQ score are his experiences during the first five years of life. These experiences lead the young black child to do poorly on IQ tests in part because he does not appreciate the nature of a problem.

A recent study of urban black children showed that the IQ distribution had two peaks. There was a large proportion of children with IQ scores around 60 and a much larger group whose distribution was normal and similar to that of white populations. The examiners felt that the

very low IQ scores were a product of failure to understand the problem; failure to know what to do; failure to appreciate a test was being administered. This argument finds support in a recent study by Dr. Francis Palmer of the City University of New York. Dr. Palmer administered mental tests to middle and lower class black children from Harlem. However, each examiner was instructed not to begin any testing with any children until she felt that the child was completely relaxed, and understood what was required of him. Many children had five, six and even seven hours of rapport sessions with the examiner before any questions were administered. Few psychological studies have ever devoted this much care to establishing rapport with the child. Dr. Palmer found very few significant differences in mental ability between the lower and middle class populations. This is one of the first times such a finding has been reported and it seems due, in part, to the great care taken to insure that the child comprehended the nature of the test questions and felt at ease with the examiner.

We can quickly dismiss Jensen's suggestion that compensatory education is not likely to help black children. The value of Head Start or similar remedial programs has not yet been adequately assessed. It is not reasonable to assume that compensatory education has failed merely because eight weeks of a Head Start program organized on a crash basis failed to produce stable increases in IQ score. The flaws in this logic are overwhelming. It would be nonsense to assume that feeding animal protein to a seriously malnourished child for three days would lead to a permanent increase in his weight and height, if after 72 hours of steak and eggs he was sent back to his malnourished environment. It *may be* that compensatory education is of little value, but this idea has not been tested in any adequate way up to now.

Finally, it is important to realize that the genetic constitution of a population does not produce a specific level of mental ability; rather it sets a range of mental ability. Thus genetic factors are likely to be most predictive of proficiency in mental talents that are extremely difficult to attain, such as creative genius in mathematics or music, not relatively easy skills. Learning to read, write or add are easy skills, well within the competence of all children who do not have serious brain damage. Therefore, it is erroneous to suggest that genetic differences between human populations could be responsible for failure to master school related tasks. Ninety out of every 100 children, black, yellow or white, are capable of adequate mastery of the intellectual requirements of our schools. Let us concentrate on the conditions that will allow this latent competence to be actualized with maximal ease.

REFERENCES

Gottesman, I. I. Biogenetics of race and class. In M. Deutsch, I. Katz, and A. R. Jensen (Eds.), *Social class, race, and psychological development.* New York: Holt, Rinehart & Winston, 1968.

Palmer, F., unpublished research reported at a colloquium at Harvard University, November, 1968.

38.
behavior-genetic analysis
and its biosocial consequences

jerry hirsch

As a psychology student I was taught that a science was founded on the discovery of lawful relations between variables. During my student days at Berkeley, the true psychological scientist was preoccupied with the major learning theories. We read, studied, and designed experiments to test the theories of Thorndike, Guthrie, Hull and Tolman. Many of their verbally formulated laws of behavior were replaced by the mathematical models that have since come into vogue.

Afterwards I learned empirically the truth of what might be the most general of all behavioral laws, the Harvard law of animal behavior: "Under the most carefully controlled experimental conditions the animals do as they damn please." Still later I discovered the low esteem in which post World War II psychology was held by two of the best minds this century has seen. In 1946, John Dewey, eighth president of the American Psychological Association, wrote to discourage young Robert V. Daniel from studying psychology at Harvard:

Psychology . . . is on the whole, in my opinion, the most inept and backwards a tool as there is. It is much of it actually harmful because of wrong basic postulates—maybe not all stated, but actually there when

Reprinted from *Seminars in Psychiatry*, 1970, 2 (1), 89–105. By permission of the author and Henry M. Stratton.
Invited address presented to the XIXth International Congress of Psychology, London, England, July 30, 1969, and dedicated to Prof. Th. Dobzhansky on his 70th birthday.
This work was prepared with the support of Mental Health Training Grant 1 TO1 10715–04 BLS for Research Training in the Biological Sciences.

one judges from what they do—the kind of problems attacked and the way they attack them (5).

On the final page of the last book written before his death in 1951 Ludwig Wittgenstein, perhaps the most influential of the founders of modern philosophical analysis, observed:

The confusion and barrenness of psychology is not to be explained by calling it a "young science"; its state is not comparable with that of physics, for instance, in its beginning. (Rather with that of certain branches of mathematics. Set theory.) For in psychology there are experimental methods and conceptual confusion. (As in the other case conceptual confusion and methods of proof.)

The existence of the experimental method makes us think we have the means of solving the problems which trouble us; though problem and method pass one another by (34).

LAWS OF GENETICS

It was then while overcome by feelings of disenchantment (obviously without laws behavior study could never be science) that I embraced genetics. There was true science. My passion became even more intense when I realized that, like thermodynamics, genetics had three laws: segregation, independent assortment and the Hardy-Weinberg law of population equilibria. What a foundation they provided for my beloved individual differences.

Since both my teaching and research involved considerable work with *Drosophila*, I knew and would recount to my classes in somewhat elaborate detail the story of Calvin Bridge's classic experiments on sex determination as a function of a ratio between the sex chromosomes and the autosomes. As the important discoveries in human cytogenetics were made throughout the 1950's and 60's and "abnormalities" like Klinefelter's, Turner's and Down's syndromes and the violence-prone males with an extra Y chromosome became genetically comprehensible, I began to realize that the so-called laws of genetics were no more universal than the so-called laws of behavior. Every one of the above-mentioned clinical conditions involved, at the very least, a violation of Mendel's law of segregation. Of course, so did Bridge's experiments, but it had been too easy to rationalize them as clever laboratory tricks.

BEHAVIORISM

Over the past two decades the case against behaviorist extremism has been spelled out in incontrovertible detail. The behaviorists committed many sins: they accepted the mind at birth as Locke's *tabula rasa*, they advocated an empty-organism psychology, they asserted the uniformity postulate of no prenatal individual differences; in short they epitomized typological thinking. Many times we have heard quoted the famous boast by the first high priest of behaviorism, John B. Watson:

> Give me a dozen healthy infants, well-formed, and my own specified world to bring them up in, and I'll guarantee to take any one at random and train him to become any type of specialist I might select—doctor, lawyer, artist, merchant-chief' and yes, even beggar-man and thief, regardless of his talents, penchants, tendencies, abilities, vocations, race of his ancestors.

However, it is only when we read the next sentence, which is rarely, if ever, quoted, that we begin to understand how so many people might have embraced something intellectually so shallow as radical behaviorism. In that all important next sentence Watson explains:

> I am going beyond my facts and I admit it, but so have the advocates of the contrary and they have been doing it for many thousands of years (33, p. 104).

RACISM

Who were the advocates of the contrary and what had they been saying? It is difficult to establish the origins of racist thinking, but certainly one of its most influential advocates was Joseph Arthur de Gobineau, who published a four-volume *Essay on the inequality of the human races (10)* in the mid-1850s. De Gobineau preached the superiority of the white race, and among whites it was the Aryans who carried civilization to its highest point. In fact, they were responsible for civilization wherever it appeared. Unfortunately, de Gobineau's essay proved to be the major seminal work that inspired some of the most perverse developments in the intellectual and political history of our civilization. Later in his life, de Gobineau became an intimate of the celebrated German composer, Richard Wagner. The English-born Houston Stewart Chamberlain, who emigrated to the Continent, became a devoted admirer of both de Gobineau and Wagner. In 1908, after Wagner's death, he married Wagner's daughter, Eva, settled in and supported Germany against England during World War I, becoming a naturalized German citizen in 1916.

In the summer of 1923, an admirer who had read Chamberlain's writings, Adolf Hitler, visited Wahnfried, the Wagner family home in Bayreuth where Chamberlain lived. After their meeting, Chamberlain wrote to Hitler: "My faith in the Germans had never wavered for a moment, but my hope . . . had sunk to a low ebb. At one stroke you have transformed the state of my soul!" (14). We all know the sequel to that unfortunate tale. I find that our modern scientific colleagues, whether they be biological or social scientists, for the most part, do not know the sad parallel that exists for the essentially political tale I have so far recounted. The same theme can be traced down the main stream of biosocial science.

Today not many people know the complete title of Darwin's most famous book: *On the Origin of Species by Means of Natural Selection or the Preservation of Favored Races in the Struggle for Life*. I find no evidence that Darwin had the attitudes we now call racist. Unfortunately many of his admirers, his contemporaries, and his successors were not as circumspect as he. In Paris in 1838, J.E.D. Esquirol first described a form of mental deficiency later to become well known by two inappropriate names unrelated to his work. Unhappily one of these names, through textbook adoption and clinical jargon, puts into wide circulation a term loaded with race prejudice. Somewhat later (1846 and 1866), E. Seguin described the same condition under the name "furfuracious cretinism" and his account has only recently been recognized as "the most ingenious description of physical characteristics . . ." (2).

Unhappily that most promising scientific beginning was ignored. Instead the following unfortunate events occurred: In 1866, John Langdon Haydon Down published the paper entitled "Observations of an ethnic classification of idiots" (6)

. . . making a classification of the feeble-minded, by arranging them around various ethnic standards—in other words, framing a natural system to supplement the information to be derived by an inquiry into the history of the case.

I have been able to find among the large number of idiots and imbeciles which comes under my observation, both at Earlswood and the out-patient department of the Hospital, that a considerable portion can be fairly referred to one of the great divisions of the human family other than the class from which they have sprung. Of course, there are numerous representatives of the great Caucasian family. Several well-marked examples of the Ethiopian variety have come under my notice, presenting the characteristic malar bones, the prominent eyes, the puffy lips, and retreating chin. The woolly hair has also been present, although not always black nor has the skin acquired pigmentary deposit. They have been specimens of white negroes, although of European descent.

Some arrange themselves around the Malay variety, and present in their soft, black, curly hair, their prominent upper jaws and capacious mouths, types of the family which people the South Sea Islands.

Nor have there been wanting the analogues of the people who with shortened foreheads, prominent cheeks, deep-set eyes, and slightly apish nose, originally inhabited the American Continent.

The great Mongolian family has numerous representatives, and it is to this division, I wish, in this paper, to call special attention. A very large number of congenital idiots are typical Mongols. So marked is this, that when placed side by side, it is difficult to believe that the specimens compared are not children of the same parents. The number of idiots who arrange themselves around the Mongolian type is so great, and they present such a close resemblance to one another in mental power, that I shall describe an idiot member of this racial division, selected from the large number that have fallen under my observation.

The hair is not black, as in the real Mongol, but of a brownish colour, straight and scanty. The face is flat and broad, and destitute of prominence. The cheeks are roundish, and extended laterally. The eyes are obliquely placed, and the internal canthi more than normally distant from one another. The palpebral fissure is very narrow. The forehead is wrinkled transversely from the constant assistance which the levatores palpebrarum derive from the occipito-frontalis muscle in the opening of the eyes. The lips are large and thick with transverse fissures. The tongue is long, thick, and is much roughened. The nose is small. The skin has a slightly dirty yellowish tinge and is deficient in elasticity, giving the appearance of being too large for the body.

> *The boy's aspect is such that it is difficult to realize that he is the child of Europeans, but so frequently are these characters presented, that there can be no doubt that these ethnic features are the result of degeneration.*

And he means degeneration from a higher to a lower race. The foregoing represents a distasteful but excellent example of the racial hierarchy theory and its misleadingly dangerous implications. That was how the widely-used terms Mongolism and Mongolian idiocy entered our "technical" vocabulary. For the next century, this pattern of thought is going to persist and occupy an important place in the minds of many leading scientists.

ALLEGED JEWISH GENETIC INFERIORITY

In 1884, Francis Galton, Darwin's half cousin, founder of the Eugenics movement and respected contributor to many fields of science, wrote to the distinguished Swiss botanist, Alphonse de Candolle: "It strikes me that the Jews are specialized for a parasitical existence upon other nations, and that there is need of evidence that they are capable of fulfilling the varied duties of a civilized nation by themselves" (27, p. 209). Karl Pearson, Galton's disciple and biographer, echoed this opinion 40 years later during his attempt to prove the undesirability of Jewish immigration into Britain: ". . . for such men as religion, social habits, or language keep as a caste apart, there should be no place. They will not be absorbed by, and at the same time strengthen the existing population; they will develop into a parasitic race . . ." (28, p. 125).

Beginning in 1908 and continuing at least until 1928, Karl Pearson collected and analyzed data in order to assess "the quality of the racial stock immigrating into Great Britain . . ." (25, p. 33). He was particularly disturbed by the large numbers of East European Jews, who near the turn of the century began coming from Poland and Russia to escape the pogroms. Pearson's philosophy was quite explicitly spelled out:

> *Let us admit . . . that the mind of man is for the most part a congenital product, and the factors which determine it are racial and familial; we are not dealing with a mutable characteristic capable of being moulded by the doctor, the teacher, the parent or the home environment (28, p. 124).*
>
> *The ancestors of the men who pride themselves on being English today were all at one time immigrants; it is not for us to cast the first stone against newcomers, solely because they are newcomers. But the test for immigrants in the old days was a severe one; it was power, physical and mental, to retain their hold on the land they seized. So came Celts, Saxons, Norsemen, Danes and Normans in succession and built up the nation of which we are proud. Nor do we criticize the alien Jewish immigration simply because it is Jewish; we took the alien Jews to study, because they were the chief immigrants of that day and material was readily available (28, p. 127).*

His observations led him to conclude: "Taken *on the average*, and regarding both sexes, this alien Jewish population is somewhat inferior physically and mentally to the native population" (28, p. 126).

ALLEGED BLACK GENETIC INFERIORITY

Quite recently there has appeared a series of papers disputing whether or not black Americans are, in fact, genetically inferior to white Americans in intellectual capacity. The claims and counterclaims have been given enormous publicity in the popular press in America. Some of those papers contain most of the fallacies that can conceivably be associated with this widely misunderstood problem.

The steps toward the intellectual cul-de-sac into which this dispute leads and the fallacious assumptions on which such "progress" is based are the following: (1) A trait called intelligence, or anything else, is defined and a testing instrument for the measurement of trait expression is used; (2) the heritability of that trait is estimated; (3) races (populations) are compared with respect to their performance on the test of trait expression; (4) when the races (populations) differ on the test whose heritability has now been measured, the one with the lower score is genetically inferior, Q.E.D.

The foregoing argument can be applied to any, single trait or to as many traits as one might choose to consider. Therefore, analysis of this general problem does *not* depend upon the particular definition and test used for this or that trait. For my analysis I shall pretend that an acceptable test exists for some trait, be it height, weight, intelligence, or anything else. (Without an acceptable test, discussion of the "trait" remains unscientific.)

Even to consider comparisons between races, the following concepts must be recognized: (1) the genome as a mosaic, (2) development as the expression of one out of many alternatives in the genotype's norm of reaction, (3) a population as a gene pool, (4) heritability is not instinct, (5) traits as distributions of scores, and (6) distributions as moments.

Since inheritance is particulate and not integral, the genome, genotype or hereditary endowment of each individual is a unique mosaic—an assemblage of factors many of which are independent. Because of the lottery-like nature of both gamete formation and fertilization, other than monozygotes no two individuals share the same genotypic mosaic.

NORM OF REACTION

The ontogeny of an individual's phenotype (observable outcome of development) has a norm or range of reaction not predictable in advance. In most cases the norm of reaction remains largely unknown; but the concept is nevertheless of fundamental importance, because it saves us from being taken in by glib and misleading textbook clichés such as "heredity sets the limits but environment determines the extent of development within those limits." Even in the most favorable materials only an approximate estimate can be obtained for the norm

of reaction, when, as in plants and some animals, an individual genotype can be replicated many times and its development studied over a range of environmental conditions. The more varied the conditions, the more diverse might be the phenotypes developed from any one genotype. Of course, different genotypes should not be expected to have the same norm of reaction; unfortunately psychology's attention was diverted from appreciating this basic fact of biology by a half century of misguided environmentalism. Just as we see that, except for monozygotes, no two human faces are alike, so we must expect norms of reaction to show genotypic uniqueness. That is one reason why the heroic but ill-fated attempts of experimental learning psychology to write the "laws of environmental influence" were grasping at shadows. Therefore, those limits set by heredity in the textbook cliché can never be specified. They are plastic within each individual but differ between individuals. Extreme environmentalists were wrong to hope that one law or set of laws described universal features of modifiability. Extreme hereditarians were wrong to ignore the norm of reaction.

Individuals occur in populations and then only as temporary attachments, so to speak, each to particular combinations of genes. The population, on the other hand, can endure indefinitely as a pool of genes, maybe forever recombining to generate new individuals.

INSTINCTS, GENES AND HERITABILITY

What is heritability? How is heritability estimated for intelligence or any other trait? Is heritability related to instinct? In 1872, Douglas Spalding demonstrated that the ontogeny of a bird's ability to fly is simply maturation and not the result of practice, imitation or any demonstrable kind of learning. He confined immature birds and deprived them of the opportunity either to practice flapping their wings or to observe and imitate the flight of older birds; in spite of this, they developed the ability to fly. For some ethologists this deprivation experiment became the paradigm for proving the innateness or instinctive nature of a behavior by demonstrating that it appears despite the absence of any opportunity for it to be learned. Remember two things about this approach: (1) the observation involves experimental manipulation of the conditions of experience during development, and (2) such observation can be made on the development of one individual. For some people the results of a deprivation experiment now constitute the operational demonstration of the existence (or non-existence) of an instinct (in a particular species).

Are instincts heritable? That is, are they determined by genes? But what is a gene? A gene is an inference from a breeding experiment. It is recognized by the measurement of individual differences—the recognition of the segregation of distinguishable forms of the expression of some trait among the progeny of appropriate matings. For example, when an individual of blood type AA mates with one of type BB, their offspring are uniformly AB. If two of the AB offspring mate, it is found that the A and B gene forms have segregated during reproduction and recombined in their progeny to produce all combinations of A and B: AA, AB, and BB. Note that the only operation involved in such a study is *breeding* of one or more generations and then at an appropriate time of life, observation of the separate individuals born in each generation— controlled breeding with experimental material or pedigree analysis of the appropriate families with human subjects. In principle, only one (usually brief) observation is required. Thus we see that genetics is a science of *differences,* and the breeding experiment is its fundamental operation. The operational definition of the gene, therefore, involves observation in a breeding experiment of the segregation among several individuals of distinguishable differences in the expression of some trait from which the gene can be inferred. Genetics does not work with a single subject, whose development is studied. (The foregoing, the following, and all discussions of genetic analysis presuppose sufficiently adequate control of environmental conditions so that all observed individual differences have

developed under the same, homogeneous environmental conditions, conditions never achieved in any human studies.)

How does heritability enter the picture? At the present stage of knowledge, many features (traits) of animals and plants have not yet been related to genes that can be recognized individually. But the role of large numbers of genes, often called polygenes and in most organisms still indistinguishable one from the other, has been demonstrated easily (and often) by selective breeding or by appropriate comparisons between different strains of animals or plants. Selection and strain crossing have provided the basis for many advances in agriculture and among the new generation of research workers are becoming standard tools for the experimental behaviorist. Heritability often summarizes the extent to which a particular population has responded to a regimen of being bred selectively on the basis of the expression of some trait. Heritability values vary between zero and plus one. If the distribution of trait expression among progeny remains the same no matter how their parents might be selected, then heritability has zero value. If parental selection does make a difference, heritability exceeds zero, its exact value reflecting the parent-offspring correlation. Or more generally, as Jensen says: "The basic data from which . . . heritability coefficients are estimated are correlations among individuals of different degrees of kinship" (*18*, p. 48). Though, many of the heritabilities Jensen discusses have been obtaind by comparing mono- and de-zygotic twins (*17*).

A heritability estimate, however, is a far more limited piece of information than most people realize. As was so well stated by Fuller and Thompson: "heritability is a property of populations and not of traits" (*9*). In its strictest sense, a heritability measure provides for a given population an estimate of the proportion of the variance it shows in trait (phenotype) expression which is correlated with the segregation of the alleles of independently acting genes. There are other more broadly conceived heritability measures, which estimate this correlation and also include the combined effects of genes that are independent and of those that interact. Therefore, heritability estimates the proportion of the total phenotypic variance (individual differences) shown by a trait that can be attributed to genetic variation (narrowly or broadly interpreted) in some particular population at a single generation under one set of conditions.

The foregoing description contains three fundamentally important limitations which have rarely been accorded sufficient attention: (1) The importance of limiting any heritability statement to a specific population is evident when we realize that a gene, which shows variation in one population because it is represented there by two or more segregating alleles, might show no variation in some other population because it is uniformly represented there by only a single allele. Remember that initially such a gene could never have been detected by genetic methods in the second population. Once it has been detected in some population carrying two or more of its segregating alleles, the information thus obtained might permit us to recognize it in populations carrying only a single allele. Note how this is related to heritability: the trait will show a greater-than-zero heritability in the segregating population but zero heritability in the non-segregating population. This does *not* mean that the trait is determined genetically in the first population and environmentally in the second!

Up to now my discussion has been limited to a single gene. The very same argument applies for every gene of the polygenic complexes involved in continuously varying traits like height, weight and intelligence. Also, only *genetic* variation has been considered—the presence or absence of segregating alleles at one or more loci in different populations.

(2) Next let us consider the ever-present environmental sources of variation. Usually from the Mendelian point of view, except for the genes on the segregating chromosomes, everything inside the cell and outside the organism is lumped together and can be called environmental variation: cytoplasmic constituents, the maternal effects now known to be so important, the early experience effects studied in so many psychological

laboratories, and so on. None of these can be considered unimportant or trivial. They are ever present. Let us now perform what physicists call a Gedanken, or thought, experiment. Imagine Aldous Huxley's *Brave New World* or Skinner's *Walden II* organized in such a way that every individual is exposed to precisely the same environmental conditions. In other words, consider the extreme, but *un*realistic, case of complete environmental homogeneity. Under those circumstances the heritability value would approach unity, because only genetic variation would be present. Don't forget that even under the most simplifying assumptions, there are over 70 trillion potential human genotypes—no two of us share the same genotype no matter how many ancestors we happen to have in common *(16)*. Since mitosis projects our unique genotype into the nucleus, or executive, of every cell in our bodies, the individuality that is so obvious in the human faces we see around us must also characterize the unseen components. Let the same experiment be imagined for any number of environments. In each environment heritability will approximate unity but each genotype *may* develop a different phenotype in every environment and the distribution (hierarchy) of genotypes (in terms of their phenotypes) must not be expected to remain invariant over environments.

(3) The third limitation refers to the fact that because gene frequencies can and do change from one generation to the next, so will heritability values or the magnitude of the genetic variance.

Now let us shift our focus to the entire genotype or at least to those of its components that might co-vary at least partially with the phenotypic expression of a particular trait. Early in this century Woltereck *(7)* called to our attention the norm-of-reaction concept: the same genotype can give rise to a wide array of phenotypes depending upon the environment in which it develops. This is most conveniently studied in plants where genotypes are easily replicated. Later Goldschmidt *(11)* was to show in *Drosophila* that, by careful selection of the environmental conditions at critical periods in development, various phenotypes ordinarily associated with specific gene mutations could be produced from genotypes that did not include the mutant form of those genes. Descriptively, Goldschmidt called these events *phenocopies*—environmentally produced imitations of gene mutants or phenotypic expressions only manifested by the "inappropriate" genotype if unusual environmental influences impinge during critical periods in development, but regularly manifested by the "appropriate" genotype under the usual environmental conditions.

In 1946, the brilliant British geneticist J.B.S. Haldane (12) analyzed the interaction concept and gave quantitative meaning to the foregoing. For the simplest case but one, that of two genotypes in three environments or, for its mathematical equivalent, that of three genotypes in two environments, he showed that there are 60 possible kinds of interaction. Ten genotypes in 10 environments generate 10 (144) possible kinds of interaction. In general m genotypes in n environments generate $\dfrac{(mn)!}{m!n!}$ kinds of interaction. Since the characterization of genotype-environment interaction can only be ad hoc and the number of possible interactions is effectively unlimited, it is no wonder that the long search for general laws has been so unfruitful.

For genetically different lines of rats showing the Tryon-type "bright-dull" difference in performance on a learning task, by so simple a change in environmental conditions as replacing massed-practice trials by distributed-practice trials, McGaugh, Jennings and Thompson (23) found that the so-called dulls moved right up to the scoring level of the so-called brights. In a recent study of the open-field behavior of mice, Hegmann and DeFries (13) found that heritabilities measured repeatedly in the same individuals were unstable over two successive days. In surveying earlier work they commented: "Heritability estimates for repeated measurements of behavioral characters have been found to increase (Broadhurst & Jinks, 1961), decrease (Broadhurst & Jinks, 1966), and fluctuate randomly (Fuller & Thompson, 1960) as a function of repeated testing" (p. 27).

Therefore, to the limitations on heritability due to population, situation and breeding generation, we must now add developmental stage, or, many people might say, just plain unreliability! The late and brilliant Sir Ronald Fisher, whose authority Jensen cites (18, p. 34) indicated how fully he had appreciated such limitations when he commented: "the so-called coefficient of heritability, which I regard as one of those unfortunate short-cuts which have emerged in biometry for lack of a more thorough analysis of the data" (8, p. 217). The plain facts are that in the study of man a heritability estimate turns out to be a piece of "knowledge" that is both deceptive and trivial.

THE ROOTS OF ONE MISUSE OF STATISTICS

The other two concepts to be taken into account when racial comparisons are considered involve the representation of traits in populations by distributions of scores and the characterization of distributions by moment-derived statistics. Populations should be compared only with respect to one trait at a time and comparisons should be made in terms of the moment statistics of their trait distributions. Therefore, for any two populations, on each trait of interest, a separate comparison should be made for every moment of their score distributions. If we consider only the first four moments, from which are derived the familiar statistics for mean, variance, skewness, and kurtosis, then there are four ways in which populations or races may differ with respect to any single trait. Since we possess 23 independently assorting pairs of chromosomes, certainly there are at least 23 uncorrelated traits with respect to which populations can be compared. Since comparisons will be made in terms of four (usually independent) statistics, there are $4 \times 23 = 92$ ways in which races can differ. Since the integrity of chromosomes is *not* preserved over the generations, because they often break apart at meiosis and exchange constituent genes, there are far more than 23 independent hereditary units. If instead of 23 chromosomes we take the 100,000 genes man is now estimated to possess (24, p. IX) and we think in terms of their phenotypic trait correlates, then there may be as many as 400,000 comparisons to be made between any two populations or races.

A priori, at this time we know enough to expect no two populations to be the same with respect to most or all of the constituents of their gene pools. "Mutations and recombinations will occur at different places, at different times, and with differing frequencies. Furthermore, selection pressures will also vary" (16, p. 1441). So the number and kinds of differences between populations now waiting to be revealed in "the more thorough analysis" recommended by Fisher literally staggers the imagination. It does not suggest a linear hierarchy of inferior and superior races.

Why has so much stress been placed on comparing distributions only with respect to their central tendencies by testing the significance of mean differences? There is much evidence that many observations are not normally distributed and that the distributions from many populations do not share homogeneity of variance. The source of our difficulty traces back to the very inception of our statistical tradition.

There is an unbroken line of intellectual influence from Quetelet through Galton and Pearson to modern psychometrics and biometrics. Adolphe Quetelet (1796–1874), the Belgian astronomer-statistician, introduced the concept of "the average man"; he also applied the normal distribution, so widely used in astronomy for error variation, to human data, biological and social. The great Francis Galton followed Quetelet's lead and then Karl Pearson elaborated and perfected their methods. I know of nothing that has contributed more to impose the typological way of thought on, and perpetuate it in, present-day psychology than the feedback from these methods for describing observations in terms of group averages.

There is a technique called composite photography to the perfection of which Sir Francis Galton contributed in an important way. Some of Galton's best work in this field was done by combining—

literally averaging—the separate physiognomic features of many different Jewish individuals into his composite photograph of "the Jewish type." Karl Pearson, his disciple and biographer, wrote: "There is little doubt that Galton's Jewish type formed a landmark in composite photography . . ." (27, p. 293). The part played by typological thinking in the development of modern statistics and the way in which such typological thinking has been feeding back into our conceptual framework through our continued careless use of these statistics is illuminated by Galton's following remarks: "The word generic presupposes a genus, that is to say, a collection of individuals who have much in common, and among whom medium characteristics are very much more frequent than extreme ones. The same idea is sometimes expressed by the word typical, which was much used by Quetelet, who was the first to give it a rigorous interpretation, and whose idea of a type lies at the basis of his statistical views. No statistician dreams of combining objects into the same generic group that do not cluster towards a common centre; no more can we compose generic portraits out of heterogeneous elements, for if the attempt be made to do so the result is monstrous and meaningless" (27, p. 295). The basic assumption of a type, or typical individual, is clear and explicit. They used the normal curve and they permitted distributions to be represented by an average because, even though at times they knew better, far too often they tended to think of races as discrete, even homogeneous, groups and individual variation as error.

It is important to realize that these developments began before 1900, when Mendel's work was still unknown. Thus at the inception of biosocial science there was no substantive basis for understanding individual differences. After 1900, when Mendel's work became available, its incorporation into biosocial science was bitterly opposed by the biometricians under Pearson's leadership. Galton had promulgated two "laws": his Law of Ancestral Heredity (1865) (27) and his Law of Regression (1877) (27). When Yule (35) and Castle (4) pointed out how the Law of Ancestral Heredity could be explained in Mendelian terms, Pearson (26) stubbornly denied it. Mendel had chosen for experimental observation seven traits, each of which, in his pea-plant material, turned out to be a phenotypic correlate of a single gene with two segregating alleles. For all seven traits one allele was dominant. Unfortunately Pearson assumed the universality of dominance and based his disdain for Mendelism on this assumption. Yule (36) then showed that without the assumption of dominance, Mendelism becomes perfectly consistent with the kind of quantitative data on the basis of which it was being rejected by Pearson. It is sad to realize that Pearson never appreciated the generality of Mendelism and seems to have gone on for the next 32 years without doing so.

TWO FALLACIES

Now we can consider the recent debate about the meaning of comparisons between the "intelligence" of different human races. We are told that intelligence has a high heritability and that one race performs better than another on intelligence tests. In essence we are presented with a racial hierarchy reminiscent of that pernicious "system" which John Haydon Langdon Down used when he misnamed a disease entity "mongolism."

The people who are so committed to answering the nature-nurture pseudo-question (Is heredity or environment more important in determining intelligence?) make two conceptual blunders. (1) Like Spalding's question about the instinctive nature of bird flight, which introduced the ethologist's deprivation experiment, their question about intelligence is, in fact, being asked about the development of a single individual. Unlike Spalding and the ethologists, however, they do not study development in single individuals. Usually they test groups of individuals at a single time of life. The proportions being assigned to heredity and to environment refer to the relative amounts of the variance between individuals comprising a population, not how much of whatever enters into the development of the observed expression

of a trait in a particular individual has been contributed by heredity and by environment respectively. They want to know how instinctive is intelligence in the development of a certain individual, but instead they measure differences between large numbers of fully, or partially, developed individuals. If we now take into consideration the norm-of-reaction concept and combine it with the facts of genotypic individuality, then there is no general statement that can be made about the assignment of fixed proportions to the contributions of heredity and environment either to the development of a single individual, because we have not even begun to assess his norm of reaction, or to the differences that might be measured among members of a population, because we have hardly begun to assess the range of environmental conditions under which its constituent members might develop!

(2) Their second mistake, an egregious error, is related to the first one. They assume an inverse relationship between heritability magnitude and improvability by training and teaching. If heritability is high, little room is left for improvement by environmental modification. If heritability is low, much more improvement is possible. Note how this basic fallacy is incorporated directly into the title of Jensen's article "How much can we boost IQ and scholastic achievement?" (18). That question received a straightforward, but fallacious, answer on his page 59: "The fact that scholastic achievement is considerably less heritable than intelligence . . . means there is potentially much more we can do to improve school performance through environmental means than we can do to change intelligence. . . ." Commenting on the heritability of intelligence and "the old nature-nurture controversy" one of Jensen's respondents makes the same mistake in his rebuttal: "This is an old estimate which many of us have used but we have used it to determine what could be done with the variance left for the environment." He then goes on "to further emphasize some of the implications of environmental variance for education and child rearing" (3, p. 419).

High or low heritability tells us absolutely nothing about how a given individual might have developed under conditions different from those in which he actually did develop. Heritability provides no information about norm of reaction. Since the characterization of genotype-environment interaction can only be ad hoc and the number of possible interactions is effectively unlimited, no wonder the search for general laws of behavior has been so unfruitful, and *the* heritability of intelligence or of any other trait must be recognized as still another of those will-o-the-wisp general laws. And no magic words about an interaction component in a linear analysis-of-variance model will make disappear the reality of each genotype's unique norm of reaction. Such claims by Jensen or anyone else are false. Interaction is an abstraction of mathematics. Norm of reaction is a developmental reality of biology in plants, animals and people.

In Israel, the descendants of those Jews Pearson feared would contaminate Britain are manifesting some interesting properties of the norm of reaction. Children of European origin have an average IQ of 105 when they are brought up in individual homes. Those brought up in a Kibbutz on the nursery rearing schedule of 22 hours per day for 4 or more years have an average IQ of 115. In contrast, the mid-Eastern Jewish children brought up in individual homes have an average IQ of only 85, Jensen's danger point. However, when brought up in a Kibbutz, they also have an average IQ of 115. That is, they perform the same as the European children with whom they were matched for education, the occupational level of parents and the Kibbutz group in which they were raised (3, p. 420). There is no basis for expecting different overall results for any population in our species.

SOME PROMISING RECENT DEVELOPMENTS

The power of the approach that begins by thinking first in terms of the genetic system and only later in terms of the phenotype (or behavior) to be analyzed is now being demonstrated by an accumulating and impressive body of evidence. The rationale of that approach derives directly from the particulate nature of the gene, the mosaic nature of the genotype and the manner in which heredity breaks apart and gets reassembled in being passed on from one generation to the next. We now have a well-articulated picture of the way heredity is shared among biological relatives.

That madness runs in families has been known for centuries. The controversy has been over whether it was the heredity or the environment supplied by the family that was responsible for the madness. Franz Kallmann and some others collected large amounts of data in the 1940s and 1950s showing that monozygotic twins were much more concordant than dizygotic twins. Since David Rosenthal of NIMH has provided some of the best criticism of the incompleteness, and therefore inconclusiveness, of the twin-study evidence for the role of heredity in schizophrenia, Rosenthal's own recent findings become especially noteworthy.

He has divided foster-reared children from adoptive homes into two groups: those with a biological parent who is schizophrenic and those without a schizophrenic biological parent. It was found by Rosenthal, (31) and by Heston (15) in a completely independent but similar study, that the incidence of schizophrenia was much greater among the biological children of schizophrenics. Most significantly, combining the two studies, the risk of schizophrenia in offspring is four to five times greater if a biological parent is schizophrenic. Still other recent studies support the Rosenthal and the Heston findings. Both Karlson (19) and Wender (30) found a high incidence of schizophrenia in the foster-reared relatives of schizophrenics.

Thinking genetically first in terms of biological relationship has already paid off in the analytical detail revealed as well as in the mere demonstration of concordance with respect to diagnostic category. Lidz and co-workers (20) reported marked distortions in communicating among many of the non-hospitalized parents of schizophrenic hospital patients. McConaghy, (22) using an objective test of thought disorder, assessed the parents of 10 schizophrenic patients and compared them to a series of control subjects. Sixty per cent of the patients' parents, including at least one parent in every pair, registered test scores in the range indicative of thought disturbance. In contrast, less than 10 per cent of the controls had such scores.

The major features of McConaghy's findings have since been replicated by Lidz and co-workers (21). More recently Phillips and co-workers (29) studied 48 relatives of adult schizophrenics and 45 control subjects using a battery of tests to assess thought disorder. They found cognitive disorders to be much more frequent among the relatives of schizophrenics; 17 of 18 parents registered "pathological" scores, even though their social behavior had never been diagnosed as pathological.

In 1962, Anastasopoulos and Photiades (1) assessed susceptibility to LSD-induced "pathological reactions" in the relatives of schizophrenic patients. After studying 21 families of patients and 9 members of two control families, they reported ". . . it was almost invariable to find reactions to LSD in one of the parents, and often in one or more of the siblings and uncles and aunts, which were neither constant nor even common during the LSD-intoxication of healthy persons."

Analogous work has been done studying the responses of the relatives of patients with depressive disorders using anti-depressant drugs like imipramine (Tofranil) or an MAO inhibitor. Relatives tend to show a response pattern similar to that of their hospitalized relations.

Some very interesting human behavior-genetic analyses are currently being done on these affective disorders by George Winokur and his colleagues in St. Louis (30). Out of 1075 consecutive admissions to a psychiatric hospital, 426 were diagnosed as primary affective disorders. So far, these appear to fall into two subtypes, the first of which shows manic episodes; some first-degree relatives show similar manifestations. The other subtype is characterized by depressive episodes and lack of concordance among close relatives. Furthermore, evidence is now accumulat-

ing implicating a dominant factor or factors on the X-chromosome in the manic subtype: (1) the condition is considerably more prevalent in females than in males; (2) the morbid risk among siblings of male probands is the same for males and females, but the morbid risk among siblings of female probands is quite different—sisters of female probands are at a 21 per cent risk while their brothers are only at a 7.4 per cent risk. More detailed study in several appropriately chosen family pedigrees suggests that there is a dominant gene on the short arm of the X-chromosome. The condition has so far shown linkage with color-blindness and the Xg blood groups, both of which are loosely linked on the short arm of the X-chromosome.

To examine the structure of the phenotypic variation in a trait whose development is in no obvious way influenced by environment and which, though ostensibly a simple trait, has been sufficiently well-analyzed phenotypically to reveal its interesting complexity, we have chosen to study dermatoglyphics, or fingerprints, in my laboratory. For his doctoral dissertation, R. Peter Johnson is making these observations on both parents and offspring in individual families. His preparatory survey of the previous literature revealed one study which reported data on a cross-sectional sample of 2000 males (32). Scoring them on all ten fingers with respect to four distinguishable pattern types, the following data reveal the interesting but sobering complexity that exists in such a "simple" trait: the same type of pattern was shown on all 10 fingers by 12 per cent, on 9 of 10 fingers by 16 per cent, and on 8 of 10 fingers by 10 per cent of the men. In addition, 5 per cent of the men showed all four pattern types. This included 1 per cent of the individuals who had all four pattern types on a single hand.

While probably everybody has heard that there are some unusual hospitalized males who carry two Y chromosomes are rather tall, and prone to commit crimes of violence, few people know that when a comparison was made between the first-order relatives of both the Y-Y chromosome males and control males hospitalized for similar reasons (but not carrying two Y chromosomes), there was a far greater incidence of a family history of crime among the controls. In this control group there were over six times as many individual first-order relatives convicted and many, many times the number of convictions.

In summary, the relationship between heredity and behavior has turned out to be one of neither isomorphism nor independence. Isomorphism might justify an approach like naive reductionism, independence a naive behaviorism. Neither one turns out to be adequate. I believe that in order to study behavior, we must understand genetics quite thoroughly. Then, and only then, can we as psychologists forget about it intelligently.

REFERENCES

1. Anastasopoulos, G., and Photiades, H.: Effects of LSD-25 on relatives of schizophrenic patients. J. Ment. Sci. *108*:95–98, 1962.

2. Benda, C. E.: "Mongolism" or "Down's syndrome." Lancet. *1*:163, 1962.

3. Bloom, B. S.: Letter to the editor. Harvard Educ. Rev. *39*:419–421, 1969.

4. Castle, W. E.: The laws of heredity of Galton and Mendel, and some laws governing race improvement by selection. Proc. Amer. Acad. Arts Sci. *39*:223–242, 1903.

5. Dewey, J.: Correspondence with Robert V. Daniel, 19 November, 1946. J. Hist. Ideas *20*:570, 1959.

6. Down, J. L. H.: Observations on an ethnic classification of idiots. London Hospital Reports, 1866. Reprinted in McKusick, V. A. (Ed.): Medical genetics, 1961. J. Chron. Dis. *15*:432, 1962.

7. Dunn, L. C.: A Short History of Genetics. New York, McGraw-Hill, 1965.

8. Fisher, R. A.: Limits to intensive production in animals. Brit. Agr. Bull. *4*:217–218, 1951.

9. Fuller, J. L., and Thompson, W. R.: Behavior Genetics. New York, Wiley, 1960.

10. de Gobineau, J. A.: Essai sur l' inégalité des races humaines. Rééd. intégrale en 1 vol., avec une préface de Hubert Juin. Paris, P. Belfond, 1967.

11. Goldschmidt, R. B.: Theoretical Genetics. Berkeley, University of California Press, 1955, p. 257.

12. Haldane, J. B. S.: The interaction of nature and nurture. Ann. Eugen. *13*:197–205, 1946.

13. Hegmann, J. P., and DeFries, J. C.: Open-field behavior in mice: Genetic analysis of repeated measures. Psychon. Sci. *13*: 27–28, 1968.

14. Heiden, K.: Der Führer. London, 1944, p. 198. Cited in Bullock, A.: Hitler: A Study in Tyranny. Harmondsworth, Penguin, 1962, p. 80.

15. Heston, L. L.: Psychiatric disorders in foster home reared children of schizophrenic mothers. Brit. J. Psychiat. *112*:819–825, 1966.

16. Hirsch, J.: Behavior genetics and individuality understood: behaviorism's counterfactual dogma blinded the behavioral sciences to the significance of meiosis. Science *142*:1436–1442, 1963.

17. Jensen, A. R.: Estimation of the limits of heritability of traits by comparison of monozygotic and dizygotic twins. Proc. Nat. Acad. Sci. *58*:149–156, 1967.

18. Jensen, A. R.: How much can we boost IQ and scholastic achievement? Harvard Educ. Rev. *39*:1–123, 1969.

19. Karlsson, J. L.: The Biologic Basis of Schizophrenia. Springfield. Ill., Charles C Thomas, 1966.

20. Lidz, T., Cornelison, A., Terry, D., and Fleck, S.: Intrafamilial environment of the schizophrenic patient: VI. The transmission of irrationality. AMA Arch. Neurol. Psychiat. *79*:305–316, 1958.

21. Lidz, T., Wild, C., Schafer, S., Rosman, B., and Fleck, S.: Thought disorders in the study of schizophrenic patients: A study utilizing the Object Sorting Test. Psychiat. Res. *1*:193–200, 1962.

22. McConaghy, N.: The use of an object sorting test in elucidating the hereditary factor in schizophrenia. J. Neurol, Neurosurg. Psychiat. 22:243, 1959.

23. McGaugh, J. L., Jennings, R. D., and Thompson, C. W.: Effect of distribution of practice on the maze learning of descendants of the Tryon maze bright and maze dull strains. Psychol. Rep. *9*:147–150, 1962

24. McKusick, V. A.: Mendelian Inheritance in Man: Catalogs of Autosomal Dominant, Recessive, and X-Linked Phenotypes. Baltimore, Johns Hopkins Press, 1966.

25. Pastore, N.: The Nature-Nurture Controversy. New York King's Crown Press (Columbia University), 1949.

26. Pearson, K.: On a generalized theory of alternative inheritance, with special reference to Mendel's laws. Phil. Trans. Roy. Soc. London *A203*:53–86, 1904.

27. Pearson, K.: The Life, Letters and La-

bours of Francis Galton, Vol. II: Researches of Middle Life. Cambridge, Cambridge University Press, 1924.

28. Pearson, K.: and Moul, M.: The problem of alien immigration into Great Britain, illustrated by an examination of Russian and Polish Jewish children. Ann. Eugen. 1: 5–127, 1925.

29. Phillips, J. E., Jacobson, N., and Turner, W. J.: Conceptual thinking in schizophrenics and their relatives. Brit. J. Psychiat. 111:823–829, 1965.

30. Rose, R. J., Department of Psychology, University of Indiana, private communication, 1969.

31. Rosenthal, D., Wender, P. H., Kety, S. S., Schulsinger, F., Welner, J., and Østergaard, L.: Schizophrenics' offspring reared in adoptive homes. J. Psychiat. Res. 6:377–391, 1968.

32. Waite, H.: Association of fingerprints. Biometrika 10:421–478, 1915.

33. Watson, J. B.: Behaviorism. Chicago, University of Chicago Press, 1959.

34. Wittgenstein, L.: Philosophical Investigations (ed. 2). Translated by Anscombe, G. E. Oxford, Blackwell, 1963, p. 232.

35. Yule, G. U.: Mendel's laws and their probable relation to inter-racial heredity. New Phytologist 1:193–207, 222–238, 1902.

36. Yule, G. U.: On the theory of inheritance of quantitative compound characters on the basis of Mendel's laws—A preliminary note. Report 3rd Int. Conf. Genetics p. 140–142, 1906.

39.
how to talk back to a statistic

darrell huff

Not all the statistical information that you may come upon can be tested with the sureness of chemical analysis or of what goes on in an assayer's laboratory. But you can prod the stuff with five simple questions, and by finding the answers avoid learning a remarkable lot that isn't so.

WHO SAYS SO?

About the first thing to look for is bias—the laboratory with something to prove for the sake of a theory, a reputation, or a fee; the newspaper whose aim is a good story; labor or management with a wage level at stake.

Look for conscious bias. The method may be direct mistatement or it may be ambiguous statement that serves as well and cannot be convicted. It may be selection of favorable data and suppression of unfavorable. Units of measurement may be shifted, as with the practice of using one year for one comparison and sliding over to a more favorable year for another. An improper measure may be used: a mean where a median would be more informative (perhaps all too informative), with the trickery covered by the unqualified word "average."

Look sharply for unconscious bias. It is often more dangerous. In the charts and predictions of many statisticians and economists in 1928 it operated to produce remarkable things. The cracks in the economic structure were joyously overlooked and all sorts of evidence was adduced and statistically supported to show that we had no more than entered the stream of prosperity.

Reprinted from Darrell Huff, *How To Lie with Statistics*. Pictures by Irving Geis. By permission of W. W. Norton & Company, Inc. Copyright 1954 by Darrell Huff and Irving Geis.

It may take at least a second look to find out who-says-so. The who may be hidden by what Stephen Potter, the *Lifemanship* man, would probably call the "O.K. name." Anything smacking of the medical profession is an O.K. name. Scientific laboratories have O.K. names. So do colleges, especially universities, more especially ones eminent in technical work. The writer who proved a few chapters back that higher education jeopardizes a girl's chance to marry made good use of the O.K. name of Cornell. Please note that while the data came from Cornell, the conclusions were entirely the writer's own. But the O.K. name helps you carry away a misimpression of "Cornell University says. . . ."

When an O.K. name is cited, make sure that the authority stands behind the information, not merely somewhere alongside it.

You may have read a proud announcement by the Chicago *Journal of Commerce*. That publication had made a survey. Of 169 corporations that replied to a poll on price gouging and hoarding, two-thirds declared that they were absorbing price increases produced by the Korean war. "The survey shows," said the *Journal* (look sharp whenever you meet those words!), "that corporations have done exactly the opposite of what the enemies of the American business system have charged." This is an obvious place to ask, "Who says so?" since the *Journal of Commerce* might be regarded as an interested party. It is also a splendid place to ask our second test question:

HOW DOES HE KNOW?

It turns out that the *Journal* had begun by sending its questionnaires to 1,200 large companies. Only fourteen per cent had replied. Eighty-six per cent had not cared to say anything in public on whether they were hoarding or price gouging.

The *Journal* had put a remarkably good face on things, but the fact remains that there was little to brag about. It came down to this: Of 1,200 companies polled, nine per cent said they had not raised prices, five per cent said they had, and eighty-six per cent wouldn't say. Those that had replied constituted a sample in which bias might be suspected.

Watch out for evidence of a biased sample, one that has been selected improperly or—as with this one—has selected itself. Ask the question we dealt with in an early chapter: Is the sample large enough to permit any reliable conclusion?

Similarly with a reported correlation: Is it big enough to mean anything? Are there enough cases to add up to any significance? You cannot, as a casual reader, apply tests of significance or come to exact conclusions as to the adequacy of a sample. On a good many of the things you see reported, however, you will be able to tell at a glance—a good long glance, perhaps—that there just weren't enough cases to convince any reasoning person of anything.

WHAT'S MISSING?

You won't always be told how many cases. The absence of such a figure, particularly when the source is an interested one, is enough to throw suspicion on the whole thing. Similarly a correlation given without a measure of reliability (probable error, standard error) is not to be taken very seriously.

Watch out for an average, variety unspecified, in any matter where mean and median might be expected to differ substantially.

Many figures lose meaning because a comparison is missing. An article in *Look* magazine says, in connection with Mongolism, that "one study shows that in 2,800 cases, over half of the mothers were 35 or over." Getting any meaning from this depends upon your knowing something about the ages at which women in general produce babies. Few of us know things like that.

Here is an extract from the *New Yorker* magazine's "Letter from London" of January 31, 1953.

The Ministry of Health's recently published figures showing that in the week of the great fog the death rate for Greater London jumped by twenty-eight hundred were a shock to the public, which is used to regarding Britain's unpleasant climatic effects as nuisances rather than as killers. . . . The extraordinary lethal properties of this winter's prize visitation. . . .

But how lethal *was* the visitation? Was it exceptional for the death rate to be that much higher than usual in a week? All such things do vary. And what about ensuing weeks? Did the death rate drop below average, indicating that if the fog killed people they were largely those who would have died shortly anyway? The figure sounds impressive, but the absence of other figures takes away most of its meaning.

Sometimes it is percentages that are given and raw figures that are missing, and this can be deceptive too. Long ago, when Johns Hopkins University had just begun to admit women students, someone not particularly enamored of coeducation reported a real shocker: Thirty three and one-third per cent of the women at Hopkins had married faculty members! The raw figures gave a clearer picture. There were three women enrolled at the time, and one of them had married a faculty man.

A couple of years ago the Boston Chamber of Commerce chose its American Women of Achievement. Of the sixteen among them who were also in *Who's Who*, it was announced that they had "sixty academic degrees and eighteen children." That sounds like an informative picture of the group until you discover that among the women were Dean Virginia Gildersleeve and Mrs. Lillian M. Gilbreth. Those two had a full third of the degrees between them. And Mrs. Gilbreth, of course, supplied two-thirds of the children.

A corporation was able to announce that its stock was held by 3,003 persons who had an average of 660 shares each. This was true. It was also true that o the two million shares of stock in the corporation three men held three-quarters and three thousand persons held the other one-fourth among them.

If you are handed an index, you may ask what's missing there. It may be the base, a base chosen to give a distorted picture. A national organization once showed that indexes of profits and production had risen much more rapidly after the depression than an index of wages had. As an argument for wage increases this demonstration lost its potency when someone dug out the missing figures. It could be seen then that profits had been almost bound to rise more rapidly in percentage than wages simply because profits had reached a lower point, giving a smaller base.

Sometimes what is missing is the factor that caused a change to occur. This omission leaves the implication that some other, more desired, factor is responsible. Figures published one year attempted to show that business was on the upgrade by pointing out that April retail sales were greater than in the year before. What was missing was the fact that Easter had come in March in the earlier year and in April in the later year.

A report of a great increase in deaths from cancer in the last quarter-century is misleading unless you know how much of it is a product of such extraneous factors as these: Cancer is often listed now where "causes unknown" was formerly used; autopsies are more frequent, giving surer diagnoses; reporting and compiling of medical statistics are more complete; and people more frequently reach the most susceptible ages now. And if you are looking at total deaths rather than the death rate, don't neglect the fact that there are more people now than there used to be.

DID SOMEBODY CHANGE THE SUBJECT?

When assaying a statistic, watch out for a switch somewhere between the raw figure and the conclusion. One thing is all too often reported as another.

As just indicated, more reported cases of a disease are not always the same thing as more cases of the disease. A straw-vote victory for a candidate is not always negotiable at the polls. An expressed preference by a "cross section" of a magazine's readers for articles on world affairs is no final proof that they would read the articles if they were published.

Encephalitis cases reported in the central valley of California in 1952 were triple the figure for the worst previous year. Many alarmed residents shipped their children away. But when the reckoning was in, there had been no great increase in deaths from sleeping sickness. What had happened was that state and federal health people had come in in great numbers to tackle a long-time problem; as a result of their efforts a great many low-grade cases were recorded that in other years would have been overlooked, possibly not even recognized.

It is all reminiscent of the way that Lincoln Steffens and Jacob A. Riis, as New York newspapermen, once created a crime wave. Crime cases in the papers reached such proportions, both in numbers and in space and big type given to them, that the public demanded action. Theodore Roosevelt, as president of the reform Police Board, was seriously embarrassed. He put an end to the crime wave simply by asking Steffens and Riis to lay off. It had all come about simply because the reporters, led by those two, had got into competition as to who could dig up the most burglaries and whatnot. The official police record showed no increase at all.

"The British male over 5 years of age soaks himself in a hot tub on an average of 1.7 times a week in the winter and 2.1 times in the summer," says a newspaper story. "British women average 1.5 baths a week in the winter and 2.0 in the summer." The source is a Ministry of Works hot-water survey of "6,000 representative British homes." The sample was representative, it says, and seems quite adequate in size to justify the conclusion in the San Francisco *Chronicle's* amusing headline: BRITISH HE'S BATHE MORE THAN SHE'S.

The figures would be more informative if there were some indication of whether they are means or medians. However, the major weakness is that the subject has been changed. What the Ministry really found out is how often these people said they bathed, not how often they did so. When a subject is as intimate as this one is, with the British bath-taking tradition involved, saying and doing may not be the same thing at all. British he's may or may not bathe oftener than she's; all that can safely be concluded is that they say they do.

Here are some more varieties of change-of-subject to watch out for.

A back-to-the-farm movement was discerned when a census showed half a million more farms in 1935 than five years earlier. But the two counts were not talking about the same thing. The definition of farm used by the Bureau of the Census had been changed; it took in at least 300,000 farms that would not have been so listed under the 1930 definition.

Strange things crop out when figures are based on what people say—even about things that seem to be objective facts. Census reports have shown more people at thirty-five years of age, for instance, than at either thirty-four or thirty-six. The false picture comes from one family member's reporting the ages of the others and, not being sure of the exact ages, tending to round them off to a familiar multiple of five. One way to get around this: ask birth dates instead.

The "population" of a large area in China was 28 million. Five years later it was 105 million. Very little of that increase was real; the great difference could be explained only by taking into account the purposes of the two enumerations and the way people would be inclined to feel about being counted in each instance. The first census was for tax and military purposes, the second for famine relief.

Something of the same sort has happened in the United States. The 1950 census found more people in the sixty-five-to-seventy age group than there were in the fifty-five-to-sixty group ten years before. The difference could not be accounted for by immigration. Most of it could be a product of large-scale falsifying of ages by people eager to collect social security. Also possible is that some of the earlier ages were understated out of vanity.

Another kind of change-of-subject is represented by Senator William Langer's cry that "we could take a prisoner from Alcatraz and board him at the Waldorf-Astoria cheaper. . . ." The North Dakotan was referring to earlier statements that it cost eight dollars a day to maintain a prisoner at Alcatraz, "the cost of a room at a good San Francisco hotel." The subject has been changed from total maintenance cost (Alcatraz) to hotel-room rent alone.

The *post hoc* variety of pretentious nonsense is another way of changing the subject without seeming to. The change of something *with* something else is presented as *because of.* The magazine *Electrical World* once offered a composite chart in an editorial on "What Electricity Means to America." You could see from it that as "electrical horsepower in factories" climbed, so did "average wages per hour." At the same time "average hours per week" dropped. All these things are long-time trends, of course, and there is no evidence at all that any one of them has produced any other.

And then there are the firsters. Almost anybody can claim to be first in something if he is not too particular what it is. At the end of 1952 two New York newspapers were each insisting on first rank in grocery advertising. Both were right too, in a way. The *World-Telegram* went on to explain that it was first in full-run advertising, the kind that appears in all copies, which is the only kind it runs. The *Journal-American* insisted that total linage was what counted and that it was first in that. This is the kind of reaching for a superlative that leads the weather reported on the radio to label a quite normal day "the hottest June second since 1949."

Change-of-subject makes it difficult to compare cost when you contemplate borrowing money either directly or in the form of installment buying. Six per cent sounds like six per cent—but it may not be at all.

If you borrow $100 from a bank at six per cent interest and pay it back in equal monthly installments for a year, the price you pay for the use of the money is about $3. But another six per cent loan on the basis sometimes called $6 on the

$100, will cost you twice as much. That's the way most automobile loans are figured. It is very tricky.

The point is that you don't have the $100 for a year. By the end of six months you have paid back half of it. If you are charged $6 on the $100, or six per cent of the amount, you really pay interest at nearly twelve per cent.

Even worse was what happened to some careless purchasers of freezer-food plans in 1952 and 1953. They were quoted a figure of anywhere from six to twelve per cent. It sounded like interest, but it was not. It was an on-the-dollar figure and, worst of all, the time was often six months rather than a year. Now $12 on the $100 for money to be paid back regularly over half a year works out to something like forty-eight per cent real interest. It is no wonder that so many customers defaulted and so many food plans blew up.

Sometimes the semantic approach will be used to change the subject. Here is an item from *Business Week* magazine.

> *Accountants have decided that "surplus" is a nasty word. They propose eliminating it from corporate balance sheets. The Committee on Accounting Procedure of the American Institute of accountants says: . . . Use such descriptive terms as "retained earnings" or "appreciation of fixed assets."*

This one is from a newspaper story reporting Standard Oil's record-breaking revenue and net profit of a million dollars a day.

> *Possibly the directors may be thinking some time of splitting the stock for there may be an advantage . . . if the profits per share do not look so large. . . .*

DOES IT MAKE SENSE?

"Does it make sense?" will often cut a statistic down to size when the whole rigmarole is based on an unproved assumption. You may be familiar with the Rudolf Flesch readability formula. It purports to measure how easy a piece of prose is to read, by such simple and objective items as length of words and sentences. Like all devices for reducing the imponderable to a number and substituting arithmetic for judgment, it is an appealing idea. At least it has appealed to people who employ writers, such as newspaper publishers, even if not to many writers themselves. The assumption in the formula is that such things as word length determine readability. This, to be ornery about it, remains to be proved.

A man named Robert A. Dufour put the Flesch formula to trial on some literature that he found handy. It showed "The Legend of Sleepy Hollow" to be half again as hard to read as Plato's *Republic*. The Sinclair Lewis novel *Cass Timberlane* was rated more difficult than an essay by Jacques Maritain, "The Spiritual Value of Art." A likely story.

Many a statistic is false on its face. It gets by only because the magic of numbers brings about a suspension of common sense. Leonard Engel, in a *Harper's* article, has listed a few of the medical variety.

> *An example is the calculation of a well-known urologist that there are eight million cases of cancer of the prostate gland in the United States —which would be enough to provide 1.1 carcinomatous prostate glands for every male in the susceptible age group! Another is a prominent neurologist's estimate that one American in twelve suffers from migraine; since migraine is responsible for a third of chronic headache cases, this would mean that a quarter of us must suffer from disabling headaches. Still another is the figure of 250,000 often given for the number of multiple sclerosis cases; death data indicate that there can be, happily, no more than thirty to forty thousand cases of this paralytic disease in the country.*

Hearings on amendments to the Social Security Act have been haunted by various forms of a statement that makes sense only when not looked at closely. It is an argument that goes like this: Since life expectancy is only about sixty-three years, it is a sham and a fraud to set up a social-security plan with a re-tirement age of sixty-five, because virtu-ally everybody dies before that.

You can rebut that one by looking around at people you know. The basic fallacy, however, is that the figure refers to expectancy at birth, and so about half the babies born can expect to live longer than that. The figure, incidentally, is from the latest official complete life table and is correct for the 1939–1941 period. An up-to-date estimate corrects it to sixty-five-plus. Maybe that will produce a new and equally silly argument to the effect that practically everybody now lives to be sixty-five.

Postwar planning at a big electrical-appliance company was going great guns a few years ago on the basis of a de-clining birth rate, something that had been taken for granted a long time. Plans called for emphasis on small-ca-pacity appliances, apartment-size refrig-erators. Then one of the planners had an attack of common sense: He came out of his graphs and charts long enough to notice that he and his co-workers and his friends and his neighbors and his former classmates with few exceptions either had three or four children or planned to. This led to some open-minded investigating and charting—and the company shortly turned its emphasis most profitably to big-family models.

The impressively precise figure is something else that contradicts common sense. A study reported in New York City newspapers announced that a working woman living with her family needed a weekly pay check of $40.13 for adequate support. Anyone who has not suspended all logical process while read-ing his paper will realize that the cost of keeping body and soul together can-not be calculated to the last cent. But there is a dreadful temptation; "$40.13" sounds so much more knowing than "about $40."

You are entitled to look with the same suspicion on the report, some years ago, by the American Petroleum Industries Committee that the average yearly tax bill for automobiles is $51.13.

Extrapolations are useful, particularly in that form of soothsaying called fore-casting trends. But in looking at the figures or the charts made from them, it is necessary to remember one thing con-stantly: The trend-to-now may be a fact, but the future trend represents no more than an educated guess. Implicit in it is "everything else being equal" and "present trends continuing." And some-how everything else refuses to remain equal, else life would be dull indeed.

For a sample of the nonsense inherent in uncontrolled extrapolation, consider the trend of television. The number of sets in American homes increased around 10,000% from 1947 to 1952. Project this for the next five years and you find that there'll soon be a couple billion of the things, Heaven forbid, or forty sets per family. If you want to be even sillier, begin with a base year that is earlier in the television scheme of things than 1947 and you can just as well "prove" that each family will soon have not forty but forty thousand sets.

A Government research man, Morris Hansen, called Gallup's 1948 election forecasting "the most publicized statisti-cal error in human history." It was a paragon of accuracy, however, compared with some of our most widely used estimates of future population, which have earned a nationwide horselaugh. As late as 1938 a presidential commission loaded with experts doubted that the U. S. population would ever reach 140 million; it was 12 million more than that just twelve years later. There are textbooks published so recently that they are still in college use that predict a peak population of not more than 150 mil-lion and figure it will take until about 1980 to reach it. These fearful underesti-mates came from assuming that a trend would continue without change. A simi-lar assumption a century ago did as badly in the opposite direction because it assumed continuation of the popula-tion-increase rate of 1790 to 1860. In his second message to Congress, Abraham Lincoln predicted the U. S. population would reach 251,689,914 in 1930.

Not long after that, in 1874, Mark Twain summed up the nonsense side of extrapolation in *Life on the Mississippi.*

In the space of one hundred and seventy-six years the Lower Missis-

sippi has shortened itself two hundred and forty-two miles. That is an average of a trifle over one mile and a third per year. Therefore, any calm person, who is not blind or idiotic, can see that in the Old Oölitic Silurian Period, just a million years ago next November, the Lower Mississippi River was upward of one million three hundred thousand miles long, and stuck out over the Gulf of Mexico like a fishing rod. And by the same token any person can see that seven hundred and forty-two years from now the Lower Mississippi will be only a mile and three-quarters long, and Cairo and New Orleans will have joined their streets together, and be plodding comfortably along under a single mayor and a mutual board of aldermen. There is something fascinating about science. One gets such wholesale returns of conjecture out of such a trifling investment of fact.

REVIEW QUESTIONS

1. How does Wechsler operationally define intelligence? Why is intelligence not merely the sum of intellectual abilities?
2. What two contributions did Spearman make to the study of intelligence testing?
3. Jensen states "the fact that a reasonable hypothesis has not been rigorously proved does not mean that it should be summarily dismissed." What is the "reasonable hypothesis" he is referring to and how does he suggest we test it?
4. What is the concept of "regression toward the mean" as discussed by Jensen.
5. Kagan states that Jensen's essay "contains a pair of partially correct empirical generalizations wedded to a logically incorrect conclusion." What does Kagan say are the partially correct generalizations and

what does he feel is the logical error?
6. What is the difference between mother-child interaction in low- and upper-class homes as discussed by Kagan?
7. What is the difference between the genotype and phenotype? What is a gene according to Hirsch?
8. Try to summarize for yourself the relationship between heredity and behavior as discussed by Hirsch.
9. A newspaper reports more reported cases of a disease for this year than ten years ago. Does this necessarily mean that now the disease is occurring more frequently? What other possible explanations are there?
10. What does Huff mean by his questions "Did Somebody Change the Subject?" Look through today's newspaper and see if you can find examples of this.

part eight
learning and
memory

My first exposure to programed learning
was a textbook that presented the intricacies
of human neuroanatomy. I distinctly remember
that I hated the book at the start. The endless
repetition and the extremely small
amount of material presented in each
question proved tedious and frustrating.
I think most students have a similar reaction
to their initial exposure to a programed text.

By the same token, as one proceeds
through the book and the sense of learning
and accomplishment increase, the experience
becomes more and more pleasant. There
can be little doubt that the programed approach
is solidly established in educational practice
and will, no doubt, be prominent for some
time to come. The selection by Hilgard
and Bower (#40) discusses the basic
programing techniques and presents
several research questions the answers to
which will presumably improve the
technique even more.

Superstitious behavior is behavior that
accompanies the performance of a response
and which is not necessary for the production
of reinforcement. Perhaps an example will
help to make things clearer. A compulsive
gambler may go through a long ritual of
touching his nose, rubbing his stomach, etc.,
before depositing his coin in the slot
machine. All that is really necessary, of

course, is that the coin be deposited and the lever pulled to produce the reinforcement (the jackpot win). The ritual activity occurring before has no effect on the probability or producement of reinforcement, so it can be classified as superstitious behavior. I remember once asking a class for examples of superstitious behavior from their own lives and a student replied "making the sign of the cross before shooting a foul shot in a basketball game."

The example is a good one in that it can be used to illustrate an additional aspect of superstitious behavior. The efficacy of the act on the religious level is, of course, beyond the scope of science. Personally, however, I have always felt that the divine being has "more important" things to be concerned with than basketball games (with the possible exception when Notre Dame is involved). On a psychological level the behavior may or may not be superstitious depending upon whether it alters the probability of reinforcement (putting the ball in the basket). If such behavior calms the shooter or increases his self-confidence and helps his accuracy, then it should not be classified as a superstition. It is increasing the probability of reinforcement. Psychologists have studied superstitious behavior in animals and one of the earliest studies by B. F. Skinner (#41) is reprinted here.

Students often fail to see how the principles of classical conditioning and operant learning operate in their day-to-day living. In many cases, they use these very techniques without being aware of them. Azrin and his colleagues (#42) present an interesting attempt to influence the content of conversation through reinforcement. After reading the experiment, the reader should try the basic technique in a conversation with a friend. You will be able to see firsthand some of the

problems with this type of research as mentioned in the article.

Anyone who has experienced an upset stomach or a headache before a big exam knows that psychosomatic illnesses can be as painful and distressing as "real" illnesses. Neal E. Miller's article "Psychosomatic Effects of Specific Types of Training" (#43), illustrates the role of learning in such illnesses and the underlying physiological mechanisms.

Questions about memory have interested psychologists for as long as there have been psychologists. Techniques or methods of memorizing that increase the extent and effectiveness of recall are obviously important and valuable for any student. Gordon H. Bower and Michal C. Clark (#44) scientifically tested the effectiveness of a technique recommended by mnemonists and found it extremly effective. In addition to increasing the amount of material retained, mnemonic devices also sometimes make studying more fun.

Most psychologists on a theoretical level divide memory into two kinds or aspects: short and long term. Short-term memory is our immediate memory of events that have just transpired. Long-term memory refers to our ability to recall material that has been previously stored. An example of short-term memory occurs when an experimenter gives you a series of five numbers to remember and asks you immediately after the series is given for the numbers. If the experimenter then prevents you from active rehearsal of the series by giving you, for example, some other task to perform, it is then necessary to utilize long-term memory, or storage, to recall the series. Psychologists use the term consolidation to refer to the process by which short-term memories pass into or are stored in long-term memory.

There is a great deal of evidence that memories recently stored (recently consolidated) are much more susceptible to disruption than memories that have been in permanent memory storage for long periods of time. A person receiving a severe blow to the head in an automobile accident often cannot remember the events that immediately preceded the actual incident. One explanation for this is that the blow somehow interfered with the consolidation process and events occurring immediately before the trauma were not stored properly. Electroconvulsive shock (ECS) is also known to interfere with consolidation. Human patients who have received this therapy often complain of memory difficulties. A systematic study of the effects of ECS on memory is presented as the concluding selection (#45).

40.
programed learning

ernest r. hilgard
and gordon h. bower

Attention to programed learning began with the introduction of the *teaching machine* as a technological aid, although, as we shall see, the essence of programing does not reside in the particular kind of equipment used. The first of these machines was developed by Sidney L. Pressey at Ohio State University many years ago (Pressey, 1926, 1927). While originally developed as a self-scoring machine to facilitate the taking and scoring of objective examinations, the machine soon demonstrated its ability to actually teach. The student reads the question presented in the aperture of the machine, selects an answer from among several alternatives, and then presses the button corresponding to this chosen answer. If he is correct, the next question appears in the slot; if he has made a mistake, the original question remains. The machine counts his errors but the tape does not move on to the next question until the right button has been pressed. Because the student knows that he is correct when the question moves, he has immediate information (reinforcement, feedback) and thus he learns while testing himself. Because the machine has counted his errors, his score can be read off as soon as he has finished taking the test. This machine of Pressey's did not become popular, although a number of studies by him and his students showed it to be effective as a teaching device.

A new forward push was given to the idea of automatic self-instruction by the publication of a paper by Skinner (1954), whose operant conditioning work had al-

Reprinted from Ernest R. Hilgard and Gordon H. Bower, *Theories of Learning*, Third Edition, New York, pp. 554–561. Copyright © 1966. Abridgment reprinted by permission of Appleton-Century-Crofts, Educational Division, Meredith Corporation.

ready given him authority in the field of learning. The time was now right, and work on teaching machines and programed learning flourished shortly thereafter. Now it is a very large-scale international scientific, educational, and commercial enterprise. Skinner's machine differed from Pressey's chiefly in that the student was not given alternatives to choose from, but instead was asked to write his own response in the spaces provided, and then, as a printed tape advanced, the correct answer appeared for comparison with what he had written. He thus "emitted" his own response to be "reinforced" by the comparison response. A further difference is involved, in that the material is so planned that it is not essentially a review of partially learned material, but rather a "program" in which the responses of the learner are "shaped" as he learns. We shall return to the problems of programming after considering another set of technological aids.

Far more complex instructional devices have been developed beyond those of Pressey and Skinner. Quite different sets of devices were developed somewhat earlier in the U.S. Air Force. Lumsdaine, who had a prominent role in the development, has given a description of some of them (Lumsdaine, 1959). For example, in one arrangement a step-by-step film projection is used to teach a technician how to operate a piece of electronic equipment. A single demonstrational segment appears on the screen until the learner has mastered it. He then presses the button to bring on the next illustration, and so on, until he has learned the complete operation. Modern electronic computers have been brought into the picture, occasionally to combine slide projection, motion picture projection, and other materials within the program for a single learner, occasionally to make possible the management of learning for a group of learners. The flexibility provided makes possible almost any arrangement that the investigator desires, as long as the costs can be met.

The essence of learning by means of a teaching machine lies not in the machinery but in the material to be presented, and it has been found that properly designed programed books can serve about the same purpose as the simpler forms of teaching machines. The simple machines are sometimes derogated as "mechanical page turners" because they do little more than the student can as well do for himself. Obviously the more complex machines do much more than this, but the teasing of the simple machine is intended to point to the importance of the program over the technology. The programed book is not to be confused with the earlier "workbook" in common educational use; the "workbook" was primarily a place to practice on examples of what had been taught by the teacher or a textbook, but the program is designed to do the teaching itself. Hence the program necessarily must begin with what the learner already knows, and it then adds to this by supplying answers that are at first *hinted at* or *prompted* in order to make the correct answers highly probable. These answers, once "reinforced," are then overlearned through their repeated use as new material is grafted on that already learned. It is evident that the person who constructs a program must be aware of the *organization of knowledge*, both its logical organization and its psychological organization, in order to build knowledge and understanding in this way. The programer does his best to anticipate what will happen, but in practice he corrects the programs through tryout until the program can be mastered by its intended learners with a minimum of errors, usually in one run through the program. The results of the learning are then tested by a conventional-type examination to see if the material has indeed been mastered and can be applied appropriately in new contexts.

In order to correct misapprehensions about programing being just another form of mass education, Skinner (1958) made the case for a similarity between programed instruction and individual tutoring. He pointed out several resemblances to a tutor:

1. A good tutor begins where the pupil is, and does not insist on moving beyond what the pupil can comprehend.
2. A good tutor moves at the rate that is consistent with the ability of the pupil to learn.
3. A good tutor does not permit false answers to remain uncorrected.
4. A good tutor does not lecture; instead by his hints and questioning he helps the pupil to find and state answers for himself.

According to Skinner, these qualities are all found in a good program.

Varieties of Programing. The type of program advocated by Skinner, that which moves step by step through a single set of materials, has come to be called *linear programing.* Another type, commonly associated with the name of Norman Crowder, is called a *branching program.*[1] In the programed books which use this method (e.g., Crowder and Martin, 1961), multiple-choice answers are provided, and the answers the student selects direct him to a different page in the book. The book is thus a "scrambled one" which is read most irregularly. The correct answer leads to a page on which the next bit of instruction is given, with new alternatives. An incorrect answer is pointed out, with some comments as to why this might have been selected, and then the learner is sent back to make another choice. Crowder believes that students who are ill-prepared should always have a way to go back to simpler materials, and if well-prepared should be able to bypass some of the material; hence his later developments provide for these alternative paths through the material. Linear programs of

---

[1]Another name is *intrinsic* programing. Although this is Crowder's own name for his program (e.g., Crowder, 1959), it is less descriptive than *branching.*

a more modern sort also provide for some kind of review for those who wish to go back to earlier parts of the program, and some kind of skipping for those ready to go ahead (Markle, 1963). Computer-based programs provide the maximum amount of flexibility in these respects, including alternative paths and different examples for those who may need them. Thus programing is no more a single line of development than the teaching machine is a single type of equipment.

Some Problems Within Programed Learning. The literature on programed learning has been building up at an accelerated rate, so that a review at this time would soon be outmoded. Still a few of the pressing problems can be highlighted, with some illustrations of the results of investigation.

Schramm (1964a), having reviewed some 165 papers on programed learning, was able to summarize some of the generalizations that could be made from the research reports at that time. Because his summaries, and a number of others,[2] are readily available, what he reports will be digested without references to the original sources. He begins by asking the general question, do students learn from programed instruction? The answer is clearly in the affirmative, but we need more information to know whether or not programed instruction is a more efficient form of instruction than other forms that we now use. Of 36 reports comparing programs with conventional classroom instruction (at all levels from primary school to college and adult education) the general summary is that 17 showed superiority for programed over conventional instruction, 18 showed no significant difference, and but 1 showed a final superiority for the conventional classroom method. While such a summary has its defects, there is little doubt that programing is an educational method to be taken seriously.

[2]For example, Coulson (1961), Galanter (1959), Hanson (1963), Lumsdaine (1961, 1962, 1963, 1964), Lumsdaine and Glaser (1960), Schramm (1964b), Smith and Moore (1962).

With respect to more analytical problems of the program, Schramm considers a number of questions which have troubled programers:

1. *Is the ordered sequence essential?* The assumption in most programs is that the substance in the form of "frames" is arranged in an optimum order for learning, the later knowledge being built upon the earlier. Even something as plausible as this can be questioned on the basis of research findings. Of five studies comparing the immediate and delayed post-test results of an ordered sequence with a random ordering, three showed no difference, one showed an immediate advantage for the ordered sequence, but none on a delayed test, and only one showed clear advantage for the ordered sequence! In a different kind of experiment, but not unrelated, Mager (1961) permitted some electronics students to do their own sequencing by asking questions. They were highly motivated, and learned what was required, but their orders of presentation were very different from the orders in which the topics would typically have been programed.

2. *Are short steps to be preferred?* The typical Skinnerian program moves in small steps, leading the students along very gradually. While, with a few exceptions, studies have come out favorable to small steps, some kind of compromise may be better. Thus Maccoby and Sheffield (1961) found an advantage in a gradual increase in the size of step in a demonstrational film sequence before interrupting for practice.

3. *What form of response is to be preferred?* Skinner favored a response constructed by the learner, hence "emitted" by him, rather than some other form of response, such as selecting from a group of multiple-choice possibilities. The research results are confusing, usually with no significant difference between constructed and multiple-choice responses, and often no difference between overt and covert (thinking) responses. In some cases, presenting the word normally sought as a reply, underlined for emphasis, works as well as having the student actually write the response himself, and this, of course, saves the student a

great deal of time (when it works). The research is beginning to sharpen those circumstances under which one form of response is better than another, and the differential effects on long-term retention. In any case, dogmatic assertions are inappropriate in view of the varied findings.

4. *Is immediate knowledge of results helpful?* In the theory of programed learning no principle taken over from the laboratory has had more prominence than "reinforcement" or "feedback," in the form of immediate knowledge of results. While the results are generally favorable to knowledge of results, they are not universally so; delay may not matter, and confirmatory knowledge on but a fraction of the trials (corresponding to "intermittent reinforcement") may be just as effective as every-trial feedback. It may be that in well-cued programs there are so few errors that the learner knows he is correct when he catches the cue, without any external verification.

As in laboratory types of reinforcement, some cue other than a fully informative one may be used. Such cues have been compared with the informative type of feedback in which the correct answer is given as reinforcement. Apparently trinkets, small monetary rewards, or flashing lights can be used to reinforce correct responses in programed learning, with results not significantly different from the more usual informative feedback.

It should be pointed out that what is learned is not limited to the response that eventually appears in the space provided for responses, for this response, like other cues used for reinforcement, is designed to reinforce the behavior that leads to the response. This behavior presumably depends upon the comprehension of a line of thought. To make this clear, consider a program designed in true-false style, so that all blanks can be filled in by either "yes" or "no." Such a program could teach, but it would be teaching something besides how to emit "yes" and "no." This means that a program should not be judged by examining the tape to see what answers occur on it; such an appraisal could be very mis-

leading. It would be something like judging an arithmetic test by seeing a set of numerical answers to its questions, without inquiring what the operations were that these answers served to check.

5. *Should the learner set his own pace?* One of the intuitively appealing features of programed instruction is that it recognizes individual differences in the learner, and each learner is free to move through the program at his own pace. The results are, however, not unequivocally in favor of self-pacing. Schramm found two studies in which self-pacing was indeed better than external pacing, but he located eight others in which no significant differences were found. These included presentations by teaching machines, programed texts, television and films. An interesting conjecture by Frye (1963) was that self-pacing would prove more advantageous for heterogenous groups of students than for more homogeneous ones, a result which he found to be the case. He reasoned that for students of equal background and ability, self-pacing would not be necessary to meet individual differences in rate of learning.

While many other comparisons have been made (linear vs branching programs, sex differences, the use of explanations supplementing informative feedback, programs as supplementary to textbook material vs teaching by program alone, having more than one student use the same program and discuss their answers) the foregoing questions, with their tentative answers, help orient us to the place of programing in relation to learning theory.

It is often supposed that programs are appropriate chiefly for materials that can be learned by "drill," that is, materials subject to rote learning, such as number combinations, vocabulary, geographical locations. This is a mistake; in fact, the programed method is cumbersome for teaching such materials and is better adapted to more complexly structured bodies of materials in which what is learned later depends upon what has been learned before. A quite satisfactory programed book exists on teaching the appreciation of poetry (Reid, Ciardi, and Perrine, 1963), and programing has been used to train for creativity and problem-solving (Crutchfield, 1965). It is evident that the programing method is not limited to any one kind of subject-matter.

There remain the questions about the extent to which programing has been adopted in school systems, and what its success has been when used in a wholesale fashion. The most informative report to date is another one edited by Schramm (1964b), which reports on experiences in four widely separated geographical locations: Manhasset, New York; Denver, Colorado; Chicago, Illinois; and Provo, Utah. The Manhasset experience (Herbert and Foshay, 1964) is that of a junior high school that pioneered in introducing programs, but after three years of sympathetic encouragement by the principal, only one program, having to do with English grammar, remained in regular use. The Denver schools spent three years in which they made their own programs in grammar, Spanish, French, and one on the constitution (Schramm, 1964c). While they interpret this experience as valuable, they believe that in the future they will use more commercial programs. In one of the studies on the advantages of individualization of instruction, a comparison was made of which students, according to ability level, profited most from the program on English usage. The hope of programing is that individual differences will be reduced, but this was not found to be the case: the students who profited most were the superior ones, although they complained most about the programs. The least able students (in the so-called modified classes) learned more from regular class instruction than

from the programs. The report on experiences in the Chicago area (Thelen and Ginther, 1964) draws some generalizations from a number of different tryouts of programed learning. The authors conclude that programed materials used by themselves are likely to satisfy neither pupils nor teachers; the programs will have to be more fully appropriate to a pupil's individual needs, and some kinds of reward beyond the program's self-contained feedback will have to be provided for the pupil working alone with a program. Individualized instruction—each pupil moving at his own rate—conflicts with the notion of "teaching a class," and makes it difficult to use the other enriching experiences open to the teacher and pupil. Thus far the programs have failed "to turn education into a meaningful inquiry by the students." The experiences in the Brigham Young University Laboratory School (Edling, 1964) are among the more encouraging. The school has operated since 1959 on what is called a Continuous Progress Plan, whereby the student moves through the school at his own rate, and is thus unusually well prepared for the use of programed instruction. Even in this favorable setting it is clear that programed materials will be used to supplement rather than supplant present teaching methods and materials. The need for better and more widely ranging programs is evident. Programs use teacher time as well as save it; teachers will probably have to be given more clerical help than is usually provided them if many programs are adopted.

REFERENCES

Crowder, N., and Martin, G. (1961) Trigonometry. Garden City: Doubleday.

Crowder, N. A. (1959) Automatic tutoring by means of intrinsic programming. In E. H. Galanter (Editor), *Automatic teaching: The state of the art.* New York: Wiley, 109–116.

Edling, J. V. (1964) Programmed instruction in a "continuous progress" school—Provo, Utah. In W. Schramm (Editor), *Four case studies of programmed instruction.* New York: Fund for the Advancement of Education, 65–94.

Frye, C. H. (1963) *Group vs individual*

pacing in programmed instruction. Portland, Ore.: Oregon State System of Higher Education.

Herbert, J., and Foshay, A. W. (1964) Programed instruction in the Manhasset Junior High School. In W. Schramm (Editor) *Four case studies of programed instruction.* New York: Fund for the Advancement of Education.

Lumsdaine, A. A. (1959) Teaching machines and self-instructional materials. *Audiovisual Communica. Rev.,* 7, 163–172.

Maccoby, N., and Sheffield, F. D. (1961) Combining practice with demonstration in teaching complex sequences: Summary and interpretations. In A. A. Lumsdaine (Editor), *Student response in programmed learning: A Symposium.* Washington, D.C.: Natl. Acad. of Sci., 77–85.

Mager, R. F. (1961) On the sequencing of instructional content. *Psychol. Reports, 9,* 405–413.

Markle, S. M. (1963) Programming '63: The straight line bends. In *Programmierter unterricht und Lehrmaschinen.* Report of International Conference on Programmed Instruction and Teaching Machines. Berlin: Pädagogische Arbeitstelle, Secretariat Pädogogisches Zentrum, 368–386.

Pressey, S. L. (1926) A simple apparatus which gives tests and scores—and teaches. *Sch. and Soc., 23,* 373–376.

Pressey, S. L. (1927) A machine for automatic teaching of drill material. *Sch. and Soc., 25,* 549–552.

Reid, J. M., Ciardi, J., and Perrine, L. (1963) *Poetry: A closer look.* New York: Harcourt, Brace & World.

Schramm, W. (1964a) *The research on programmed instruction: An annotated bibliography.* Washington, D.C.: U.S. Office of Education (OE–34034).

Schramm, W. (Editor) (1964b) *Four case studies of programmed instruction.* New York: Fund for the Advancement of Education.

Schramm, W. (1964c) Programmed instruction in Denver. In W. Schramm (Editor), *Four case studies of programmed instruction.* New York: Fund for the Advancement of Education, 29–40.

Skinner, B. F. (1954) The science of learning and the art of teaching. *Harvard educ. Rev., 24,* 86–97.

Skinner, B. F. (1958) Teaching machines. *Science, 128,* 969–977.

Thelen, H., and Ginther, J. R. (1964) Experiences with programmed materials in the Chicago area. In W. Schramm (Editor) (1964b) *Four case studies of programmed instruction.* New York: Fund for the Advancement of Education, 41–62.

41.
"superstition" in the pigeon

b. f. skinner

To say that a reinforcement is contingent upon a response may mean nothing more than that it follows the response. It may follow because of some mechanical connection or because of the mediation of another organism; but conditioning takes place presumably because of the temporal relation only, expressed in terms of the order and proximity of response and reinforcement. Whenever we present a state of affairs which is known to be reinforcing at a given drive, we must suppose that conditioning takes place, even though we have paid no attention to the behavior of the organism in making the presentation. A simple experiment demonstrates this to be the case.

A pigeon is brought to a stable state of hunger by reducing it to 75 percent of its weight when well fed. It is put into an experimental cage for a few minutes each day. A food hopper attached to the cage may be swung into place so that the pigeon can eat from it. A solenoid and a timing relay hold the hopper in place for five sec. at each reinforcement.

If a clock is now arranged to present the food hopper at regular intervals *with no reference whatsoever to the bird's behavior,* operant conditioning usually takes place. In six out of eight cases the resulting responses were so clearly defined that two observers could agree perfectly in counting instances. One bird was conditioned to turn counter-clockwise about the cage, making two or three turns between reinforcements. Another repeatedly thrust its head into one of the upper corners of the cage. A third developed a "tossing" response, as if placing its head beneath an invisible bar and lifting it repeatedly. Two birds developed a pendulum motion of the head and body, in which the head was extended forward and swung from right to left with a sharp movement followed by a somewhat slower return. The body generally followed the movement and a few steps might be taken when it was extensive. Another bird was conditioned to make incomplete pecking or brushing movements directed toward but not touching the floor. None of these responses appeared in any noticeable strength during adaptation to the cage or until the food hopper was periodically presented. In the remaining two cases, conditioned responses were not clearly marked.

The conditioning process is usually obvious. The bird happens to be executing some response as the hopper appears; as a result it tends to repeat this response. If the interval before the next presentation is not so great that extinction takes place, a second "contingency" is probable. This strengthens the response still further and subsequent reinforcement becomes more probable. It is true that some responses go unreinforced and some reinforcements appear when the response has not just been made, but the net result is the development of a considerable state of strength.

With the exception of the counter-clockwise turn, each response was almost always repeated in the same part of the cage, and it generally involved an orientation toward some feature of the cage. The effect of the reinforcement was to condition the bird to respond to some aspect of the environment rather than merely to execute a series of movements. All responses came to be repeated rapidly between reinforcements—typically five or six times in 15 sec.

The effect appears to depend upon the

Reprinted by permission from *Journal of Experimental Psychology*, 1948, *38* (2), 168–172. Published by the American Psychological Association.

rate of reinforcement. In general, we should expect that the shorter the intervening interval, the speedier and more marked the conditioning. One reason is that the pigeon's behavior becomes more diverse as time passes after reinforcement. A hundred photographs, each taken two sec. after withdrawal of the hopper, would show fairly uniform behavior. The bird would be in the same part of the cage, near the hopper, and probably oriented toward the wall where the hopper has disappeared or turning to one side or the other. A hundred photographs taken after 10 sec., on the other hand, would find the bird in various parts of the cage responding to many different aspects of the environment. The sooner a second reinforcement appears, therefore, the more likely it is that the second reinforced response will be similar to the first, and also that they will both have one of a few standard forms. In the limiting case of a very brief interval the behavior to be expected would be holding the head toward the opening through which the magazine has disappeared.

Another reason for the greater effectiveness of short intervals is that the longer the interval, the greater the number of intervening responses emitted without reinforcement. The resulting extinction cancels the effect of an occasional reinforcement.

According to this interpretation the effective interval will depend upon the rate of conditioning and the rate of extinction, and will therefore vary with the drive and also presumably between species. Fifteen sec. is a very effective interval at the drive level indicated above. One min. is much less so. When a response has once been set up, however, the interval can be lengthened. In one case it was extended to two min., and a high rate of responding was maintained with no sign of weakening. In another case, many hours of responding were observed with an interval of one min. between reinforcements.

In the latter case, the response showed a noticeable drift in topography. It began as a sharp movement of the head from the middle position to the left. This movement became more energetic, and eventually the whole body of the bird turned in the same direction, and a step or two would be taken. After many hours, the stepping response became the predominant feature. The bird made a well defined hopping step from the right to the left foot, meanwhile turning its head and body to the left as before.

When the stepping response became strong, it was possible to obtain a mechanical record by putting the bird on a large tambour directly connected with a small tambour which made a delicate electric contact each time stepping took place. By watching the bird and listening to the sound of the recorder it was possible to confirm the fact that a fairly authentic record was being made. It was possible for the bird to hear the recorder at each step, but this was, of course, in no way correlated with feeding. The record obtained when the magazine was presented once every min. resembles in every respect the characteristic curve for the pigeon under periodic reinforcement of a standard selected response. A well marked temporal discrimination develops. The bird does not respond immediately after eating, but when 10 or 15 or even 20 sec. have elapsed it begins to respond rapidly and continues until the reinforcement is received.

In this case it was possible to record the "extinction" of the response when the clock was turned off and the magazine was no longer presented at any time. The bird continued to respond with its characteristic side to side hop. More than 10,000 responses were recorded before "extinction" had reached the point at which few if any responses were made during a 10 or 15 min. interval. When the clock was again started, the periodic presentation of the magazine (still without any connection whatsoever with the bird's behavior) brought out a typical curve for reconditioning after periodic reinforcement, shown in Figure 1. The record had been essentially horizontal for 20 min. prior to the beginning of this curve. The first reinforcement had some slight effect and the second a greater effect. There is a smooth positive acceleration in rate as the bird returns to the rate of responding which prevailed when it was reinforced every min.

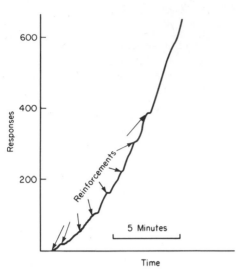

Figure 1. "Reconditioning" of a superstitious response after extinction. The response of hopping from right to left had been thoroughly extinguished just before the record was taken. The arrows indicate the automatic presentation of food at one-min. intervals without reference to the pigeon's behavior.

When the response was again extinguished and the periodic presentation of food then resumed, a different response was picked up. This consisted of a progressive walking response in which the bird moved about the cage. The response of hopping from side to side never reappeared and could not, of course, be obtained deliberately without making the reinforcement contingent upon the behavior.

The experiment might be said to demonstrate a sort of superstition. The bird behaves as if there were a causal relation between its behavior and the presentation of food, although such a relation is lacking. There are many analogies in human behavior. Rituals for changing one's luck at cards are good examples. A few accidental connections between a ritual and favorable consequences suffice to set up and maintain the behavior in spite of many unreinforced instances. The bowler who has released a ball down the alley but continues to behave as if he were controlling it by twisting and turning his arm and shoulder is another case in point. These behaviors have, of course, no real effect upon one's luck or upon a ball half way down an alley, just as in the present case the food would appear as often if the pigeon did nothing—or, more strictly speaking, did something else.

It is perhaps not quite correct to say that conditioned behavior has been set up without any previously determined contingency whatsoever. We have appealed to a uniform sequence of responses in the behavior of the pigeon to obtain an over-all net contingency. When we arrange a clock to present food every 15 sec., we are in effect basing our reinforcement upon a limited set of responses which frequently occur 15 sec. after reinforcement. When a response has been strengthened (and this may result from one reinforcement), the setting of the clock implies an even more restricted contingency. Something of the same sort is true of the bowler. It is not quite correct to say that there is no connection between his twisting and turning and the course taken by the ball at the far end of the alley. The connection was established before the ball left the bowler's hand, but since both the path of the ball and the behavior of the bowler are determined, some relation survives. The subsequent behavior of the bowler may have no effect upon the ball, but the behavior of the ball has an effect upon the bowler. The contingency, though not perfect, is enough to maintain the behavior in strength. The particular form of the behavior adopted by the bowler is due to induction from responses in which there is actual contact with the ball. It is clearly a movement appropriate to changing the ball's direction. But this does not invalidate the comparison, since we are not concerned with what response is selected but with why it persists in strength. In rituals for changing luck the inductive strengthening of a particular form of behavior is generally absent. The behavior of the pigeon in this experiment is of the latter sort, as the variety of responses obtained from different pigeons indicates. Whether there is any unconditioned behavior in the pigeon appropriate to a given effect upon the environment is under investigation.

The results throw some light on incidental behavior observed in experiments in which a discriminative stimulus is frequently presented. Such a stimulus has reinforcing value and can set up superstitious behavior. A pigeon will often develop some response such as turning, twisting, pecking near the locus of the discriminative stimulus, flapping its wings, etc. In much of the work to date in this field the interval between presentations of the discriminative stimulus has been one min., and many of these superstitious responses are short-lived. Their appearance as the result of accidental correlations with the presentation of the stimulus is unmistakable.

42.
the control of
the content of conversation
through reinforcement

nathan h. azrin, w. holz,
roger ulrich,
and israel goldiamond

The present study is an attempt to replicate an investigation by Verplanck (1955). In that investigation, psychology students were reported as able to exert strong control over the casual conversations of other people by selectively reinforcing a certain type of opinion-statement and extinguishing all other types of statements. To produce reinforcement, the student E paraphrased or agreed with each opinion of the S. Conversely, to produce extinction, the student E openly disagreed with the opinions or simply said nothing. Each S was studied for 30 minutes. For some groups of Ss, 10 minutes of extinction were preceded and followed by 10 minutes of reinforcement. For other groups, a 10-minute period of reinforcement was preceded and followed by 10 minutes of extinction.

The results of this experiment were quite dramatic. Within this brief 30-minute period, "All Ss increased their rate of stating opinions, regardless of the topic of conversation, its setting, or S's particular relationship with the E." (Verplanck, 1955, p. 673).

From the theoretical view, this study is one of the very few successful attempts to reinforce human verbal behavior in a free-operant situation. From a more practical view, this study seemed

Reprinted by permission from *Journal of the Experimental Analysis of Behavior*, 1961, 4, 25–30. Copyright 1961 by the Society for the Experimental Analysis of Behavior, Inc.

This investigation was supported by a grant from the Psychiatric Training and Research Fund of the Illinois Department of Public Welfare.

ideal as a laboratory exercise for a class of college graduate students. No special laboratory apparatus was needed other than a clock or watch which permitted the students to record the number of opinions and statements at 1-minute intervals. No laboratory space was needed because the experiment had been conducted in informal settings, such as a cafeteria or dormitory, or even over a telephone. Other advantages were the brief period of time required (30 minutes) and the apparent simplicity of the procedure. For example, after adequate instruction, "Of the 17 students who undertook the experiment, all were able to collect one or two sets of data as the design demanded." (Verplanck, 1955, p. 669).

CLASS EXPERIMENT I

Unlike the original study, a class composed of graduate students rather than undergraduates was used here. Of the 16 students, 11 either majored or minored in psychology. Before replicating this experiment, these students had received intensive instruction in the principles of operant conditioning, and had been tested on their knowledge. Further, each student read Verplanck's original study and was examined on his knowledge of it, and the procedure was discussed and rehearsed in detail in class. Two procedures were used. Half of the students conducted 10 minutes of extinction followed by 10 minutes of reinforcement, which was followed by another 10 minutes of extinction. The other half of the students reversed the procedure: reinforcement—

extinction—reinforcement. Reinforcement consisted of the student E's agreement with the opinions of the subject. Extinction consisted of saying nothing. As in the original study, the student Es were instructed to say nothing at any time other than when agreeing with expressed opinions.

The results here were quite similar to those of the original study. Out of 15 students, 14 reported a higher frequency of opinions during the reinforcement period than during extinction. An application of the test by Wilcoxin for paired replicates[1] to these results showed that they were statistically significant well below the .0001 level. As was also true of the original study, the frequency of statements other than opinions did not change greatly.

Except for one student who could not complete the experiment, none of the students reported any difficulty either in conducting the experiment, defining the responses, scoring the behavior, or obtaining the expected results. However, the one student reported that he was unable to maintain a conversation without actively participating in the conversation, alhough such participation clearly violated the prescribed procedure. Also, he found it difficult to categorize the conversation into opinion vs. statements while simultaneously attending to his watch for purposes of timing. After six attempts, this one student reported that he was unable to complete the experiment according to the required procedure. After class discussion of his difficulties, eight of the other students stated that they had had similar difficulties, previously unmentioned, and were thereby forced to deviate appreciably from the stated procedure. The most frequently stated difficulties were: (1) the S walked out during extinction; (2) the E was forced to actively participate by nodding, smiling, or asking questions; (3) the S was aware of the recording; (4) E made errors in timing; and, finally, (5) E became too interested in the subject of conversation to concentrate on the recording of opinions.

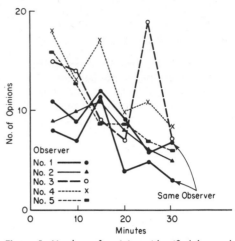

Figure 1. Number of opinions identified by each of five observers listening to the same tape. Observer No. 1 (heavy lines) listened to the conversation a second time after an interval of 2 hours.

During this class discussion, one student mentioned that he had taken a tape recording of his own experiment. A second student was therefore assigned to analyze the tape to determine the reliability of the recording. After several attempts, this second observer reported that he could not discriminate between the reinforcement and extinction periods, since the E had been actively participating throughout. A comparison of the frequency of opinions and statements between the two observers revealed little or no correspondence.

Because of this apparent difficulty in categorizing verbal behavior as an opinion or a statement, the following study was conducted.[2] A 30-minute tape recording was taken of a conversation in which the speaker knew that his opinions and statements were being recorded. Five students from this same class, including the original E, then listened to the recording individually and recorded the numbers of opinions and statements made. To minimize errors in timing, the five observers noted the behavior in terms of 5-minute rather than 1-minute intervals.

Figure 1 presents the number of opinions recorded by the five observers. It

[1]This test was used in all statistical comparisons in this paper.

[2]Mr. R. Teague assisted in the collection of the data for this aspect of the study.

shows that during each 5-minute interval, the number of opinions differed greatly among observers. The minimum and maximum is in a ratio of about 2 to 1 for each 5-minute period. More surprising is the difference found between the E's original scoring and his own later scoring from the tape recording only 2 hours later. (See dark lines in Figure 1.)

CLASS EXPERIMENT II

The many difficulties reported by the first class in replicating the original experiment, as well as the surprising lack of reliability in identifying the responses, might be interpreted simply as differences in the types of students used. A second class was therefore given the same experiment, but was not given the original article to read. Furthermore, they were not told that the study had ever been done before. As in the original study by Verplanck, this class was composed largely of undergraduates who had been instructed and tested on the principles of reinforcement. The procedure followed for this second class was the same as that followed in the previous class. There were successive 10-minute periods of reinforcement—extinction—reinforcement. However, extinction was defined as disagreement rather than as silence. Verplanck had found that disagreement was as effective as silence in decreasing the response, and the present results support these findings. Of the 12 students who completed the study, 11 found that disagreement (described as extinction) produced a lower frequency of opinions than did agreement (described as reinforcement). This difference was again statistically significant at below the .001 level. Again, the students reported no serious difficulty.

These results pose somewhat of a dilemma. Despite seemingly great unreliability in identifying an opinion, and despite the numerous difficulties the first class of students mentioned, agreement with opinions is reported almost unanimously to produce a higher frequency of opinions than does silence or disagreement with the opinions. This procedure also seems to work as well for undergraduates as for graduate students.

CLASS EXPERIMENT III

An analysis of the results of the previous classes revealed some apparent relationship between the student's understanding of reinforcement principles and his reported results. For example, those students who were frequently absent from class and who revealed relatively little knowledge of reinforcement on their class exams usually reported relatively little effect of reinforcement upon opinions. At least two reasons might account for this failure: either these students did not follow the appropriate procedure, or they had no firm expectations about the results. To evaluate this second possibility, a third class of undergraduates was assigned to the same experiment, but this class had not read the original article. Half of the students conducted consecutive 10-minute periods of reinforcement—extinction—reinforcement, and the other half conducted periods of extinction—reinforcement—extinction. Again, reinforcement consisted of agreeing with each opinion, whereas extinction consisted of silence. This experiment was conducted during and after classroom instruction on the principles of reinforcement. The results were virtually the same as those in the previous class: 44 out of 47 students reported a greater frequency of opinions during reinforcement than during extinction (P < .001). One month later, following classroom discussion of emotions, essentially the same experiment was assigned to these students except that periods of disagreement were used instead of periods of silence. Verplanck had found that silence and disagreement were functionally identical in producing a decrease of opinions. However, the effect of disagreement was discussed in the present class in terms of catharsis rather than in terms of extinction, as in Verplanck's class and in the second class of the present experiment. The students were told that catharsis is the release of emotion, and that such release could be obtained by agreeing with an individual, so that a relative state of tranquility followed in which there was little reason for stating strong opinions. Conversely, disagreement was described as preventing catharsis, so that an increase of emotionally charged opinions followed. These comments about catharsis were intended to produce a bias toward obtaining an increase in the frequency of opinions rather than the decrease that was reported by Verplanck and that was obtained in the previous class in the present study.

Figure 2 compares the mean number of opinions reported by the students of this third class with the number reported by the students of the second class under the two sets of response bias. According to Figure 2, the procedure of disagreement produced an increase of opinions when identified as catharsis but a decrease when identified as extinction. Statistically, the difference in the number of opinions between agreement and disagreement for each class, as well as the difference between the two disagreement periods, is significant at well below the .001 level. Allegedly, the procedure of disagreeing with the subjects' opinions was the same for both classes. Therefore, the actual procedures used appeared to be almost irrelevant for obtaining the above changes in opinions. Rather, the same procedures of disagreeing with opinions have resulted in diametrically opposite effects because of the response bias given to the experimenters.

It will be recalled that the first class of graduate students had reluctantly admitted to various procedural difficulties. By coincidence, a student was enrolled in this third class who was also employed as a research assistant in a psychology laboratory. This student employee was assigned to question the other students informally and outside of class as to how they had conducted their experiments. The other students had no knowledge of this arrangement. Out of 19 students questioned, consisting of almost one-half of the class, 12 stated that they fabricated part or all of the data. This admission of "dry-running" was readily made when the student was asked by the employee, "I'm having trouble with my experiment; can you tell me how you did yours?" Five of the remaining seven students questioned stated that they had deviated greatly from the prescribed procedure. Only two out of nineteen students stated that they had

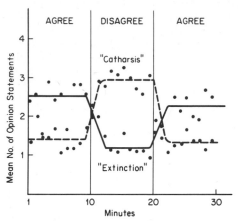

Figure 2. The effect of the expectation of experiments upon the results obtained. One group of **Es** (dashed line) was told that disagreement was expected to produce an increase because of catharsis. The other group of **Es** (solid line) was told that disagreement (the same procedure) would produce a decrease of opinion.

followed the prescribed procedure. Consequently, an attempt at an exact replication seemed pointless, since the data reports themselves were probably fabricated.

Granted that students may not be competent investigators, the question still remained whether or not more experienced investigators could demonstrate the control of casual conversation by reinforcement. The study was therefore repeated by four experienced investigators. Each of these four investigators had (1) advanced psychology training—a Ph.D. or M.A.; (2) skill in shaping animal behavior; (3) a healthy respect for negative results; and (4) practice in defining opinions. Verplanck (personal communication) considers these four crieria as essential in guaranteeing the success of the reinforcement procedure. In order to maximize the likelihood of success, a sequence of agreement—disagreement—agreement was used to avoid the expected difficulties in maintaining silence. Out of 12 attempts, not one of the four E's could complete his experiment. It may be recalled that the procedure requires that the E restrict himself to agreement (or disagreement) of opinions, and stipulates no questions, statements, nods, smiles, or other types of interaction. The reason for forbidding such behavior proved to be obvious: E's reaction, however subtle, could often be seen to exert profound but uncontrolled effects upon the conversation of the subject. In the absence of any reaction by the four Es, however, all of the twelve Ss terminated the conversation within 10 minutes by leaving the room where the conversation was taking place.

The above results indicate that the successful reinforcement of opinions by student experimenters in casual conversation seems open to serious question. Out of a sincere attempt to produce such reinforcement, procedural difficulties emerged, also unreliability in identifying the response, results that were a function of E's expectations, and, finally, evidence of extensive falsification of the data. These findings have implications for the conduct of research in operant conditioning. Operant-conditioning procedures have generally been characterized by a high degree of control. In order to avoid unreliability, the response is usually defined very simply and precisely. In order to ensure proper programming of the procedure, automatic apparatus is used. Printed records of the responses are also obtained by automatic means to eliminate bias from the E's expectations. These and other precautions have been used, not because of any inherent fascination with "artificial" situations or with complex equipment, but because empirical considerations have demanded such control. The importance of extending the procedures of operant conditioning to "real-life" situation should not be allowed to override the elementary considerations of experimental control.

It would be incorrect to conclude from this study that control over verbal behavior through reinforcement is not possible. Indeed, the existence of such control seems demonstrated by the degree to which the reports of the experimenters could be modified. Certainly, if the situation could be structured in such a manner that the E is not expected or required to speak, there would seem to be a reasonable basis for selective reinforcement. However, the present findings indicate that different procedures will be needed before free-operant conditioning can be validly extended to the control of casual conversation. More important, these findings emphasize the necessity of objective programming and recording in the study of verbal conditioning. In the absence of such objectivity, the results of studies in verbal conditioning may be more of a reflection of the experimenter's expectations and theories than of the subject's behavior.

REFERENCE

Verplanck, W. S. The control of the content of conversation: reinforcement of statements of opinion. *J. abnorm. soc. Psychol.*, 1955, *55*, 668–676.

43.
psychosomatic effects
of specific types of training

neal e. miller

INSTRUMENTAL LEARNING OF VISCERAL RESPONSES

Can the visceral responses involved in psychosomatic symptoms be directly modified by learning? The traditional view has been that such responses, mediated by the autonomic nervous system, are subject only to classical conditioning, which means that they can be reinforced only by unconditioned stimuli innately able to elicit the specific response to be learned. The following experiments show that this traditional view is wrong; visceral responses are subject to instrumental learning. This instrumental learning is much more flexible than classical conditioning, because the reward used as reinforcement does not need to be capable of eliciting the response to be learned. The reward strengthens any immediately preceding response, which means that a given response may be reinforced by a variety of rewards or that a given reward may be used to reinforce a variety of responses.

My formulation of learning theory (Miller & Dollard, 1941; Miller, 1951, 1959) has not made any distinction between the mechanisms of classical conditioning and instrumental learning, and hence, has demanded that those visceral responses that are subject to classical conditioning should also be subject to instrumental learning. It was only about a decade ago, however, that I started to work experimentally on this problem. A few of the earlier attempts have been

Reprinted by permission from *Annals* of The New York Academy of Sciences, 1969, *159* (article 3), 1025–1040. © 1969 The New York Academy of Sciences. Abridged by permission of the author.

Supported by U.S. Public Health grant MH-13189 from the National Institute of Mental Health.

described elsewhere (Miller, 1966), and I refer to this early work, showing tantalizing but inconclusive results, only to emphasize that scientific research is not always a parade of easy successes. One of the sources of difficulty was the firm conviction of my students and research assistants that I was assigning them an impossible problem. Another was the fact that I sometimes used rewards that had strong unconditioned effects, so that any instrumental learning was obscured by classical conditioning. Finally, I thought that learning would be easier in the normal, uncurarized state, so that it would be logical to demonstrate the phenomena first with normal animals before trying to rule out possible mediation via overt skeletal responses by paralyzing them with curare. Actually, learning appears to be easier for curarized animals, perhaps because "noise" from skeletal movement is eliminated. Finally, there were a host of minor technical problems to overcome.

In the first experiment, Carmona and I (1967) rewarded the spontaneous salivation of uncurarized, thirsty dogs with water, which did not elicit any obvious unconditioned changes in salivation. When we rewarded bursts of spontaneous salivation, the dogs learned to salivate progressively more, and when we rewarded pauses without salivation, they learned to salivate progressively less. There were no obvious skeletal responses such as chewing or panting to mediate the salivation, but the dogs rewarded for increases seemed to show more general activation, while those rewarded for decreases seemed to be more drowsy.

Concurrently, Jay Trowill (1967) was showing great courage and ingenuity in persisting in wrestling with the problem of rewarding changes in the heart rate of curarized animals. Eventually, we hit on a fruitful procedure. Rats were paralyzed by intraperitoneal injections of curare and respirated via a face mask at a rate that Trowill found, by trial-and-error, would hold the heart rate constand at an approximately normal rate for the two-to-four hour duration of an experiment. Half of the rats were rewarded by electrical stimulation of the medial forebrain bundle in the hypothalamus whenever their heart rate was above normal; the other half were rewarded whenever it was slightly below normal. The two groups showed highly reliable changes in the rewarded direction, but the difference was small.

Next, DiCara and I (1967) showed that, by first rewarding small changes in the desired direction and then setting the criteria at progressively more difficult levels, we could shape the rats to learn much larger changes, averaging 20%, in heart-rate increases or decreases. We also showed that reliably greater changes in the rewarded direction occurred to the time-in stimulus, which indicated when reward would be delivered, than to the time-out one.

Finally, follow-up tests showed that instrumentally learned changes in heart rate can be retained for at least a three-month period without further practice (DiCara & Miller, 1968c).

SPECIFICITY OF VISCERAL LEARNING

In the preceding studies, the fact that the same reward could be used to produce changes in opposite directions rules out the interpretation that all of the learning was produced by the classical conditioning of any unconditioned effect that the reward might have had. The fact that the rats were completely paralyzed by curare rules out any mediation via instrumentally learned, overt skeletal responses. It is possible, however, that what was being learned was either a general pattern of activation or the initiation of impulses from the motor cortex that would have produced vigorous skeletal movement had the motor endplates not been paralyzed by curare. Perhaps such central impulses were learned and had either an innate or a conditioned effect on heart rate. Such possibilities

made it highly desirable to discover whether or not a different visceral response could be instrumentally learned, and to determine the specificity of such learning. Therefore, Ali Banuazizi and I (1968) performed experiments comparing the instrumental learning of intestinal contractions with that of heart rate.

Intestinal contractions were recorded via a little balloon on the end of a blunt hypodermic needle thrust 4 cm beyond the anal sphincter into the large intestine. The rats were deeply paralyzed with curare and rewarded by direct electrical stimulation of the brain. Both intestinal contractions and heart rate were recorded for each of 12 rats, half of which were rewarded for changes in one response and the other half for changes in the other. Each of the foregoing two groups was divided into two subgroups, one of which was rewarded for increases and the other for decreases. Every tenth trial was a test trial during which the reward circuit was turned off for the first 10 seconds of the time-in stimulus so that responses could be measured without any selective or interfering factors that might have been introduced if the trials had been terminated and the rewarding brain stimulation administered as soon as the criterion was met. At the end of the 10-second recording interval, the response counters were turned off and the reward circuit was turned on, so that reinforcement was delayed rather than omitted. Training consisted of 500 learning trials during approximately four hours.

The objectively recorded intestinal contraction scores are presented in Figure 1. It can be seen that when increases or decreases, respectively, in spontaneous intestinal contraction are rewarded, changes in the appropriate direction are produced. But when a different response, heart rate, is rewarded, intestinal contractions are unaffected. Figure 2 shows that when increases or decreases, respectively, in heart rate are rewarded, the rate changes in the appropriate direction. But when changes in intestinal contractions are rewarded, no changes in heart rate are produced. The learning is specific to the type of response that is rewarded.

The learning shown in Figures 1 and

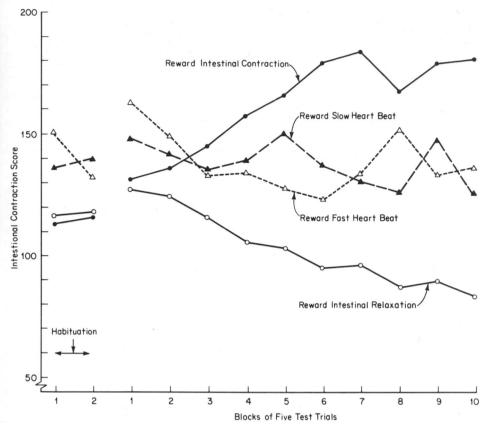

Figure 1. Rewarding increases or decreases, respectively, in spontaneous contractions of the intestine produces changes in the appropriate direction, but rewarding a different response, heart rate, produces no changes in intestinal contractions. (From Miller & Banuazizi, 1968)

2 is not merely the product of group averages, but is characteristic of individual rats. The changes in the rewarded direction were reliable beyond the .001 level for each of 11 out of 12 rats; the twelfth rat was a little poorer, showing changes in the rewarded direction that were reliable only at the .05 level. For 11 out of 12 rats the changes in the score for the rewarded response (as shown by the correlation of the score on each test trial with the ordinal number of that trial) was greater than the change in the score for the nonrewarded response. The twelfth rat was the one that had shown the poorest learning. For the group as a whole, the better the rewarded response was learned, the less

change occurred in the nonrewarded one. The hypothesis that both the intestinal and cardiac responses were mediated by some general reaction, such as arousal, struggling, or a shift in the sympathetic-parasympathetic balance, would predict exactly the opposite result.

VASOMOTOR LEARNING

In order to see whether yet a different kind of response is subject to instrumental learning, Leo DiCara and I (1968b) used the same general procedures of the preceding studies in an experiment on the learning of vasoconstriction or vasodilatation of the rat's tail as measured by a photoelectric plethysmograph. In the

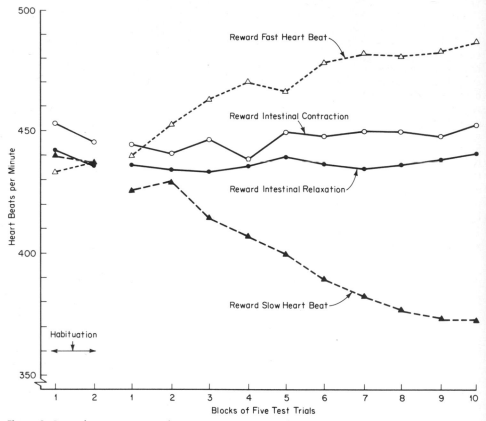

Figure 2. Rewarding increases or decreases, respectively, in heart rate produces changes in the appropriate direction, but rewarding a different response, intestinal contractions, produces no changes in heart rate. (From Miller & Banuazizi, 1968)

first experiments, which were done at Yale in the summer of 1966, each of the two rats rewarded for vasoconstriction learned reliable (p < .01) constriction, while the one rat rewarded for vasodilatation learned reliable (p < .01) dilatation. In a more recent replication performed at Rockefeller University, four out of four rewarded for vasoconstriction learned it, while four out of four rewarded for vasodilatation learned that opposite response.

The next question was whether a more specific vasomotor response can be learned. Can the rat learn to make a peripheral response of the blood vessels independent of general changes in heart rate and blood pressure, and can he learn to make these vascular changes specific to a given structure?

In order to try to answer these questions, Dr. DiCara and I (1968b) decided to try a bold, and perhaps foolish, experiment. We obtained photoelectric plethysmographs from both ears of the curarized rat and hooked the individual amplifier for each ear to a bridge circuit, so that we could record differential changes in the two ears. Half of the rats were rewarded for relatively greater vasoconstriction (which could also be relatively less vasodilatation) in the right ear, and the other half were rewarded for changing the balance of the two ears in the opposite direction. To our amazement and delight, five out of five rats rewarded for a bilateral change in vasomotor balance in one direction showed it, and five out of five rewarded for a change in the opposite direction showed it. While we have not yet analyzed the data in complete detail, a sign test shows that results of this kind would be expected by chance less than one time in a thousand. These results appear to indicate that peripheral vasomotor changes, which could not be produced by any general changes in heart rate or blood pressure, can be learned, and that such responses can be specific to a given structure, or at least to a given side of the rat. Since the innervation of the vessels in the rat's ears is primarily sympathetic, this result suggests that the sympathetic nervous system may have a greater capacity for specificity than has usually been attributed to it.

KIDNEY FUNCTIONS

The purpose of the next experiment (Miller and DiCara, 1968) was to determine whether a glandular response, formation of urine by the kidney, can be modified by instrumental learning in the curarized rat. In order to eliminate the influence of the bladder, chronic catheters were placed in it and the bladder walls secured around them by surgical silk. To control fluid load, the rats had catheters implanted into the jugular veins. As in preceding experiments, they were paralyzed by curare, maintained on artificial respiration, and rewarded by direct electrical stimulation of the brain. Small drops of urine bridged a tiny gap between a hypodermic needle immediately above a surgical needle below, and activated a counter via an electronic relay.

In order to secure fast enough rate of urine formation so that changes could be recorded and rewarded promptly, rats were loaded via the venal catheter with 10 ml of Ringer's solution during the hour before the training began, and their waterloads were kept constant throughout training by injection of ½ ml of Ringer's solution for each ½ ml of urine collected. Glomerular filtration was measured by the use of ^{14}C-labeled inulin, and the rate of renal blood flow by the use of tritiated p-aminohippuric acid (PAH). These tracers were injected via the venal catheter during the preloading procedure.

The instrumental learning of increased or decreased rates of urine formation,

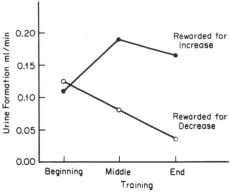

Figure 3. Instrumental learning of changes in rate of urine formation. (From Miller & DiCara, 1968)

respectively, is shown in Figure 3. Seven out of the seven rats rewarded for increases showed them, and seven out of seven rewarded for decreases showed them. That this learning was independent of changes in peripheral blood pressure is demonstrated by Figure 4, which shows that there is a great overlap between the two groups in the change of blood pressure recorded from the tail, but no overlap in the changes in urine formation. A similar analysis shows that the effect was on urine formation rather than on heart rate.

Figure 5 shows that the training procedure produced changes in glomerular filtration rate, in renal blood flow, and in osmolarity. Since the changes in blood flow were not accompanied by changes in heart rate or blood pressure, they must have been the effect of local vasomotor changes. The previous experiment showed that vasomotor changes affecting a peripheral structure, the ear, can be instrumentally learned: the present experiment shows that vasomotor changes affecting an internal organ, the kidney, can be learned.

BLOOD PRESSURE

Although no systematic changes in blood pressure were observed during training for changes in urine formation, Dr. DiCara and I (1968d) have recently completed an experiment in which increases or decreases, respectively, of more

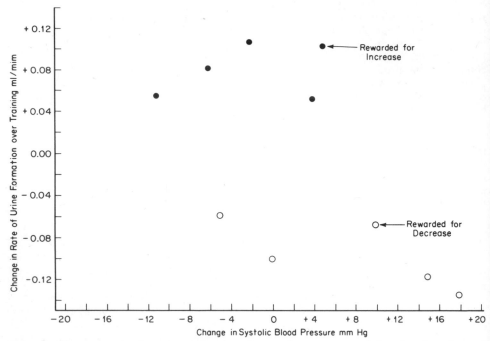

Figure 4. Changes in urine formation as function of type of response rewarded, rather than change in blood pressure. (From Miller & DiCara, 1968)

than 20 mm mercury were produced by rewarding the appropriate changes by direct electrical stimulation of the brain. The rats were paralyzed by curare and the blood pressure was recorded by a chronic catheter into the abdominal aorta. Five out of six rats rewarded for increases learned an increase, and six out of six rewarded for decreases learned a decrease.

ESCAPE AND AVOIDANCE LEARNING OF VISCERAL RESPONSES

In all of the preceding experiments on curarized rats, the reward was direct electrical stimulation of the medial forebrain bundle. Is there anything unique about this kind of reward, which might make it succeed where all other rewards will fail to produce visceral learning? In order to answer this question, Leo DiCara and I (1968a) performed an experiment in which curarized rats received a warning signal, which was followed after five

seconds by brief pulses (150 msec) of mild electric shock (0.3 ma) delivered to the tails once every three seconds. If the rat made the correct change (an increase in heart rate for half of the rats and a decrease for the other half), he turned off the shock and the warning signal; if he made the correct heart-rate change during the five-second period of grace, he turned off the warning signal and avoided receiving the shock. For half of the rats the warning signal was a tone and the irrelevant cue was a flashing light; for the other half the roles of these cues was reversed. Positive trials with warning signals, negative trials with the irrelevant cue, and blank test trials, during which heart rate was measured but no stimulus was presented, were given a randomized sequence.

Every tenth positive trial throughout training was a special test trial, during the five seconds of which both the criterion and shock circuits were turned off so that heart rate could be measured

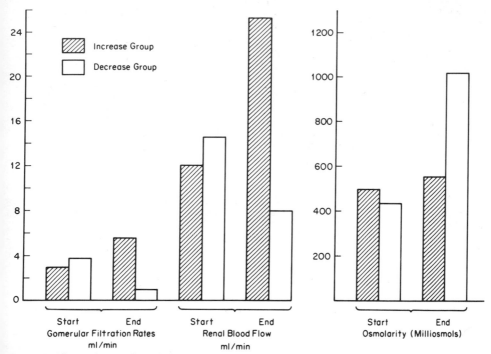

Figure 5. Effects of rewarding different rates of urine formation on glomerular filtration, renal blood flow, and osmolarity. (From Miller & DiCara, 1968)

for the same constant interval for each type of trial throughout training without any possible contaminating effects from having the shock signal turned off or the shock turned on. At the end of the five-second interval, the scoring circuit was turned off, the criterion was turned on, and the procedure continued as though this had been the beginning of a regular positive trial.

The results are shown in Figure 6. It can be seen that the rats rewarded by escape or avoidance for increasing their heart rates learned to increase them, while those rewarded by escape or avoidance for decreasing their heart rates learned to decrease them. Each of the 12 individual rats changed in the predicted direction; t-tests for the reliability of the changes of individual rats yielded one nonsignificant difference, three beyond the 0.1 level, and eight beyond .001 level.

While part of the learning was a general change in base line, as indicated by

the blank trials, in each of the two groups the rats showed highly reliable ($p < .004$) additional changes in the correct direction, which was an increase for one group and a decrease for the other, during the signal for shock. Since these highly reliable changes occurred to the

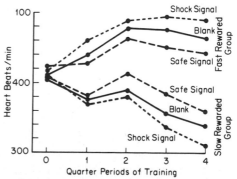

Figure 6. Changes in heart rate during avoidance training. (From Miller & DiCara, 1968a)

shock signal before the time for delivery of shock, and turned off the shock signal and shock circuit, they are avoidance responses.

In order to shape the response, to produce larger changes, and also to control for possible effects of different frequencies of electric shock by holding these relatively constant, the criterion was progressively increased throughout training. Therefore, an increase in the number of successful avoidances cannot be used as an additional indication of avoidance learning. Additional evidence for avoidance learning during training is given by the progressively increasing size of the difference between the blank trials and the shock-signal test trials. Suitable trend-tests (Winer, 1962, 298) show that this increase in difference is reliable both for the slow and the fast groups ($f = 3.7$ and 5.2; $< .02$ and $.01$, respectively; df $= 4$, 50).

During the negative stimulus, both groups showed a reliable change in the opposite direction, toward the original starting level. This last result shows that the stimulus not associated with shock did not function solely as a neutral stimulus, but, instead, as an inhibitory stimulus or safe signal. This result, of course, is analogous to the one originally reported for conditioning by Pavlov (1927) and more recently by Rescorla and Lo-Lordo (1965). Since the rats were always safe in the absence of a shock signal, the only additional function of the negative stimulus (in comparison to a blank trial) was to predict that no onset of a shock signal (followed by a five-second period of grace) was imminent. Nevertheless, there was a difference between the responses during the safe signal and the blank trials that was highly reliable (p $< .01$) for both the fast and the slow groups.

Since the rats in each group responded reliably in the reinforced direction to the shock signal and reliably in the opposite direction to the safe signal, it is clear that the instrumental-training procedure had brought the heart rate under discriminative stimulus control.

Additional analyses show that the results cannot be accounted for in terms of the number and duration of shocks.

Electromyographic records show that the curare produced complete paralysis of the gastrocnemius muscle, lasting for at least one hour after the end of the training.

In an experiment quite similar to ours on heart rate, Ali Banuazizi (1968) has shown that rats can learn to either increase or decrease, respectively, their intestinal contractions in order to escape and/or avoid punishment. He used extinction trials at the end of training as his most critical measure. During this trial, both the group that had been rewarded for an increase and the group that had been rewarded for a decrease showed a highly reliable difference in the expected direction between the scores during the presentation of the positive stimulus and those during either the presentation of the negative stimulus or the blank trials (p $< .001$).

These results, along with the fact that Miller and Carmona (1967) were able to use water as a reward to change the rate of salivation of thirsty noncurarized dogs, indicate that the instrumental learning of visceral responses is not limited to a peculiar type of reward such as electrical stimulation of the brain.

TRANSFER FROM CURARIZED TO NONCURARIZED STATE: IMPLICATIONS FOR MEDIATIONAL HYPOTHESIS

In one of the earlier papers (Miller & DiCara, 1967), we raised the possibility that "subjects learned to send out from the motor cortex central impulses for skeletal responses, such as struggling, and that these impulses elicited innate or classically conditioned changes in heart rate." If the changes in heart rate were not directly learned instrumentally but instead were mediated via the learning of central impulses to skeletal muscles, we would expect movements of such muscles to appear if the heart-rate training transferred from the curarized to the noncurarized state. For this reason, DiCara and I (1968e) have studied such transfer.

We have found that learned increases and decreases in heart rate, adding up to a total difference of 20%, do indeed transfer to the noncurarized state. But such differences as were found in the recordings of movement and breathing in the noncurarized state fell into a pattern that could not easily explain the differences in heart rate. For example, differences in respiration during the noncurarized test were decreasing, while those in heart rate were increasing. In view of the work summarized by Ehrlich and Malmo (1967) on the vigor of muscular movement required to affect heart rate in the rat, we believe that it is extremely unlikely that any impulses for skeletal muscles could have been involved that were great enough to mediate the observed changes in heart rate. Furthermore, it is difficult to think of different skeletal movements that might mediate each of the different specific changes that we have secured in visceral responses such as heart rate, intestinal contractions, formation of urine by the kidney, blood pressure, and differential vasomotor responses of the two ears. Similarly, it is difficult to conceive of enough different thoughts, each of which would elicit a different one of these visceral responses indirectly, by each inducing a different emotional state innately eliciting a specific visceral response. If one conceives of specific thoughts eliciting specific visceral responses in any more direct way, the hypothesis becomes indistinguishable from the ideomotor theory of voluntary movement (James, 1890).

LEARNING IN NONCURARIZED STATE

It will be remembered that the original experiment with Carmona showed that an instrumental-training procedure could be used to modify the rate of salivation in normal dogs. This learning was much slower than that secured in our later experiments on other responses with curarized rats. Recently, DiCara and I have been training some rats in the noncurarized state. Our preliminary results indicate that with the normal rat, the learning of certain responses such as heart rate and blood pressure definitely is possible, but that it probably is considerably harder than similar learning with the curarized rat. Our "hunch" is that one of the main reasons for this

difficulty is the noise introduced by skeletal movements; however, other factors may also be involved.

Furthermore, a considerable number of studies on human subjects, recently summarized by Kimmel (1967), show that heart rate and the galvanic skin response can be modified by instrumental conditioning procedures. While the earlier studies of this kind were not completely convincing by themselves, the total picture is convincing in the light of the results on animals.

IMPLICATIONS FOR LEARNING THEORY, PSYCHOSOMATIC SYMPTOMS, AND BEHAVIOR THERAPY

Our results on visceral learning remove one of the strongest arguments that has been used for the hypothesis that classical conditioning and instrumental learning are two basically different processes involving different neural mechanisms. They also remove one of the reasons for considering the autonomic nervous system to be behaviorally inferior to and independent from the cerebrospinal one. As I have pointed out elsewhere (Miller, 1966), neuroanatomical and neurophysiological evidence against such a distinction has been accumulating for some time. Visceral functions are clearly represented at the highest level of the brain, the cerebral cortex.

The fact that visceral responses are subject to instrumental learning means that the reinforcement of changes in them is not limited to unconditioned stimuli that elicit as an unconditioned response the specific change to be learned. Instead, it is highly probable that they can be modified by any one of the great variety of rewards and punishments that are known to be capable of producing the learning of skeletal responses. Psychiatrists commonly refer to such rewards as secondary gains. It is clearly possible for the visceral responses involved in psychosomatic symptoms to be learned as well as to be innately elicited in the hierarchy of responses to a strong emotion such as fear. The degree to which psychosomatic symptoms, and the individual differences in profiles studied by Lacey and Lacey (1958, 1962), actually are learned will depend, of course, on the degree to which suitable conditions for reinforcement are present in the life of the individual. This remains to be determined by clinical research.

The instrumental learning of visceral responses also opens up interesting new therapeutic possibilities. By recording such responses and immediately rewarding first small and then larger changes, it should be possible to teach a well-motivated patient to change undesirable visceral responses to more desirable ones. Since other experiments from our labora-

tory (Carmona, 1967) have shown that the voltage of brain waves of curarized rats can be increased by rewarding increases, or decreased by rewarding decreases, it is even conceivable that in some cases the responses reflected in abnormal EEG activity can be modified by learning. The degree to which these theoretical possibilities will have practical utility remains to be determined by clinical tests; it certainly should be exceedingly worthwhile to give them a thorough trial.

REFERENCES

Banuazizi, A. 1968. Ph.D. Thesis. Yale University. New Haven, Conn.

Carmona, A. 1967. Trial-and-error learning of the voltage of the cortical EEG activity. Ph.D. Thesis. Yale Univ. New Haven, Conn.

DiCara, L. V. & N. E. Miller. 1968a. Changes in heart rate instrumentally learned by curarized rats as avoidance responses. J. Comp. Physiol. Psychol. 65:8–12.

DiCara, L. V. & N. E. Miller. 1968b. Instrumental learning of vasomotor responses by rats: learning to respond differentially in the two ears. Science 159:1485–1486.

DiCara, L. V. & N. E. Miller. 1968c. Long-term retention of instrumentally learned heart rate changes in the curarized rat. Commun. Behav. Biol. Part A. 2:19–23.

DiCara, L. V. & N. E. Miller. 1968d. Instrumental learning of systolic blood pressure responses by curarized rats: Dissociation of cardiac and vascular changes. Psychosom. Med. 30:489–494.

DiCara, L. V. & N. E. Miller. 1968e. Transfer of instrumentally learned heart rate changes from curarized to noncurarized state: Implications for a mediational hypothesis. J. Comp. Physiol. Psychol. (In press.)

Ehrlich, D. J. & R. B. Malmo. 1967. Electrophysiological concomitants of simple operant conditioning in the rat. Neuropsychologia 5:219–235.

James, W. 1890. Principles of Psychology. II:26. Reprinted 1950. Dover Publications. New York, N. Y.

Kimmel, H. D. 1967. Instrumental conditioning of autonomically mediated behavior. Psychol. Bull. 67:337–345.

Lacey, J. I. & B. C. Lacey. 1958. Verification and extension of the principle of autonomic response stereotypy. Amer. J. Psychol. 71:50–73.

Lacey, J. I. & B. C. Lacey. 1962. The law of initial value in the longitudinal study of autonomic constitution: Reproducibility of autonomic responses and response patterns over a four-year interval. Ann. N. Y. Acad. Sci. 98:1257–1290.

Miller, N. E. 1951. Comments on multiple-process conceptions of learning. Psychol. Rev. 58:375–381.

Miller, N. E. 1959. Liberalization of basic S-R concepts. Extensions to conflict behavior, motivation and social learning. In Psychology: A Study of a Science. S. Koch, Ed. Study I. 2:196–292. McGraw-Hill Book Co. New York, N. Y.

Miller, N. E. 1966. Experiments relevant to learning theory and psychopathology. In Proceedings of the XVIII International Congress of Psychology. Moscow, USSR. In press.

Miller, N. E. & A. Banuazizi. 1968. Instrumental learning by curarized rats of a specific visceral response, intestinal or cardiac J. Comp. Physiol. Psychol. 65:1–7.

Miller, N. E. & A. Carmona. 1967. Modification of a visceral response, salivation in thirsty dogs, by instrumental training with water reward. J. Comp. Physiol. Psychol. 63: 1–6.

Miller, N. E. & L. V. DiCara. 1967. Instrumental learning of heart-rate changes in curarized rats: shaping, and specificity to discriminative stimulus. J. Comp. Physiol. Psychol. 63:12–19.

Miller, N. E. & L. V. DiCara. 1968. Instrumental learning of urine formation b rats; changes in renal blood flow. Amer. Physiol. 215:677–683.

Miller, N. E. & J. Dollard. 1941. Social learning and imitation. Yale Univ. Pres New Haven, Conn. (Also available in Yal Univ. Press paperback.)

Myers, A. K. 1956. The effects of pre

dictable vs. unpredictable punishment in the albino rat. Ph.D. Thesis. Yale Univ. New Haven, Conn.

Pavlov, I. P. 1927. Conditioned Reflexes. G. V. Anrep, Trans. Oxford Univ. Press. London, England. Reprinted 1960. Dover Publications. New York, N. Y.

Rescorla, R. A. & V. LoLordo. 1965. In-hibition of avoidance behavior. J. Comp. Physiol. Psychol. 59:406–413.

Trowell, J. A. 1967. Instrumental conditioning of the heart rate in the curarized rat. J. Comp. Physiol. Psychol. 63:7–11.

Winer, B. J. 1962. Statistical Analysis in Experimental Design. McGraw-Hill Book Co., New York, N. Y.

44.
narrative stories
as mediators
for serial learning

gordon h. bower
and michal c. clark

A technique recommended by mnemonists (e.g., Young & Gibson, 1962) for learning serial lists is the "chaining" method, whereby S is enjoined to construct a narrative story around the critical words to be remembered. The critical words are to be woven into the story in the order they are to be recalled, and these words should be emphasized in some manner, e.g., by vocal stress, pausing, or by making them the main actors or objects in the narrative. The prescriptions permit a wide latitude in constructive details (e.g., the number of critical words per sentence) depending upon the ease of organizing the particular list of words to be learned. A common additional prescription is that S should try to visualize the scenes he is constructing for linking the successive words.

Such procedures request that S generate very many contextual verbal responses. And it is not at all obvious why these should aid memory rather than compete or interfere with recall of the critical words. Further, a prior study by Jensen & Rohwer (1963) found no effect of sentence mediators (linking words n and n + 1) upon rote learning by the serial anticipation method. However, the Jensen and Rohwer study had several features not conducive to showing verbal mediation effects: (a) successive linking sentences were unrelated and were provided by E only on the first trial, and (b) the Ss were mental retardates learning a picture series.

Reprinted by permission from *Psychosomatic Science*, 1969, *14* (4), 181–182.

This research was supported by Grant MH-13950 to the first author from the National Institute of Mental Health.

For several reasons, then, our initial study with the chaining technique was done simply to see whether it "worked" efficiently in circumstances for which it plausibly might be efficient. These circumstances were (a) self-paced exposure to the complete serial list, (b) the critical recall units were content words (nouns), and (c) S had a large number of lists to learn and remember, so that massive interference and forgetting would normally be expected for control Ss not using the narrative chaining technique.

METHOD

Each S studied and recalled 12 successive serial lists consisting of 10 concrete nouns chosen to be apparently unrelated. All Ss were run individually; they first received general instructions for the serial learning task. The Narrative Ss were then briefly instructed on the mnemonic technique, as follows: "A good way to learn a list of items is to make up a story relating the items to one another. Specifically, start with the first item and put it in a setting which will allow other items to be added to it. Then, add the other items to the story in the same order as the items appear. Make each story meaningful to yourself. Then, when you are asked to recall the items, you can simply go through your story and pull out the proper items in their correct order."

The Narrative S was handed the first list of 10 words and told to make up his story. He did not have to say his story aloud, and he could take as long as he needed. When S was finished, he handed the list back to E (who recorded the time taken by S), and then S immediately recalled the serial list just studied. Then the second through twelfth lists were gone through in the same way. For each Narrative S, a yoked Control S was run who received the 12 lists in the same order, each for a study-time equal to that taken by the Narrative. S The Control S was told simply to study and learn each serial list, and he also did an immediate recall of each list just after he had studied it. After the twelfth list had been studied and immediately recalled, S was asked to recall the first list again, then the second list, and all subsequent lists. The cue for recall of a list was the first word in that list; S was asked to recall the remaining nine words of that list in their correct order.

The Ss were 24 undergraduates fulfilling a service requirement for their introductory psychology course. Alternate Ss were assigned to be in the Narrative vs yoked Control condition. Each pair of Ss received the 12 lists in a different order within the day.

RESULTS

The times taken by the Narrative Ss to construct their story varied from 40 sec to 199 sec with a grand mean of 104 sec. Fifty-seven per cent had times between 1 and 2 min. These times grew shorter over the first four lists, as though Ss were becoming more proficient at concocting their stories.

Neither group experienced any difficulty in the immediate recall test that followed study of a list. Median percentages recalled were 99.9% and 99.1% for the Narrative and Control Ss, respectively. However, the differential learning and/ or forgetting for the Narrative Ss showed up strongly in their later recall, when S tried to recall all 12 lists. The median percentages of words recalled in their correct list and correct absolute position are shown in Figure 1 for the two groups for the 12 lists. There is a tremendous difference, with the Narrative Ss recalling six to seven times more than their yoked Controls. There was no overlap in recall scores of the two groups on any list; the average of the median scores was 93% for the Narrative Ss vs 13% for their yoked Controls.

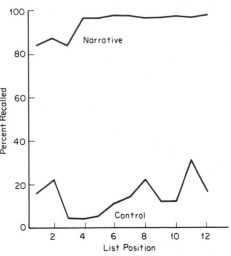

Figure 1. Medium percentages recalled over the 12 lists.

The picture is much the same if one scores recall leniently, counting a word correct regardless of the order or intended list in which it was recalled. For Control Ss the list words have simply become unavailable, whereas this has been prevented in some way by the narrative-story constructions.

There are small effects due to list order apparent in Figure 1, an improvement over early lists for Narrative Ss, and a slight serial-position curve for Control Ss. These are ancillary findings of no interest here.

We next examined the relationship between study-time on a list and later recall of that list. First, for each S, recall of the six lists with his longer study times was compared to recall of the six lists with his shorter study times. In this within-S comparison, there was no suggestion of a short vs long difference in recall for either the Narrative or Control Ss. This may have been because variation of an S's study times was relatively small. Second, over the 12 Ss by 12 lists in each condition, the 144 cases were divided at the median study time, and average recall scores computed for the shorter vs longer times. For the Narrative Ss, average recall for the lists with the shorter study times was 88% vs 92%

TABLE 1. Sample Stories

A LUMBERJACK DARTed out of a forest, SKATed around a HEDGE past a COLONY of DUCKs. He tripped on some FURNITURE, tearing his STOCKING while hastening toward the PILLOW where his MISTRESS lay.

A VEGETABLE can be a useful INSTRUMENT for a COLLEGE student. A carrot can be a NAIL for your FENCE or BASIN. But a MERCHANT of the QUEEN would SCALE that fence and feed the carrot to a GOAT.

One night at DINNER I had the NERVE to bring my TEACHER. There had been a FLOOD that day, and the rain BARREL was sure to RATTLE. There was, however, a VESSEL in the HARBOR carrying this ARTIST to my CASTLE.

for the lists with the longer study times. For the Control Ss, average recall was 12% for the shorter-time and 41% for the longer-time lists; these differ significantly, indicating that Control Ss yoked with fast Narrative Ss recalled less than those yoked with slow Narrative Ss.

These comparisons reveal that recall of Control Ss was affected by study time, while that of Narrative Ss was not. However, this effect of study time on Control Ss is still far from accounting for the main effect of the narrative elaboration. (Incidentally, Control Ss always felt that they had more than enough time to learn each list—until the final recall tests.)

Stories were taken from a few Narrative Ss after their final recall; a sample of these are shown in Table 1 with the 10 critical words capitalized. These have a certain "stream of consciousness" sense and unity about them, and they are not bad solutions to the task of connecting 10 unrelated nouns in a specified order.

DISCUSSION

We think the effect in this experiment is *probably* due to thematic organization. The person generates meaningful sentences to relate successive words, and he tries to relate successive sentences of his generated text around some central theme or action imagery. The sentences and themes from successive lists are different and probably are kept distinct from one another in memory. The first-word cue prompts recall of the theme, and from that the person appears to *reconstruct* the sentences and pull out the critical words. The reconstruction appears to be hierarchical, from theme to sentences to critical words. We would presume that this thematic organization affects learning and that it also reduces interference between the many lists S is learning. Further studies of this effect could yield more useful information by recording Ss' total verbal behavior ("thinking aloud") at study and at recall.

A remarkable aspect of the performance of Narrative Ss is that they rarely intruded nonlist words in their recall (less than .5 per S). One might first suppose that this discrimination between critical vs context words was based on form class, since all critical words were concrete nouns. But a glance at the sample stories in Table 1 shows (a) some context words are nouns; and (b) some critical words are used as verbs or adjectives in the stories. The basis for this high level discrimination between critical and context words added by S remains somewhat of a mystery.

REFERENCES

Jensen, A. R., Rowher, W. D., Jr. Verbal mediation in paired-associate and serial learning. Journal of Verbal Learning & Verbal Behavior, 1963, *1*, 346–352.

Young, M. N., & Gibson, W. B. *How to develop an exceptional memory.* Hollywood, California: Wilshire Book Co., 1962.

45.
memory disturbances after electroconvulsive therapy
influence of an interpolated electroconvulsive shock on retention of memory material

börje cronholm
and lars molander

PROBLEM

The aim of the present investigation is to study the influence of an electroconvulsive shock (ECS) on retention of memory material learnt one hour before shock. We have also studied the effect in the same respect of a dose of Evipan given one hour after learning.

EARLIER INVESTIGATIONS

It is well known that memory material learnt some time before an ECS will be forgotten to an abnormal extent. Most of the psychological methods used to study retrograde amnesia after an ECS in man do not seem to be either sensitive or reliable enough to be used to study possible differences between influence on retention by an ECS when induced by different methods, under different conditions or in different groups of individuals.—For a review see *Cronholm & Lagergren* (1959).

A priori it seems just as reasonable to assume that a dose of Evipan given after learning will facilitate or hamper retention. Several investigations have shown the disturbing influence of activity on retention of memory material, and that sleep immediately after learning improves retention (see *Woodworth & Schlossberg* (1954). It is thus possible that if sleep (or at least drowsiness) is medically induced shortly after learning, retention will be better than when the patient remains awake. On the other hand, *Leukel* (1957) found that anesthetization of rats by means of sodium pentothal 1 min. after each trial during maze learning slowed the rate of habit acquisition. Anesthetization 30 min. after learning had no such effect, however. He concludes that sodium pentothal has the effect of attenuating a "consolidation" process following each experimental trial.

PRESENT INVESTIGATIONS

General Procedure

A number of patients for whom electroconvulsive therapy (ECT) was prescribed (or could at least be considered) were examined with two parallel forms of three memory tests on two successive days. (In two cases the interval was two days). Reproduction was studied immediately after learning and six hours later. The two forms of the tests were used alternatively at the first and at the second examination.

Three groups of patients were examined.

In Group I the possible influence on retention of an ECS (in combination with Evipan (hexobarbital sodium), Skopyl (methscopolamine nitrate) and Celocurin (suxamethonium iodide) was studied.

In Group II the possible influence on retention of Evipan (in combination with Skopyl) was studied.

In Group III the possible influence of repeating the same test procedure on succeeding days was studied. This group served as a control relative to Groups I and II.

Reprinted by permission from *Acta Psychiatrica et Neurologica Scandinavica*, 1961, *36*, 83–90.

TABLE 1. Test Results

	GROUP I					
	1. Exam. No Medical Interference		2. Exam. ECS (+ Evipan) 1 Hour After Learning		Difference	
	Mean	s	Mean	s	Mean	t
The 30 Word Pair Test						
Correct answers immediately (A)	19.1	4.2	18.6	5.2	0.4	—
Correct answers 6 hrs later (B)	12.1	4.1	5.9	4.2	6.2	5.68[c]
Forgetting (A-B)	6.9	3.5	12.7	4.7	−5.8	4.71[c]
The 20 Figure Test[a]						
Correct answers immediately (A)	16.3	2.5	16.1	2.9	0.3	—
Correct answers 6 hrs later (B)	14.4	2.6	9.6	4.6	4.8	4.76[c]
Forgetting (A-B)	1.9	1.1	6.4	3.5	−4.6	4.58[c]
The 15 Letter-Symbol Test						
Correct answers immediately (A)	8.2	3.9	9.9	3.2	−1.9	2.10
Correct answers 6 hrs later (B)	3.8	3.2	1.8	1.6	2.1	3.31[b]
Forgetting (A-B)	4.4	2.3	8.2	2.8	−3.8	5.29[c]

[a] Without correction for guessing.
[b] $0.0001 < p < 0.01$.
[c] $p \leq 0.001$.

Material

For the investigation we chose in-patients at the Psychiatric Department, Karolinska sjukhuset, with a relatively mild disturbance, which in most cases had a depressive colouring. The patients should be "testable," that is, they should agree to the examination and have a good motivation for it. If these criteria were satisfied we found it permissible to include even patients with a mild schizophrenic residual state, alcoholism or abuse of barbiturates. Each group comprised 16 patients, 10 women and 6 men.

In Group I the patients' ages ranged from 26–55 years (M = 39.6 years). The diagnoses were psychoneurosis 9 (in one case with mental deficiency), psychogenic depression 2 (in one case with abuse of barbiturates), mild endogenous depression 3, mild schizophrenic residual state (with abuse of barbiturates) 1 and psychopathic personality 1. 3 of the patients had received ECT earlier, the minimum interval was one year.

In Group II the patients' ages ranged from 27–53 years (M = 38.0 years). The diagnoses were psychoneurosis 6, psychogenic depression 4, mild endogenous depression 4, torticollis spastica 1 and psychopathic personality 2 (in one case with alcoholism). 4 of the patients had received ECT earlier; the minimum interval was one year. 10 patients received ECT after the examination.

In Group III the patients' ages ranged from 26–56 years (M = 40.3 years). The diagnoses were psychoneurosis 8, psychogenic depression 4 (in one case with alcoholism), mild endogenous depression 2, psychopathic personality 1 and neurocirculatory asthenia 1. 5 patients had received ECT earlier; the minimum interval was about eleven months. 9 patients received ECT after the examination.

The groups seem to be fairly equal as regards age and mental state, in spite of the varying clinical diagnoses.

Psychological Methods

The 30 word pair and the 20 figure tests, described by *Cronholm & Molander*

	GROUP II						GROUP III					
1. Exam. No Medical Interference		2. Exam. Evipan 1 Hour After Learning		Difference		1. Exam. No Medical Interference		2. Exam. No Medical Interference		Difference	
Mean	s	Mean	s	Mean	t	Mean	s	Mean	s	Mean	t
18.8	5.8	17.5	6.7	1.3	—	17.3	5.3	17.7	5.4	−0.4	—
12.3	6.4	10.8	6.9	1.7	1.74	11.9	6.3	11.6	5.1	0.3	—
6.4	2.4	6.8	3.7	−0.4	—	5.3	3.0	6.1	3.8	−0.8	—
17.4	2.2	16.2	3.2	1.3	—	17.1	3.4	16.1	2.8	0.9	—
14.8	4.3	13.7	3.1	1.1	—	15.3	3.4	13.4	2.9		3.96[b]
2.7	2.7	2.5	1.6	0.2	—	1.8	1.5	2.8	2.1	−0.9	—
8.1	3.7	9.3	3.9	−1.1	—	8.2	3.4	8.3	3.2	−0.1	—
4.0	2.8	3.4	3.3	0.6	—	4.3	3.2	3.9	3.3	0.4	—
4.1	2.8	5.8	3.3	−1.7	—	3.9	1.9	4.4	1.9	−0.6	—

(1957), and the 15 letter-symbol pair test, described by *Cronholm & Blomquist* (1959), were used. The method of administration was the same as described in these papers; the only difference in procedure was that we studied reproduction immediately and six hours after learning instead of immediately and three hours after learning. The reason for this was that in Groups I and II we wished to carry out the second study of reproduction late enough to ensure that the most acute effects of ECS and the Evipan dose had disappeared. The order of the tests was always the same: first the figure, then the word pair and last the letter-symbol pair test.

The learning and the first examination required about 20 min. and the second examination about 10 min.

In all the tests the number of items recalled immediately is denoted immediate reproduction and that recalled three hours later is denoted delayed reproduction. The difference between these two scores is denoted forgetting.

Experimental Procedure

In all groups there was no medical interference between learning and reproduction six hours later on the first day of examination. The results thus served as controls on the results achieved during the second day of examination, where the procedure differed in the different groups.

Group I. On the second day of examination, learning started one hour before an ECS was induced. Siemens Konvulsator III (*v. Braunmühl* (1951) was used for electroshock treatment. ECS was induced with unidirectional electric impulses, the apparatus was adjusted to gains 7–8 and the current was applied for 1.9–5.4 sec. depending on age. In all cases a major seizure was induced. About forty-five minutes before an ECS was induced the patients received 0.25 mg Skopyl intramuscularly. Immediately before treatment they were given intravenously a dose of Evipan (5 mg/kg body weight) and of Celocurin (in men

TABLE 2. Statistical Analysis of Mean Group Differences (M_d) Between Test Performances at the First and Second Day of Examination

	Analysis of Variance M_d and s in Group				t-Value for the Differences Between M_d in Group		
	I	II	III	F	I-II	I-III	II-III
The 30 Word Pair Test							
Correct answers	0.4	1.3	−0.4	0.71	—	—	—
immediately (A)	**3.8**	**4.8**	**3.2**				
Correct answers	6.2	1.7	0.3	6.51[c]	2.39[b]	4.18[d]	0.79
6 hrs later (B)	**4.2**	**5.9**	**3.5**				
Forgetting (A-B)	−5.8	−0.4	0.8	8.45[d]	3.51[c]	3.29[c]	0.31
	4.7	**3.7**	**3.5**				
The 20 Figure Test[a]							
Correct answers	0.3	1.3	0.9	0.85	—	—	—
immediately (A)	**2.0**	**2.3**	**2.2**				
Correct answers	4.8	1.1	1.9	6.24[c]	3.03[c]	2.59[b]	0.96
6 hrs later (B)	**3.9**	**2.7**	**1.8**				
Forgetting (A-B)	−4.6	0.2	0.9	9.64[d]	3.90[d]	3.14[c]	1.15
	3.9	**2.8**	**2.3**				
The 15 Letter-Symbol Test							
Correct answers	−1.9	−1.1	−0.1	1.10	—	—	—
immediately (A)	**3.4**	**3.0**	**2.6**				
Correct answers	2.1	0.6	0.4	1.90	—	—	—
6 hrs later (B)	**2.4**	**3.6**	**3.2**				
Forgetting (A-B)	3.8	1.7	0.6	4.86[b]	1.76	3.60[c]	1.02
	2.8	**3.7**	**2.0**				

Note: The standard deviations of M_d (s) are given in bold.
[a] Without correction for guessing.
[b] $0.01 < p \leq 0.05$.
[c] $0.001 < p < 0.01$.
[d] $p \leq 0.001$.

1.5 mg and in women 1 mg/kg body weight) (see *Holmberg & Thesleff* (1952). At the examination five hours after ECS the patients displayed as a rule a slight elevation of mood compared with their emotional state at the first examination. Some of them, however, complained of headache and nausea.

Group II. On the second day of examination the same doses of Skopyl and Evipan were given at the same times relative to learning as in Group I. No ECS was given. It is highly improbable that Skopyl influences memory performances but to be able to compare performances in this group and in Group I we found it desirable to make conditions as similar as possible. As Celocurin causes some discomfort and as it is still more improbable that this drug influences memory performances, we refrained from giving it in this group. After the injection of Evipan the patients became markedly somnolent and some fell asleep for a short while. At the examination five hours later the patients' mental state was the same as before the injections, and many of them expressed their satisfaction with the relaxing effect of the injection.

Group III. In this group there was no medical interference between learning and reproduction six hours later, neither on the first nor on the second day of examination.

Statistical Methods

To examine whether the mean test results at the first and second day of examination differ significantly we have made use of Fisher's t-test for paired sets of measurements (see *Guilford* (1950)

formula 9.41). To examine whether these mean differences are significantly dissimilar between the groups we have first applied an analysis of variance (see, e.g. *Guilford* (1950) p. 236 ff.). When the variance ratio F proved significant below the 0.05 level we also made use of Fisher's t-test for uncorrelated means (see *Guilford* (1950) formula 9.39).

Results

The test results in all three groups are seen from Table 1. The results of analysis of variance and the t-tests of the differences between the mean group differences in scores at the first and second day of examination are seen from Table 2.

DISCUSSION

It is seen from Table 1 that the test results at the first day of examination are rather similar in the three groups. The pre-treatment level of performance could thus be regarded as uniform in the groups. The scores on immediate reproduction differ only insignificantly at the first and second day of examination in all groups.

In all three tests performances were much worse six hours after learning at the second day of examination in Group I, where an ECS was interpolated one hour after learning. The same holds true of the scores for forgetting. In the other groups there were only small differences between these performances at the first and second day of examination. The only exception is that delayed reproduction was significantly worse in the figure test at the second day of examination in Group III, where exactly the same procedure was repeated on both days.

It is seen from Table 2 that the change from the first to the second day of examination in scores for delayed reproduction and forgetting differ significantly between Group I and the other groups in the word pair and the figure tests. In the letter-symbol pair test, however, there is a significant difference only as regards forgetting between Groups I and III.

In line with earlier investigations the study has shown that an ECS has a considerable, adverse effect on the retention of recently learnt memory material. When Evipan was given at the same time after learning it had no effect on retention and thus the effect in the group who had an ECS could be ascribed to the ECS itself. A possible source of error is that the impairment of the general state, with headache and nausea in some cases, might have influenced the results adversely. However, the patients worked with good motivation and such impairment of the general state was neither marked nor present in all cases. Further, *Cronholm & Molander* (1957) found no impairment in any other tests than memory tests six hours after an ECS. It is thus improbable that this factor is of any importance.

Neither the hypothesis of impaired nor of improved retention after a dose of Evipan could be confirmed. It is still possible that a greater dose, or a dose given sooner after learning. may have some effect, however. The great differences between performances in the word pair and the figure tests when an ECS was interpolated after learning, and when it was not, indicate a high sensitivity of the tests to the influence of an ECS. Thus they could be expected to be useful in studies of possible differences between the influence of an ECS on retention when different methods are used or when conditions differ otherwise.

SUMMARY

In three groups of patients, reproduction of memory material immediately and six hours after learning were studied under different conditions by means of the 30 word pair, the 20 figure and the 15 letter-symbol pair tests. Each group consisted of 16 in-patients at the Psychiatric Department, Karolinska sjukhuset, all with a relatively mild mental disturbance. They were all considered "testable," they agreed to the examination and were well motivated. In one group an ECS in combination with Evipan (hexobarbital sodium), Skopyl (methscopolamine nitrate) and Celocurin (suxamethonium iodide) was given one hour after learning, in another group Evipan was given one hour after learning (in combination with Skopyl). In both groups performances were compared with performances in the same individuals when there was no medical interference between learning and delayed reproduction. In the third group the same procedure with no medical interference was repeated on succeeding days. In the word pair and the figure tests forgetting was much greater when an ECS was given one hour after learning than when there was no medical interference or when Evipan (and Skopyl) only was given. Evipan in itself could not be shown to have any effect on forgetting.

REFERENCES

von Braunmühl, A. (1951): Ein neues Gerät für die Heilkrampfbehandlung mittels elektrischen Stromes. Fortschr. Neurol. & Psychiat. *19*, 325–332.

Cronholm, B., & L. Molander (1957): Memory disturbances after electroconvulsive therapy. 1. Conditions 6 hours after electroshock treatment. Acta psychiat. scand. *32*, 280–306.

Cronholm, B., & C. Blomquist (1959): Memory disturbances after electroconvulsive therapy. 2. Conditions one week after a series of treatments. Acta psychiat. scand. *34*, 18–25.

Cronholm, B., & A. Lagergren (1959): Memory disturbances after electroconvulsive therapy. 3. An experimental study of retrograde amnesia after electroshock treatment. Acta psychiat. scand. *34*, 283–310.

Guilford, J. P. (1950): Fundamental statistics in psychology and education. New York.

Holmberg, G., & S. Thesleff (1952): Succinyl-choline-iodide as a muscular relaxant in electroshock therapy. Am. J. Psychiat. *108*, 842–846.

Leukel, F. (1957): A comparison of the effects of ECS and anesthesia on acquisition of the maze habit. J. Comp. Physiol. Psychol. *50*, 300–306.

Woodworth, R. S., & H. Schlossberg (1954): Experimental Psychology. New York, Holt.

REVIEW QUESTIONS

1. What is the difference between linear programing and branching programing? What are some of the advantages of branching programing?

2. Under what circumstances would self-pacing be more advantageous than external pacing?

3. In the Skinner article, what behavior by the pigeon was necessary for the production of reinforcement?

4. How would you define "superstitious behavior"? Try to think of a few examples from your own life.

5. What was the reinforcement used by Azrin and his colleagues in their study? How did they try to extinguish the behavior?

6. The Azrin article contains the statement "It would be incorrect to conclude that control over verbal behavior through reinforcement is not possible." What does the article indicate can be concluded?

7. Why was Neal Miller concerned as to whether learned increases and decreases in heart rate would transfer from the curarized to the non-curarized state?

8. What new therapeutic possibilities does the fact of instrumental learning of visceral responses present?

9. What do Bower and Clark mean by thematic organization and how do they use this concept to explain their finding?

10. How did Cronholm and his colleagues rule out the possibility that headache and nausea were responsible for the adverse effect on memory?

11. What effect did Evipan have on forgetting and why was this result important?

part nine
personality and maladjustment

Behavior therapy has its foundations in laboratory experiments conducted primarily with animals. As an approach to the treatment of human problems, it is distinctive in its concern with overt symptoms rather than underlying causes. Suppose, for example, that a college student seeks professional advice because a sexual fetish he has developed is causing him anxiety. A more traditional therapist would try to determine what event(s) in the student's previous life might have led to the problem. Considerable time could also be spent discussing the client's early childhood experiences which may have led to a predisposition toward this particular fetish. Once the underlying causality is explored and at least partially understood, the therapist tries to help the patient in the understanding of his behavior and might suggest practical measures that will lead to a reduction in the anxiety.

The same student seeking therapy from a behavior therapist would be treated in an entirely different manner. There would be little or no concern with the underlying causes. The behavior therapist assumes that the anxiety is caused by the very fact that the student is engaging in the sexual fetish behavior. The immediate objective is to stop the behavior; and once this is accomplished, the theory is that the anxiety will also cease. Engaging in the behavior would be extinguished by using the basic, laboratory-derived principles of classical conditioning and operant conditioning. The student might, for example, be presented with the fetish object and a few seconds later with a painful electric shock. In time, through classical conditioning the fetish object would become a conditioned stimulus (the CS) for fear (the conditioned response) rather than the previous sexual arousal. The unconditioned stimulus (the UCS) in this example is, of course, the painful electric shock.

As Joseph Wolpe (#46) says in the introduction to his article: "The foremost task of the clinician is always the relief of suffering, and his effectiveness in accomplishing it depends upon the potency of the methods he uses." This, then, is the core of the disagreement between therapists of different theoretical orientations: which therapeutic technique is the most effective in helping to relieve human suffering. On the surface, it seems an easy matter to evaluate which type of therapy is the most effective and then to practice it exclusively. Wolpe (a behavior therapist) points up the many problems involved in such an evaluation and in the process compares the relative success of behavior therapy and psychoanalysis in the "relief of suffering." Articles #47 and #48 are good examples of how behavior therapists attack human problems. The reader should be able to get some feel for the behavior therapy approach from these two examples.

An old joke among psychologists is that "the neurotic builds castles in the sky and the psychotic lives in them." The joke points up an admittedly oversimplified, but nevertheless true, distinction between neurosis and psychosis. The neurotic remains in touch with reality and usually does not require hospitalization. He is simply unhappy in his existence and does not have a satisfying interaction with his environment. The psychotic, on the other hand, loses contact with reality and usually requires hospitalization because he cannot manage his own affairs in the world. John Dollard and Neal E. Miller try to answer the question "What Is a Neurosis?" (#49). The article discusses the important question of why symptoms come about and what purpose they serve in neurotic behavior.

The question of dream interpretation has fascinated mankind for centuries. Freud, in his theoretical formulation, assigned great importance to dream content. In the dream state, the Id was thought to be relatively free from censorship by the Ego and Superego and, as a result, it was during this time that the therapist could get some of his best insights into what the patient's strongest Id desires were. Gay Gaer Luce summarizes a wealth of dream research in her excellent review entitled "The Meaning of Dreams" (#50). The article is a beautiful example of how physiology and psychology can combine to study behavior with extremely profitable results. The article answers a number of interesting questions. Do some people never dream? What is the neural basis for dreams? How do experiences just before falling asleep affect subsequent dream material? What is the role of sexual motivation in dream content? The student might find it necessary and profitable to reread article #28 before attempting #50. Both articles are from the same source, and the latter selection assumes the background information contained in the earlier article.

Neil E. Miller's article (#43) presented in Part Eight, "Learning and Memory," considered possible underlying mechanisms of psychosomatic illnesses. The final selection in Part Nine (#51) is a case report by James L. Mathis of a psychosomatic illness pushed to the extreme of death.

46.
the comparative clinical status
of conditioning therapies
and psychoanalysis

joseph wolpe

The germinal cause of the convocation of this conference is the presence of a vast problem: how to lift the burden of suffering that neurosis imposes on humanity. The foremost task of the clinician is always the relief of suffering, and his effectiveness in accomplishing it depends upon the potency of the methods he uses.

Whatever the problem at issue, the clinical status of a method, or of a principle that generates methods, is, or should be, assessed on several criteria. The primary criteria relate directly to the well-being of the patient. Is the suffering alleviated? If so, how quickly, how completely, and how enduringly? And how free is the accomplishment from disadvantageous sequelae? Secondary criteria are the amount of time and effort demanded of the therapist, and the cost of the treatment to the patient.

Let us scrutinize the application to the neuroses of the primary criteria of the clinical status of treatments. Almost invariably, what motivates the patient to come to us in the first place is the presence of various kinds of suffering and disability, which frequently, on investigating his case, we may find even more widespread than he may initially have been able to verbalize. It is both inevitable and reasonable that the patient will ultimately appraise his therapy in terms of the relief that he will experience—just as he would if his suffering were

due to an organic disease. The indispensability of this yardstick is recognized by anybody with a medical background, and the different aspects of it were very helpfully systematized by Knight (1941) when he proposed his criteria for evaluating the outcome of psychoanalytic therapy. The criteria he put forth were five—symptomatic improvement, increased productiveness, improved adjustment and pleasure in sex, improved interpersonal relationships, and ability to handle ordinary psychological conflicts and reasonable reality stresses. Every treated case can be assessed with these criteria in mind. But it is important to realize that only one of them is *always* relevant, and that is symptomatic improvement, because neuroses vary with regard to interference with functions. For example, a man with neurotic anxieties in group situations may have a completely satisfying sex life, and a man with sexual anxieties may be productive and happy at work and altogether at ease in social situations.

Having said that symptomatic improvement is the only criterion of improvement of neuroses that must be taken into account in every case, I must make my meaning clear. Baldly stated, symptomatic improvement simply means that the patient has less discomfort. Discomfort can be diminished in a variety of ways. One method consists of the use of appropriate drugs. Although drugs are a valuable *aid* to treatment of many cases, for several reasons it is unsatisfactory to base treatment solely on them. The alleviation of symptoms is often only partial, there may be side effects, there are risks of toxicity and addiction, and, above all, the need for treatment may well continue indefinitely. Psychoanalysts and conditioning therapists are at one in comparing

Excerpts reprinted from Joseph Wolpe, Andrew Salter, and L. J. Reyan (Eds.), *The Conditioning Therapies: The Challenge in Psychotherapy*, New York, 1964, pp. 5–16. Copyright © 1964 by Holt, Rinehart and Winston, Inc. Reprinted by permission of Holt, Rinehart and Winston, Inc.

this with treating a slipped spinal disc with analgesics; they rightly disparage it, favoring the superior therapeutic objective of removing the underlying state of affairs upon which the symptoms depend. In other words, they both advocate aiming at a *radical* cure of neurosis, to render the patient free from his symptoms without the use of drugs or other means of palliation. Among other palliative measures I include taking the patient away from a disturbing environment, or manipulating the environment so as to ameliorate stressful features. Clearly, if the underlying basis of his symptoms were to be removed, the patient would be symptom-free without drugs in all circumstances in which symptoms were previously evoked. The crucial question, then, in comparing the clinical status of the conditioning therapies with that of psychoanalysis is: how effective is each of them in achieving this result?

While directing our minds to this practical question, we must be aware that at bottom the conflict is one of *concepts*. The comparison is not between this and that batch of methods that are merely empirically different, like some of the remedies for warts, but between two different conceptions of the nature of neurosis, each of which generates methods of treatment consistent with it. The different theories of neurosis suggest different requirements for recovery, and therefore different therapeutic maneuvers. In carrying out appropriate therapeutic maneuvers one is in fact performing operations that test predictions from the respective theories. As always in science, a theory becomes questionable when its predictions fail to be supported by experience.

PSYCHOANALYTIC THERAPY

With the foregoing as orientation we may proceed to evaluate the clinical status of psychoanalytic therapy. The conception of neurotic symptoms that leads to this therapy is that they are the consequences of emotional forces that have been repressed, taking the form of compromises between partial discharges of these forces and various defenses resist-

ing their discharge. In 1922 Freud put it in the following words:

> *The neuroses are the expression of conflicts between the ego and such of the sexual impulses as seem to the ego incompatible with its integrity or with its ethical standards. . . . Symptoms are in the nature of compromise-formations between the repressed sexual instincts and the repressive ego instincts. . . .*

Although some analysts may protest that this statement is out of date, modern deviators from Freud, such as Horney, Fromm, and Alexander, differ from him mainly in the direction of ascribing greater importance to unconscious conflicts related to the immediate situation of the patient. The core of the theory remains, and with it, quite naturally, a broad basis of agreement upon what needs to be done in therapy, this being a logical deduction from the theory. The psychoanalytic objective is to overcome a neurosis by making repressed impulses conscious, using various tactics to overcome the resistances that oppose this. Munroe (1955) has said that the crux of the therapeutic process not only for Freud, but also for Adler, Horney, Fromm, and Sullivan "may be stated as the development of insight," not mere intellectual insight, but "the actual *experiencing* of aspects of one's personality which have been made defensively unconscious." This whole matter has been discussed more fully in another context (Wolpe, 1961a).

We need to consider to what extent the therapeutic procedures based on psychoanalytic theory have been effective in bringing about recovery from neurosis. It must be said at once that the evidence available is remarkable for its paucity, considering that psychoanalysis has been practiced for sixty years. It is also remarkable that, as far as I have been able to discover, not a single individual psychoanalyst has ever published a statistical survey of his own practice. Is it unreasonable to ask if this may be at least partly because they have not been very happy with their results?

In respect to those results that have been published, we are constantly faced with the problem whether or not, in assessing a case as improved, criteria such as Knight's have been applied by the analyst. I have again and again seen cases claimed as successes of analytic psychotherapy that would certainly be rated failures on Knight's criteria. For example, a young woman's analysis by a Freudian analyst was terminated despite only slight diminution of severe interpersonal anxiety reactions on the grounds that she had graduated to "emotional maturity," and that her dreams had changed. In another case, a Sullivan-oriented therapist discharged as recovered a man with marked anxiety reactions to aggressive behavior of others, on the criterion that the patient "now fully accepts himself and his reactions," even though the anxiety reactions were as strong as ever. That at least some analysts should favorably evaluate such outcomes need not surprise us when we consider the criteria they themselves set for terminating a psychoanalysis. The criteria used by a number of analysts were given by Wilder in his famous paper, "Facts and Figures on Psychotherapy" (1945). The criteria most frequently stated by the analysts were "the patient's ability to accept freely his sexuality, freedom in social relations and freedom from disturbance in work." Other criteria were insight, acceptance of heterosexuality, solution of the internal conflict, receding of childhood transference, substantial working through of the Oedipus constellation, and freedom from symptoms. Wilder's comment is, "It is interesting to note that freedom from symptoms as a criterion plays a minor role."

It seems fair to conclude that, in at least some cases judged by psychoanalysts as recovered, Knight's criteria are not complied with, and there is not the relief from suffering that is our main interest here. However, this need not deflect us from the comparison we wish to make. We can be generous and suppose that, by and large, where recovery has been claimed, Knight's criteria *would have been* satisfied.

The older statistical studies were tabulated in 1941 by Knight. They comprise reports from the Berlin Psychoanalytic Institute, the Chicago Psychoanalytic Institute, the Menninger Clinic, the London Psychoanalytic Clinic, and a small group of cases reported by Kessel and Hyman. Out of a total of 534 cases listed as "psychoneuroses," 242 were either apparently cured or much improved. This is a success rate of 45 percent of the total number of patients, and 63.2 percent if patients who had less than six months of therapy are excluded (see Table 1, p. 367). Knight himself remarked that those thus excluded "represent an important group of failures."

For many years no further statistical data were published. However, a few years ago, the American Psychoanalytic Association appointed its now famous Fact-Gathering Committee to survey the results of psychoanalytic practice. The chairman of this committee, Dr. Harry I. Weinstock, subsequently stated at a lecture at the Maudsley Hospital, London, that his association made *no claims of therapeutic usefulness for psychoanalytic methods* (Eysenck, 1960). In March 1962, Dr. Morris W. Brody, of Temple University, revealed some details (Brody, 1962). (See also Masserman, 1963.) Of 595 patients who undertook analysis, 306 were regarded as having been "completely analyzed." Of the latter number, 210 were followed up after completing their analyses, and 126 of them, or 60 percent, were stated to have been cured or greatly improved. This percentage is not much more than would be expected of simple traditional therapy (Wilder, 1945), but when one looks more closely the picture is even less impressive. If the percentage of favorable results is viewed with reference to the total number of patients treated by the analysts (and not only those "completely analyzed"), the success rate is less (see Table 1). Alternatively, considering only the completely analyzed cases, it seems to be a controversion of the psychoanalytic theory of neurosis if 40 percent of the analyses that were rated complete did not effect marked improvement, let alone complete recovery. If that theory accorded with reality, would not "complete analysis" remove the whole basis of the patient's neurosis?

But even at the figure of 60 percent

apparently cured or much improved—even then, as Wilder noted, the results do not show any definite superiority over the results obtained in hospitals or clinics or by psychotherapists employing the various conventional methods. The fact that so much effort, more than 600 hours (Masserman, 1963) for each markedly improved case in the series, was needed to produce such undistinguished results raises the startling question whether psychoanalytic therapy introduces features into therapy that actually impede recovery!

THE CONDITIONING THERAPIES

Now let us consider the conditioning therapies. These methods stem from the conception that neuroses are persistent unadaptive habits that have been conditioned (that is, learned). If this conception is correct, the fundamental overcoming of a neurosis *can* consist of nothing but deconditioning—or undoing the relevant habit patterns.

The most characteristic and common feature of neurotic habits is anxiety. There is persuasive evidence, both experimental and clinical, that the great majority of neuroses are fundamentally conditioned autonomic responses (Wolpe, 1958). The individual has persistent habits of reacting with anxiety to situations that, objectively, are not dangerous. Typical stimuli to which the response of anxiety may be regarded as neurotic are the sight of a bird, the interior of an elevator, asking a favor, or receiving a compliment. Experimentally it is possible to condition an animal to respond with anxiety to any stimulus one pleases merely by arranging for that stimulus, on a number of occasions, to appear in an appropriate time relation to the evocation of anxiety; and by manipulating various factors one can obtain an emotional habit that is utterly refractory to extinction in the ordinary way (Wolpe, 1948, 1958). In human neuroses one can usually elicit a history of similar kinds of conditioning. Human neuroses, too, are characterized by the same remarkable resistance to extinction. Since neurotic reactions are, as a rule, autonomic reactions first and foremost,

this resistance is in keeping with Gantt's observations of the great refractoriness of cardiovascular conditioned responses to extinction.

It is implicit in conditioning theory that recovery from neurosis should be achieved by applying the learning process in a reverse direction: whatever undesirable behavior has been learned may be unlearned. In experiments performed about fourteen years ago I demonstrated in cats that had been made neurotic experimentally how this unlearning can be brought about (Wolpe, 1948, 1958). Anxiety reactions had been strongly conditioned to a small confining cage and to other stimuli, and could not be made to extinguish despite repeated exposure to the stimuli. The anxiety response habits could, however, be overcome in piecemeal fashion by counterposing feeding to weak anxiety responses. At first, stimuli distantly similar to the conditioned stimuli were used, until anxiety decreased to zero, and then, step by step, stimuli closer in resemblance to the original conditioned stimuli were introduced, until even the strongest eventually lost its power to evoke anxiety. These findings led to the framing of the reciprocal inhibition principle of psychotherapy, which is that *if a response inhibitory of anxiety can be made to occur in the presence of anxiety-evoking stimuli it will weaken the bond between these stimuli and the anxiety.*

Experience with human neuroses indicates that the principle has quite general validity; in addition to feeding, a good many other kinds of responses,[1] each of which, empirically, appears to inhibit anxiety, have been successfully used to weaken neurotic anxiety-response habits and related neurotic habits. The reciprocal inhibition principle also affords an explanation for the therapeutic effects of interviewing as such (which is seemingly the main basis of the successes of the traditional therapies) and for so-called spontaneous recoveries.

[1]Gellhorn and Loofbourrow (1963) present a number of modern instances of reciprocally inhibitory relationships between reactions in both the somatic and the autonomic nervous systems. (See also Gellhorn, 1961.)

I have described elsewhere (1958) the deliberate therapeutic use of a considerable range of anxiety-inhibiting responses. I shall briefly review those most widely employed—assertive, relaxation, and sexual responses.

Assertive responses are used where there is a need to overcome neurotic anxieties that arise irrationally in the course of interpersonal relationships—such anxieties as prevent a person from expressing his opinions to his friends lest they disagree, or from reprimanding inefficient underlings. The essence of the therapist's role is to encourage appropriate assertiveness, the outward expression, wherever it is reasonable and right to do so, of the feelings and action tendencies that anxiety has in the past inhibited. In other words, the therapist instigates "acting out." Each act of assertion to some extent reciprocally inhibits the anxiety, and in consequence somewhat weakens the anxiety response habit. The assertion required is not necessarily aggressive, and behavior in accordance with affectionate and other feelings may need to be instigated. The maneuvers involved are largely similar to those described by Salter (1949), though the rationale upon which he bases them is different.

Relaxation responses were first used on a scientific basis by Jacobson (1939), who demonstrated that they have autonomic accompaniments opposite to those of anxiety. His method of intensive training in relaxation for use in the life situation, though of great value, is rather cumbersome. More economical and clearly directed use of relaxation is made in the technique known as *systematic desensitization* (Wolpe, 1958, 1961b). Lang reports its use in the context of snake phobias, but its range of application is very wide indeed.[2] The therapist

has to identify the categories of stimuli to which the patient reacts with anxiety, and then rank the stimuli of each category in order of intensity of evoked anxiety. In the course of about six interviews the patient is given training in relaxation in parallel with this. When the preliminaries have been completed, the patient is made to relax as deeply as possible (in some cases under hypnosis), and then instructed to imagine the weakest of the anxiety-evoking stimuli for a few seconds. The instruction is repeated at short intervals, and if the response to the stimulus has been weak initially, it declines, on repetition, to zero. Under these circumstances, what apparently happens is that on each occasion the relaxation inhibits the anxiety, to some extent, and somewhat weakens the anxiety-evoking potential of the stimulus concerned. With repetition this potential is brought down to zero.

Recent studies have demonstrated:

—that the effects of desensitization are due to the procedure itself and not to suggestion or transference (Wolpe, 1962; Lang, pp. 47–48);
—that after one or two sessions it can be predicted with virtual certainly whether a patient will respond to this treatment or not; and
—that in phobias with independently measurable parameters, such as acrophobia, the numbers of therapeutic operations involved show consistent mathematical relationships to the stages of decrement of the phobia (Wolpe, 1963) that are suggestively similar to the psychophysical law proposed by Stevens (1962).

Sexual responses are used to inhibit anxiety responses conditioned to sexual situations. By manipulating the conditions of sexual approaches so that anxiety is never permitted to be strong, reciprocal inhibition of anxiety by sexual arousal is effected, and the anxiety response habit is progressively weakened. It is usually possible to overcome im-

---

[2]Some people are erroneously under the impression that this method is effective only for classical phobias. The word "phobia" refers to clearly defined stimulus sources of neurotic anxiety. The conditioning therapist differs from his colleagues in that he *seeks out the* precise stimuli to anxiety, and finds himself able to break down almost every neurosis into what are essentially *phobic systems*. Their subject matter extends far

beyond the classical phobias, and includes such contents as neurotic fears of incurring obligations, of being watched, or of receiving praise. (See Wolpe, 1964.)

potence or premature ejaculation in a few weeks. Sexual responses have generally only a secondary role in the treatment of frigidity (Lazarus, 1963b).

The question is, how effective are these and related techniques in procuring the recovery of neurotic patients in terms of Knight's criteria?

Using the whole range of available methods according to their indications, I have reported between 1952 and 1958 three series of results embracing 210 neurotic patients. Every patient in whom the reciprocal inhibition techniques had been given a fair trial was included in the series. Nearly 90 percent of these patients were rated on Knight's criteria as either apparently cured or much improved after an average of about 30 therapeutic interviews. The cases were unselected in the sense that no case diagnosed as neurotic was ever refused treatment. Psychotics and psychopaths were not accepted for treatment unless by error of diagnosis.

Until recently, there were no other studies involving considerable numbers of patients, although numerous accounts had been published describing the successful treatment of individuals or small groups. One noteworthy small group comprised 18 cases of phobias in children treated by Lazarus (1959). All the patients recovered in a mean of 9.5 sessions; follow-up from six months to two and a half years showed no relapses. Lazarus has recently analyzed his results with reciprocal inhibition therapies. His findings[3] have been summarized in a mimeographed paper as follows: In the course of about 4 years the *total* number of patients who consulted him was 408. Of these, 321 (or 78 percent) derived "definite and constructive benefit according to certain specified criteria which are unusually stringent." Hussain reports 95 percent of 105 patients whom he treated by a direct approach involving hypnosis apparently recovered or much improved. Recently, I received from the Hospital for Mental and Nervous Diseases at St. John's, Newfoundland, a report by Drs. Alastair Burnett and Ed-

mond Ryan of the treatment of 100 neurotic patients on learning theory principles. The usual treatment period was five weeks. The evaluation of outcome was on Knight's criteria. Substantial improvement occurred in almost every case (Burnett, 1962). Twenty-five of the patients were followed up over a year or more, and fifteen of these (60 percent) were then either apparently cured or much improved. Another 32 percent were rated "moderately improved." As the outcome of five weeks of therapy this is quite noteworthy. Burnett and Ryan express the view that these methods make effective psychotherapy available for the first time to "fairly large numbers of rural, unsophisticated patients who have limited formal education."

In Table 1, the results of the two largest and most characteristic behavior therapy series are compared with those of the two major psychoanalytic series discussed above.

A critical question is, of course, the durability of the results obtained by conditioning methods. The answer appears to be that they are practically always long-lasting. In 1958 I was able to report only one relapse among forty-five patients who had been followed up for periods ranging from two to seven years. Published communication from other conditioning therapists indicates that their experience is essentially the same. Furthermore, whenever resurgence of symptoms has occurred, and could be investigated, it has always been found to be related to specific events that could clearly have reconditioned the neurotic emotional habit. Learning theory predicts that *unless* there are intervening events that directly recondition neurotic reactions, recovery from neurosis that is radical in the sense defined earlier in this paper will be lasting, no matter by what maneuvers it has been obtained. There are facts that bear out this prediction. I elsewhere reported (Wolpe, 1961a) a survey of follow-up studies on neurotic patients who, with various therapies, other than psychoanalysis, had either recovered or improved markedly. Of 249 patients followed up from two to fifteen years only 4 had relapsed. This finding is not only in line with condi-

---

[3]These have since been published (Lazarus, 1963a). See Table 1.

TABLE 1. Comparative Results

Series	No. of Cases	Apparently Cured or Much Improved (Recoveries)	Percentage Recoveries
Psychoanalytic Therapy			
Collected series of psychoneuroses (Knight, 1941)			
a. Over 6 months' therapy	383		63.2
		242	
b. Total cases	534		45.3
Psychoanalytic Fact-gathering Committee (Brody, 1962)			
a. Completely analyzed cases	210	126	60
b. Total cases	595	(184)	(31)[a]
Behavior Therapy			
Wolpe (1958)	210	188	89.5[b]
Lazarus (1963)	408	321	78.0[b]

[a] This percentage is calculated from data of the Fact-Gathering Committee of the American Psychoanalytic Association, as follows. It is granted that the whole "completely analyzed" group of 306 would have shown the 60% recovery rate found in the 210 who were followed up, giving 184 recoveries for 306 patients. These would appear to be the sum total of patients claimed as apparently cured or much improved out of the whole group of 595, which includes 289 who discontinued analysis (Brody, 1962; Masserman, 1963).

[b] Lazarus included in his series **every** neurotic patient—even if he had seen him only once. Wolpe counted only those to whom the available techniques had actually been applied. When treatment was ineffective, this was generally established in 15–30 sessions.

tioning theory, but also directly contrary to the expectations of the psychoanalytic theory of neurosis.

CONCLUSIONS

The comparison I have presented is, of course, not based on data emanating from a controlled study on matched patients. Such a study, which should include an untreated group of patients similarly matched, is obviously desirable. Nevertheless, I submit that the evidence justifies now substituting behavior therapy for psychoanalysis in the training of therapists, and not temporizing until absolute proof has been provided. There are some who favor waiting for a study on matched groups of patients on the ground that the inferior results of psychoanalysis may be attributable to the psychoanalysts having to treat more difficult cases. There are several reasons for thinking this unlikely. In the first place, while conditioning therapists as a rule undertake treatment of all cases of neurosis, psychoanalysts are often very selective, and surely do not refuse those whom they believe they could *easily*

help. Second, conditioning therapists frequently overcome neuroses that have been unsuccessfully treated by psychoanalysis, and often for many years. Third, in private practice, the individual medical practitioner tends to send *all* his neurotic cases to a favored psychotherapist, whether analyst or not. Fourth, it is at least tangentially relevant that, as already noted, psychoanalysts often profess a disinterest in symptomatic recovery, claiming that they aim at something "deeper," such as radical personality change. It may, however, be noted parenthetically that the analysts often represent this alleged deep kind of change as being *prerequisite* to durable freedom from symptoms, a proposition that evidence I have quoted flatly contradicts.

The present position is clear. As far as the evidence goes, conditioning therapies appear to produce a higher proportion of lasting recoveries from the distress and disability of neurosis than does psychoanalysis. Even if a controlled study were to show an equal, or even higher, percentage of recovery for psychoanalysis, the time it requires would remain incomparably greater, and conditioning therapy would therefore still deserve preference. The possible public health implications are great. A psychotherapist who uses behavioristic techniques can handle over ten times as many patients per year as the therapist who employs psychoanalysis, and with greater hope of success for each patient. Effective treatment has thus become possible for many more victims of neurotic disturbance—and at much less expense than psychoanalysis requires.

REFERENCES

Brody, M. W. Prognosis and results of psychoanalysis. In J. H. Nodine and J. H. Moyer (Eds.), *Psychosomatic medicine.* Philadelphia: Lea & Febiger, 1962.

Burnett, A. Personal communication, 1962.

Burnett, A., & Ryan, E. *The outpatient treatment of neuroses by reciprocal inhibition methods.* In mimeograph, St. John's Hospital, Newfoundland, 1962.

Eysenck, H. J. *Behaviour therapy and the neuroses.* New York: Pergamon, 1960.

Freud, S. *Collected papers.* Vol. 5 London: Hogarth, 1950. (Encyclopedia article on psychoanalysis written in 1922).

Gellhorn, E. Prolegomena to a theory of emotions. *Perspec. Biol. Med.,* 1961, 4, 403–436.

Gellhorn, E., & Loofbourrow, G. N. *Emotions and emotional disorders.* New York: Harper, 1963.

Jacobson, E. *Progressive relaxation.* Chicago: U. Chicago Press, 1939.

Knight, R. P. Evaluation of the results of psychoanalytic therapy. *Amer. J. Psychiat.,* 1941, 98, 434–446.

Lazarus, A. A. The elimination of children's phobias by deconditioning. *Med. Proc.,* 1959, 5, 261–265.

Lazarus, A. A. The results of behavior therapy in 126 cases of severe neurosis. *Behav. Res. Ther.* 1963, 1, 69–80 (a).

Lazarus, A. A. The treatment of chronic frigidity by systematic desensitization. *J. nerv. ment. Dis.* 1963, 136, 272–278 (b).

Masserman, J. H. Ethology, comparative biodynamics, and psychoanalytic research. In J. Scher (Ed.), *Theories of the mind.* New York: Free Press, 1963.

Munroe, R. *Schools of psychoanalytic thought.* New York: Holt, Rinehart, and Winston, 1955.

Salter, A. *Conditioned reflex therapy.* New York: Farrar, Straus, 1949, and Capricorn Books, Putnam's Sons, 1961.

Stevens, S. S. The surprising simplicity of sensory metrics. *Amer. Psychol.,* 1962, 17, 29–39.

Wilder, J. Facts and figures on psychotherapy. *J. clin. Psychopath.,* 1945, 7, 311–347.

Wolpe, J. *An approach to the problem of neurosis based on the conditioned response.* M.D. thesis, University of the Witwatersrand, 1948.

Wolpe, J. *Psychotherapy by reciprocal inhibition.* Stanford: Stanford U. Press, 1958.

Wolpe, J. The prognosis in unpsychoanalyzed recovery from neurosis. *Amer. J. Psychiat.,* 1961, 117, 35–39 (a).

Wolpe, J. The systematic desensitization treatment of neuroses. *J. nerv. ment. Dis.,* 1961, 132, 189–203 (b).

Wolpe, J. Isolation of a conditioning procedure as the crucial psychotherapeutic factor. *J. nerv. ment. Dis.,* 1962, 134, 316–329.

Wolpe, J. Quantitative relations in the systematic desensitization treatment of phobias. *Amer. J. Psychiat.,* 1963, 119, 1062–1068.

Wolpe, P. Behavior therapy in complex neurotic states. *Brit. J. Psychiat.,* 1964, 110, 28–34.

47.
a new treatment of constipation by conditioning: a preliminary report

c. quarti and j. renaud

translated and adapted
by moneim a. el-meligi

INTRODUCTION

Today, constipation is one of the most widespread functional disorders. Its varied causes include irregularity of alimentary habits, functional disorders of the gall-bladder or—more often—the psychosomatic correlates of certain modes of contemporary living, as in the case of city dwellers who lead lives which are physically sedentary yet subject to continual stress. Whatever its cause, constipation is basically a disorder of intestinal motility, presenting in a variety of forms: spastic, paretic, or as an irregularity in the alternation of the phases of contraction and relaxation in the intestinal muscle.

The consequences of constipation are

Reprinted from Cyril M. Franks (Ed.), *Conditioning Techniques in Clinical Practice and Research*, New York: Springer, 1964, pp. 219–227.

It is a pleasure to acknowledge the many clarifications of the medical aspects of this paper provided by my colleagues at the New Jersey Neuro-Psychiatric Institute, Drs. McMillan, de Bernard and Kanther. Dr. Habiba Wassef was particularly helpful in the translation of the paper with respect to medical terminology. My gratitude goes to Dr. Franks for drawing my attention to the potential importance of this paper and for his editing of the final manuscript. We are grateful to the authors of the article and the editor of La Clinique (Paris) for permission to translate and reproduce this paper. The original reference is as follows "Note préliminaire sur un nouveau traitement des constipations par réflexe conditionnel" La Clinique (Paris), 57, 1962, 577–583.

as different as their causes and all are to be deplored. The "maladie des laxatifs" may be considered as the least serious. It occurs following a long period, during which the patient exhausts the pharmacopoeia, passing from one group of laxatives to another. As laxatives are substituted and doses are increased, the process of elimination becomes progressively artificial, deviating more and more from the normal physiologic pattern, due to exhaustion of the liver cells, irritation of the gall bladder or interference with the reflex system of intestinal motility.

Treatment of constipation therefore calls for a therapy aimed at the cause rather than the symptom. It should make use of the natural resources of the organism, avoiding the use of any medication which, because of the complexity of the mechanism of defecation in its temporal sequence, may exert an untimely pharmacological action. The goal of treatment should be to restore the normal physiological functioning of the mechanism of defecation, not by artificially stimulating defecation, but by re-educating the intestinal motility and helping it regain its own harmony.

PHYSIOLOGICAL BASIS OF DEFECATION

To facilitate the presentation of the techniques to be utilized in our method of re-education, a brief physiological account seems to be in order.

Movements of the alimentary canal, responsible for the transfer of the contents from the esophagus through the stomach, small intestines, and finally to the anus, are under the co-ordinated control of the nervous system. The prerequisites for a normal passage are:

(a) Adequate food intake, both quantitatively and qualitatively. This food intake is, in itself, an important stimulant for intestinal motility. The rate of passage also depends on the state of fluidity and viscosity of the intestinal contents, which in turn depend on the type of foods consumed (bringing us to the psychological implications of alimentary habits), the intestinal juices and bile (the flow of the latter being under the reflex control of the nervous system).

(b) Well co-ordinated intestinal movements. Three types of intestinal movements are responsible for the progression of the intestinal contents, namely: segmentary, pendular and peristaltic. The first two are attributed to intrinsic nervous reflexes and are modified by extrinsic sympathetic and vagal activity. Peristalsis is produced by extrinsic nervous impulses; it is a mass reflex response that may encompass the entire length of the intestines, and is dependent upon the co-ordinated action of certain medullary centers and abdomino-pelvic autonomic pathways.

The average time for the passage of chyme from the stomach to the anus is about 24 hours. Serious irritation of the gastric mucosa produces a "mass reflex" represented by an active peristaltic wave which reduces the duration to a few minutes. The stimulus for this reflex is the entry of food into the stomach, which explains the healthy habit of having the first bowel movement in the morning after breakfast, thereby evacuating the digestive products of the previous day.

(c) The act of defecation begins with the passage of feces across the pelvirectal flexure where local sphincter-like thickening of the circular muscle fibres exists. The sphincter presumably relaxes and feces enter the rectum, whose lumen immediately reacts by slight constriction or dilatation, depending on the size of the fecal mass, so as to produce an active resistance which will now be the stimulus for the final expulsive movements. Distention of the rectum by sudden entry of feces gives rise to a perineal

sensation, often agreeable, and a conscious desire to defecate. If this desire is acceded to, a co-ordinated reflex is set up, emptying every part of the bowel from the middle of the transverse colon to the anus; the diaphragm descends, the glottis is closed, the abdominal muscles and levator ani contract, waves of peristalsis pass over the distal part of the colon, the sphincter ani are relaxed and the feces are evacuated through the narrow anal canal. The reflex centers for defecation are situated in the medulla and in the spinal cord corresponding to the sacral segments 2, 3, and 4.

NEUROPHYSIOLOGICAL CHANGES IN CONSTIPATION

The rectum initially presents the physiological phenomenon of adaptation, which is also the ultimate end of all physio-pathological changes in constipation. It ceases to respond to the presence of the fecal mass in its lumen, either due to paretic relaxation of the rectal wall instead of maintaining an active resistance to the pressure exerted by the feces, or to failure of the pressure and stretch receptors to respond to their specific stimulus. On the other hand, the phenomenon of adaptation may take place normally in instances of refrain from defecation, when circumstances are unfavorable at the moment the desire is experienced. In this way, certain modes of existence, serving only to increase these unfavorable conditions, become a common cause of constipation. The resulting rectal stasis sets up the colo-colic reflex producing reflex inhibition of intestinal motility and peristalsis. The vicious circle, characteristic of chronic constipation, is thereby established.

RESTORATION OF NORMAL PHYSIOLOGICAL RHYTHM TO THE INTESTINAL PASSAGE

The physiological rhythm of the bowel motions should first be obtained, at which point the vicious circle will be interrupted. Laxatives may succeed in overcoming rectal inertia, once in a while, by strong stimulation reaching above the threshold of its wall receptors.

The afferent component of the defecation reflex is associated with a special conscious sensation, "the desire to defecate." This characteristic indicates the exact moment at which the reflex commences, and aids in the physiologic timing of any therapeutic procedure.

According to the laws of conditioning of the nervous system, it is possible to establish almost any reflex at will, including that of defecation. Conditioning consists of subordinating acts and signals. In other words, if a neutral stimulus or signal is repeatedly applied a few seconds before the basic unconditioned stimulus which elicits a precise organic reaction, the initially neutral stimulus will finally replace the unconditioned stimulus and will of itself elicit the reaction. The reaction becomes conditioned to the neutral stimulus which will therefore be called a conditioned stimulus. Almost any stimulus, suitably employed, may become a conditioned stimulus, viz. internal or external afferent impulses, the conscious or physiological notion of time or even the disappearance of a stimulus.

Conditioned reflexes may be simple or chain-like, with overlapping of one reflex with the other, since the acquired conditional quality may be transferred from one stimulus to the next, giving rise to conditioning of the 1st, 2nd, 3rd order and so forth. This process is known by Soviet scientists as summation.

The conditioned reflex depends for its appearance on the formation of new functional connections in the central nervous system in accordance with precise laws, of which the following are of interest to us:

(a) For a conditioned stimulus to retain its new properties, it should be reinforced periodically by following it with the basic unconditioned stimulus.

(b) A conditioned stimulus repeated without reinforcement will, after a variable interval of time, lead to weakening and, finally, extinction of the conditioned reflex. However, extinction is never complete because the pathway will always remain.

(c) Under similar experimental conditions, visceral conditioned responses develop more rapidly and are more lasting than responses conditioned within other systems. This phenomenon is attributed to the functional differences existing between the corresponding visceral or cortical sensory areas of the brain. Recording the action potentials evoked by sensory stimulation of both areas shows that, in the former, the potential persists much longer even after cessation of the stimulation.

(d) Though all sensory stimuli reach the cerebral cortex few are retained, the rest are ignored. It can therefore be assumed that, in the same manner, selection is made from different stimuli sharing the same sensory field. This capacity to make a selection is a function of the affect, and the process which leads to it is called motivation. The totality of motivations ranges in intensity from the very instinctive act to the highest intellectual activity. Instinctive behavior is produced by an essential "primitive" affective stimulus; and the more behavior becomes emotionally free, i.e., intellectualized, the less pronounced becomes the participation of the affective quality. Nevertheless, all mental acts comprise an affective component; the more marked this component is, viz. motivation, the more rapid and lasting the conditioning will be. In other words, the more emotionally charged is the material to be learned, the more the learning process is effective.

The neurophysiological basis for the above is as follows.

It is known that the same association areas and fibres in the frontal lobes permit the transmission and spread of the emotional charge to the corresponding areas in the brain with which they are functionally synergistic. Therefore, the frontal lobes produce a certain "quantum" of energy comprising an intellectual and an affective component, the ratio of which will depend on the functional associations engaged at the moment of production of this energy.

There exist two pathways for the reflexion of the cortico-subcortical afferents. The first is essentially cortico-thalamic; a given sensory stimulation takes place through intra-cortical associations, produced by the impulses received through the diffuse thalamic system. This implies very little, if any, of a vegetative, affective or "primitive" type of response.

The second is more complex; in addition to the preceding pattern we have the regions that play a paramount role in the emotional life, namely, the limbic system. This system, apart from the functional characteristics mentioned above, is closely related to the hypothalamus and, through it, to the neurovegetative expressions of affectivity, its primitive or instinctive aspects. This implies also the participation of the reticular alerting system which brings about the massive intervention of *cortical activity*. When stimulated, the activating effect of both the hypothalamus and the reticular formation is so great that the reappearance of the extinguished conditioned reflexes could be brought about without further reinforcement and sometimes could even be sustained several months.

(e) Finally, there is the role played by electric stimulation in methods of training. According to certain authors, the most minor electric shock serves as a necessary reinforcement for obtaining rapid and durable associations. The mechanism by which this phenomenon is produced is yet unknown. It may be due either to the emotional charge contained in the defense reflex provoked by the shock, or to an inherent power in the electricity itself. The only evidence available in this respect is from the experiments of Vinogradova and Sokolov who demonstrated that the response evoked by a new stimulus differs from that produced by the same stimulus associated with an electric shock.

RE-EDUCATION OF THE MECHANISM OF DEFECATION USING THE LAWS OF CONDITIONING

Because of an awareness of the act of defecation, the subject is conscious of the moment at which the defecation reflex is set up. The stimulus that elicits this reflex is the passage of the fecal mass through the pelvi-rectal flexure or, in the case of chronically constipated subjects, the stimulation of the wall of the rectum. We are going to designate this stimulation the absolute or unconditioned stimulus and we will associate with it a signal or conditioned stimulus.

Since defecation is accompanied by a mass reflex in the colon, associating the conditioned stimulus with the sensation of defecation will also mean associating the colic reflex with the conditioned stimulus. Repetition of the conditioned stimulus in association with the unconditioned stimulus would make it possible, after a certain period of time, for the former alone to elicit not only the defecation mechanism but also the accompanying reflex colonic contractions.

The conditioned stimulus should have a slight affective quality and, if possible, be of a pleasant nature lest sympathetic reactions interfere with the elicited processes. It is also thought useful to utilize electrical means of stimulation because of the empirical importance of this modality in conditioning.

The apparatus used (Figure 1) is transsistorized and generates a current modifiable so as to provoke a sensation which is almost pleasant. The subject is stimulated by two electrodes which are applied on each side of the lumbar spine and secured on the abdomen by a strap (Figure 2). The apparatus is visible to the subject and has a switch which permits him to change the intensity of stimulation at will. In practice, individual differences in sensitivity and resistance of the skin are very wide.

The subject to be re-educated continues to take his usual laxatives so as to produce one bowel movement per day. As he goes to the toilet he puts on the apparatus, starts operating it prior to defecation and stops the electric stimulation as soon as his evacuation is terminated. Should the desire continue, and should evacuation reoccur while still on the toilet, stimulation should be resumed each time. Since the characteristics of the stimulation maintain an affective state that we may call "pre-emotional awakening," it is very important that the subject thinks of the association taking place within him. An association is thus facilitated between the conditioned stimulus and the evacuation reflex.

Gradually the subject should reduce the quantity of laxatives until eventually he will no longer take any and will go to the toilet even without having the desire to defecate. Once conditioning has been established, which generally happens after 20 to 30 applications, the electrical stimulation alone produces defecation accord-

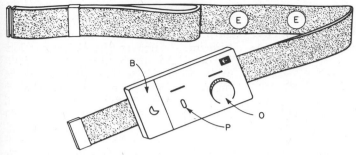

Figure 1. Apparatus used in the conditioned stimulus. E, Electrodes; O, On-off switch and intensity control; P, Pilot; B, Battery compartment.

ing to the individual rhythm of digestion.

The second step is for the subject to utilize the principle of vertical synthesis, going to the toilet every day at a given hour (preferably after breakfast in order to benefit from the morning gastro-colic response). Thus, one gets conditioning of the second order, the chosen hour becomes the conditioned stimulus and finally the patient can dispense with the apparatus altogether.

It is advisable in periods of nervous or physical stress to reinforce the reflex by resuming the use of the apparatus for a few days. In principle, a normally developed subject can practice his own re-education without special guidance; in practice it is preferable that the overall management be the responsibility of the treating physician. The physician is best able to assess progress, supervise the tapering off of laxatives and determine the moment when re-education has been accomplished.

The following are three illustrative case reports:

Case 1

An unconstipated subject used as a control. The object of this experiment is to demonstrate the instigation of defecation by electric stimulation in a healthy woman of 38 years. Her intestinal passage was normal apart from ordinary irregularities and transitory periods of constipation which had never necessitated the use of laxatives. During the first ten applications daily evacuations took place at all times, though never in the morning. On the morning of the eleventh day, as the subject was manipulating the apparatus to prepare the electrodes, she was

suddenly seized by quite intense tenesmus and straining. The feeling was not distinct enough to lead her to the toilet, but a feeling of heaviness and of intestinal movements persisted until her attention was diverted by another activity.

From the 20th day the subject decided to try one application without having any desire to defecate, in the morning and on an empty stomach. The preliminary operations (preparation of the saline solution to moisten the electrodes, fixing the belt, and so forth) were sufficient to trigger a pressing need, followed by normal defecation. After twelve days the subject had conditioned herself to evacuate at a fixed hour. A few days later, the process of vertical synthesis having been extended, seeing the apparatus, or even hearing or pronouncing its name, would be sufficient to elicit the sensation of the need to defecate. Naturally, her voluntary inhibition could control these phe-

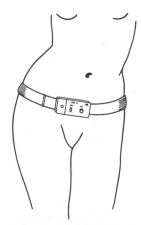

Figure 2. Position of the apparatus in use.

nomena, which we point out here only for their physiological importance. It should be noted that the technique was also effective during her periods of transitory constipation.

Case 2

M.M., a young woman of 34 years, suffering from dysmenorrhea and migraine, of a nervous temperament but otherwise quite balanced. Occasional periods of constipation appeared to be principally related to her mode of living, her menstrual cycle and her emotional state. She did not go spontaneously to the toilet except when her daily life imposed on her a physical and nervous hyperactivity. This occurred at a regular rate of three to four times per week.

During this period of conditioning she could, thanks to nightly laxatives, evacuate, on the average, of once every two days. After a week, a sort of "reverse" conditioning took place, the apparatus becoming indispensable to her. On the one hand, in spite of her absent-mindedness, she would never leave it at home when she went out all day; on the other hand, should she feel the need to go to the toilet under circumstances that made it impossible to use the apparatus, this circumstance would immediately cut off the need.

After 21 days, either seeing the instrument or just talking about it would make her feel some intestinal movements, but without distinctive need. On the 26th day, following a bulky movement on the previous day, we advised her to try the method without feeling the need to defecate. She had some mild abdominal pains, passed a great deal of flatus and experienced a sensation of "evacuation" but no bowel movement.

The following day a very positive result ensued without any desire to defecate. She described the event as follows: . . . "after about thirty seconds of electric stimulation, without any effort on my behalf, and without preliminary sensations of any sort, defecation happened precipitously." Since then positive results were obtained each day.

Case 3

M.R., a woman of 36 years, suffering

since she was 30 from hepatic insufficiency which severely restricted her diet and intake of laxatives and certain other medicines. Moreover, she had megacolon. She managed to go to the toilet about twice per week through the effects of mucilages. Being a simple-minded woman, she could not relate to us precise physical or psychic phenomena other than the fact that, after only eight days, she had already cut down by half the dose of laxatives necessary for a normal evacuation. To avoid irregularity in the progress of the treatment we waited 30 days before encouraging her to go to the toilet and administer the stimulation without a desire to defecate. She had had her mucilage the previous evening. The result was very positive.

Later, among the trials with or without laxative, some failed and some succeeded. The ultimate result of all these more or less successful trials was that the patient was able to go regularly to the toilet three or four times per week, without laxatives but always with the apparatus. For reasons which could not be readily ascertained it was not possible to establish second order conditioning in her case.

CONCLUSION

We have thus demonstrated that the principles of conditioning may be practically applied in the treatment of constipation. Bowel evacuation represents but one among the many activities of the human organism which can be conditioned. In man, such conditioning is easily brought about without a complicated apparatus. The present method is of significance for several reasons: it is convenient, easy and simple; the principle of "visceral re-education" may be extended to a wide variety of other diseases of a largely functional nature; it helps us to understand some of the mechanisms which govern our physiological existence. Finally, it is suggested that the general approach represents a most important medical attitude: confidence in the mechanisms of re-adaptation and in the fundamental tendency to revert to normal functioning that is inherent in every living organism.

48.
application of operant conditioning to reinstate verbal behavior in psychotics

wayne isaacs, james thomas, and israel goldiamond

In operant conditioning, behavior is controlled by explicitly arranging the consequences of the response, the explicit consequence being termed reinforcement. For example, a lever-press by a rat activates a mechanism which releases food. If the rat has been deprived of food, lever-pressing responses will increase in frequency. If this relationship between food and response holds only when a light is on, the organism may discriminate between light on and light off, that is, there will be no lever-pressing responses when the light is turned off, but turning it on will occasion such responses. From this simple case, extensions can be made to more complicated cases which may involve control of schedules of reinforcement. These procedures have recently been extended to the study of psychopharmacology (5), controlled production of stomach ulcers (4), obtaining psychophysical curves from pigeons (3),

Reprinted by permission from *Journal of Speech and Hearing Disorders*, 1960, 25, (1), 8–12.
This report stems from projects connected with a weekly seminar on operant conditioning conducted at the hospital by the third author. Responsibility for the authorship and the *post hoc* analysis is the third author's; the first two authors are responsible for application of experimentally based procedures to shape the verbal behaviors of the patients.

The authors wish to express their appreciation to Dr. Leonard Horecker, Clinical Director of Anna State Hospital, and to Dr. Robert C. Steck, Hospital Superintendent, for their encouragement and facilitation of the project. This investigation was supported in part by a grant from the Psychiatric Training and Research Fund of the Illinois Department of Public Welfare.

conditioning cooperative behavior in children (2), programming machines which teach academic subjects (11), analyzing the effects of noise on human behavior (1), and decreasing stuttering (7), to mention a few examples.

The following account is a preliminary report of the use of operant conditioning to reinstate verbal behavior in two hospitalized mute psychotics. Patient A, classified as a catatonic schizophrenic, 40, became completely mute almost immediately upon commitment 19 years ago. He was recorded as withdrawn and exhibiting little psychomotor activity. Patient B, classified as schizophrenic, mixed type, with catatonic features predominating, was 43, and was committed after a psychotic break in 1942, when he was combative. He completely stopped verbalizing 14 years ago. Each S was handled by a different E (experimenter). The E's were ignorant of each other's activities until pressed to report their cases. This study covers the period prior to such report.

CASE HISTORIES

Patient A

The S was brought to a group therapy session with other chronic schizophrenics (who were verbal), but he sat in the position in which he was placed and continued the withdrawal behaviors which characterized him. He remained impassive and stared ahead even when cigarettes, which other members accepted, were offered to him and were waved before his face. At one session, when E removed cigarettes from his pocket, a package of chewing gum accidentally fell out. The S's eyes moved toward the gum and then returned to their usual position.

This response was chosen by E as one with which he would start to work, using the method of successive approximation (9). (This method finds use where E desires to produce responses which are not present in the current repertoire of the organism and which are considerably removed from those which are available. The E then attempts to 'shape' the available behaviors into the desired form, capitalizing upon both the variability and regularity of successive behaviors. The shaping process involves the reinforcement of those parts of a selected response which are successively in the desired direction and the nonreinforcement of those which are not. For example, a pigeon may be initially reinforced when it moves its head. When this movement occurs regularly, only an upward movement may be reinforced, with downward movement not reinforced. The pigeon may now stretch its neck, with this movement reinforced. Eventually the pigeon may be trained to peck at a disc which was initially high above its head and at which it would normally never peck. In the case of the psychotic under discussion, the succession was eye movement, which brought into play occasional facial movements, including those of the mouth, lip movements, vocalizations, word utterance, and finally, verbal behavior.)

The S met individually with E three times a week. Group sessions also continued. The following sequence of procedures was introduced in the private sessions. Although the weeks are numbered consecutively, they did not follow at regular intervals since other duties kept E from seeing S every week.

Weeks 1, 2. A stick of gum was held before S's face, and E waited until S's eyes moved toward it. When this response occurred, E as a consequence gave him the gum. By the end of the second week, response probability in the presence of the gum was increased to such an extent that S's eyes moved toward the gum as soon as it was held up.

Weeks 3, 4. The E now held the gum before S, waiting until he noticed movement in S's lips before giving it to him. Toward the end of the first session of the third week, a lip movement spontaneously occurred, which E promptly re-inforced. By the end of this week, both lip movement and eye movement occurred when the gum was held up. The E then withheld giving S the gum until S spontaneously made a vocalization, at which time E gave S the gum. By the end of this week, holding up the gum readily occasioned eye movement toward it, lip movement, and a vocalization resembling a croak.

Weeks 5, 6. The E held up the gum, and said, 'Say gum, gum,' repeating these words each time S vocalized. Giving S the gum was made contingent upon vocalizations increasingly approximating gum. At the sixth session (at the end of Week 6), when E said, 'Say gum, gum,' S suddenly said, 'Gum, please.' This response was accompanied by reinstatement of other responses of this class, that is, S answered questions regarding his name and age.

Thereafter, he responded to questions by E both in individual sessions and in group sessions, but answered no one else. Responses to the discriminative stimuli of the room generalized to E on the ward; he greeted E on two occasions in the group room. He read from signs in E's office upon request by E.

Since the response now seemed to be under the strong stimulus control of E, the person, attempt was made to generalize the stimulus to other people. Accordingly, a nurse was brought into the private room; S smiled at her. After a month, he began answering her questions. Later, when he brought his coat to a volunteer worker on the ward, she interpreted the gesture as a desire to go outdoors and conducted him there. Upon informing E of the incident, she was instructed to obey S only as a consequence of explicit verbal requests by him. The S thereafter vocalized requests. These instructions have now been given to other hospital personnel, and S regularly initiates verbal requests when nonverbal requests have no reinforcing consequences. Upon being taken to the commissary, he said, 'Ping pong,' to the volunteer worker and played a game with her. Other patients, visitors, and members of hospital-society-at-large continue, however, to interpret nonverbal requests and to reinforce them by obeying S.

Patient B

This patient, with a combative history prior to mutism, habitually lay on a bench in the day room in the same position, rising only for meals and for bed. Weekly visits were begun by E and an attendant. During these visits, E urged S to attend group therapy sessions which were being held elsewhere in the hospital. The E offered S chewing gum. This was not accepted during the first two visits, but was accepted on the third visit and thereafter. On the sixth visit, E made receipt of the gum contingent upon S's going to the group room and so informed S. The S then altered his posture to look at E and accompanied him to the group room, where he seated himself in a chair and was given the gum. Thereafter, he came to this room when the attendants called for him.

Group Sessions 1–4. Gum reinforcement was provided for coming to the first two weekly sessions, but starting with the third, it was made contingent upon S's participation in the announced group activity. The group (whose other members were verbal) was arranged in a semicircle. The E announced that each S would, when his turn came, give the name of an animal. The E immediately provided gum to each S who did so. The S did not respond and skipped his turn three times around. The same response occurred during the fourth session.

Group Session 5. The activity announced was drawing a person; E provided paper and colored chalk and visited each S in turn to examine the paper. The S had drawn a stick figure and was reinforced with gum. Two of the other patients, spontaneously and without prior prompting by E, asked to see the drawing and complimented S. Attendants reported that on the following day, S, when introduced to two ward visitors, smiled and said, 'I'm glad to see you.' The incident was followed by no particular explicit consequences.

Group Session 6. The announced activity was to give the name of a city or town in Illinois. The S, in his turn, said, 'Chicago.' He was reinforced by E, who gave him chewing gum, and again two members of the group congratulated him

for responding. Thereafter, he responded whenever his turn came.

After the tenth session in the group, gum reinforcement was discontinued. The S has continued to respond vocally in the situations in which he was reinforced by E but not in others. He never initiates conversations, but he will answer various direct questions in the *group sessions*. He will not, however, respond vocally to questions asked *on the ward*, even when put by E.

DISCUSSION

Both S's came from special therapy wards of patients selected because of depressed verbal behavior and long stay in the hospital; tranquilizing drugs were not used. The extent to which reinstatement of verbal behavior was related to the special treatment offered the patients in the special wards set up for them cannot readily be assayed. Among the special treatments accorded them were group therapy sessions. Nevertheless, the similarities between the pattern of reacquisition of verbal behavior by the patients and the patterns of learning encountered in laboratory studies suggest that the conditioning procedures themselves were involved in the reinstatement of verbal behavior.

In the case of Patient A, the speaking response itself was gradually shaped. The anatomical relation between the muscles of chewing and speaking probably had some part in E's effectiveness. When a word was finally produced, the response was reinstated along with other response members of its class, which had not been reinforced. The economy of this process is apparent, since it eliminates the necessity of getting S to produce *every* desired response in order to increase his repertoire. In this case, E concentrated on one verbal response, and in reinstating it, reinstated verbal responses in general. On the stimulus side, when the response came under the stimulus control of E, the stimulus could be generalized to other members of E's class of discriminative *stimuli*, namely, people. This may have relevance for the clinical inference of the importance for future interpersonal relations of prior identification with some person. In the case of Patient B, the stimulus control involved a *given setting*, the rooms where he had been reinforced. The discrimination of E in one case, and not in the other, may be explained in terms of the establishment of operant discrimination, which also involves extinction (9). Operant discrimination is established when a response in the presence of S^D, a discriminative stimulus, is reinforced, and a response in the presence of S^Δ, a stimulus other than S^D, is not. After some time, the response will occur when S^D is presented, but not when S^Δ is presented; the response discriminates S^D from S^Δ, it having been extinguished when S^Δ was presented. In the case of Patient A, E was with S on the ward, in the group room, and privately. Reinforcement occurred in all occasions. But S was on the ward (and other rooms) without E, and therefore without reinforcement for those responses which were occasioned by the ward and which only E reinforced. Hence, these responses would extinguish in the ward alone, but would continue in the presence of E, defining discrimination of E from other stimuli. In the case of Patient B, this process may have been delayed by the fact that E and the other patients reinforced only in a specific room. It will be recalled that attendants rather than E brought S to the group room.

Interestingly, in the group sessions, when Patient B emitted the responses which E reinforced, other psychotic patients also reinforced Patient B. They were thereby responding, on the occasion of S's responses (discriminative stimuli for them), in the same way that E did. The term *identification*, used as a label here, shares some behavioral referents with the term as used in the preceding paragraph and might be explained behaviorally in terms of the *generalized reinforcer* (10). These behaviors by the patients are similar to behaviors reported in client-centered group sessions, where clients increase in reflective behaviors as counseling progresses, and in psychoanalytic group sessions, where patients increasingly make analytic interpretations of each other. Here, the patients are also behaving like the therapist. While this parallel lends itself to the facetious

thought that operant group sessions may produce operant conditioners, it does suggest that psychotics are behaving, with regard to responses by the major source of reinforcement in the group, according to the same laws which govern such group behaviors of nonhospitalized Ss.

The various diagnostic labels applied to psychotics are based to a considerable extent upon differences between responses considered abnormal, for example, hallucinations, delusions of persecution, and the like. The therapeutic process is accordingly at times seen in terms of eliminating the abnormal behaviors or states. Experimental laboratory work indicates that it is often extremely difficult to *eliminate* behavior; extinction is extremely difficult where the schedule of reinforcement has been a variable interval schedule (6), that is, reinforcement has been irregular, as it is in most of our behaviors. Such behaviors persist for considerable periods without reinforcement. Experimental laboratory work has provided us quite readily with procedures to *increase* responses. In the case of psychotics, this would suggest focusing attention on whatever *normal* behaviors S has; an appropriate operant, no matter how small or insignificant, even if it is confined to an eye movement, may possibly be raised to greater probability, and shaped to normal behavior (8). Stated otherwise, abnormal behaviors and normal behaviors can be viewed as reciprocally related, and psychotics as exhibiting considerable abnormal behavior, or little normal behavior. Normal behavior probability can be increased by decreasing probability of abnormal behaviors, or abnormal behaviors can be decreased by the controlled increase of normal behaviors. This preliminary report suggests that a plan of attack based upon the latter approach may be worth further investigation.

SUMMARY

Verbal behavior was reinstated in two psychotics, classified as schizophrenics, who had been mute for 19 and 14 years. The procedures utilized involved application of operant conditioning. The relationship of such procedures, based on controlled laboratory investigations with men and animals, to procedures based on clinical practice with human patients was discussed and was considered as

directing our attention to shaping and increasing the probability of what normal behaviors the psychotic possesses.

REFERENCES

1. Azrin, N. H., Some effects of noise on human behavior. *J. exp. Anal. Behavior,* 1958, *1,* 183–200.

2. Azrin, N. H., and Lindsley, O. R., The reinforcement of cooperation between children. *J. abnorm. (soc.) Psychol.,* 52, 1956, 100–102.

3. Blough, D. S., A method for obtaining psychophysical thresholds from the pigeon. *J. exp. Anal. Behavior,* 1958, *1,* 31–44.

4. Brady, J. V., Ulcers in 'executive' monkeys. *Sci. Amer.,* 1958, *199*(4), 95–100.

5. Dews, P. B., The effects of chlorpromazine and promazine on performance on a mixed schedule of reinforcement. *J. exp. Anal. Behavior,* 1958, *1,* 73–82.

6. Ferster, C. B., and Skinner, B. F., *Schedules of Reinforcement.* New York: Appleton-Century-Crofts, 1957.

7. Flanagan, B., Goldiamond, I., and Azrin, N. H., Operant stuttering: the control of stuttering behavior through response-contingent consequences. *J. exp. Anal. Behavior,* 1958, *1,* 173–178.

8. Goldiamond, I., Research which can be done in a mental hospital. Address delivered to Illinois State Mental Hospitals Conference, Giant City State Park, Ilinois, 1958.

9. Keller, F., and Schoenfeld, W., *Principles of Psychology.* New York: Appleton-Century-Crofts, 1950.

10. Skinner, B. F., *Science and Human Behavior.* New York: Macmillan, 1953.

11. Skinner, B. F., Teaching machines, *Science,* 1958, *128,* 969–977.

49.
what is a neurosis?

john dollard
and neal e. miller

Most people, even scientists, are vague about neurosis. Neither the neurotic victim nor those who know him seem able to state precisely what is involved. The victim feels a mysterious malady. The witness observes inexplicable behavior. The neurotic is mysterious because he is *capable* of acting and yet he is *unable* to act and enjoy. Though physically capable of attaining sex rewards, he is anesthetic; though capable of aggression, he is meek; though capable of affection, he is cold and unresponsive. As seen by the outside witness, the neurotic does not make use of the obvious opportunities for satisfaction which life offers him.

TO BE EXPLAINED:
MISERY, STUPIDITY, SYMPTOMS

The therapist confronts a person who is miserable, stupid (in some ways) and who has symptoms. These are the three major factors to be accounted for. Why is he miserable, in what curious way is he stupid, and whence arise the symptoms? The waiting room of every psychiatric clinic is crowded with patients showing these common signs.

Neurotic Misery Is Real

Neurotic misery is real—not imaginary. Observers, not understanding the neurotic conflict, often belittle the suffering of neurotics and confuse neurosis with malingering. Neurotic habits are forced upon an individual by peculiar conditions of life and are not cheap attempts to escape duty and responsibility. In most

Reprinted by permission from John Dollard and Neal E. Miller, *Personality and Psychotherapy*, New York, pp. 12–22. Copyright 1950 by McGraw-Hill Inc. Used by permission of McGraw-Hill Book Company.

cases the misery is attested by many specific complaints. These complaints or symptoms differ with each category of neurosis but sleeplessness, restlessness, irritability, sexual inhibitions, distaste for life, lack of clear personal goals, phobias, headaches, and irrational fears are among the more common ones.

At times the depth of the misery of the neurotic is concealed by his symptoms. Only when they are withdrawn does his true anguish appear. Occasionally the misery will be private, not easily visible to outside observers because friends and relatives are ringed around the neurotic person and prevent observation of his pain. In still other cases, the neurotic person is miserable but apathetic. He has lost even the hope that complaining and attracting attention will be helpful. However this may be, *if the neurotic takes the usual risks of life* he is miserable. He suffers if he attempts to love, marry, and be a parent. He fails if he tries to work responsibly and independently. His social relations tend to be invaded by peculiar demands and conditions. Neurotic misery is thus often masked by the protective conditions of life (as in childhood) and appears only when the individual has to "go it on his own."

Conflict Produces Misery. Suffering so intense as that shown by neurotics must have powerful causes, and it does. The neurotic is miserable because he is in conflict. As a usual thing two or more strong drives are operating in him and producing incompatible responses. Strongly driven to approach and as strongly to flee, he is not able to act to reduce either of the conflicting drives. These drives therefore remain dammed up, active, and nagging.

Where such a drive conflict is conscious there is no problem in convincing anyone why it should produce misery. If we picture a very hungry man confronting food which he knows to be poisoned, we can understand that he is driven on the one hand by hunger and on the other by fear. He oscillates at some distance from the tempting food, fearing to grasp but unable to leave. Everyone understands immediately the turmoil produced by such a conflict of hunger and fear.

Many people remember from their adolescence the tension of a strong sex conflict. Primary sex responses heightened by imaginative elaboration are met by intense fear. Though usually not allowed to talk about such matters, children sometimes can, and the misery they reveal is one of the most serious prices exacted of adolescents in our culture. That this conflict is acquired and not innate was shown by Margaret Mead in her brilliant book, "Coming of Age in Samoa" (1928). It is also agonizingly depicted in a novel by Vardis Fisher (1932).

Our third example of conscious conflict shows anger pitted against fear. In the early part of the war, an officer, newly commissioned from civilian life and without the habits of the professional soldier, was sent to an Army post. There he met a superior officer who decided to make an example of some minor mistake. The ranking officer lectured and berated the subordinate, refusing to let him speak and explain his behavior. He made him stand at attention against the wall for half an hour while this lecture was going on. The new-made officer quaked in fearful conflict. He detected the sadistic satisfaction which his superior got in dressing him down. He had never so much wanted to kill anyone. On the other hand, the junior officer felt the strong pressure of his own conscience to be a competent soldier and some real fear about what the consequence of assault might be. We met him shortly after this episode, and he still shook with rage when he described the experience. There was no doubt in his mind but that bearing strong, conflicting drives is one of the most severe causes of misery.

Repression Causes Stupidity

In each of the above cases, however, the individual could eventually solve his conflict. The hungry man could find nourishing food; the sex-tortured adolescent could eventually marry; the new officer could and did avoid his punishing superior.

With the neurotic this is not the case. He is not able to solve his conflict even with the passage of time. Though obviously intelligent in some ways, he is stupid in-so-far as his neurotic conflict is concerned. This stupidity is not an over-all affair, however. It is really a stupid area in the mind of a person who is quite intelligent in other respects. For some reason he cannot use his head on his neurotic conflicts.

Though the neurotic is sure he is miserable and is vocal about his symptoms, he is vague about what it is within him that could produce such painful effects. The fact that the neurotic cannot describe his own conflicts has been the source of great confusion in dealing with him either in terms of scientific theory or in terms of clinical practice. Nor can the therapist immediately spot these areas of stupidity. Only after extensive study of the patient's life can the areas of repression be clearly identified. Then the surprising fact emerges that the competing drives which afflict the neurotic person are not labeled. He has no language to describe the conflicting forces within him.

Without language and adequate labeling the higher mental processes cannot function. When these processes are knocked out by repression, the person cannot guide himself by mental means to a resolution of his conflict. Since the neurotic cannot help himself, he must have the help of others if he is to be helped at all—though millions today live out their lives in strong neurotic pain and never get help. The neurotic, therefore, is, or appears to be, stupid because he is unable to use his mind in dealing with certain of his problems. He feels that someone should help him, but he does not know how to ask for help since he does not know what his problem is. He may feel aggrieved that he is suffering, but he cannot explain his case.

Symptoms Slightly Reduce Conflict

Although in many ways superficial, the symptoms of the neurotic are the most obvious aspects of his problems. These are what the patient is familiar with and feels he should be rid of. The phobias, inhibitions, avoidances, compulsions, rationalizations, and psychosomatic symptoms of the neurotic are experienced as a nuisance by him and by all who have to deal with him. The symptoms cannot be integrated into the texture of sensible social relations. The patient, however, believes that the symptoms *are* his disorder. It is these he wishes to be rid of and, not knowing that a serious conflict underlies them, he would like to confine the therapeutic discussion to getting rid of the symptoms.

The symptoms do not solve the basic conflict in which the neurotic person is plunged, but they mitigate it. They are responses which tend to reduce the conflict, and in part they succeed. When a successful symptom occurs it is reinforced because it reduces neurotic misery. The symptom is thus learned as a habit. One very common function of symptoms is to keep the neurotic person away from those stimuli which would activate and intensify his neurotic conflict. Thus, the combat pilot with a harrowing military disaster behind him may "walk away" from the sight of any airplane. As he walks toward the plane his anxiety goes up; as he walks away it goes down. "Walking away" is thus reinforced. It is this phobic walking away which constitutes his symptom. If the whole situation is not understood, such behavior seems bizarre to the casual witness.

Conflict, Repression, and Symptoms Closely Related

In the foregoing discussion we have "taken apart" the most conspicuous factors which define the neurosis and have separately discussed conflict, stupidity, and misery. We hope that the discussion has clarified the problem even at the expense of slightly distorting the actual relationships. In every human case of neurosis the three basic factors are closely and dynamically interrelated. The conflict could not be unconscious and insoluble were it not for the repressive factors involved. The symptoms could not exist did they not somewhat relieve the pressure of conflict. The mental paralysis of repression has been created by the very same forces which originally imposed the emotional conflict on the neurotic person.

THE CASE OF MRS. A

We are presenting the facts about Mrs. A[1] for two reasons: (1) as background material on a case from which we will draw many concrete examples throughout the book; (2) as a set of facts from which we can illustrate the relationships between misery and conflict, stupidity and repression, symptoms and reinforcement. The reader will understand, of course, that the sole function of this case material is to give a clear exposition of principles by means of concrete illustrations; it is *not* presented as evidence or proof.

The Facts. Mrs. A was an unusually pretty twenty-three-year-old married woman. Her husband worked in the offices of an insurance company. When she came to the therapist she was exceedingly upset. She had a number of fears. One of the strongest of these was that her heart would stop beating if she did not concentrate on counting the beats.

The therapist, who saw Mrs. A twice a week over a three-month period, took careful notes. The life-history data that we present were pieced together from the patient's statements during a total of 26 hours. The scope of the material is necessarily limited by the brevity of the treatment. The treatment had to end

---

[1]We are allowed to present and analyze the material on Mrs. A through the kindness of a New York colleague, a man so remarkable as to provide this laboriously gathered material and yet be willing to remain anonymous to aid in the complete disguise of the case.

when a change in the husband's work forced her to move to another city.

Her first neurotic symptoms had appeared five months before she came to the psychiatrist. While she was shopping in a New York store, she felt faint and became afraid that something would happen to her and "no one would know where I was." She telephoned her husband's office and asked him to come and get her. Thereafter she was afraid to go out alone. Shortly after this time, she talked with an aunt who had a neurotic fear of heart trouble. After a conversation with this aunt, Mrs. A's fears changed from a fear of fainting to a concern about her heart.

Mrs. A was an orphan, born of unknown parents in a city in the upper South. She spent the first few months of life in an orphanage, then was placed in a foster home, where she lived, except for a year when she was doing war work in Washington, until her marriage at the age of twenty.

The foster parents belonged to the working class, had three children of their own, two girls and a boy, all of them older than the patient. The foster mother, who dominated the family, was cruel, strict, and miserly toward all the children. She had a coarse and vulgar demeanor, swore continually, and punished the foster child for the least offense. Mrs. A recalls: "She whipped me all the time —whether I'd done anything or not."

The foster mother had imposed a very repressive sex training on the patient, making her feel that sex was dirty and wrong. Moreover, the foster mother never let the patient think independently. She discouraged the patient's striving for an education, taking her out of school at sixteen when the family could have afforded to let her go on.

Despite the repressive sex training she received, Mrs. A had developed strong sexual appetites. In early childhood she had overheard parental intercourse, had masturbated, and had witnessed animal copulation. When she was ten or twelve, her foster brother seduced her. During the years before her marriage a dozen men tried to seduce her and most of them succeeded.

Nevertheless, sex was to her a dirty, loathesome thing that was painful for her to discuss or think about. She found sexual relations with her husband disgusting and was morbidly shy in her relations with him.

The patient had met her husband-to-be while she was working as a typist in Washington during the war. He was an Army officer and a college graduate. Her beauty enabled the patient to make a marriage that improved her social position; her husband's family were middle-class people. At the time of treatment Mrs. A had not yet learned all the habits of middle-class life. She was still somewhat awkward about entertaining or being entertained and made glaring errors in grammar and pronunciation. She was dominated, socially subordinated, and partly rejected by her husband's family.

When they were first married, Mr. and Mrs. A lived with his parents in a small town north of New York City and commuted to the city for work. Mrs. A had an office job there. Later, they were able to get an apartment in New York, but they stayed with the in-laws every week end. Although she described her mother-in-law in glowing terms at the beginning of the treatment, Mrs. A later came to express considerable hostility toward her.

When she came to the psychiatrist, Mrs. A was in great distress. She had to pay continual attention to her heart lest it stop beating. She lived under a burden of vague anxiety and had a number of specific phobias that prevented her from enjoying many of the normal pleasures of her life, such as going to the movies. She felt helpless to cope with her problems. Her constant complaints had tired out and alienated her friends. Her husband was fed up with her troubles and had threatened to divorce her. She could not get along with her foster mother and her mother-in-law had rejected her. She had no one left to talk to. She was hurt, baffled, and terrified by the thought that she might be going crazy.

Analysis in Terms of Conflict, Repression, Reinforcement

We have described Mrs. A as of the moment when she came to treatment.

The analysis of the case, however, presents the facts as they were afterward ordered and clarified by study.

Misery. Mrs. A's misery was obvious to her family, her therapist, and herself. She suffered from a strong, vague, unremitting fear. She was tantalized by a mysterious temptation. The phobic limitations on her life prevented her from having much ordinary fun, as by shopping or going to the movies. Her husband and mother-in-law criticized her painfully. She feared that her husband would carry out his threat and divorce her. She feared that her heart would stop. She feared to be left all alone, sick and rejected. Her friends and relatives pitied her at first, then became put out with her when her condition persisted despite well-meant advice. Her misery, though baffling, was recognized as entirely real.

Conflict. Mrs. A suffered from two conflicts which produced her misery. The first might be described as a sex-fear conflict. Thanks to childhood circumstances she had developed strong sex appetites. At the same time strong anxieties were created in her and attached to the cues produced by sex excitement. However, she saw no connection between these remembered circumstances and the miserable life she was leading. The connective thoughts had been knocked out and the conflict was thus unconscious. The presence of the sexual appetites showed up in a kind of driven behavior in which she seemed to court seduction. Her fear was exhibited in her revulsion from sexual acts and thoughts and in her inability to take responsibility for a reasonable sexual expressiveness with her husband. The conflict was greatly intensified after her marriage because of her wish to be a dutiful wife. Guilt about the prospect of adultery was added to fear about sex motives.

Mrs. A was involved in a second, though less severe, conflict between aggression and fear. She was a gentle person who had been very badly treated by her mother-in-law. Resentful tendencies arose in her but they were quickly inhibited by fear. She attempted to escape the anger-fear conflict by exceptionally submissive behavior, putting up meekly with slights and subordination and protesting her fondness for the mother-in-law. She was tormented by it nevertheless, especially by feelings of worthlessness and helplessness. She felt much better, late in therapy, when she was able to state her resentment and begin to put it into effect in a measured way. (After all, she had the husband and his love, and if the mother-in-law wanted to see her son and prospective grandchildren she would have to take a decent attitude toward Mrs. A.)

Stupidity. Mrs. A's mind was certainly of little use to her in solving her problem. She tried the usual medical help with no result. She took a trip, as advised, and got no help. Her symptoms waxed and waned in unpredictable ways. She knew that she was helpless. At the time she came for therapy she had no plans for dealing with her problem and no hope of solving it. In addition to being unable to deal with her basic problems, Mrs. A did many things that were quite unintelligent and maladaptive. For example, in spite of the fact that she wanted very much to make a success of her marriage and was consciously trying to live a proper married life, she frequently exposed herself to danger of seduction. She went out on drinking parties with single girls. She hitchhiked rides with truck drivers. She was completely unaware of the motivation for this behavior and often unable to foresee its consequences until it was too late. While her behavior seems stupid in the light of a knowledge of the actual state of affairs, there were many ways in which Mrs. A did not seem at all stupid —for example, when debating with the therapist to protect herself against fear-producing thoughts. She then gave hopeful evidence of what she could do with her mind when she had available all the necessary units to think with.

Repression. Mrs. A gave abundant evidence of the laming effects of repression. At the outset she thought she had no sex feelings or appetites. She described behavior obviously motivated by fear but could not label the fear itself. The closest she came was to express the idea that she was going insane. Further, Mrs. A thought she had an organic disease and clung desperately to this idea, inviting any kind of treatment so long as it did not force her to think about matters which would produce fear. Such mental gaps and distortions are a characteristic result of repression. They are what produce the stupidity.

Symptoms. Mrs. A's chief symptoms were the spreading phobia which drove her out of theaters and stores and the compulsive counting of breaths and heartbeats. These symptoms almost incapacitated her. She had lost her freedom to think and to move.

Reinforcement of Symptoms. An analysis of the phobia revealed the following events. When on the streets alone, her fear of sex temptation was increased. Someone might speak to her, wink at her, make an approach to her. Such an approach would increase her sex desire and make her more vulnerable to seduction. Increased sex desire, however, touched off both anxiety and guilt, and this intensified her conflict when she was on the street. When she "escaped home," the temptation stimuli were lessened, along with a reduction of the fear which they elicited. Going home and, later, avoiding the temptation situation by anticipation were reinforced. Naturally, the basic sex-anxiety conflict was

not resolved by the defensive measure of the symptom. The conflict persisted but was not so keen.

The counting of heartbeats can be analytically taken apart in a similar way. When sexy thoughts came to mind or other sex stimuli tended to occur, these stimuli elicited anxiety. It is clear that these stimuli were occurring frequently because Mrs. A was responding with anxiety much of the time. Since counting is a highly preoccupying kind of response, no other thoughts could enter her mind during this time. While counting, the sexy thoughts which excited fear dropped out. Mrs. A "felt better" immediately when she started counting, and the counting habit was reinforced by the drop in anxiety. Occasionally, Mrs. A would forget to count and then her intense anxiety would recur. In this case, as in that of the phobia, the counting symptom does not resolve the basic conflict—it only avoids exacerbating it.

Thus Mrs. A's case illustrates the analysis of neurotic mechanisms made in the earlier part of the chapter. Conflict produced high drives experienced as misery; repression interfered with higher mental processes and so with the intelligent solution of the conflict; the symptoms were learned responses which were reinforced by producing some reduction in the strength of drive. We will discuss later how higher mental life can be restored and how actions which *will* resolve the poisonous conflict can be made to occur.

50.
the meaning of dreams

gay gaer luce

Unleashed from reason and detached from circumstance, the play of dreams is armed with terrible freedom. In all history and every recorded culture the mysterious and evanescent dream has been taken seriously. Strategic dream interpretations have altered the course of nations, as did Joseph with the fat kine and lean. Oracles dreamed the future. By pagan dream-rites the sick were healed. Lincoln's dream of death seemed a harbinger of his fate. American Indians enacted their dreams. During the reign of terror and superstition from the 12th through the 17th century, Western Europeans fought an international conspiracy of witches, and the seriousness of the dream was evident in the Malleus, guide and handbook to every judge of the Inquisition, at a time when dreams might mean burning. Dreams also inspired poetry in Coleridge, fiction in Robert Louis Stevenson, and Kekule, the organic chemist, is said to have deciphered the arrangement of atoms in the benzene ring by a dream of a snake eating its tail. The skillful man, said Emerson, reads his dreams for self-knowledge. Although dream books including codes for gamblers and advice on all aspects of practical life are abundant on newsstands today, we tend to probe dreams for insight into the dreamer.

Dramatic, recurrent, universal to mankind, the dream is nevertheless an experience that people cannot share. The dream that is communicated is a memory from a sleeping state and the extent to which people must distort their dreams can be estimated by the imperfect court testimonies of witnesses who are attempting to report real events truthfully. There have been a number of attempts

Reprinted from *Current Research on Sleep and Dreams*, Public Health Service Publication No. 1389, pp. 96–103.

to ascertain the memory span for dreams. One, an initial study in the University of Chicago, by Drs. Edward Wolpert and Harry Trosman, showed that volunteers could remember dreams if awakened at the end of REM periods, but not several minutes later. Like the trace of the evanescent neutrino, the dream had to be captured at once or it evaporated.

A psychiatrist, whose patients were awakened in his laboratory, compared the immediate narratives with the patients' daytime recollection, and found that the morning versions were palpably different. Similar discrepancies were noted at the Institute for Dream Research in Miami, Fla., when monitored records from laboratory awakenings were compared with the written accounts by the same volunteers at home (Hall and Van de Castle, 1964.) The laboratory narratives were long and incoherent and less intense than the tightly organized home reports. There is no means of checking a dream report against a dream. However embroidered and shaped, however censored and skewed, we have only human recall for evidence. Until recently the dreams reported were usually the last of the night, just before awakening.

With today's electrical recording equipment it has been possible to sample the night's dreams. Customarily, volunteers will spend several nights in the laboratory, adjusting, while the investigator obtains EEG recordings that roughly indicate the individual's timing and spacing of dreams. He can predict when the subject will begin dreaming and approximately how long each dream period will last, awakening the subject toward the end of a segment.

Is there any relation between the several dreams of a night? Freud suspected that sequences of dreams elaborated the same motive, timidly at first and then more distinctly. Franz Alexander postulated that successive dreams were connected in pairs, and that a night's preoccupation was clarified by the repetition of a theme. Drs. Harry Trosman, Allan Rechtschaffen, William Offenkrantz, and Edward Wolpert studied 2 young men for 32 nights. Well over a hundred dreams were collected and analyzed, but only on one night did a subject have four dreams directly related in theme and content. The lack of continuity found in an earlier study by Dement and Wolpert did not outlaw the suggestion that a sustained emotional tone and recurrent items might pervade the night, and continuity was observed by Offenkrantz and Rechtschaffen (Offenkrantz and Rechtschaffen, 1963).

The possibility that dreams might have predictable and characteristic differences at different times of night was pursued by Dr. Paul P. Verdone, who found that the initial dreams seemed to revolve around current events, whereas dreams of childhood and past events occurred later, coinciding with the time of the person's lowest temperature. The longer a person had been asleep the more vivid and emotional his dream reports, the easier his recall. Then, after about 7 hours of sleep, the volunteers began once more dreaming of current elements in their lives. Work in progress at NIMH may illuminate the interesting correlation between low temperature and dreams of past events, and may determine whether the particularly vivid dreams are associated with time of day, time in bed, or body temperature (Verdone, 1965).

As a great many researchers have demonstrated, the REM dreams are not islands of imagination on a dark river of oblivion, for when people have been wakened between REM periods they have offered wisps, thoughts, fragments, and images. Perhaps these provide continuity among the REM dreams of the night. Drs. Allan Rechtschaffen, Gerald Vogel, and Gerald Shaikun have collected intermediate recollections from subjects and found that these non-REM elements resembling day-dreams or imagistic thought may be interwoven into the REM content, demonstrating some continuity in the thematic fabric of the night. It is interesting that people talk throughout their night of sleep, and not only during REM dreams (Rechtschaffen, Goodenough, and Shapiro, 1962). Studies of sleep talking indicate that it is a common occurrence and that it changes in tone, growing more expressive and emotional during REM periods.

INFLUENCING DREAM CONTENT

Dreaming animals and people are incorrigibly wrapped up in their private worlds and are usually hard to awaken. Freud and others have postulated that the dream protects a person from awakening and that outside events may simply be incorporated in the dream. While working at the University of Chicago, Dement and Wolpert tested dreaming volunteers with lights, sounds, water. The stimulus was identifiably incorporated in only 20–60 percent of the dreams, but perhaps more of the dreams did interweave the outside disturbances in transmuted or symbolic form. (Dement and Wolpert, 1958.) By objective assessment, however, Berger did find outside events highly incorporated in dreams (Berger, 1963).

The fact that we may not incorporate outside events into our dreams 100 percent of the time does not mean that we don't interweave these events some of the time. After applying heat or cold to sleeping subjects, investigators have obtained thermal references in only about 25 percent of the subsequent dreams. Because the incidence has been low in some well designed studies, there has been a tendency to feel that external events do not influence dream content very much. Similarly, bodily states such as hunger and thirst, have produced little impact on reported dreams (Dement and Wolpert, 1958). However, thirsty subjects, deprived of food and liquids, and then given a spicy meal before sleep, have referred to thirst to a degree that suggests a definite somatic influence on the actual dream content (Bokert, 1965).

There have been a number of attempts to manipulate the content of dreams. Dr. Johann Stoyva of Langley Porter Institute, San Francisco, assigned several volunteers dream topics by posthypnotic suggestion. When awakened and asked their dreams, only one or two dreams would contain these preassigned elements, which were instructions to dream of climbing a tree, etc. The notable effect, even with a well seasoned laboratory volunteer, was a reduction in the amount of dreaming (Stoyva, 1962).

Manipulations of dreaming behavior have interested many researchers, for individuals differ greatly in their responsiveness, perhaps indicating far-reaching constitutional and psychological endowments that would be useful to define. In studies already cited, some volunteers were able to hear and remember tape-recorded numbers while dreaming, sometimes incorporating them into their dreams; others could be motivated to press switches when entering a dream period or respond to signals. Rechtschaffen, at the University of Chicago, has paid volunteers to increase or decrease their amount of dreaming with a small effect on the amount of time spent in REM. (Rechtschaffen and Verdone, 1964.) In each instance one might expect that individuals divide sharply in their responsiveness. Dr. Martin Orne, and his associates at the Institute of the Pennsylvania Hospital, have been conducting a program of studies on hypnosis, and in a recent pilot study find that deeply hypnotizable subjects can act upon suggestions delivered during dream periods, whereas less hypnotizable people will not follow sleep instruction. During sleep, with no prior hypnotic suggestion, volunteers were told that the word "pillow" would make the pillow seem uncomfortable and they should move it; the word "itch" would cause their noses to itch until they scratched. When the instructions came during REM dreaming, the deeply hypnotizable subjects did indeed move their pillows and scratch their noses. The others either gave no response or awakened. This difference in suggestibility, evident in sleep and waking, is a curious phenomenon (Cobb et al., 1965). People differ quite as sharply in their ability to remember dreams.

DREAM RECALL

Ten years ago it was possible for a person who remembered dreaming every night to look with pity on the impoverished soul whose nights were devoid of imagination—the person who said, "I never dream." Now it seems clear that we all dream about the same amount, every night. Why do some people not remember? There have been many speculations on this point. Patients in analysis, motivated by questioning, begin to remember dreams. Personality differences have been discovered in which introspective people have seemed to recall dreaming most easily. The question of dream recall prodded Drs. Donald Goodenough, Arthur Shapiro, and their associates at the New York Downstate Medical Center into a long program of studies. Many factors were at play. For instance, the faster a person awakened the more fully he would describe a dream, so the mode of awakening mattered (Shapiro et al., 1963). However, individuals differed in the amount of noise that would awaken them. Those who normally remembered dreaming at home would awaken quickly in the laboratory, after a horrendous 80 decibel blast, and recite a rich dream narrative. People who rarely remembered dreaming at home, when aroused into wakefulness often thought they had been awake and thinking the whole time. One young man delivered a bizarre narrative about sitting in class popping pennies into a vending machine and striking oil —yet asserted he was thinking. He could control his dream, he explained, in the manner of a daydream, and he was aware of sounds in the room, such as the air conditioner. This kind of explanation and a wealth of other data suggest that there might be distinct physiological differences; some people dreaming at a lighter than normal level of sleep and thinking themselves awake, while others dream in a deeper than normal stage of sleep and lose their dreams in the long process of awakening. But there seems to be another kind of forgetting as well, possibly repression (Shapiro et al., 1964; Goodenough et al.).

DREAM INTENSITY

Some guidelines have emerged during the last few years for estimating the emotionality of a dream from physiological measures. Dr. Frederick Snyder of NIMH and others have correlated physiological changes with dream content. One sign that suggests an intense dream is highly irregular respiration, like the breathing of a person in terrible anxiety or impatience. Dr. Charles Fisher of Mount Sinai Hospital has shown that penile erections accompany almost all dreaming periods in males, from birth on, and dreams that are not accompanied by erection or which have sudden detumescence appear to be dreams of terrible anxiety, of violence and body mutilation. Some thousands of nights have now been dreamed away in sleep laboratories, and many investigators have observed physical symptoms that suggested an intense dream, only to find out when they awakened the person that he did not remember, or only gave a vague and bland story.

STIMULATION BEFORE SLEEP

Investigators at the New York Downstate Medical Center are currently watching the physiological symptoms and EEG configurations of volunteers who have been exposed to films before sleep. On one night there is a pleasant, neutral travelog. On other nights there is either an anthropological documentary showing birth or initiation rites, both quite disturbing. In a preliminary study of 10 people, Drs. Herman A. Witkin and Helen B. Lewis found evidence that the elements of the presleep film were identifiably incorporated into the dreams of that night. By interview techniques and prior clinical information, the investigators have been able to connect the way the person dreamed about the material with significant events in his personal life. The subjects were transit workers, telephone engineers, bakers, airplane factory workers, and others who normally sleep during the day, and who had not been exposed to theories of psychology. Further studies using these films may discriminate between those people whose inability to recall dreams is related to physiology, and those who cannot remember disturbing experiences.

Many people have wondered whether a film seen just before sleep has an influence on one's dreams. Many parents have asked themselves this question as their small children gave rapt attention to a TV drama of monsters, or crime and violence, just before bedtime. In studies of the impact of mass media on children, some social scientists have postulated a direct influence on behavior. Dr. David Foulkes, when at the University of Chicago, sought another approach and looked for the influence of presleep stimuli on dreams. From its roots in a sociological interest, the study then took on quite an independent aspect. Adult volunteers watched two different films on two separate nights before retiring in the laboratory. These were network telecasts, one a typical western, the other a romantic comedy. By sifting the dreams for incorporation of the previous TV material, the investigator found direct influence in about 5 percent of the dreams. However, when he analyzed the emotional qualities of the dreams he found that the dreams following the western were far more vivid, imaginative, and highly charged than the dreams following the comedy. The results of this study do not conflict with the Downstate study, for the investigators used the kind of films a person might normally watch before bedtime. Witkin and Lewis employed traumatic and bloody films among theirs and were particularly interested in the metaphors by which an individual might transform material. For instance, a dream of taking cake from a bag appeared to be easily connected to the birth film the subject had seen a few hours earlier.

We know a great deal more about dreaming today than we did in Freud's time. We know more about the amount of dreaming in individuals of specified age, physiological changes that occur at the same time, the effects of drugs, some of the neurophysiological events. We can evoke behavior in dreaming and compare responsiveness and recall. We find that recall differs as the night wears on, improving toward morning. We may soon understand the biochemistry that triggers dreaming. All of our observations about the need to dream, the intensity of dreams, and how their incidence varies with illness are bound to be refined. But the meaning of dreams?

Grand and confident theories become more difficult to compose as the data accumulate, for today's theories require predictability, demonstrations that the relationships between dream and dreamer are not subject to the varying interpretations of investigators. Many of the dream reports obtained in the laboratories over the last 10 years differ from the types of dreams analyzed by Freud and others, yet many investigators feel that some of those early intuitive analyses were, in some sense, true. What beast is loosed at night from the cage of civilization to stalk through stark and perplexing dramas, perhaps cloaked in innocuous symbolism? How are these figments related to the day past, to the core of the personality, or to random noises in the bedroom? Does an obsessional nightmare relate to neurosis or physiological changes, are there dreams characteristic of health, and dreams bespeaking illness? These are important questions, and the modern dream hunter is equipped with new tools for exploring, but the dream reports are still memories and we do not yet have methods of checking the speaker's veracity from outside.

CLASSIFYING DREAMS

Some years ago, before the advent of electronically tracked dreaming, some of these questions were attacked very differently—with methods a sociologist might use to classify the attitudes of people toward a sensitive issue such as birth control. Here, hopefully, statistics might be used on a large sample of questionnaires to filter out the small lies and obfuscations of individuals and reveal the general attitudes of people in different socioeconomic or regional groups. By amassing a truly enormous number of dream reports and applying statistical analyses, the Dream Research Institute of Miami, Fla., has been finding out the general kinds of dream content that typify certain groups of people: normal college youngsters, the physically ill, mentally ill, the aged, and people of particular ethnic groups.

The institute, founded and directed by Dr. Calvin Hall, is probably the largest repository of dream narratives in the world, its files containing some 30,000 dreams. Among these are 5,000 dreams collected from other countries and cultures, from Australians, Peruvians, Nigerians, Mexicans, and many others. Many of these dreams have been broken down into components, classified, and subjected to statistical procedures. If this method can render the distinctive dream patterns of a specific culture or distinguish between the mentally ill and the healthy, a dream report may become a diagnostic aid. Among other things, it may help a doctor foresee an impending mental breakdown, the onset of an acute episode, suicidal tendencies. It may provide us with useful insight into other cultures and in the differences in outlook between the sexes (Hall, 1951–64).

This empirical evaluation of dream content is based on a systematic categorization of each element or event. Dr. Hall and his associates have first classified items that occur most frequently: the kinds of characters that appear in dreams and their relationship to the dreamer, the setting, the objects, the dreamer's emotions, lucky or unfortunate events. Out of these analyses, they have developed manuals that might be used by a therapist, for instance, in analyzing a patient's dreams and judging whether these included more than a normal number of fearful events. Although this large scale normative study is still in progress, the manuals offer some guides for judgment by citing the distribution of the categories of dream events for specific populations. For instance, an analysis of 1,182 dreams reported by young men and women suggested that about 2 out of 5 dreams are fearful, often containing a sequence in which the dreamer is pursued. A similar assay implied that for every dream of good fortune, a person may have seven dreams of misfortune. The dreamer is more often the victim than beneficiary. Questionnaires filled out by students who contributed dreams indicated that they felt only about a quarter of their dreams were pleasant.

An analysis of 7,000 dreams shows up one notable difference between men and women. Men tend to dream about men, in general, but women dream equally of men and women (Hall and Domhoff, 1963).

A recent study of the dreams of 60 nurses suggests that women's physiological cycles may influence their dreams. A tentative assay of dreams before and during menstruation shows that women may dream of waiting for something, a bus, or train, during the premenstrual period, whereas dreams of destruction seem to occur during the first days of the cycle.

The institute's new sleep laboratory is unusual in the sense that it is located in a residential house and has little of the laboratory aura. Here, while attempting to obtain a representative dream sample from 25 healthy young unmarried men, the investigators hope to detect and correct the kinds of censorship and bias that have entered the dream reports collected outside the laboratory. As this empirical work continues on a grand scale, people continue to ask what do dreams mean. Are they wishes, unspoken or unadmitted by day? Are they a safety valve? Does unemotional, toneless dreaming indicate schizophrenia? Does one solve "problems" in dreams?

The task of interpreting dreams has grown no smaller now that we can clock them, collect more of them, try to manipulate them. Today's accumulation of data has instigated a few very tentative speculations, for dreams, their images, sensations, emotions, are physically part of us, and the blue rhinoceros that stalks the salon of our dream reveals something of our nature. The images must come from somewhere.

SPECULATIONS ABOUT THE NEURAL BASIS FOR DREAMS

Some investigators have speculated that they are made up of memories and are activated in the hippocampus, a neurol formation that curls across the center of the brain like two horseshoes joined at the middle and curving toward the temples, ending in the amygdala. This region has been thought to act as a clearinghouse for memory, a stage before memories are filed for storage. Lesions of the hippocampus or amygdala will cause a loss of short-term memory. During the EEG phase that corresponds to the dream period, animal studies have shown bursts of rhythmic activity from the hippocampus—theta activity that spreads to a

part of the brain that participates in awareness or attention. Perhaps this is the episode we call a dream. However, a simple kaleidoscope of images, memories, thoughts, would not explain the cold sweat of terror we suffer in a nightmare or the pleasurable involvement we sometimes experience. It would not explain why inconsistent images, the trivial intermixed with the momentous, appear to have some meaning we cannot explain. One very tentative explanation has been offered. In a word, it says that motivational centers within the brain are activated during dreaming and that these centers may structure our dreams. This is a familiar hypothesis. It was suggested by Freud in evolving a theory about the latent content of dreams.

Today, an anatomical hypothesis has been phrased by Dr. Raul Hernandez-Peon, and while it is emphatically tentative, it suggests a neural background for the significance of dreams, indeed perhaps explaining man's centuries of profound interest in dream symbols. A hypnogenic system extending from the front of the brain toward the spinal cord overlaps with a portion of the hypothalamus where stimulation evokes signs of pleasure—a center, one might say, for positive reinforcement and a positive component of motivation. Reactions of abhorrence have also been produced by stimulating another area in the hypothalamus, a center, roughly speaking, of punishment or negative reinforcement. Motivation, as we think of it, may be based on the sensations of pleasure or punishment attaching to certain acts or impulses. Pleasure or pain can be evoked by directly stimulating the brain, but like sleep and wakefulness, they are induced by stimulation from the outside world, by monotony, or sudden noises, that send their impulses up the spinal cord. Similarly, they can be induced, like voluntary sleep or waking, by impulses descending from the cortex, internally generated. It is quite plausible to think of this motivational system as active during sleep, and if so, it might be the editor, the shaping power behind our dreams. During our wakeful hours, especially in youth, we learn to suppress the behaviors and even thoughts for which we are usually punished. By maturity, we hardly pay attention to this constant suppression of antisocial impulses.

In waking life, when the vigilance system is active and dominant, our neural apparatus is energetically holding down these punished impulses. The fact that a region of negative reinforcement lies close to the arousal system gives some encouragement to this conjecture. During sleep, however, this very system that inhibits our punished impulses may be suppressed, itself by the activity of the hypnogenic system. Are repressed impulses now released in a manner resembling the release that comes with certain depressants like alcohol or anesthesias? If this be the case, the punished impulses could now emerge and place their positive or negative weight upon the welter of images that have been activated in this dreaming state of sleep. It is unnecessary to belabor the point that the most punished impulses of the child are those behaviors and curiosities directed by basic drives. If these are the suppressed factors that structure the otherwise incomprehensible mélange of dream material—they are indeed the elements of latent dream content, phrased somewhat differently by Freud.

This is a complicated speculation and built upon an enormous amount of anatomical and behavioral data. Although it may be unfair to cite the hypothesis so simply, it may indicate the new threshold over which dream interpretation—the question of meaning—may be moving. Neurophysiologists are beginning to suggest that dreams may be shaped by drives in an organization that brain research may soon begin to elucidate. A dream is a psychological phenomenon. It cannot be understood by physics. The act of dreaming, however, is both a psychological and a physical process, determined by our structure and the learning imposed upon our very cells.

DRIVE MECHANISMS IN REM

Freud might be privately amused to see the implications of some recent research. The intensive sleep studies of Dr. Charles Fisher at Mount Sinai Hospital in New York, suggest that the strong sexual motivation underlying dreams, as Freud saw them, might be even stronger than Freud supposed. Preceding every REM period, from infancy onward, males have penile erections. This does not mean they have overtly sexual dreams; indeed, what would such a dream be for an infant? Sexual activity, however, is part of our survival equipment and something toward which much learning must be applied, step by step. The REM sleep, in which erections occur, begins very early —in premature babies, perhaps in the womb. The function of REM activity, as Dement has suggested, may be that of a primitive core activity, a rhythm in the rudimentary brain into which all later motivation and learning interlocks, a first practice in the body learning that occurs with development. It is during this predominant phase of sleep that the infant first exercises his limbs, sucks, and smiles. This may represent a first practice in the effectors of the great drive forces for survival. Perhaps erections are involved in the body-brain learning process of the infant. Their existence suggests that sexual drive mechanisms develop from the start and are subject to influence by very early training. The function of such drive discharge in adult sleep is unexplained and could be purely vestigial. But in adults, they are connected with dream content. The interesting dream is the exception, the REM period that is not accompanied by erection or in which there is rapid detumescence. Data so far suggest that these are dreams of intense anxiety, often including body mutilation (Fisher et al., 1965).

The fact that there may be a strong connection between drives, dreams, and the covert symbolism of dreams does not give us a direct handle for the interpretation of specific dreams in relation to their dreamers, but it opens up new avenues of exploration that may not have seemed relevant to dream interpretation 10 years ago. By using tools now being developed in neurophysiological and physiological research, we now begin to look at the process by which dreams are formed. Here we may begin to find some of the complex but lawful processes by which living experience accrues in the brain and is transmuted into that most private experience, the dream. The anatomy of dreaming, as we may learn from animals, may divulge some of the roots of fantasy, revealing the way in which emotional learning encrusts event and sensory experience. From young children in various stages of maturation we may hope to learn about the impact of environment in its larger ramifications. The development of new analytic tools for reading brain wave rhythms and the accumulation of data allowing us to localize their sources may give us a kind of Geiger counter on the dreaming mind and its responses to our manipulations from outside. Slowly we may learn how to disentangle the components of dreams. The findings and speculations mentioned here contribute to the disentangling. If the dream memory is to provide an understanding of an individual personality, to be useful in therapy or aid in diagnosis, we should be able to differentiate physiological cycles, from cultural idiosyncrasies, and from immediate events—seeing the pervasive style and shaping that is given to the dream by an individual. Since dreams are formed by physical processes, and since illness, mental or physical, presumably comes from alterations within our cells, it does not seem impossible that

dreams might provide diagnosticians of the future with warning signals.

At present we have to rely upon intuitions and education sharpened by the mounting data. Science cannot encompass all life at one gulp, and life is the stuff dreams are built upon. Each of us in a private universe weaves together a myriad of experiences, important, and trivial—daily routine, learning, automatic responses of hunger or breathing, and moments as transient as an eyeblink. Embedded in the central nervous system, shaped by learning, these are the tools of conscious behavior. By day it all seems purposeful and real, the actuality confirmed by others, but the unsharable dream, for the most part, leaves no more impression on memory than the shadow of a leaf falling over a stone. Since we tend to recall the unusual, and for yet unexplained reasons do sometimes remember some figment from an implausible mirror-image world, we have throughout history concentrated upon these few gleanings and singled them out for the game of interpretation. Today, at least, we may sample the whole gamut, perhaps seeing them as the processes of all mammal minds and not interpreting them as a harbinger of external world events.

REFERENCES

Berger, R. J. Experimental modification of dream content by meaningful verbal stimuli. *Brit. J. Psychiat.*, 1963, 109:722–740.

Cobb, J. Evans, F., Gustafson, L., O'Connell, D. N., Orne, M., and Shor, R. Specific motor responses during sleep to sleep-administered meaningful suggestion: an exploratory investigation. *Percept. Mot. Skills*, 1965, 20:629–636.

Dement, W. C., and Wolpert, E. A. The relationship of eye movement, body motility, and external stimuli to dream content. *J. Exp. Psychol.*, 1958, 55:543–553.

Fishbein, W., Schaumberg, H., and Weitzmann, E. D. Rapid eye movements during sleep in dark reared kittens. *APSS*, 1965, Washington, D.C.

Goodenough, D. R., Lewis, H. B., Shapiro, A., and Sleser, I. Some factors affecting recall of dreams after laboratory awakenings. Reprint.

Hall, C. What people dream about. *Scientific American*, 1951, 184:60–63.

Hall, C. S. A cognitive theory of dream symbols. *J. Gen. Psychol.*, 1953, 48:169–186.

Hall, C. S. A cognitve theory of dreams. *J. Gen. Psychol.*, 1953, 49:273–282.

Hall, C. S. *The Meaning of Dreams.* New York: Dell, 1959.

Hall, C. S. Strangers in dreams: an empirical confirmation of the Oedipus complex. *J. Personality*, 1963, 31:336–345.

Hall, C. S. Slang and dream symbols. *Psychoanalysis and Psychoanalytic Review,* 1964. In press.

Hall, C., and Domhoff, B. A ubiquitous sex difference in dreams. *J. Abnor. & Soc. Psych.*, 1963, 66:278–280.

Hall, C., and Van de castle, R. L. A comparison of home and monitored dreams. *APSS*, 1964, Palo Alto.

Offenkrantz, W., and Rechtschaffen, A. Clinical studies of sequential dreams. I. A patient in psychotherapy. *Arch. Gen. Psychiat.*, 1963, 8:497–508.

Rechtschaffen, A., Goodenough, D. R., and

Shapiro, A. Patterns of sleep talking. *Arch. Gen. Psychiat.*, 1962, 7:418–426.

Rechtschaffen, A., and Verdone, P. Amount of dreaming: Effect of incentive, adaptation to laboratory, and individual differences. *Percept. Mot. Skills*, 1964, 19:947–958.

Shapiro, A., Goodenough, D. R., Biederman, I., and Sleser, I. Dream recall and the physiology of sleep. *J. App. Physiol.*, 1964, 19.

Shapiro, A., Goodenough, D. R., and Gryler, R. B. Dream recall as a function of method of awakening. *Psychosom. Med.*, 1963, 25:174–180.

Stoyva, J. The effect of suggested dreams on the length of rapid eye movement periods. *APSS*, 1962, Chicago.

Verdone, P. P. Variables related to the temporal reference of manifest dream content. *Percept. Mot. Skills*, 1965, 20:1253–1268.

51.
a sophisticated version
of voodoo death:
report of a case

james l. mathis

The belief that death could be produced by magical means was an unquestionable part of man's early culture. (1) Many such cases have been reported in primitive societies. Although modern man has coined the term "psychophysiological reactions" to cover these phenomena when they occur in his advanced society, actual deaths from such causes are infrequently reported. The case to be presented may represent a sophisticated version of "voodoo death."

Cannon stated that voodoo death resulted when all body forces were mobilized and maintained for an action which never came. (2) He felt that the death was primarily due to prolonged overstimulation of the adrenals by the sympathetic nervous system. Richter, however, felt that the demise was due to a complete "giving up," a feeling of utter hopelessness and helplessness, in effect, a parasympathetic death. (3) Zoological experts have observed this in the deaths of wild animals who find themselves suddenly caged in an apparently hopeless situation. (4) The thin veneer of civilized intellect covering man's primitive emotions serves as an armor to prevent vulnerability to this type of influence. It is suggested that when this armor proves too thin, modern man may also succumb, albeit less directly and more slowly, than did his less sophisticated predecessors.

CASE REPORT

Mr. X, age 53, was admitted on Jan. 7, 1960 with severe bronchial asthma. He was transferred from his hometown hos-

Reprinted by permission from *Psychosomatic Medicine*, March-April, 1964, *XXVI* (2), 104–107.

pital where he had been admitted 2 days previously in a semicomatose condition. Routine measures had failed to abort the attack. After 2 weeks' hospitalization he was discharged symptom-free on bronchodilators and expectorants.

He was next admitted on July 13, 1960, in a similar condition. In the interim he had been hospitalized in private institutions 6 times. Three attacks had resulted in loss of consciousness and epileptic-like convulsions for which he was given Dilantin. Non-specific t-wave changes on an EKG had led to digitalization, although no signs of cardiac failure were noted by examination or history. These medications were continued, and some small nasal polyps were removed under local anesthesia. He improved rapidly and following a thorough work-up, he was discharged with diagnoses of bronchial asthma and mild obstructive emphysema. He went directly from the hospital to his mother's home. In a few hours he was wheezing again, and in less than 48 hr. he was readmitted by ambulance in a near-terminal condition. Medical management aborted the attack, but the patient became extremely depressed and voiced feelings of utter futility and hopelessness. Psychiatric consultation advised transfer to its service on Aug. 4, 1960.

Medical management was continued with the addition of Tofranil, 100 mg. daily. The asthma remained under control and the depression rapidly improved. On Aug. 11, he was given a pass, but returned early from a visit to his mother's home where he noted rapidly increasing wheezing. Shortly after entering the ward, his breathing began to improve.

On Aug. 17, X was given another pass, with strict instructions for his activities. He was to visit his wife, but was to avoid all contact with his mother. He returned in excellent spirits after 24 hrs. with no signs of asthma. He was now willing to discuss the possible relationship of his asthma to maternal influence. In addition to this type of psychotherapy, plans for a future entry into business were eagerly discussed. With one exception he remained in excellent spirits; the exception was that he retained grave doubts of escaping his physical disability permanently.

X was seen for a 30-min. interview at 5 p.m. on August 23. Some dental work had been completed that day, and he was in excellent physical and mental condition. At 6:35 p.m. he was found gasping for breath, cyanotic and semicomatose. He was pronounced dead at 6:55 p.m. A complete autopsy reported the cause of death as acute right ventricular dilatation and bronchial asthma. The bronchial tubes were markedly constricted and filled with extremely tenacious mucus.

The history of X's illness is unusually reminiscent of descriptions of psychological (voodoo) death. He was the third child in a sibship of five. All except the youngest, who is mentally retarded, are successful, educated people. X did not complete the eighth grade, partially because he was given the responsibility for keeping the incompetent younger brother out of trouble, a role which he did not like, but which he filled well. He complained many times that his mother never showed him the gratitude and appreciation he deserved for his care of this brother. He described his mother as a wonderful lady who made all the family decisions correctly and who never met a situation she could not control.

The father, a traveling salesman rarely home, died when X was in his early teens. Since the older brother was in college, X became the man of the household. He lived with his mother and worked in local filling stations until 31 years of age. Two marriages during this period rapidly ended in divorce. Both failures were predicted by his mother.

At age 31, he bought a nightclub in a moderate-sized city. His mother helped him finance the business and continued to keep the accounts of what proved to be a very successful venture. During his one year of military service, she ran the club efficiently and profitably by herself.

At age 38 X married a well-educated school teacher 10 years his junior. He was now a respected and successful businessman, but he saw himself as an ignorant and inadequate man, extremely fortunate to marry an esteemed woman of whom his mother approved. His wife resented the dependency X felt toward his demanding and disdainful mother, but the marriage otherwise was described as ideal. A son was born, the business prospered, and life was uncomplicated until November 1959. At this time he received a profitable offer for his business. His mother became distraught when informed of the proposed transaction. When, with much indecision and misgiving, and with the support of his wife, he decided to accept the offer, his mother said, "Do this and something dire will happen to you." Two days later he had his first mild spell of wheezing.

X had no previous history of respiratory difficulty of any kind. He and his wife agreed that he had not had a common cold in about 10 years. He consulted his physician and was given some capsules which decreased this wheezing and cough to an acceptable level for the next several weeks. Relations with his mother remained strained.

On Jan. 2, 1960, the sale of his business was completed. The next day his asthma was much worse. Two days later he was rushed to the hospital via ambulance, and on January 7 he was transferred to the V.A. hospital. Upon completion of the sale his mother had become very angry and had repeatedly reminded him of her prediction of dire results. She had used the words, "Something will strike you."

Numerous hospitalizations, asthmatic attacks 3-4 times per week, three convulsions, and the apparent inability of the medical profession to help him, dovetailed into X's growing idea that mother was right again. The depression for which psychiatric consultation was sought was marked by his frequent protestations of the hopelessness of his condition. A hopeful sign appeared when he was able consciously to see some connection between the asthmatic attacks and contact with his mother. However, he did not forget that mother had previously proven infallible; in fact, he reminded me of this on the afternoon of his death.

This last interview was primarily concerned with his plans to reinvest the capital from the sale of his business. The desirability of excluding his mother from the new venture and whether or not she would resent this were discussed. He expressed the belief that he was "allergic" to his mother, but could not understand how this had developed so late in life. No attempt was made, and this was also true of past interviews, to approach the problem on other than a very superficial level. The interview ended with X reaffirming his fear of his mother's prediction.

In reconstructing the events of his death, it was found that X had called his mother shortly after 5:30 p.m. His wife, present in the mother's home at the time, confirmed the story. X had told his mother that he had concrete plans to reinvest his money in another business which would not require her intervention. He expressed optimism for his future health. His mother made no attempt to dissuade him, but ended the conversation with a statement to the effect that regardless of how he or the doctors felt, he should remember her warning and be prepared for her prediction of "dire results." Give or take a few minutes, X was dead within the hour.

DISCUSSION

Psychophysiological conditions are known to be present in a large percentage of medical patients, but the possibility that emotional factors may contribute in a major way to an illness is not often considered. Psychological death, whether by the weird incantations of a primitive shaman or by the malevolent wish of a thwarted mother, is a difficult thing for a scientifically trained physician to accept. Whatever name is given, it seems evident that such things may occur in a more complex although less dramatic form in our modern civilization.

The influence of the mother's death wish in this case can be regarded at least as a triggering mechanism for the asthmatic attacks. X may have interpreted the prophecy as a sign that mother was lost and reconciliation impossible. This might explain the further aggravation and intensity of the attacks, and the fatal attack could be regarded as the final event in a chain of circumstances in which mother's prophecy played a major precipitating and sustaining role.

In a summary of the psychogenic factors in bronchial asthma, French and Alexander state: "Firstly, the asthmatic attack is a reaction to the danger of separation from the mother, and secondly, the attack is a sort of equivalent of an inhibited and repressed cry of anxiety and rage, and thirdly, the sources of danger of losing the mother are due to some temptation to which the patient is exposed." (5)

In a study of a hospitalized medical population Schmale was impressed by the depression which followed a real or symbolic loss of or separation from an important person in individuals with life-long unsupported dependency needs and rejection. (6) The question arose as to why such patients developed physiological symptoms rather than pure psychological depression. X poses a similar problem. Also unanswered is whether the asthma developed as a "voodoo-like" response to the mother's threat and continued to be aggravated to the point of death, or whether it developed from other causes and was aided and nurtured by the perceived hopelessness of the situation.

Passive-dependent individuals such as Mr. X are not rare. They are highly suggestible people. When a situation arises which threatens a loss of dependency gratifications, real or symbolic, these people may develop physical illness and serious depression. In the case presented the mother's suggestion of "dire results" was direct and verbal. More often than one realizes it may be implied or even fantasied by the victim and it may be well to investigate the frequency with which this actually occurs.

If this case represents the sudden development of a previously nonexistent and eventually fatal disease due to "voodoo-like" suggestion, then it may be that much of the voodoo death of folklore was also psychologically provoked through physiological mechanisms different from those described by Cannon and Richter; that is, through development of psychosomatic disease.

REFERENCES

1. Frazer, J., and Gaston, T. H. *The New Golden Bough*. Criterion Books, New York, 1959.
2. Cannon, W. B. Voodoo death. *Psychosom. Med. 19*:182, 1957.
3. Richter, C. On the phenomenon of sudden death in animals and men. *Psychosom. Med. 19*:191, 1959.
4. Personal communication from Warren Thomas, D. V. M., Director, Lincoln Park Zoo, Oklahoma City, Oklahoma.
5. French and Alexander. Psychogenic factors in bronchial asthma. *Psychosomatic Medicine Monographs* II and IV, 1941.
6. Schmale, A. H., Jr. Relation of separation and depression to disease. I. a report on a hospitalized medical population. *Psychosom. Med. 20*:259, 1958.

REVIEW QUESTIONS

1. What does Wolpe say is the foremost task of the clinician? What are some of the problems inherent in the evaluation of therapeutic success?
2. A student is a homosexual and this is causing him great anxiety. How would a therapist in the analytic tradition approach this problem? Contrast this type of therapy with that of a behavior therapist handling the same problem. Which approach do you think would be the most successful and why?
3. Describe how "systematic desensitization" might be used to help a person with a snake phobia.
4. What were the conditioned and the unconditioned stimuli in the study by Quarti and Renaud?
5. What was used as the original reinforcer in the study by Isaac and his colleagues? What became the reinforcer after the original reinforcer was no longer given to the two patients?
6. Are normal or abnormal behaviors more important in the treatment of psychotics according to the Isaac article?
7. What do Dollard and Miller say that symptoms can accomplish for the neurotic and how do they do this?
8. What do Dollard and Miller mean by their statement that "repression causes stupidity"?
9. What conceivably happens to antisocial impulses when we are awake and how does this change when we are asleep? What does this tell you about your own dreams and what could the content of your dreams indicate about your personality?
10. A friend tells you that he never dreams. What is a more likely explanation according to recent evidence?
11. How does Mathis hypothesize that the mother's death wish influenced asthmatic attacks in his case of voodoo death?

part ten
prejudice

The answer to the question of whether
prejudice is innate or learned has dramatic
implications for our society. If prejudice is
truly innate, there would be little hope for
our society to live together peacefully in racial
harmony. Psychologists have traditionally
thought that prejudiced behavior was learned
behavior. The usual explanation is that
parents (either consciously or unconsciously)
and society in general teach the young that
certain other members of the society are
inferior because of skin color, religious beliefs,
etc. The situation is thought to be analogous
to the way a child learns to fear snakes,
for example. A very young child will
approach a snake and fondle it with no
signs of fear. The same child at age 3 or 4,
after several trips to the zoo where his parents
have told him about the "horrors" of
snake bite and after he has seen two or
three jungle movies, will show tremendous
fear of snakes.

   The learned explanation for prejudiced
behavior is still prevalent today, and
there has been little evidence to contradict
this view. Presumably one of the primary
situations in which white children learn
prejudiced attitudes against blacks is in the
school setting. This would be particularly true
in a totally segregated school system. The
Supreme Court desegregation ruling of
1954 was hailed by many "liberals" as the
beginning of the end of racial prejudice in the

United States. There can be little doubt now in the early 1970s that this was not to be the case. One could argue strongly that the Court's decision was never fully implemented, and this partially explains the current racial tension in the United States. Stuart W. Cook (#52) outlines a series of research questions, the answers to which would provide a firm basis for evaluating whether even total school integration would substantially reduce racial prejudice in this country. He discusses the kinds and quantity of attitude change that we can expect from interracial contact and has some insightful comments about prejudiced behavior in general. Cook's article was published in 1957, and he concludes with a plea to psychologists to do the kinds of research he has been describing. While there are certainly some exceptions, there can be little doubt that psychologists have generally failed to provide answers to the important questions Cook raises. One can only speculate whether the same questions will still be around in the early 1980s. Perhaps the "new generation" of psychologists will do a better job than their predecessors; at least, one can hope that this will be the case.

The rapid and effective way in which black leaders in the United States were able to develop and cement the concept of black identity in the black community came as somewhat of a surprise to most psychologists. In a classic study of racial self-awareness, it was found that approximately one-third of the Negro children tested said that a white rather than a brown doll looked like them. This denial of racial identity and supposed confused self-image was thought to be a general characteristic of blacks in this country. Subsequent and more recent research has, however, indicated that the extent of black identity was probably greatly underestimated. Several methodological flaws in the original studies were corrected in the selection presented here (#53). The study

also points out an important lesson for anyone trying to apply psychological findings to current social problems. A certain amount of caution and prudence are obviously necessary.

Stuart W. Cook (#52) pointed out in his article that a person's stated opinion in the area of race relations is frequently not a reliable basis for prediction of behavior. One cannot always trust, then, a person's verbal report of his racial attitudes. Joseph B. Cooper, in "Emotion in Prejudice" (#54), reports on a technique for evaluating racial attitudes without having to depend upon the subject's verbal report. It is interesting to speculate whether refinement of Cooper's basic technique could be used to detect racial prejudice that even the subject himself was unaware of. It is one thing for a person to express positive attitudes toward a racial minority when he knows that he dislikes the group immensely, but quite a different matter when a person truly feels that he isn't prejudiced and an electrophysiological measure indicates that this may not be the case.

According to the scapegoat theory of prejudice, the prejudiced person is assumed to be apprehensive about directly aggressing toward the real source of his hostility and, therefore, tends to aggress in indirect forms and/or against substitute objects. This is known as displaced aggression and the student should be able to observe many examples of this in his daily life. Often an extremely prejudiced college student is merely displacing the aggression toward a minority group when in reality the source of the frustration is his parents, but he is hesitant to agress against them for any of a variety of reasons. Donald Weatherly (#55) subjected the scapegoat theory to experimental verification. Even though he was measuring anti-Semitism, presumably the same sorts of processes are operating in other kinds of racial prejudice as well.

Prejudice against women has certainly achieved notoriety in the popular press recently. Women's Liberation groups exist in most major cities and their membership rolls are growing daily. Naomi Weisstein is a psychologist, and she has strong words for psychologists and what could be called the "psychology of women" (#56). She concludes her paper with the following: "It is clear that until social expectations for men and women are equal, until we provide equal respect for both men and women, our answers to this question will simply reflect our prejudices." The question she is referring to is whether immutable differences exist between men and women apart from differences in their genitals.

52.
desegregation:
a psychological analysis

stuart w. cook

I want to talk with you about a psychologist's view of a major social change which is taking place in this country. I am referring to the series of events in the South which have followed the Supreme Court's decisions against segregation in public schools.

As *citizens* we may consider the Court's rulings wise or unwise, we may applaud or condemn specific actions taken in the South, we may find the ferment and the turmoil and the apparently inconsistent reactions in the South fascinating or confusing, or both. But as *psychologists* our approach must be to consider, on the one hand, whether our available knowledge can contribute to an understanding of what is going on, and, on the other hand, to seek in the changing situation opportunities for research which will increase our understanding of the process of change in relations between social groups.

I believe that even in the present rather primitive state of social psychology, we do have knowledge which would suggest a different interpretation of events than everyday common sense provides. Take, for instance, the recent vote in Virginia, in which residents of that state, by a two-to-one majority, approved a plan which will make possible the transformation of public schools into what are technically private schools in order to evade the Supreme Court ruling. A correspondent of the *New York Times*, in commenting on the vote, drew the con-

clusion that much of the South will not accept racially integrated schools and that desegregation there will have to be a slow evolutionary process. I am doubtful that this is the correct interpretation; I will shortly suggest another possibility.

Or—what about the school strikes? During the first weeks of desegregation in Washington and in Baltimore white children went on strike. Does this bode ill for future relations between white and Negro students in desegregated schools in those communities? The obvious interpretation is that the students struck because of their antagonism to association with Negroes. But is this interpretation correct?

And, on a much larger scale—what are the long-range implications of the fact that schools are being desegregated in many communities, and probably sooner or later throughout the South? Many interpreters have seen in this event the beginning of the end of racial segregation in the South. How realistic an expectation is this?

I don't know, with any certainty, the answers to these questions. In fact, my main argument is going to be that the significance of the Supreme Court's decision, from the standpoint of a *science of psychology,* is that it provides a rare opportunity to acquire more of the kind of knowledge we need in order to make better interpretations of such matters than is now possible.

First, however, I want to indicate that I think we already know enough to suggest alternative—though not necessarily correct—interpretations for each of the points I have just mentioned.

Take the Virginia vote. My expectation would be that when school desegregation does take place in Virginia it will be with as little unpleasantness as there has been in places like Washington, Bal-

Reprinted from *American Psychologist*, 1957, *12* (1), 1–8, 12–13. Published by the American Psychological Association. Abridged by permission of the author.

Address of the President at the annual meeting of the New York State Psychological Association, New York, New York, January 28, 1956.

timore, and St. Louis, which have already undergone desegregation. I do not mean to say that I doubt that the people of Virginia are opposed to desegregation; on the contrary, I think the vote is a very clear expression of that opposition. But I do not think it provides a basis for predicting what their behavior will be when school desegregation is initiated. I would guess that, if similar votes had been taken in other communities before desegregation was started, the balloting would have been about the same.

I base my interpretation on a number of studies which suggest that, in the area of race relations, stated opinion is frequently not a reliable basis for prediction of behavior. The classic example, of course, is the study in which LaPiere (6), after traveling throughout the United States with a Chinese couple, wrote to the hotels and restaurants which they had visited, asking if the establishment would accept Chinese as guests. What he found was that over 90 per cent of the respondents (all of whom actually had served the Chinese couple) said they would not do so. Saenger's (9) interviews with white women in New York City made the same point. Individuals who had been seen buying goods from Negro salesgirls denied that they would do so.

At it happens, we have *direct* evidence that stated opposition to school desegregation in Southern communities does not necessarily lead to hostile *action* once desegregation has been initiated.

For example, Bower and Walker (1) in interviews with a cross section of the population of Washington, D.C., in June, 1954, found that 52 per cent of the white respondents thought the Supreme Court decision was bad, only 24 per cent thought it was good, and another 24 per cent was neutral. In other words, among those who had definite opinions, feeling was two to one against the decision—the same proportion as the Virginia vote. Yet desegregation took place the following fall. According to Bower and Walker, the first gradual change-over worked so well that the school superintendent decided to speed the process a bit and authorized a large-scale transfer: at this point there was a brief strike by junior and senior high school students, which collapsed after a few days when it received little support from the adult community. Except for this brief strike, desegregation proceeded without incident. When the same sample of respondents were reinterviewed toward the end of the school year, even among those who had disapproved of the Supreme Court decision, 39 per cent conceded that desegregation was going "very well" or "fairly well," and only 29 per cent said it was going "not so well" or "badly."

Or take the story of Tucson, Arizona, as reported by Edward and Marianne Dozier in Schools in Transition, a series of community studies edited by Williams and Ryan (11). In the spring of 1950 a bill to make school desegregation compulsory was presented directly to the voters of the state, and was rejected. During this election the Tucson superintendent of schools publicly supported the bill; he received a number of anonymous letters and telephone calls condemning his stand. A year later the state legislature passed a bill permitting desegregation, but not requiring it. The Tucson schools were desegregated at the beginning of the next school term—and at this time there was no public protest from anyone in the community. Other examples of this same sort could be cited.

As for the school strikes—my guess is that, far from being an omen of continuing trouble, they will leave almost no trace. I would predict that if after a few months you looked at interracial associations and attitudes within the schools in towns in which there had been strikes and others which desegregated at the same time without any student strikes, you would find few, if any, differences. I base this interpretation not only on the principle I mentioned in connection with the Virginia vote—that expressed opposition is not necessarily a reliable indicator of future behavior—but on a question as to whether strikes really do reflect widespread student opposition to desegregation. Two of the most widely publicized strikes have been in Washington and Baltimore. But in Washington only 2 per cent, and in Baltimore only 3 per cent, of the total student body stayed out of school. Bower, Walker, and Mendelsohn (1, 7) interviewed 100 student strikers in

Washington and concluded, briefly, that "nothing specific seemed to have started the strike and students participated mostly because other students were in it." Although the strikers repeated rumors about attacks by Negroes on white students, when they were asked what made them stay out of school, the most frequent answer did not refer to the ostensible issues but to the influence of their friends and schoolmates. Many were carrying schoolbooks and lunch boxes, and had clearly set out for school as usual; they were drawn into the strike along the way, and one may speculate that they participated as much for the adventure as for reasons having to do with segregation or desegregation.

What about the expectation that the end of school segregation will lead to sweeping changes in the pattern of race relations in the South—and, specifically, that it will mean the end of all segregation? In expressing some reservations about this I do not mean for one moment to underestimate the importance of the Supreme Court decisions; I share the general judgment that they constitute a major historic event. But I think there is a tendency to overestimate the probable effects of the change in school patterns, both among liberals who *hope* that desegregation of schools will lead to desegregation in all aspects of life, and among many Southerners who *fear* that it will. One of the clearest findings of studies of the relation between intergroup contact and attitude change is that, while individuals rather quickly come to accept and even approve of association with members of another social group in situations of the type where they have experienced such association, this approval is not likely to be generalized to other situations unless the individuals have quite close personal relationships with members of the other group. Thus, for example, Harding and Hogrefe (4) found that white salesgirls in Philadelphia department stores who worked in departments where there were Negro salesgirls were more likely than those in all-white departments to express willingness to work with Negroes, but were no more willing to have Negroes as neighbors or as friends. A particularly dramatic example of the extent to which behavior may be limited to a specific situation is Minard's description (8) of a mining community in West Virginia where white and Negro miners work amicably together in mixed teams, sometimes with a Negro supervising white workers, but separate at the mine shaft and lead their aboveground lives in complete segregation— living in separate neighborhoods, eating in separate restaurants, participating jointly in no activities save those in the union hall. And one need only look around any Northern community to see that unsegregated schools do not necessarily lead to unsegregated living.

That this kind of compartmentalization occurs also when schools are newly desegregated is evidenced by the descriptions of a number of border communities, in the Williams and Ryan book (11). In community after community they report that, although relations between white and Negro students within the schools are matter-of-fact and even friendly, the two groups go their separate ways outside of school. The example is given of a white mother, at first reluctant to send her children to a mixed school, who found that her children liked the school and their Negro teachers. She became perfectly tolerant about the classroom situation, but did not want her children to eat in the school cafeteria or play with Negro students off the school grounds. Time will tell, of course, whether over a period of years school desegregation will gradually extend to desegregation in other areas of living, but there seems no reason to expect an immediate sweeping change.

THE NEED FOR AN ANALYTICAL SCHEMA

These few examples are more than enough to show how our present understanding of social relations leads us to question the more obvious common sense interpretations which are usually offered. We look for meanings other than those which appear on the face of things and, by taking a more comprehensive view of the determinants of human action, less often assume direct correspondence between stated opinion and other kinds of behavior. Such an approach suggests alternative and probably more accurate interpretations of specific events. But, to be most useful, psychological science must go beyond explanations of specific phenomena, and provide a schema within which a range of events can be organized and understood. Can social psychology provide such a framework for viewing the present scene?

My answer—as you may guess—is "yes" and "no." To elaborate this, I must distinguish between two aspects of the events following on the Supreme Court decision: first, those having to do with the decision of policy makers whether to accept the Court's ruling and desegregate the schools; second, those having to do with what happens once desegregation has been initiated. On questions of the second sort—the process and the effects of desegregation—we have a considerable body of relevant information, and, I think, the beginnings of an organized analytical approach. Within this schema we have a basis for at least tentative predictions and for identifying with some certainty the kinds of situations in which research could provide answers to crucial questions. On the first aspect—that of the process of deciding whether to desegregate—we have much less to draw upon; I should say we are in a position of having to develop simultaneously both a systematic approach and ways of testing the hypotheses which grow out of this approach.

ATTITUDE CHANGES FOLLOWING INTERGROUP CONTACT

Let me start with the area in which I think our knowledge and our thinking are relatively far along. After the last war, a number of psychologists and sociologists interested in attitude change turned their attention to problems of intergroup relations. They developed a consensus that some of the most important determinants of attitude change toward other social groups were to be found in the experience of face-to-face contact with members of those groups. At first, they tended to the optimistic view that such personal contact with members of another group was sure to

be a powerful influence toward *favorable* attitude change.

However, in spite of the considerable number of studies which found such a relationship, some did not. A much earlier study by Horowitz (5)—and one of the most interesting in the present context—had already reported that attitudes toward Negroes of white boys in racially mixed schools in New York City differed little from attitudes of white boys in segregated schools in Tennessee and in Georgia.

Additional research on the relationship between intergroup contact and changes in attitude gave rise to a variation of the old chicken-and-egg question: A number of studies had found contact with members of an ethnic group other than one's own associated with favorable attitudes toward that ethnic group. But which came first—the contact or the favorable attitude? This methodological difficulty led to an interest in situations of so-called involuntary contact—on the job, in public housing, in the armed forces, etc.—that is, in situations where the individual is in a setting where there are members of another social group, but he is there not because of a desire to associate with that group but because of a strong push or pull from some other source.

Also, it proved helpful to distinguish between mere physical presence of members of different ethnic groups in a common situation, on the one hand, and the occurrence of interaction between them, on the other. We are now thinking in terms of the following schema: Individuals from two ethnic groups encounter one another involuntarily in some situation. This encounter may or may not lead to interaction, depending on the characteristics of the individuals involved and on the nature of the situation. When it does, the interaction may vary in amount and quality and this variation, in turn, influences the type of attitude change which takes place.

The Influence of Conditions Under Which Contact Occurs. When we raise the question, "What does the nature of the contact situation have to do with the outcome of the experience?", the need to identify the dimensions in terms of which contact situations can be described becomes apparent.

Here are three examples of what I mean. One of the characteristics of a contact situation is the extent to which it offers the opportunity for the participants to get to know one another—labeled, for short, its *acquaintance potential*. There is great variation in the extent to which the characteristics of individuals are revealed during contact. You may encounter an elevator operator, for example, twice a day for years, without communication about anything other than the weather. A contrasting situation—that of living as neighbors—does not impose comparable limitations on the areas over which communication may take place and individuality emerge.

A second characteristic of contact situations has to do with the way in which they define the *relative status* of participants belonging to the two ethnic groups. For example, in a given work situation, Negroes may have only menial jobs while white persons are in skilled or supervisory positions; in another work situation, Negroes and whites may be doing the same kinds of jobs.

My third example of a dimension along which contact situations differ involves the nature of the *social norm* toward contact of one ethnic group with another. In some situations, the general expectation of persons in authority and of most of the participants may be that friendly association between members of the two groups is appropriate; in other situations, even though for some reason members of the two groups are present, the general feeling on the part of at least one of the groups may be that any unnecessary mingling should be avoided.

I have time this afternoon to examine the implications of only one of these three concepts for our thinking about the outcomes of desegregation in the public schools of the South—the social norm regarding interaction with the other group. Several studies have pointed to the significance of this variable.

Thus, Minard (8), in the study I have already mentioned of the behavior of white workers in coal mines where they worked with Negroes on an unsegregated basis, and of the same workers in the segregated communities where the mines were located, estimated that about three-fifths of the men adapted their behavior, without apparent conflict, to the generally accepted practices in the specific situation —even to the extent of sitting next to Negroes in the mine bus but sitting in the white section when they transfer to the public bus.

The perceived norm with regard to contact also has wider effects. In a study of relationships within biracial public housing projects (12), we found that white housewives differed not only in the extent of their association with Negroes in the project but in their views as to whether other white women in the project approved of associating with Negroes. We found that those who believed that the other white women in the project approved of such association showed much more favorable attitudes toward Negroes than did those who believed that the other white women disapproved of such association. With minor exceptions, this influence of the perceived social norm showed up regardless of whether the women lived in integrated or in building-segregated projects, or of whether they had much or little contact with Negroes: those who believed the other white women in the project approved of interracial association were more favorable in their attitudes toward Negroes than were the comparable white housewives who thought such association was not approved.

The question may, of course, be raised whether perception of the social climate is not itself a function of one's own attitude. The investigators in this study concluded that, while the white housewife's own attitude might color to some extent her interpretation of the views of other women in the project, on the whole the perceptions of social climate were based on more or less objective evidence.

The cumulative weight of these and other studies highlights the effect of what is generally referred to as the social climate or social atmosphere. What they tell us is that interracial contacts take place in a social context in which the individual is responding not only to persons from another ethnic group but also to what he believes would be judged proper in such relationships by those whose social approval he needs and seeks. This, of course, is a familiar and pervasive characteristic of human behavior. The fact that it operates generally below the level of conscious awareness and is often accompanied by the production of beliefs and feelings which rationalize otherwise incomprehensible behavior gives it a prominent place in the study of social relations.

Nevertheless not enough progress has been made with the task of studying analytically the effect of social climate on the outcomes of intergroup contact. Some effort has been made to identify factors contributing to it. It seems possible to distinguish several components: first, positions taken publicly by individuals or groups who carry an aura of moral authority or of extremely high prestige (for example, the Supreme Court, the President of the United States, church figures); second, the attitudes and behavior of the general population of the community or the region; third, the statements and practices of persons in authority in the particular situation such as the employer or the school superintendent; and fourth, the behavior, expectations, beliefs, etc., of other members of one's own group with whom one is in direct personal association.

It would be of great interest to know, for instance, the relative weight of a position taken by a powerful but distant authority such as the Supreme Court as compared with the norms of the face-to-face group in influencing an individual's reaction to new experiences of interracial contact. And it would be of interest to know what effect a face-to-face group norm that is in conflict with the position taken by the powerful but distant authority has on the interpretation of the latter's action and how this bears on the individual's reaction to novel contact experiences. Do Southerners, for instance, more than others, perceive the anti-segregation decisions as a political—in the low sense of the term—act rather than as a truly juridical one? And do individuals who so perceive the decisions react differently to contact experiences than do

those who believe the Supreme Court justices were honestly and faithfully attempting to abide by strictly constitutional considerations?

In cases where the norm of the immediate group differs from that held by the larger population, we need to know which one is more likely to be followed. And, since the other members of one's immediate group in a situation of intergroup contact are themselves subject to the influences of the contact experience, we need to study changes in the face-to-face group norm itself.

The Supreme Court decisions, and the events which have followed them, provide a rare opportunity for studying questions of this sort. We are, in effect, presented with a ready-made laboratory in which, on the one hand, the position of national figures—notably, of course, of the Court itself—has become prominent and is a constant, but where individual communities present a wide range of variation in terms of the position taken by state and city political leaders, local school authorities, and the residents. Studies of border communities in which school desegregation has already taken place, as reported by Williams and Ryan (11), show an enormous range in this respect. In Cairo, Illinois, for instance, desegregation was initiated reluctantly, as the result of threats that the state would withhold financial aid and of legal action by the NAACP; the local school authorities, apparently the entire white population, and much of the Negro population, appeared to be opposed to desegregation. At the other extreme, Carlsbad, New Mexico, operating under a permissive state law, began to desegregate its schools two years before the Supreme Court decision was actually handed down. All important segments of the community seemed to support the move. The superintendent of schools advocated it; the board of education favored the change on the basis of monetary savings; teachers and principals, on the whole, were not opposed; the Ministerial Alliance cooperated; community leaders in general took the position that times were changing, and "we might as well go along with it since we can't stop it"; the white high school students voted for integration at the high school level. There are still other communities—such as Hoxie, Arkansas—where the school authorities favor desegregation on economic grounds but general community opinion is strongly opposed.

This wide variation among communities provides a striking opportunity—one which it is probably not possible to create under laboratory conditions, and which is not likely to be again duplicated on such a scale in our lifetime—for studying the effects on social change of differences in social norms, and the relative influence of different sources of norms.

Were we able to utilize this real-life laboratory, I would find of especial interest the community which desegregates its schools while all the sources of social climate save those at the national level oppose the step and, where possible, act to limit its effect. It is in such communities that I suspect we may see the really dramatic developments. Under the influence of the social norms which prevail at the outset, the schoolroom contact may seem for some time to be without effect. Then at some later period—and I could not guess how much later—there will be a time during which change in the relationships between white and Negro students proceeds at what will seem an unexpectedly rapid pace. Behind this, if I am right, will lurk unrecognized the influence of a changed social norm among the students themselves. It seems to be often the case that the basis for a shift in norms develops well in advance of the shift itself. When, for some reason, the new norm crystallizes in the perceptions of members of a group they may show very suddenly behavior for which in fact they had been individually ready for some time. A factor which may help encourage such a development in school desegregation is the general readiness of adolescents to rebel against adult authority.

The Influence of Characteristics of Individuals Who Are in Contact. So much for this illustration of the need to think in terms of characteristics of the contact situation when analyzing the outcomes of involuntary presence in inter-

group contact situations. Let me mention more briefly another class of variables which seem important: namely, characteristics of the individuals who are in contact. They are of interest from two quite different points of view. First, each group constitutes part of the contact situation for the other group. Characteristics which are relevant from this point of view may be thought of as "characteristics of the individual as object" or "characteristics of the object-group." Second, each group may be looked at as potential changers as a result of the contact. Characteristics which are relevant from this point of view I shall refer to as "characteristics of the individual as subject" or "characteristics of the subject-group."

To the extent that learning about the other group takes place in intergroup contact, it follows that the characteristics of the individuals with whom contact takes place may have an effect on the outcome. With specific reference to the interethnic character of the contact, two aspects of the characteristics of object individuals seem likely to be of particular importance: the extent to which the individuals differ from the commonly held stereotypes about the object group; and the extent to which they resemble the subject individuals in terms of background characteristics, interests, etc.

It seems likely that the great variety of patterns which are appearing in the course of the shift to desegregated schools may give rise to situations which differ in this respect. For example, Valien's report on the process of desegregation in Cairo, Illinois *(11)*, notes that, because of a variety of community pressures, middle- and upper-class Negro children remained in segregated schools, and only children of the lowest socioeconomic group enrolled in the formerly white schools. Many of these children were below average in intellectual ability, had had poor records in the Negro schools, and did not do well in their new schools; according to the report, they tended, because of this selective process, to confirm the white stereotypes that Negroes are stupid and lazy. On the other hand, there will certainly be other communities where the children of the better-educated Negro families will enter mixed schools. While it will admittedly be difficult to identify in advance situations where the Negro children in a mixed school will tend to conform to the derogatory stereotypes and others where they will not, examination of the characteristics of residential neighborhoods should make it possible to identify schools where each of these situations is likely to occur. Comparisons of attitudes and behavior of white children in the two types of schools should throw considerable light on the importance of characteristics of the object individuals in determining attitudes.

When we consider the individuals in the contact situation as *subjects*, we regard them from a somewhat different point of view. Focusing now upon the attitude changes they may undergo, we would like to know why some change more and others less; some in one direction, others in another. Two classes of personal variables may be thought of as likely to influence the individual's reaction to intergroup contact: the nature and intensity of initial attitudes toward the object group, and aspects of personality or character structure which may predispose one to hostile reactions toward members of outgroups.

The few studies which have attempted to take account of initial attitudes have emerged with a striking diversity of conclusions. Two studies in public housing projects *(3, 12)* found that white housewives who said they were initially unfavorable to Negroes were *more* likely to report favorable attitude changes than were those who reported themselves as being originally favorable. Another study *(10)*, of white residents of a block into which Negroes had moved, reported exactly the opposite finding: those who were relatively favorable toward Negroes at the time the first Negro family was about to move in became more favorable after the Negroes had been living there a few weeks; those who were initially unfavorable had become still more unfavorable.

All of these studies took into account simply differences in the degree of favorableness or unfavorableness of the attitudes rather than the particular constellation of beliefs and feelings. It may be, however, that there are other differences in attitudes which make them more or less resistant to change. It has sometimes been stated, for example, that there are at least two distinct constellations of attitudes in the South. According to one, Negroes are gentle, fun-loving, jolly, but childlike and irresponsible; this attitude is said to have a warm, affectionate component; one is fond of Negroes, but just doesn't consider them intellectually and socially the same class of human being as oneself. The second, apparently quite different, attitude constellation is dominated by apprehension of the Negro as potentially dangerous, animal-like, and sexually uncontrolled. It is likely, of course, that the two constellations may often exist simultaneously in the same individual.

If these observations of differences in *kinds* of attitudes are correct, it is reasonable to ask whether they differ in the extent to which they can be changed by experience with Negroes. For example, if there is really an attitude which is made up of friendly feelings in combination with unrealistic beliefs about Negroes and a caste feeling that they are a different order of being (and from my personal experience, I believe there is), is it possible that experience with Negroes in a situation where at least officially they are defined as equals might correct the beliefs and gradually eradicate the caste feelings, without destroying the friendliness? Or would the disappearance of the caste distinction result in a threat to self-esteem which would generate hostility? To my knowledge, there are no studies on attitude constellations of this sort, and the outcome should be quite instructive.

The Research Potential in School Desegregation. Many of these questions can be studied as well in situations of involuntary contact in the North as in desegregated schools in the South. Why then do I emphasize the importance of research in Southern schools? Partly, it is because of the scale on which desegregation is taking place in the South. It is estimated that more than 150,000 Negro children who formerly attended segregated schools are now in mixed classes for the first time. Since in most of the newly mixed schools Negro children are in the minority, it seems safe to estimate that about half a million white children are for the first time having contact with Negroes in school.

From the point of view of research, the significance of change on such a scale is the probability that contact between Negro and white children will occur under a great variety of conditions and that this would make it possible to find contrasts which highlight the variable one is interested in studying. Moreover, the fact that the change is occurring in so many schools and so many communities means that similar combinations of variables will be repeated, thus making it possible to replicate studies and so check the findings.

The situation also presents a second advantage. Because of the gradualness of the increase in the number of situations of involuntary contact in the North, it is difficult to find comparable or contrasting situations in which interracial contact is about to occur for the first time. Almost all studies have been carried out in situations where whites and Negroes were already in contact at the time of the investigation; initial attitudes had to be recalled by the respondents or inferred by the investigators on the basis of indirect evidence. In contrast, the fact that thousands of children in hundreds of southern communities will be attending mixed schools for the first time offers an unprecedented opportunity for research which can get direct evidence of initial attitude and in which the process of attitude change can be traced rather than inferred.

There is still another advantage—namely, the possibility of checking findings which seem fairly well substantiated in Northern studies, in settings where the over-all milieu is quite different. For example, it seems quite well established that, under certain combinations of circumstances—such as those obtaining in interracial public housing projects in the North—actual physical proximity of residence of whites to Negroes is an important determinant of favorableness of attitudes toward them. Would this finding

hold in the quite different setting of a mixed school in a Southern town: will the white children who happen to be seated close to Negro children associate with them more, and become more friendly with them, than those who are seated farther away? Here I predict rather confidently that the answer will be yes. . . .

WILL THE NEEDED RESEARCH BE DONE?

I should like to be able to conclude my comments with the statement that the type of research I have been describing was being done or might soon get under way. Social scientists are agreed on the unparalleled opportunity which the situation presents. It seems inconceivable in the face of this that we should not make a major effort to utilize the opportunity. But as yet, with minor exceptions, we have available only a collection of case histories of school systems where desegregation has been initiated. Without detracting from their obvious value, it is clear that they can not give us the evidence in the form we need it if our understanding of social change is to be advanced. Nevertheless, with the exception of research on some aspects of desegregation in Washington carried out by Bower of American University and Walker of Howard University, and a few small-scale and isolated investigations supported by funds from the Society for the Psychological Study of Social Issues (2, 7), I know of no systematic work in progress or in prospect. And, worse yet, I am afraid the die has been cast and that little or no research is to be done.

Wherein lies the trouble? In view of the interest among social scientists, why do they not go ahead? The answer is that field research of the sort required necessitates funds for research expenses and these are not available. Government agencies which sponsor research have felt they could not incur the enmity of congressmen who might reduce support for their research as a whole. But what about foundations? To my knowledge, the major foundations having interests in this area have all been asked for assistance and the answer has been uniformly nega-tive. Why this is so I, of course, do not know. I trust it may be only a coinci-dence that the recent congressional in-vestigations of foundations were chaired by a southern congressman quite op-posed to social change. If it is not, it is quite understandable, although regretta-ble, that such investigations should have led to a more cautious appraisal of the wisdom of supporting research on con-troversial subjects.

It is a small consolation, but comfort-ing, nevertheless, to feel that we under-stand the events of this dramatic period in American history well enough to be able to conceive a fruitful research at-tack upon their meaning for social rela-tions in general. That this attack is not to be prosecuted is a scientific tragedy of the first order. Being possessed of a great faith in the determination and in-genuity of my scientific colleagues, I can only hope that the tragedy may yet be averted.

REFERENCES

1. Bower, R. T., & Walker, H. Early im-pacts of desegregation in D.C. Mimeo-graphed, Bureau of Social Science Research, The American University, Washington, D.C.

2. Crockett, H. J., Jr. A study of some factors affecting the decision of Negro high school students to enroll in previously all-white high schools, St. Louis, 1955. Un-published manuscript, Washington Univer-sity, St. Louis, Missouri.

3. Deutsch, M. & Collins, Mary Evans. *Interracial housing: a psychological evalu-ation of a social experiment.* Minneapolis: Univer. of Minnesota Press, 1951.

4. Harding, J., & Hogrefe, R. Attitudes of white department store employees toward Negro co-workers. *J. soc. Issues, 8,* 1, 1952.

5. Horowitz, E. L. The development of attitudes toward the Negro. *Archives of Psy-chology,* No. 194. New York: Columbia Univer., 1936.

6. LaPiere, R. T. Attitudes vs. actions. *Social forces,* 1934, *XIII,* 230–237.

7. Mendelsohn, H. The "student strike" as a sociopsychological reaction to desegre-gation. Mimeographed, Bureau of Social Sci-ence Research, The American University, Washington, D.C., 1955.

8. Minard, R. D. Race relationships in the Pocahontas coal field. *J. soc. Issues, 8,* 1, 1952.

9. Saenger, G., & Gilbert, Emily. Cus-tomer reactions to the integration of Negro sales personnel. *Int. J. Opin. and Attitude Res., 4,* 1950, 57–76.

10. Taylor, I. Personal communication.

11. Williams, R. M., Jr., & Ryan, Mar-garet W. (Eds.) *Schools in transition: com-munity experiences in desegregation.* Chapel Hill: Univer. of North Carolina Press, 1954.

12. Wilner, D. M., Walkley, Rosabelle Price, & Cook, S. W. *Human relations in interracial housing: a study of the contact hypothesis.* Minneapolis: Univer. of Minne-sota Press, 1955.

53.
reported magnitude of self-misidentification among negro children—artifact?

herbert j. greenwald and don b. oppenheim

Clark and Clark (1947), in a classic study of racial self-awareness, found that 33% of Negro children (39% of northern Negro children) said that a white rather than a brown doll looked like them. In Horowitz (1939), misidentifications were 42% (which dropped to 17% when a more reliable test was used). In Goodman (1946), misidentifications were 60%, in Morland (1958), 32%, and in Morland (1963), 54%. These studies, the Clarks' in particular, have had strong impact. For example, those prior to 1954 played a role in the United States Supreme Court desegregation ruling. The results might also lead psychologists to pursue such mediating factors as "denial of racial identity" and "confused self-image."

However, certain methodological aspects of these studies merit consideration. In the Clark and Clark, Horowitz, and Morland studies the Negro children were given a choice of only two skin colors (e.g., white versus dark brown). But in the Clarks' study, 80% of the light-skinned Negro children misidentified themselves, compared to only 23% for medium- and dark-skinned children.

Reprinted by permission from *Journal of Personality and Social Psychology*, 1968, 8 (1), 49–52. Published by the American Psychological Association.

This study was conducted in 1961 when both authors were in Goodwin Watson's social psychology course at Columbia University. They wish to express their appreciation for the assistance given to them by the nurseries and to Abraham Blum, Ralph Rosnow, and Roberta Marmer for their comments on the manuscript. Writing was partially supported by Boston University Grant GRS Ps-145.

Perhaps the lighter-skinned children were objectively correct: the white doll actually may have resembled their skin color more than the dark doll. And the Clarks' study, the only one which tabulated responses by Negro children's skin color, did not compare Negroes' responses with those of whites, although some of the later studies did make this comparison.

Perhaps the misidentification results are misleading. In studies employing only two alternatives, the responses of light-skinned Negro children may have been forced artifactually. Moreover, a certain percentage of children in any race may have an erroneous picture of themselves. The authors hoped to clarify these issues.

METHOD

The authors' study followed the Clarks', with six basic changes: (a) Three dolls were used, dark brown, mulatto, and white (instead of dark brown and white); (b) white children's responses were also obtained; (c) all subjects were from the north where misidentification has been found to be greatest; (d) the dolls were identical except for skin color (including the hair); (e) the questions were more open-ended (e.g., "Is there a doll that . . . ?" instead of "Give me the doll that . . ."); (f) the investigators were white (the Clarks are Negro).

Subjects and Experimental Procedure. Subjects were 75 nursery school children, 39 Negro and 36 white. Most were 4 or 5 years old, a few were as young as 3. Of the Negro children, 21 were male, 18 were female, and among the white children, 21 were male and 15 were female. Subjects were interviewed in integrated and nonintegrated nursery schools in Manhattan and New Rochelle (a suburb of New York City).

After initial contact with each child at play the child was brought into a separate play room by the nursery teacher and the friendly contact was continued after the teacher excused herself. The child was asked to point to a doll, clad in diapers, in answer to each question. The first question was, "Is there a doll that you like to play with best?" The other eight questions, which also began, "Is there a doll that . . ." were in sequence: ". . . you don't want to play with?" ". . . is a good doll?" ". . . is a bad doll?" ". . . is a nice color?" ". . . is not a nice color?" ". . . looks like a white child?" ". . . looks like a colored child?" and the critical question, ". . . looks like you?" Responses were scored in one of five ways: one, two, all (three) dolls, none of the dolls, or no answer. The last three answers, because they were noncommittal, were tabulated as "evasive." Each experimenter rated the Negro children's skin color independently. Nine Negro children were classified as light-skinned, 16 as medium, and 14 as dark. The Negro children were judged to be from the lower and middle classes, while all the whites appeared to be middle class. Two subjects in different subgroups were reinterviewed to check the reliability of the interview.

RESULTS

Reliability of the Findings. The two experimenters' judgments of Negro children's skin color agreed completely, as did the reinterviews. Judgments about socioeconomic status matched with one exception. The conclusions were similar for boys and girls, and regardless of whether the nursery was or was not integrated. These categories were pooled to aid clarity of presentation.

Responses to the eight preliminary questions (e.g., "Is there a doll that is a good doll?") are given in Table 1. Both Negro and white children rejected the colored dolls. This pattern is perhaps most clearly seen when the eight questions are categorized into four groups as in Table 1: it was the white doll

which was preferred for play (68% versus 21% for the Negro dolls), was thought to be good (69% versus 21%), and was believed to have a nice color (75% versus 20%).[1] (These percentages sum to 100% when the evasive responses are included.)

Moreover, just as the other researchers had found, the dolls' skin colors were accurately labeled by the children. Mean accuracy, for the two questions asking which doll was white and which colored, was 89% for the colored dolls and 84% for the white doll. (The Negro children were slightly more accurate.)[2]

These similarities to the previous researchers' results on the initial questions indicate high reliability over time, despite the intervening 20 years. (The Clarks' data had been gathered in 1939–1941, the present data in 1961.) And the similarity of the Negro and white children's answers suggests internal consistency. Apparently, then, different samples and sample sizes, the difference of an entire generation, the use of different dolls,

---

[1] These figures combine both Negro and white children's responses. Negro children's preference for white dolls was further corroborated by the difficulty in locating Negro dolls in the highly populated Negro areas of New York City. And only a few doll manufacturers were found who made both Negro and white dolls. None manufactured a doll of mulatto color. Three all-plastic dolls from the same mold were purchased, two white and one dark brown. One white doll was painted a "mulatto color" by a doll hospital. Then each doll was painted to be identical to each other except for body skin color. The non-factory-produced color of the mulatto doll, light grayish-brown, may have affected subjects' responses (see discussion).

[2] Westie's (1964, p. 992) hypothesis that Negro children may have preferred the white doll because of greater familiarity with it could not be checked with the present data since Negro dolls were still relatively uncommon (see ftn. 1). Nor could a second hypothesis be checked, that preschool children may not be able to understand the term, "Negro," since the present study used the term "colored doll." However, the Clarks' (1947, p. 172) data indicated that the majority of Negro children as young as 3 years were able to correctly identify the "Negro doll."

TABLE 1. Negro and White Children's Responses to Initial Questions About Racial Dolls, in Percentages[a]

Question	Doll[b]	Negro Children (N = 39)	White Children (N = 36)	Clarks' Results (N = 253)
Play preference				
1. Doll want to play with best	D	28	22	32
	M	13	4	—
	W	56	63	67
2. Doll don't want to play with	D	14	31	
	M	56	51	
	W	12	4	
Goodness evaluation				
3. Doll that is good	D	35	20	38
	M	15	3	—
	W	50	69	59
4. Doll that is bad	D	21	26	59
	M	59	51	—
	W	10	3	17
Color preference				
5. Doll that is a nice color	D	31	18	38
	M	8	8	—
	W	56	71	60
6. Doll that is not a nice color	D	17	37	
	M	62	57	
	W	13	3	
Color accuracy				
7. Doll that looks like a white child	D	5	0	5
	M	3	17	—
	W	90	78	94
8. Doll that looks like a colored child	D	73	54	93
	M	19	33	—
	W	5	6	6

[a] To aid clarity of presentation evasive answers are not included.
[b] D = dark brown doll, M = Mulatto doll, W = white doll.

and also white examiners did not bring about appreciably different answers to these basic questions.

Children's Misidentification of Themselves. However, changes occurred with regard to the critical question—which doll looked like them. As Table 2 shows, only 13% of the Negro children misidentified themselves in the present sample, compared to 39% among the Clarks' northern Negro children (33% in their total sample). As hypothesized, the mulatto doll did play a role in reducing the percentage of misidentifications. As Table 2 indicates, of the light-skinned Negro children only 11% misidentified themselves (i.e., reported that the white doll looked like them) in the present study —whereas 80% did in the Clarks' study. This reduction of incorrect responses was

highly significant ($x^2 = 83.37$, $df = 2$, $p < .0001$).[3] The results are similar to Horowitz' (1939) report of only 17% misidentifications. Interestingly, the number of misidentifications among medium-colored Negroes remained about the same (25% in the present study, 26% in the Clarks' study), but dark-skinned Negroes no longer misidentified themselves (compared to 19% misidentification in the Clarks' results). Perhaps this was because 50% of the dark-skinned Negro children were now able to identify with the mulatto doll.

[3] If the single light-skinned Negro child who identified himself with the white doll was objectively correct, then the overall misidentification among Negroes would be only 10%. Some of the Negro and white children's misidentification was due to inaccurate labeling of the skin colors.

On the other hand, misidentification among the white children was 44%. That is, it appeared whites were more likely than Negroes to make errors when matching themselves with a skin color (see Table 2, $x^2 = 16.29$, $df = 2$, $p <$ .0001). However, the authors' procedure may have artifactually contributed to the whites' misidentifications. Perhaps the mulatto doll was also an appropriate choice for some white children—those who were darker skinned. Unfortunately, this problem was not anticipated and no measures of white children's skin color were obtained. If the whites' selections of a mulatto doll (25%) are viewed as appropriate choices, then the picture changes considerably. The white children's misidentification would drop to 19%, resembling Morland's (1963) finding of 14% misidentification among white children. While still sizable, a fifth of the sample, this 19% of whites' misidentification would not be significantly different from the Negroes' 13% misidentification ($x^2 = 0.05$, $df = 1$, p nonsignificant).

"Evasive" Responses. "Evasive" responses were tabulated when an answer was noncommittal. However, there wasn't much "evasiveness," 6% for Negro children and 8% for white children overall. Most evasiveness occurred in response to questions about which doll was preferred for play and which dolls were good or bad, especially when the questions had a negative implication (e.g., "Is there a doll that is bad?"). Interestingly, the critical question in this study, subjects' identification of themselves with one of the dolls, did not elicit much evasiveness. Perhaps this question is not as disturbing to subjects as it might appear.

DISCUSSION

These results suggest that Negro children's misidentification in the previous studies, particularly the Clarks', may have been due to an artifact inadvertently introduced by having given Negro subjects a forced choice between two starkly contrasting skin colors, dark brown and white. By including an in-between (mu-

TABLE 2. Percentage of Negro and White Children's Selections of the Doll Which Looked Like Them[a]

Results	Negro Children by Skin Color			Total Negro Children	White Children
	Lt.	Med.	Dk.		
Present study[b,c]					
Doll color					
Dark brown	22	50	43	41	**19**
Mulatto	**56**	**19**	**50**	**38**	**25**
White	11	25	0	13	**47**
N	9	16	14	39	36
Clarks' study					
Doll color					
Dark brown	20	73	81	63	
White	80	26	19	33	
N	46	126	79	253	

[a] To aid clarity of presentation evasive answers are not included.

[b] White children misidentified themselves more than Negro children in the present study ($X^2 = 16.29$, **df = 2, p < .0001**) But see text for possible artifact. It appears that whites and Negroes may have misidentified themselves to about the same extent.

[c] To aid comparison with the Clarks' study, results for the mulatto doll and the white children are in bold

latto) color the light-skinned Negro children had a more appropriate color with which to match themselves.[4] Also, white children misidentified themselves to about the same degree as did the Negro children (perhaps even more so). This suggests that a certain amount of misidentification may occur among children regardless of race. Since recent replications of the Clarks' approach (choice of only two skin colors) have continued to produce sizable misidentification among Negro children, it appears likely that the present study's finding of more appropriate self-identification was due to improvement in the experimental design rather than to changes in the phenomenon under investigation. The authors conclude that Negro children do not manifest an unusual tendency to misidentify themselves. However, the similarity of the evaluative responses in all the studies

[4]It seems reasonable to expect a larger number of light-skinned Negroes in the north, through intermarriage. This may explain why the Clarks found more identification with the white doll among Negro children in the north (39% overall) than in the south (29% overall).

corroborates the unpopularity of Negro's skin color among children.

The mulatto doll received especially adverse evaluations. For example, only 13% of the Negro, and 4% of the white children preferred to play with the mulatto doll, while the dark doll was chosen by 28% and 22%, respectively (see Table 1). Similar responses occurred for the "goodness" and color-preference questions. Perhaps the doll's color, light grayish-brown (see Footnote 2), was a factor. If so, the evaluative responses should be interpreted with caution, although both the color accuracy and self-identification responses for the mulatto doll seemed appropriate.

Two fundamental methodological issues were interestingly illustrated in this study: the striking misinterpretations which can arise when (a) subjects' response range is restricted, and (b) no base line is available with which to compare the results. In the first instance, providing a more continuous response range improved the precision of subjects' responses. And in the second instance, the Clarks' implicit independent variable (subjects' race) had a "missing level" (white children). With inclusion of the latter for comparison a clearer perspective emerged for viewing both the direction and the magnitude of the Negro children's responses.

REFERENCES

Clark, K. B., & Clark, M. P. Racial identification and preference in Negro children. In T. M. Newcomb & E. L. Hartley (Eds.), *Readings in social psychology*, N. Y.: Holt, 1947. Pp. 169–178.

Goodman, M. E. Evidence concerning the genesis of interracial attitudes. *American Anthropologist*, 1946, 48, 624–630.

Horowitz, R. Racial aspects of self-identification in nursery school children. *Journal of Psychology*, 1939, 7, 9–99.

Morland, J. K. Racial recognition by nursery school children in Lynchburg, Virginia. *Social Forces*, 1958, 37, 132–137.

Morland, J. K. Racial self-identification: A study of nursery school children. *American Catholic Sociological Review*, 1963, 24, 231–242.

Westie, F. R. Race and ethnic relations. In R. E. L. Faris (Ed.), *Handbook of modern sociology*, Chicago: Rand McNally, 1964. Pp. 576–618.

54.
emotion in prejudice
physiological tests support the thesis that prejudicial attitudes are attended by relatively strong emotion

joseph b. cooper

Attitudes are viewed psychologically as learned sets, preparations for action toward particular stimulus objects. Although some attitudes are referred to as prejudicial, the specific characteristics which social psychologists agree upon as essential criteria for judging whether or not an attitude is prejudical are not fully understood.

One of the characteristics most investigators agree upon as an essential criterion for designating an attitude as prejudicial is level of emotionality. In fact some psychologists (1) have gone so far as to define prejudice as ". . . an emotional attitude." Gordon Allport (2) has stated this thesis operationally in the following way: "We tend to become emotional when a prejudice is threatened with contradiction."

Grounds for the thesis that prejudicial attitudes are supported by emotion are not especially convincing when viewed empirically. It may be that the thesis is acceptable to many psychologists partly because there seems to be no contradictory evidence. What supporting evidence there is has come principally from two sources. First, when a person verbally expresses a strong negative or positive attitude toward some human group, or defends such an attitude in the face of contradiction, he commonly displays behavior which is interpreted by others as emotional. Second, emotionally charged

Reprinted from *Science*, August 7, 1959, 130 (3371), 314–318. Copyright 1959 by the American Association for the Advancement of Science. Abridged by permission of the author.

words and phrases used in attitude scales are often selected by subjects as descriptive of their attitudes toward certain human groups (3). "Attitude scale" refers to any paper-and-pencil device to which subjects individually respond either by placing a given stimulus group (for example, ethnic or national) at some position on a preference continuum, or by checking a statement which is descriptive of the individual subject's feeling toward a given stimulus group.

If it is true that prejudicial attitudes are supported by emotion, it should be possible to detect the presence of emotion by physiological means as well as by attitude scale content analysis and overt behavior observation. Attitude scale "content analysis" is a procedure whereby statements which are descriptive of many possible feelings toward stimulus groups are categorized according to psychological meaning, that is, such meaning categories as emotional strength, type of emotion, cognitive state, and so forth. By "overt behavior observation" is meant observing humans react, and recording their reactions in accordance with certain categories; for example, emotional and nonemotional responses are tabulated. To our knowledge, physiological measurement has not been used to test the thesis that prejudicial attitudes which are subjected to verbal contradiction are supported by relatively high levels of emotionality (4).

It is known that emotion involves widespread physiological changes which have the effect of mobilizing the body to meet emergency. The galvanic skin response is regarded as a reasonably valid index of such physiological changes. When this response indicates a decrease in skin resistance, the inference is drawn that physiological mobilization has increased. Upon the basis of such an increase in physiological mobilization, the further inference is drawn that the level of emotion has increased. For a given subject, galvanic skin responses will provide an ordinal index of emotional level. That is, one measurement may be said to be greatest, another next greatest, and so on to that which is least. However, the response affords no information with respect to the cognitive direction an emotion may take. That is to say, the skin response does not distinguish scorn from fear, rage from joy.

This article (5) describes three exploratory studies, each designed to test the validity of the thesis that prejudicial attitudes are supported by relatively high levels of emotionality.

RESPONSES TO VERBAL CONTRADICTION OF POSITIVE AND NEGATIVE ATTITUDES

In the first study (6) college students were asked to rate and rank 20 alphabetically listed ethnic and national groups in terms of preference. Subjects rated each group independently by checking one of six graded preference categories: "like intensely" to "dislike intensely." They ranked the groups by designating the group liked best, next best, and so on, to the group liked least. The groups were: Argentines, Austrians, Canadians, Chinese, English, French, Germans, Greeks, Indians (India), Irish, Italians, Japanese, Jews, Mexicans, Negroes, Filipinos, Poles, Russians, Swedes, Turks. Interest did not reside in the particular named groups, but rather in each subject's negative and positive attitude-indicating responses to groups as groups.

Of 126 subjects, 26 confirmed the validity of their highest and lowest rankings (positions 1 and 20) by also rating those groups high and low, respectively. It was assumed that extreme rankings which were confirmed by extreme ratings identified prejudicial attitudes. Twenty of these 26 subjects were

subsequently available for individual laboratory sessions.

The equipment used to measure galvanic skin responses was a Stoelting psychogalvanoscope. With this equipment, resistance changes were indicated by a dial needle which reflected "units of resistance." Deflection magnitudes could not be directly compared from subject to subject since subjects balanced in at different response (resistance) levels. However, for a given subject in a given session, magnitudes of needle deflections could be directly compared. Thus, for a given subject, it was possible to obtain both ordinal and interval values of several possible emotion-evoking stimuli. That is, for a given subject, not only could his galvanic skin response magnitudes be ordered to ranks, but they could be assigned quantitative values which permitted their conversion to ratios. Because needle excursions varied not only in space covered but also in duration, the responses were estimated as the product of needle deflection multiplied by time. This was the procedure followed in this study. During the presentation of a stimulus by the experimenter the equipment operator observed two things, needle deflection and time. If and when the needle passed the fifth calibration mark (the pin was at 35 maximum) he started his stop watch. He stopped his watch when the needle came to the fifth calibration mark on its return.

Four brief evaluation statements were composed for use in the individual experimental sessions. Each was designed so that the name of any group could be inserted into it. Two of the statements could be used to place any inserted group name in a derogatory light, and the other two to place any inserted group name in a complimentary light. For a given subject, the name of his most liked group was inserted into one of the derogatory statements, and the name of his most disliked group was inserted into one of the complimentary statements. The names of the groups that the subject ranked in positions 10 and 11 were inserted into the two remaining statements—one derogatory and one complimentary. The order of presentation of the statements and the insertion of ranked (as confirmed by ratings) group names was randomized from subject to subject. The equipment operator had no way of knowing either the content or strength of the subject's scaled attitude toward any group.

One of the derogatory statements was: "People can be divided into two groups: the good and the bad. Close to the bottom of the list are the ———. They certainly can be said to have caused more trouble for humanity than they are worth." One of the complimentary statements was: "The world over, no single group of people has done as much for us, for our civilization, as the ———. The world will undoubtedly come to recognize them as honest, wise and completely unselfish." The other statements were similar to these.

After a subject had been balanced in, a trial statement which incorporated the name of the group the subject had ranked in position 9 was read. Following this the four critical statements were read.

Since galvanic skin response raw scores could not be directly compared from subject to subject, each subject's laboratory session was treated as an independent experiment. That is, intrasubject rather than intersubject comparisons were made. Thus, 20 separate experiments were conducted. The problem was reduced to determining in how many experiments the critical stimuli evoked relatively greater responses than did the neutral stimuli. The data were analyzed in two ways.

In the first analysis, each subject's skin responses to the names of the groups he had ranked in positions 10 and 11 were averaged. It was then determined by simple inspection whether or not responses evoked by critical stimuli (those relating to most liked and most disliked groups) were larger or smaller than the mean of the responses to the noncritical stimuli. It will be noted that for 14 of the subjects, skin responses were greater to derogatory statements containing the names of liked groups than to statements containing the names of groups toward which they had expressed a relative attitude of neutrality. The binomial test indicated a probability of .059. This provided minimal evidence for the thesis that positive (that is, favorable) prejudicial attitudes are supported by relatively great emotionality. However, for 19 of the 20 subjects, galvanic skin responses were greater to complimentary statements containing the names of disliked groups than to those containing the names of neutrals. In this instance $p < .001$. Thus, substantial support for the thesis that negative (that is, unfavorable) prejudicial attitudes are supported by relatively great emotionality was provided by this result.

The second analysis was purely descriptive. Ratios for each subject's skin responses were computed for the following: neutral attitude response (rank position 10) to neutral attitude response (rank position 11), positive attitude response to mean neutral attitude response, and negative attitude response to mean neutral attitude response. When these three distributions of ratios were compared, one significant observation emerged. The ratios of neutral to neutral stimulus-evoked responses clustered around unity; the variability was relatively slight. For both the negative attitude and positive attitude stimulus-evoked responses to neutral stimulus-evoked responses, the ratio variability was clearly much greater. This lends support to the contention that the group name stimulus was principally responsible for response magnitude, rather than the evaluation statement itself.

RESPONSES TO VERBAL CONTRADICTIONS OF NEGATIVE ATTITUDES—PARTIAL REPLICATION

The second study (7) was designed as a partial replication of the first. In view of the fact that in the first study only one of 20 subjects failed to respond to a negative attitude stimulus with greater emotionality than to the mean of neutral stimuli, it was apparent that further study of this relationship was warranted. Thus, the second study dealt only with negative prejudicial attitudes.

The same rating and ranking scales that were used in the first study were administered to 176 college students. Of

these, 31 gave extremely low ratings to
the groups they ranked lowest. Twenty-
three of these subjects were subsequently
available for skin response sessions.

A self-recording galvanic skin response
unit of a Keeler polygraph was used in
place of the dual-indicator Stoelting
psychogalvanoscope. This polygraph is
equipped with a kymograph which carries chart paper at a uniform rate beneath a recording pen. Skin response
magnitude may be calculated by measuring the area under the curve between
two given points.

Four 18-word complimentary statements were so constructed that the name
of a selected group could be inserted as
the second word. One of the statements
was: "The ——— have demonstrated to
the rest of the world that their excellence
is justly and honestly earned."

Subjects were individually escorted into
the laboratory room by the experimenter.
Rapport was established by introducing
the subject to the equipment operator,
and briefly describing the equipment and
the manifest purpose of the experiment.
After the subject was comfortably seated
in a specially designed chair, directions
were read by the experimenter. The directions included a statement instructing
the subject to refrain from overtly verbalizing about any of the statements. Subjects were urged to "concentrate on the
statement, imagining how you feel about
it or how you would respond." This control was introduced with the intention
of reducing the possibility that part of
the measured affectivity might be a function of preparing, responding, and listening to one's own speech in a social setting. The subject was seated facing the
experimenter, slightly to the right of the
equipment and operator. His position was
such that he could see both the equipment and the operator but could not
observe the pen tracings.

The equipment operator then attached
palmar electrodes. While the experimenter
read the directions, the equipment operator began balancing the subject into the
bridge circuit. After balancing in had
been accomplished, the operator nodded
to the experimenter, who, after a pause
of about 10 seconds, began reading the
first statement. The first statement was

the same for each subject and contained
the name of the group the subject had
placed in rank preference position 9. This
was for the purpose of validating the
skin response base line which had been
established for the subject. Into the three
remaining statements were inserted the
names of the groups the subject had
ranked at positions 10, 11, and 20. The
orders of presentations of both the group
names and the statements were randomized from subject to subject.

The same data analyses were made in
this study as in the first. Each subject's
galvanic skin responses to his rank position 10 and 11 stimuli were averaged.
This mean magnitude was then compared
with the magnitude of his response to the
statement containing the name of his
20th rank position. In 20 of the 23 cases,
responses were greater to statements containing the subject's most disliked groups.
The binomial test indicated $p < .001$.
Thus, this finding confirmed its counterpart in the first study.

Ratios for each subject's galvanic skin
responses were computed as follows: response for the statement containing the
group name of rank position 20 (disliked)
to the mean response for preference positions 10 and 11 (neutrals), and the response for rank position 10 to the
response for rank position 11. When
these ratios were rank distributed the
same pattern that was found in the first
study appeared. The ratios of negative to
neutral stimulus-evoked responses were
widely distributed, whereas those of
neutral to neutral were relatively restricted. This tends to confirm the results of the first study, which led to the
inference that the group name stimulus
is an independent variable of importance
in determining skin response magnitude.

ATTITUDES PREDICTED FROM SKIN RESPONSE MEASUREMENTS—REVERSE DESIGN

In the third study (8) the basic design
of the first and second studies was reversed. Subjects were first measured for
galvanic skin responses to complimentary
statements in reference to nine ethnic
and national groups. At a later time these
subjects were administered an attitude

scale containing the names of the same groups. From skin response records, predictions were made with reference to subjects' scale-measured attitudes. The basic prediction was: an excessive galvanic skin response to a complimentary statement concerning a group identifies that group as the object of a negative prejudicial attitude. In this study, subjects were not first screened and selected upon the basis of attitude scale results. Nothing was known of a subject's attitudes prior to his coming to the laboratory.

Seventy-two college student subjects were individually measured for galvanic skin response. Nineteen did not respond sufficiently for scoring, leaving a total N of 53. Approximately 1 week after the skin response measurements had been completed, these 53 subjects were administered a paired comparison attitude scale containing the names of the groups which had been used as stimulus objects in the skin response sessions. The paired comparison scale was so devised that the name of each stimulus object (in this case, a group) was paired once with every other. A subject's preference for each stimulus object could thus be assigned a score by counting the number of times the stimulus object was selected in preference to its paired opposite.

The Keeler polygraph was again used. Individual galvanic skin response sessions differed from those of the second study in four minor ways. First, the number of complimentary statements was increased from three to nine. Second, group names were reduced from 20 to 9 and scaled by paired comparisons. Third, statements were not randomized, and only three of the group names were positionally rotated from subject to subject. Fourth, the experimenter not only read the statements but operated the equipment as well.

The order of presentation of the nine statements was the same for each subject. Final balancing in was achieved by reading a preliminary statement which referred to the Irish. The names of three groups (Japanese, Jews, and Mexicans), minorities in the population from which the sample was drawn, were successively rotated from subject to subject into the statements which had positions 3, 5, and 7. It was suspected that one or another of these groups would later be scale-identified by some of the subjects as objects of strong negative attitudes. The rotation of these names was intended as a safeguard against possible positional effects.

The paired comparison attitude scale contained the following group names: Austrians, Canadians, English, Germans, Irish, Japanese, Jews, Mexicans, Poles, and Swedes. These names were randomly paired so that each appeared once with every other. Each subject circled the name of the group he preferred in each pair. The highest possible score for any group was 9 and the lowest was 0. The median test-retest Spearman rank correlation coefficient was .96.

Again, the hypothesis to be tested was: relatively strong prejudicial attitudes are supported by relatively high levels of emotion. According to the hypothesis, group name stimuli which elicit the greatest amounts of emotionality should identify those groups as objects of relatively strong prejudicial attitudes as confirmed by attitude scaling. Four analyses of the data were made.

The first analysis was restricted to data elicited by the three positionally rotated group names: Japanese, Jews, and Mexicans. By inference from the hypothesis, it was predicted that a subject whose galvanic skin response to one of these groups was above his mean galvanic skin response would rank that group below the median. The accuracy of the prediction was tested by the chi square test for two independent samples (9). For Japanese, Jews and Mexicans, the chi squares were, respectively, 8.54, 6.73, and 9.43. In each case $p < .005$. For most subjects, then, a relatively great skin response identified a group as relatively low on the paired comparison scale.

The second analysis dealt with data elicited by all nine group name stimuli. It was predicted that in most instances the group name stimulus which elicited the greatest skin response would be ranked below the paired comparison scale median. As it turned out, the group name stimulus which elicited the greatest skin response was ranked below the paired comparison rank median by 43 of

TABLE 1.   Galvanic Skin Response (GSR) and Paired-Comparison (P-C) Ranks for Stimulus Groups. GSR Rank 1 Indicates Least Response by Sample. P-C Rank 1 Indicates Best Liked by Sample

Stimulus Group	GSR Rank	P-C Rank
Swedes	1	2
Canadians	2	1
Austrians	3	5
English	4	4
Poles	5	7
Germans	6	3
Japanese	7	6
Jews	8	9
Mexicans	9	8

the 53 subjects. The binomial test result was: $Z = - 4.41$, $p < .001$.

The third analysis was the same as the second except for one modification.

Instead of the single greatest galvanic skin response, the two greatest were identified and the same prediction was made with respect to both being ranked below the paired comparison median. Of the 53 subjects, 41 ranked both below the paired comparison scale median. The binomial test was again applied: $Z = - 3.85$, $p < .001$.

The fourth analysis was directed to the relationship between the sample's attitude consensus toward the nine groups and the magnitude of galvanic skin responses which the group names elicited. The nine stimulus groups were ranked according to both skin response magnitude and paired comparison position. As predicted by inference from hypothesis, a positive relationship was found. The rank orders of these two variables are shown in Table 1. The Spearman rank coefficient was .82, $p < .01$ (10).

REFERENCES AND NOTES

1. R. Dewey and W. J. Humber, *The Development of Human Behavior* (Macmillan, New York, 1951).

2. G. Allport, *The Nature of Prejudice* (Addison-Wesley, Cambridge, Mass., 1954).

3. B. M. Kramer, *J. Psychol.* 27, 289 (1949).

4. R. E. Rankin and D. T. Campbell, *J. Abnormal Social Psychol.* 51, 30 (1955). White subjects' galvanic skin responses were greater to a Negro than to a white experimenter.

5. I wish to thank the following individuals: my former students D. N. Singer, H. E. Siegel, and D. A. Pollock for their assistance in designing and conducting the studies; Sidney Siegel for statistical advice; J. L. McGaugh for critical reading of the manuscript; and G. E. Kemp for preparation of figures.

6. J. B. Cooper and D. N. Singer, *J. Social Psychol.* 44, 241 (1956).

7. J. B. Cooper and H. E. Siegel, *J. Psychol.* 42, 149 (1956).

8. J. B. Cooper and D. A. Pollock, *J. Social Psychol.* In press.

9. S. Siegel, *Nonparametric Statistics* (McGraw-Hill, New York, 1956).

10. Since the levels of significance were clearly substantial, adjustment of significance level was not made.

55.
anti-semitism
and the expression
of fantasy aggression

donald weatherley

According to the scapegoat theory of prejudice, the manner in which a person copes with his aggressive urges has an important bearing on the degree to which he exhibits prejudicial reactions toward members of minority groups. The prejudiced person is assumed to be apprehensive about directly aggressing toward the real instigators of his hostility and as a consequence tends to express aggression in indirect forms and/or against substitute objects—i.e., he displaces aggression. This tendency to displace aggression is considered an important factor in producing and maintaining ethnic prejudice (e.g., Dollard, Doob, Miller, Mowrer, & Sears, 1939).

If there is in fact a functional relationship between a tendency to displace aggression and degree of prejudice we should expect to find that intolerant persons have a greater tendency than tolerant persons to displace aggression. Studies bearing directly on this proposition (Berkowitz, 1959; Lindzey, 1950) have produced inconclusive results. The pertinence of these studies to the scapegoat theory involves the assumption that prejudice is but one aspect of a more general tendency to displace aggression on the part of intolerant individuals. As Lindzey

Reprinted by permission from *Journal of Abnormal and Social Psychology*, 1961, 62 (2), 454–457. Published by the American Psychological Association.

This paper is based on a doctoral dissertation done at Stanford University. The work was done while the author was on active duty in the Army Medical Service Corps, enrolled in the Army Senior Psychology Training Program.

The author gratefully acknowledges the aid given by J. K. Adams, Robert Sears, and C. L. Winder.

(1950) first suggested, however, the prejudiced person may be one who has acquired a specific tendency to displace aggression *selectivity* toward members of certain minority groups. Thus, for example, the highly anti-Semitic individual may have a strong tendency to displace aggression onto Jews, but may not necessarily show other evidence of a strong tendency to displace aggression. The present study was designed to test this hypothesis.

Subjects differing in degree of anti-Semitism were compared with respect to their readiness to express experimentally aroused aggression in subsequent fantasy productions. By a special manipulation of the instructions for the fantasy measure, it was possible to obtain measures of aggression expressed toward fantasy characters with Jewish or non-Jewish names. As a test of the hypothesis that High A-S subjects have a greater specific tendency than Low A-S subjects to displace aggression selectively onto Jews, it was predicted that as a function of aggression arousal: High A-S subjects should express more fantasy aggression toward Jewish-named characters than Low A-S subjects; and High A-S subjects, as compared with Low A-S subjects, should direct more aggression toward fantasy characters with Jewish names than toward characters with non-Jewish names. The second prediction, it can be seen, refers to an interaction between the variables of A-S level and character name.

METHOD

Subjects and Procedure

The data were obtained from 100 male, non-Jewish college students, selected on the basis of extremely high and extremely low scores on the Levinson Anti-Semitism (A-S) Scale. Twenty-five High A-S subjects and 25 Low A-S subjects were subjected to an aggression arousing situation, and a specially designed fantasy test was then administered. Control subjects, individually matched with the angered subjects on the basis of A-S scale scores, took the fantasy test without prior aggressional arousal.

The data were collected in small group sessions. In Arousal group sessions aggression arousal was accomplished by making highly insulting and depreciating comments to the subjects in the course of administering a brief paper-and-pencil task to them. The insulting was done by the author. Immediately after this procedure a different experimenter administered the fantasy test. The situation was arranged so that the subjects would not perceive a relationship between the aggression arousing situation and the subsequent fantasy test. Following the fantasy test and before the subjects were told of the deception employed, they were asked to complete an open-ended questionnaire that gave them an opportunity to express hostility toward the author.

The same procedure was followed for the control subjects, with the exception that the paper-and-pencil task was administered in a friendly, nonprovoking manner.

A more complete description of this procedure has been reported elsewhere (Weatherley, 1956).

Fantasy Test

Eight original pencil sketches, each depicting four male figures involved in an ambiguous situation, were successively projected on a screen for 20 seconds in constant order in all sessions. The subjects were given 4 minutes to write a story about each picture.

In addition to the usual group TAT instruction (McClelland, Atkinson, Clark, & Lowell, 1953) the subjects were given the age, name, and occupation of a fictional character at the time each picture was shown. They were instructed to tell what was happening to that character in their story about the picture. Four characters were named and described to the subjects. Thus each character was presented twice in the series of pictures.

Two of the characters were given Jewish sounding names: Sam Goldblatt and Herb Rosen. The other two characters were called Ken Taylor and Jim Brooks. These were considered non-Jewish names. The choice of names was based on empirical results reported elsewhere (Weatherley, 1956). Each character was not only named, but described to the subjects as either a 28-year-old college graduate student or a 16-year-old high school student. Each of these two descriptions was combined equally often with Jewish and non-Jewish names.

Analysis of Fantasy Data

For each subject, a count was made of the number of aggressive acts directed toward each of the four characters which the subjects had been told to include in their stories. From this count, two total scores were derived for each subject. These scores corresponded to the total number of aggressive acts directed toward Jewish and non-Jewish characters, respectively. The data were then reduced to difference scores by subtracting the two scores of each control subject from the comparable scores obtained by his matched partner in the Arousal group. Since the Arousal and Control groups differed only in that the former was subjected to an aggression arousing experience prior to taking the fantasy test, these A-C difference scores reflected the net effect of aggression arousal on fantasy aggression.

RESULTS

Effectiveness of Aggression Arousal

The questionnaire administered immediately after the fantasy test and before the subjects were told of the deception provided one basis for comparing the reactions of the angered subjects with that of control subjects. As evaluated by three raters, 65% of the Arousal group subjects were judged to have expressed hostility toward the experimenter who had insulted them, while none of the subjects in the Control group did so. (There was not a significant difference within the Arousal group between High and Low

A-S subjects on this measure.) In addition to this questionnaire, at the end of the Arousal group sessions the subjects were asked to describe in writing how they had felt when insulted earlier in the session. All but 6 of the 50 Arousal group subjects admitted that they had felt angered by the comments of the experimenter. In addition, all of these subjects stated that they did not perceive a relationship between the aggression arousing situation and the subsequent fantasy test. Thus both in the report of their subjective feelings and in an objective measure of hostility expressed, the Arousal group subjects gave convincing evidence that aggression arousal had been effective.

Effect of Aggression Arousal upon Fantasy Aggression

The net effect of aggression arousal upon fantasy aggression is reflected in the A-C mean differences reported in Table 1. It can be seen that for High A-S subjects, aggression arousal produced a slight increase in fantasy aggression toward Jewish-named characters and a slight decrease in aggression toward characters with non-Jewish names. Neither of these A-C means differed significantly from zero. They did, however, differ significantly ($p < .05$) from one another when a one-tailed test was used.

For Low A-S subjects aggression arousal resulted in a very significant decrease in fantasy aggression directed toward Jewish-named characters ($t = 3.85$; $p < .001$) but only a slight, non-significant decrease in aggression directed toward non-Jewish characters. These two A-C means also differed significantly ($p < .05$) from one another.

As the findings reported above suggest, aggression arousal did have a differential effect upon the fantasy aggression of High and Low A-S subjects. It resulted in a significant difference ($p < .01$) between High and Low A-S subjects in the amount of aggression directed toward fantasy characters with Jewish names. An analysis of variance of the A-C difference scores also revealed a significant interaction ($F = 8.35$; $p < .01$) between the variables of anti-Semitism and "Jewishness" of the characters selected as targets of fantasy aggression. These obtained differences between High and Low A-S subjects were in accord with the predictions made.[1]

TABLE 1. A-C Mean Differences in Number of Aggressive Acts toward Characters with Jewish and Non-Jewish Names

Object of Aggression	Pairs of High A-S Subjects (N = 25)	Pairs of Low A-S Subjects (N = 25)	t between Means
Jewish Characters	.28	−2.04	3.05[c]
Non-Jewish Characters	−.56	−.68	.19
t between Means	1.81[a]	2.26[b]	

[a] $p < .05$, using a one-tailed test.
[b] $p < .05$.
[c] $p < .01$.

DISCUSSION

Despite evidence that the aggression arousing situation was successful in making the subjects angry, it did not result in a significant increase in fantasy aggression—none of the A-C means was significantly positive. Displacement of aggression in fantasy form was thus not formally demonstrated to have occurred. In general the reverse was true, especially in the case of the Low A-S subjects. Lindzey (1950), however, was able to demonstrate an increase in the fantasy aggression of both tolerant and intolerant individuals following a frustrating situation. This discrepancy between Lindzey's results and the present findings suggests that situational factors may play an im-

[1]The procedure of comparing High and Low A-S subjects in terms of A-C differences insures that any significant differences between them are a function of aggression arousal. It is of interest, nevertheless, to examine the data for possible differences in fantasy aggression between High and Low A-S subjects under control conditions. An analysis of variance of the fantasy data obtained from the Control group indicated that the High and Low A-S subjects who were not subjected to the aggression arousal situation did not differ significantly in the amount of fantasy aggression they directed toward the four fantasy characters.

portant role in determining the net effect of aggression arousal upon subsequent, indirect expressions of aggression.

In contrast to the frustration procedure used by Lindzey, the present study used a technique that evoked anger directed toward an easily identified instigator, implicitly involved strong sanctions against counteraggression, and evoked anger in subjects to an extent that made it relatively easy for them to recognize their own hostile feelings. Factors such as these may well have led to inhibiting influences upon subsequent fantasy aggression, in the angered subjects. In any event, the results dramatically demonstrated that aggression arousal did produce differences in reaction to the subsequent fantasy test.

In terms of the hypothesis under study, an important finding was that aggression arousal resulted in the High A-S subjects directing significantly more aggression toward Jewish characters than they did toward non-Jewish characters. This finding suggests that highly anti-Semitic persons do tend to select Jews over non-Jews as targets for aroused aggression. Furthermore, as predicted, it was shown that High and Low A-S subjects differed reliably in this respect. Also as predicted, High A-S subjects directed significantly more aggression toward the Jewish-named characters than did the Low A-S subjects as a function of aggression arousal. These results then support the hypothesis that persons high in anti-Semitism have a greater specific tendency then persons low in anti-Semitism to displace aggression selectively onto Jews.

Another aspect of the data serves to underscore the specific nature of the differences found between prejudice groups. High and Low A-S subjects did not differ significantly as a function of aggression arousal in the amount of aggression expressed toward the non-Jewish characters. The implication is that at least in a situation where Jewish objects are available as targets for aggression, the High A-S subject is not any more likely than the Low A-S subject to direct aroused aggression toward non-Jewish substitute objects. This finding argues against an explanation of prejudice as representing

merely one facet of a more general tendency to displace aggression diffusely.

So far, Low A-S subjects have been discussed only in connection with the differences found between prejudice groups. However, the reaction of the Low A-S subjects to the aggression arousing situations deserves attention in its own right. Low A-S subjects in the Arousal group directed significantly less aggression toward the Jewish-named characters than did their matched partners in the Control group. Thus they showed a definite inhibition of postarousal fantasy aggression with respect to Jewish-named characters. Even more noteworthy is the fact that as a function of aggression arousal Low A-S subjects directed significantly less aggression toward Jewish-named characters than they did toward the non-Jewish characters. This differential response to the fantasy characters is the reciprocal of that found in the case of High A-S subjects. In effect, the tolerant subjects gave evidence of a specific tendency to avoid expressing aroused aggression toward Jews.

This finding challenges the traditional image of the very tolerant individual as one who is a biasfree neutral in his reactions to minority group members. The Low A-S subjects clearly demonstrated a response bias when angered that was consonant with their expressed attitudes of extreme tolerance. The finding agrees with the proposition that extreme attitudes in any direction are likely to entail an appreciable emotional involvement. True emotional neutrality, in the case of prejudice as with any other dimension of attitude, may be found most often in persons who lie between the positive and negative extremes.

SUMMARY

In order to test a hypothesis derived from the scapegoat theory of prejudice, two groups of male college students, chosen on the basis of extremely high and extremely low scores on the Levinson Anti-Semitism Scale, were subjected to an aggression arousing situation. Following aggression arousal a specially designed fantasy test was administered, which yielded measures of aggression expressed toward fantasy characters with Jewish or non-Jewish names. Control subjects, matched with Arousal group subjects on the basis of A-S scale scores, took the fantasy test without prior aggression arousal.

Aggression arousal produced significant differences in the fantasy aggression of High and Low A-S subjects. The nature of these differences supported the hypothesis that persons high in anti-Semitism have a greater specific tendency than persons low in anti-Semitism to displace aggression selectivity onto Jews. In addition, evidence was obtained suggesting that individuals very low in anti-Semitism have a specific tendency to avoid expressing aroused aggression toward Jews.

REFERENCES

Berkowitz, L. Anti-Semitism and the displacement of aggression. *J. abnorm. soc. Psychol.*, 1959, *59*, 182–187.

Dollard, J., Doob, L. W., Miller, N. E., Mowrer, O. H., & Sears, R. R. *Frustration and aggression.* New Haven: Yale Univer. Press, 1939.

Lindzey, G. An experimental examination of the scapegoat theory of prejudice. *J. abnorm. soc. Psychol.*, 1950, *45*, 296–309.

McClelland, D. C., Atkinson, J. W., Clark, R. A., & Lowell, E. L. *The achievement motive.* New York: Appleton-Century-Crofts, 1953.

Weatherley, D. A. An investigation of the relationship between anti-Semitism and displacement, projection, and inhibition of aggression. Unpublished doctoral dissertation, Stanford University, 1956.

56.
psychology constructs the female, or the fantasy life of the male psychologist

naomi weisstein

It is an implicit assumption that the area of psychology which concerns itself with personality has the onerous but necessary task of describing the limits of human possibility. Thus when we are about to consider the liberation of women, we naturally look to psychology to tell us what "true" liberation would mean: what would give women the freedom to fulfill their own intrinsic natures. Psychologists have set about describing the true natures of women with a certainty and a sense of their own infallibility rarely found in the secular world. Bruno Bettelheim, of the University of Chicago, tells us (1965) that "We must start with the realization that, as much as women want to be good scientists or engineers, they want first and foremost to be womanly companions of men and to be mothers." Erik Erikson of Harvard University (1964), upon noting that young women often ask whether they can "have an identity before they know whom they will marry, and for whom they will make a home," explains somewhat elegiacally that "Much of a young woman's identity is already defined in her kind of attractiveness and in the selectivity of her search for the man (or men) by whom she wishes to be sought . . ." Mature womanly fulfillment, for Erikson, rests on the fact that a woman's ". . . somatic design harbors an 'inner space' destined to bear the offspring of chosen men, and with it, a biological,

psychological, and ethical commitment to take care of human infancy!" Some psychiatrists even see the acceptance of woman's role by women as a solution to societal problems. "Woman is nurturance . . . ," writes Joseph Rheingold (1964), a psychiatrist, at Harvard Medical School, ". . . anatomy decrees the life of woman . . . when women grow up without dread of their biological functions and without subversion by feminist doctrine, and therefore enter upon motherhood with a sense of fulfillment and altruistic sentiment, we shall attain the goal of a good life and a secure world in which to live it." (p. 714)

These views from men who are assumed to be experts reflect, in a surprisingly transparent way, the cultural consensus. They not only assert that a woman is defined by her ability to attract men, they see no alternative definitions. They think that the definition of a woman in terms of a man is the way it should be; and they back it up with psychosexual incantation and biological ritual curses. A woman has an identity if she is attractive enough to obtain a man, and thus, a home; for this will allow her to set about her life's task of "joyful altruism and nurturance."

Business certainly does not disagree. If views such as Bettelheim's and Erikson's do indeed have something to do with real liberation for women, then seldom in human history has so much money and effort been spent on helping a group of people realize their true potential. Clothing, cosmetics, home furnishings, are multi-million dollar businesses: if you don't like investing in firms that make weaponry and flaming gasoline, then there's a lot of cash in "inner space."

This is a revised and expanded version of "Kinder, Kuche, Kirche as Scientific Law: Psychology Constructs the Female," Boston, New England Free Press, 1968. Copyright 1970 Naomi Weisstein. Reprinted by permission of the author.

Sheet and pillowcase manufacturers are concerned to fill this inner space:

> Mother, for a while this morning, I thought I wasn't cut our for married life. Hank was late for work and forgot his apricot juice and walked out without kissing me, and when I was alone I started crying. But then the postman came with the sheets and towels you sent, that look like big bandana handkerchiefs, and you know what I thought? That those big red and blue handkerchiefs, are for girls like me to dry their tears on so they can get busy and do what a housewife has to do. Throw open the windows and start getting the house ready, and the dinner, maybe clean the silver and put new geraniums in the box. Everything to be ready for him when he walks through that door. (Fieldcrest 1966; emphasis added.)

Of course, it is not only the sheet and pillowcase manufacturers, the cosmetics industry, the home furnishings salesmen who profit from and make use of the cultural definitions of man and woman. The example above is blatantly and overtly pitched to a particular kind of sexist stereotype: the child nymph. But almost all aspects of the media are normative, that is, they have to do with the ways in which beautiful people, or just folks, or ordinary Americans, or extraordinary Americans should live their lives. They define the possible; and the possibilities are usually in terms of what is male and what is female. Men and women alike are waiting for Hank, the Silva Thins man, to walk back through that door.

It is interesting but limited exercise to show that psychologists and psychiatrists embrace these sexist norms of our culture, that they do not see beyond the most superficial and stultifying media conceptions of female nature, and that their ideas of female nature serve industry and commerce so well. Just because it's good for business doesn't mean it's wrong. What I will show is that it is wrong; that there isn't the tiniest shred of evidence that these fantasies of servitude and childish dependence have any-

thing to do with women's true potential; that the idea of the nature of human possibility which rests on the accidents of individual development of genitalia, on what is possible today because of what happened yesterday, on the fundamentalist myth of sex organ causality, has strangled and deflected psychology so that it is relatively useless in describing, explaining or predicting humans and their behavior. It then goes without saying that present psychology is less than worthless in contributing to a vision which could truly liberate—men as well as women.

The central argument of my paper, then, is this. Psychology has nothing to say about what women are really like, what they need and what they want, essentially because psychology does not know. I want to stress that this failure is not limited to women; rather, the kind of psychology which has addressed itself to how people act and who they are has failed to understand, in the first place, why people act the way they do, and certainly failed to understand what might make them act differently.

The kind of psychology which has addressed itself to these questions divides into two professional areas: academic personality research, and clinical psychology and psychiatry. The basic reason for failure is the same in both these areas: the central assumption for most psychologists of human personality has been that human behavior rests on an individual and inner dynamic, perhaps fixed in infancy, perhaps fixed by genitalia, perhaps simply arranged in a rather immovable cognitive network. But this assumption is rapidly losing ground as personality psychologists fail again and again to get consistency in the assumed personalities of their subjects (Block, 1968). Meanwhile, the evidence is collecting that what a person does and who he believes himself to be, will in general be a function of what people around him expect him to be, and what the overall situation in which he is acting implies that he is. Compared to the influence of the social context within which a person lives, his or her history and "traits," as well as biological makeup, may simply be random variations, "noise" superimposed on the true signal which can predict behavior.

Some academic personality psychologists are at least looking at the counter evidence and questioning their theories; no such corrective is occurring in clinical psychology and psychiatry. Freudians and neo-Freudians, Adlerians and neo-Adlerians, classicists and swingers, clinicians and psychiatrists, simply refuse to look at the evidence against their theory and practice. And they support their theory and their practice with stuff so transparently biased as to have absolutely no standing as empirical evidence.

To summarize: the first reason for psychology's failure to understand what people are and how they act is that psychology has looked for inner traits when it should have been looking for social content; the second reason for psychology's failure is that the theoreticians of personality have generally been clinicians and psychiatrists, and they have never considered it necessary to have evidence in support of their theories.

THEORY WITHOUT EVIDENCE

Let us turn to this latter cause of failure first: the acceptance by psychiatrists and clinical psychologists of theory without evidence. If we inspect the literature of personality, it is immediately obvious that the bulk of it is written by clinicians and psychiatrists, and that the major support for their theories is "years of intensive clinical experience." This is a tradition started by Freud. His "insights" occurred during the course of his work with his patients. Now there is nothing wrong with such an approach to theory *formulation*; a person is free to make up theories with any inspiration which works: divine revelation, intensive clinical practice, a random numbers table. But he is not free to claim any validity for his theory until it has been tested and confirmed. But theories are treated in no such tentative way in ordinary clinical practice. Consider Freud. What he thought constituted evidence violated the most minimal conditions of scientific rigor. In *The Sexual Enlightenment of Children* (1963), the classic document which is supposed to demonstrate empir-

ically the existence of a castration complex and its connection to a phobia, Freud based his analysis on the reports of the father of the little boy, himself in therapy, and a devotee of Freudian theory. I really don't have to comment further on the contamination in this kind of evidence. It is remarkable that only recently has Freud's classic theory on the sexuality of women—the notion of the double orgasm—been actually tested physiologically and found just plain wrong. Now those who claim that fifty years of psychoanalytic experience constitute evidence enough of the essential truths of Freud's theory should ponder the robust health of the double orgasm. Did women, until Masters and Johnson (1966), believe they were having two different kinds of orgasm? Did their psychiatrists cow them into reporting something that was not true? If so, were there other things they reported that were also not true? Did psychiatrists ever learn anything different than their theories had led them to believe? If clinical experience means anything at all, surely we should have been done with the double orgasm myth long before the Masters and Johnson studies.

But certainly, you may object, "years of intensive clinical experience" is the only reliable measure in a discipline which rests for its findings on insight, sensitivity, and intuition. The problem with insight, sensitivity, and intuition, is that they can conform for all time the biases that one started out with. People used to be absolutely convinced of their ability to tell which of their number were engaging in witchcraft. All it required was some sensitivity to the workings of the devil.

Years of intensive clinical experience is not the same thing as empirical evidence. The first thing an experimenter learns in any kind of experiment which involves humans is the concept of the "double blind." The term is taken from medical experiments, where one group is given a drug which is presumably supposed to change behavior in a certain way, and a control group is given a placebo. If the observers or the subjects know which group took which drug, the result invariably comes out on the positive side for the new drug. Only when it is not known which subject took which pill, is validity remotely approximated. In addition, with judgments of human behavior, it is so difficult to precisely tie down just what behavior is going on, let alone what behavior should be expected, that one must test again and again the reliability of judgments. How many judges, blind, will agree in their observations? Can they replicate their own judgments at some later time? When, in actual practice, these judgment criteria are tested for clinical judgments, then we find that the judges cannot judge reliably, nor can they judge consistently: they do no better than chance in identifying which of a certain set of stories were written by men and which by women; which of a whole battery of clinical test results are the products of homosexuals and which are the products of heterosexuals (Hooker, 1957), and which, of a battery of clinical test results *and* interviews (where questions are asked such as "Do you have delusions?" Little & Schneidman, 1959) are products of psychotics, neurotics, psychosomatics, or normals. Lest this summary escape your notice, let me stress the implications of these findings. The ability of judges, chosen for their clinical expertise, to distinguish male heterosexuals from male homosexuals on the basis of three widely used clinical projective tests—the Rorschach, the TAT, and the MAP—was *no better than chance*. The reason this is such devastating news, of course, is that sexuality is supposed to be of fundamental importance in the deep dynamic of personality; if what is considered gross sexual deviance cannot be caught, then what are psychologists talking about when they, for example, claim that at the basis of paranoid psychosis is "latent homosexual panic"? They can't even identify what homosexual anything is, let alone "latent homosexual panic."[1] More

frightening, expert clinicians cannot be consistent on what diagnostic category to assign to a person, again on the basis of both tests and interviews; a number of normals in the Little & Schneidman study were described as psychotic, in such categories as "schizophrenic with homosexual tendencies" or "schizoid character with depressive trends." But most disheartening, when the judges were asked to rejudge the test protocols some weeks later, their diagnoses of the same subjects on the basis of the same protocol differed markedly from their initial judgments. It is obvious that even simple descriptive conventions in clinical psychology cannot be consistently applied; that these descriptive conventions have any explanatory significance is therefore, of course, out of the question.

As a graduate student at Harvard some years ago, I was a member of a seminar which was asked to identify which of two piles of a clinical test, the TAT, had been written by males and which by females. Only four students out of twenty identified the piles correctly, and this was after one and a half months of intensively studying the differences between men and women. Since this result is below chance—that is, this result would occur by chance about four out of a thousand times—we may conclude that there is finally a consistency here; students are judging knowledgeably within the context of psychological teaching about the differences between men and women; the teachings themselves are simply erroneous.

You may argue that the theory may be scientifically "unsound" but at least it cures people. There is no evidence that it does. In 1952, Eysenck reported the results of what is called an "outcome of therapy" study of neurotics which showed that, of the patients who received psychoanalysis the improvement rate was 44%; of the patients who re-

---

[1]It should be noted that psychologists have been as quick to assert absolute truths about the nature of homosexuality as they have about the nature of women. The arguments presented in this paper apply equally to the nature of homosexuality; psychologists know nothing about it; there is no more evidence for the "naturalness" of

heterosexuality than for the "naturalness" of homosexuality. Psychology has functioned as a pseudo-scientific buttress for our cultural sex-role notions, that is, as a buttress for patriarchal ideology and patriarchal social organization: women's liberation and gay liberation fight against a common victimization.

ceived psychotherapy the improvement rate was 64%; and of the patients who received no treatment at all the improvement rate was 72%. These findings have never been refuted; subsequently, later studies have confirmed the negative results of the Eysenck study. (Barron & Leary, 1955; Bergin, 1963; Cartwright and Vogel, 1960; Truax, 1963; Powers and Witmer, 1951). How can good clinicians and psychiatrists, then, in all good conscience, continue to practice? Largely by ignoring these results and being careful not to do outcome-of-therapy studies. The attitude is nicely summarized by Rotter (1960; quoted in Astin, 1961): "Research studies in psychotherapy tend to be concerned with psychotherapeutic procedure and less with outcome . . . to some extent, it reflects an interest in the psychotherapy situation as a kind of personality laboratory." Some laboratory.

THE SOCIAL CONTENT

Thus, since clinical experience and tools can be shown to be worse than useless when tested for consistency, efficacy, agreement, and reliability, we can safely conclude that theories of a clinical nature advanced about women are also worse than useless. I want to turn now to the second major point in my paper, which is that, even when psychological theory is constructed so that it may be tested, and rigorous standards of evidence are used, it has become increasingly clear that in order to understand why people do what they do, and certainly in order to change what people do, psychologists must turn away from the theory of the causal nature of the inner dynamic and look to the social context within which individuals live.

Before examining the relevance of this approach for the question of women, let me first sketch the groundwork for this assertion.

In the first place, it is clear (Block, 1968) that personality tests never yield consistent predictions; a rigid authoritarian on one measure will be an unauthoritarian on the next. But the reason for this inconsistency is only now becoming clear, and it seems overwhelmingly to have much more to do with the social situation in which the subject finds himself than with the subject himself.

In a series of brilliant experiments, Rosenthal and his co-workers (Rosenthal and Jacobson, 1968; Rosenthal, 1966) have shown that if one group of experimenters has one hypothesis about what they expect to find, and another group of experimenters has the opposite hypothesis, both groups will obtain results in accord with their hypotheses. The results obtained are not due to mishandling of data by biased experimenters; rather, somehow, the bias of the experimenter creates a changed environment in which subjects actually act differently. For instance, in one experiment, subjects were to assign numbers to pictures of men's faces, with high numbers representing the subject's judgment that the man in the picture was a successful person, and low numbers representing the subject's judgment that the man in the picture was an unsuccessful person. The experimenters read the same set of instructions to two groups of subjects, and were required to say nothing else than what was in the instructions. One group of experimenters was told that the subjects tended to rate the faces high; another group of experimenters was told that the subjects tended to rate the faces low. Each group of experimenters was instructed to follow precisely the same procedure: they were required to read to subjects a set of instructions, and to *say nothing else*. For the 375 subjects run, the results showed clearly that those subjects who performed the task with experimenters who expected high ratings gave high ratings, and those subjects who performed the task with experimenters who expected low ratings gave low ratings. How did this happen? The experimenters all used the same words; it was something in their conduct which made one group of subjects do one thing, and another group of subjects do another thing.

The concreteness of the changed conditions produced by expectation is a fact, a reality: even with animal subjects, in two separate studies (Rosenthal & Fode, 1960; Rosenthal & Lawson, 1961), those experimenters who were told that rats learning mazes had been especially bred for brightness obtained better learning from their rats than did experimenters believing their rats to have been bred for dullness. In a very recent study, Rosenthal & Jacobson (1968) extended their analysis to the natural classroom situation. Here, they tested a group of students and reported to the teachers that some among the students tested "showed great promise." Actually, the students so named had been selected on a random basis. Some time later, the experimenters retested the group of students: those students whose teachers had been told that they were "promising" showed real and dramatic increments in their IQ's as compared to the rest of the students. Something in the conduct of the teachers towards who the teachers believed to be the "bright" students, made those students brighter.

Thus, even in carefully controlled experiments, and with no outward or conscious difference in behavior, the hypothesis we start with will influence enormously the behavior of another organism. These studies are extremely important when assessing the validity of psychological studies of women. Since it is beyond doubt that most of us start with notions as to the nature of men and women, the validity of a number of observations of sex differences is questionable, even when these observations have been made under carefully controlled conditions. Second, and more important, the Rosenthal experiments point quite clearly to the influence of social expectation. In some extremely important ways, people are what you expect them to be or at least they behave as you expect them to behave. Thus, if women, according to Bettelheim, want first and foremost to be good wives and mothers, it is extremely likely that this is what Bruno Bettelheim, and the rest of society, want them to be.

There is another series of brilliant social psychological experiments which point to the overwhelming effect of social context. These are the obedience experiments of Stanley Milgram (1965) in which subjects are asked to obey the orders of unknown experimenters, orders which carry with them the distinct possibility that the subject is killing somebody.

In Milgram's experiments, a subject is told that he is administering a learning experiment, and that he is to deal out shocks each time the other "subject" (in reality, a confederate of the experimenter) answers incorrectly. The equipment appears to provide graduated shocks ranging upwards from 15 volts through 450 volts; for each of four consecutive voltages there are verbal descriptions such as "mild shock," "danger, severe shock," and, finally, for the 435 and 450 volt switches, a red XXX marked over the switches. Each time the stooge answers incorrectly the subject is supposed to increase the voltage. As the voltage increases, the stooge begins to cry in pain; he demands that the experiment stop; finally, he refuses to answer at all. When he stops responding, the experimenter instructs the subject to continue increasing the voltage; for each shock administered the stooge shrieks in agony. Under these conditions, about 62.5% of the subjects administered shock that they believed to be possibly lethal.

No tested individual differences between subjects predicted how many would continue to obey, and which would break off the experiment. When forty psychiatrists predicted how many of a group of 100 subjects would go on to give the lethal shock, their predictions were orders of magnitude below the actual percentages; most expected only one-tenth of one per cent of the subjects to obey to the end.

But even though *psychiatrists* have no idea how people will behave in this situation, and even though individual differences do not predict which subjects will obey and which will not, it is easy to predict when subjects will be obedient and when they will be defiant. All the experimenter has to do is change the social situation. In a variant of Milgram's experiment, two stooges were present in addition to the "victim"; these worked along with the subject in administering electric shocks. When these two stooges refused to go on with the experiment, only ten per cent of the subjects continued to the maximum voltage. This is critical for personality theory. It says that behavior is predicted from the social situation, not from the individual history.

Finally, an ingenious experiment by Schachter and Singer (1962) showed that subjects injected with adrenalin, which produces a state of physiological arousal in all but minor respects identical to that which occurs when subjects are extremely afraid, became euphoric when they were in a room with a stooge who was acting euphoric, and became extremely angry when they were placed in a room with a stooge who was acting extremely angry.

To summarize: If subjects under quite innocuous and non-coercive social conditions can be made to kill other subjects and under other types of social conditions will positively refuse to do so; if subjects can react to a state of physiological fear by becoming euphoric because there is somebody else around who is euphoric or angry because there is somebody else around who is angry; if students become intelligent because teachers expect them to be intelligent, and rats run mazes better because experimenters are told the rats are bright, then it is obvious that a study of human behavior requires, first and foremost, a study of the social contexts within which people move, the expectations as to how they will behave, and the authority which tells them who they are and what they are supposed to do.

BIOLOGICALLY BASED THEORIES

Two theories of the nature of women, which come not from psychiatric and clinical tradition, but from biology, can be disposed of now with little difficulty. The first biological theory of sex differences argues that since females and males differ in their sex hormones, and sex hormones enter the brain (Hamburg & Lunde in Maccoby, 1966), there must be innate differences in "nature." But the only thing this argument tells us is that there are differences in physiological state. The problem is whether these differences are at all relevant to behavior. Recall that Schachter and Singer (1962) have shown that a particular physiological state can itself lead to a multiplicity of felt emotional states, and outward behavior, depending on the social situation.

The second theory is a form of biological reductionism: sex-role behavior in some primate species is described, and it is concluded that this is the "natural" behavior for humans. Putting aside the not insignificant problem of observer bias (for instance, Harlow, 1962, of the University of Wisconsin, after observing differences between male and female rhesus monkeys, quotes Lawrence Sterne to the effect that women are silly and trivial, and concludes that "men and women have differed in the past and they will differ in the future"), there are a number of problems with this approach.

The most general and serious problem is that there are no grounds to assume that anything primates do is necessary, natural, or desirable in humans, for the simple reason that humans are not nonhumans. For instance, it is found that male chimpanzees placed alone with infants will not "mother" them. Jumping from hard data to ideological speculation researchers conclude from this information that *human* females are necessary for the safe growth of human infants. It would be as reasonable to conclude, following this logic, that it is quite useless to teach human infants to speak, since it has been tried with chimpanzees and it does not work.

One strategy that has been used is to extrapolate from primate behavior to "innate" human preference by noticing certain trends in primate behavior as one moves phylogenetically closer to humans. But there are great difficulties with this approach. When behaviors from lower primates are directly opposite to those of higher primates, or to those one expects of humans, they can be dismissed on evolutionary grounds—higher primates and/or humans grew out of that kid stuff. On the other hand, if the behavior of higher primates is counter to the behavior considered natural for humans, while the behavior of some lower primate is considered the natural one for humans, the higher primate behavior can be dismissed also, on the grounds that it has diverged from an older, prototypical pattern. So either way, one can select those behaviors one wants to prove as innate for humans. In addition, one does not know whether the sex-role behavior exhibited is dependent on the phylogenetic rank, or on the environmental conditions (both physical and social) under which different species live.

Is there then any value at all in primate observations as they relate to human females and males? There is a value but it is limited: its function can be no more than to show some extant examples of diverse sex-role behavior. It must be stressed, however, that this is an extremely limited function. The extant behavior does not begin to suggest all the possibilities, either for non-human primates or for humans. Bearing these caveats in mind, it is nonetheless interesting that if one inspects the limited set of existing non-human primate sex-role behaviors, one finds, in fact, a much larger range of sex-role behavior than is commonly believed to exist. "Biology" appears to limit very little; the fact that a female gives birth does not mean, even in non-humans, that she necessarily cares for the infant (in marmosets, for instance, the male carries the infant at all times except when the infant is feeding [Mitchell, 1969]); "natural" female and male behavior varies all the way from females who are much more aggressive and competitive than males (e.g. Tamarins, see Mitchell, 1969) and male "mothers" (e.g., Titi monkeys, night monkeys, and marmosets, see Mitchell, 1969)[2] to submissive and passive females and male antagonists (e.g., rhesus monkeys).

But even for the limited function that primate arguments serve, the evidence has been misused. Invariably, only those primates have been cited which exhibit exactly the kind of behavior that the proponents of the biological basis of human female behavior wish were true for humans. Thus, baboons and rhesus monkeys are generally cited: males in these groups exhibit some of the most irritable and aggressive behavior found in primates, and if one wishes to argue that females are naturally passive and submis-sive, these groups provide vivid examples. There are abundant counter examples, such as those mentioned above (Mitchell, 1969); in fact, in general, a counter example can be found for every sex-role behavior cited, including, as mentioned in the case of marmosets, male "mothers."

But the presence of counter examples has not stopped florid and overarching theories of the natural or biological basis of male privilege from proliferating. For instance, there have been a number of theories dealing with the innate incapacity in human males for monogamy. Here, as in most of this type of theorizing, baboons are a favorite example, probably because of their fantasy value: the family unit of the hamadryas baboon, for instance, consists of a highly constant pattern of one male and a number of females and their young. And again, the counter examples, such as the invariably monogamous gibbon, are ignored.

An extreme example of this maiming and selective truncation of the evidence in the service of a plea for the maintenance of male privilege is a recent book, *Men in Groups* (1969) by a man who calls himself Tiger.[3] The central claim of this book is that females are incapable of honorable collective action because they are incapable of "bonding" as in "male bonding." What is "male bonding"? Its surface definition is simple: ". . . a particular relationship between two or more males such that they react differently to members of their bonding units as compared to individuals outside of it" (pp. 19–20). If one deletes the word male, the definition, on its face, would seem to include all organisms that have any kind of social organization. But this is not what Tiger means. For instance, Tiger asserts that females are incapable of bonding; and this alleged incapacity indicates to Tiger that females should be restricted from public life. Why is bonding an exclusively male behavior? Because, says Tiger, it is seen in male primates. All male primates? No, very

---

[2]All these are lower-order primates, which makes their behavior with reference to humans unnatural, or more natural; take your choice.

[3]Schwarz-Belkin (1914) claims that the name was originally *Mouse*, but this may be a reference to an earlier L. Tiger (putative).

few male primates. Tiger cites two examples where male bonding is seen: rhesus monkeys and baboons. Surprise, surprise. But not even all baboons: as mentioned above, the hamadryas social organization consists of one-male units; so does that of the Gelada baboon. (Mitchell, 1969). And the great apes do not go in for male bonding much either. The "male bond" is hardly a serious contribution to scholarship; one reviewer for *Science* has observed that the book ". . . shows basically more resemblance to a partisan political tract than to a work of objective social science," with male bonding being ". . . some kind of behavioral phlogiston" (Fried, 1969, p. 884).

In short, primate arguments have generally misused the evidence; primate studies themselves have, in any case, only the very limited function of describing some possible sex-role behavior; and at present, primate observations have been sufficiently limited so that even the range of possible sex-role behavior for non-human primates is not known. This range is not known since there is only minimal observation of what happens to behavior if the physical or social environment is changed. In one study (Itani, 1963), different troops of Japanese macaques were observed. Here, there appeared to be cultural differences. Males in 3 out of the 18 troops observed differed in their amount of aggressiveness and infant-caring behavior. There could be no possibility of differential evolution here; the differences seemed largely transmitted by infant socialization. Thus, the very limited evidence points to some plasticity in the sex-role behavior of non-human primates; if we can figure out experiments which massively change the social organization of primate groups, it is possible that we might observe great changes in behavior. At present, however, we must conclude that, since non-human primates are too stupid to change their social conditions by themselves, the "innateness" and fixedness of their behavior is simply not known. Thus, even if there were some way, which there isn't, to settle on the behavior of a particular primate species as being the "natural" way for humans, we would not know whether or not this were simply some function of the present social organization of that species. And finally, once again it must be stressed that even if non-human primate behavior turned out to be relatively fixed, this would say little about our behavior. More immediate and relevant evidence, i.e. the evidence from social psychology, points to the enormous plasticity in human behavior, not only from one culture to the next, but from one experimental group to the next. One of the most salient features of human social organization is its variety; there are a number of cultures where there is at least a rough equality between men and women (Mead, 1949). In summary, primate arguments can tell us very little about our "innate" sex-role behavior; if they tell us anything at all, they tell us that there is no one biologically "natural" female or male behavior, and that sex-role behavior in non-human primates is much more varied than has previously been thought.

In brief, the uselessness of present psychology with regard to women is simply a special case of the general conclusion: one must understand social expectations about women if one is going to characterize the behavior of women.

How are women characterized in our culture, and in psychology? They are inconsistent, emotionally unstable, lacking in a strong conscience or superego, weaker, "nuturant" rather than productive, "intuitive" rather than intelligent, and, if they are at all "normal," suited to the home and the family. In short, the list adds up to a typical minority group stereotype of inferiority (Hacker, 1951): if they know their place, which is in the home, they are really quite lovable, happy, childlike, loving creatures. In a review of the intellectual differences between little boys and little girls, Eleanor Maccoby (1966) has shown that there are no intellectual differences until about high school, or, if there are, girls are slightly ahead of boys. At high school, girls begin to do worse on a few intellectual tasks, such as arithmetic reasoning, and beyond high school, the achievement of women now measured in terms of productivity and accomplishment drops off even more rapidly. There are a number of other, non-intellectual tests which show sex differences; I chose the intellectual differences since it is seen clearly that women start becoming inferior. It is no use to talk about women being different but equal; all of the tests I can think of have a "good" outcome and a "bad" outcome. Women usually end up at the "bad" outcome. In light of social expectations about women, what is surprising is not that women end up where society expects they will; what is surprising is that little girls don't get the message that they are supposed to be stupid until high school; and what is even more remarkable is that some women resist this message even after high school, college, and graduate school.

My paper began with remarks on the task of the discovery of the limits of human potential. Psychologists must realize that it is they who are limiting discovery of human potential. They re-

fuse to accept evidence, if they are clinical psychologists, or, if they are rigorous, they assume that people move in a context-free ether, with only their innate dispositions and their individual traits determining what they will do. Until psychologists begin to respect evidence, and until they begin looking at the social contexts within which people move psychology will have nothing of substance to offer in this task of discovery. I don't know what immutable differences exist between men and women apart from differences in their genitals; perhaps there are some other unchangeable differences; probably there are a number of irrelevant differences. But it is clear that until social expectations for men and women are equal, until we provide equal respect for both men and women, our answers to this question will simply reflect our prejudices.

REFERENCES

Astin, A. W., The functional autonomy of psychotherapy. *American Psychologist*, 1961, *16*, 75–78.

Barron, F. & Leary, T., Changes in psychoneurotic patients with and without psychotherapy. *J. Consulting Psychology*, 1955, *19*, 239–245.

Bregin, A. E., The effects of psychotherapy: negative results revisited. *Journal of Consulting Psychology*, 1963, *10*, 244–250.

Bettelheim, B., The Commitment required of a woman entering a scientific profession in present day American society. *Woman and the Scientific Professions*. The MIT symposium on American Women in Science and Engineering, 1965.

Blook, J., Some reasons for the apparent inconsistency of personality. *Psychological Bulletin*, 1968, *70*, 210–212.

Cartwright, R. D. & Vogel, J. L., A comparison of changes in psychoneurotic patients during matched periods of therapy and no-therapy. *Journal of Consulting Psychology*, 1960, *24*, 121–127.

Erikson, E., Inner and outer space: reflections on womanhood. *Daedalus*, 1964, *93*, 582–606.

Eysenck, H. J., The effects of psychotherapy: an evaluation. *Journal of Consulting Psychology*, 1952, *16*, 319–324.

Fieldcrest—Advertisement in the *New Yorker*, 1965.

Fried, M. H., "Mankind excluding wom-

an", review of Tiger's *Men in Groups. Science*, *165*, 1969, pp. 883–884.

Freud, S., *The Sexual Enlightenment of Children*. Collier Books Edition, 1963.

Goldstein, A. P. & Dean, S. J., *The investigation of Psychotherapy: Commentaries and Readings*. New York: John Wiley & Sons, 1966.

Hamburg, D. A. & Lunde, D. T., Sex hormones in the development of sex differences in human behavior. In Maccoby, ed., *The Development of Sex Differences*, pp. 1–24. Stanford University Press, 1966.

Hacker, H. M., Women as a minority group. *Social Forces*, 1951, *30*, 60–69.

Harlow, H. F., The heterosexual affectional system in monkeys. *The American Psychologist*, 1962, *17*, 1–9.

Hooker, E., Male Homosexuality in the Rorschach. *Journal of Projective Techniques*, 1957, *21*, 18–31.

Itani, J., Paternal care in the wild Japanese monkeys, *Macaca fuscata*. In C. H. Southwick (Ed.) *Primate Social Behavior*. Princeton: Van Nostrand, 1963.

Little, K. B. & Schneidman, E. S., Congruences among interpretations of psychological and anamestic data. *Psychological Monographs*, 1959, *73*, 1–42.

Maccoby, Eleanor E., Sex differences in intellectual functioning, in Maccoby, ed., *The development of sex differences*, pp. 25–55. Stanford University Press, 1966.

Masters, W. H. & Johnson, V. E., *Human Sexual Response*. Boston: Little Brown, 1966.

Mead, M., *Male and Female: A Study of the sexes in a changing world*. New York: William Morrow, 1949.

Milgrim, S., Some Conditions of Obedience to Authority. *Human Relations*, 1965a, *18*, 57–76.

Milgram, S., Liberating effects of group pressure. *Journal of Personality and Social Psychology*, 1965b, *1*, 127–134.

Mitchell, G. D. "Paternalistic behavior in primates." *Psychological Bulletin* 1969, *71*, 399–417.

Powers, E. & Witmer, H., *An experiment in the prevention of delinquency*, New York: Columbia University Press, 1951.

Rheingold, J., *The fear of being a woman*. New York: Grune & Stratton, 1964.

Rosenthal, R., On the social psychology of the psychological experiment: The experimenter's hypothesis as unintended determinant of experimental results. *American Scientist*, 1963, *51*, 268–283.

Rosenthal, R., *Experimenter effects in Behavioral Research*. New York: Appleton-Century Crofts, 1966.

Rosenthal, R. & Jacobson, L., *Pygmalion in the classroom: teacher expectation and pupil's intellectual development*. New York: Holt, Rinehart & Winston, 1968.

Rosenthal, R. & Lawson, R., A longitudinal study of the effects of experimenter bias on the operant learning of laboratory rats. Unpublished Manuscript, Harvard University, 1961.

Rosenthal, R. & Fode, K. L., The effect of experimenter bias on the performance of the albino rat. Unpublished manuscript Harvard University, 1960.

Rotter, J. B., Psychotherapy. *Annual Review of Psychology*, 1960, *11*, 381–414.

Schachter, S. & Singer, J. E., Cognitive, social and physiological determinants of emotional state. *Psychological Review*, 1962, *69*, 379–399.

Schwarz-Belkin, M., "Les Fleurs de Mal," in *Festschrift for Gordon Piltdown*. New York: Ponzi Press, 1914.

Tiger, L., *Men in Groups*. New York: Random House, 1969.

Truax, C. B., Effective ingredients in psychotherapy: an approach to unraveling the patient-therapist interaction. *Journal of Counseling Psychology*, 1963, *10*, 256–263.

REVIEW QUESTIONS

1. Give several examples illustrating Cook's point that in the area of race relations stated opinion is frequently not a reliable basis for prediction of behavior.

2. You are put in charge of an integrated housing project. What predictions would you make about the attitudes of the residents toward members of other races? What does Cook mean by perceived social norm and how would this affect attitudes?

3. What two methodological criticisms did Greenwald and Oppenheim offer of earlier studies?

4. Greenwald and Oppenheim state "misidentification among the white children was 44%." What is a possible explanation for this finding?

5. When the galvanic skin response indicates a decrease in skin resistance, what inferences are made about the emotional state? What can be said about the cognitive direction of emotion from a galvanic skin response?

6. You have a strong dislike for Mexican-Americans. Someone expresses a complimentary statement about them. What would you expect your galvanic skin response to be? You also have neutral feelings toward Jews in the United States and you hear a complimentary statement about them. How would this affect the galvanic skin response?

7. What is meant by the scapegoat theory of prejudice? Give an example from your own experience which either confirms or denies the theory.

8. How did subjects who were low in anti-Semitism respond to the aggression arousing situation? What challenge does this offer to the traditional image of the very tolerant individual being one who is a bias-free neutral in his reactions to minority group members?

9. What two explanations does Naomi Weisstein offer for psychology's failure to understand what people are and how they act?

10. What are "social expectations" and how do they influence a woman's role in our society?

part eleven
aggressive behavior

As Ulrich, Hutchinson, and Azrin (#57) point out, the causes for most human aggression are "so complex and difficult to understand that the problem of controlling them sometimes seems insoluble." The complexity of human aggression has lead psychologists to the study of aggressive behavior in animals where better experimental control may be accomplished. Hopefully, the principles derived from these laboratory studies will at some time be applicable with beneficial results to the control of human aggression.

It is fairly easy to induce aggression in animals. Intraspecies, interspecies, and aggression toward inanimate objects can be elicited through the application of pain. Two snakes, for example, can live peacefully together for long periods of time with no aggressive behavior. Applying electric shocks to these same two animals in their living cage very quickly leads to a situation where the two animals begin to strike and bite each other. The fact of pain-elicited aggression in animals should give us some insight into the causes of human aggresson. Physical punishment used by parents and society as a whole, of course, causes pain. While the punishment applied may succeed in stopping the organism from further performance of a particular response, there is also the distinct possibility that new, even less desirable aggressive responses may appear. The animal studies also show dramatically that the aggression need not be directed toward the actual source of the punishment. Innocent bystanders may be attacked with great vigor even though they have nothing to do with the delivery of the punishment.

Though the problems are great, psychologists certainly study aggression on the human level as well. A classic study of human aggression, performed by Stanley Milgram (#58), points out among other things the powerful influence that authority figures can have. Male subjects were persuaded to apply what they thought were severe shocks to a fellow human being all in the interest of science. Subjects continued to apply the shocks even though the supposed victim was pounding on the wall of the room in which he was bound to an electric chair. Subjects continued to apply the severe shocks at great upset to themselves—they were observed to sweat, tremble, stutter, bite their lips, groan, and dig their fingers into their flesh—all the while, of course, continuing to apply the shocks.

This kind of research certainly makes some of the aggression we read about daily in our newspapers easier to understand. Authority figures, such as army officers and high-ranking police officials who in any sense advocate unjustified violent acts by their subordinates, should not be surprised when such activity occurs and goes to such extremes as police brutality and the massacre of civilians in a war zone. The authority figure must realize his inherent power over his followers and act responsibly. The prominent campus revolutionary who in many instances is an extremely powerful authority figure cannot advocate in the heat of a speech that "the university must be destroyed" and not expect violent, irresponsible activity on the part of his followers. Authority figures seem to be able to legitimize some behaviors that an individual would never undertake on his own.

The question of whether violence on the movie and television screen leads to increased violence in the audience prompted Leonard Berkowitz and Russell G. Geen to undertake research (#59) in this area. While the study showed that film violence could be an important cue for "real-life" violence, the situation is not quite as simple as is sometimes thought. Film violence did not seem to lead to open aggression against just anyone, but seemed to increase aggression toward particular targets possessing "aggression-eliciting cue properties."

Alan E. Gross, a Wisconsin colleague of mine, feels strongly that psychologists in general, and social psychologists in particular, should make every effort to do research in a "real-world" setting rather than remaining exclusively in the laboratory. He and Anthony N. Doob took the study of frustration and aggression to six intersections in Palo Alto and Menlo Park, California (#60). The measure of aggression in this study was the amount of "horn-honking" in a frustrating situation. Two of the driver-subjects had to be excluded from the study because they were not content with merely horn-honking—they hit the back bumper of the experimental car!

57.
pain-elicited aggression

roger e. ulrich,
ronald r. hutchinson,
and nathan h. azrin

Although any exact description of aggression will vary from species to species, as it is generally used it refers to fighting and means the act of initiating an attack. As such, fighting has always been an important problem for human beings, and it has long constituted an important research area for scientists of various disciplines. Often, however, the causes for most human aggression remain so complex and difficult to understand that the problem of controlling them sometimes seems insoluble. Since other animals besides man fight their own kind, scientists have been able to study aggression in other species, thus explaining the considerable amount of research done on aggression using animal Ss. Although most of the early studies on aggression were descriptive in nature (Davis, 1933; Hall & Klein, 1952; Zuckerman, 1932), there has recently been a trend toward a more exact laboratory analysis of the phenomenon and those factors which produce it (Masserman, 1964; Scott, 1958).

One such factor which has long been suspected as a probable cause of aggression is the variable pain. Little children are admonished not to hurt the "doggy" because it might make him bite. Wounded

Reprinted by permission from *The Psychological Record*, 1965, *15*, 111–126. By permission of the authors.

This paper is a slightly modified version of one presented at the Grinnell Behavior Science Institute, conducted at Grinnell College during the summer of 1964. The majority of the research reported in this paper has been supported by Research Grants from the National Institute of Mental Health, United States Public Health Service and the Psychiatric Training and Research Fund of the Illinois Department of Public Welfare.

animals suffering pain are known to be more apt to attack than they would be under more normal circumstances. Indeed, actual research has shown that in the common grey mouse painful stimulation is a primary factor in the early appearance of aggression (Scott & Fredericson, 1951). It has also been demonstrated that domestic rats will attack each other when painfully stimulated with electric foot-shock. This phenomenon was first noted by O'Kelly and Steckle (1939), and Daniel (1943) later found essentially the same results. Other investigations have shown that foot-shock elicits fighting behavior in wild rats (Covain, 1949) and domestic mice (Tedeschi, et al., 1959) as well as in domestic rats (Ulrich, 1961). It is the purpose of this paper to review the research describing the conditions under which pain aggression occurs with the hope that a systematic organization of the data may lead to a better understanding of the phenomenon.

DEFINITION OF PAIN AND AGGRESSION

The first objective in any scientific analysis of behavior is to describe accurately the behavioral phenomenon we wish to investigate. The term "aggression" will be used as defined above. Pain, as it is used in the present review, is synonymous with aversive stimulation and incorporates those variables from which organisms have been observed in the past to escape. Making pain contingent upon a response will lower the future probability of its occurrence. A good example of the pain-aggression phenomenon is contained in a study by Ulrich and Azrin (1962). In it, paired rats were placed in an experimental chamber and observations were made of their behavior prior to the presentation of foot-shock. At no time during this period did any aggression appear. However, soon after shock was delivered, a drastic change took place in the rats' behavior. They would suddenly face each other in an upright position, and with mouths open they would strike out at one another.

So far most of the research on fighting has employed human observers to record the aggressive behavior. Fighting responses are recorded by an observer depressing a microswitch for any striking or biting movement of either or both animals toward the other. Reliability checks run by having different observers simultaneously record the fighting behavior have shown that the characteristic pattern of the fighting response is sufficiently clear to allow for accurate recording (Ulrich & Azrin, 1962). Recent experiments, however, have employed automatic techniques for the recording of pain-elicited aggression (Azrin, Hutchinson & Sallery, 1964). Monkeys placed in a special chair in a loosely restrained position would attack a cloth ball following the onset of shock. The string by which the ball was suspended was attached to a switch which closed when the ball was pulled. The results obtained by this automatic method of recording fighting behavior were found to agree very closely with those obtained in the observation of the same experiment by a human being who closed a microswitch whenever the monkey was making contact with the inanimate object.

GENERALITY OF PAIN-ELICITED AGGRESSION

Intra-Species Aggression

In addition to rats, paired snakes, turtles, chickens, (Azrin & Hutchinson, 1963) and hamsters (Ulrich & Azrin, 1962) have all been found to react to electric shock with sudden attack movements. Placing a gopher snake and a rat snake together without shock resulted in exploratory behavior with neither snake attending to the other. Once shock was delivered, however, both snakes immediately responded by striking at each other

with mouths wide open. Such striking movements frequently resulted in one of the snakes being bitten. Turtles' reactions to shock, although much slower, do eventually result in attacks toward each other. The general reaction of paired chickens to shock is also one of attack. However, as is also true with monkeys, there is a greater tendency between chickens for one subject to become the dominant partner than that observed in rats. Delivery of shock to a pair of hamsters produced a type of stereotyped fighting posture and attack similar to that of the rats. The only differences were that these fighting responses could be consistently elicited at lower intensities of shock than was required for the rats; and that the hamsters persisted longer in their fighting. (Ulrich & Azrin, 1962). This persistence in fighting beyond the moment of shock presentation was also observed in cats (Ulrich, Wolff & Azrin, 1964) and in squirrel monkeys (Azrin, Hutchinson & Hake, 1963). Furthermore, both cats and monkeys often fought until forcibly separated, and unless precautions were taken they would frequently inflict serious physical injury.

Inter-Species Aggression

Pain-elicited aggression has also been found between different species. Snakes, raccoons, opossums, monkeys (Azrin, 1964), rats, hamsters (Ulrich & Azrin, 1962) and cats (Ulrich, Wolff & Azrin, 1964) have all been observed to attack members of different species as a function of aversive stimulation. In most instances the topography of the interspecies fighting response is the same as that observed between members of the same species. What differences do appear seem to be a function of such variables as the relative size of the two subjects and the amount of reciprocal fighting. For example, rats, when shocked, will consistently exhibit aggression towards hamsters as will the hamster toward the rat (Ulrich & Azrin, 1962), whereas reciprocal attacks by the rat with respect to snakes, opossums, cats and monkeys are infrequent. A possible reason for this lack of aggression of the rat toward the snake is the fact that the snake strikes so swiftly. Although rats have occasionally been observed to assume the stereotyped shock-induced fighting posture in the presence of cats (Ulrich, Wolff & Azrin, 1964), such behavior has at best always been short-lived and thus difficult to investigate further.

Another example of a modification in the attack response of an animal fighting a member of a different species was observed when rats were paired with guinea pigs. In the first place, all the attacking was done by the rat which assumed a semi-crouching position with the forepaws raised only slightly off the floor, a posture which differed slightly from the stereotypical position. Since the guinea pig never stood upright, the crouching position of the rat brought its head to the level of the guinea pig's head. In this case, the otherwise inflexible and stereotyped fighting position of the rat appeared to be modified by the position of the guinea pig. During these attacks the guinea pig's only reaction was to withdraw (Ulrich & Azrin, 1962).

Aggression toward inanimate objects. Another aspect of pain-elicited aggression which has received considerable study is the extent to which aversive stimulation will produce attack at inanimate objects. Casual observation has indicated that numerous animals, including man, will occasionally, when hurt, strike out toward the inanimate environment. As mentioned previously, monkeys, when aversively stimulated, will consistently attack inanimate objects such as a stuffed doll or even a round ball (Azrin, Hutchinson & Sallery, 1964). This attack was not found to be a random thrashing out at the environment, as evidenced by the fact that selective attacks were made upon cloth-covered objects to the exclusion of a metal box when these objects were simultaneously available.

Besides monkeys, other species such as raccoons and opossums have been observed to attack inanimate objects as a function of aversive stimulation (Azrin, 1964). Our own laboratory experience with rats on Sidman avoidance (Sidman, 1953) has been that rats will often bite the projecting response bar shortly after the delivery of a shock. However, when an insulated doll was placed with a rat while shock was being delivered, no attack toward the doll was attempted. Similarly, no attack movements were made toward either a conducting doll or a recently deceased rat. Dolls moved rapidly about the chamber also failed to induce fighting. Fighting responses were elicited only when the dead rat was moved about the chamber on a stick. The fact that certain stimulus objects and not others will be attacked in the presence of shock indicates that additional research is needed to determine the stimulus characteristics necessary for the elicitation of pain-aggression.

DEVELOPMENT OF PAIN-ELICITED AGGRESSION

Since pain-elicited aggression appears to have many characteristics of unconditioned behavior, a question naturally arises concerning the relations which might exist between such aggression and age or age-related factors such as hormone activity and prior history of aggression. The results of recent studies concerned with this question (Hutchinson, Ulrich & Azrin, 1964) have demonstrated that several age-related factors are important determinants of aggressive behavior. In a study conducted to discover whether shock-elicited aggression changed as a function of age and prior social history, it was found that fighting increased as a direct function of age regardless of whether Ss were housed in community cages or were kept in isolation. These findings indicated that prior social exposure to other Ss was not critical for the development of aggressive behavior. However, it was noted that although fighting increased with age, Ss raised in community cages fought more than those raised in isolation. In another experiment, conducted to determine whether castration could influence aggression, it was found that castration produced a lowered fighting probability in adult Ss irrespective of whether it was performed before or after sexual maturation. It is possible that the relationship between increased age and increased aggression mentioned above may be due to such a factor as androgen level (Hutchinson, Ulrich & Azrin, 1964).

AGGRESSION AS A FUNCTION OF ELECTRIC-SHOCK

The earliest of the various studies dealing with the pain-aggression relationship were those which analyzed the exact aspects of painful stimuli necessary for the elicitation of aggression. The stimulus most frequently used to elicit fighting was electric foot-shock. The various parameters of the shock variables studied were shock intensity, shock frequency, shock duration and shock consistency.

Shock Intensity

For example, it was found that fighting between rats occurred as a non-monotonic function of shock intensity. Increasing the shock intensity from 0 to 2 ma. produced an increased frequency of fighting; at still higher intensities (3–5 ma.) the rate of fighting was found to decrease. Lower intensities produced a fighting response of less vigor and longer latency. The slight decrease in fighting behavior at the highest intensity (5 ma.) appeared to be partly a consequence of the debilitating effects of shock. The optimal current intensity for eliciting fighting was approximately 2 ma. At lower intensities the shock did not seem to be painful to the rat, while at higher intensities the shock appeared to be debilitating and generated competing behavior (Ulrich & Azrin, 1962). Tedeschi et al. (1959) also found that 2 to 3 ma. intensity was optimal for producing fighting between mice.

Shock Frequency

The elicitation of the fighting reflex was found to occur as a direct function of the frequency of shock presentations. The more often the shock was presented, the more often the Ss fought. However, when shock was made so frequent as to be continuous, the fighting decreased and much of the rat's behavior appeared to be directed toward escape from the experimental chamber. This "escape" behavior appeared to interfere somewhat with the usual fighting. The lower rate of fighting observed at the lower fre-

quencies of shock presentation was apparently due to the fact that the rats, during the longer interval between shocks, frequently assumed positions other than the stereotyped fighting posture. The optimum frequency of shock presentation for eliciting fighting between rats thus appears to be approximately 30 to 40 shocks per minute (Ulrich & Azrin, 1962). However, lower frequencies have been found to be equally effective in species whose fighting tends to persist long after the shock has been presented. (Azrin, Hutchinson & Hake, 1963).

Shock Duration

Fighting was also found to be a direct function of the duration of the shocks. The longer the duration of shock, the greater was the probability of fighting. Continual delivery of foot-shocks, however, partially reversed this relation. The very brief shock durations became progressively more effective during continued shock presentation; and the longer shock durations became less effective as a session progressed (Azrin, Ulrich, Hutchinson & Norman, 1964). Gross observation of the rats indicated that the longer shock durations gave ample opportunity for the rats to acquire postures and movements, such as jumping, which reduced the receipt of shock. These escape attempts appeared to compete with the fighting reaction. The briefer shock durations did not appear to produce these marked escape attempts. It was also observed that the longer shock durations may have indirectly reduced the likelihood of fighting by physically weakening the rats.

Shock Consistency

The consistency of the shock presentation was found to be critical. Failure to scramble the polarity of the electrified grids produced inconsistency in fighting. Several investigations of shock-produced fighting appear to have used a type of shock circuit in which alternative bars of the floor grids were wired in parallel. Such a design permits the animal to avoid shocks by standing on bars of the same polarity and may account for the frequent failure of shock to elicit fighting behavior reported by other investigators (Miller, 1948; Richter, 1950;).

Shock Location

Another form of aversive stimulation which has proven an effective elicitor of fighting is electrode shock. In one study (Ulrich & Azrin, 1962) electrodes were implanted beneath a fold of skin on the back of a single rat. A harness and swivel arrangement allowed the rat complete freedom to move about. When a 0.5 sec. duration shock was delivered at an intensity of 2 ma. only a spasmodic movement of the rat resulted if no other rat was present. When the shock was delivered in the presence of a second rat, the stimulated rat usually assumed the stereotyped posture and initiated the attack.

OTHER TYPES OF PAIN STIMULI

Another experiment in the study mentioned above showed that fighting in response to aversive foot-heat could be obtained by placing paired rats in an experimental chamber on a preheated thin metal floor. The heated floor appeared to elicit fighting in much the same manner as a continuously electrified floor grid. Although cold, intense noise and air blasts have not as yet proved effective as consistent elicitors of the fighting response, it is felt that further investigation of the effects of these variables as they relate to pain-elicited aggression is desirable.

INTERACTION OF OTHER VARIABLES WITH PAIN-ELICITED FIGHTING

Other variables studied in relation to pain-elicited fighting have been sex, chamber size, the number of rats in the chamber, length of session, sensory impairment and the Ss' orientation at the moment of shock.

Sex. Sex as a variable in the elicitation of fighting by foot-shock showed that the same type of fighting that occurred between males also occurred between females. Sexual behavior between the male and the female was, in fact, completely displaced by the elicitation of fighting behavior (Ulrich & Azrin, 1962).

Chamber size. The amount of fighting between rats in response to shock was found to depend critically upon the amount of floor space. When the floor space was small (6 × 6 in.) the fighting response was elicited by approximately 90% of the shocks. On larger floor areas, the number of fighting responses decreased; with the largest floor studied (24 × 24 in.) only 2% of the shocks elicited fighting. It thus appears that when the rats were confined so as to remain only a few inches apart, the shock was likely to cause them to turn and lunge at each other. At the larger distances, the rats largely ignored each other. (Ulrich & Azrin, 1962).

Number of rats. Unconditioned fighting also resulted when more than two rats were shocked. When 2, 3, 4, 6 or 8 rats were simultaneously given footshock the same stereotyped fighting reaction occurred, two or more rats often attacking a single rat (Ulrich & Azrin, 1962).

Length of session. In order to discover the effects of numerous shocks over an extended session, Ulrich and Azrin (1962) delivered frequent shocks (every 1.5 sec.) to a pair of rats for an uninterrupted period of 7½ hours. It was found that the fighting reflex proved extremely resistant to fatigue. During the first 2,400 presentations (1 hr.) of the shock, fighting was elicited after 82% of the shocks. After 7,200 presentations of shock (3rd hour), fighting still occurred after 70% of the shocks. Only during the last 1.5 hours, after 6 hours and nearly 15,000 shocks, did the consistency of elicitation drop below 40%. By this time the rats were damp with perspiration and appeared to be weakened physically. By the end of the 7.5 hours approximately 10,000 fighting responses had been elicited.

Sensory impairment. In order to test the role played by visual stimuli animals were blinded and shocked. Although blinding decreased the fighting it did not eliminate it. Rats whose eyes were removed fought more than rats who were simply hooded. The reason for this was related to the fact that the hoods covered the rats' whiskers, thereby eliminating another source of sensory reception which appears to be related to fighting (Flory, Ulrich & Wolff, 1964).

Ss' orientation. Another factor affecting the probability of fighting is the Ss' orientation toward each other at the moment of the shock. It has been noted in several experiments (Brierton, Stachnik & Ulrich, 1964; Ulrich & Azrin, 1962) that the Ss will occasionally slip out of the fighting posture and assume other positions. It was also apparent in these experiments that fighting in response to shock was more likely if the animals were facing each other at the moment of shock delivery.

CONDITIONED AGGRESSION

Respondent Conditioned Aggression

So far we have discussed the effects of aversive stimulation as an elicitor of aggression prior to any specific conditioning. It is possible, however, that aggressive behavior might be conditioned according to Pavlovian principles. For example, if one were to pair consistently a neutral stimulus with an aversive unconditioned stimulus, it is possible that the neutral stimulus would eventually become a conditioned stimulus eliciting a conditioned response similar to that originally elicited by the unconditioned stimulus. In an experiment conducted by Ulrich (1962) concerning this question it was found that fighting which was originally elicited by the unconditioned stimulus alone eventually appeared in its absence although in a somewhat modified form. Two animals, isolated at 18 days of age and brought together only for the daily experimental sessions, were placed in a chamber with two naive animals. Their behavior in this situation was very dramatic. Any move or noise by any other animal would immediately elicit the fighting posture and occasional striking responses. This continued for two days in a manner very similar to that reported by O'Kelly and Steckle (1939). The occurrence of this behavior

can best be explained by the principles of classical conditioning. The only time these animals had been together since age 18 days was in a situation where shock was presented every 3 seconds. Always associated with the shock was the other animal whose shock-elicited fighting and other varied movements inevitably preceded another shock. The other animal, which originally was simply a neutral stimulus later became, through consistent pairing with shock, a conditioned stimulus capable of producing the long enduring conditioned fighting behavior observed in the second chamber.

Other studies concerned with classically conditioning the fighting response have paired a buzzer with the shock and observed the number of fighting responses eventually made to the buzzer alone. Azrin & Hutchinson (1963) found that both monkeys and chickens will occasionally attack following the onset of the buzzer. Similar research with paired rats has shown that the fighting posture can be more readily elicited by the conditioned stimulus than the actual striking motions although the striking movements do sometimes occur (Brierton, Ulrich, & Wolff, 1964). On several occasions rats have been removed from the chamber in which they were conditioned and placed in another chamber nearby. Following their placement in the second chamber the conditioned stimulus was presented, and they immediately assumed the stereotyped posture. Although these findings show that fighting can be elicited not only by the aversive unconditioned stimulus, but also occasionally by conditioned stimuli, it is felt that the inconsistency of such elicitation necessitates further research into the question of classically conditioned aggression.

Operant Conditioned Aggression

A study, often referred to, which conditioned fighting according to operant principles, is that of Miller (1948). In this study paired rats were placed in a chamber and shocked. When the Ss happened to approach each other in a sparring position similar to that used by rats when fighting, the shock was abruptly turned off. After a minute without the shock the current was again turned on, and the animals were given another trial, and it was reported that this technique proved very effective for producing aggressive behavior. A situation which is analogous to this experimentally contrived environment may be seen in the natural habitat where the source of aversive stimulation is often another animal. One way in which the attacked S can eliminate the aversive contingencies provided by the attacker is to leave the situation. The flight response in this case is negatively reinforced by the termination of the attack. A second way of eliminating the aversive circumstances would be to destroy or immobilize the individual who is responsible for them. However, if we return to our earlier discussion of pain-elicited aggression we will recall that simply presenting an aversive unconditioned stimulus produced aggressive attacks even though the organism being attacked did not deliver the painful stimulus nor was the painful stimulus eliminated following attack behavior. Such findings suggest that the conditioned fighting found by Miller (1948) would have eventually occurred even if no reinforcement through shock termination had been given. Thus, we see that the effectiveness of operant reinforcement of fighting using escape procedures is weakened by our knowledge of the fact that aversive stimulation alone produces fighting.

PERSISTENCE OF SHOCK-ELICITED AGGRESSION

Certainly the findings from these studies on pain-elicited and conditioned aggression raise some interesting questions concerning the use of aversive stimulation in a social situation. Since we know that painful stimulation produces aggression between paired animals prior to any specific conditioning it might be asked "can animals be kept from fighting in a situation where they are together and are both receiving the pain stimulus?" The most recent studies of pain-elicited fighting have attempted to answer this question. For example, Ulrich and Craine (1964) conducted an experiment to determine if paired rats could be conditioned not to fight when presented with electric shock by reinforcing

nonaggressive responses with shock removal and allowing all aggressive responses to produce further shock. The procedure involved placing paired rats in an experimental chamber and presenting continuous shock after 60 sec. had elapsed, until a non-fighting response occurred, whereupon the shock was immediately terminated for another 60 sec. Following this 60-sec. period the shocks were again presented and the same procedure was repeated. A record was kept of the amount of time the Ss spent in fighting. It was found that the amount of time spent fighting during the later sessions was actually greater than that observed at the beginning. This increase in fighting occurred in spite of the fact that shock was terminated following nonaggressive responses and continued following aggressive responses.

Such findings imply that pain-elicited aggression can not be suppressed in spite of reinforcement for other behaviors. Other studies have proven however, that environmental experiences can alter innate or unlearned response patterns (Beach & Jaynes, 1954, Farris, 1963), indicating that possible explanations for the failure to suppress fighting, as mentioned above, should be considered. Indeed further study by Ulrich and Craine (1964) did show that under certain circumstances fighting between paired rats in response to shock could be suppressed. In the initial procedure used to eliminate pain-elicited aggression the continuation of shock was solely contingent upon aggression although its termination was related to a number of different responses. The animals, for example, could move away from each other in several directions. One animal might simply lower to the floor as the other jumped back toward an opposite wall, or both might fall away from each other onto their backs. In short, the escape, i.e. non-aggressive, response was not specific. A procedure incorporating a specific escape response was thus tried.

Two rats with a long history of stable performance in a discriminated avoidance situation were used along with 1 naive rat and 1 small rat-sized rubber dummy. The avoidance animals had been conditioned to press a bar which produced a period of 20 sec. of no shock. If the bar was not pressed, brief (.5 sec.) shocks (1 ma.) occurred every 5 sec. A signal was always presented 2 sec. prior to the shock. During this probe each animal was run for a typical 4-hour session with the exception of the final 30 min., during which either a naive rat or a small dummy was added to the chamber.

It was found that no major change in avoidance behavior took place as a result of the dummy being added to the chamber. Furthermore, no attack movements were observed to be made toward the dummy. In contrast, when a live rat was placed with the previously trained animal, there occurred a sharp drop-off in the number of avoidance responses. Visual observation indicated that in the social situation with a second live animal, bar pressing had been replaced with fighting behavior. In fact, during the first two sessions, the Ss fought after almost every shock. In the subsequent sessions, however, the actual fighting fell off rapidly to an average of 10 fighting responses per session. On the other hand, during the same period, the escape-avoidance responding did not return to the single S rate. It appeared that the reason for this lack of recovery in bar pressing was related again to the fighting phenomenon. In the single S situation the avoidance animals tended to remain near the bar and only occasionally following a response did they move away. However, after a bar press in the presence of another live S the avoidance animal would frequently return to the naive animal and reassume the stereotyped posture. This posture was maintained until the pre-shock stimulus appeared, whereupon the avoidance animal would return to the bar and press it, then return again to the naive animal, thus apparently lowering the probability of bar pressing. This preoccupation with the naive animal appeared to be one of the factors responsible for the lower frequency of avoidance responding.

Further studies investigating the interaction between fighting and avoidance have shown that simply placing naive Ss in a chamber and allowing their shock-induced random movements to produce a bar press, which in turn terminates shock, will eventually bring about avoidance behavior in both paired and single Ss. Single Ss, however, performed consistently better in such a situation than the paired Ss. Single Ss received fewer shocks, responded at higher rates and learned the bar pressing response quickly whereas the paired Ss received more shocks and responded at lower rates. It was apparent in these studies that the poor avoidance behavior which occurred in the social setting was related to the high incidence of shock-elicited aggression (Ulrich, Stachnik, Brierton & Mabry, 1964).

CONCLUSIONS

Certainly psychological research provides us with numerous examples of the use of aversive stimulation in conditioning and the control such stimulation exerts over behavior has been shown in many cases to be quite powerful. Electric shocks, (Holz, Azrin, & Ulrich, 1963) loud sounds, (Azrin, 1958), and strong lights (Schoenfeld, 1947) have all been found to decrease the subsequent frequency of the responses which they have followed. Conversely, a number of responses have been conditioned entirely on the basis of escape from or reduction of these same aversive stimulus conditions (Azrin, 1958; Keller, 1941; Mowrer, 1940). Typically, the experimental procedures used in these studies have involved the presentation of the aversive stimulus to a single organism rather than to a pair or to a group of Ss. The use of aversive stimulation for the control of human Ss, however, is seldom if ever used outside of a social context. The fact that pain-elicited aggression was found to interfere noticeably with both the acquisition and maintenance of operant behavior indicates that at least certain conditioning procedures, which employ aversive stimuli and which have proven effective in exerting control over single Ss, will not exert the same control when more than one S is in the experimental environment. Perhaps the most important thing about pain-elicited aggression is that it is a general response to aversive stimulation. Furthermore, it is felt that the greatest implications suggested by the findings which relate aversive stimulation to fighting pertain to the use of punishment in a social setting. Since physical punishment is by definition the delivery of aversive stimulation following a response, it may be expected that social aggression will occur as an elicited reaction to such punishment. Thus, our main objective of eliminating a response by punishment may have the completely unexpected effect of producing aggression by the punished organism. Also important is the fact that under this elicited aggression the punished S can be expected to attack other nearby Ss even though they

had nothing to do with delivering the punishment. Although other studies have shown that the probability of aggression will increase if the aggression results in favorable consequences such as an increase of food (Reynolds, Catania, & Skinner, 1963; Skinner, 1959; Ulrich, Johnston, Richardson & Wolff, 1963), a decrease in painful stimulation (Miller, 1948), access to a female by a male (Tinbergen, 1951) or maintenance of territorial privileges (Tinbergen, 1951; 1953), the present pain-aggression reaction does not originate from such operant reinforcement since no favorable consequences are apparent.

REFERENCES

Azrin, N. H. Some effects of noise on human behavior. *J. exp. Anal. Behav.*, 1958, 1, 183–199.

Azrin, N. H. Aggression. Paper presented at APA, Los Angeles, 1964.

Azrin, N. H. & Hutchinson, R. R. Unpublished study, 1963.

Azrin, N. H., Hutchinson, R. & Hake, D. Pain-induced fighting in the squirrel monkey. *J. exp. Anal. Behav.*, 1963, 6, 620–621.

Azrin, N. H., Hutchinson, R. R. & Sallery, R. D. Pain-aggression toward inanimate objects. *J. exp. Anal. Behav.*, 1964, 7, 3, 227–233.

Azrin, N. H., Ulrich, R. E., Hutchinson, R. R. & Norman, D. G. Effect of shock-duration on shock-induced fighting. *J. exp. Anal. Behav.*, 1964, 7, 9–11.

Beach, F. A. & Jaynes, J. Effects of early experience upon the behavior of animals. *Psychol. Bull.*, 1954, 51, 239–263.

Brierton, G. R., Stachnik, T. J. & Ulrich, R. E. Unpublished study, 1964.

Brierton, G. R., Ulrich, R. E. & Wolff, P. C. Unpublished study, 1964.

Covain, M. R. Rate of emotional stress in the survival of adrenalectomized rats given replacement therapy. *J. clin. Endocrinol.*, 1949, 9, 678.

Daniel, W. J. An experimental note on O'Kelley-Steckle reaction. *J. comp. Psychol.*, 1943, 35, 267–268.

Davis, F. C. The measurement of aggressive behavior in laboratory rats. *J. genet. Psychol.*, 1933, 43, 213–217.

Farris, H. D. Behavioral development, social organization and conditioning of courting behavior in the Japanese quail (*Coturnix coturnix japonica*). Unpublished doctoral dissertation, Michigan State Universtiy, 1963.

Flory, R. K., Ulrich, R. E. & Wolff, P. C. Effects of visual deprivation on fighting behavior. *Psychol. Rec. In press*.

Hall, C. S. & Klein, S. J. Individual differences in aggressiveness in rats. *J. comp. Psychol.*, 1942, 33, 371–383.

Holz, W. C., Azrin, N. H. & Ulrich, R. E. Punishment of temporally spaced responding *J. exp. Anal. Behav.*, 1963, 6, 115–122.

Hutchinson, R., Ulrich, R. E. & Azrin, N. H. Effects of age and age related factors on reflexive aggression. *J. comp. physiol. Psychol. In press*.

Keller, F. S. Light aversion in the white rat. *Psychol. Rec.*, 1941, 4, 235–250.

Masserman, J. H. *Behavior and neurosis.* Chicago: University of Chicago Press, 1964.

Miller, W. E. Theory and experiment relating psychoanalytic displacement in stimulus-response generalization. *J. abnorm. soc. Psychol.*, 1948, 43, No. 2, 155–178.

Mowrer, O. H. An experimental analogue of "regression" with incidental observations on "reaction-formation." *J. abnorm. soc. Psychol.*, 1940, 35, 56–87.

O'Kelley, L. E. & Steckle, L. C. A note on long-enduring emotional responses in the rat. *J. Psychol.*, 1939, 8, 125–131.

Reynolds, G. S., Catania, A. C. & Skinner, B. F. Conditioned and unconditioned aggression in pigeons. *J. exp. Anal. Behav.*, 1963, 1, 73–75.

Richter, C. P. Domestication of the Norway rat and its implications for the problem of stress. In Harold G. Wolff, *et al.* (Eds.), *Life stress and bodily disease.* Chap. ii, pp. 19–47. Assoc. for Research in Nervous and Mental Diseases, Vol. 29. Baltimore: William & Wilkins Co., 1950.

Shoenfeld, W. N. Unpublished study, 1947.

Scott, J. P. *Aggression.* Univer. of Chicago Press, 1958.

Scott, J. P. & Fredericson, E. The causes of fighting in mice and rats. *Psychol. Zol.* 1951, *24,* 273–309.

Sidman, M. Avoidance conditioning with brief shock and no exteroceptive warning signal. *Science,* 1953, *118,* 157–158.

Skinner, B. F. An experimental analysis of certain emotions. *J. exp. Anal. Behav.,* 1959, *2,* 264.

Tedeschi, R. E., Tedeschi, D. H., Mucha, A., Cook, L., Mattis, P. A. & Fellows, E. J. Effects of various centrally acting drugs on fighting behavior of mice. *J. pharm. exp. Therapeutics,* 1959, *125,* 28–31.

Tinbergen, N. *The study of instinct.* Oxford: Clarendon Press, 1951.

Tinbergen, N. *Social behavior in animals.* London: Methuen, 1953.

Ulrich, R. E. Reflexive fighting in response to aversive stimulation. *Dissert. Abstr.,* 1961, *22,* 4421.

Ulrich, R. E. Unpublished study, 1962.

Ulrich, R. E. & Azrin, N. H. Reflective fighting in response to aversive stimulation. *J. exp. Anal. Behav.,* 1962, *5,* 511–520.

Ulrich, R. E. & Craine, W. H. Behavior: Persistence of shock-induced aggression. *Science,* 1964, *143,* 971–973.

Ulrich, R. E., Johnston, M., Richardson, J. & Wolff, P. C. The operant conditioning of fighting behavior in rats. *Psychol Rec.,* 1963, *13,* 465–470.

Ulrich, R. E., Stachnik, T. J., Brierton, G. R. & Mabry, J. H. Fighting and avoidance reactions in response to aversive stimulation. Submitted to *J. exp. Anal. Behav.*

Ulrich, R. E., Wolff, P. C. & Azrin, N. H. Shock as an elicitor of intra- and inter-species fighting behavior. *Animal Behav.,* 1964, *12,* 14–15.

Zuckerman, S. *The social life of monkeys and apes.* London: Kegan Paul, New York: Harcourt Brace, 1932.

58.
behavioral study of obedience

stanley milgram

Obedience is as basic an element in the structure of social life as one can point to. Some system of authority is a requirement of all communal living, and it is only the man dwelling in isolation who is not forced to respond, through defiance or submission, to the commands of others. Obedience, as a determinant of behavior, is of particular relevance to our time. It has been reliably established that from 1933–45 millions of innocent persons were systematically slaughtered on command. Gas chambers were built, death camps were guarded, daily quotas of corpses were produced with the same efficiency as the manufacture of appliances. These inhumane policies may have originated in the mind of a single person but they could only be carried out on a massive scale if a very large number of persons obeyed orders.

Obedience is the psychological mechanism that links individual action to political purpose. It is the dispositional cement that binds men to systems of authority. Facts of recent history and observation in daily life suggest that for many persons obedience may be ,a deeply ingrained behavior tendency, indeed, a prepotent impulse overriding training in ethics, sympathy, and moral conduct. C. P. Snow (1961) points to its importance when he writes:

> When you think of the long and gloomy history of man, you will find more hideous crimes have been committed in the name of obedience than have ever been committed in

the name of rebellion. If you doubt that, read William Shirer's "Rise and Fall of the Third Reich." The German Officer Corps were brought up in the most rigorous code of obedience . . . in the name of obedience they were party to, and assisted in, the most wicked large scale actions in the history of the world [p. 24].

While the particular form of obedience dealt with in the present study has its antecedents in these episodes, it must not be thought all obedience entails acts of aggression against others. Obedience serves numerous productive functions. Indeed, the very life of society is predicated on its existence. Obedience may be ennobling and educative and refer to acts of charity and kindness, as well as to destruction.

GENERAL PROCEDURE

A procedure was devised which seems useful as a tool for studying obedience (Milgram, 1961). It consists of ordering a naive subject to administer electric shock to a victim. A simulated shock generator is used, with 30 clearly marked voltage levels that range from 15 to 450 volts. The instrument bears verbal designations that range from Slight Shock to Danger: Severe Shock. The responses of the victim, who is a trained confederate of the experimenter, are standardized. The orders to administer shocks are given to the naive subject in the context of a "learning experiment" ostensibly set up to study the effects of punishment on memory. As the experiment proceeds the

Reprinted by permission from *Journal of Abnormal and Social Psychology*. 1963, 67 (4), 371–378. Published by the American Psychological Association.

This research was supported by a grant (NSF G-17916) from the National Science Foundation. Exploratory studies conducted in 1960 were supported by a grant from the Higgins Fund at Yale University. The research assistance of Alan C. Elms and Jon Wayland is gratefully acknowledged.

TABLE 1. Distribution of Age and Occupational Types in the Experiment

Occupations	20–29 Years n	30–39 Years n	40–50 Years n	Percentage of Total (Occupations)
Workers, skilled and unskilled	4	5	6	37.5
Sales, business, and white-collar	3	6	7	40.0
Professional	1	5	3	22.5
Percentage of total (age)	20	40	40	

Note: Total **N** = 40.

naive subject is commanded to administer increasingly more intense shocks to the victim, even to the point of reaching the level marked Danger: Severe Shock. Internal resistances become stronger, and at a certain point the subject refuses to go on with the experiment. Behavior prior to this rupture is considered "obedience," in that the subject complies with the commands of the experimenter. The point of rupture is the act of disobedience. A quantitative value is assigned to the subject's performance based on the maximum intensity shock he is willing to administer before he refuses to participate further. Thus for any particular subject and for any particular experimental condition the degree of obedience may be specified with a numerical value. The crux of the study is to systematically vary the factors believed to alter the degree of obedience to the experimental commands.

The technique allows important variables to be manipulated at several points in the experiment. One may vary aspects of the source of command, content and form of command, instrumentalities for its execution, target object, general social setting, etc. The problem, therefore, is not one of designing increasingly more numerous experimental conditions, but of selecting those that best illuminate the *process* of obedience from the sociopsychological standpoint.

RELATED STUDIES

The inquiry bears an important relation to philosophic analyses of obedience and authority (Arendt, 1958; Friedrich, 1958; Weber, 1947), an early experimental study of obedience by Frank (1944), studies in "authoritarianism" (Adorno, Frenkel-Brunswik, Levinson, & Sanford, 1950; Rokeach, 1961), and a recent series of analytic and empirical studies in social power (Cartwright, 1959). It owes much to the long concern with *suggestion* in social psychology, both in its normal forms (e.g., Binet, 1900) and in its clinical manifestations (Charcot, 1881). But it derives, in the first instance, from direct observation of a social fact; the individual who is commanded by a legitimate authority ordinarily obeys. Obedience comes easily and often. It is a ubiquitous and indispensable feature of social life.

METHOD

Subjects

The subjects were 40 males between the ages of 20 and 50, drawn from New Haven, Conn., and the surrounding communities. Subjects were obtained by a newspaper advertisement and direct mail solicitation. Those who responded to the appeal believed they were to participate in a study of memory and learning at Yale University. A wide range of occupations is represented in the sample. Typical subjects were postal clerks, high school teachers, salesmen, engineers, and laborers. Subjects ranged in educational level from one who had not finished elementary school, to those who had doctorate and other professional degrees. They were paid $4.50 for their participation in the experiment. However, subjects were told that payment was simply for coming to the laboratory, and that the money was theirs no matter what happened after they arrived. Table 1 shows the proportion of age and occupational types assigned to the experimental condition.

Personnel and Locale

The experiment was conducted on the grounds of Yale University in the elegant interaction laboratory. (This detail is relevant to the perceived legitimacy of the experiment. In further variations, the experiment was dissociated from the university, with consequences for performance.) The role of experimenter was played by a 31-year-old high school teacher of biology. His manner was impassive, and his appearance somewhat stern throughout the experiment. He was dressed in a gray technician's coat. The victim was played by a 47-year-old accountant, trained for the role; he was of Irish-American stock, whom most observers found mild-mannered and likable.

Procedure

One naive subject and one victim (an accomplice) performed in each experiment. A pretext had to be devised that would justify the administration of electric shock by the naive subject. This was effectively accomplished by the cover story. After a general introduction on the presumed relation between punishment and learning, subjects were told:

> But actually, we know very little about the effect of punishment on learning, because almost no truly scientific studies have been made of it in human beings.
>
> For instance, we don't know how much punishment is best for learning —and we don't know how much difference it makes as to who is giving the punishment, whether an adult learns best from a younger or an older person than himself—or many things of that sort.
>
> So in this study we are bringing together a number of adults of different occupations and ages. And we're asking some of them to be teachers and some of them to be learners.
>
> We want to find out just what effect different people have on each other as teachers and learners, and also what effect punishment will have on learning in this situation.
>
> Therefore, I'm going to ask one of you to be the teacher here tonight and the other one to be the learner.
>
> Does either of you have a preference?

Subjects then drew slips of paper from a hat to determine who would be the teacher and who would be the learner in the experiment. The drawing was rigged so that the naive subject was always the teacher and the accomplice always the learner. (Both slips contained the word "Teacher.") Immediately after the drawing, the teacher and learner were taken to an adjacent room and the learner was strapped into an "electric chair" apparatus.

The experimenter explained that the straps were to prevent excessive movement while the learner was being shocked. The effect was to make it impossible for him to escape from the situation. An electrode was attached to the learner's wrist, and electrode paste was applied "to avoid blisters and burns." Subjects were told that the electrode was attached to the shock generator in the adjoining room.

In order to improve credibility the experimenter declared, in response to a question by the learner: "Although the shocks can be extremely painful, they cause no permanent tissue damage."

Learning Task. The lesson administered by the subject was a paired-associate learning task. The subject read a series of word pairs to the learner, and then read the first word of the pair along with four terms. The learner was to indicate which of the four terms had originally been paired with the first word. He communicated his answer by pressing one of four switches in front of him, which in turn lit up one of four numbered quadrants in an answer-box located atop the shock generator.

Shock Generator. The instrument panel consists of 30 lever switches set in a horizontal line. Each switch is clearly labeled with a voltage designation that ranges from 15 to 450 volts. There is a 15-volt increment from one switch to the next going from left to right. In addition, the following verbal designations are clearly indicated for groups of four switches going from left to right: Slight Shock, Moderate Shock, Strong Shock, Very Strong Shock, Intense Shock, Extreme Intensity Shock, Danger: Severe Shock. (Two switches after this last designation are simply marked XXX.)

Upon depressing a switch: a pilot light corresponding to each switch is illuminated in bright red; an electric buzzing is heard; an electric blue light, labeled "voltage energizer," flashes; the dial on the voltage meter swings to the right; various relay clicks are sounded.

The upper left-hand corner of the generator is labeled Shock Generator, Type ZLB, Dyson Instrument Company, Waltham, Mass. Output 15 Volts–450 Volts.

Details of the instrument were carefully handled to insure an appearance of authenticity. The panel was engraved by precision industrial engravers, and all components were of high quality. No subject in the experiment suspected that the instrument was merely a simulated shock generator.[1]

Sample Shock. Each naive subject is given a sample shock on the shock generator, prior to beginning his run as teacher. This shock is always 45 volts, and is applied by pressing the third switch of the generator. The shock is applied to the wrist of the naive subject, and has its source in a 45-volt battery wired into the generator. This further convinces the subject of the authenticity of the generator.

Shock Instructions. The subject is told to administer a shock to the learner each time he gives a wrong response. Moreover—and this is the key command—the subject is instructed to "move one level higher on the shock generator each time the learner flashes a wrong answer." He is also instructed to announce the voltage level before administering a shock. This serves to continually remind subjects of

[1] A related technique, making use of a shock generator, was reported by Buss (1961) for the study of aggression in the laboratory. Despite the considerable similarity of technical detail in the experimental procedures, both investigators proceeded in ignorance of the other's work. Milgram provided plans and photographs of his shock generator, experimental procedure, and first results in a report to the National Science Foundation in January 1961. This report received only limited circulation. Buss reported his procedure 6 months later, but to a wider audience. Subsequently, technical information and reports were exchanged. The present article was first received in the Editor's office on December 27, 1961; it was resubmitted with deletions on July 27, 1962.

the increasing intensity of shocks administered to the learner.

Preliminary and Regular Run. Pretests revealed that the procedure of reading words and administering shocks requires some practice before it can be handled smoothly. Therefore, immediately preceding the regular run, the teacher is given a preliminary series of 10 words to read to the learner. There are 3 neutral words in the practice series (i.e., words that the learner answers correctly), so that shocks are administered for 7 of the words, with the maximum shock at 105 volts (moderate shock). Almost all subjects master the procedure by this time the preliminary run is over.

Subjects are then presented with a second list, and are told that the procedure is the same as for the first list; the experimenter adds, however:

When you get to the bottom of the list, repeat it over again, and continue giving shocks, until the learner has learned all the pairs correctly.

The experimenter instructs the subject to,

start from 15 volts and increase the shock level one step each time the learner gives a wrong answer.

Feedback from the Victim. In all conditions the learner gives a predetermined set of responses to the word pair test, based on a schedule of approximately three wrong answers to one correct answer. In the present experimental condition no vocal response or other sign of protest is heard from the learner until Shock Level 300 is reached. When the 300-volt shock is administered, the learner pounds on the wall of the room in which he is bound to the electric chair. The pounding can be heard by the subject. From this point on, the learner's answers no longer appear on the four-way panel.

At this juncture, subjects ordinarily turn to the experimenter for guidance. The experimenter instructs the subject to treat the absence of a response as a wrong answer, and to shock the subject according to the usual schedule. He advises the subjects to allow 5–10 seconds before considering no response as a wrong answer, and to increase the shock level one step each time the learner fails to respond correctly. The learner's pounding is repeated after the 315-volt shock is administered; afterwards he is not heard from, nor do his answers reappear on the four-way signal box.

Experimenter Feedback. At various points in the experiment the subject may turn to the experimenter for advice on whether he should continue to administer shocks. Or he may indicate that he does not wish to go on. It was important to standardize the experimenter's responses to these inquiries and reactions.

If the subject indicated his unwillingness to go on, the experimenter responded with a sequence of "prods," using as many as necessary to bring the subject into line.

> *Prod 1: Please continue* or *go on.*
> *Prod 2: The experiment requires that you continue.*
> *Prod 3: It is absolutely essential that you continue.*
> *Prod 4: You have no other choice, you must go on.*

The prods were always made in sequence: Only if Prod 1 has been unsuccessful, could Prod 2 be used. If the subject refused to obey the experimenter after Prod 4, the experiment was terminated. The experimenter's tone of voice was at all times firm, but not impolite. The sequence was begun anew on each occasion that the subject balked or showed reluctance to follow orders.

Special Prods. If the subject asked if the learner was liable to suffer permanent physical injury, the experimenter said:

> *Although the shocks may be painful, there is no permanent tissue damage, so please go on. [Followed by Prods 2, 3, and 4 if necessary.]*

If the subject said that the learner did not want to go on, the experimenter replied:

> *Whether the learner likes it or not, you must go on until he has learned all the word pairs correctly. So please go on. [Followed by Prods 2, 3, and 4 if necessary.]*

Dependent Measures

The primary dependent measure for any subject is the maximum shock he administers before he refuses to go any further. In principle this may vary from 0 (for a subject who refuses to administer even the first shock) to 30 (for a subject who administers the highest shock on the generator). A subject who breaks off the experiment at any point prior to administering the thirtieth shock level is termed a *defiant* subject. One who complies with experimental commands fully, and proceeds to administer all shock levels commanded, is termed an *obedient* subject.

Further Records. With few exceptions, experimental sessions were recorded on magnetic tape. Occasional photographs were taken through one-way mirrors. Notes were kept on any unusual behavior occurring during the course of the experiments. On occasion, additional observers were directed to write objective descriptions of the subjects' behavior. The latency and duration of shocks were measured by accurate timing devices.

Interview and Dehoax. Following the experiment, subjects were interviewed; open-ended questions, projective measures, and attitude scales were employed. After the interview, procedures were undertaken to assure that the subject would leave the laboratory in a state of well being. A friendly reconciliation was arranged between the subject and the victim, and an effort was made to reduce any tensions that arose as a result of the experiment.

RESULTS

Preliminary Notions

Before giving an account of the experimental results, it is instructive to consider how persons predict others will perform when commanded to administer powerful shocks to another person. Fourteen Yale seniors, all psychology majors, were provided with a detailed description of the experimental situation. They were asked to reflect carefully on it, and to predict the behavior of 100 hypothetical subjects. More specifically, they were instructed to plot the distribution of obedience of "100 Americans of diverse occupations, and ranging in age from 20 to 50 years," who were placed in the experimental situation.

There was considerable agreement among the respondents on the expected behavior of hypothetical subjects. All respondents predicted that only an insignificant minority would go through to the end of the shock series. (The estimates ranged from 0 to 3%; i.e., the most "pessimistic" member of the class predicted that of 100 persons, 3 would continue through to the most potent shock available on the shock generator—450 volts.) The class mean was 1.2%. The question was also posed informally to colleagues of the author, and the most general feeling was that few if any subjects would go beyond the designation Very Strong Shock.

Result of Experiment I

Subjects Accept Situation. With few exceptions subjects were convinced of the reality of the experimental situation, that they were administering shocks to another person, and the most potent shocks were extremely painful. In the post-experimental interview subjects were asked: "How painful to the learner were the last few shocks that you administered to him?" Subjects were instructed to indicate their answers on a printed 14-point scale ranging from "Not at all painful" to "Extremely painful." The modal response was 14 (Extremely painful) with the mean at 13.42.

Signs of Extreme Tension. Many subjects showed signs of nervousness in the experimental situation, and especially upon administering the more powerful shocks. In a large number of cases the degree of tension reached extremes that are rarely seen in sociopsychological laboratory studies. Subjects were observed to sweat, tremble, stutter, bite their lips, groan, and dig their fingernails into their flesh. These were characteristic rather than exceptional responses to the experiment.

One sign of tension was the regular occurrence of nervous laughing fits. Fourteen of the 40 subjects showed definite signs of nervous laughter and smiling.

The laughter seemed entirely out of place, even bizarre. Full-blown, uncontrollable seizures were observed for 3 subjects. On one occasion we observed a seizure so violently convulsive that it was necessary to call a halt to the experiment. The subject, a 46-year-old encyclopedia salesman, was seriously embarrassed by his untoward and uncontrollable behavior. In the post-experimental interviews subjects took pains to point out that they were not sadistic types, and that the laughter did not mean they enjoyed shocking the victim.

Distribution of Scores. It had been conjectured that persons would not, in general, agree to administer shocks beyond the level designated as Very Strong Shock. The distribution of maximum shocks for this experiment is shown in Table 2. The obtained distribution of scores deviates radically from the prediction.

Upon command of the experimenter, each of the 40 subjects went beyond the expected breakoff point. No subject stopped prior to administering Shock Level 20. (At this level—300 volts—the victim kicks on the wall and no longer provides answers to the teacher's multiple-choice questions.)

Of the 40 subjects, 5 refused to obey the experimental commands beyond the 300-volt level. Four more subjects administered one further shock, and then refused to go on. Two broke off at the 330-volt level, and 1 each at 345, 360, and 375 volts. Thus a total of 14 subjects defied the experimenter. It is instructive to reprint their remarks at the point of defiance, as transcribed from the tape recordings:

[0124] I think he's trying to communicate, he's knocking. . . . Well it's not fair to shock the guy . . . these are terrific volts. I don't think this is very humane. . . . Oh, I can't go on with this; no, this isn't right. It's a hell of an experiment. The guy is suffering in there. No, I don't want to go on. This is crazy. [Subject refused to administer more shocks.]

[0123] He's banging in there. I'm gonna chicken out. I'd like to continue,

but I can't do that to a man. . . .
I'm sorry I can't do that to a man.
I'll hurt his heart. You take your
check. . . . No really, I couldn't do it.

These subjects were frequently in a highly agitated and even angered state. Sometimes, verbal protest was at a minimum, and the subject simply got up from his chair in front of the shock generator, and indicated that he wished to leave the laboratory.

Of the 40 subjects, 26 obeyed the orders of the experimenter to the end, proceeding to punish the victim until they reached the most potent shock available on the shock generator. At that point, the experimenter called a halt to the session. (The maximum shock is labeled 450 volts, and is two steps beyond the designation: Danger: Severe Shock.) Although obedient subjects continued to administer shocks, they often did so under extreme stress. Some expressed reluctance to administer shocks beyond the 300-volt level, and displayed fears similar to those who defied the experimenter; yet they obeyed.

After the maximum shocks had been delivered, and the experimenter called a halt to the proceedings, many obedient subjects heaved sighs of relief, mopped their brows, rubbed their fingers over their eyes, or nervously fumbled cigarettes. Some shook their heads, apparently in regret. Some subjects had remained calm throughout the experiment, and displayed only minimal signs of tension from beginning to end.

DISCUSSION

The experiment yielded two findings that were surprising. The first finding concerns the sheer strength of obedient tendencies manifested in this situation. Subjects have learned from childhood that it is a fundamental breach of moral conduct to hurt another person against his will. Yet, 26 subjects abandon this tenet in following the instructions of an authority who has no special powers to enforce his commands. To disobey would bring no material loss to the subject; no punishment would ensue. It is clear from the remarks and outward behavior of

TABLE 2. Distribution of Breakoff Points

Verbal Designation and Voltage Indication	Number of Subjects for Whom This Was Maximum Shock
Slight Shock	
15	0
30	0
45	0
60	0
Moderate Shock	
75	0
90	0
105	0
120	0
Strong Shock	
135	0
150	0
165	0
180	0
Very Strong Shock	
195	0
210	0
225	0
240	0
Intense Shock	
255	0
270	0
285	0
300	5
Extreme Intensity Shock	
315	4
330	2
345	1
360	1
Danger: Severe Shock	
375	1
390	0
405	0
420	0
XXX	
435	0
450	26

many participants that in punishing the victim they are often acting against their own values. Subjects often expressed deep disapproval of shocking a man in the face of his objections, and others denounced it as stupid and senseless. Yet the majority complied with the experimental commands. This outcome was surprising from two perspectives: first, from the standpoint of predictions made in the questionnaire described earlier. (Here, however, it is possible that the remoteness of the respondents from the actual situation, and the difficulty of conveying to them the concrete details of the experiment, could account for the serious underestimation of obedience.)

But the results were also unexpected to persons who observed the experiment in progress, through one-way mirrors. Observers often utttered expressions of disbelief upon seeing a subject administer more powerful shocks to the victim. These persons had a full acquaintance with the details of the situation, and yet systematically underestimated the amount of obedience that subjects would display.

The second unanticipated effect was the extraordinary tension generated by the procedures. One might suppose that a subject would simply break off or continue as his conscience dictated. Yet, this is very far from what happened. There were striking reactions of tension and emotional strain. One observer related:

> I observed a mature and initially poised businessman enter the laboratory smiling and confident. Within 20 minutes he was reduced to a twitching, stuttering wreck, who was rapidly approaching a point of nervous collapse. He constantly pulled on his earlobe, and twisted his hands. At one point he pushed his fist into his forehead and muttered: "Oh, God, let's stop it." And yet he continued to respond to every word of the experimenter, and obeyed to the end.

Any understanding of the phenomenon of obedience must rest on an analysis of the particular conditions in which it occurs. The following features of the experiment go some distance in explaining the high amount of obedience observed in the situation.

1. The experiment is sponsored by and takes place on the grounds of an institution of unimpeachable reputation, Yale University. It may be reasonably presumed that the personnel are competent and reputable. The importance of this background authority is now being studied by conducting a series of experiments outside of New Haven, and without any visible ties to the university.

2. The experiment is, on the face of it, designed to attain a worthy purpose—advancement of knowledge about learning and memory. Obedience occurs not as an end in itself, but as an instrumental element in a situation that the subject construes as significant, and meaningful. He may not be able to see its full significance, but he may properly assume that the experimenter does.

3. The subject perceives that the victim has voluntarily submitted to the authority system of the experimenter. He is not (at first) an unwilling captive impressed for involuntary service. He is taken the trouble to come to the laboratory presumably to aid the experimental research. That he later becomes an involuntary subject does not alter the fact that, initially, he consented to participate without qualification. Thus he has in some degree incurred an obligation toward the experimenter.

4. The subject, too, has entered the experiment voluntarily, and perceives himself under obligation to aid the experimenter. He has made a commitment, and to disrupt the experiment is a repudiation of this initial promise of aid.

5. Certain features of the procedure strengthen the subject's sense of obligation to the experimenter. For one, he has been paid for coming to the laboratory. In part this is canceled out by the experimenter's statement that:

> Of course, as in all experiments, the money is yours simply for coming to the laboratory. From this point on, no matter what happens, the money is yours.[2]

6. From the subject's standpoint, the fact that he is the teacher and the other man the learner is purely a chance consequence (it is determined by drawing lots) and he, the subject, ran the same risk as the other man in being assigned the role of learner. Since the assignment of positions in the experiment was achieved by fair means, the learner is deprived of any basis of complaint on this count. (A similar situation obtains in Army units, in which—in the absence of volunteers—a particularly dangerous

[2]Forty-three subjects, undergraduates at Yale University, were run in the experiment without payment. The results are very similar to those obtained with paid subjects.

mission may be assigned by drawing lots, and the unlucky soldier is expected to bear his misfortune with sportsmanship.)

7. There is, at best, ambiguity with regard to the prerogatives of a psychologist and the corresponding rights of his subject. There is a vagueness of expectation concerning what a psychologist may require of his subject, and when he is overstepping acceptable limits. Moreover, the experiment occurs in a closed setting, and thus provides no opportunity for the subject to remove these ambiguities by discussion with others. There are few standards that seem directly applicable to the situation, which is a novel one for most subjects.

8. The subjects are assured that the shocks administered to the subject are "painful but not dangerous." Thus they assume that the discomfort caused the victim is momentary, while the scientific gains resulting from the experiment are enduring.

9. Through Shock Level 20 the victim continues to provide answers on the signal box. The subject may construe this as a sign that the victim is still willing to "play the game." It is only after Shock Level 20 that the victim repudiates the rules completely, refusing to answer further.

These features help to explain the high amount of obedience obtained in this experiment. Many of the arguments raised need not remain matters of speculation, but can be reduced to testable proportions to be confirmed or disproved by further experiments.[3]

The following features of the experiment concern the nature of the conflict which the subject faces.

10. The subject is placed in a position

[3] A series of recently completed experiments employing the obedience paradigm is reported in Milgram (1964).

in which he must respond to the competing demands of two persons: the experimenter and the victim. The conflict must be resolved by meeting the demands of one or the other; satisfaction of the victim and the experimenter are mutually exclusive. Moreover, the resolution must take the form of a highly visible action, that of continuing to shock the victim or breaking off the experiment. Thus the subject is forced into a public conflict that does not permit any completely satisfactory solution.

11. While the demands of the experimenter carry the weight of scientific authority, the demands of the victim spring from his personal experience of pain and suffering. The two claims need not be regarded as equally pressing and legitimate. The experimenter seeks an abstract scientific datum; the victim cries out for relief from physical suffering caused by the subject's actions.

12. The experiment gives the subject little time for reflection. The conflict comes on rapidly. It is only minutes after the subject has been seated before the shock generator that the victim begins his protests. Moreover, the subject perceives that he has gone through but two-thirds of the shock levels at the time the subject's first protests are heard. Thus he understands that the conflict will have a persistent aspect to it, and may well become more intense as increasingly more powerful shocks are required. The rapidity with which the conflict descends on the subject, and his realization that it is predictably recurrent may well be sources of tension to him.

13. At a more general level, the conflict stems from the opposition of two deeply ingrained behavior dispositions: first, the disposition not to harm other people, and second, the tendency to obey those whom we perceive to be legitimate authorities.

REFERENCES

Adorno, T., Frenkel-Brunswik, Else, Levinson, D. J., & Sanford, R. N. The authoritarian personality. New York: Harper, 1950.

Arendt, H. What was authority? In C. J. Friedrich (Ed.), Authority. Cambridge: Harvard Univer. Press, 1958. Pp. 81–112.

Binet, A. La suggestibilité. Paris: Schleicher, 1900.

Buss, A. H. The psychology of aggression. New York: Wiley, 1961.

Cartwright, S. (Ed.) Studies in social power. Ann Arbor: University of Michigan Institute for Social Research, 1959.

Charcot, J. M. *Oeuvres complètes.* Paris: Bureaux du Progrès Médical, 1881.

Frank, J. D. Experimental studies of personal pressure and resistance. *J. gen. Psychol.*, 1944, *30*, 23–64.

Friedrich, C. J. (Ed.) *Authority.* Cambridge: Harvard Univer. Press, 1958.

Milgram, S. Dynamics of obedience. Washington: National Science Foundation, 25 January 1961. (Mimeo)

Milgram, S. Some conditions of obedience and disobedience to authority. *Hum. Relat.*, 1964. In press.

Rokeach, M. Authority, authoritarianism, and conformity. In I. A. Berg & B. M. Bass (Eds.), *Conformity and deviation.* New York: Harper, 1961. Pp. 230–257.

Snow, C. P. Either-or. *Progressive*, 1961 (Feb.), 24.

Weber, M. *The theory of social and economic organization.* Oxford: Oxford Univer. Press, 1947.

59.
film violence
and the cue properties
of available targets

leonard berkowitz
and russell g. geen

According to a number of experiments, the display of aggression on the movie or television screen is more likely to increase than reduce the probability of aggressive behavior by members of the audience (Bandura & Walters, 1963; Berkowitz, 1962, 1964, 1965; Berkowitz & Rawlings, 1963; Walters, Thomas & Acker, 1962). This heightened likelihood of aggression is not always apparent, however. If the audience regards the depicted aggression as being unwarranted or morally wrong, inhibitions will be aroused. Such restraints against hostility can weaken the intensity of the aggressive actions shown by the audience members, or may even cause them to avoid displaying any overt hostility at all (Berkowitz & Rawlings, 1963).

There is some question as to what the specific role of the witnessed hostility is. Bandura and Walters (1963) generally prefer to emphasize two processes in accounting for film-engendered aggression: imitative learning and inhibitory and disinhibitory effects (cf. p. 60). By watching the actions of another person, they state, "the observer may acquire new responses that did not previously exist in his repertory." In addition, the observed model's behavior may also either arouse or weaken the audience's inhibitions against particular actions. Thus, according to this analysis, witnessed hostility

Reprinted by permission from *Journal of Personality and Social Psychology*, 1966, 3 (5), 525–530. Published by the American Psychological Association.

This study was carried out by RGG under LB's supervision as part of a project sponsored by Grant G-23988 from the National Science Foundation to the senior author.

presumably gives rise to a persistent action tendency, a readiness to display aggression toward *anyone*. If certain persons are attacked rather than other people, the former supposedly have produced a disinhibition against aggression, for example, by somehow reminding the observer that hostility toward these people is permissible. (As the reader will recognize, the Bandura-Walters analysis is reminiscent of the classic scapegoat theory of prejudice. This latter doctrine also contends that the frustrated or prejudiced person is ready to attack just anyone and aggresses against those groups who are visible and safe to attack.)

But while modeling and inhibition effects are undoubtedly important, filmed violence may also serve to elicit aggressive responses from the observer (Berkowitz, 1962, 1964). The depicted aggression may increase the probability of attacks upon *particular targets*, depending upon the aggression-evoking cue properties of these objects. Observed aggression presumably is likely to have aggressive consequences as a function of: the strength of the observer's previously acquired aggressiveness habits; the association between the witnessed event and both the situations in which the observer had learned to act aggressively, and the postobservation setting; and the intensity of the guilt and/or aggression-anxiety also aroused by the observed violence (Berkowitz, 1962, p. 238). Putting it simply, this reasoning implies that the aggressiveness habits activated by witnessed hostility are often only in "low gear," so to speak. Other appropriate, aggression-evoking cues must be present before the observed violence can lead to strong aggressive responses by the observer. These cues are stimuli in the post-observation situation which have some association with the depicted event, or which may be connected with previous aggression-instigating situations. Thus, a person who sees a brutal fight may not himself display any detectable aggression immediately afterwards, even if his inhibitions are relatively weak, unless he encounters stimuli having some association with the fight. (Returning to the problem of scapegoating, this analysis maintains that the victimized groups evoke hostile responses from people who are ready to act aggressively; these groups have appropriate cue properties as well as being safe and visible targets—cf. Berkowitz, 1962; Berkowitz & Green, 1962).

Although there is considerable evidence that is consistent with this formulation (cf. Berkowitz, 1964), attempts to apply it to the consequences of movie aggression have led to somewhat ambiguous results (Berkowitz, 1965). Male college students were either angered or treated in a neutral fashion by a person who had been labeled either as a college boxer or a speech major. After this, the subjects witnessed either a prize fight or neutral film scene. It was found that the anger instigator received the greatest volume of aggression when the subjects had seen the prize fight and the anger instigator was said to be a college boxer; his label-induced association with the aggressive scene could have caused him to elicit aggressive responses from the men who were ready to act aggressively. However, there was also an indication that the label "boxer" could have strengthened the person's cue value for aggression regardless of the nature of the film witnessed by the subjects. This latter finding confirms the importance of the available target's cue value for aggression. But in the context of this study it raises a question as to whether the target's association with the observed violence had contributed to his aggression-eliciting properties. The present experiment is another test of the eliciting-cue hypothesis. This time, however, the association with the aggressive scene is varied by means of the available target's name rather than his supposed role.

METHOD

Subjects

The subjects were 88 male undergraduates at the University of Wisconsin. Seventy-two of these people had volunteered from sections of the introductory psychology course in order to earn points counting toward their final grade. The remaining 16 subjects were recruited from an introductory sociology course several weeks later without offering any grade-increasing inducements and were distributed evenly among the eight treatment groups.

Procedure

Three independent variables were arranged in a 2 × 2 × 2 factorial design so that some subjects would be (a) angered, (b) by a person having a name-mediated association, (c) with an aggressive scene. When each subject arrived at the laboratory he was met by a peer (actually the experimenter's accomplice) and the experimenter. The first experimental treatment was carried out by asking the two men what their names were. For half of the cases the accomplice identified himself as *Kirk* Anderson while for the remaining men he said his name was *Bob* Anderson.

Following this, the experimenter said the experiment involved the administration of a mild electric shock and gave the subject an opportunity to withdraw from the study if he so desired. He then showed the men two rooms, one containing various sorts of apparatus which, he said, were instruments for giving and receiving electric shocks, and the second containing a motion picture projector and screen. In this latter room the experimenter described the experiment as dealing with problem-solving ability under stress. One person, and the experimenter indicated that the subject was to take this role, would have to work on a problem knowing the other person (the accomplice) would judge the quality of his solution. The accomplice would evaluate the subject's performance by giving the subject from 1 to 10 electric shocks; the poorer the solution the greater the number of shocks that the subject was to receive.

The accomplice then left to go into the room containing the electrical apparatus, and the subject was given his problem: to suggest how an automotive service station could attract new customers. Five minutes later the experimenter returned, picked up the subject's written solution, and strapped the shock electrode onto the subject's arm. He then left the room again, ostensibly to bring the subject's work to the other person for judging. One minute later the accomplice in the adjoining room administered either one shock (*nonangered* condition) or seven shocks (*angered* condition) to the subject. After waiting 30 seconds, the experimenter returned to the subject, asked him how many shocks he had received, and then administered a brief questionnaire on which the subject rated his mood on four separate scales.[1]

While the subject was responding to this form, the experimenter recalled the accomplice. Then as soon as the subject had finished, the experimenter said he would show the two men a brief film in order to study the effects of a diversion upon problem-solving effectiveness. Half of the subjects (*aggressive movie* condition) saw the fight scene from the movie *Champion*. The experimenter introduced this 7-minute film clip by giving them the "justified aggression" synopsis. According to earlier findings (Berkowitz & Rawlings, 1963), this context seems to lower inhibitions against aggression. Further, in the *aggressive movie-Kirk* condition the experimenter casually but pointedly remarked that the first name of the movie protagonist was the same as that of the other person, that is, the accomplice. This was done to make sure that there was a name-mediated connection between the experimenter's confederate and the witnessed violence when the accomplice was said to be "Kirk Anderson." The other

[1]The one shock given to the men in the nonangered conditions could have introduced a ceiling effect limiting the number of shocks administered in these conditions by defining what was the appropriate number. Contrary to this possibility, however, questionnaire findings indicate that the subjects receiving one shock were much less hostile toward the confederate than subjects getting seven shocks.

half of the subjects were shown an equally long and exciting movie of a track race between the first two men to run the mile in less than 4 minutes.

Upon conclusion of the 7-minute film clip, the experimenter again sent the accomplice from the room with instructions to write his solution to the sale-promotion problem. The subject was informed that he would be given the other person's solution and then was to evaluate it by shocking the other person from 1 to 10 times. Five minutes later the experimenter brought the subject a written problem solution saying this was the other person's work but which was actually previously constructed to be standard for all conditions. He told the subject to shock the other person as many times as he thought appropriate. The experimenter then went to the control room to record the number and duration of the shocks supposedly being given to the accomplice.[2] After waiting 30 seconds, the experimenter returned to the experimental room and gave the subject the final questionnaire on which the subject indicated how much he liked the accomplice. When this form was completed the experimenter explained the deceptions that had been practiced upon the subject and asked him not to discuss the experiment with anyone else for the remainder of the semester.

RESULTS

Effectiveness of the Experimental Manipulations

Since the experiment depended upon the proper registering of the accomplice's name, the final questionnaire asked each

[2]Earlier studies in our program employed total shock duration as one of the aggression measures. Since this score obviously has a high positive correlation with number of shocks, we here experimented with another measure, mean shock duration. Our results with this score proved quite disappointing. There were negative correlations between shock number and the mean duration of each shock in six of the eight conditions, suggesting that a "law of least effort" may have been operating to some extent, and that this could have restricted the utility of the duration measure.

TABLE 1. Mean Rating of Felt Anger

Accomplice's Name	Aggressive Film		Track Film	
	Angered	Non-angered	Angered	Non-angered
Kirk	7.36a	11.27b	7.27a	10.55b
Bob	6.00a	12.09b	7.27a	11.27b

Note: The lower the score the greater the felt anger. Cells having a subscript in common are not significantly different (at the .05 level) by Duncan multiple range test.

subject to write down "the other person's" name. All 88 men were correct.

There also were several checks of the success of the anger induction. First, each subject was asked how many shocks he had received and, again, each person correctly recalled the number of shocks given to him. More directly relevant to the arousal of emotion, after receiving the shocks each subject also rated his mood on a brief four-item questionnaire. The only item yielding a significant effect by analysis of variance was the measure of how "angry" or "placid" the subject felt; the men given seven shocks reported themselves as being reliably angrier than the men shocked only once. There were no other significant differences. Table 1 presents the mean anger rating in each of the eight experimental conditions.

We might also note at this time the significant main effects for anger-non-anger on the final questionnaire. In comparison to the men getting only one shock, those people receiving seven shocks expressed a significantly lower preference for the accomplice as a partner in any subsequent experiment, indicated a reliably weaker desire to know the accomplice better, and were significantly more opposed to him as a possible roommate.

TABLE 2. Mean Number of Shocks Given to Accomplice

Accomplice's Name	Aggressive Film		Track Film	
	Angered	Non-angered	Angered	Non-angered
Kirk	6.09a	1.73c	4.18b	1.54c
Bob	4.55b	1.45c	4.00b	1.64c

Note: Cells having a subscript in common are not significantly different (at the .05 level) by Duncan multiple range test.

All in all, there can be little doubt that the seven shocks had made the subjects angry with the experimenter's accomplice. The findings obtained with these ratings and the earlier mood reports, also suggest that the confederate's name had not influenced either the subjects' level of felt anger or their attitudes toward this person.

Test of the Aggression-Evoking-Cue Hypothesis

The primary measure of aggression in this experiment was the number of shocks administered by each subject. As we had expected, the men displaying the greatest number of aggressive responses were those who had seen the prize-fight film after they were provoked and who then had an opportunity to attack their frustrater named "Kirk Anderson." The accomplice's name had apparently caused him to be associated with the violent scene so that he could then elicit strong overt hostility from the people who, being angered, were primed to act aggressively. These subjects gave a significantly greater number of shocks than the men in any of the other conditions. The mean number of shocks in each condition is given in Table 2.

Other Questionnaire Findings

We have already summarized the major findings obtained with the final questionnaire, administered after the subjects had given the accomplice the electric shocks; in general, at the end of the experiment the subjects still disliked the accomplice more after having received seven shocks from him than after getting only one shock. Aside from this, however, the pattern of condition differences obtained with the questionnaire data did not resemble the findings obtained with the shock measure. Many of the men could have become somewhat anxious or guilty after administering the electrical punishment. This reaction might have then affected the questionnaire responses—either decreasing or intensifying the verbal expressions of hostility (cf. Berkowitz, 1962, Ch. 8).

But we can make an assumption here that seems warranted in the light of other findings. Those people experiencing a strong instigation to aggression may display persistently strong aggressive responses over time, responses that are not quickly altered by anxiety-guilt reactions (cf. Berkowitz & Holmes, 1960, cited in Berkowitz, 1962, p. 96). Thus, if the final questionnaire ratings are, at least in part, expressions of hostility, the condition in which the strongest aggressive response tendencies had been activated should exhibit the highest positive correlation between shock number and questionnaire ratings. In order to test this reasoning four product-moment correlations were computed in each of the eight conditions: between the number of shocks given by each subject and his verbal expression of hostility on each of the four hostility items in the final questionnaire. A mean correlation was then obtained for each condition after first employing the r to z transformation. The results are shown in Table 3.

While none of the condition differences are statistically reliable, the general pattern is consistent with the shock data and our theoretical expectations. First, combining the four angered and the four nonangered groups, we find that 62.5% of the 16 correlations in the strongly provoked groups were positive but only 25% of the relationships in the nonangered conditions were in this direction ($x^2 = 4.58$, $p = .05$, if we treat the correlations within a group as independent events). Thus, strong anger arousal tended to produce relatively persistent hostile tendencies; the people exhibiting comparatively strong open aggression on the first occasion generally expressed a high level of aggression the next time measurements were obtained shortly afterwards.

Turning now to the specific theoretical expectations, Table 3 also shows that the condition having the highest mean positive correlation was the one predicted to have the strongest aggressive responses: the angered-aggressive film-Kirk group. The strong activation of aggression in this condition resulting from the combination of provocation and aggression-eliciting cues led to longer lasting aggressive response tendencies as well as the high volume of electrical attacks upon the accomplice.

TABLE 3. Mean Product-Moment Correlation Between Shock Number and Subsequent Questionnaire Hostility

Accomplice's Name	Aggressive Film		Track Film	
	Angered	Non-angered	Angered	Non-angered
Kirk	.37(4)[a]	—.09(1)	—.18(2)	—.15(1)
Bob	—.16(1)	—.27(1)	.10(3)	—.01(1)

[a] The numbers in parentheses refer to the number of positive correlations of the four computed in each condition. One of the four positive correlations in the aggressive film-angered-Kirk condition attained statistical significance while none of the four remaining significant r's were positive.

These effects of the name attributed to the accomplice raised a further question. Did the name "Kirk" serve as an aggression-evoking cue after the subjects had seen Kirk Douglas being beaten in part because of prior attitudes? Disliked objects may have the cue properties enabling them to elicit aggressive responses from people who are ready to act aggressively (Berkowitz, 1962; Berkowitz & Green, 1962). It is conceivable, then, that the present college students had some negative attitudes toward the name "Kirk" and/or the actor Kirk Douglas which generalized to the accomplice, "Kirk Anderson." These attitudes could have facilitated the expression of open hostility toward Kirk Anderson. An additional investigation was conducted as an examination of this possibility. A sample of 44 male university students comparable to those who participated in the experiment was given a list of 14 masculine and feminine first names and was asked to indicate how much they liked or disliked each name on a 7-point scale. The results demonstrated that there were no particularly strong feelings connected with the name Kirk. Although the subjects tended to rate the name on the negative side of the scale (mean rating = 4.50), this mean rating was not significantly different from the neutral point ($p = .22$, one-tailed test).

These subjects, however, did tend to associate the name Kirk with Kirk Douglas. When asked on a subsequent form to write down what family names came to mind in response to each of the 17 first names, 40 of the 44 respondents listed the patronym "Douglas" after the first name Kirk. But while Kirk may be connected with a particular person, this individual is not necessarily disliked. This is indicated by the findings of a third questionnaire on which the respondents rated their attitudes toward each of 14 public figures. Kirk Douglas obtained a mean rating of 3.75 on the 7-point scales used in this instrument, a mean score which again is not significantly different from the neutral point.

DISCUSSION

All in all, the above findings lend comparatively clear support to the theoretical analysis upon which the present study was based. Observed aggression, we have shown, does not necessarily lead to open aggression against anyone. Particular targets are most likely to be attacked, and these are objects having appropriate, aggression-eliciting cue properties. In the present case the target's cue value is derived from a label-mediated association with the witnessed aggressive scene—or more specifically, with the victim of the observed hostility. Having this association, the target evokes aggressive responses from the audience members who are primed to act aggressively and whose restraints against aggression are fairly weak.

But assuming the essential validity of this analysis, we can also raise a number of important unanswered questions. For one thing, did the accomplice draw the greatest number of aggressive responses from the people in the angered-aggressive film-Kirk group because of his connection with aggression *generally*, or because he was most closely associated with the *victim* of the observed violence? It is conceivable that an object's aggressive cue properties are derived fundamentally from the object's connection with aggressive behavior, whether these acts are given or received. Thus, if college boxers tend to draw stronger hostility than do speech majors, as seems to be the case (Berkowitz, 1965), this may be due to the former role's closer association with fighting in general. The same point can perhaps be made with regard to the presumed aggression-eliciting properties of

disliked people. Here again the disliked object may somehow be associated with aggression.

A second question has to do with the frequently exciting nature of observed aggression. In addition to their specific content, violent scenes typically are fairly exciting. This excitement means, of course, that there is a relatively strong arousal state within the observer, and this high arousal level might well contribute to the strength of the aggressive responses elicited in the situation. There is a suggestion to this effect in the data summarized in Table 2. Looking at the mean number of shocks delivered to the accomplice "Bob," we can see that the angered subjects seeing the prize fight did not express reliably stronger hostility than the men witnessing the exciting track race. Other experiments have obtained a much more substantial difference when the same aggressive scene was compared with a less arousing neutral film (e.g., Berkowitz & Rawlings, 1963). The exciting nature of the prize fight might have contributed to the condition differences obtained in the earlier research. Whether this is true or not, however, film-engendered differences in degree of arousal cannot account for the present findings. The aggressive scene was probably not more exciting when the accomplice's name was Kirk than when he was called Bob. For that matter, as is shown in Table 1, the subjects did not feel greater anger toward Kirk than toward Bob.[3]

[3]An experiment by the present writers, conducted after this article went to press, indicates that associations with nonaggressive, exciting scenes do not increase the available target's aggressive cue properties. Subjects were made to be angry with a confederate, whose name in some cases was said to be either "Landy" or "Bannister," and then either saw the track race film or sat still for an equivalent time. For the people shown the track film the confederates never connected him either with the winner or loser in the observed race. The confederate did *not* receive more shocks after the track film than after the no-film treatment and regardless of whether or not his name connected him with the track film did not do so. The important association evidently is with an aggressive scene.

REFERENCES

Bandura, A., & Walters, R. H. *Social learning and personality development.* New York: Holt, Rinehart, & Winston, 1963.

Berkowitz, L. *Aggression: A social psychological analysis.* New York: McGraw-Hill, 1962.

Berkowitz, L. Aggressive cues in aggressive behavior and hostility catharsis. *Psychological Review,* 1964, 71, 104–122.

Berkowitz, L. Some aspects of observed aggression. *Journal of Personality and Social Psychology,* 1965, 2, 359–369.

Berkowitz, L., & Green, J. A. The stimulus qualities of the scapegoat. *Journal of Abnormal and Social Psychology,* 1962, *64,* 293–301.

Berkowitz, L., & Rawlings, E. Effects of film violence on inhibitions against subsequent aggression. *Journal of Abnormal and Social Psychology,* 1963, *66,* 405–412.

Walters, R. H., Thomas, E. L., & Acker, C. W. Enhancement of punitive behavior by audio-visual displays. *Science,* 1962, *136,* 872–873.

60.
status of frustrator
as an inhibitor
of horn-honking responses

anthony n. doob
and alan e. gross

A. INTRODUCTION

Subjects may consciously attempt to present themselves in a favorable manner, they may cooperate with the experimenter or interviewer, and their reactions may be affected by the measurement process itself. In reviewing a number of such problems, Webb et al. (6, pp. 13–27) point out that some of these sources of contamination can be avoided when field data are collected from people who are unaware that they are subjects participating in an experiment. Although field procedures can reduce demand and reactivity effects, experimental manipulations outside of the laboratory may gain realism at the expense of control. The study reported here is an attempt to investigate unobtrusively some effects of frustration in a naturalistic setting without sacrificing experimental control.

Modern automobile traffic frequently creates situations which closely resemble classical formulations of how frustration is instigated. One such instance occurs when one car blocks another at a signal-controlled intersection. Unlike many traffic frustrations, this situation provides a clearly identifiable frustrator and a fairly typical response for the blocked driver: sounding his horn. Horn honking may function instrumentally to remove

Reprinted by permission from *The Journal of Social Psychology*, 1968, 76, 213–218. Published by The Journal Press.

We wish to thank Tina Fox and Mike Rosenberg, the observers in the field experiment, and Lorraine Soderstrum of Foothill College, Los Altos Hills, California, who made her class available for the questionnaire experiment. The first author was supported by a Public Health Service Predoctoral Fellowship.

the offending driver and emotionally to reduce tension. Both kinds of honks may be considered aggressive, especially if they are intended to make the frustrator uncomfortable by bombarding him with unpleasant stimuli.

One factor that is likely to affect aggressive responses is the status of the frustrator (2, 3). The higher a person's status, the more likely it is he will have power to exercise sanctions, and although it is improbable that a high status driver would seek vengeance against a honker, fear of retaliation may generalize from other situations where aggression against superiors has been punished.

Aggression is not the only kind of social response that may be affected by status. High status may inhibit the initiation of any social response, even a simple informational signal. Although it is difficult in the present study to distinguish informational from aggressive motivation, it is hypothesized that a high status frustrator will generally inhibit horn honking.

B. METHOD

One of two automobiles, a new luxury model or an older car, was driven up to a signal controlled intersection and stopped. The driver was instructed to remain stopped after the signal had changed to green until 15 seconds had elapsed, or until the driver of the car immediately behind honked his horn twice. Subjects were the 82 drivers, 26 women and 56 men, whose progress was blocked by the experimental car. The experiment was run from 10:30 a.m. to 5:30 p.m. on a Sunday, in order to avoid heavy weekday traffic.

1. Status Manipulation

A black 1966 Chrysler Crown Imperial hardtop which had been washed and polished was selected as the high status car.[1] Two low status cars were used: a rusty 1954 Ford station wagon and an unobtrusive gray 1961 Rambler sedan. The Rambler was substituted at noon because it was felt that subjects might reasonably attribute the Ford's failure to move to mechanical breakdown. Responses to these two cars did not turn out to be different, and the data for the two low status cars were combined.

2. Location

Six intersections in Palo Alto and Menlo Park, California, were selected according to these criteria: (a) a red light sufficiently long to insure that a high proportion of potential subjects would come to a complete stop behind the experimental car before the signal changed to green, (b) relatively light traffic so that only one car, the subject's, was likely to pull up behind the experimental car, and (c) a narrow street so that it would be difficult for the subject to drive around the car blocking him. Approximately equal numbers of high and low status trials were run at each intersection.

3. Procedure

By timing the signal cycle, the driver of the experimental car usually managed to arrive at the intersection just as the light facing him was turning red. If at least one other car had come to a complete stop behind the experimental car before the signal had turned green, a trial was counted, and when the light changed, an observer started two stop watches and a tape recorder. Observers were usually stationed in a car parked close to the intersection, but when this was not feasible, they were concealed from view in the back seat of the ex-

[1] We have labeled this operation a "status manipulation" because a large expensive car is frequently associated with wealth, power, and other qualities which are commonly regarded as comprising high status. However, it could be argued that Chrysler is potentially inhibiting not because it is a status symbol, but because of some other less plausible attribute (e.g., physical size).

perimental car. High and low status trials were run simultaneously at different intersections, and the two driver-observer teams switched cars periodically during the day. Drivers wore a plaid sport jacket and white shirt while driving the Chrysler, and an old khaki jacket while driving the older car.

a. Dependent Measures. At the end of each trial, the observer noted whether the subject had honked once, twice, or not at all. Latency of each honk and estimated length of each honk were recorded and later double-checked against tape recordings.

b. Subject Characteristics. Immediately after each trial, the observer took down the year, make, and model of the subject's car. Sex and estimated age of driver, number of passengers, and number of cars behind the experimental car when the signal changed were also recorded.

C. RESULTS AND DISCUSSION

Eight subjects, all men, were eliminated from the analysis for the following reasons: four cars in the low status condition and one in the high status condition went around the experimental car; on one trial the driver of the experimental car left the intersection early; and two cars in the low status condition, instead of honking, hit the back bumper of the experimental car, and the driver did not wish to wait for a honk. This left 38 subjects in the low status condition and 36 in the high status condition.

Although the drivers of the experimental cars usually waited for 15 seconds, two of the lights used in the experiment were green for only 12 seconds; therefore 12 seconds was used as a cutoff for all data. There were no differences attributable to drivers or intersections.

The clearest way of looking at the results is in terms of the percentage in each condition that honked at least once in 12 seconds. In the low status condition 84 per cent of the subjects honked at least once, whereas in the high status condition, only 50 per cent of the subjects honked ($x^2 = 8.37$, $df = 1$, $p < .01$).

TABLE 1. Field Experiment (Mean Latency of First Honk in Seconds)

Frustrator	Sex of Driver	
	Male	Female
Low status	6.8 (23)	7.6 (15)
High status	8.5 (25)	10.9 (11)

Note: Numbers in parentheses indicate the number of subjects.

Another way of looking at this finding is in terms of the latency of the first honk. When no honks are counted as a latency of 12 seconds, it can be seen in Table 1 that the average latency for the new car was longer for both sexes. ($F = 10.71$, $p < .01$).

Thus, it is quite clear that status had an inhibitory effect on honking even once. It could be argued that status would have even greater inhibitory effects on more aggressive honking. Although one honk can be considered a polite way of calling attention to the green light, it is possible that subjects felt that a second honk would be interpreted as aggression.[2]

Forty-seven per cent of the subjects in the low status condition honked twice at the experimental car, as compared to 19 per cent of the subjects in the high status condition ($x^2 = 5.26$, $df = 1$, $p < .05$.) This difference should be interpreted cautiously because it is confounded with the main result that more people honk generally in the low status condition. Of those who overcame the inhibitions to honk at all, 56 per cent in the low status condition and 39 per cent in the high status condition honked a second time, a difference which was not significant. First-honk latencies for honkers

TABLE 2. Number of Drivers Honking Zero, One, and Two Times

Frustrator	Honking in 12 Seconds		
	Twice	Once	Never
Low status	18	14	6
High status	7	11	18

Note: Overall $\chi^2 = 11.14$, **p** $< .01$.

[2]Series of honks separated by intervals of less than one second were counted as a single honk.

were about equal for the two conditions. The overall findings are presented in Table 2.

Sex of driver was the only other measure that was a good predictor of honking behavior. In both conditions men tended to honk faster than women ($F = 4.49$, $p < .05$). The interaction of status and sex did not approach significance ($F = 1.17$). These data are consistent with laboratory findings (1) that men tend to aggress more than women.

Most experiments designed to study the effects of frustration have been carried out in the laboratory or the classroom, and many of these have employed written materials (2, 5).

It is undoubtedly much easier to use questionnaires, and if they produce the same results as field experiments, then in the interest of economy, they would have great advantage over naturalistic experiments. However, over 30 years ago, LaPiere warned that reactions to such instruments "may indicate what the responder would actually do when confronted with the situation symbolized in the question, but there is no assurance that it will" (4, p. 236).

In order to investigate this relationship between actual and predicted behavior, an attempt was made to replicate the present study as a questionnaire experiment. Obviously, the most appropriate sample to use would be one comprised of motorists sampled in the same way that the original drivers were sampled. Because this was not practicable, a questionnaire experiment was administered in a junior college classroom.

Subjects were 57 students in an introductory psychology class. Two forms of critical item were included as the first of three traffic situations on a one-page questionnaire: "You are stopped at a traffic light behind a black 1966 Chrysler (gray 1961 Rambler). The light turns green and for no apparent reason the driver does not go on. Would you honk at him?" If subjects indicated that they would honk, they were then asked to indicate on a scale from one to 14 seconds how long they would wait before honking. Forms were alternated so that approximately equal numbers of subjects received the Chrysler and Rambler versions. Verbal instructions strongly emphasized that subjects were to answer according to what they actually thought they would do in such a situation. No personal information other than sex, age, and whether or not they were licensed to drive was required.

After the questionnaire had been collected, the class was informed that different kinds of cars had been used for the horn-honking item. The experimenter then asked subjects to raise their hands when they heard the name of the car that appeared in the first item of their questionnaire. All subjects were able to select the correct name from a list of four makes which was read.

One subject (a female in the high status condition) failed to mark the honk latency scale, and another subject in the same condition indicated that she would go around the blocking car. Both of these subjects were eliminated from the analysis, leaving 27 in the high status condition and 28 in the low status condition. The results were analyzed in the same manner as the latency data from the field experiment. Means for each condition broken down by sex are presented in Table 3. Males reported that they thought that they would honk considerably sooner at the Chrysler than at the Rambler, whereas this was slightly reversed for females (interaction of sex and status $F = 4.97$, $p < .05$). Eleven subjects, six males in the low status condition and five females in the high status condition indicated that they would not honk within 12 seconds.

TABLE 3. Questionnaire Experiment (Mean Latency of Honking in Seconds)

Frustrator	Sex of Subject	
	Male	Female
Low status	9.1 (18)	8.2 (10)
High status	5.5 (13)	9.2 (14)

Note: Numbers in parentheses indicate the number of subjects.

It is clear that the behavior reported on the questionnaire is different from the behavior actually observed in the field. The age difference in the samples may account for this disparity. Median estimated age of subjects in the field was 38, compared to a median age of 22 in the classroom. In order to check the possibility that younger males would indeed honk faster at the high status car, the field data were reanalyzed by age. The results for younger males, estimated ages 16 to 30, fit the general pattern of the field results and differed from the results of the classroom experiment. In the field, young males honked sooner at the Rambler than at the Chrysler ($t = 2.74$, $df = 11$, $p < .02$).

Unfortunately, because these two studies differed in both sample and method, it is impossible to conclude that the differences are due to differences in the method of collecting data. However, it is clear that questionnaire data obtained from this often used population of subjects do not always correspond to what goes on in the real world.

REFERENCES

1. Buss, A. H. Instrumentality of aggression, feedback, and frustration as determinants of physical aggression. *J. of Personal. & Soc. Psychol.*, 1966, *3*, 153–162.

2. Cohen, A. R. Social norms, arbitrariness of frustration, and status of the agent in the frustration-aggression hypothesis. *J. Abn. & Soc. Psychol.*, 1955, *51*, 222–226.

3. Hokanson, J. E., & Burgess, M. The effects of status, type of frustration and aggression on vascular processes. *J. Abn. & Soc. Psychol.*, 1962, *65*, 232–237.

4. LaPiere, R. T. Attitudes vs. actions. *Social Forces*, 1934, *13*, 230–237.

5. Pastore, N. The role of arbitrariness in the frustration-aggression hypothesis. *J. Abn. & Soc. Psychol.*, 1952, *47*, 728–731.

6. Webb, E. J., Campbell, D. T., Schwartz, R. D., & Sechrest, L. Unobtrusive Measures: Nonreactive Research in the Social Sciences. Chicago, Ill.: Rand McNally, 1966.

REVIEW QUESTIONS

1. How does shock intensity, shock frequency, shock duration, and shock consistency affect fighting behavior in animals?

2. Define conditioned aggression and try to give an example of this on the human level.

3. What does pain-elicited aggression imply about the use of physical punishment in our society?

4. What sorts of evidence does Milgram present indicating that the subjects thought they were actually shocking the victim?

5. Do you think you would have been one of the subjects in the Milgram study who applied all of the severe shocks? What factors does Milgram list which resulted in the great amount of obedience and how do you think these would have influenced you?

6. What experimental finding(s) led Berkowitz and Geen to their conclusion that observed aggression does not necessarily lead to open aggression against anyone? What can observed aggression lead to?

7. Summarize the Bandura and Walters formulation of the influence of witnessed hostility and how is this similar to the scapegoat theory of prejudice?

8. Why do Doob and Gross feel that a high-status frustrator is likely to be the target of less aggressive behavior?

9. Why did Doob and Gross try to do the same study using questionnaire data in a laboratory setting? What did the results of the questionnaire experiment lead them to conclude about behavior in the real world and behavior in a laboratory setting?

index

71 72 73 74 7 6 5 4 3 2 1